Public transit is an essential component of a sustainable future, but how to design a system that meets accessibility needs given finite budgets? Curtis and Scheurer offer help in the form of a sophisticated yet practical tool for analyzing transit accessibility. They demonstrate its use with a fascinating comparison across four continents that yields insightful lessons for planners.

Susan Handy, University of California, Davis, USA

This is a unique and comprehensive sourcebook in the field of transport and urban planning. If you want to understand how cities and metropolitan areas around the globe are performing in terms of public transport accessibility, and what opportunities there are to improve it, read this book.

Karst Geurs, University of Twente, the Netherlands

PLANNING FOR PUBLIC TRANSPORT ACCESSIBILITY

Bringing together a comparative analysis of the accessibility by public transport of 23 cities spanning four continents, this book provides a "hands-on" introduction to the evolution, rationale and effectiveness of a new generation of accessibility planning tools that have emerged since the mid-2000s. The Spatial Network Analysis for Multimodal Urban Transport Systems (SNAMUTS) tool is used as a practical example to demonstrate how city planners can find answers as they seek to improve public transport accessibility. Uniquely among the new generation of accessibility tools, SNAMUTS has been designed for multi-city comparisons. A range of indicators are employed in each city including: the effectiveness of the public transport network; the relationship between the transport network and land use activity; who gets access within the city; and how resilient the city will be. The cities selected enable a comparison between cities by old world–new world; public transport modes; governance approach; urban development constraints. The book is arranged along six themes that address the different planning challenges cities confront. Richly illustrated with maps and diagrams, this volume acts as a comprehensive sourcebook of accessibility indicators and a snapshot of current policy making around the world in the realm of strategic planning for land use–transport integration and the growth of public transport. It provides a deeper understanding of the complexity, opportunities and challenges of twenty-first-century accessibility planning.

Carey Curtis is Professor in City Planning and Transport at Curtin University, Australia. She is Visiting Professor at University of Amsterdam. Her research interests cover land use planning and transport planning, including a focus on city form and structure, transit oriented development, personal travel behaviour, accessibility planning, institutional barriers to sustainable transport, governance and transport policy. She has published over 90 papers, book chapters and books including *Institutional Barriers for Sustainable Transport* (2012) with Nicholas Low, and *Transit Oriented Development: Making it Happen* (2009) with John Renne and Luca Bertolini.

Jan Scheurer is a Senior Research Associate at Curtin University, Australia and RMIT University, Australia/Spain. Trained in architecture and sustainability policy, his research straddles the gaps between urban design and spatial planning, transport policy, user behaviour and mobility culture. He has been an activist for sustainable transport in several parts of the world since 1989 and lives nomadically, but regularly sets anchor in Amsterdam, Barcelona, Melbourne and Perth.

To Professor Paul Mees OAM (1961–2013)

Paul started this research project with us and his insights into urban public transport networks not only launched our appetite to understand cities further, but to follow in his footsteps in trying to improve cities with this knowledge. We miss him immensely.

PLANNING FOR PUBLIC TRANSPORT ACCESSIBILITY

An International Sourcebook

CAREY CURTIS AND JAN SCHEURER

LONDON AND NEW YORK

First published 2016
by Routledge

2 Park Square, Milton Park, Abingdon, Oxfordshire OX14 4RN
52 Vanderbilt Avenue, New York, NY 10017

Routledge is an imprint of the Taylor & Francis Group, an informa business

First issued in paperback 2020

British Library Cataloguing in Publication Data
A catalogue record for this book is available from the British Library

Library of Congress Cataloging-in-Publication Data
Names: Curtis, Carey, author. | Scheurer, Jan, author.
Title: Planning for public transport accessibility : an international sourcebook / by Carey Curtis and Jan Scheurer.
Description: Burlington, VT : Ashgate, 2016. | Includes bibliographical references and index.
Identifiers: LCCN 2015033101
Subjects: LCSH: Local transit—Case studies. | Urban transportation—Planning.
Classification: LCC HE4211 .C87 2016 | DDC 388.4—dc23
LC record available at http://lccn.loc.gov/2015033101

ISBN: 978-1-4724-4724-1 (hbk)
ISBN: 978-0-367-66836-5 (pbk)

Typeset in Constantia
by Apex CoVantage, LLC

Contents

Preface

How can cities improve public transport accessibility so that all residents and employees can have an alternative choice of transport to the car? What are the most effective infrastructure interventions to make? This book is the culmination of an international research project seeking an answer to these questions in the field of transport and urban planning. The purpose is to provide a comprehensive sourcebook of richly illustrated spatial accessibility indicators, visualised by maps and diagrams, together with a snapshot of current policy making around the world in the realm of strategic planning for land use–transport integration and the growth of public transport.

A sample of 23 cities spanning four continents provides the source for our analysis. The cities selected present a mix of New World, European and wealthy Asian cities to enable a comparison between cities which embraced public transport accessibility as a real transport mode choice many decades ago, and recent newcomers. The cities have also been selected in order to provide a mix of different public transport modes, a range of different governance approaches, a range of different geographical or policy-induced urban development constraints. In this way it is possible to interrogate a rich set of variables. The narrative of the book is arranged along six key themes which address the different planning challenges cities confront and cities are grouped according to these themes.

This is a new approach to understanding public transport accessibility in urban transport and planning where there has been an absence of such knowledge. The book is addressed to researchers, practitioners and policy shapers interested in gaining a deeper understanding of the complexity, opportunities and challenges of twenty-first-century accessibility planning.

Carey Curtis and Jan Scheurer

Acknowledgements

The research and writing of this book has been the collaborative work of both authors whose partnership precedes the current research grant from which the material is drawn. A three-year Australian Research Council Grant (DP110104884) enabled the study of the cities analysed in this book. The research team also included Paul Mees (Chief Investigator, RMIT), Oscar Thomson, Sarah Taylor, Elizabeth Taylor, David Robertson, Sevilla Furness-Holland, Stefanie Knippenkötter (Research Assistants), Kristen Bell (PhD Scholar at RMIT) and Roger Mellor (PhD Scholar at Curtin University) and we thank them for their questions, challenges to our thinking, humour and companionship at various cities around the world. To Oscar in particular for his diligence in mapping and data collection – without him our task would have been much harder.

A large body of like-minded individuals with a keen interest in sustainable mobility and accessibility planning have supported this research along its journey. We would like to thank you all! In particular:

- The members of the European Union COST Action TU1002: Accessibility Tools in Planning Practice for their interest in our accessibility tool and the stimulating discussions – in particular – Dr Marco te Brömmelstroet and Prof Luca Bertolini (University of Amsterdam); Dr Enrica Papa (University of Ghent); Dr Wendy Tan (University of Groningen); Dr Cecilia Silva (University of Porto); Prof Angela Hull (Heriot Watt University); Prof Anssi Joutsiniemi (Tampere University of Technology); Prof Gebhard Wulfhorst and Mr Benjamin Büttner (Technical University Munich); Dr Anders Larsson (University of Gothenburg); Dr Dimitris Milakis (TU Delft).

- Dr Thomas Straatemeier of Goudappel Coffeng in the Netherlands for the opportunity to work on the Randstad region and providing Jan with an 'artist in residence' spot.

- Prof Kay Axhausen and Dr Alexander Erath from the Future Cities Laboratory, ETH Zurich who saved the Singapore analysis by providing land use data from their own research. The Land Transport Authority, Singapore and Urban Redevelopment Authority, Singapore for giving permission to use this data.

- Prof Gordon Price and Prof Anthony Perl, Simon Fraser University, Vancouver.

- Dr Craig Townsend, Mr Chris Harding and Ms Annelise Grube-Cavers, Concordia University, Montreal.

- Dr Andrea Broaddus, UC Berkeley and University College London.

- Prof Carsten Gertz, Dr Philine Gaffron, Ms Sonja Löwa and Mr Marcus Peter, Technical University of Hamburg.

- Mr Pau Noy, LAPTP, Barcelona, Prof Francesc Robusté and Mr Hugo Badia, CENIT, Universitat Politècnica de Catalunya.

- Mr Patrick Driscoll, Dr Morten Skou Nicolaisen, Ms Mette Jensen, Aalborg Universitet and Dr Thomas Sick Nielsen, DTU, Copenhagen.

- Dr Monica Menendez and Dr Noriko Otsuka, ETH Zurich, Dr Felix Laube, Zurich/Copenhagen.
- Prof Guenter Emberger, TU Vienna.
- Merten Nefs, Vereniging Delta-metropool.
- Dr Michelle Zeibots, UTS, Sydney.
- Prof Jago Dodson and Prof Neil Sipe, Griffith University, Brisbane.
- Prof Michael Taylor, University of Adelaide.
- Dr John Stone, Prof Kim Dovey, Mr Ian Woodcock and Dr Alison Barr, University of Melbourne.
- Prof Peter Newman, Dr Annie Matan, Dr Roman Trubka, Dr Cole Hendrigan, Dr James McIntosh, Curtin University; Prof Jeff Kenworthy, University of Frankfurt and Curtin University.
- Mr David Mayes, Mr Richard Smithers, Mr Stuart Outhred, Mr Damon Rao, Ms Anne Laing, City of Melbourne.
- The Association of European Schools of Planning (AESOP) Transport Research Group for their enduring interest in our presentations on SNAMUTS over the years as we struggled to develop ideas and present them coherently in 15 minutes! In particular (in addition to the COST team) Prof Petter Naess from Norwegian University of Life Sciences (NMBU) and Prof Akkie van Nes from TU Delft and University College Bergen.

We thank Valerie Rose at Ashgate for her enthusiasm for the project and for her patience and support in seeing the book through to publication.

Carey Curtis and Jan Scheurer

In addition to our joint acknowledgements we each have personal things we want to acknowledge.

I would like to thank my fellow author Jan. We have worked together now for many years – meeting first as members of the Fremantle Bicycle User Group and then taking turns to 'own' Babbaganoush, the cat. Our friendship cemented as we both got interested in accessibility – for me with what I thought would be a relatively easy question to answer – 'how can you compare three station precincts by their accessibility to the region?' Well it turned out the answer was more complex and the questions grew and grew! From here SNAMUTS developed with planning practice work in Perth and Melbourne and eventually the inspiration for the global study of cities. As with any good partnership we offer different and complementary skills – Jan's ability with fine detail and modelling complemented my contribution of strategic overview and application and as narrator to practitioners. That we both analyse in colour also helps! The research grant succeeded, but with serious budget cuts, and without Jan's bohemian lifestyle the fieldwork would not have been possible.

I thank my close colleagues in the Department of Urban and Regional Planning at Curtin University – Shane Greive, Paul Cozens, Dave Hedgcock, Garry Middle and Diana MacCallum – who did their best to support me in difficult times and to protect my time (against the odds) so that I could honour the research contract.

On a more personal note I acknowledge my partner David for his support. To my son Janni – well you were always telling me I should catch the bus to work – now here's the evidence as to just how challenging that task is! You and your generation have a mission – other cities in this book show that cities can offer great public transport accessibility.

Carey Curtis

I have little to add to Carey's wonderful description of the refreshingly non-linear evolution of our collaboration, which now spans a good decade and a half and is certain to embark on many more academic adventures in the future. Thanks! My gratitude also goes to my colleagues at RMIT University's Centre for Urban Research (CUR), who have provided me with an academic base since 2005 across a plethora of research grants, consultancy and short-term teaching contracts as well as periods of transition between funding sources. Thanks particularly to Serena Lim and Yani Iskandar for holding the administrative side of things together. At the other end of the continent, I was privileged to maintain a similar base at the Curtin University Sustainability Policy Institute (CUSP) – thank you to everyone and especially to Prof Peter Newman and Prof Jeff Kenworthy, whose inspiring work on global cities played no small part in encouraging me to embark on a mission of international fieldwork and comparative analysis of my own. More recently, RMIT Europe in Barcelona has become a welcoming host, and community, for the completion of this book.

Many friends and relatives supported my extensive travel, both in terms of stimulating exchanges and local expertise on a research topic that ultimately affects the daily life of most, and in terms of logistics. I am indebted particularly for the free accommodation and hospitality provided during field research and book writing stints by Valerie and Rüdiger (Seattle), Craig and Buk (Montreal), Bron and Ben (New York City), Ilse, Ulrich, Birgit, Olaf and Johnny (Hamburg), Maarten and Eva (Amsterdam), Marieke and Pjotr (Utrecht), Roland (Cologne), John and Susan (Edinburgh), Brenden, Valérie and Lee (Barcelona), Felix and Marcus (Zurich), Maria Miguel (Vienna), Linn and Sebastian (Munich), Anke and Alfred (Garmisch-Partenkirchen), Dave and Andrew (Perth), Ian, Flavia, Yamini and Nica (Melbourne), Margx (Sydney), and Odette and Jason (Wellington). Thanks too to my housemates (when I was still residentially settled) for enduring many long nights and days of nerding in their midst (interspersed, of course, with the odd social event to restore sanity!) – especially Sarah, Luke, Steven and Juliette in Melbourne, and Jana, Jett and all the other mansionistas in Fremantle.

Jan Scheurer

1 Introduction

What Is Accessibility Planning and Why Does It Matter?

Cities of the developed and developing world are facing major problems with ever increasing car congestion, rising fuel prices and the need to stem carbon emissions. In response many city planners and politicians are confronting the challenge of how to provide public transport to a standard which offers a viable alternative to the car. This challenge has several dimensions: establishing the most effective infrastructure interventions to make – both spatially and temporally – that enhance accessibility; considering how to link public transport infrastructure with urban development as a means of improving spatial accessibility; finding cost-effective solutions.

A major stumbling block in improving public transport accessibility is the lack of strategic overview. In our work to date (see, for example, Curtis and Scheurer, 2010; Curtis et al, 2013) we have noted that while city planners are prepared to embrace the challenge, they lack the technical planning support tools capable of supporting their endeavours. Accessibility tools provide one solution. Designed well, these tools can offer a means of measuring, visualising, and facilitating a stakeholder dialogue about efforts to better integrate transport and land use planning in contemporary cities. Such efforts have led to a variety of narratives on how such integration goals can be achieved in the specific local context of each city or city-region, and assist in the challenges set by the sustainability agenda and the transition to a low-carbon future. A critical overarching theme in this process is the reassessment of the role of public transport systems in the mobility mix of cities, and the imperative to increase the role of public transport modes for urban movement and accessibility particularly where current patterns of car use appear wasteful or excessive.

Historically, planning for urban public transport has seen a number of phases (Schaeffer and Sclar, 1975). Each phase has been the result, on the one hand, of the transport modes available at that time and the urban development needs of the city, and on the other hand, the result of transport policy choices made by bureaucrats and elected officials. Early cities relied on walking as the means of transport and city form was dictated accordingly. With the introduction of horse-powered buses and tramways in the early industrial age cities were able to expand, but for the most part remained compact with resultant health and sanitation problems. The development of suburban railways in the late nineteenth century facilitated greater spatial expansion of settlements, a favoured policy response to the ills of the industrial city, where railway owners were also land developers. The rise of the private motor car in the 1950s saw a significant further expansion of urban boundaries and investment in public transport was all too often abandoned as cities pursued the 'modern age'. Public transport was often relegated to a 'welfare option', deemed only necessary to supply a skeleton service to serve those not able to afford a car or unable to drive.

Since the 1980s there has been a paradigm shift towards sustainable mobility – a response to environmental and later social concerns of urban development, namely the carbon intensity, pollution effects, spatial and socio-economic inequities associated with individual motorised transport (Whitelegg, 1997). A result of these concerns has been a renewed interest in the role of urban public transport. Cities throughout the world are at different stages in the development of their urban public transport systems for the twenty-first century. Some have made astounding progress as they embrace the environmental and economic imperative to keep cities functioning with less reliance on private cars. Others remain tardy, unwilling to recognise that a transport system based on the car as the primary mode is on a collision course with the future resilience of cities. In either case, resource availability dictates that decisions about improving public transport accessibility must be carefully considered beyond simply choosing to keep investing in the car at the expense of public transport, particularly where the total transport budget is finite.

New accessibility tools can assist decision making. Their use can help answer critical planning questions. How should the city develop in future – what is the most suitable urban form to optimise public transport accessibility – polycentric/monocentric, contiguous/dispersed, concentrated and/or decentralised? How should we invest in public transport infrastructure – what are the public transport modes, and their interplay, that deliver the best accessibility outcomes under what physical conditions? What should the focus of operational resources be on – the top-performing routes (by patronage) or a spread to increase network coverage (Walker, 2012)?

This book provides a 'hands-on' introduction to the evolution, rationale and effectiveness of a new generation of accessibility planning tools that have emerged since the mid-2000s. The Spatial Network Analysis for Multimodal Urban Transport Systems (SNAMUTS) tool, one such tool developed by the authors, is used as a practical example to demonstrate how city planners can find answers to the questions that arise as they seek to improve the accessibility of their city by public transport.

Uniquely among the new generation of accessibility tools, SNAMUTS has been designed for multi-city comparisons. A range of indicators are employed in each city. Each indicator is designed to measure key aspects of the system, including the effectiveness of the public transport network itself; the relationship between the transport network and land use activity; who gets access within the city; and how resilient the city is. The latter indicator addresses where future opportunities for growth and potential bottlenecks may be located. For each city, these indicators are set against the background of their differing historical development, urban geography and settlement form, spatial configuration of public transport networks and their institutional governance, and strategic plans for the future.

RESEARCH APPROACH

This book draws on a major research project which set out to provide a national benchmark for public transport accessibility in Australian cities by analysing the experience of a range of international cities. For us, integral to our concept of public transport accessibility is the need to consider the accessibility of the transport network and the accessibility of place (the opportunities different places provide to those using the network). This approach lies at the heart of new ideas of land use–transport integration, whereby cities are developed so that public transport can support people's daily activities as an alternative to the car, and also that land use (activity) can support public transport (by optimising patterns of patronage).

Our interest was in whether an accessibility tool could be employed to deliver comparable outputs for cities and regions with different cultures and histories concerning the evolution and state of the built environment as well as planning and transport policies and institutions. If this could be achieved, then the knowledge could inform Australian policy shapers, and ideally benchmarks could be set for improvements to urban public transport aimed at offering a quality service to all (where currently only between 5 and 10 per cent of trips are made by public transport in Australian metropolitan areas). The challenge was how to design an accessibility tool to address the performance of all relevant transport modes and land use trends within a specific urban or regional environment – bearing in mind the considerable differences in public transport service. We were also interested in how an accessibility tool could be communicated and utilised effectively among a broad range of stakeholders with varying degrees of influence and articulation in the political process and public arena. This book demonstrates the ability of accessibility tools to do just that. Further, we dream that citizens will take up an interest in the question of just how accessible their city is by public transport, especially compared to the car, and use this book as a resource to seek improvements.

STRUCTURE OF THE BOOK

While accessibility analysis is not new, there is an emerging range of new tools. These have been designed to address contemporary urban planning and transport issues. Many tools remain in the ivory towers of researchers, a limited few have been taken up in planning practice (te Brömmelstroet et al, 2014), and of those, some have been successfully utilised to inform future development and infrastructure investment (Curtis et al, 2013; Curtis and Scheurer, 2010). In Chapter 2 we take the reader through the key network theory and best practice concepts informing the design of the SNAMUTS tool. The eight component indicators are explained alongside practical questions emerging from the introductory discussion. Our aim is to provide the explanations in layman's terms, thus making the language of transport accessibility accessible to both professionals and interested citizens in terms that align with everyday experience of getting around their city.

Chapters 3 to 8 are organised around six themes consistent with the key questions about planning for public transport in different situations across the globe. Each chapter also features an accessibility profile of each city, illustrated with SNAMUTS maps of each core indicator.

Chapter 3 explores the theme of continuity and change in the Australasian cities of Perth, Melbourne, Sydney, Adelaide, Brisbane and Auckland. These cities are by and large characterised by a low-density, horizontally dispersed urban form, strong central cities and high rates of urban growth. Public transport networks are anchored by long-standing radial suburban rail systems and a post-war policy history of prioritising the needs of car-based transport over those of public transport. In recent years, pressures from rising petrol prices, increasing road congestion, a resurgence of public transport usage and a shifting preference particularly of younger generations towards inner urban living have begun to influence the policy focus on the potential of public transport to capture a much greater share of the urban travel market.

Chapter 4 continues with the analysis of New World cities. The theme of stagnation and aspiration paints the picture for a sample of North American cities which share some similarities with their Australian counterparts in terms of their generally high growth rates and the prevalence of post-war, low-density suburban form. There are also some differences in public transport supply, particularly the absence of historically grown suburban rail networks that make a significant contribution to urban mobility in much of the US and Canada. Hence, most contemporary North American public transport networks are the outcome of recent retrofits with high-capacity infrastructure elements. The selection of the four cities – Seattle, Portland, Montreal and Vancouver – reflects the breadth of approaches found across the continent, where city planners seek to establish a new role for public transport in cities that had embraced automobility like no others during a now fading phase of their evolution.

From the New World cities we move to the Old World established cities. In Chapter 5 the theme is 'more with less' exploring the relationship between fostering efficiency in a public transport system and achieving accessibility outcomes. European cities follow a range of approaches to designing and managing the public transport–land use context, owing to their varying cultural and historical characteristics as well as varying governance arrangements and planning traditions. The four cities selected – Hamburg, Munich, Porto and Edinburgh – provide an overview of these different approaches. Munich, in less than 50 years, has transitioned from a public transport system based primarily on radial suburban rail and urban trams to one where an expansive metro system designed for the needs of the post-war city forms the backbone of movement, supplemented by trams and buses in a lean, integrated multimodal network. Hamburg's approach has a greater complexity, characterised by the need to adapt pre-existing rapid transit systems during post-war reconstruction and the inability to complete the post-war metro expansion program that had served as the rationale for closing the tram system. Edinburgh represents another extreme. The city openly encouraged different public transport operators to compete for passengers in the same network segments, creating a heavily serviced bus system designed to minimise transfers between services. Porto's bus network is similarly structured to Edinburgh's, but has seen a gradual transformation towards greater multimodal integration when a new light rail system was introduced at the beginning of this century.

Staying with Europe, Chapter 6 follows the theme 'eclipsing the car'. Drawing on the cities of Copenhagen, Zurich, Vienna and Barcelona, it becomes evident that there have been dedicated efforts to rein in the role of the car for urban mobility and that this has been underpinned by redirection of resources. Copenhagen has a well-performing, though in a European comparison somewhat underutilised, public transport system whose main competitor in inner urban areas is the bicycle rather than the car – bicycle use is higher than in any other major city except Amsterdam. In Zurich, a metropolitan region with a pronounced dispersed–concentrated settlement structure, departure from a program of urban freeway and metro building in the 1970s led to a strategy to optimise and upgrade existing suburban rail, tram and trolleybus networks into a superbly organised multimodal system. In Vienna, public transport developed as a majority mode through well-targeted infrastructure investments aimed at optimising transport tasks and transport modes. In Barcelona, there has been a strategy to gradually reduce the role of the car in the very dense inner area in favour of improved public transport, expanded pedestrianisation and the reintroduction of the bicycle.

Chapter 9 brings Asian cities into the analysis with a theme of 'transit-dominance' in an examination of Singapore and Hong Kong. The extraordinarily rapid growth of high-capacity urban rail systems, now mirrored in many cities across mainland China and other developing Asian countries, has generated a significant land use–transport integration trend and generated accessibility outcomes that will profoundly shape the future form of cities on this most populated continent.

Up to this point the accessibility analysis has focussed mainly on cities developed at the metropolitan scale. In Chapter 8 we examine a settlement trend that has emerged in many urban agglomerations as they grow and begin to merge and overlap geographically. Clusters of self-contained, monocentric cities evolve into multi-centred wider urban regions with growing degrees of regional interdependency and cross-commuting, a process aided by the establishment of high-speed rail or other fast public transport links. We use the example of the Dutch Randstad, a polycentric region comprised of the major centres of Amsterdam, Den Haag, Rotterdam, Utrecht and many smaller cities.

Finally Chapter 9 brings together the analysis to enable a reflection on policy questions of importance to planners including the public transport mix and infrastructure that can deliver the best accessibility outcomes; the type of urban form and structure that can optimise accessibility by public transport; the operational input and efficiency.

2 Spatial Network Analysis for Multimodal Urban Transport Systems (SNAMUTS)

Understanding the Indicators

INTRODUCTION

In order to understand the accessibility analysis of cities presented in the following chapters it is important to explain the construct and rationale behind each indicator used. The starting point for developing an accessibility tool is to take the perspective of an everyday user of a city's land use–transport system. Everyday users make, and are often constrained by, long-term decisions about where their everyday activities take place, for example, the location of home, workplace, schools and the homes of regular social contacts such as family members or close friends. These locations generally change infrequently, and for many people, the spatial arrangement of these anchor activities will influence any changes they are in a position to make. Individuals also make many short-term, discretionary decisions about activities: where to go shopping, where to socialise away from home, where to engage in recreational pursuits, and how often any of these things occur. A critical premise of accessibility research is to recognise the impact that urban structure and the available transport networks have on the location and distribution of these activities. Everyday users are more likely to frequent activities and places that they perceive as convenient to access. To the extent that such destinations form clusters where a significant number or variety of activities are contained within relatively small areas, we can begin to understand a city as a composition of 'activity hotspots' or sub-centres, forming the hubs or nodes of a network in which transport infrastructures act as the links or edges.

People, especially in wealthy and relatively compact cities or parts of cities, are also likely to have a choice of transport modes to get around. They can draw on the services of overlapping, sometimes complimentary and sometimes competing networks for private motorised transport, public transport, walking and cycling. For public transport to assume a significant role in the mobility mix of a city it must offer a viable alternative for as many travel purposes as possible. It must be well aligned with the land uses it serves. The most significant factor in attracting choice travellers to a public transport network is its ability to offer an equivalent to the 'go anywhere, anytime' convenience usually associated with the private car, or at a smaller spatial range with non-motorised modes. In large cities, the best way to achieve this is usually to configure public transport as a multimodal network that allows travel along geographical desire lines, at service frequencies high enough to not require timetable consultation, and with seamless transfers between vehicles both in terms of physical co-location and in terms of integrated ticketing and timetable coordination. The interplay of these characteristics is what is known as the 'network effect' of public transport services, where the ability of the network as a whole to provide accessibility is superior to that of the sum of its individual components (Mees, 2010a; Nielsen et al, 2005; Walker, 2012).

In understanding accessibility we need to find out the extent to which such network-based synergy has been optimised for the land use–transport context in a given city, and to pinpoint areas with room for further improvement. On this basis we have established a set of tasks and measurements that highlight the challenge of land use–transport integration from a range of perspectives:

- What is the number of public transport services required to achieve an optimal level of accessibility across the network, noting that resources may be limited?
- What is the ease of movement offered on public transport across the city and for each route? Fast and/or frequent services reduce 'spatial resistance' to the user compared to slow and/or infrequent services.
- What is the transfer intensity of the network? While transfers are a necessary component of an integrated public transport network, is there a way of measuring whether their occurrence may be excessive or underdeveloped?
- What is the percentage of residents and employees within walking-distance to public transport services at a standard that allows for both planned and spontaneous trip making across most hours of the day, seven days a week?

- What is the geographical range users can cover by way of a public transport journey within a particular time frame, and how many destinations are located within this range?

- How does the public transport network channel concentrate and disperse the travel opportunities generated by the interplay of land uses and the transport system? Where on the network do these effects result in a potential mismatch between public transport supply and potential demand?

- How well is each activity centre connected in order to attract stopovers on public transport chain journeys and encourage land use intensification to capitalise on such flows of people?

- Can the results of these indicators be calibrated to arrive at a comparative scale for public transport accessibility between different cities and within one city over a time line?

KEY ASSUMPTIONS AND DEFINITIONS OF SNAMUTS

To analyse and quantify these different aspects of accessibility performance, Spatial Network Analysis for Multimodal Urban Transport Systems (SNAMUTS) has been developed as a GIS tool operating on a database that captures the configuration and service levels of the public transport network in question. It can be used for the networks of entire metropolitan regions as well as for specifically defined subregions or corridors.

The core methodology of SNAMUTS has primarily been inspired by the Space Syntax theory (Hillier and Hanson, 1984) and by the Multiple Centrality Analysis tool (Porta et al, 2006a, 2006b). Space Syntax investigates the organising principles within built environments or movement networks and their inherent patterns of relationships. Among the resulting categories is the distinction of convex (topological) and metric shapes, a dichotomy that also constitutes the Multiple Centrality Analysis methodology as primal and dual graphs of spatial representation. In brief, the topological perspective examines the degrees of separation between a pair of objects in a spatial context or network, measured in changes of direction, passages through doors or gateways, or (in public transport networks) number of transfers. In contrast, the metric perspective examines the objects' distance from each other, expressed either in common measurements of distance (kilometres, miles) and/or by a proxy measure (travel time, travel cost, ease of movement). Operationalised for analytic output, these categories inform the concepts of *degree centrality* and *closeness centrality*, a terminology used frequently in the analysis of networks (Neal, 2013) and adopted for the SNAMUTS indicator set with some important variations (discussed below). Space syntax merges degree centrality and closeness centrality by developing concepts of integration and connectivity (Hillier, 1996). This understanding allows us to query whether a location that is functionally *well-connected* to others (spatially or visually overlapping) is also *well-integrated* with others (easy to get to and from) – or whether there are prominent mismatches between these properties, which can have a detrimental impact on a network's legibility and resilience.

This insight provides a potent vantage point for the development of an accessibility tool, particularly in a complex urban system where overlapping movement networks (such as for pedestrians, motor vehicles and off-street public transport) act partially in concert with and partially in competition to each other. Put simply, are those locations within an urban system that have the largest number and concentration of activities also the locations that can be accessed most easily? How does their accessibility by public transport differ from that by other modes? Since public transport distributes patrons through a limited number of access points (rail stations or bus stops), patrons cannot frequent intermediate land uses in the same way that pedestrians, cyclists or motorists can (albeit with some constraints regarding the availability of parking for the latter). Underground railway passengers are also visually removed from what occurs above ground in land use terms. The relationship between movement and urban form is thus a different one in public transport networks than in those for individualised modes of transport. A useful way to understand this is to see public transport access points in terms of both nodes and places (Bertolini, 1999).

Bertolini's 'node-place model' notes that while railway stations provide access to the transport network, which he defines as the 'node' element in his model, they also offer a 'place' function. So the railway station precinct can also be a destination where land use activities are available to public transport users and others. The place function, or accessibility of opportunity, is an important aspect of our inquiry and urges us to see accessibility not only in terms of 'ease of movement' or 'degrees of separation'. The extent of concentration of activities around public transport facilities, as well as within a specific travel time range to and from each destination, emerge as equally critical factors in understanding accessibility. These concepts inform the SNAMUTS measures of *network coverage* and *contour catchments*.

In the node-place model the observation that there can be 'balanced' or 'unbalanced' node-places is also important. A *balanced node-place* benefits from a good match between the level of transport network accessibility and the mix of activities (opportunities) to access within the precinct. In this way both the transport network and the place are efficiently used. An *unbalanced node* suffers from good transport network access but a limited number and range of activities, while an *unbalanced place* will be characterised by a vibrant mix and concentration of activities but poor transport network access. Further, node-places can experience stress where both node and place functions are exceptionally high, generating pressures such as transport network and interchange congestion, strong market demand for further land use intensification and increasing property values (Bertolini, 2005). To examine and quantify these dynamics, SNAMUTS returns to a concept from the Multiple Centrality Analysis toolbox known as *betweenness centrality* (Porta et al, 2006a, 2006b). This set of measures aims to assess and visualise how the distribution of land uses in a settlement area and their interdependence generate travel opportunities in accordance with the spatial configuration and service levels of the public transport network. We have also focussed specifically on the phenomena of stress and resilience in the land use–transport system by deriving a dedicated *network resilience* measure from the betweenness results.

A MATRIX OF ACTIVITY NODES

To produce a set of accessibility indicators for a land use–transport system, SNAMUTS assesses the hierarchy of central places in an urban area. Strategic planning documents can assist with the identification of district, regional or neighbourhood centres (where there are clusters of employment, retail, education or health facilities, recreational uses and/or large concentrations of residences). Extensive on-site observation and, where available, station or stop-specific public transport boarding data is used to pinpoint activity centres. A matrix of central places and nodes is compiled as each potential origin-destination pair is subjected to a GIS-based way-finding procedure. An activity centre is included if it is spatially associated with a particular public transport access point or interchange and if its walkable catchment (an 800-metre radius for rail stations and ferry ports or a 400-metre corridor around surface routes) contains an average minimum of 10,000 residents and jobs. In some cases, however, network nodes with no or weak associated land use clusters (the 'unbalanced node' archetype) are prominent within an urban area, such as where major public transport corridors follow freeways or freight rail lines without historic activity centres in their vicinity, and with limited amenity to attract the emergence of new ones. Multimodal public transport interchanges of this type are generally included in the matrix despite their often limited residential and employment catchments.

MINIMUM SERVICE STANDARD

Public transport network elements are included in the analysis where they meet a minimum level of service. The rationale relates to user amenity. To be perceived as a regular service where transport users can organise both planned and spontaneous activities, public transport must allow for a degree of flexibility in personal schedule (i.e. run at a minimum frequency) and maintain a presence throughout the day and week (i.e. have operation hours that cover most or all potential travel purposes). The minimum standard also defines an outer geographical limit to the network (as the minimum service standard is usually not upheld for intra-urban and long-distance public transport links) and so shapes the city form SNAMUTS actually analyses.

The minimum service standard SNAMUTS uses is flexible in theory. In this book, however, a uniform minimum standard is applied (SNAMUTS 23) in order to maintain the comparability of results across case study cities. This requires a service frequency of 20 minutes (or better) during the weekday inter-peak period (about 10.00 to 15.00 hours) and 30 minutes (or better) during weekend days for surface modes (bus and tram), and a 30-minute frequency on weekdays combined with service seven days a week for segregated rail and ferry modes. The differentiation in service standard between modes with or without dedicated right-of-way reflects the ability of rail stations or ferry terminals to act as anchors for urban activities and attractors for land use development in their own right, an effect that tends to be significantly weaker with surface routes, particularly on-street buses.

Many conventional models of public transport performance focus on the weekday peak hours, since this is usually the period when the capacity constraints of a network are most apparent. But in most public transport systems, this is also the period when service levels are optimised to facilitate specific trip purposes (work and school journeys). In contrast, the weekday inter-peak period offers the greatest diversity of travel purposes and, we assert, determines most critically the potential of public transport to offer a viable alternative to the 'go anywhere, anytime' convenience of the car.

STRUCTURAL INDICATORS

For each city in the database we present a set of three indicators that serve to position their size, structure and role of public transport in a broader context: the total residential population within the metropolitan area; the average settlement density of the urbanised area in residents and jobs per hectare; and the number of public transport trips per capita per year. Each of these indicators requires detailed definitions (see Appendix 1) and there is a potential for incongruity among the data as they are sourced from a large number of different agencies in different cities. These local records may utilise varying definitions for the component data sets that make up these indicators.

SERVICE INTENSITY

This indicator, derived from the network analysis, measures the operational input required to provide the service levels across the system (at the minimum service standard). The number of vehicles for each mode that are in simultaneous revenue service during the weekday inter-peak period is counted. The index is expressed relative to metropolitan population (vehicles or train sets per 100,000 residents). Note that the figures for the actual numbers of vehicles required by the operators are higher as no provision is made for service breaks at the termini, contingencies for delays or disruptions, non-revenue journeys, and for vehicles undergoing scheduled or unscheduled maintenance. Greater numbers of vehicles are also generally required to operate peak hour services.

No differentiation is made between vehicles of varying capacity or performance, since the interest is in counting travel opportunities available for the transport user. Providing passengers are not turned away for overcrowding, and discounting for the effect of different travel times, a 40-seater bus every 10 minutes offers the same number of opportunities for passengers to get from A to B as a 600-person metro train every 10 minutes along the same route. Moreover, we are interested in the operational effort required to run the service, and particularly the staff cost which in developed cities forms a significant part of the total cost of operations. Each train, tram or bus in operation generally requires one on-board staff member (the driver); exceptions include some automated rail systems and the presence of conductors on some services.

Service intensity can be interpreted in two ways. Firstly, it illustrates the generosity of an operator to provide resources, and secondly, the efficiency of their deployment. For example, higher frequencies will increase the figures while shorter travel times will reduce them, yet both approaches will result in improvements on most other SNAMUTS accessibility indicators. Thus the ratio between service intensity changes and shifts on the accessibility measures (below) can help to determine the efficacy of initiatives to expand/reduce public transport services. This duality of service largesse and service efficiency can also be observed where a dominant role for fast high-capacity modes, particularly heavy rail, will tend to depress relative service intensity figures, while a large number of high-frequency, slow-moving surface routes inflates them. The intensity figure also increases, all other factors being equal, where settlement areas are dispersed or separated by geographical barriers, thus lengthening journey distances and times between places of activity. High service intensity scores are therefore not necessarily indicative of better service, but rather are indicative of the level of resources agencies are prepared to allocate to operation.

CLOSENESS CENTRALITY

This indicator describes the spatial properties of a public transport system and relates to the metric function of networks (discussed above). It is based on a proxy index for spatial separation, or *travel impediment*. Rather than accounting for metric distance between origin and destination, this travel impediment measure takes in travel time and service frequency, since both measures are key concerns of public transport users. These inputs are derived from published timetables that form part of the regular user information provided by public transport agencies. Travel time can vary greatly in relation to metric distance, depending on the speed of the service: in many cities, a metro train on a fully segregated alignment can cover a distance of several kilometres in the same time it takes a bus to cover only one kilometre along the streets of a congested central area. Service frequency adds a travel opportunity factor to the equation: the more travel opportunities per unit of time and the shorter the duration of the journey, the lower the travel impediment. From ample experimentation with different formulas we have concluded that the most meaningful way to express the ratio of these two factors in an impediment measure is to divide the travel time in minutes by the square root of frequency in departures per hour (multiplied by four to arrive at more readable numbers).

This travel impediment measure is calculated separately for each route segment (link between two adjacent nodes) across the network. A GIS wayfinding tool then automatically determines, out of all possible paths between each pair of nodes, the path with the lowest cumulative impediment while allowing up to three transfers between different lines. Closeness centrality is shown as an average value across the network, and as an average for each activity node. Lower values indicate better performance or greater *ease of movement*. Good area-wide ease of movement is achieved in lattice-shaped networks with a multitude of transfer points; conversely, in tree-shaped networks closeness values deteriorate rapidly from centre to periphery. The two network sections of Melbourne's northeast (shown below) demonstrate how closeness centrality improved after orbital bus links were added to the radial public transport in the area and how these benefits become progressively more apparent with increasing distance from the city centre. However, this circumstance is

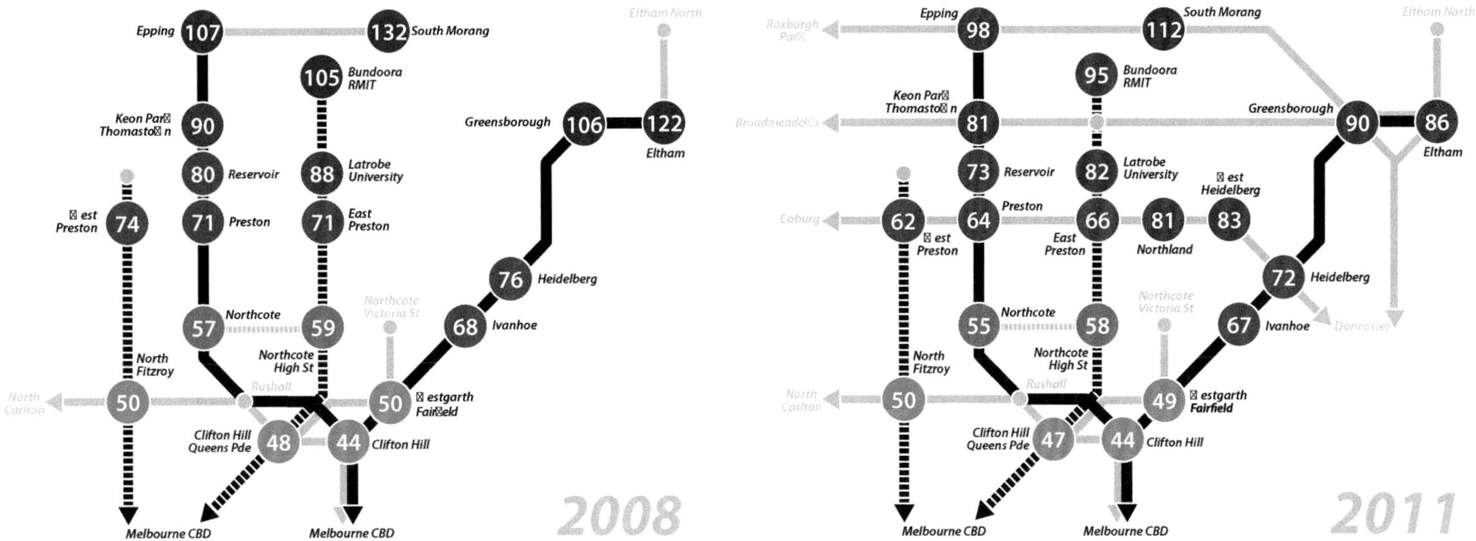

sometimes determined by urban geography or settlement patterns rather than purely by network design. Cities with more dispersed settlement patterns and more convoluted links between places of activity are at a disadvantage for public transport accessibility compared to more compact ones or ones with faster public transport systems.

DEGREE CENTRALITY

The second indicator describing the structural network properties takes a topological perspective: measuring the *degrees of separation* between each pair of nodes. Traditionally, degree centrality is used to measure the number of network paths converging in a node, for example, the number of separate streets radiating from an intersection (Neal, 2013). In a public transport network, the most meaningful way to capture this measure is by counting the number of transfers required to make the journey in question, suggesting that a node has the same degree of connection to all other nodes that are located along the same public transport lines as itself. Degree centrality, in the SNAMUTS tool, thus describes the *transfer intensity* or the *directness of journeys* along the public transport network. Use of the same GIS wayfinding tool as the closeness centrality index, the tool determines the path with the minimum number of transfers, even if this leads to a greater cumulative travel impediment value (as slower and/or lower-frequency routes are being used). Degree centrality is shown as an average value across the network and as an average for each activity node. Lower values indicate lower transfer intensity.

The index reveals hierarchical patterns in the network structure: it can pinpoint the roles that are allocated to different public transport modes, as well as the opportunities for multi-directional movement fostered by the network. In the example of Hamburg's northern suburbs (below) there are consistently low (less transfer-intensive) results at activity nodes along the radial rail lines, with the lowest scores at stations where several rail lines intersect (Barmbek and Ohlsdorf). Conversely, degree centrality values spike in activity nodes that depend on relatively short bus feeders to nearby rail stations and allow for movement in only one or two directions (Hummelsbüttel, Bergstedt,

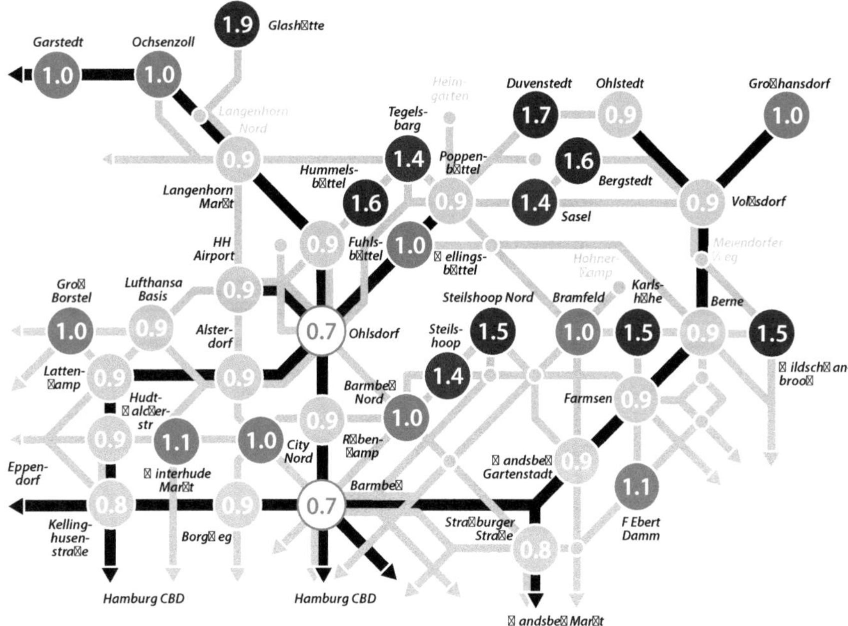

Duvenstedt and Glashütte). In other bus-only nodes, there are greater opportunities to travel in a broader range of directions, and for longer distances as the bus lines link into a number of activity nodes elsewhere in the city. Accordingly, the degree centrality results are much closer to the level found along the rail lines (Groß Borstel, Lufthansa Basis, Winterhude Markt, City Nord, Barmbek Nord and Bramfeld). A further group of nodes (Steilshoop, Karlshöhe, Tegelsbarg, Sasel) occupies an intermediate position between these extremes.

Low average degree centrality is indicative of a well-connected metropolitan network, but it can also be indicative of another type of network design encountered in several of our case study cities (the bus networks of Edinburgh, Hong Kong and Singapore). This network design aims at transfer-free connections between as many nodes and corridors as possible by offering many separate, low to mid-frequency lines. It is characterised by a flat hierarchy of modes and different types of services. In contrast, networks where most corridors are only serviced by a single, mid- to high-frequency line are configured around a greater reliance on transfers in the interest of operational efficiency, reliability and system legibility. In these networks (see Vienna and Zurich), the convenience of transfers is usually enhanced by supportive measures such as through-ticketing, timetable coordination between connecting services and their physical integration into purpose-designed transfer facilities (Nielsen et al, 2005). Average degree centrality results across the network, however, tend to climb accordingly.

NETWORK COVERAGE

This index illustrates who receives walkable access to public transport and who does not. Walkable catchments around stations and stops[1] are superimposed on a land use map and the number of residents and jobs contained within are counted. The proportion of this figure of the metropolitan total provides the network coverage result. It can be read as a proxy for the inclination of city decision-makers to supply public transport services of a certain standard to as large a pool of potential users as reasonably possible.

High network coverage can be characterised as a policy goal competing with the quest to simply maximise ridership, given that a limited pool of operational resources can be allocated to enlarge the geographical reach of the network rather than concentrate only on those routes or network segments that offer the greatest potential for patronage or mode share growth (Walker, 2012). Given that SNAMUTS measures network coverage only for services that meet or exceed the minimum standard and thus already pass a certain productivity level, network coverage should

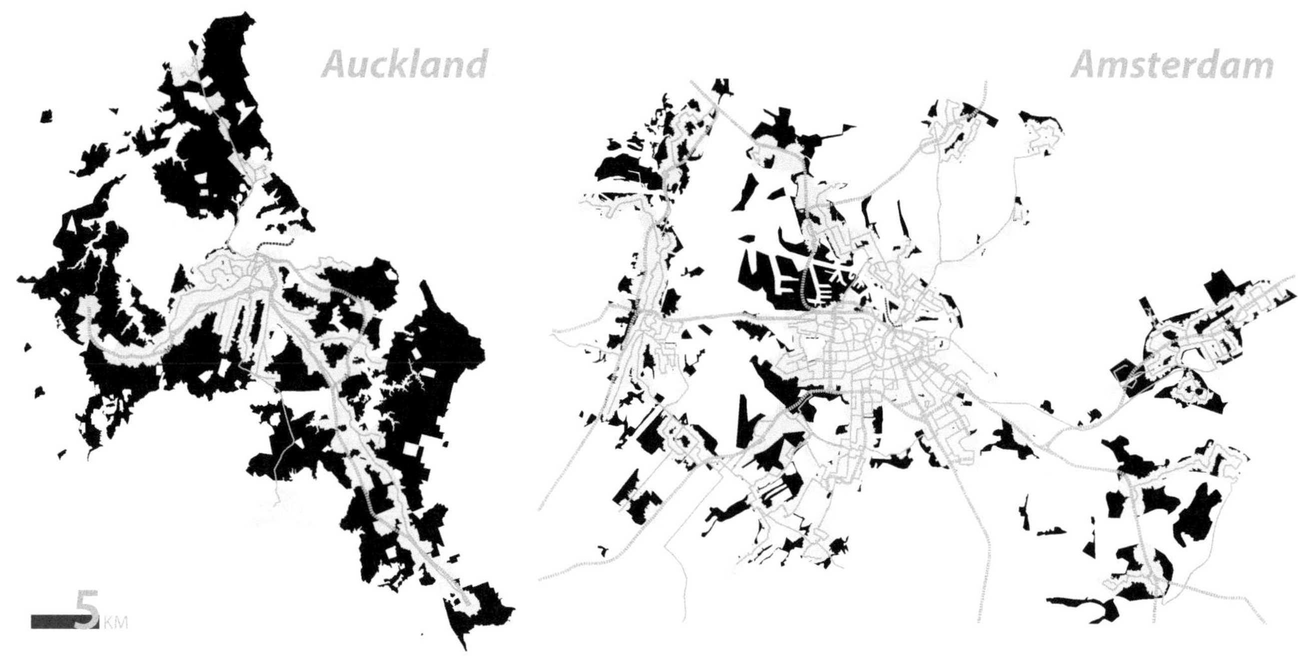

be expected to grow with increasing service intensity. However, where the goal of network coverage overrides the goal of addressing the capacity needs of the most popular services in the allocation of resources, we should expect this index to be correlated in inverse proportion with the network resilience index (discussed below).

The maps above show the metropolitan areas of Auckland, which has the lowest network coverage (33 per cent) of the case study cities, and Amsterdam, which has one of the highest (80 per cent). In Auckland, public transport at the SNAMUTS minimum standard is only provided along the most important radial corridors, leaving adjacent land serviced at a poorer standard, if at all. In Amsterdam (whose population is about 50 per cent higher than Auckland's), it extends across most of the settlement area.

THIRTY-MINUTE CONTOUR CATCHMENTS

The contour catchments index adds detail and qualification to the network coverage measure. A proportion of the total figure of metropolitan residents and jobs within walking distance to public transport is allocated by drawing a walkable catchment area specific to each activity node, consisting of the rail station radius (including, where applicable, those of neighbouring smaller stations that do not carry SNAMUTS activity node status in their own right) and/or the linear corridors of surface modes converging in the activity node. Boundaries with neighbouring activity node catchments along these corridors are determined by geographical barriers such as watercourses, or administrative borders, or simply set at the geometrical halfway point. Wherever two or more activity nodes are in such close proximity that their immediate 400/800-metre radii overlap more than marginally, the residents and jobs contained within the overlap zone are allocated in equal proportions to each activity node catchment. Importantly, the sum of residents and jobs within all activity node catchments in a metropolitan area is equal to the total network coverage figure.

The 30-minute contour catchment index counts the residents and jobs within all defined activity node catchments than can be reached from the reference point by way of a kerb-to-kerb public transport journey of 30 minutes or less (a travel time contour around each activity node). The calculation is done for the inbound and the outbound travel direction and, should the contour lines differ (travel times can vary between directions), the average of the two is used. The assessment allows for a maximum of one transfer during the 30-minute window while accounting for the average network-wide duration of a transfer (from arrival of the first vehicle to departure of the second vehicle) and requiring that both legs of the transfer journey are operated at least every 15 minutes during the reference period (weekday daytime). The contour catchment index is expressed as a percentage of the total number of metropolitan residents and jobs and is shown for each node as well as an average for all nodes. By definition, no individual nodal contour catchment score can exceed the aggregate value for network coverage.

The contour catchment is a composite indicator using parameters from several fields of inquiry and so is sensitive to manipulation of each component. Contour catchments are influenced by land use factors such as the density and concentration of urban settlement, changes to which will alter the results on this index even if the geographical extent of the contour line remains constant. They are also influenced by the speed of public transport, the configuration and density of the network and, as per our transfer definition elaborated above, the prevalence of service frequencies of 15 minutes or better. As these aspects are subject to change, the size of the contour can be expected to expand or shrink. At a broader scale, contour catchments are further influenced by the spacing of activity centres within the metropolitan area. Hence, they can also be read as a proxy measure for an agglomeration's degree of compactness or dispersal.

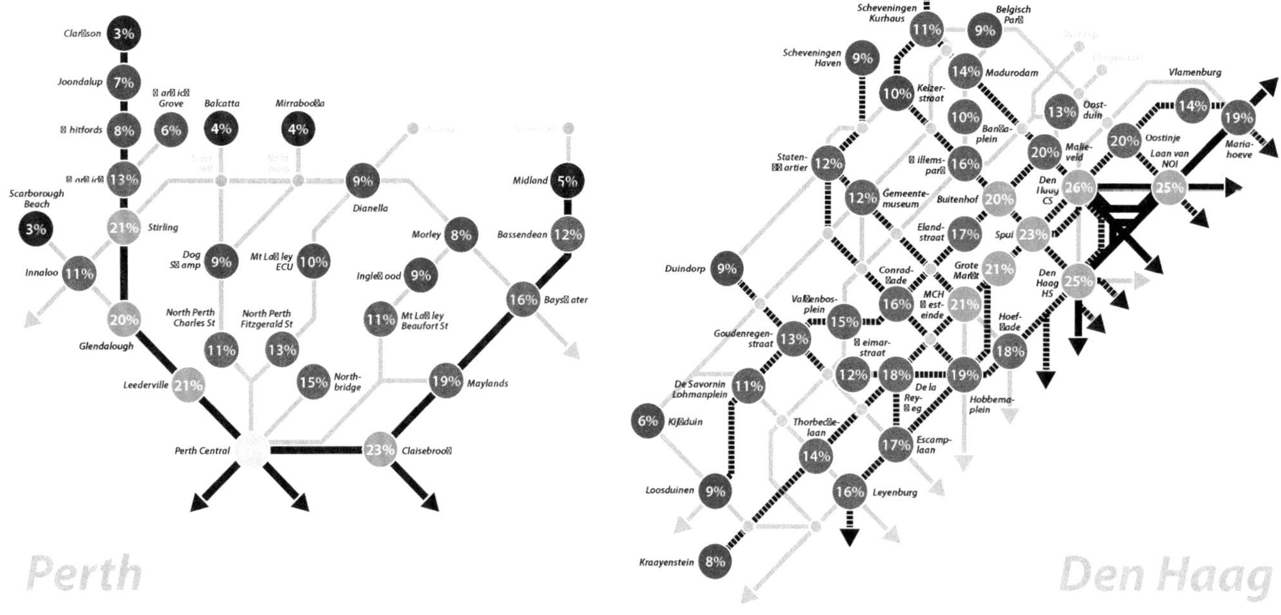

The sensitivity of the contour catchment index to travel speeds and network configuration is shown on page 16. In Perth's low-density northern suburbs, contour catchment results deteriorate much more rapidly along the slow-moving radial bus routes than along the faster-moving rail routes. This is particularly obvious when comparing the nodes where the orbital bus corridor bisects the rail lines (Stirling, Bayswater) with those where it intersects with other bus lines (Innaloo, Dianella, Morley). In contrast, Den Haag's medium-density, more multi-directional, grid-shaped surface network of trams and buses with comparable travel speeds has a more even, roughly diamond-shaped, decay from centre to periphery.

BETWEENNESS CENTRALITY

This index offers an image of the movement opportunities derived from the spatial distribution of land uses on the one hand, and the configuration and service levels of the public transport network on the other hand. The most attractive travel path between each pair of nodes is traced through all the intermediate network elements (nodes and route segments) passed along the journey. The most attractive or *preferred path* is determined by a synthesis of the approaches used in the closeness and degree centrality indexes (out of the path with the lowest cumulative travel impediment and the path with the lowest number of transfers): the path with the lower overall travel time (including transfers) is selected. Each of these paths is then weighted by two measures: First, the number of residents and jobs in the catchment area of the activity nodes at either end, following a logic of agglomeration where larger activity centres generate more travel opportunities between them than smaller ones. Second, a weighting for the travel impediment associated with the path is used, following a logic of gravity where activity centres within easy reach of each other generate more travel opportunities between them than those more remote to each other. All preferred paths across the activity node matrix are then counted, according to their weighting, at every activity node and route segment along the way. The map output illustrates the flow patterns of travel opportunities across the network. It is visually similar to a travel demand map, where passengers or vehicles are counted along particular routes or roads and then represented graphically by lines of varying thickness. But in this case, it is the *supply properties* of the network configuration that are captured. Actual travel demand can and does differ from the presence and strength of travel opportunities provided. This is because, besides the level of spatial accessibility offered, demand for public transport is also determined by the comparative availability, cost, speed, convenience and/or safety of alternative modes of transport, the extent of information available and accessible to users about the service, as well as socio-demographic and cultural factors. All of these influences are likely to vary between cities as well as for different travel purposes and geographical trip relations within the same city.

The betweenness centrality index visualises the *potential* for public transport to cater for urban movement. It shows where such 'movement energy' is concentrated and thus, to what extent an activity node or a transport corridor is located 'at the crossroads' of public transport supply – *between* other nodes, so to speak (Neal, 2013). The scale of this indicator is arbitrary but is kept to a uniform standard across all case study cities, allowing for both between-city and within-city comparisons over a time line. Two variations are represented: nodal betweenness (where the concentration of travel opportunities is measured at each activity node) and segmental betweenness (where it is measured along each route segment). Higher values indicate a greater concentration of travel opportunities.

The illustration below shows the segmental betweenness assessment of orbital bus routes introduced in Melbourne's north-eastern suburbs in 2010. The labels depict the concentration of network-wide travel opportunities attracted to each route segment.

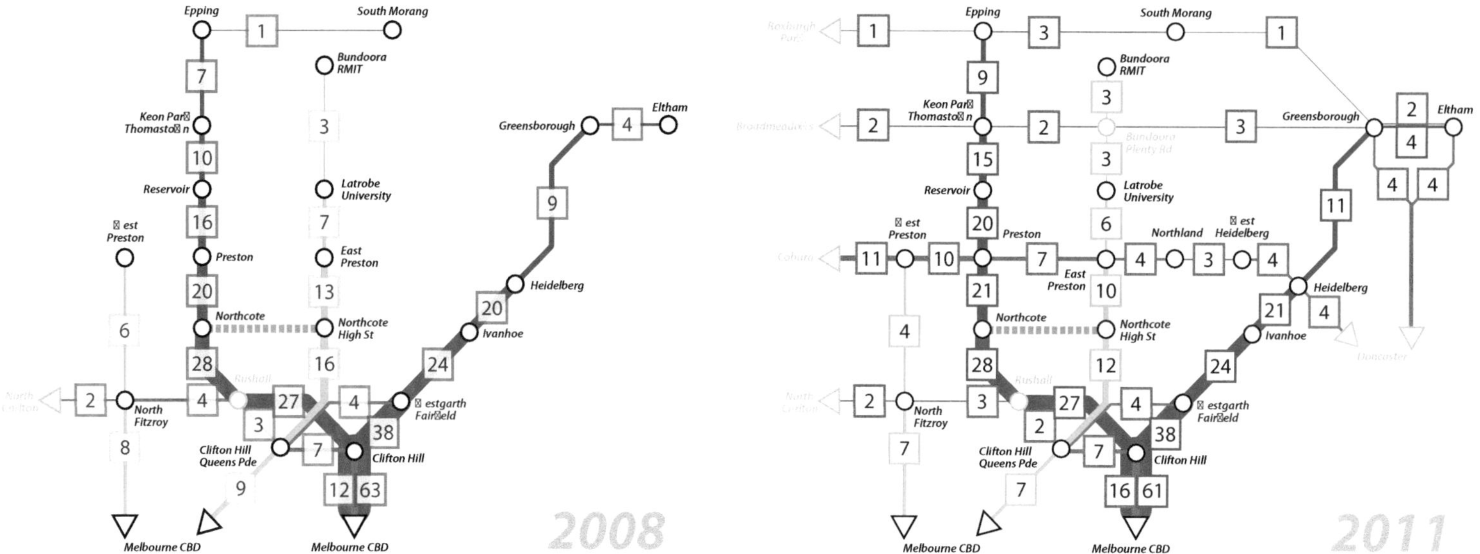

On the radial rail and tram lines, the concentration of travel opportunities increases with growing proximity to the city centre as the catchments of intermediate nodes add to their number. In the 2008 case, this increase is linear until North Fitzroy, Rushall and Clifton Hill are reached where the network is more connected and travel paths can disperse in non-radial directions. In the 2011 case, the outer segments of the rail lines are characterised by an increase in travel opportunities over 2008. This is because the new connecting bus lines add to the catchment areas of nodes such as Epping, Keon Park and Greensborough, and further because the bus lines generate new movement opportunities in their own right: They facilitate circumferential travel that previously required lengthy detours through central Melbourne, as well as provide access to two activity centres (Northland and West Heidelberg) that previously had very marginal bus services. As a result the orbital bus routes created a level of network connectivity that enabled public transport to break into new market segments while keeping congestion on the existing lines in check.

The nodal betweenness representation (shown below) for the same area and reference years, displays the betweenness values at the activity nodes at half the level of the cumulative segmental betweenness values converging there. The figures confirm that the total number of travel opportunities increased between 2008 and 2011, manifest in the average betweenness value for the 21 nodes increasing from 13.4 in 2008 to 15.9 in 2011.

This example illustrates how the betweenness centrality index can facilitate a complex, qualitative assessment of both local detail and city-wide performance of the public transport network. As a composite indicator combining parameters of land use, closeness centrality, transfer intensity and travel time, it behaves in non-linear ways: small changes in network configuration and service levels can sometimes have disproportionate effects on betweenness results. The best outcomes for accessibility and network performance are not always achieved by simply maximising betweenness scores wherever possible. Rather, it is beneficial that there is a good hierarchical fit of betweenness

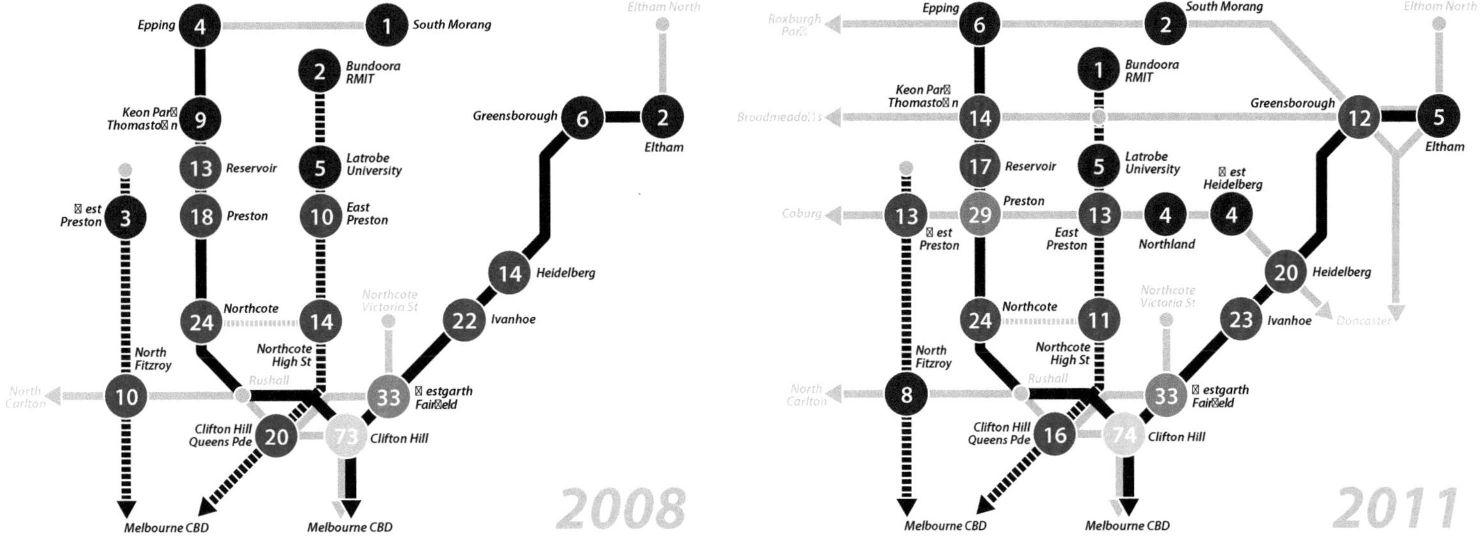

values with modal performance and capacity: rail or metro segments should typically be characterised by higher betweenness values than tram or ferry segments, and tram or ferry segments in turn by higher betweenness values than bus segments. While it is inevitable in a metropolitan area that betweenness centrality scores will be higher near the geographical centre of the network than at its periphery, it is beneficial for the decay curve of this discrepancy to be as gradual as possible to avoid excessive spikes in betweenness values in areas or on route segments where congestion is likely to occur. A stark contrast between a group of nodes with high betweenness scores and a group with low betweenness scores, with a steep performance gradient in between, may be indicative of a 'divided city' where good public transport accessibility in selected areas or corridors coexists with very poor accessibility everywhere else.

The *global betweenness index* enables meaningful comparisons between cities (while nodal betweenness is better suited to within-city analysis). This index is derived from the square root of the average number of weighted travel opportunities per pair of nodes on the network (the value which enters the betweenness count described above), divided by the total number of metropolitan residents and jobs to overcome an inherent bias of city size. The result is a proxy index for the overall 'presence' of public transport travel opportunities in a city. The key influencing parameters are: the average size of activity node catchments, indicative of the level of land use intensification around public transport infrastructures; the geographical spacing of activity nodes; the density and multi-directionality of the public transport network connecting them; and the speed and frequency of the service. This index thus rewards a dense, compact and contiguously built-up urban fabric served by a dense web of high-quality public transport links over a dispersed or disjointed settlement pattern and a patchy, slow and/or infrequent public transport network.

A scholarly debate has emerged around the relationship between urban form and public transport usage and the role of built density (Newman and Kenworthy, 1999; Mees, 2010a). This relationship is complex: the *catchment of typical path length* index attempts to capture it by compensating for the inherent pro-density bias and by isolating the component that describes the structure of the public transport network from that which describes the structure of the settlement area. This indicator calculates the length of an average public transport trip in a metropolitan area in terms of number of intermediate activity nodes traversed. The calculation is independent of their distance from one another, in either Euclidean or network terms, in order to neutralise the influence of the settlement geography on the betweenness scores. This figure is multiplied with the average walkable catchment of each activity node in terms of residents and jobs. Hence, this measure is a proxy for the number of residents and jobs travelled past on an average journey. This number will inflate if there is a strong degree of land use intensification around public transport nodes, but it will also inflate if the network is spatially configured to encourage passengers to take longer or more circuitous journeys than theoretically necessary (for example, where suburb-to-suburb travel can be done faster and with greater frequency by a rail transfer trip through the central city than by a bus that follows a more direct route). It can also indicate whether a public transport network is configured to facilitate longer trips over shorter trips – or vice versa.

Two further comparative measures presented in the city profiles concern the application of the segmental betweenness index on particular modes, and particular geographical areas. Here the interest is in the proportion of metro-wide betweenness scores that accrues on rail segments, in order to assess the extent to which a public transport system succeeds in attracting the majority of travel opportunities onto the mode with the highest performance and capacity. Further, we examine the proportion of metro-wide betweenness scores concentrated within or crossing the boundary of the CBD area, in order to assess to what extent a public transport system succeeds in diverting travel opportunities away from the area that is most likely prone to congestion. The *segmental betweenness on rail indicator* will obviously bear some relationship with the extent of heavy rail infrastructure and service offered, while the *segmental betweenness in the CBD* indicator can be expected to shrink, in relative terms, with growing overall city size.

SEGMENTAL AND NETWORK RESILIENCE

The relationship between the supply-side measure of betweenness centrality and actual, observed public transport usage can be complex. Without easy access to detailed, route and location-specific usage data it is difficult to explore empirically. An alternative is to draw a ratio between the results of the segmental betweenness index and the actual passenger capacity offered on each route segment, measured in comfortable places per hour.[2] This approach provides a comparison between the significance of a route segment for the land use–transport system (betweenness) and the level of service provided (capacity). Where this ratio appears to be well-matched the network elements can be considered *resilient*. Where the betweenness score appears to overwhelm the carrying capacity, network elements appear to be *under pressure* or *stress*. Note that such pressures are not necessarily manifest in instances of actual overcrowding of public transport vehicles or interchanges. Given the non-linearity of the betweenness – travel demand relationship (discussed above), a poor resilience score on a service with sparse patronage may be indicative of 'latent demand'. This may occur where alternative forms of travel have greater appeal than public transport, where public transport services are less legible or familiar to users than the wayfinding tool would suggest, or where demographic factors specific to particular origins and destinations depress trip-making rates. Passengers may also avoid a particular public transport service by giving preference to less convenient destinations or routes, or by foregoing travel altogether as long as they can absorb the subsequent reduction in amenity. Conversely, a good resilience score on this index is no guarantee that overcrowding will never occur on the segment; for instance, it may derive from travel generators other than residences and workplaces (Scheurer and Woodcock, 2011).

Network resilience is visualised on a network map using traffic light colours and a scale where a positive score between 0–30 (green) is considered resilient, a negative score between 0 and -30 (yellow-orange) a cause for concern and a score below -30 (red-maroon) under stress. Averages are given for the network as a whole, separately for each mode and for segments within or crossing the boundary of the CBD area.

A critical characteristic of the resilience index is the dynamic reference to public transport levels of service, in that travel impediment influences the number of travel opportunities (betweenness) offered along a particular route or route segment. For this reason, route segments are not necessarily relieved from stress on this index by simply increasing the service frequency, since the additional services also increase the travel opportunities along this route and may draw additional travel paths from alternative routes that become comparatively less attractive. Instead, the network resilience index places greater emphasis on the way the network configuration, and the role and interplay of different modes with different carrying capacities, can be optimised to mutual benefit.

NODAL CONNECTIVITY

This index measures the strength of each activity node for integration of multimodal public transport services, and by extension, the flexibility of users to move around the city on public transport. It captures the suitability of activity nodes for making transfers or breaks of journey with minimal disruption to the flow of movement. It measures how many times per hour a person can travel, in how many directions, on what size of vehicles from each node. The index multiplies the number of route segments (less one) converging in each node by the number of departures per hour, using a mode-specific weighting factor in line with average occupancy rates. Higher values indicate greater connectivity.

The nodal connectivity index expresses the attractiveness of a place for land use development that depends on good access by public transport. It can also be read as a proxy for the degree to which users can exercise a form of 'autonomous mobility' (Dowling and Kent, 2013) as they choose public transport as their principal mode of travel, similar to the experience car users have in uncongested conditions, or pedestrians and cyclists in good weather at a smaller spatial range. Can I wake up on Saturday morning and spontaneously decide to meet a friend in their favourite café in a different part of town for breakfast? Then later go to a particular craft shop in a different neighbourhood to pick up a birthday present for my niece? If the sun comes out, head to the river in the afternoon for a walk? Meanwhile ready to receive a message anytime from a visitor who's arriving in town and might want to meet for some sightseeing, possibly changing all my plans half way through the day? The nodal connectivity index can measure the extent to which public transport is capable of facilitating such planned or spontaneous chain journeys and between which cohort of origins and destinations.

SNAMUTS COMPOSITE INDEX

The composite index provides an overview of public transport accessibility in each case study city. It is comprehensive, as the index includes the results of the closeness centrality, degree centrality, contour catchment, nodal betweenness, nodal resilience and nodal connectivity indicators. Between 0 and 12 points for each component index are allocated except for the resilience index, which leads to deductions for nodal averages with negative values. Thus the highest possible composite score for an activity node is 60. The results are further moderated by an international benchmarking coefficient that includes metropolitan figures for residents and jobs, network coverage, global betweenness, catchment of typical path length, average network resilience and a factor for the degree of contiguity of the settlement area. The composite index remains cursory, however, because this calculation procedure invariably leads to subjective assumptions regarding how different component indicators are converted and weighted, and how the benchmarking coefficient is constructed. We therefore do not conceive of the composite index as a precise numerical instrument of inter-city comparison and for the same reason, refrain from presenting it as a network diagram with individual nodal values like the component indicators. Rather, we produce a scale map with nodal catchment areas shaded in traffic light colours according to performance brackets. We use it primarily as a visualisation tool to draw generalised conclusions and to engage with stakeholders in debates about public transport accessibility in the city of their concern. The other indexes enable for detailed insights to be explored as the debate unfolds in a location-specific fashion.

NOTES

1 800-metre radii rail stations around heavy ror ferry terminals; 400-metre linear corridors along surface bus or tram routes with regular stops; 400-metre catchments radii around these stations controlled-access stations or stops on surface routes such as light rail or bus rapid transit systems unless light rail infrastructure resembles that of heavy rail in operational and design terms where the catchment radius is increased to 800 metres. Adjustments are made for obvious geographical barriers such as watercourses or large transport infrastructures that cannot be entered or traversed by pedestrians.
2 'Comfortable places per hour' makes allowance for the greater comfort for standing passengers on rail vehicles than on road vehicles. It assumes a comfortable passenger load of 50 persons per standard bus, 75 persons per articulated bus, 80 persons per double-decker bus, 150 persons per tram (30 metres) and 600 persons per metro or suburban train (120 metres), making adjustments where necessary according to the specific composition of vehicle fleets, infrastructure and operational practices in each city.

3 Continuity and Change in Australasian Cities

URBAN HISTORY: LAND USE AND TRANSPORT INTEGRATION IN THE PAST

Australia's five largest capital cities, founded in the late eighteenth and early nineteenth centuries, are relative newcomers in the larger context of global urban history. Until Australia's federation in 1901, the country's six states were governed as separate colonies resulting in variation in urban growth and transport systems.

In the late nineteenth century land use and public transport planning worked in tandem. Purpose-built railways played a critical role in the major cities' urban development programs. In Perth a diametrical railway line from Fremantle to Midland opened in 1881, followed by the opening of the Perth to Armadale line in 1889 (Curtis, 2008b). Suburban development followed, pursued by private land developers. In Melbourne, the city's rapidly growing wealth led to a speculation-driven suburbanisation trend in low-rise detached houses for middle-class families as early as the 1880s. It was also facilitated by the construction of suburban railways, which met few engineering challenges in a region with a fairly uncomplicated geography and was initially undertaken by private companies (Davison, 1978; Davison and Yelland, 2004). In Sydney, early railway development was a government initiative and predominantly determined by the transport needs between the capital city and its regional hinterland. Suburban travel tasks initially took a subordinate role until the 1930s, when a purpose-built underground electric rail network was opened in the CBD and across the new Sydney Harbour Bridge to link up previously unconnected branches and provide direct access to the heart of the city (Norley, 2010; Mares, 2012).

Tram networks emerged as a competitor to the railways since the 1880s, initially using horse or cable power. In Melbourne this mode was electrified during the 1910s and 1920s and evolved into a system that, uniquely in Australasia, survived the post-war trend of conversion to bus operation. It is now one of the largest tram networks in the world. Both Melbourne's rail and tram systems have not transformed significantly in terms of network configuration since the 1930s. They remain almost exclusively radially focussed on the CBD, thus playing to their strengths predominantly within the pre-war sections of a metropolis that has more than doubled in size since 1945 (Davison, 1978; Davison and Yelland, 2004). In early twentieth-century Sydney, trams had a much more prominent role in the urban transport market than trains. However, Sydney's convoluted urban geography made for a less coherent network structure than in Melbourne, ultimately contributing to the demise of the mode in the early 1960s (Simpson, 2004; Lee, 2010; Manning, 1991). Simultaneously, trolley buses and trams were also replaced with diesel bus networks in Brisbane, Auckland and Perth, where public transport was seen largely as a job for buses until the 1980s (Curtis and Low, 2012).

Transit-oriented development (TOD) in the pre-automobile age was a market-driven process in the Australian cities. Perth's 1920s suburbs followed the early railway lines linking the central city to Armadale, Fremantle and Midland (Hemsley, 2009). In Melbourne, many middle suburban areas were not developed until the 1960s (Davison and Yelland, 2004). While post-war metropolitan plans intimated TOD (for example, Sydney's Cumberland Plan and Perth's Stephenson-Hepburn plan), little was actually implemented. Instead the primary transport mode invested in was the private car (between 70 and 80 per cent of all trips are undertaken by car in large Australian cities). Accordingly, the bulk of urban development since the 1960s has been framed around extensive low density suburban development supported by a generous high-speed road network. The turning point at which TOD started to gain traction occurred in the late 1990s and early 2000s, with most progress being made through public-private urban development partnerships (Curtis et al, 2009).

This marked a gradual shift in policy direction: away from mobility planning, where the assumption is that city dwellers access services required to support daily needs through a car-based transport system regardless of distance, and towards accessibility planning, where land use proximity is considered in order to support walking, cycling and public transport (Cervero, 1998; Vigar, 2002).

The new TOD focus has seen upgrades to the railway networks in Australian cities. Electrification of the existing railway lines in Perth and opening of two new radial rail lines (Joondalup in 1992, Mandurah in 2007) were the first attempts to stem car dependency. In Sydney and Melbourne, several underground rail lines were added since the 1980s to improve access to the CBD (Melbourne), major employment corridors and the airport (Sydney). Sydney also reintroduced light rail on a transit-focussed redevelopment corridor in the 1990s. Brisbane's suburban rail system, electrified in the 1980s, has seen several suburban extensions to service growth areas. Adelaide and Auckland are currently in the process of upgrading and electrifying their rail systems as the last major Australasian cities to do so. However, in Adelaide this project was suspended for lack of funds when only partly completed. A change of government in Australia in 2013 led to a withdrawal of Federal funding from urban public transport projects, jeopardising further progress with capital investment in recession-ridden Adelaide as well as in other Australian capitals.

THE ACCESSIBILITY CHALLENGE: LAND USE AND TRANSPORT INTEGRATION TODAY

Australasian cities have long experienced rising traffic congestion. This has led to a myopic solution with ever increasing demands for large-scale infrastructure financing to build new road space and increase the roadway capacity. It is being recognised that investment in public transport offers a significant alternative. There are opportunities for public transport to gain further market share from the car, thus reducing traffic congestion as well as addressing the social and environmental impacts associated with excessive car dependence.

Strong growth rates in public transport usage in several cities during the past five years are setting a new trend (BITRE, 2013). Australasia's public transport sector is facing a fundamental transformation as some tiers of government recognise this as a critical and desirable contribution to people's mobility. This raises a significant challenge for both public transport planners and the public transport system itself as it evolves from a dual orientation, focussed on central city job commuting and the provision of a social safety net, towards a service capable of catering for all urban passenger transport needs across metropolitan areas (Mees, 2010a).

Since the mid-1990s policy goals formulated by Federal and State Governments have begun to emphasise the desirability and importance of increasing public transport mode share (DoI VIC, 2002; DoT WA, 1995). A National Charter for Land Use Transport Integration was adopted identifying the need to integrate public transport systems directly with land use development (DTRS, 2003). The Commonwealth Government's infrastructure agency, formed in 2008, provided federal funding contributions to state urban transport infrastructure conditional on the integration of strategic land use and transport planning, and initiated a reform agenda on major cities and infrastructure planning through the Council of Australian Governments (IA, 2009). Federal action in urban public transport policy and funding, however, was terminated in 2013 by the incoming federal government, pointing to a significant partisan divide over transport policy in the political arena, and uncertainties experienced by major cities attempting to formulate long-term strategies for transport infrastructure investment.

ACCESSIBILITY PROFILE: PERTH

Perth is the capital of Western Australia, the country's largest (by land area) and most remote state. At 50,000 new residents per annum (a growth rate of 2.6 per cent), it is a fast-growing city, stretching 140 km along the Indian Ocean coast. A greater proportion of Perth's urban development originates from the rapid motorisation era after World War II than in any other major Australian city. As a consequence, the city has a generous road system and a dominance of low-density, functionally segregated urban form. Of all SNAMUTS case study cities, Perth has the lowest activity density. Public transport was neglected for several decades during the post-war period. A significant turnaround in the early 1990s resulted in the revitalisation, modernisation and expansion of the city's suburban rail system, combined with a level of multimodal integration in both physical and governance terms that is exemplary for the rest of the continent (Newman and Kenworthy, 1999; Mees, 2010a; Mees and Dodson, 2011; Curtis and Low, 2012; Mees and Groenhart, 2013).

A public agency, TransPerth, has full control of network and service planning and contracts bus operations to the private sector while rail operations remain in state government ownership. Integrated fares are based on concentric zones and predominantly collected through a smart card system.

Following patronage growth in the order of 50 per cent between 2006 and 2012, Perth's public transport usage in annual journeys per capita is now higher than in Brisbane, Adelaide and Auckland (PTA, 2013), and also the US case study cities. A bipartisan consensus informs urban infrastructure development and has led to the construction of more than 100 km of new rail lines since 1993. Plans for major inner urban road capacity expansion conceived in the 1960s were limited, first by lack of federal funding support, and later by community opposition (Alexander and MacManus, 1992). The north–south train line linking Clarkson and Mandurah is being extended north towards the urban fringe. Additional stations in growth areas are being developed along the existing line. An airport rail branch and a two-line light rail system in the inner and middle suburbs are in the planning stages, though their implementation was delayed following the withdrawal of Federal funding support.

Service Intensity

Perth's rail network is operated at minimum 15-minute service frequencies seven days a week during the daytime. This standard represents the best consistent service level found in any Australasian urban rail system, though in global terms it is relatively modest. The

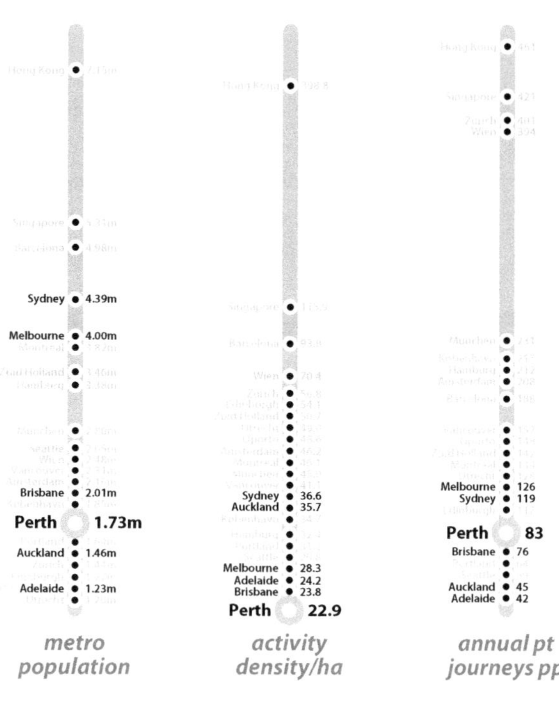

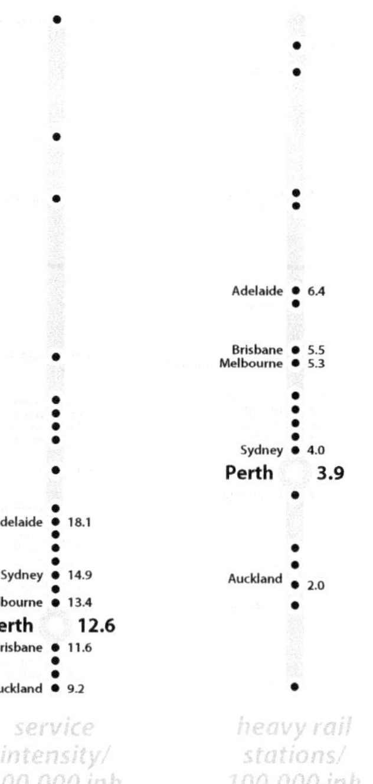

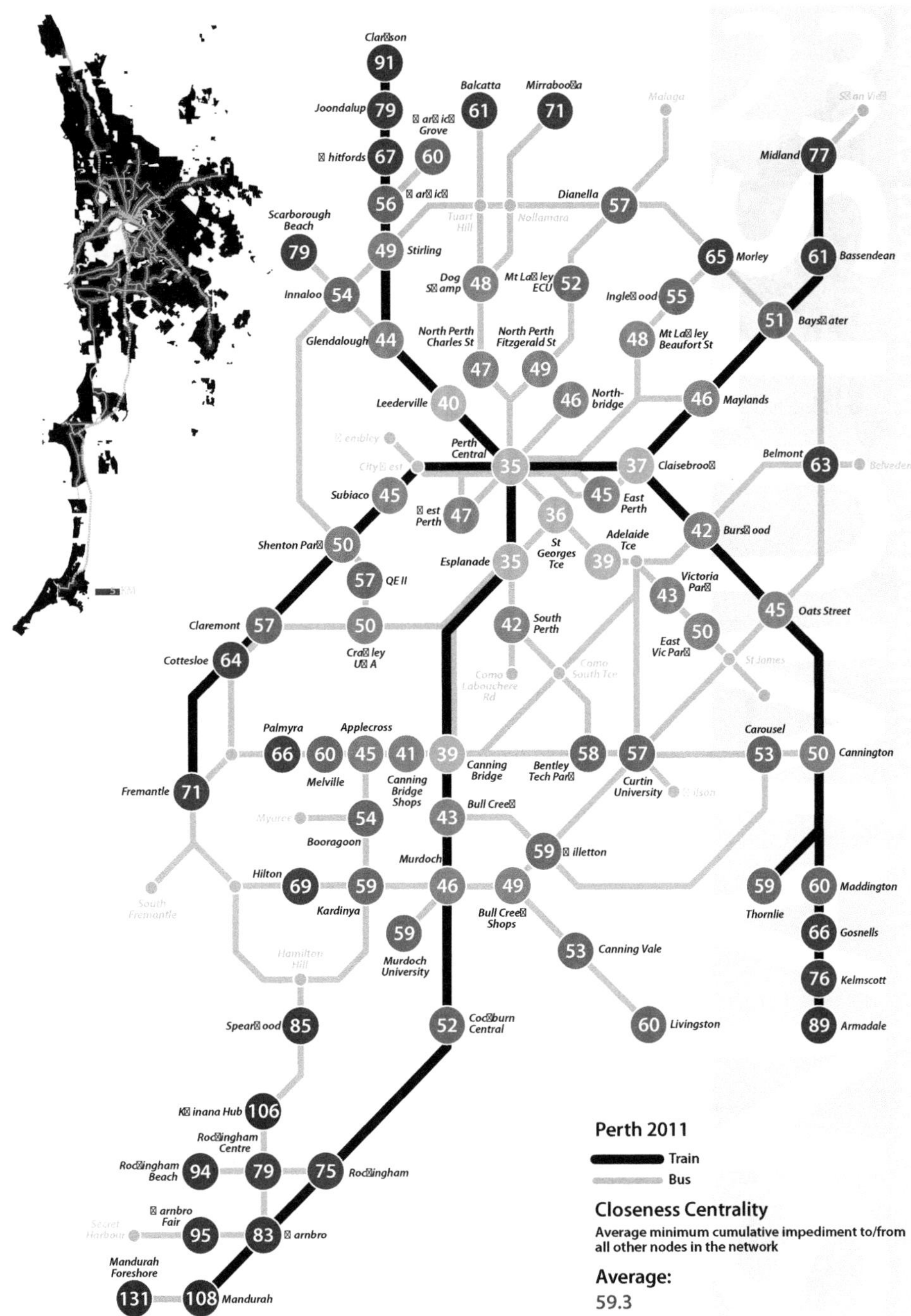

multimodal network is organised hierarchically: buses act as feeders and distributors to the rail system and service secondary inner suburban corridors. A relatively low service intensity figure results, reflecting an efficiency-driven network configuration. Simultaneously, significant spatial gaps remain between corridors of good service in this low-density metropolis. Despite the recent pace of infrastructure growth, Perth has the lowest number of rail stations relative to population of all major Australian cities. This circumstance is linked to the new rail lines' design characteristics and fast speeds, where a limited number of stations are conceived to favour bus feeder and park-and-ride access rather than pedestrian catchments.

Closeness Centrality

Perth leads its Australian peers on this index by a small margin, though the average score is still significantly poorer than in most European or Canadian cities. The network's key strength in facilitating ease of movement lies in channelling journey paths onto a rail system with a commercial speed among the highest in the sample, and where the average service frequency is higher than in other Australasian cities. The key weakness is the relative lack of compact clusters of intense urban activity outside the centre of Perth. This leads to long journey distances that discourage discretionary trips.

The network form is characterised by five radial rail lines interspersed by secondary radial bus corridors. The radial routes intersect in the middle suburbs with an orbital bus line (Circle Route). Rail stations usually have dedicated transfer facilities built to a high standard. A 'spiderweb' structure results, with a cluster of the lowest (best) closeness values in the CBD and then a wave-like spread of medium closeness values at the nodes along the Circle Route, somewhat better at intersections with rail lines and somewhat worse at

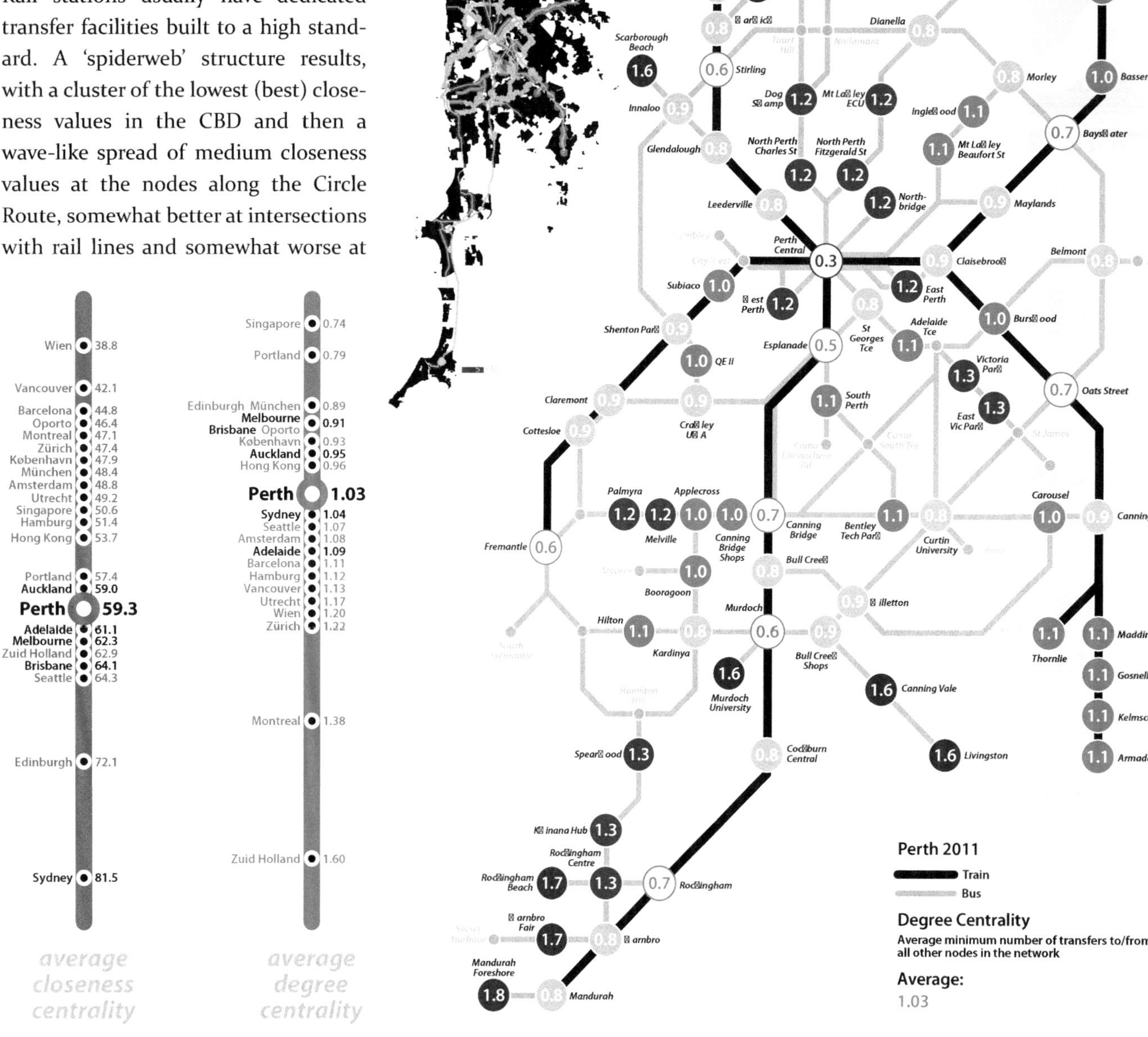

intersections with bus lines. The spacing and speed of the rail lines result in cross-suburban journeys from one rail corridor to another generally taking longer by the Circle Route than by a rail transfer trip through central Perth, but less long than by a transfer trip using radial bus lines. Outside the Circle Route, Perth's network assumes a tree-shaped character with outer suburban radial rail lines connecting to short bus feeders, with few orbital links between these corridors. In such conditions, closeness values increase quite rapidly with distance from the central city.

Degree Centrality

Perth's average performance on this index, depicting the transfer intensity of the network, is similar to Sydney's but poorer than in Brisbane, Melbourne and Auckland. With few exceptions, Perth deliberately avoids operating parallel rail and bus lines along the same corridors, opting instead for a trunk-and-feeder system with clearly differentiated tasks between rail and bus. This configuration has the effect of driving up transfer intensity and generates a group of nodes with values significantly above the average (Warwick Grove, Scarborough Beach, Livingston, Rockingham Beach). However, the superior integration of the rail network with the Circle Route and other orbital bus connections, as well as the practice of operating a transfer-free rail service from one edge of the metropolitan area to the other (Clarkson to Mandurah and Fremantle to Midland) contributes to bringing down these numbers (see the intersections between rail and Circle Route at Fremantle, Stirling, Bayswater, Oats Street and Murdoch).

Network Coverage

Perth falls below Adelaide, Melbourne and Sydney, but outperforms Brisbane and Auckland, in terms of the percentage of metropolitan residents and jobs that are situated within walking distance from public transport stations or stops serviced at the minimum standard. This can be seen in the context of lower service intensity figures. In Sydney and Melbourne, the edge over Perth on that index is of a similar margin as on the measure of network coverage, though recent improvements to the bus network in Perth have begun to narrow the gap. Perth's lower rail station density than Melbourne's and Adelaide's, most of whose rail lines originate from the late nineteenth and early twentieth centuries and have much closer station spacings than Perth's more recent north–south line, also plays a role in limiting network coverage.

Thirty-Minute Contour Catchments

Perth's activity centre users can access a similar average proportion of metropolitan residents and jobs by a way of a 30-minute public transport journey as their counterparts in Adelaide and Brisbane. This measure should be expected to fall with growing city size, giving Perth an edge over (smaller) Adelaide, perhaps related to the greater speed on its train system. Perth, however, is outperformed by (larger) Brisbane, suggesting that urban intensification in public transport–accessible locations has thus far not occurred at the scale found in its Queensland counterpart.

On this index, activity nodes along fast modes (rail system, freeway bus routes) are at an advantage, indeed the Canning Bridge interchange has the third largest contour catchment

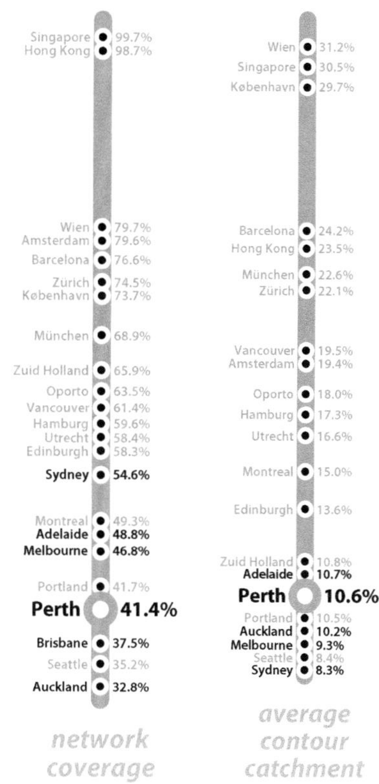

network-wide. Conversely, the index drops off quite rapidly with growing distance from the CBD for all other radial bus corridors. In the middle suburbs, the figures for Stirling (higher than its inbound neighbour, Glendalough) and to a smaller extent Shenton Park and Murdoch, show the effect of the Circle Route to expand travel contours by adding orbital directionality to the network. The network's single 'super-node' at Perth Central captures more than three quarters of the minimum-standard public transport network within a half-hour journey, representing (alongside Adelaide Central) the highest value across Australasia and illustrating the importance of the fast rail system in supporting this dispersed metropolis.

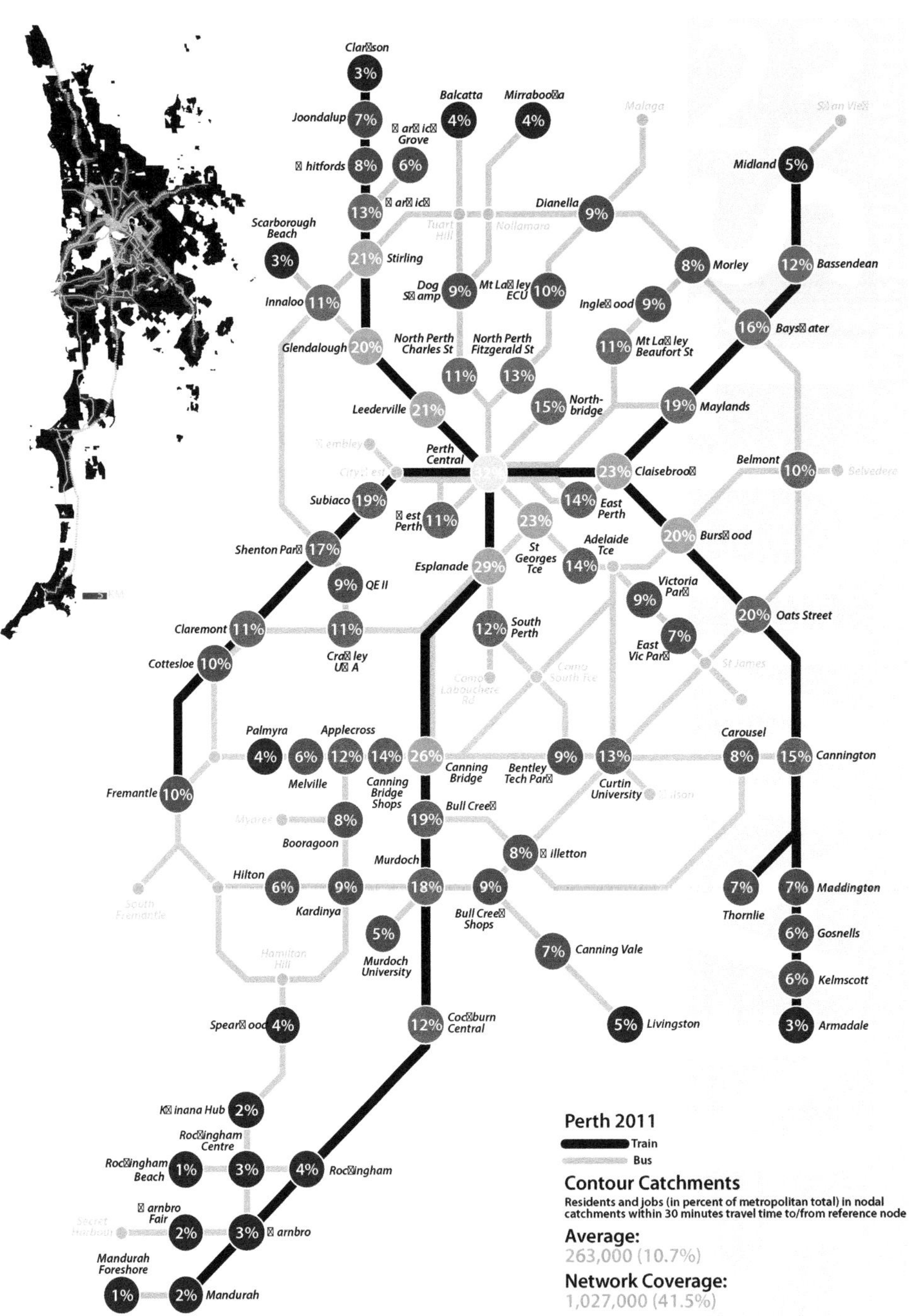

Betweenness Centrality

This index captures the geography of travel opportunities that the interplay of the public transport network and the land use system generates. Like in Sydney and Brisbane, the network stretches over a vast dispersed area compared to the number of inhabitants. As a result, the global betweenness index is more depressed than if the city were more compact. However, relative to population and jobs it represents the second highest result among the Australasian cities, outperformed only by Adelaide which has a vastly superior input of services. This illustrates the impact of the 15-minute rail frequencies and the high rail speeds on the generation of

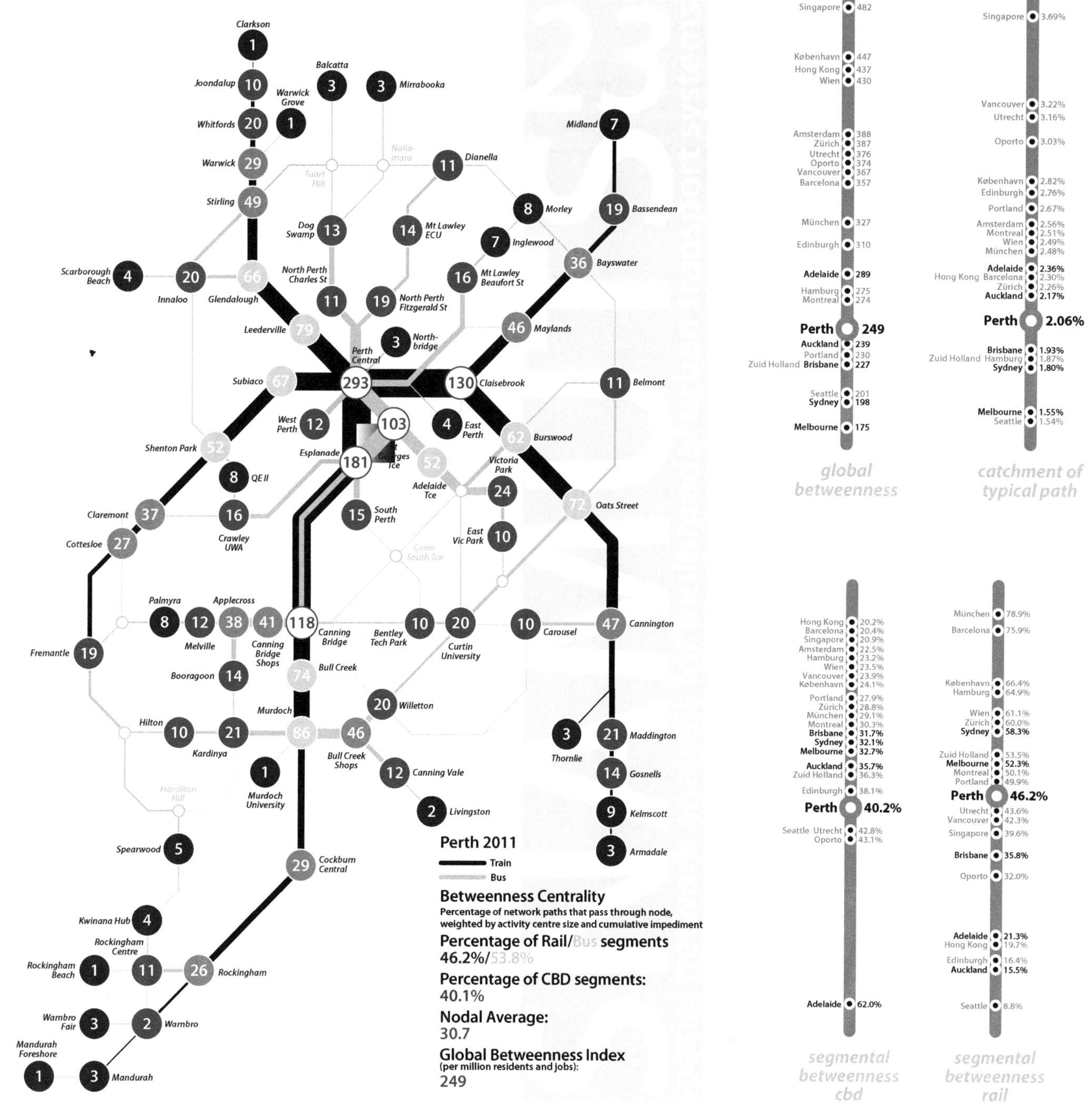

Clarkson 1
Joondalup 10
Whitfords 20
Warwick Grove 1
Warwick 29
Stirling 49
Balcatta 3
Mirrabooka 3
Nollamara
Tuart Hill
Dianella 11
Midland 7
Bassendean 19
Morley 8
Inglewood 7
Bayswater 36
Dog Swamp 13
Mt Lawley ECU 14
Mt Lawley Beaufort St 16
Scarborough Beach 4
Innaloo 20
Glendalough 66
North Perth Charles St 11
North Perth Fitzgerald St 19
Leederville 79
Maylands 46
North-bridge 3
Perth Central 293
Subiaco 67
Claisebrook 130
Belmont 11
West Perth 12
103
St Georges Tce
East Perth 4
Esplanade 181
Burswood 62
Shenton Park 52
Adelaide Tce 52
Victoria Park 24
QE II 8
Claremont 37
Crawley UWA 16
South Perth 15
Oats Street 72
East Vic Park 10
Cottesloe 27
Como South Tce
Palmyra 8
Melville 12
Applecross 38
Canning Bridge Shops 41
Canning Bridge 118
Bentley Tech Park 10
Curtin University 20
Carousel 10
Cannington 47
Fremantle 19
Booragoon 14
Bull Creek 74
Willetton 20
Hilton 10
Kardinya 21
Murdoch 86
Bull Creek Shops 46
Thornlie 3
Maddington 21
Murdoch University 1
Canning Vale 12
Gosnells 14
Hamilton Hill
Livingston 2
Kelmscott 9
Spearwood 5
Armadale 3
Cockburn Central 29
Kwinana Hub 4
Rockingham Centre 11
Rockingham Beach 1
Rockingham 26
Wambro Fair 3
Warnbro 2
Mandurah Foreshore 1
Mandurah 3
Perth 2011
Train
Bus
Betweenness Centrality
Percentage of network paths that pass through node, weighted by activity centre size and cumulative impediment
Percentage of Rail/Bus segments
46.2%/53.8%
Percentage of CBD segments:
40.1%
Nodal Average:
30.7
Global Betweenness Index
(per million residents and jobs):
249
Singapore 482
København 447
Hong Kong 437
Wien 430
Amsterdam 388
Zürich 387
Utrecht 376
Oporto 374
Vancouver 367
Barcelona 357
München 327
Edinburgh 310
Adelaide 289
Hamburg 275
Montreal 274
Perth 249
Auckland 239
Portland 230
Zuid Holland Brisbane 227
Seattle 201
Sydney 198
Melbourne 175
global betweenness
Singapore 3.69%
Vancouver 3.22%
Utrecht 3.16%
Oporto 3.03%
København 2.82%
Edinburgh 2.76%
Portland 2.67%
Amsterdam 2.56%
Montreal 2.51%
Wien 2.49%
München 2.48%
Adelaide 2.36%
Hong Kong Barcelona 2.30%
Zürich 2.26%
Auckland 2.17%
Perth 2.06%
Brisbane 1.93%
Zuid Holland Hamburg 1.87%
Sydney 1.80%
Melbourne 1.55%
Seattle 1.54%
catchment of typical path
Hong Kong 20.2%
Barcelona 20.4%
Singapore 20.9%
Amsterdam 22.5%
Hamburg 23.2%
Wien 23.5%
Vancouver 23.9%
København 24.1%
Portland 27.9%
Zürich 28.8%
München 29.1%
Montreal 30.3%
Brisbane 31.7%
Sydney 32.1%
Melbourne 32.7%
Auckland 35.7%
Zuid Holland 36.3%
Edinburgh 38.1%
Perth 40.2%
Seattle Utrecht 42.8%
Oporto 43.1%
Adelaide 62.0%
segmental betweenness cbd
München 78.9%
Barcelona 75.9%
København 66.4%
Hamburg 64.9%
Wien 61.1%
Zürich 60.0%
Sydney 58.3%
Zuid Holland 53.5%
Melbourne 52.3%
Montreal 50.1%
Portland 49.9%
Perth 46.2%
Utrecht 43.6%
Vancouver 42.3%
Singapore 39.6%
Brisbane 35.8%
Oporto 32.0%
Adelaide 21.3%
Hong Kong 19.7%
Edinburgh 16.4%
Auckland 15.5%
Seattle 8.8%
segmental betweenness rail

travel opportunities, compared to the 30-minute standard and slower services prevailing elsewhere. Perth appears to be more successful than its peers in channelling travel opportunities along the high-performance rail system, manifest in a rail share of the total betweenness score inferior only to much larger Sydney and Melbourne among its regional peers. Partly in consequence, however, the CBD share of the total betweenness score in Perth remains the second highest in the Australasian sample, reflecting the radial orientation of the rail network and the scarcity of orbital links.

Perth's result on the typical path length index is higher than in the larger cities (Sydney, Melbourne and Brisbane), primarily reflecting the ability of the fast rail network to facilitate longer journeys while providing limited attractive opportunities for shorter journeys. It is lower than in Adelaide and Auckland, however, where higher activity densities (Auckland) as well as an absence of non-radial network elements and the resulting detours combine to inflate this index.

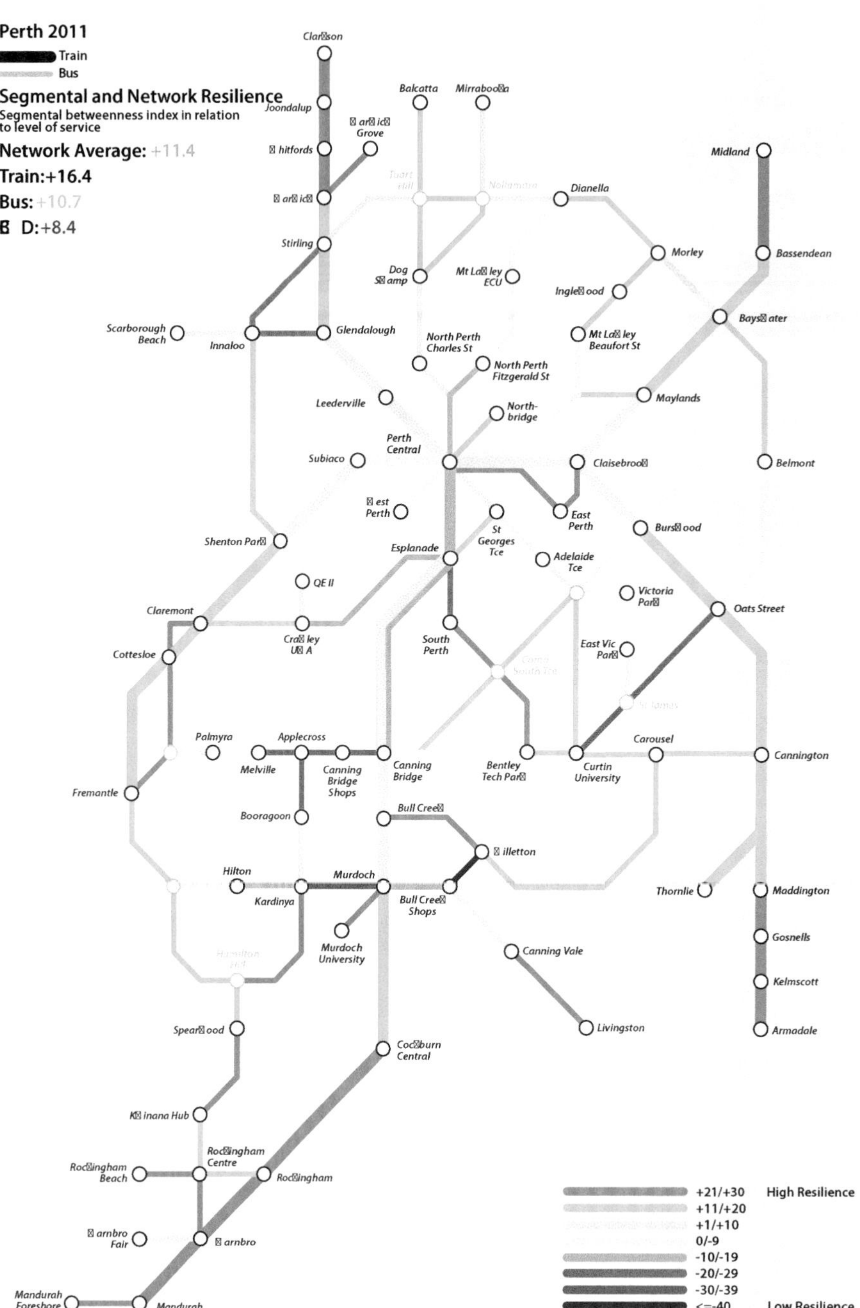

Network Resilience

Perth has the best average segmental resilience results among the Australasian cities, indicating that the distribution of transport tasks to rail and bus along a hierarchical model offers a more robust network able to accommodate further growth. However, the

network resilience index also suggests several problems. High stress values are frequently found on short bus feeder sections to rail lines (Innaloo to Stirling and Glendalough, Booragoon to Canning Bridge, Curtin University to Oats Street or Kardinya and Willetton to Murdoch). Here, the location of many rail stations away from concentrations of land use activity – much of Perth's north–south rail line is situated in a freeway median – is evident and indicates the desirability of land use strategies to focus on converting rail–bus transfer nodes to significant activity centres. In some cases (Murdoch, Stirling, Cockburn Central) this process is under way. Resilience figures also deteriorate on some radial bus corridors (Alexander Drive between central Perth and Dianella in the north-east; central Perth and Crawley-UWA in the west). Here there are plans for conversion to light rail which would greatly increase the capacity and performance of these corridors.

Nodal Connectivity

Perth's average nodal connectivity is third lowest in the global SNAMUTS sample before Adelaide and Auckland. Only Perth Central has an outstanding performance on this index. This suggests that many suburban centres as well as CBD fringe areas would require significant boosts in service levels as well as additional links in new

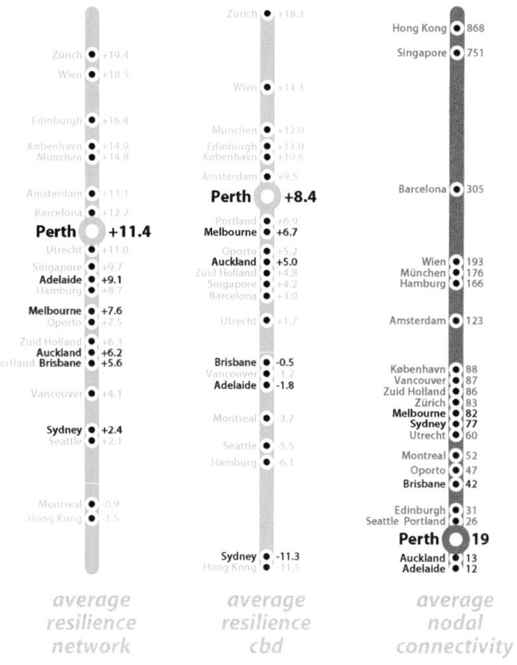

directions if they were to become genuinely attractive locations for TOD.

SNAMUTS Composite Accessibility Index and Reflections

The composite index visualises Perth's modal hierarchy by revealing a narrative of difference: rail corridors generally place their residents and jobs in a better category of overall public transport accessibility than those in bus corridors at comparable distance from the CBD. Inside the bus Circle Route some network gaps remain but generally the area is endowed with rail and bus routes at the minimum standard within walking distance of built-up areas, though usually without much multi-directionality. Clearly, the relative strength of these inner urban routes relates to their ability to capture both locally generated transport tasks and those that derive from movement needs across a broader, sub-regional context. Outside the Circle Route, there is only limited geographical network coverage – consisting of rail corridors and short bus feeders to nearby activity centres. These twin shortfalls illustrate Perth's relatively low service intensity level. While Perth has mostly average to above-average performance results among its Australasian peers, this finding suggests that performance could be improved further with the allocation of similar operational resources to the public transport system relative to population as seen in the

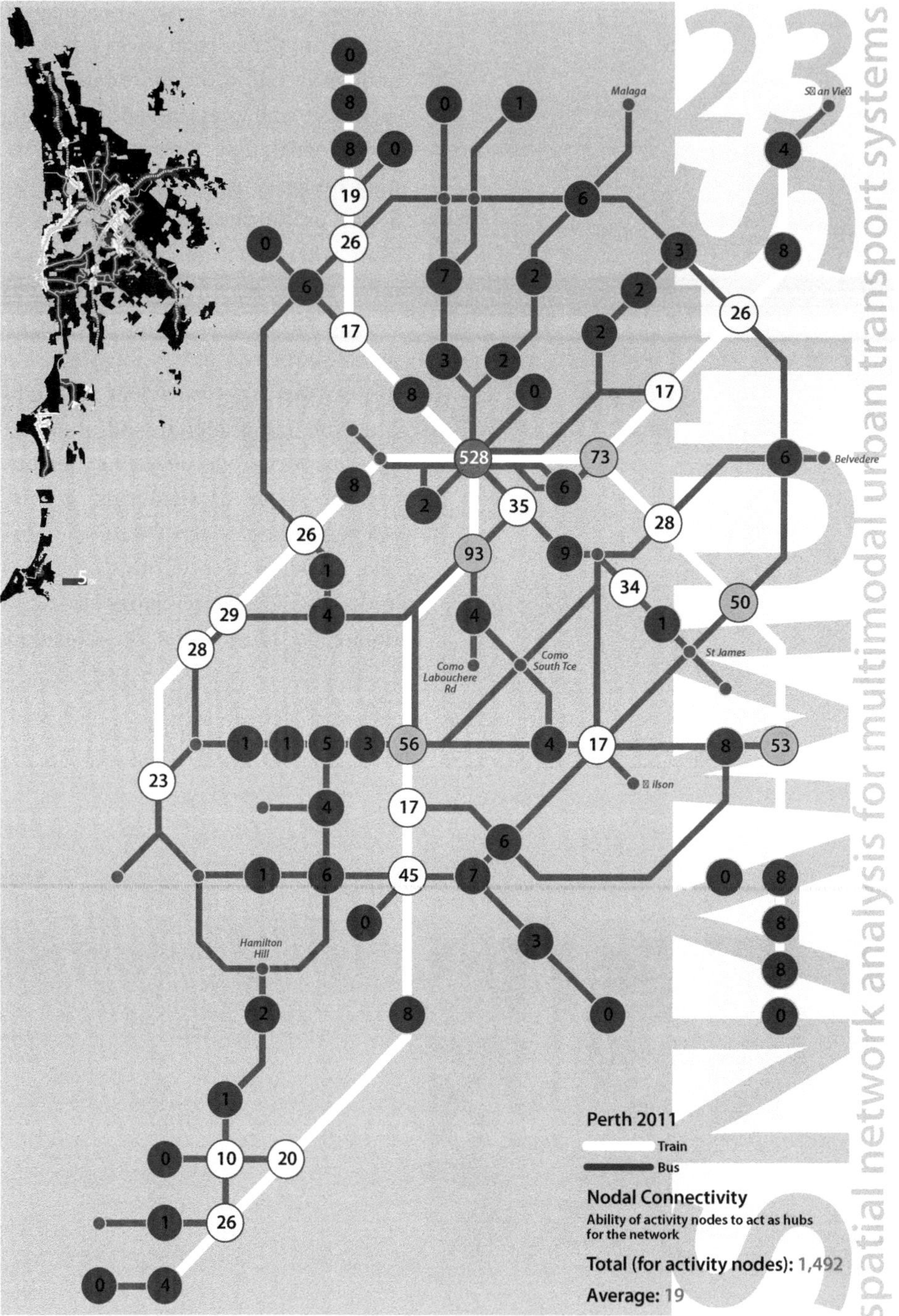

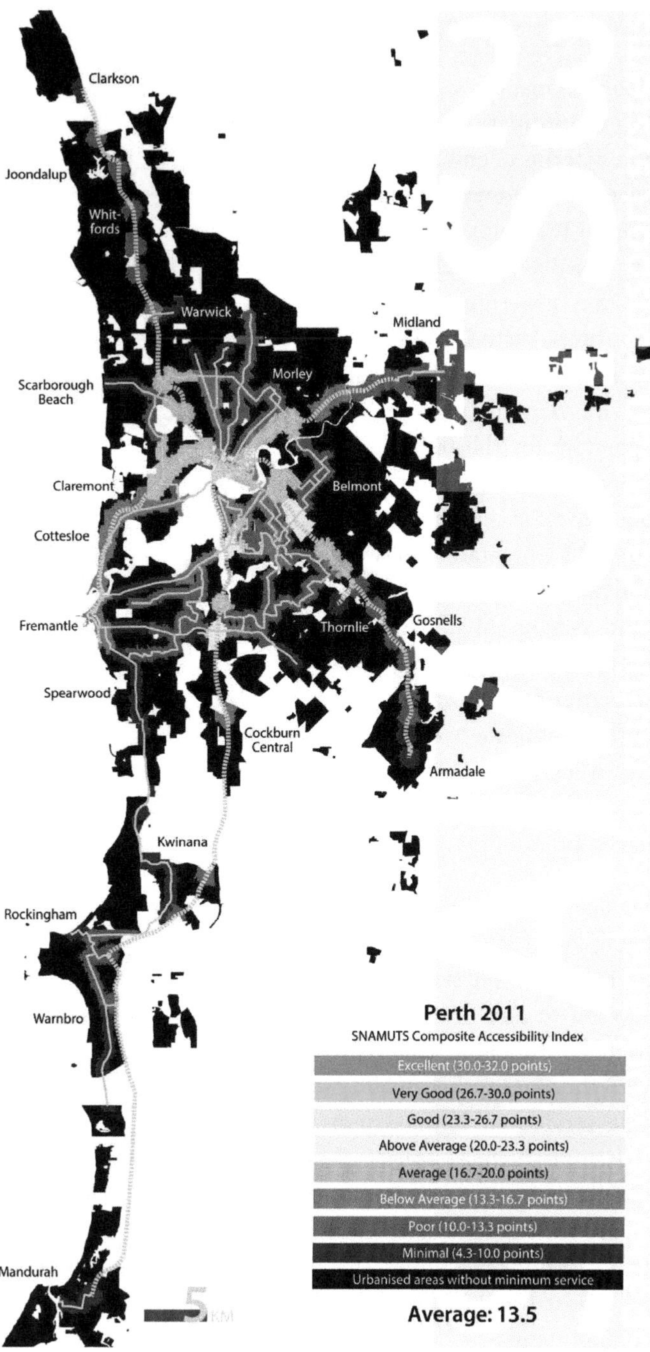

New World leaders on this index, Vancouver and Adelaide. This applies to the bus system as well as to the rail system: the composite index shows the potential of rail to spread good accessibility to areas beyond the CBD, with Canning Bridge recording the best result outside central Perth. Improvements of all-day rail frequencies towards metro standards of 10 minutes or better (for which the infrastructure already caters for) in conjunction with a greater surface network density would lay the groundwork for an urban growth strategy providing for TOD intensification of sub-centres in inner and middle suburban areas.

On the whole, Perth appears to be the best placed city in Australasia to further develop public transport into a backbone for urban mobility. There is a greater degree of bi-partisan political support for network expansion and service improvements ensuring that major long-term public transport projects survive changes of government and shifts in the collaborative relationships between federal, state and local governments. There is a long-standing tradition of and institutional basis for integrated network and service planning similar to European and Canadian best practice. Lastly, a state agency (Metropolitan Redevelopment Authority) has led innovative solutions to TOD since the 1990s and has a vital role in facilitating the intensification of TOD nodes and corridors in this low-density, spread-out metropolis.

ACCESSIBILITY PROFILE: MELBOURNE

Melbourne is Australia's second largest city at four million inhabitants in 2011, following an annual net influx of more than 80,000 people during the five preceding years. Facing few natural constraints to urban expansion besides cone-shaped Port Phillip Bay in the south and the Dandenong Ranges to the east, Melbourne's urbanised area density is lower than that of Sydney, but higher than in the smaller cities of Perth, Brisbane and Adelaide. The city has a reputation for a generous endowment with public transport infrastructure: besides a heavy rail system consisting of 11 radial trunk lines, Melbourne retains the world's largest (by track-km) first-generation tram network. It services a multitude of linear, mixed-use activity corridors along inner suburban main streets. This was a common element in Australian cities' pre-automobile settlement pattern, which trams helped to establish and which survive in a healthier condition in Melbourne than elsewhere (Goodman and Coiacetto, 2009). However, both rail and tram systems have only selectively kept pace with the expansion of the post-war city, with the consequence that the outer suburban growth belt is characterised by similar patterns of car dominance and poor public transport access as in other Australasian cities (Mees, 2000; Gleeson et al, 2003; Davison and Yelland, 2004; Mees, 2010a; Currie and Burke, 2014).

Public transport usage has grown at an extraordinary rate since about 2005 and in terms of annual trips per capita, overtaken Sydney during this period (DoT VIC, 2012). Public transport is organised as a franchise system, where a state government agency (Public Transport Victoria) oversees contractual relationships and collaborative service planning with singular private operators for the train and tram systems, and a larger number of private bus operators. Public transport fares are fully integrated between modes and are based on an electronic SmartCard system (Myki) without concurrent paper tickets. There is a two-zone structure for the network (inner and outer Melbourne), with two-hour, all-day, weekly, monthly and annual tickets available for each zone, or for both in combination.

A major piece of rail infrastructure is being constructed (Regional Rail Link), designed to physically separate rail services to and from country Victoria from metropolitan suburban services with the aim of a better and more reliable service on both systems. Other rail infrastructure projects have suffered a series of fundamental changes or reprioritisations, and were subject to a plethora of studies that yielded no robust funding or implementation commitments.

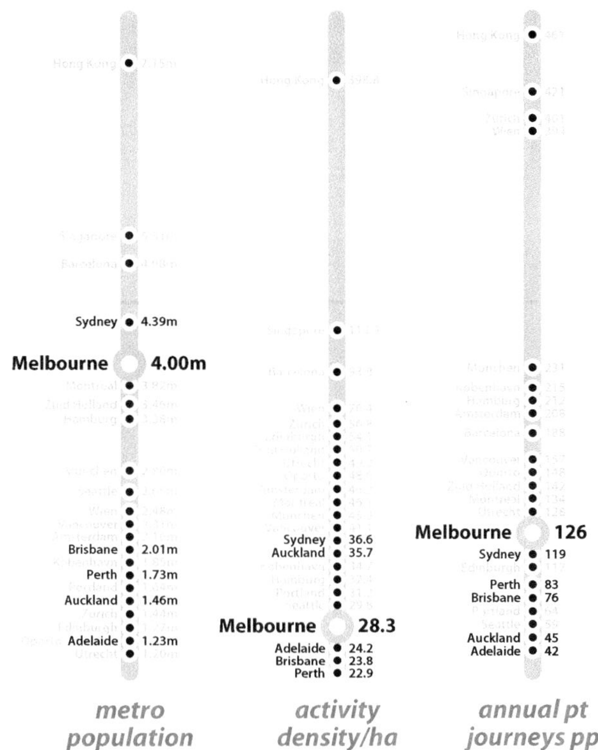

Adelaide 18.1
Sydney 14.9
Melbourne 13.4
Perth 12.6
Brisbane 11.6
Auckland 9.2

service intensity/ 100,000 inh

Adelaide 6.4
Brisbane 5.5
Melbourne 5.3
Sydney 4.0
Perth 3.9
Auckland 2.0

heavy rail stations/ 100,000 inh

Service Intensity

The majority of Melbourne's rail lines meet the SNAMUTS minimum standard; however, daytime service frequencies vary between 10 minutes (Frankston/Newport line), 15 minutes (remaining southern and eastern lines) and 20 minutes (remaining western and northern lines). On the outer branches beyond Ringwood and Dandenong, 30-minute frequencies are offered. The tram network is characterised by typical daytime frequencies between 6 and 12 minutes and some overlaps between lines in the central area, especially along Swanston Street and St Kilda Road, which form the highest-frequency tram corridor in the SNAMUTS sample. During the late 2000s, an eight-route SmartBus network was introduced on radial and orbital links in Melbourne's middle and outer suburbs offering 15-minute frequencies on weekdays and 30-minute frequencies on weekends.

Relative to population, service intensity is average among Australian cities and lower than in any European city investigated. This is despite the duplication of service generated by some parallel tram and train corridors and a relatively high presence of slow-moving surface modes in central areas. Notwithstanding the city's extensive suburban rail system, the number of rail stations relative to population occupies only a mid-field position among its Australian peers; however, Brisbane's and Adelaide's higher station density is offset by lower average service levels than in Melbourne.

Closeness Centrality

Of all Australasian cities, Melbourne has the most legible as well as the most complex public transport network in the CBD. A partially underground four-track heavy rail loop with five stations intersects with eight high-frequency tram and two bus trunk lines following specific north–south or east–west streets within the central city's rectangular pattern (Hoddle Grid). Consequently, closeness results vary little in the central area and indicate good accessibility throughout the CBD. Moving towards the periphery, however, closeness values increase, in some cases quite rapidly. This trend is exacerbated by the frequent coexistence, along the same corridors, of two sub-optimal forms of public transport access: slower but higher-frequency trams or faster but lower-frequency trains. Conversely, it is moderated by the effect of the orbital SmartBus routes which, while not yet forming a coherent network, add vital links between what were previously 'dead ends' on the rail and tram system, offering more opportunities to move along geographical 'desire lines' at acceptable service frequencies (see Chapter 2). On corridors where train frequencies approach the standard of metro services (Footscray to Caulfield) low (better) closeness centrality values extend a considerable distance from the CBD. Doncaster's impressive result is achieved by a SmartBus service to the CBD that relies on a relatively long stretch of fast motorway operation and a service frequency much higher than any suburban rail line in Melbourne.

Degree Centrality

A great majority of nodes in Melbourne show values at or near the average, which suggests that the network allows for most trips to be made with approximately one transfer. In most cases this transfer would be in the CBD area where most routes intersect (though not always in a legible location). Thus the radial nature of the rail and tram network (and of eight out of 20 minimum-service bus routes) is clearly demonstrated by this indicator. Conversely, the hierarchical configuration of public transport modes according to their performance as trunks and feeders or primary and secondary corridors remains underdeveloped despite recent progress with the introduction of orbital SmartBus routes. Few nodes have degree centrality scores much higher than the average – indicative of a feeder route relationship to the rest

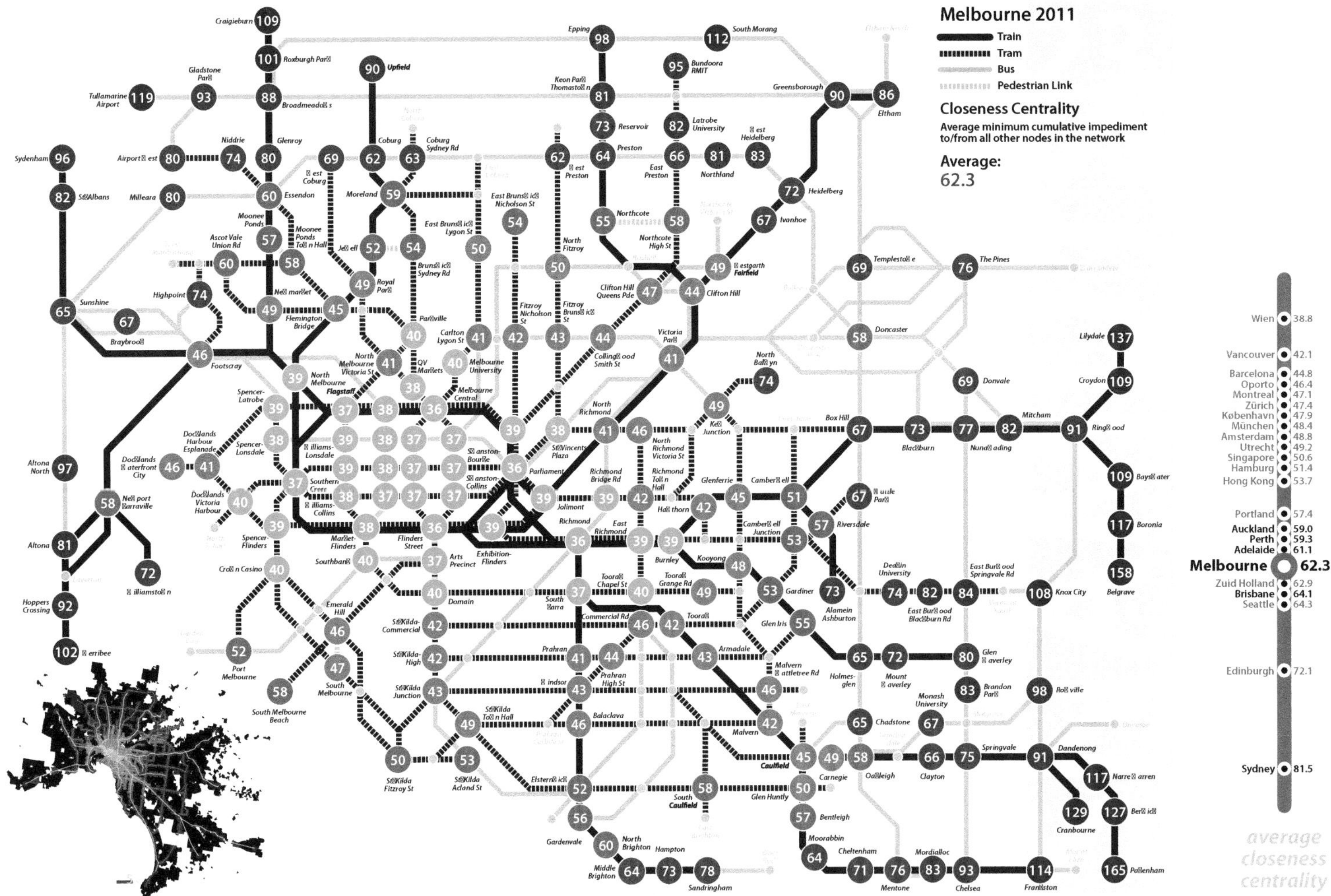

of the network. There is an absence of purpose-designed transfer facilities between rail and tram at a standard common in European or Canadian cities. The quality of train-bus or tram-bus interchanges, with a few notable exceptions, is also poor. While the orbital SmartBus network aimed at reducing transfer intensity, in practice the routes are very long and passengers would have to spend several hours in the same vehicle on significant deviations from their primary direction of movement to avoid making a transfer. There are limited opportunities for diverting travel paths away from the CBD: other than (CBD-fringe) Richmond, there is no activity node outside the city centre that matches the five city loop stations in terms of degree centrality.

Network Coverage

Despite Melbourne's extensive public transport infrastructure, the proportional coverage of residents and jobs with minimum-standard public transport services within walking distance is below Sydney and Adelaide (but above Perth, Brisbane and Auckland). Compared to Sydney, it suggests

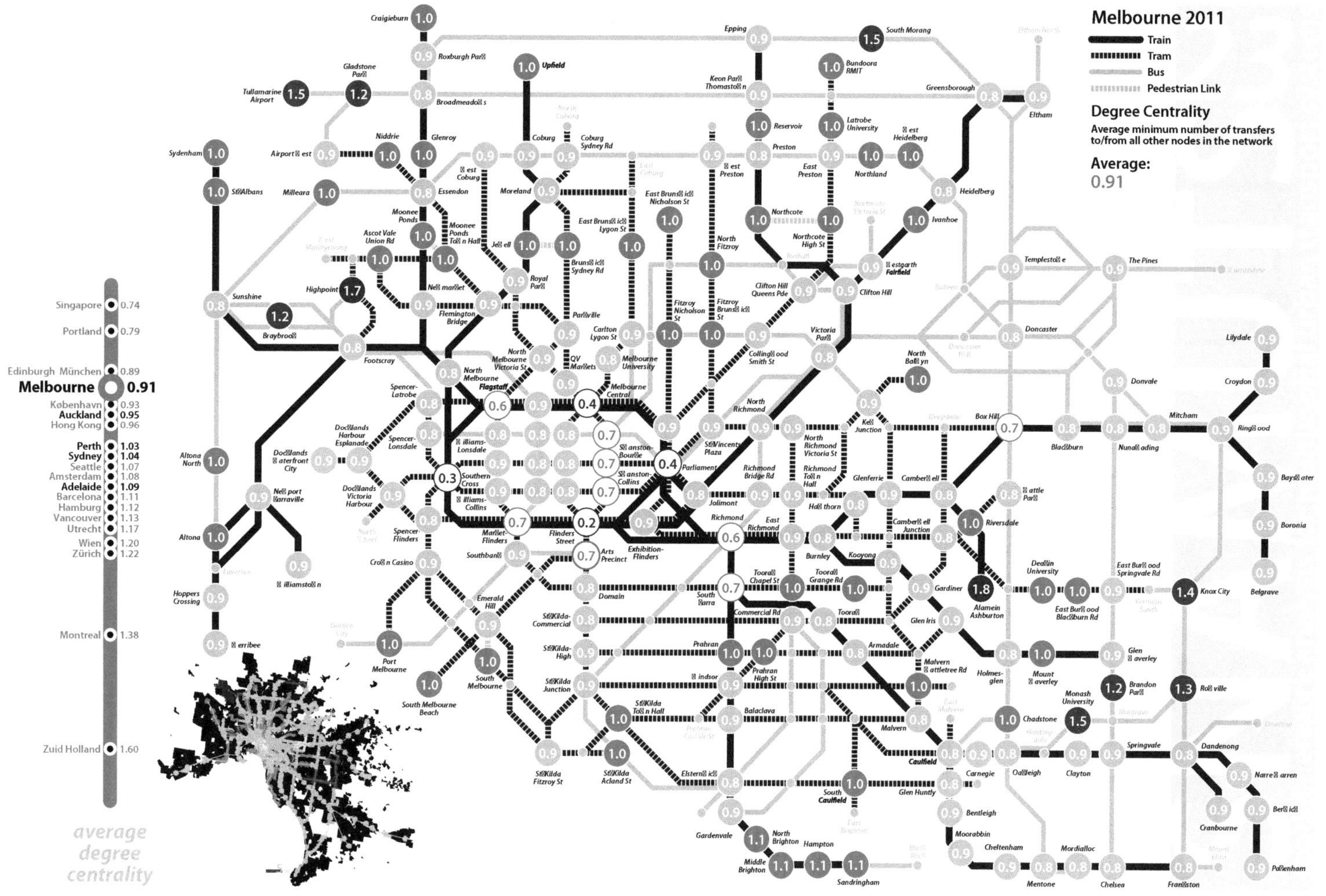

that during the last 60 years of urban growth, Melbourne had more opportunity to expand away from public transport, both in terms of available space and in terms of planning directives (or relative lack thereof). Compared to Adelaide, the correlation of lower network coverage and lower service intensity is notable.

Thirty-Minute Contour Catchments

Melbourne's public transport system shows a geographical imbalance on this index. South and east of the city centre, scores on this index in the 10–20 per cent bracket remain the norm for some distance (Elsternwick, Caulfield and Camberwell). This sector also has the only nodes outside the CBD with scores of 20 per cent and above (Richmond, South Yarra and Malvern). Conversely, in less than 2 km north of the centre few nodes have scores above 10 per cent. Throughout the entire west of the city, the same threshold is only met by North Melbourne and Footscray stations. This is related to two key factors.

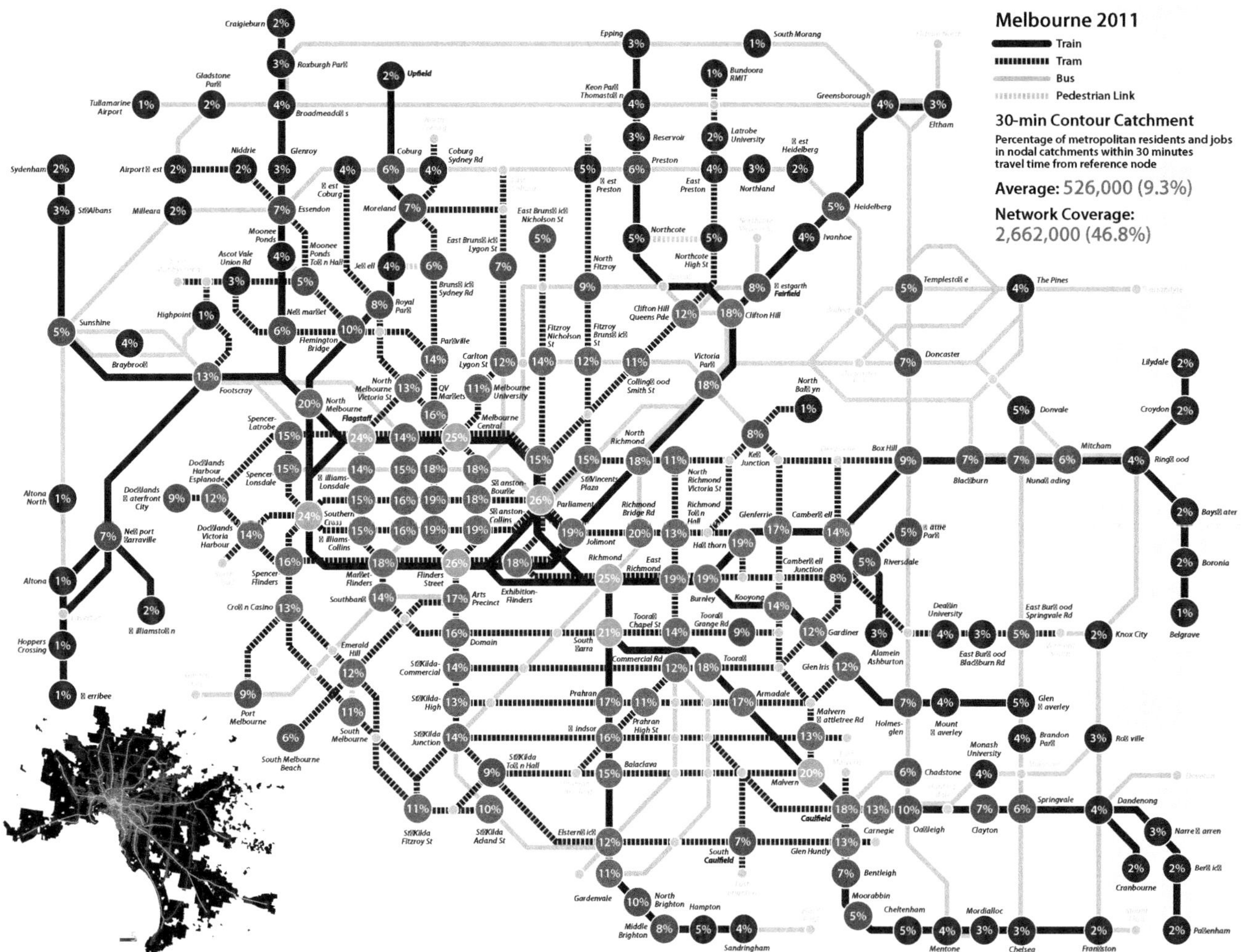

The south and east are more populous than the north and west, and the inner southern and eastern suburbs are characterised by a network structure offering greater opportunities for multi-directional movement than their northern and western counterparts. There is a relatively widespread network of both north–south and east–west routes among the surface modes, interspersed in some places by diagonal train lines. In the north, there are no frequent and full-length east–west or diagonal routes for a distance of more than 7 km between the edge of the CBD and the SmartBus 903 route connecting the outer termini of many north–south tram routes. In the west, the network is even more rudimentary.

Betweenness Centrality

Relative to population and jobs, Melbourne has the lowest global betweenness result of all SNAMUTS case study cities. This demonstrates the shortfalls of a post-war urban growth trend that largely failed to achieve an acceptable level of public transport accessibility in newly developed areas. It also illustrates that the network does not sufficiently capitalise on opportunities for distributing travel paths towards the highest-performance mode (rail), for example by using trams on secondary corridors as effective feeder services to trains on primary corridors. Instead, one of the strongest performers, rivalling the betweenness results of most rail branch lines, is the north–south corridor from Haymarket-Parkville to St Kilda Road, currently only serviced by (non-continuous) tram lines. Parts of this corridor, however, cover the alignment of a proposed north–south underground rail line providing an alternative city centre through-route for suburban rail lines converging at Footscray/North Melbourne and South Yarra/Caulfield. In the current network, the existing rail links between Footscray and Caulfield form a 'sponge' for travel opportunities due to their high level of service and close range to the central area. This raises an important question: is it preferable to strengthen this corridor further by adding another rail link, or should the benefits be distributed

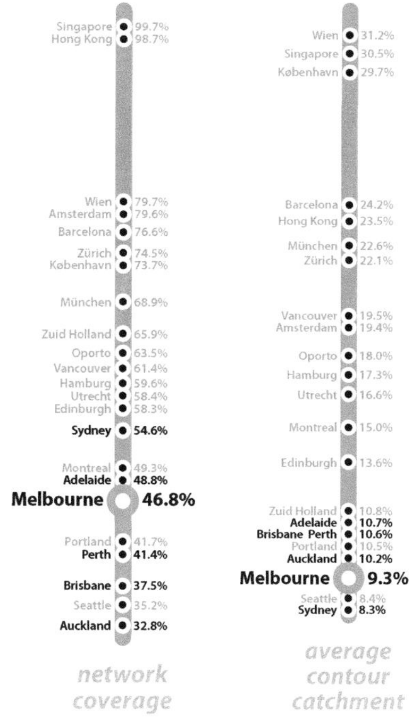

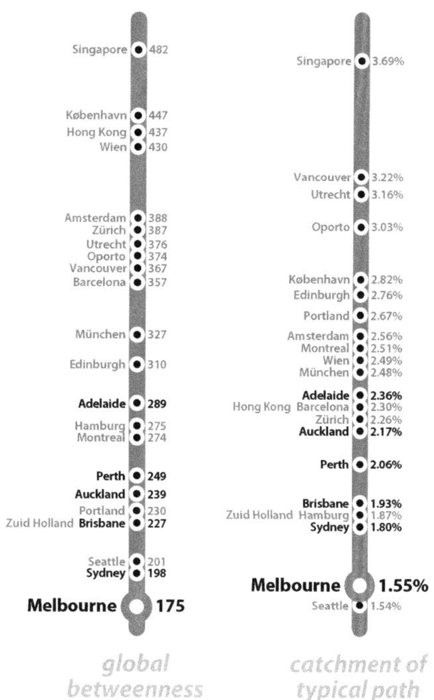

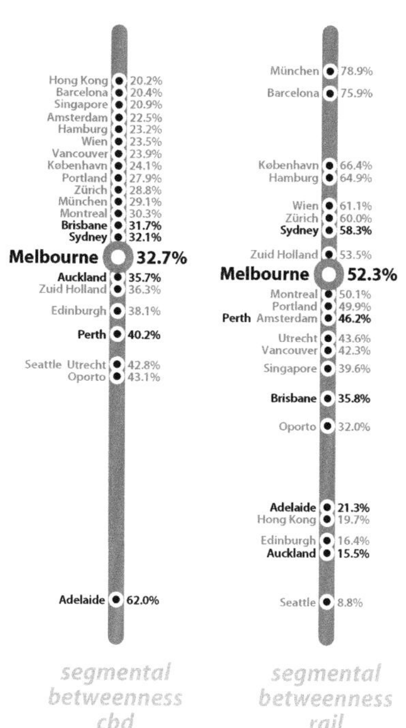

more widely over the inner area by improving service frequencies, travel speeds and network connectivity across the board? Perhaps both actions are equally important in this fast-growing city.

The importance of the CBD network components in facilitating public transport movement across the city is slightly higher in Melbourne than in Sydney or Brisbane, though in the light of the greater complexity of Melbourne's CBD network compared to its peers it is noteworthy that the difference isn't greater. Remarkably the highest nodal betweenness score is at CBD-fringe Richmond (where five major rail corridors converge) rather than stations in the CBD area. Heavy rail captures a slim absolute majority of travel opportunities in Melbourne, less than in Sydney but more than in any of the other Australasian cities.

Network Resilience

Across the network, Melbourne's resilience figures are superior to those of

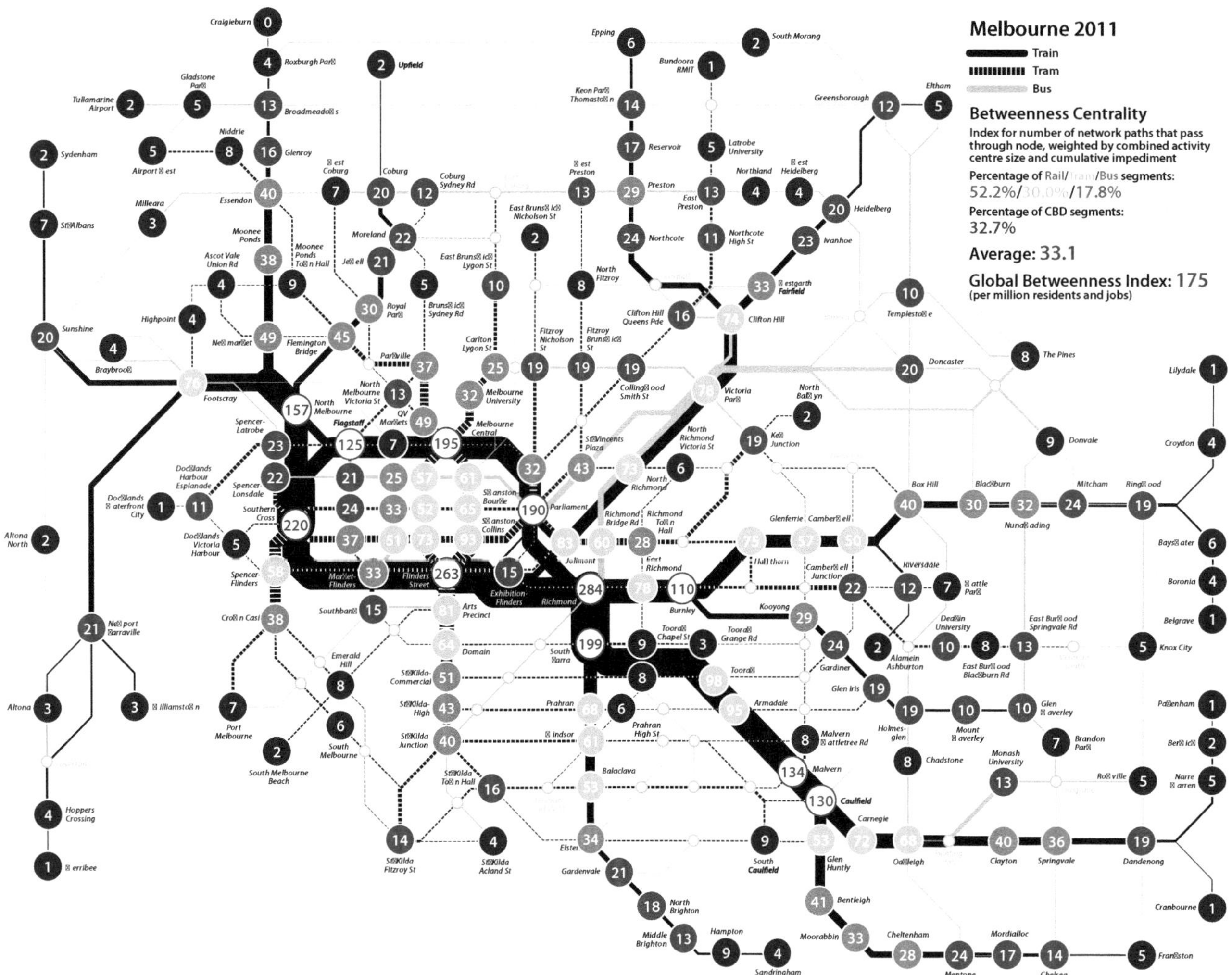

Sydney, Brisbane and Auckland, though they trail behind Perth and Adelaide. This may be a result of the relatively generous supply of public transport infrastructure and services in the CBD area, for which Melbourne records a resilience level second only to Perth in the Australasian sample. Most of Melbourne's potential 'trouble spots' on this index are located in inner and middle suburbs where network density and coherence decline markedly. The Craigieburn, Dandenong and Ringwood rail lines in particular suggest the need for a capacity boost. The Doncaster Smart Bus network along the Eastern Freeway, alongside bus route 246 along Hoddle Street between Clifton Hill and Richmond, show the poorest resilience on the network. While this may not be associated with actual overcrowding, it suggests underutilisation resulting from comparatively low public transport mode shares and/or poor legibility

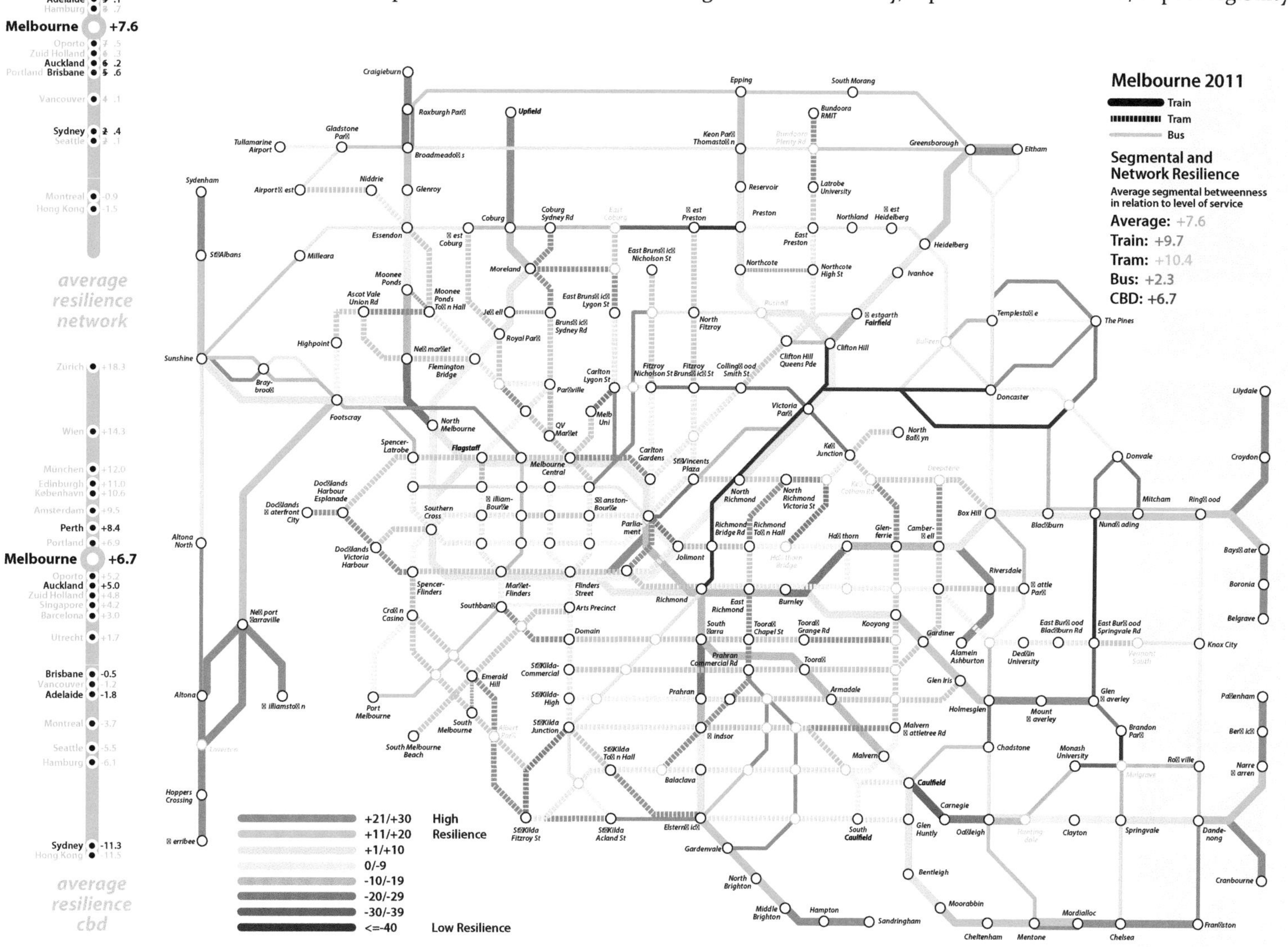

and network integration of these corridors. Poor resilience values also occur along parts of orbital bus routes 902 and 903 and the Elgin-Johnston Street bus routes – areas where the density of the network remains deficient and/or modal upgrades to light rail or bus rapid transit may be warranted in the medium term.

Nodal Connectivity

In Melbourne, 44 per cent of the combined connectivity score for all 192 nodes is captured by the 24 nodes along and within the City Loop (Hoddle Grid), underscoring the high degree of centralisation in the mostly radially configured public transport network. Elsewhere, there is a spatial imbalance on this index, as with the contour catchment index above, between the northern and western suburbs on one side and the southern and eastern suburbs on the other. Of the 53 non-CBD modes with nodal connectivity scores over 50, 39 are located in the southern and eastern suburbs while only 14 are

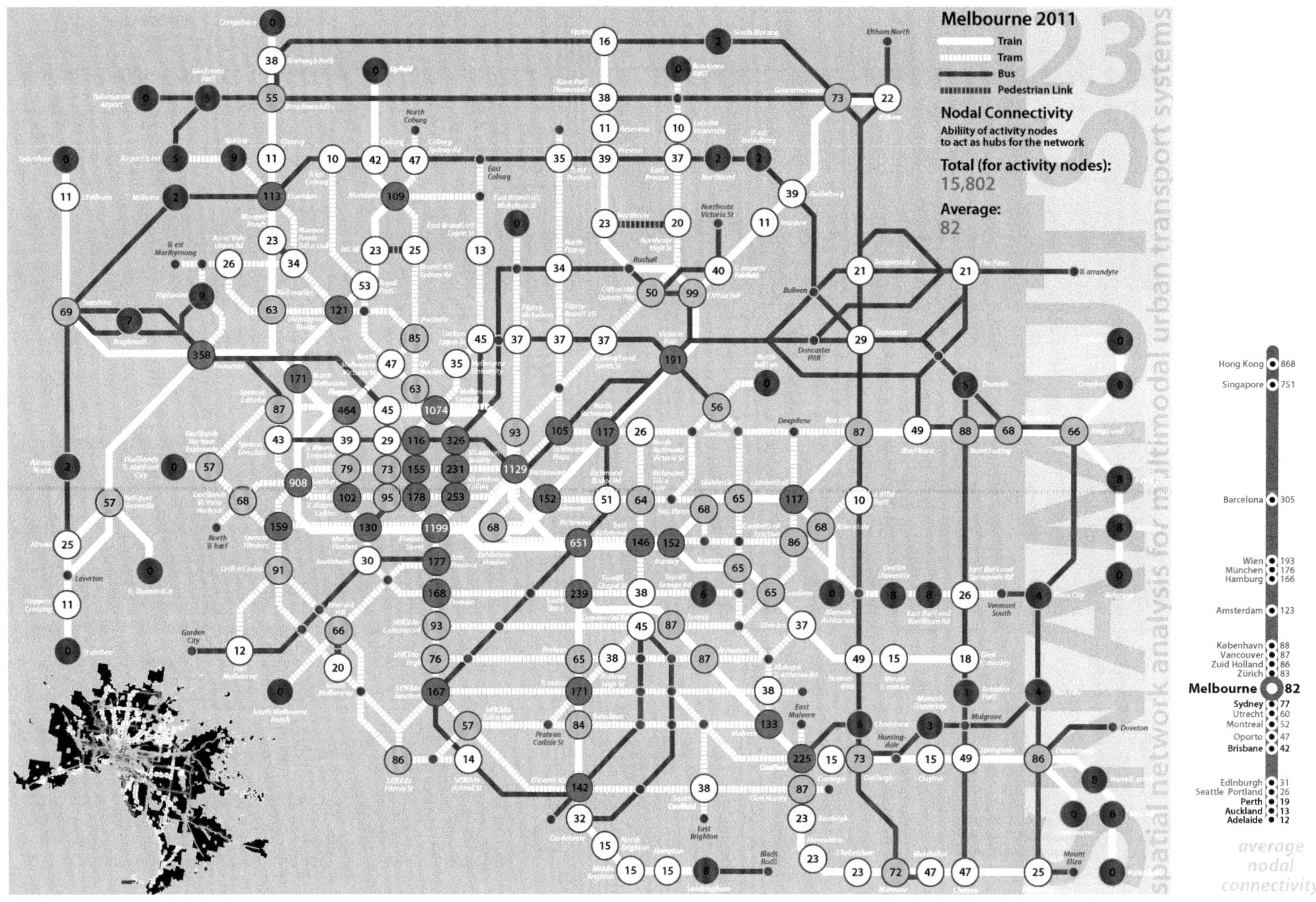

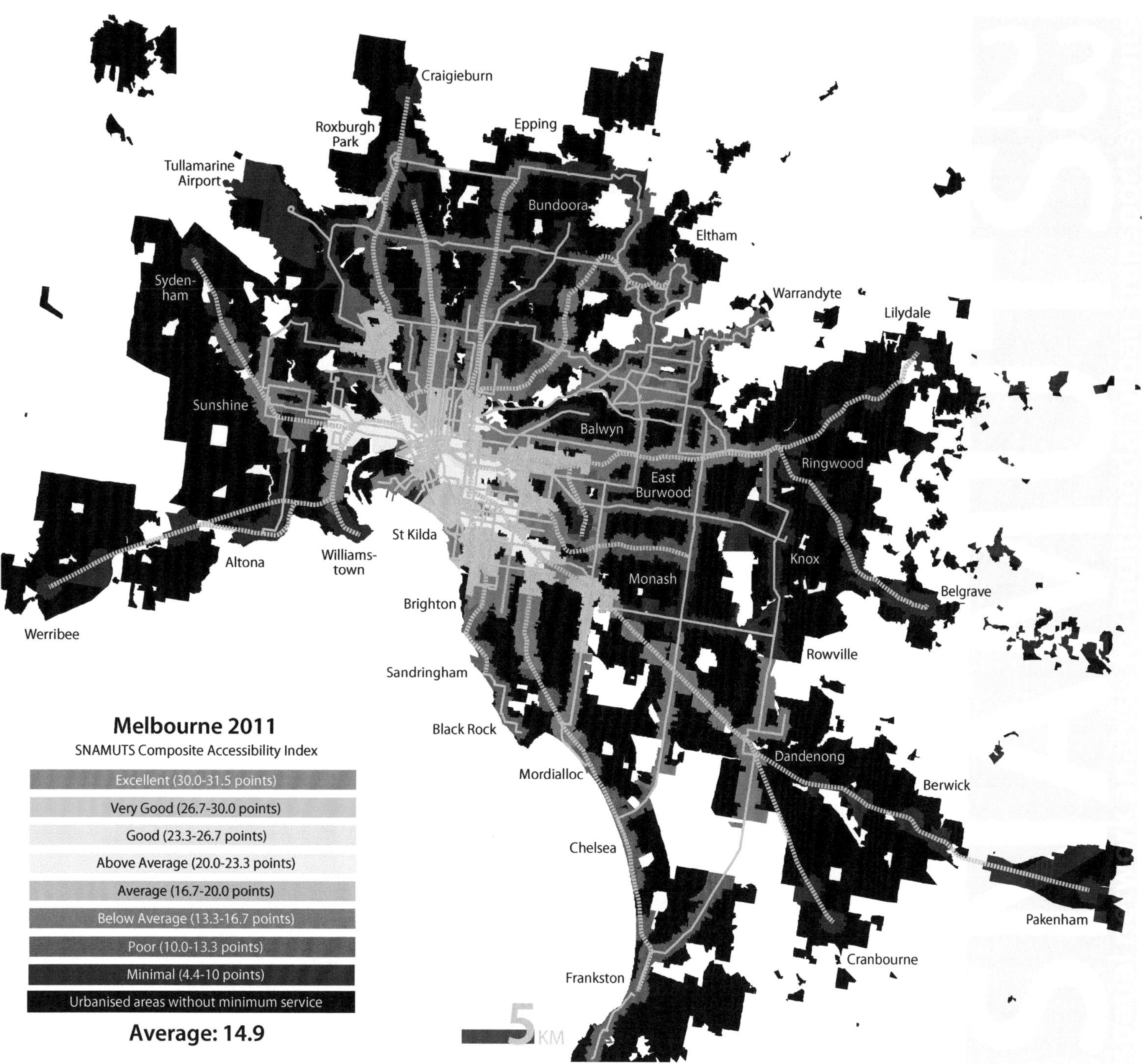

Craigieburn
Roxburgh Park
Epping
Tullamarine Airport
Bundoora
Eltham
Syden-ham
Warrandyte
Lilydale
Sunshine
Balwyn
Ringwood
East Burwood
St Kilda
Altona
Williams-town
Knox
Monash
Belgrave
Werribee
Brighton
Rowville
Sandringham
Black Rock
Dandenong
Mordialloc
Berwick
Chelsea
Pakenham
Cranbourne
Frankston
5 KM
Melbourne 2011
SNAMUTS Composite Accessibility Index
Excellent (30.0-31.5 points)
Very Good (26.7-30.0 points)
Good (23.3-26.7 points)
Above Average (20.0-23.3 points)
Average (16.7-20.0 points)
Below Average (13.3-16.7 points)
Poor (10.0-13.3 points)
Minimal (4.4-10 points)
Urbanised areas without minimum service
Average: 14.9

located in the northern and western suburbs.

SNAMUTS Composite Accessibility Index and Reflections

There is an almost gap-free coverage of public transport endowment (i.e. the presence of at least one public transport service within walking distance) across inner Melbourne, roughly as far as the pre-1960 reach of the tram network (some middle and outer suburban extensions were added more recently), as well as in the City of Manningham, where the SmartBus network was rolled out in 2010. In terms of overall public transport accessibility, however, the south-eastern inner suburbs present a patchwork mostly of average and above-average performance (in international terms) while the only northern and western locations beyond the Maribyrnong River and the City of Yarra's northern boundary with above average results are Footscray and Essendon. In the middle suburbs – the area roughly enclosed by outermost orbital SmartBus route 901 – many 'accessibility deserts' remain in the spaces between rail, tram and SmartBus corridors, while in the outer suburbs the situation deteriorates further.

Melbourne faces a challenge to address the geographical imbalances in public transport accessibility (both between the north-western and south-eastern halves of the city and between the inner, middle and outer rings) as well as to accommodate recent and expected further passenger growth. A fundamental re-think of the future role of public transport in Melbourne is needed. While the Regional Rail Link offers a step in this direction, it is only weakly embedded in a comprehensive, long-term strategy for land use and transport – it did not appear in the state government's metropolitan strategy until a funding opportunity emerged through the federal infrastructure agency (Infrastructure Australia) in 2008–09 (Mees, 2010b). This lack of strategy is also evident in more recent infrastructure proposals. In the 2014 state budget, the additional CBD rail tunnel (mentioned above), the centrepiece of a long-term network investment strategy drawn up by PTV in 2013, was abandoned in favour of a fundamentally modified alignment across Melbourne's inner south without prior consultation or explanation. Simultaneously, an underground road tollway without any significant public transport component was planned across Melbourne's inner north, as the most prominent and costly element of the State Government's infrastructure investment program, despite fierce resistance by the community and opposition parties. Recent transport plans in Melbourne appear as a collection of ad-hoc projects without transparent supporting analysis and community and stakeholder consensus on strategic directions in land use-transport planning.

ACCESSIBILITY PROFILE: SYDNEY

Sydney, Australia's largest metropolitan area of 4.39 million inhabitants (2011), records an average annual growth rate of some 55,000 people since 2006. The birthplace of European settlement in Australia, the city is configured around a large natural harbour which continues to shape significant parts of the settlement area with its multitude of bays, peninsulas and limited number of crossing points, even after two centuries of urban growth towards the hinterland. To the north and south, metropolitan Sydney is separated from the neighbouring coastal cities of Newcastle and Wollongong by two national parks forming an effective greenbelt; in the west, the Blue Mountains have a similar effect. Thus outer suburban growth

in Sydney has traditionally met greater spatial constraints than in most other Australasian cities and, in conjunction with the desirability of harbour-side living, fostered a city building tradition with higher urban densities.

An extensive suburban rail network services the metropolitan area and is operated by a state agency (City Rail). Like in other Australian cities, the majority of the network dates back to the era before the proliferation of mass car ownership, though the system continues to expand. The bus system in Sydney's inner and middle suburbs is also operated by a state government agency (Sydney Buses). It consists of a plethora of radial routes as well as a more recently introduced network of 14 radial and orbital Metrobus routes. In the western outer suburbs, several Metrobus routes are partially aligned along purpose-built bus transitways. Local services in outer Sydney, in contrast, are generally operated by private companies. Sydney Harbour and its surrounding residential areas are serviced by a ferry network centred on Circular Quay, though not all routes are operated at the 30-minute daytime frequency required for inclusion in the SNAMUTS database.

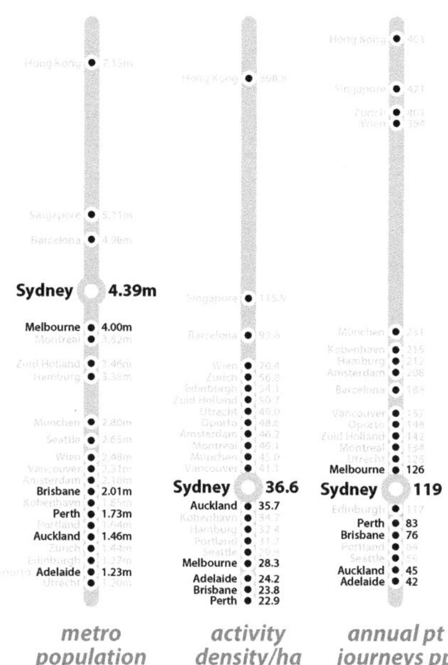

Fare integration in Sydney is far more rudimentary than in any other Australian city; as far as single-trip tickets are concerned, each transport mode maintains its own fare system that does not allow free transfers to another mode, and in the case of buses and ferries, not even to the same mode (Mees and Dodson, 2011). Fully multimodal fares (MyMulti) are only sold as periodical tickets, and these are priced much higher than the more widespread single-mode periodical tickets available from the rail operators. Sydney's ticketing system thus incurs financial disincentives against making transfers that are absent in other Australian cities.

Public transport patronage levels (annual journeys per capita) have not grown at nearly the same rate as Melbourne's in recent years. Among the New World SNAMUTS case studies, however, only the Canadian cities show greater public transport usage than Australia's two largest metropolitan centres.

Following many announcements and abandonments for public transport infrastructure projects in the last decade, a rail extension into an outer south-western urban growth corridor is under construction. A north-western rail branch line between Epping and Rouse Hill is in the planning stages. There are also plans to expand the city's single light rail line into a larger network, replacing congested bus services in the CBD and on some critical inner suburban corridors.

Service Intensity

The rail system is operated in distinct and colour-coded groups of lines, most of which run every 30 minutes during the weekday inter-peak period, while route overlaps generate 15-minute or better frequencies on the busier routes. Sydney's light rail line (built in stages since 1997 mostly on a former freight rail alignment in the inner western suburbs) is operated at 12-minute weekday inter-peak intervals by a private company. Metrobuses are serviced at minimum 15-minute frequencies, similar to Melbourne's SmartBus network and Brisbane's BUZ routes. Most other Sydney Buses routes also meet the minimum SNAMUTS standard, whereas among the privately operated bus routes in the outer suburbs, 30- or 60-minute frequencies are more common.

Relative to its slightly higher population, Sydney puts on a marginally greater number of public transport services than Melbourne. However, this difference may be associated with the far greater number of buses required to operate Sydney's network, even when comparing the combined figures for all surface modes. Melbourne's trams, with their higher passenger capacity and occupancy than buses, are likely to achieve an efficiency benefit here and reduce the operationally less than optimal oversaturation of some CBD streets with public transport vehicles. In Sydney, a total of more than 70 weekday inter-peak bus movements per hour per direction on parts of George Street and Elizabeth Street were recorded, a concentration of operational resources that has no equivalent on Melbourne's streets. Conversely, the numbers of deployed trains are quite similar in both cities, considering the difference in population. Compared to Melbourne (as well as Adelaide and Brisbane), however, Sydney has fewer train stations per capita.

Closeness Centrality

With few exceptions, Sydney's closeness centrality scores follow a relatively smooth decay gradient from the city centre outwards within the area that is covered by a relatively dense and partially multi-directional network of buses. The exceptions appear to be associated with constraining geographical features or convoluted waterfronts.

As bus network density declines, roughly beyond a line connecting Chatswood, Ryde, Burwood, Campsie and Rockdale, increases in closeness scores follow a steepening gradient, though again with a few exceptions. These concern the Parramatta rail corridor which, despite an awkward conglomerate of varying stopping patterns, is the rail trunk with the highest combined service frequency and thus offers superior conditions for public transport movement. A similar, though weaker, effect is present on the Illawarra line which offers a 10-minute frequency as far south as Sutherland. Conversely, activity centres north of the harbour fall comparatively short on this index.

In international terms, Sydney has one of the poorest network averages for closeness centrality. Ease of movement in Sydney is clearly affected by the lack of fare integration, a factor that has been considered in the analysis by making different assumptions about the attractiveness of intermodal transfers than in other cities. In addition, Sydney's geography with numerous water bodies, protected green spaces and low-density suburban areas outside the urban core, as well as relatively infrequent rail services over considerable distances, work to inflate these numbers.

Degree Centrality

Despite the rudimentary nature of fare integration, significant parts of the

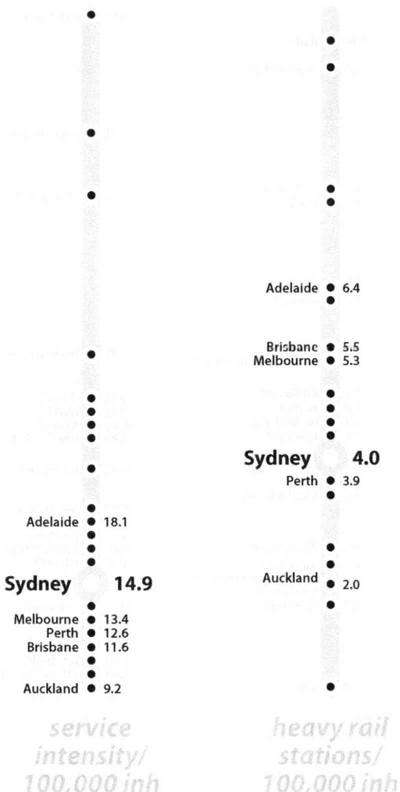

network, particularly outside the service area of Sydney Buses, are organised around transfers and a distribution of tasks between rail and bus according to the properties of each mode. This results in a number of outer suburban nodes with relatively high transfer intensity, since accessibility to and from these nodes depends on making connections at larger hubs. Some inner suburban nodes, particularly in waterfront locations in the north and east, also have only mid-range degree centrality scores, likely related to the fact that not all public transport routes that lead into the CBD provide direct connections to each other there. Town Hall scores best, relegating Sydney Central to second

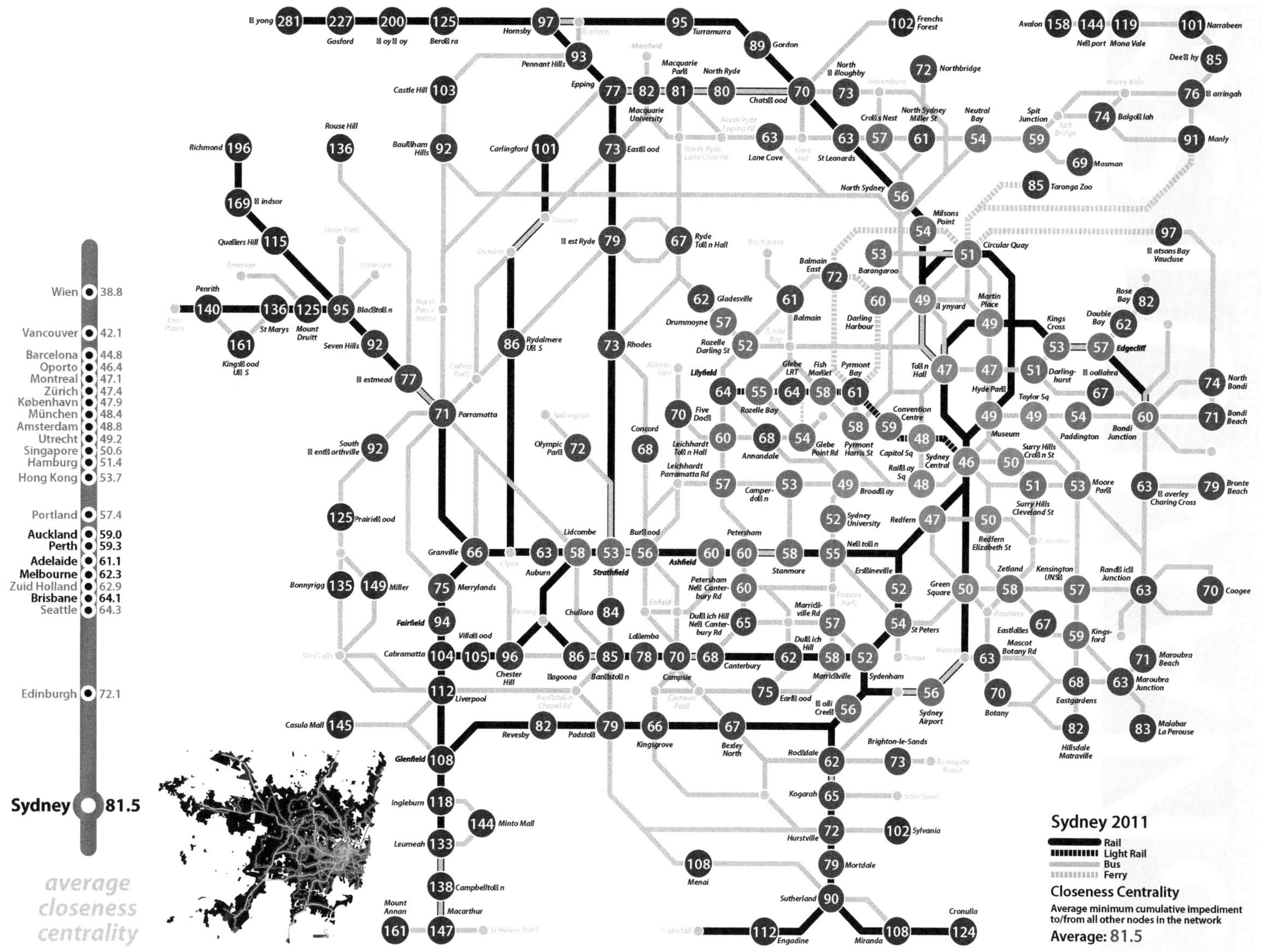

place, since this node acts as a terminus for many radial bus routes from the west, north and east. CBD-fringe node Redfern is also significant on this index, as well as the middle-suburban nodes of Burwood, Campsie and Parramatta that benefited from the improvements to the orbital bus network in recent years.

Network Coverage

Sydney's network coverage is the highest in the Australasian sample and, alongside Vancouver, the only value in a New World city to exceed 50 per cent. This relates to urban density (also higher in Sydney than in other Australasian cities) and the concentration of development around suburban rail

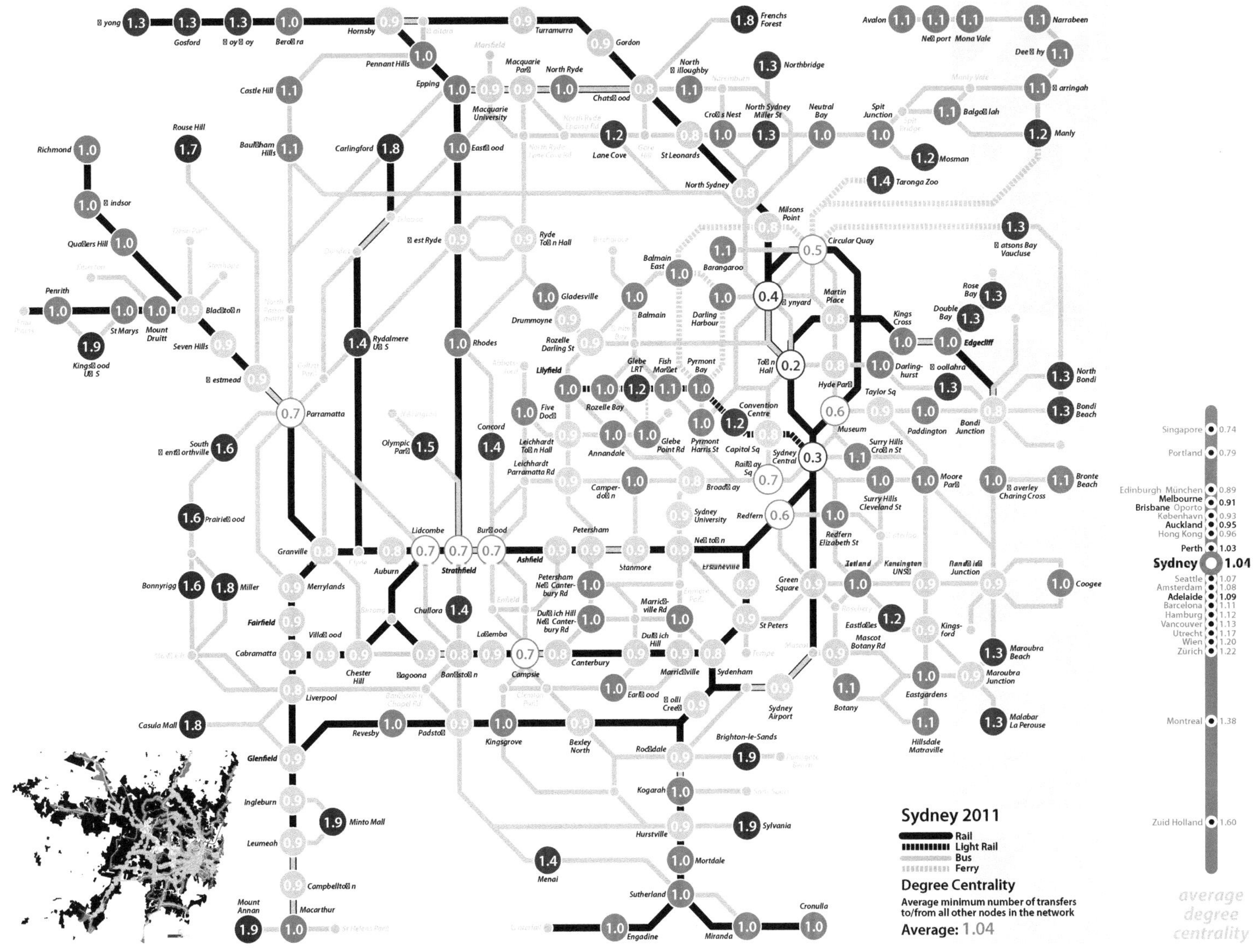

hubs, a land use policy pursued for many decades (Newman, 2009). Due to geographical barriers the overall share of dispersed suburban areas is lower than in Sydney's regional peer cities, with the exception of Auckland.

Thirty-Minute Contour Catchments

Sydney Central and Redfern are the best-performing nodes on this index. Contour catchment values drop moving north across the CBD towards the waterfront, below 20 per cent in the case of Circular Quay despite the ferry routes converging there. Along the rail network, contour catchment scores above 10 per cent prevail as far as Chatswood, Bondi Junction and to

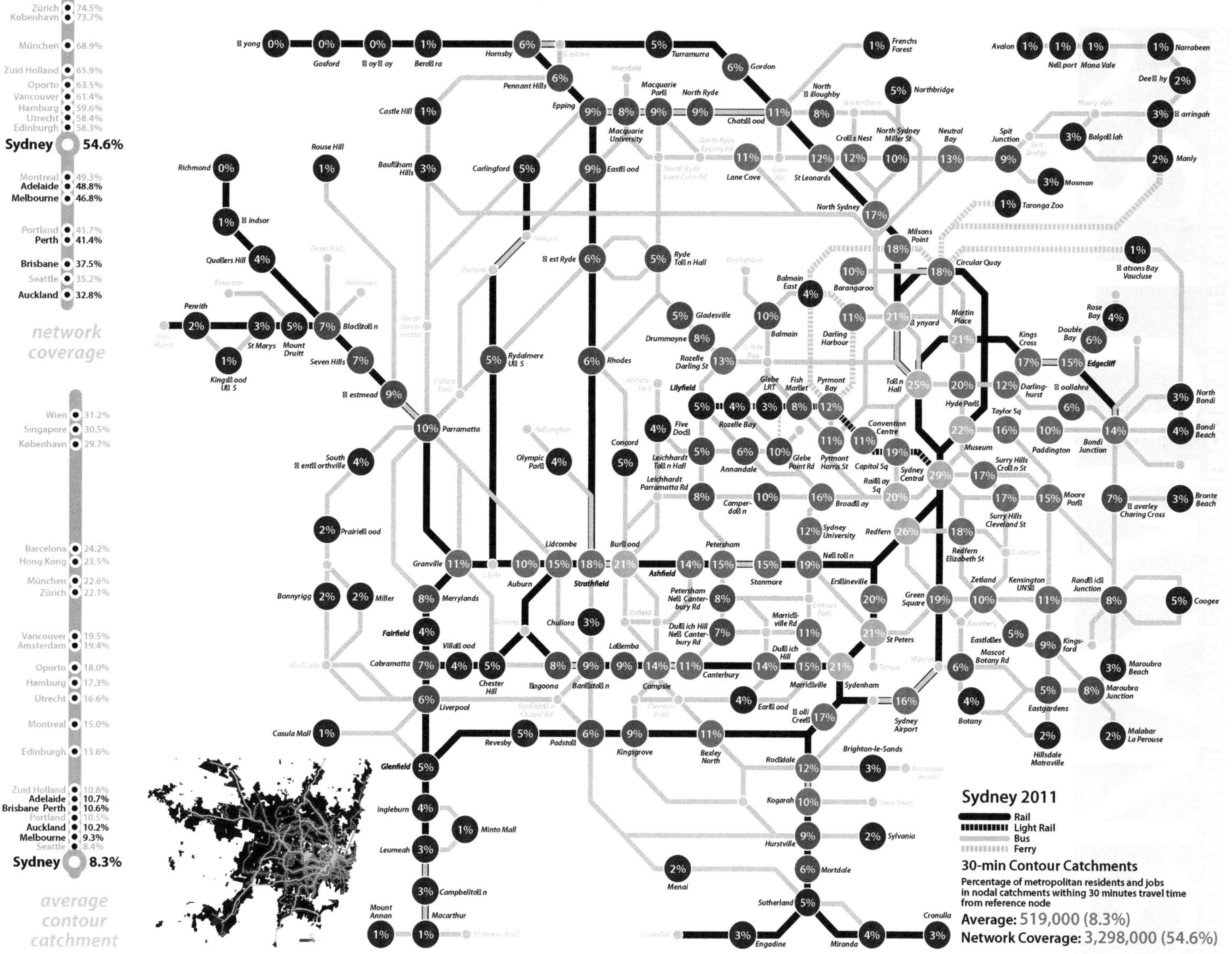

a greater distance on the western and southern sections of the system (the trunk route between Granville and the city stands out as a top performer). Conversely, there is a rapid drop in values to 10 per cent or below on the inner suburban bus network not far from the CBD fringe. The same is true for the light rail line which is disadvantaged by a lengthy detour around the peninsula of Pyrmont and Ultimo prior to reaching its more direct route through Glebe and Rozelle to Lilyfield.

Across the international sample, Sydney's average 30-minute contour catchments are the smallest in percentage terms. Again, the city's non-contiguous urban fabric in combination with relatively slow services away from the rail network and the prevalence of numerous 'missing links' between suburban nodes and corridors (even where the urban geography would allow for them) is the key cause. This is in contrast to other large SNAMUTS cities like Montreal, Barcelona, Hamburg or Munich, all of which deliver average 30-minute contour catchments at roughly two or three times Sydney's proportion.

Betweenness Centrality

Sydney's segmental betweenness index shows a pronounced division of tasks between rail and bus, in functional-hierarchical terms and even more so in geographical terms. The bulk of strategic significance for movement on the rail system is concentrated on links south and west of the CBD (the Sydney to Parramatta corridor, the Bankstown, Illawarra and Airport lines). In these areas, buses are relegated to a secondary role for more fine-grained access and for orbital and diagonal links. Such a distribution of movement opportunities in this sub-region suits the characteristics of both modes and establishes a functional hierarchy. Conversely, in the inner suburbs there is a much greater prominence of strongly performing bus corridors (along Broadway-Parramatta Road; Victoria Road; Military Road; Oxford Street; Anzac Parade) as well as many CBD streets saturated with buses. It is no surprise that proposals to convert these corridors to light or heavy rail operation regularly emerge in Sydney's transport debate. The management of bus movements along CBD streets has become a formidable challenge for the city. In contrast, the existing light rail route and the ferry system play only minor roles in generating travel opportunities. This is related to the low frequencies and slow speeds on the ferry system and the sub-optimal integration of the light rail route with areas of focussed urban development beyond the Darling Harbour-Pyrmont Bay area on the outward journey to Lilyfield.

On the global betweenness index, Sydney has the second lowest result in the world-wide sample, outperforming only Melbourne. The disjointed nature of the network, enforced partially by geography and partially by design, and the relatively long travel times and low frequencies away from a handful of key corridors are the key explanations for this. Sydney's edge over Melbourne can be attributed to Sydney's higher density and urban concentration. Half a million Sydneysiders live at residential densities of 70 per hectare or higher compared to only 100,000 in Melbourne (DPI NSW, 2010). Conversely, there are also expansive parts of the metropolitan area where the concentration of public transport travel opportunities is extremely low, similar to the peer cities. The betweenness index points to

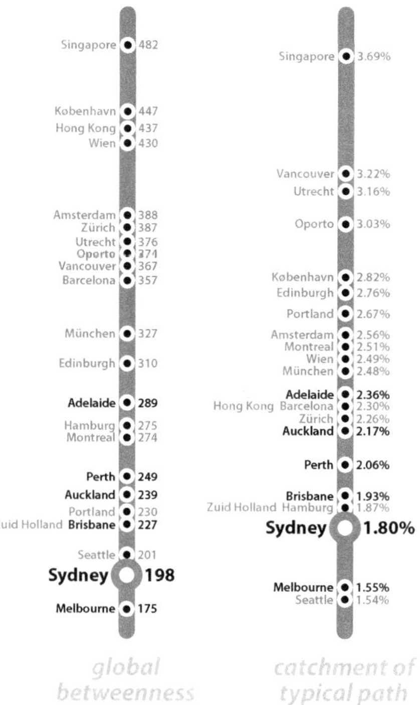

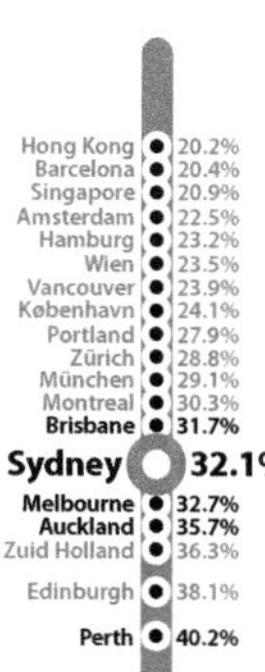

a divided city where public transport-rich inner areas and southern/western rail corridors coexist with a dearth of public transport accessibility in suburban areas and along most coastlines and waterfronts.

Network Resilience

On average, Sydney has the poorest segmental resilience result, on par with the North American rather than the Australasian cities, and the poorest value of any SNAMUTS city for segmental congestion in the CBD area. This is mostly due to a bus system under stress along the aforementioned key corridors as well as on numerous suburban feeder services. On the rail system, which is operated

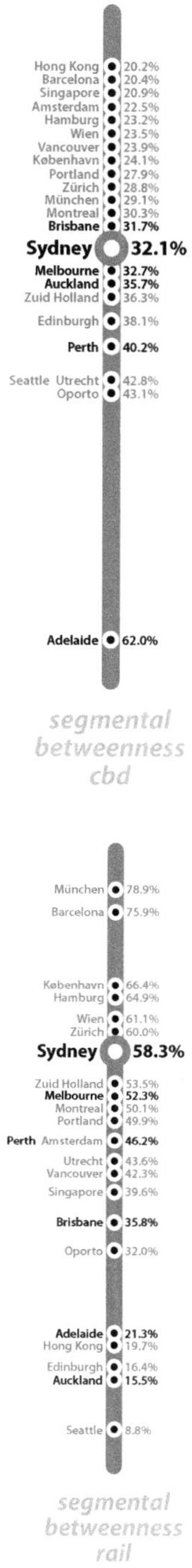

Hong Kong 20.2%
Barcelona 20.4%
Singapore 20.9%
Amsterdam 22.5%
Hamburg 23.2%
Wien 23.5%
Vancouver 23.9%
København 24.1%
Portland 27.9%
Zürich 28.8%
München 29.1%
Montreal 30.3%
Brisbane 31.7%
Sydney 32.1%
Melbourne 32.7%
Auckland 35.7%
Zuid Holland 36.3%
Edinburgh 38.1%
Perth 40.2%
Seattle Utrecht 42.8%
Oporto 43.1%
Adelaide 62.0%
segmental betweenness cbd
München 78.9%
Barcelona 75.9%
København 66.4%
Hamburg 64.9%
Wien 61.1%
Zürich 60.0%
Sydney 58.3%
Zuid Holland 53.5%
Melbourne 52.3%
Montreal 50.1%
Portland 49.9%
Perth Amsterdam 46.2%
Utrecht 43.6%
Vancouver 42.3%
Singapore 39.6%
Brisbane 35.8%
Oporto 32.0%
Adelaide 21.3%
Hong Kong 19.7%
Edinburgh 16.4%
Auckland 15.5%
Seattle 8.8%
segmental betweenness rail

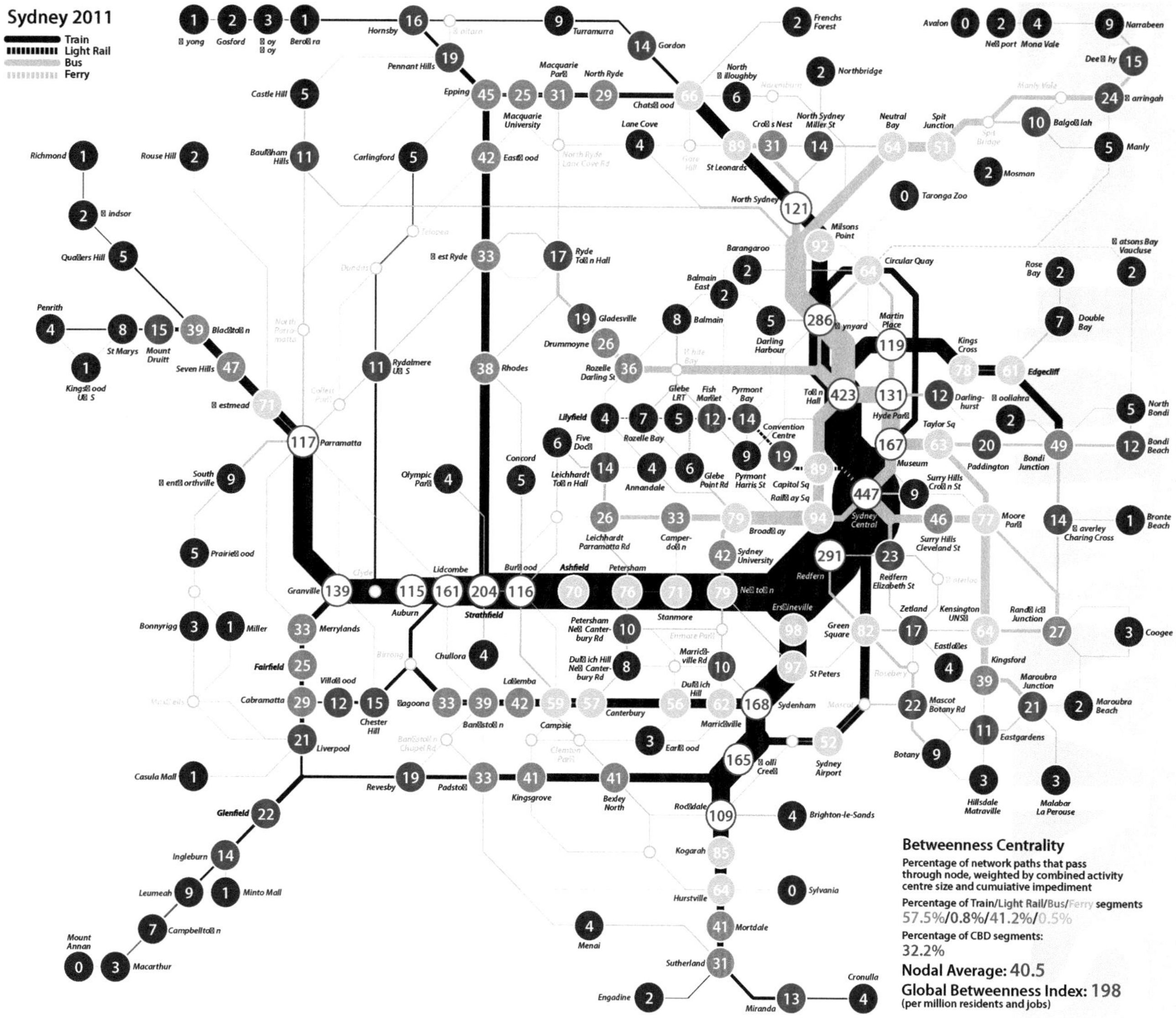

Sydney 2011
Train
Light Rail
Bus
Ferry
Betweenness Centrality
Percentage of network paths that pass through node, weighted by combined activity centre size and cumulative impediment
Percentage of Train/Light Rail/Bus/Ferry segments
57.5%/0.8%/41.2%/0.5%
Percentage of CBD segments:
32.2%
Nodal Average: 40.5
Global Betweenness Index: 198
(per million residents and jobs)

by larger (predominantly double-deck) and longer trains than those of the other Australasian cities, only the outer western trunk line between Parramatta and Strathfield may be developing a resilience problem at this stage. On the light rail route resilience figures could be enhanced if the section between Sydney Central and Pyrmont Bay, popular with tourists and casino patrons, had a frequency upgrade. Current efforts to convert some of the most congested inner-city bus corridors to the higher-capacity mode of light rail, as well as to introduce an integrated ticketing system that no longer penalises transfers, will result in some improvements to network resilience.

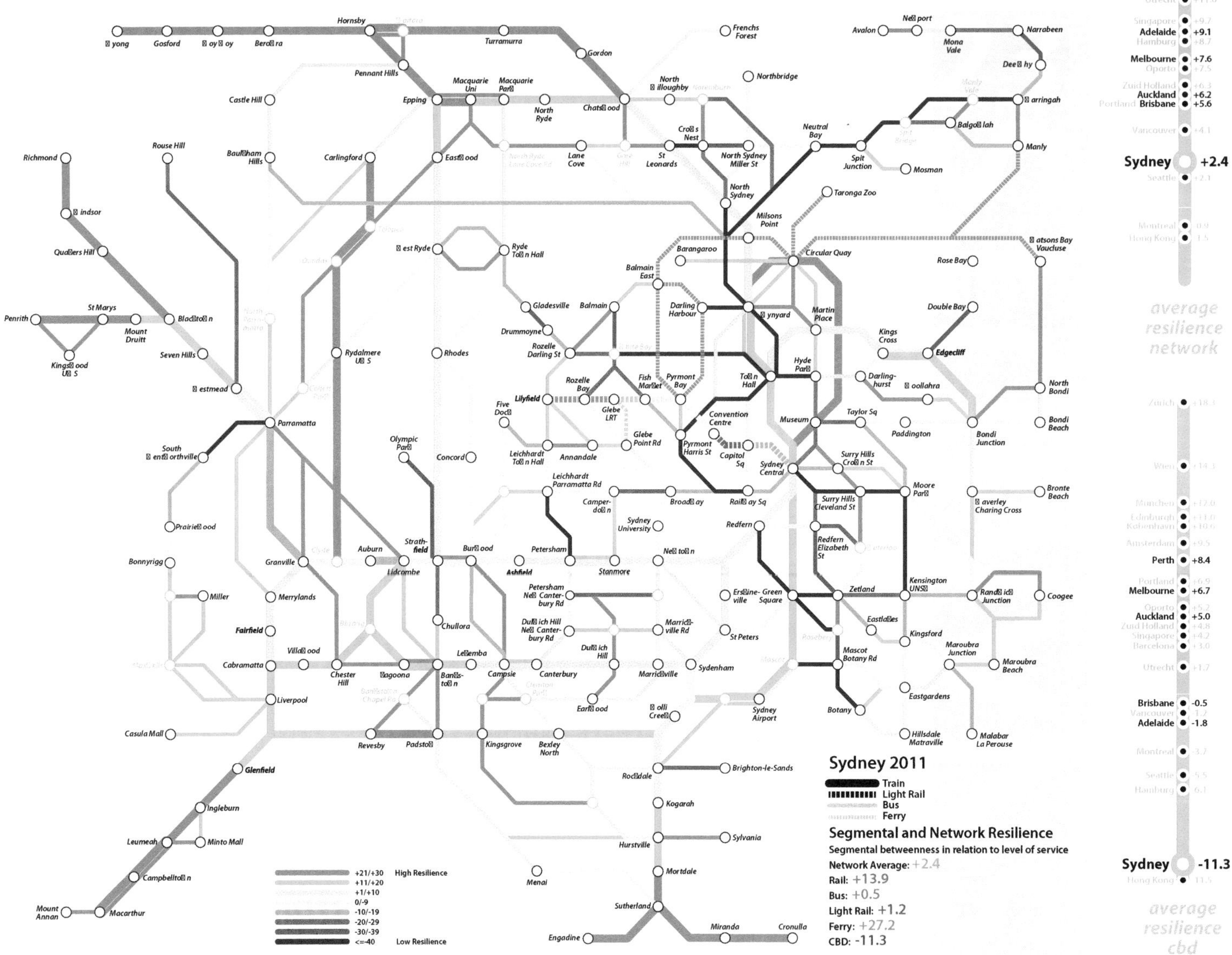

Nodal Connectivity

This index shows around 43 per cent of the total score being shared by the 10 immediate CBD nodes. Owing to the configuration of many rail-based suburban centres as public transport hubs, however, good results on this index can be found scattered around the rail system (Parramatta, Strathfield, Chatswood and Bondi Junction are the obvious examples). Along the bus-based corridors in inner Sydney, however, there are only a small number of nodes with high connectivity results, underscoring the relative isolation of

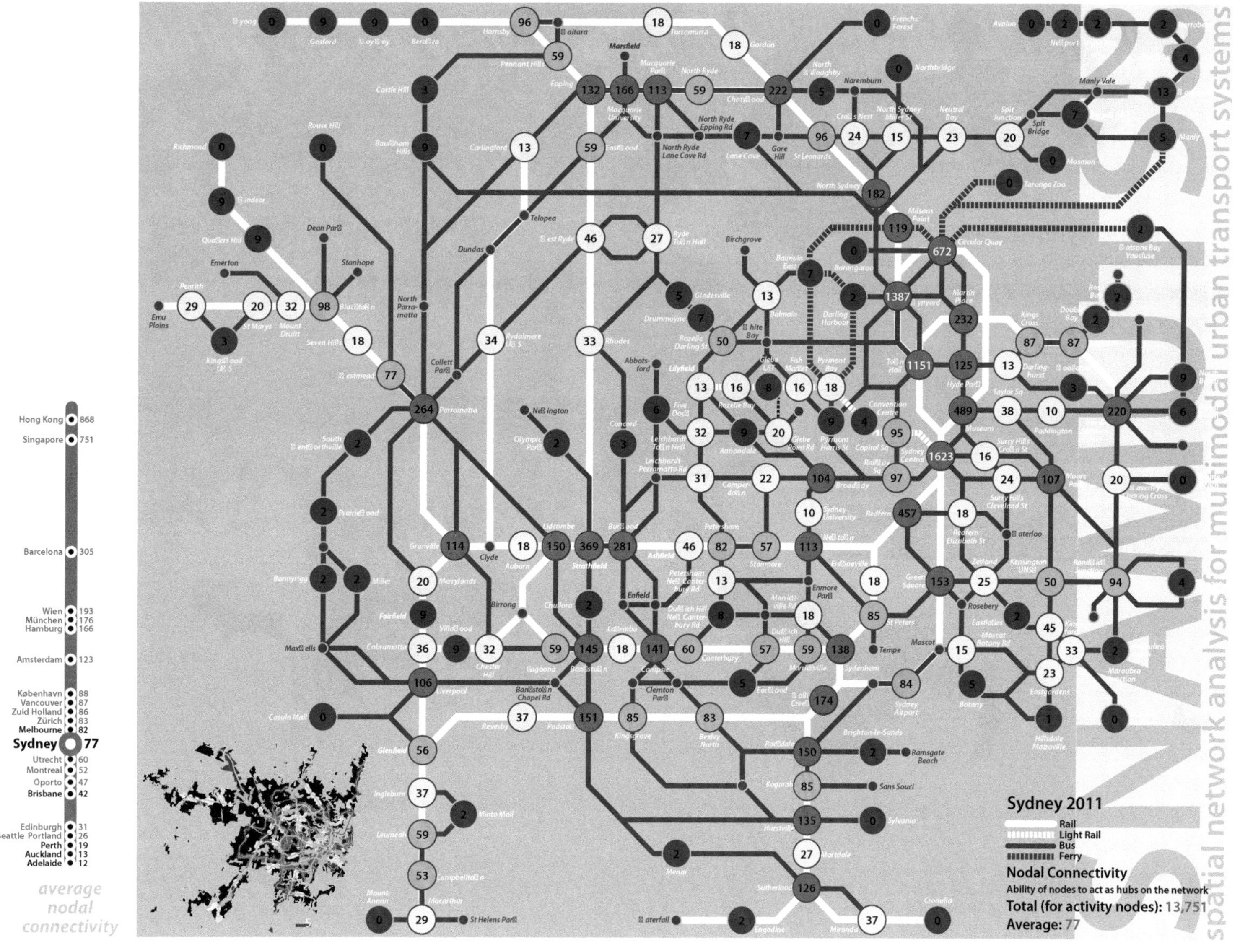

Sydney 2011
SNAMUTS Composite Accessibility Index
Excellent (30.0-31.1 points)
Very Good (26.7-30.0 points)
Good (23.3-26.7 points)
Above Average (20.0-23.3 points)
Average (16.7-20.0 points)
Below Average (13.3-16.7 points)
Poor (10.0-13.3 points)
Minimal (3.0-10 points)
Urbanised areas without minimum service
Average: 13.2
Richmond
Windsor
Berowra
Avalon
Rouse Hill
Hornsby
Penrith
Turra-mara
Dee Why
Castle Hill
St Marys
Mount Druitt
Blacktown
Manly
Parramatta
Vaucluse
Cabra-matta
Bondi Beach
Coogee
Maroubra
Glenfield
Revesby
Botany
La Perouse
Ingleburn
Campbelltown
Suther-land
Cronulla
5 KM

these locations when it comes to moving easily around the metropolitan area on public transport.

SNAMUTS Composite Accessibility Index and Reflections

An accessibility gap is apparent between Sydney's rail-based and bus-based settlement areas: above-average and good performance can be found in the central area and along the rail lines to Bondi Junction, Sydenham-Rockville and the airport. Remarkably however, there is a middle ring of rail-based suburban centres – Parramatta, Lidcombe, Strathfield, Burwood, Campsie and Chatswood – that perform better than neighbouring suburbs closer to central Sydney. Apart from the influence of fast and relatively frequent, partially express-running train services, this observation can be traced to the effect of network design: with few exceptions, there is far less physical integration between City Rail and the Sydney Buses routes in inner Sydney than there is between City Rail and the privately run bus routes in middle and outer Sydney. In the inner areas, it appears as though the two state agencies compete with one another. There also appears to be a fairly sharp boundary (roughly along the line linking Liverpool, Parramatta, Epping, Chatswood and Manly) between the relatively well-covered inner and middle areas and outer suburban Sydney, where public transport access at the SNAMUTS standard is limited to selected rail and busway corridors while leaving large tracts of urbanised land un- or underserviced. Potentially, the proposed outer suburban rail extensions will address this issue to an extent, while the recent light rail extension from Lilyfield to Dulwich Hill may add modest network connectivity in the inner west – modest because this line does not provide a convenient interchange point with the most dominant public transport corridor, the heavy rail line between central Sydney Central and Strathfield.

Overall Sydney can be characterised as the Australian city with the most inherently public transport–friendly urban form (give or take a quiet, exclusive waterfront suburb in the inner area and a comparatively modest extent of low-density urban dispersal). In practice, however, there is room for improvement by capitalising on this advantage. Integration between public transport modes remains patchy and, to the user, somewhat arbitrary, both in physical terms, in ticketing terms and in terms of institutional collaboration. Despite recent improvements (rail timetables and stopping patterns, the rollout of a network of Metrobus routes and the extension of the light rail system) there remain obsolete layers of network design and governance from the vantage point of each single mode which, in a city with mounting congestion problems, translate into inefficiencies and sub-optimal resilience seen most acutely in the city centre. Some of these shortcomings are influenced by the city's complicated geography and thus affect other modes of travel in similar ways as they affect public transport: for instance, the fragmentation of public transport fares and operation is matched by a similarly labyrinthine coexistence of different tollway operators in the road sector.

ACCESSIBILITY PROFILE: BRISBANE

Brisbane is situated at the heart of a larger agglomeration stretching more than 200 km along the Pacific Coast in south-east Queensland. In 2011, the core metropolitan region, consisting of the five municipalities of Brisbane, Ipswich, Logan, Moreton Bay and Redland, had a population of 2.01 million (annual growth of about 40,000 people since 2006), making it Australasia's third largest urban agglomeration with an urbanised area density similar to Adelaide and Perth but significantly lower than any of the remaining SNAMUTS case study cities.

Public transport across South East Queensland is coordinated by the government agency TransLink. Within the Brisbane metropolitan area the network comprises an electrified suburban rail system operated by a state agency (Queensland Rail) with an inner-city trunk line, nine suburban branches and several regional rail lines. The bus system is operated by a multitude of companies in regional concessions; the largest of these is Brisbane Transport owned by the city council. In inner Brisbane, there is a partially underground dedicated busway system on three significant corridors. Brisbane Council also operates frequent ferry services along the Brisbane River, which meanders through the CBD and adjacent inner suburbs, breaking up the central area into a series of peninsulas.

TransLink has a zonal fare structure and an electronic ticketing system (though pricier paper tickets are also available) based on single journeys with an automatic weekly cap for regular commuters. Investment in Brisbane's public transport system continues with the rollout of more high-frequency bus routes, the extension of dedicated busway routes and two new suburban rail branches in the middle and outer suburbs.

Brisbane's public transport patronage has not grown to the same magnitude as that in Perth or Melbourne in recent years, and was overtaken in terms of annual trips per capita by Perth. However, Brisbane's usage figures still compare favourably with Adelaide, Auckland and the US case study cities.

Service Intensity

Rail services in metropolitan Brisbane operate on a standardised 30-minute frequency during the weekday interpeak period, and have only limited sections of trunk routes where two or more lines combine towards shorter headways. Within the bus system, there is a core network known as BUZ running minimum 15-minute services on weekdays and 30-minute services on weekends. On the dedicated busways, many of these (and other) routes overlap, generating very high frequencies along some sections (including more than 100 buses per hour per direction across CBD-edge Victoria Bridge).

Comparatively and in relation to population size, Brisbane has the second lowest level of service intensity (before Auckland) in the Australasian sample. This is despite Brisbane's strong reliance on buses, which usually drives up this figure. Brisbane's rail station density relative to population reflects the origins of most of its rail system in the late nineteenth and early twentieth century with short station spacings to facilitate walkable access and is second only to Adelaide in the Australasian sample.

Closeness Centrality

The high-frequency busway network is chiefly responsible for generating a core group of 20 activity nodes with uniformly good closeness performance. On the suburban rail corridors, however, there is a steep gradient of deteriorating nodal scores from centre to periphery due to low frequencies and

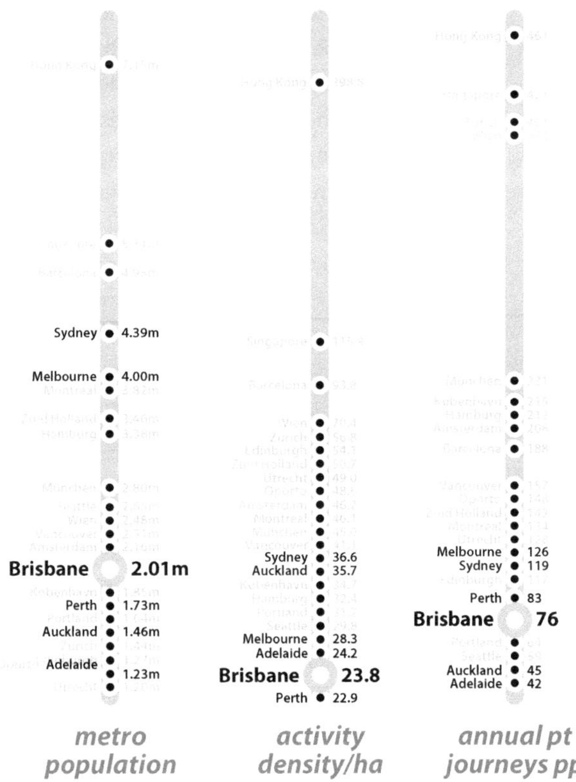

Adelaide 18.1
Sydney 14.9
Melbourne 13.4
Perth 12.6
Brisbane 11.6
Auckland 9.2

service intensity/ 100,000 inh

Adelaide 6.4
Brisbane 5.5
Melbourne 5.3
Sydney 4.0
Perth 3.9
Auckland 2.0

heavy rail stations/ 100,000 inh

(with the exception of the Beenleigh line, which has some express services) all-station stopping patterns. Some nodes predominantly, or exclusively, accessible by ferry along or across the Brisbane River also perform more poorly on this index than the neighbours, with the prevailing reason being the (by necessity) limited reach of the ferry system and the (also mostly by necessity) limited number and sub-optimal location of transfer points to other modes.

The combination of these factors produces a city with vast contrasts in terms of public transport ease of movement. The results suggest that outside the central area, South Brisbane and the busway corridors, public transport movement may be perceived as quite onerous. Brisbane's average closeness performance shares with Seattle the poorest result among the (mostly) fare-integrated SNAMUTS cities.

Degree Centrality

Activity nodes with the best degree centrality scores are associated with the CBD and inner southern busway system, and the bus corridor between Fortitude Valley and the CBD core. The poorest scores are found at several ferry nodes.

In Brisbane, unlike in Perth, there is no obvious modal hierarchy between rail and bus at the SNAMUTS minimum standard, where buses would act as feeders to radial rail lines and in turn reduce the number of bus movements in the centre. Rather, rail and bus trunk lines run parallel to one another in some locations, and the network of each mode appears able to function, in principle, independently of the other. This situation may be inherited from the era before integrated fares and network planning (prior to 2008). The coexistence of both systems also reflects the lion share of recent infrastructure investment in bus rapid transit (BRT) rather than rail projects, and is facilitated by the high-capacity bus thoroughfare and terminals created as part of this busway system in inner Brisbane. A number of lower-frequency classic bus feeder networks to rail do exist in suburban areas; however, these do not meet the minimum standard required for inclusion in the SNAMUTS analysis.

Network Coverage

Brisbane's extent of network coverage is inferior to that of any other major Australian city. Within the global SNAMUTS sample, only Seattle and Auckland provide less extensive network coverage. In Brisbane, a reasonable degree of area-wide coverage in the inner suburbs contrasts with sparse coverage in middle and outer suburbs, where only a relatively small number of rail, busway and on-street bus corridors leave significant spatial gaps and little if any connectivity among them. Some centres identified as high-order in the metropolitan strategy (QLD DIPT, 2009), such as Springfield and Capalaba, had no public transport services at the minimum standard at all in 2011 (Springfield has since been connected to the rail network).

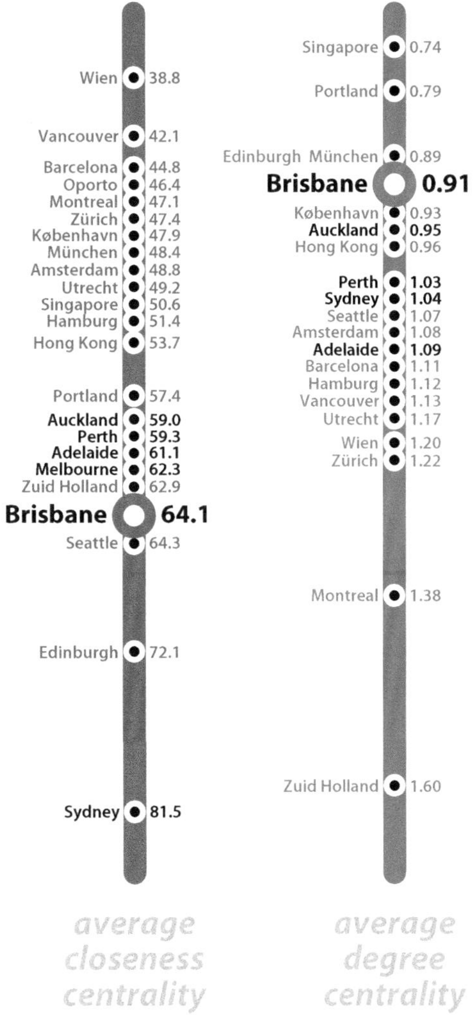

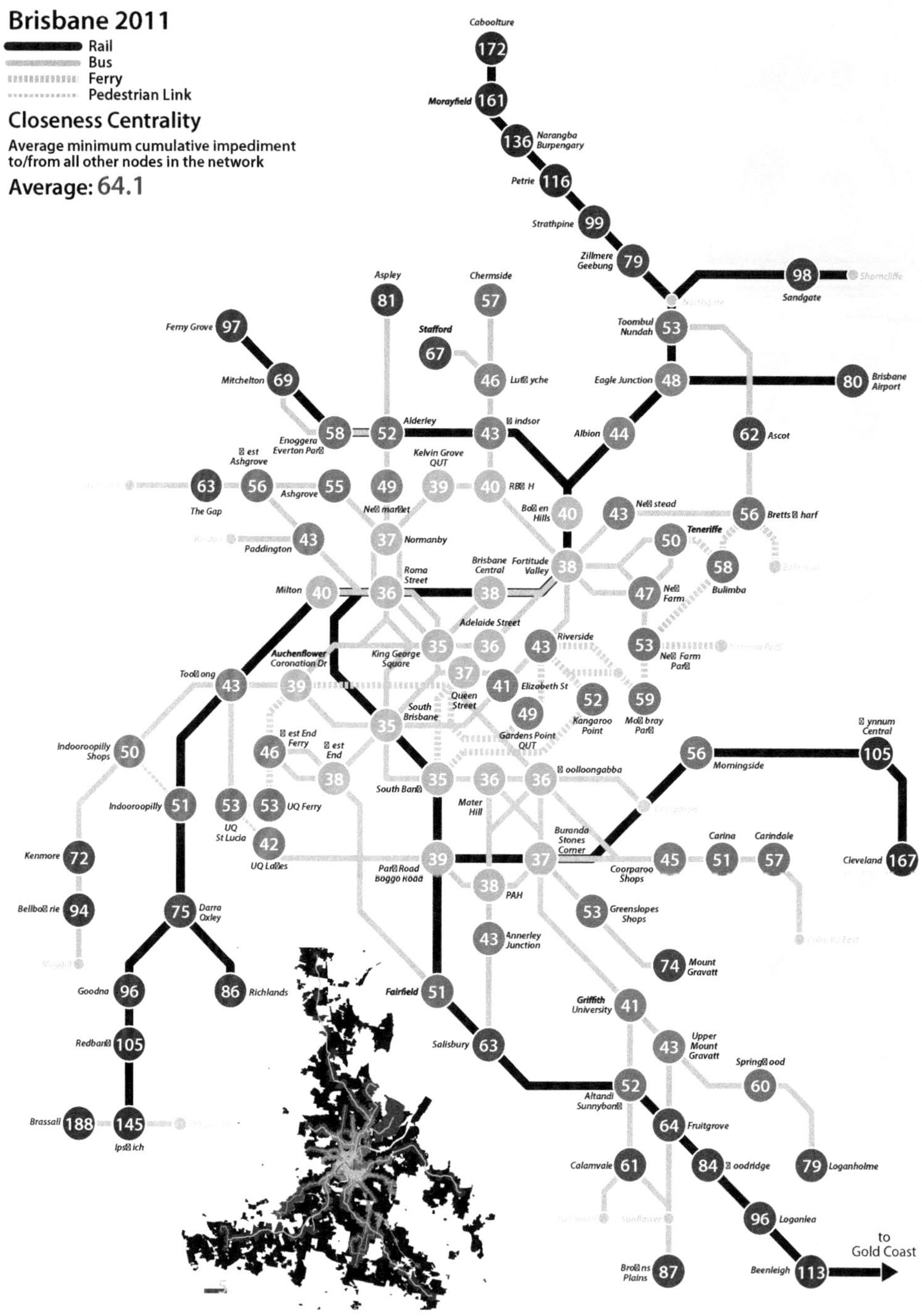

Brisbane 2011

Rail
Bus
Ferry
Pedestrian Link

Closeness Centrality

Average minimum cumulative impediment to/from all other nodes in the network

Average: 64.1

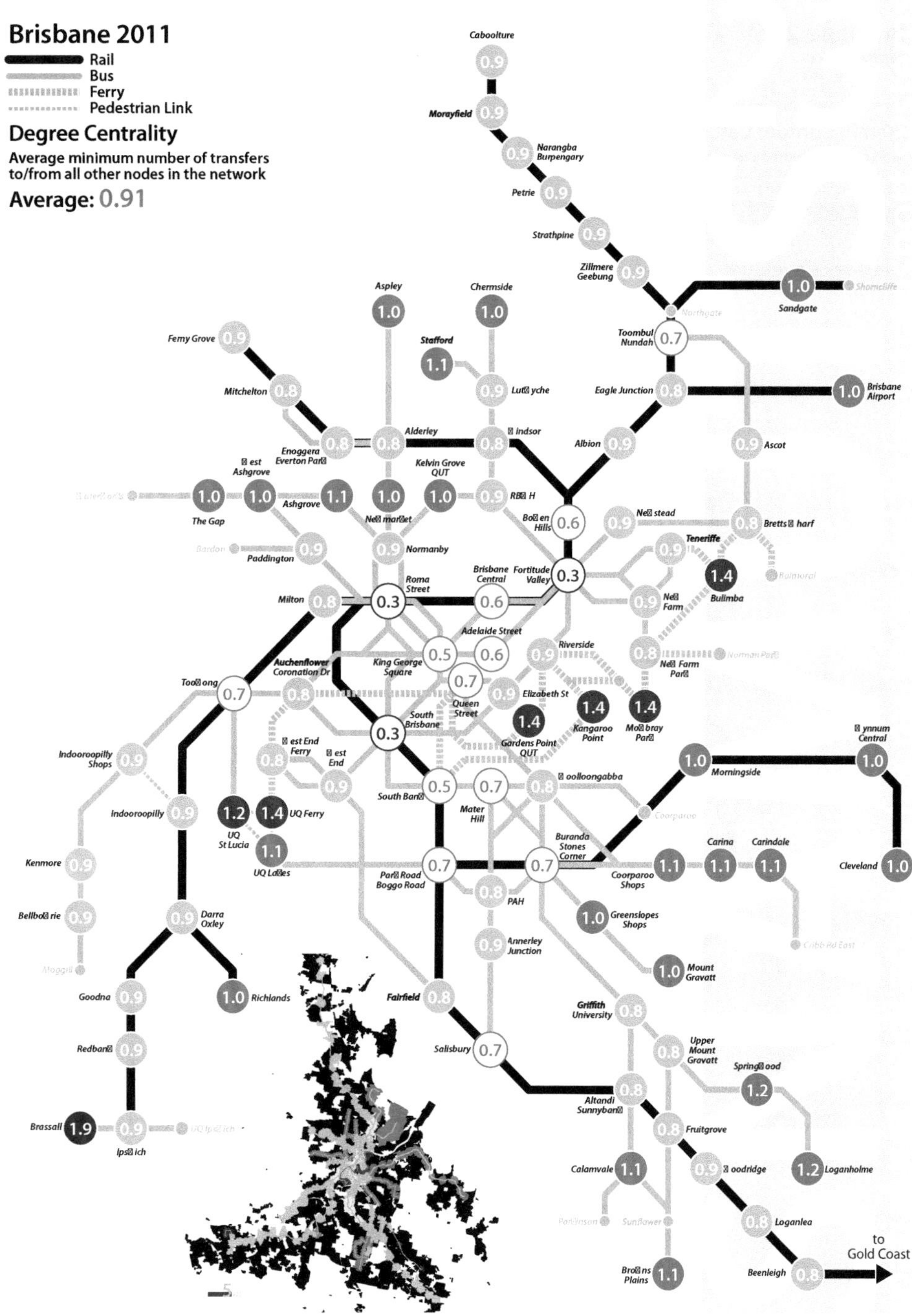

Thirty-Minute Contour Catchments

The average 30-minute public transport contour catchment for a Brisbane activity node reaches a similar percentage of metropolitan residents and jobs as its counterparts in Perth and Adelaide. In conjunction with Brisbane's lower network coverage, this suggests that Brisbane's network is more compact. This circumstance is aided by Brisbane's greater concentration of residents in the central area, where nearly 42,000 people live within 2 km of Queen Street mall, compared to only 17,000 and 26,000, respectively, in Adelaide and Perth (ABS, 2012), with demonstrable effects favourable to public transport on residents' mode choice (Kamruzzaman et al, 2014). In Perth, there is a greater focus on fast, high-frequency rail lines as the backbone of the network, stretching as far as the settlement fringe. In Adelaide, higher service intensity generates greater bus network density, but the low speed of buses prevents this from translating into larger contour catchments than in Brisbane. A similar constraint limits the contours of Brisbane's on-street suburban bus corridors. These do not tend to offer service levels at the SNAMUTS minimum standard beyond the boundaries of the City of Brisbane. The short station spacings and near-absence of express services result in far lower operational speeds on the rail system than in Perth or Sydney. In addition the suburban busway towards Loganholme is characterised by a very small number of stations and associated limitation to geographical reach.

Betweenness Centrality

Of the four smaller Australasian cities, Brisbane records the lowest global betweenness measure relative to population and jobs, indicating a weaker average presence of public transport travel opportunities for its citizens than

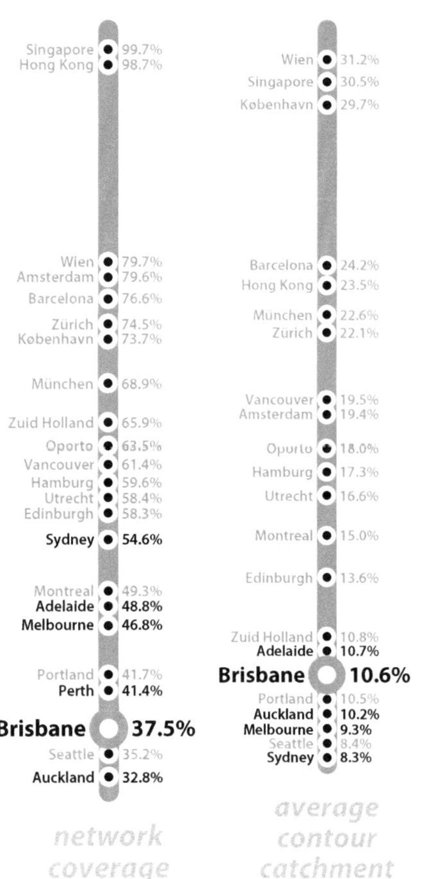

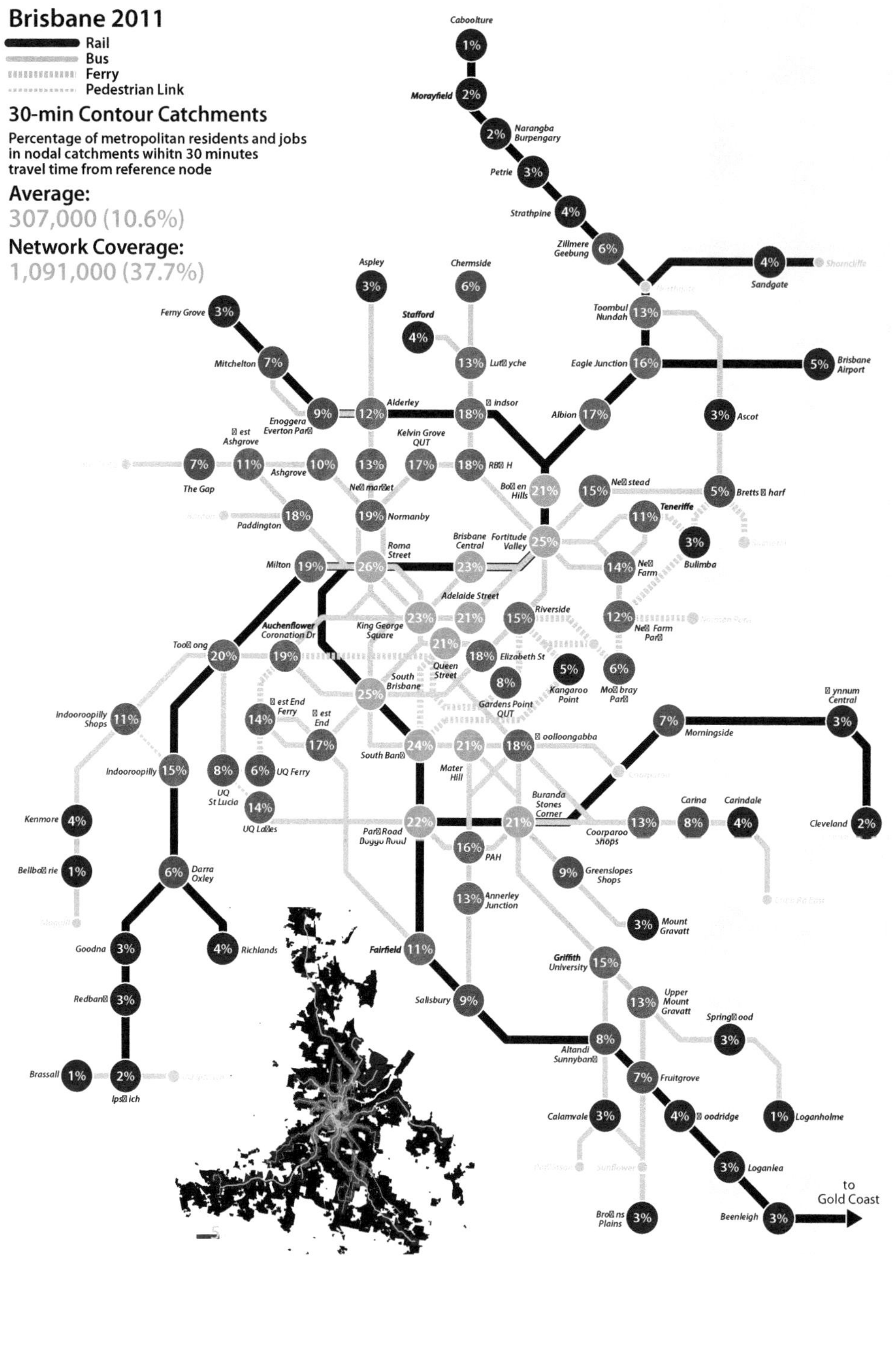

Brisbane 2011

Rail
Bus
Ferry
Pedestrian Link

30-min Contour Catchments

Percentage of metropolitan residents and jobs in nodal catchments wihitn 30 minutes travel time from reference node

Average:
307,000 (10.6%)

Network Coverage:
1,091,000 (37.7%)

elsewhere. The distribution of nodal betweenness values, like in Melbourne, shows a node outside the immediate CBD area as the peak performer (South Brisbane-Cultural Centre), suggesting that the greatest concentration of public transport travel opportunities in Brisbane occurs in the South Bank area. This observation is also linked to Brisbane focussing the lowest share of travel opportunities among all Australasian cities on the CBD.

The bus system clearly dominates the rail system on this index, though much of the total betweenness score is concentrated on a limited number of busway segments which, moreover, are not consistently well integrated with concentrations of land use within walking distance. In comparison, Perth has a significantly higher heavy rail share among travel opportunities than Brisbane, due to a network that aligns the roles of rail and bus more closely to their performance hierarchy.

Brisbane's typical path length catchment, while modest in an international context, is higher than in Melbourne and Sydney but lower than in the smaller Australasian cities, despite Brisbane's significantly greater concentration of land use activities in the central area compared to Perth or Adelaide. This effect is compensated by the network's weakness in facilitating longer journeys, owing to the low frequencies on the rail system, the limited geographical reach of the high-frequency busways, and the sub-optimal integration of rail, bus and ferry modes.

Network Resilience

On average across the network, Brisbane has the second poorest level of network resilience among the Australasian cities after Sydney. The key reason is the high reliance on buses, which despite their high frequency on a network of dedicated busways offer only a limited capacity to move passengers in relation to the significance of these lines for the network. Segmental congestion effects in the SNAMUTS sense are also apparent on some on-street bus routes that feed into the busway network where service frequency is closer to Australasian standard practice at 15 or 20 minutes. In contrast, the rail lines, whose spatial integration with the bus system remains deficient, are barely affected by network stress.

These findings illustrate a system constraint associated with bus rapid transit (BRT) routes, especially those that also combine elements of on-street running. Their role as trunks for an expansive network of suburban feeder routes produces extremely high frequencies, travel speeds and hence travel opportunities which inflate the numerator of the segmental resilience figure; however, the capacity of the vehicles

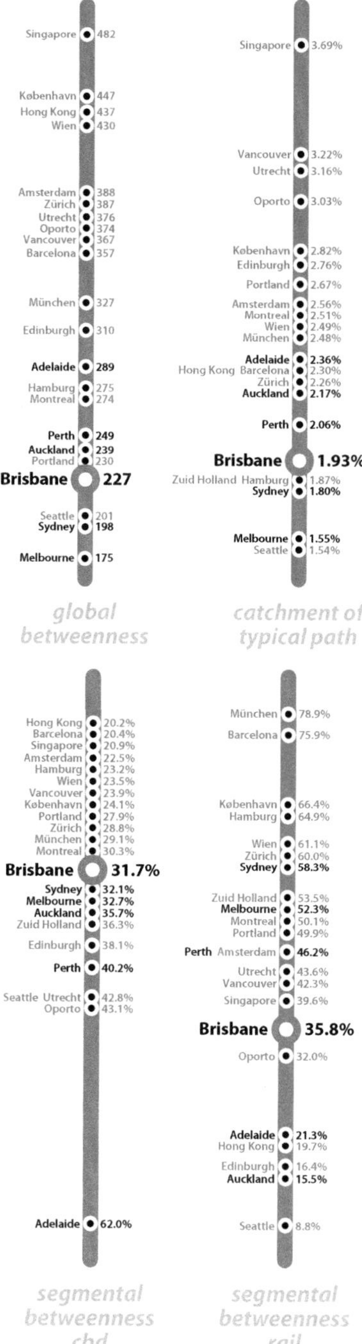

(most buses in Brisbane are of standard length) in the denominator remains low and results in the system falling victim to its own success. To alleviate this situation, it is critical to establish a greater degree of integration between rail and bus, with frequency boosts to rail lines and the creation of user-friendly rail-bus interchanges facilitating a distribution of transport tasks between the two modes that is better aligned to their differing performance.

Nodal Connectivity

Brisbane's best-connected activity node, mirroring the betweenness performance, is South Brisbane-Cultural Centre rather than any of the immediate CBD nodes (though Roma Street and King George Square occupy second and third place). Good nodal connectivity performance, and by extension the attractiveness of locations for TOD intensification, as well as a user perception of easy public transport access for both planned and spontaneous journeys, is generally limited to the corridor between the CBD (Roma Street) and the Woolloongabba/Buranda area where rail and busway lines run parallel, as well as Fortitude Valley which acts as a northern CBD fringe gateway for rail and on-street bus lines. On average, Brisbane outperforms Perth, Adelaide and Auckland on this index, but trails the remainder of the global sample with the exception of Edinburgh and the US cities.

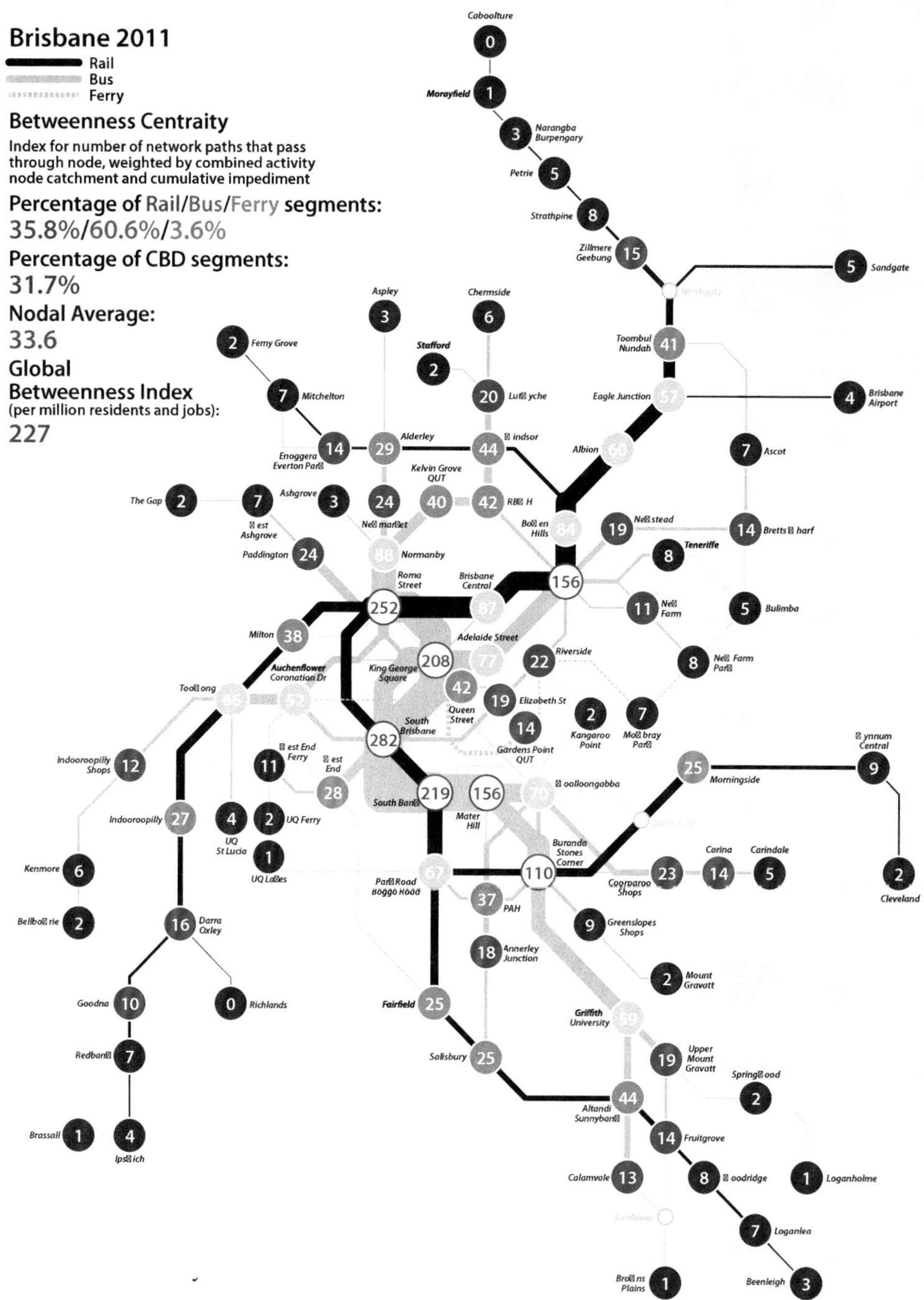

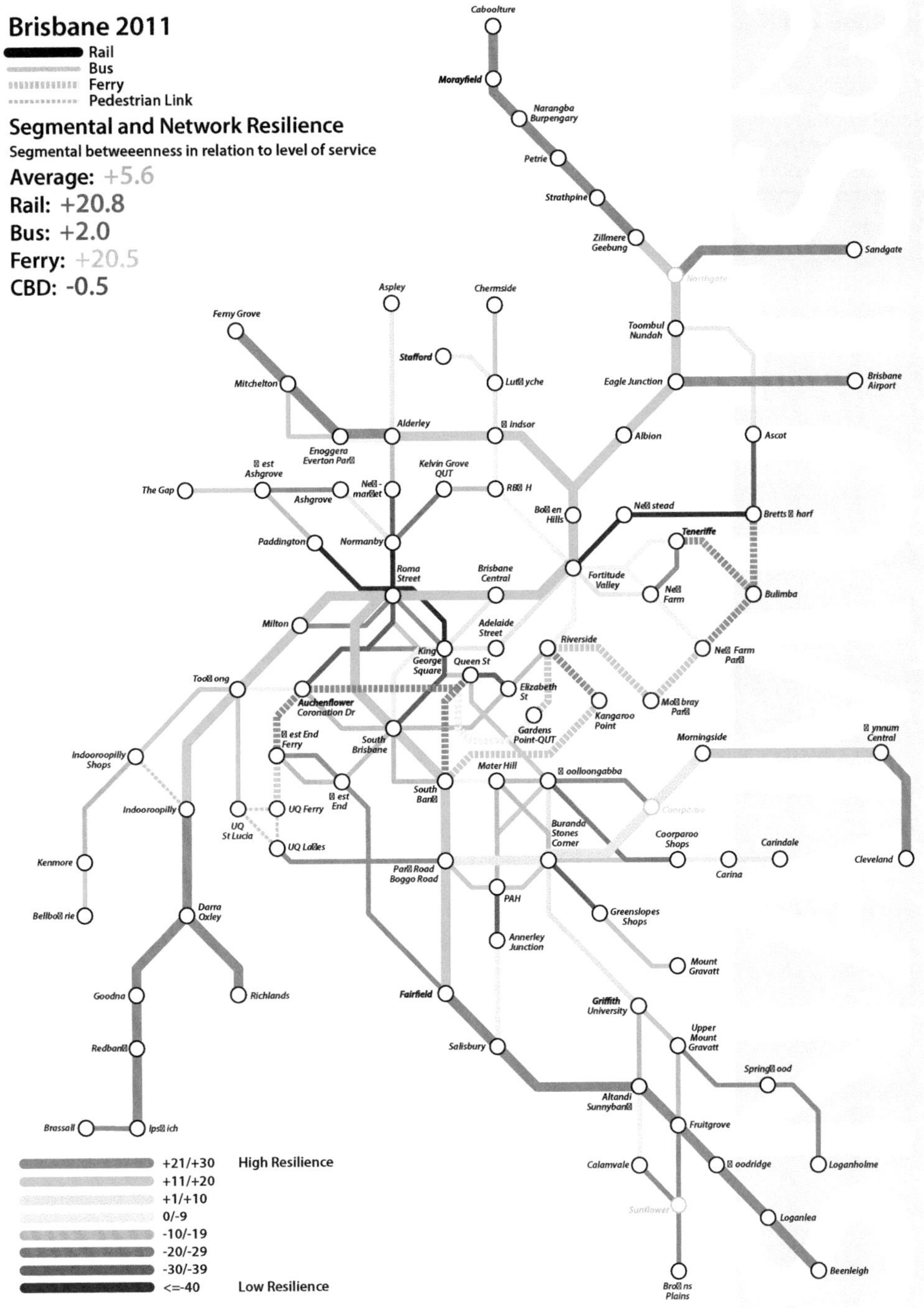

Brisbane 2011

Rail
Bus
Ferry
Pedestrian Link

Segmental and Network Resilience

Segmental betweeenness in relation to level of service

Average: +5.6
Rail: +20.8
Bus: +2.0
Ferry: +20.5
CBD: -0.5

+21/+30 High Resilience
+11/+20
+1/+10
0/-9
-10/-19
-20/-29
-30/-39
<=-40 Low Resilience

SNAMUTS Composite Accessibility Index and Reflections

The most public transport–accessible area in Brisbane is at South Bank, whereas the CBD across the river shows an interesting zoning pattern that sees composite accessibility gradually drop with growing proximity to the river from a peak along the rail and busway corridor at Roma Street, King George Square, Brisbane Central and Fortitude Valley. In accessibility terms, the Brisbane River appears to generate something like a

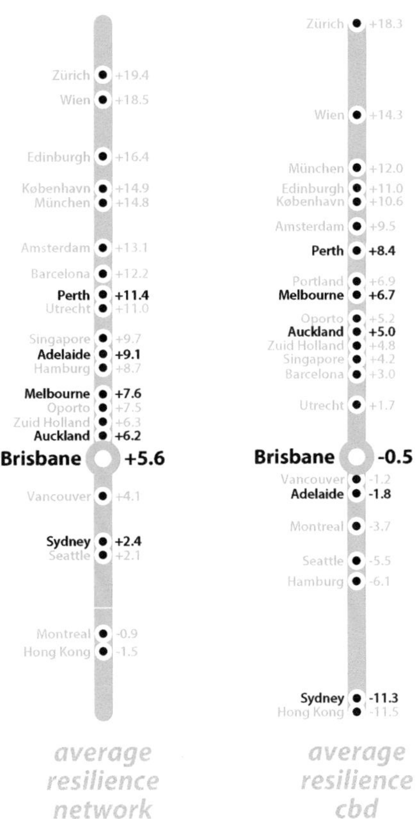

peripheral corridor within the inner area. The waterborne public transport routes that follow it from UQ to Balmoral constitute the best ferry service found in any case study city other than Hong Kong. The land-based public transport network, however, does not overcome the divide in the urban fabric associated with the river by making the most of existing crossings and of co-locating multimodal interchanges there.

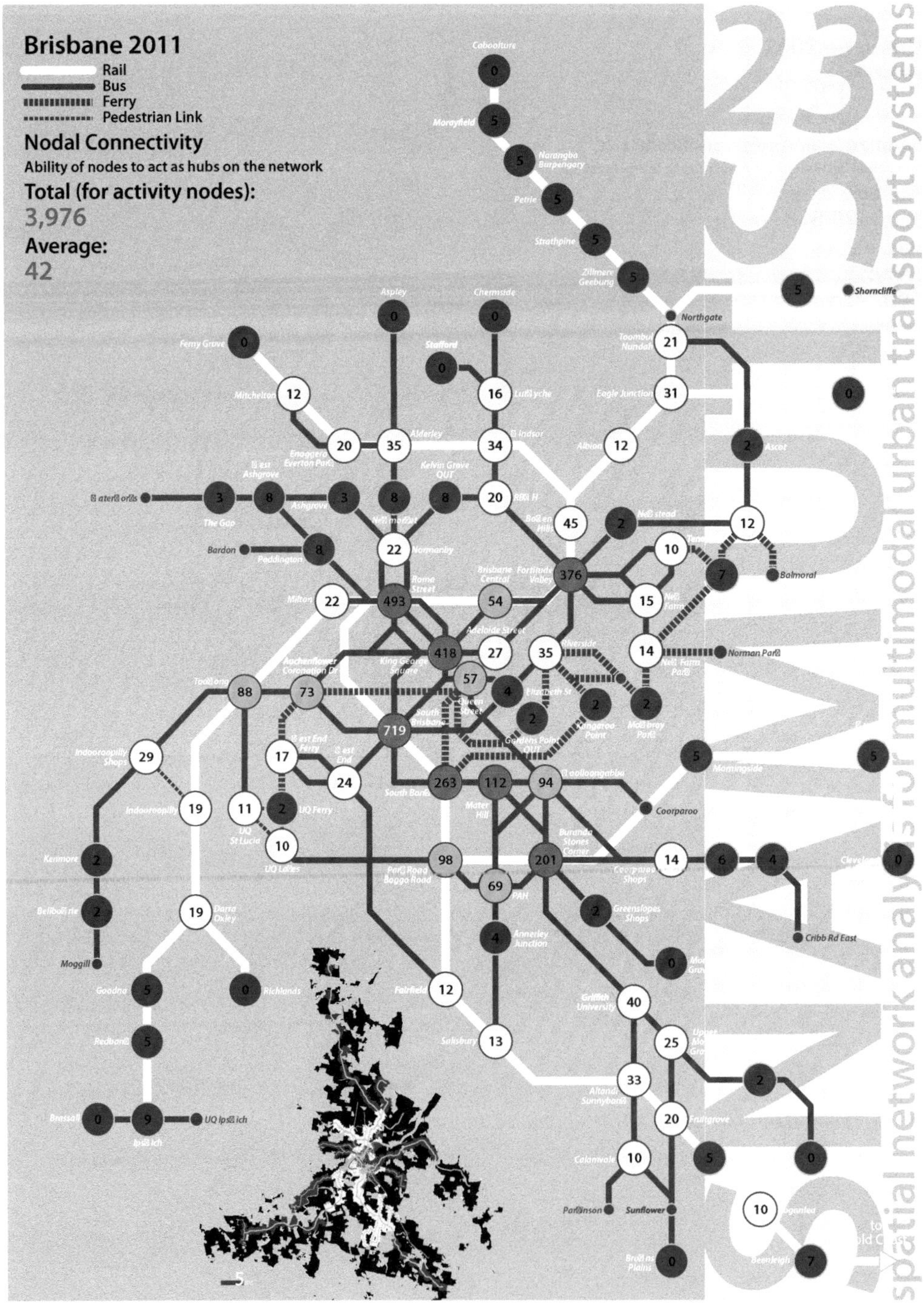

Brisbane 2011
Rail
Bus
Ferry
Pedestrian Link
Nodal Connectivity
Ability of nodes to act as hubs on the network
Total (for activity nodes): 3,976
Average: 42

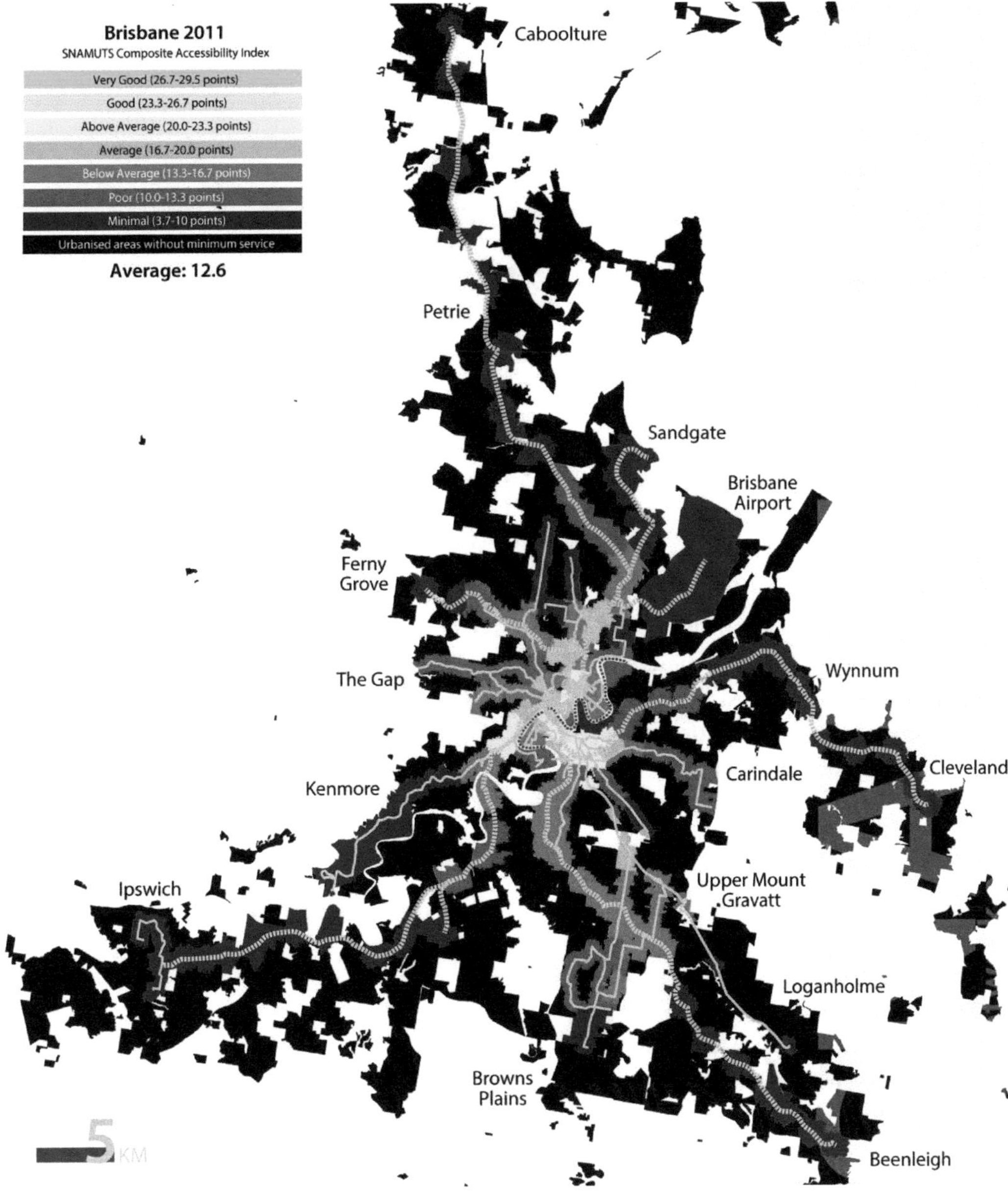

Beyond this limited high-accessibility zone in South Brisbane, the upper CBD and Fortitude Valley, composite scores drop quite rapidly in most corridors. Across the four municipalities outside the City of Brisbane (Moreton Bay, Ipswich, Redlands and Logan) the only composite accessibility categories are 'minimal' and 'without minimum service'. To improve this, it is vital for Brisbane to operate its rail spines, the principal public transport access routes for the suburban municipalities, at 15-minute or better frequencies (introduced on the Ferny Grove branch line in 2011, post analysis), and to reconfigure the bus system to service a greater number of suburban interchanges at a similar standard, thus providing greater choices of routes for a larger proportion of travellers.

ACCESSIBILITY PROFILE: ADELAIDE

Adelaide is the smallest of the six major Australasian cities and in recent years the slowest growing at less than 25,000 residents annually. The city is bordered by a coastline to the west, which runs in a relatively un-convoluted north–south direction over a distance of more than 60 km. Most of the urbanised area is located on a flat coastal plain, whose width varies from less than 10 km in the south to more than 20 km in the north. The eastern boundary of this plain is formed by the Adelaide Hills which contain extensive areas of protected open space, are penetrated by a limited number of transport routes and make up an effective urban growth boundary. Adelaide's urban density is comparable to that of Perth and Brisbane, but below that of Melbourne, Sydney, Auckland and other cities studied.

The public transport system is managed by a government agency (Adelaide Metro) which also operates the city's four suburban rail trunk lines and single tram line. Bus operations are contracted to private companies. There is a 12-km dedicated radial busway corridor in the city's north-east (O-Bahn) using vehicle guidance technology. Fares are flat – there are single and daily zone-free, multiple-transfer tickets, but no periodical tickets – and fully integrated between modes. Annual public transport usage per capita, however, is at the low end of the SNAMUTS scale. While Adelaide has no inner-urban motorways, there is a dense network of wide and relatively uncongested arterial roads and generous parking provision in the CBD.

Current public transport projects include the electrification, extension and capacity upgrade of the southern rail line linking central Adelaide and Noarlunga-Seaford. Similar projects on other suburban rail lines have currently stalled due to funding shortfalls; these include a tram-train project on the Port Adelaide line with several suburban on-street extensions.

Service Intensity

Adelaide has a comprehensive bus network on inner urban corridors with guaranteed service frequencies of 15 minutes all day on weekdays, and 30 minutes during evenings and weekends (GO Zones). While most of this network is radial and offers few cross-suburban movement opportunities at the same standard, it helps boost Adelaide's service intensity to the highest level among its Australasian peers and is also reflected in a relatively large extent of geographical network coverage (see below). Another reason for Adelaide's high service intensity figure is the strong reliance on buses (using slower-moving, smaller vehicles) over rail (faster-moving, larger vehicles). This is despite the highest supply of rail stations relative to population of all non-European cities in the sample.

Closeness Centrality

On this index, Adelaide shows an average performance that is quite typical for an Australasian city. The grid structure of the network in the central city, though not as legible as Melbourne's, produces an even distribution of good closeness values in the CBD. In suburban areas, the best results are associated with the high-frequency O-Bahn route to Paradise and Modbury (Tea Tree Plaza) and the tram and bus corridor to Glenelg, while the standard 30-minute frequency of the rail system

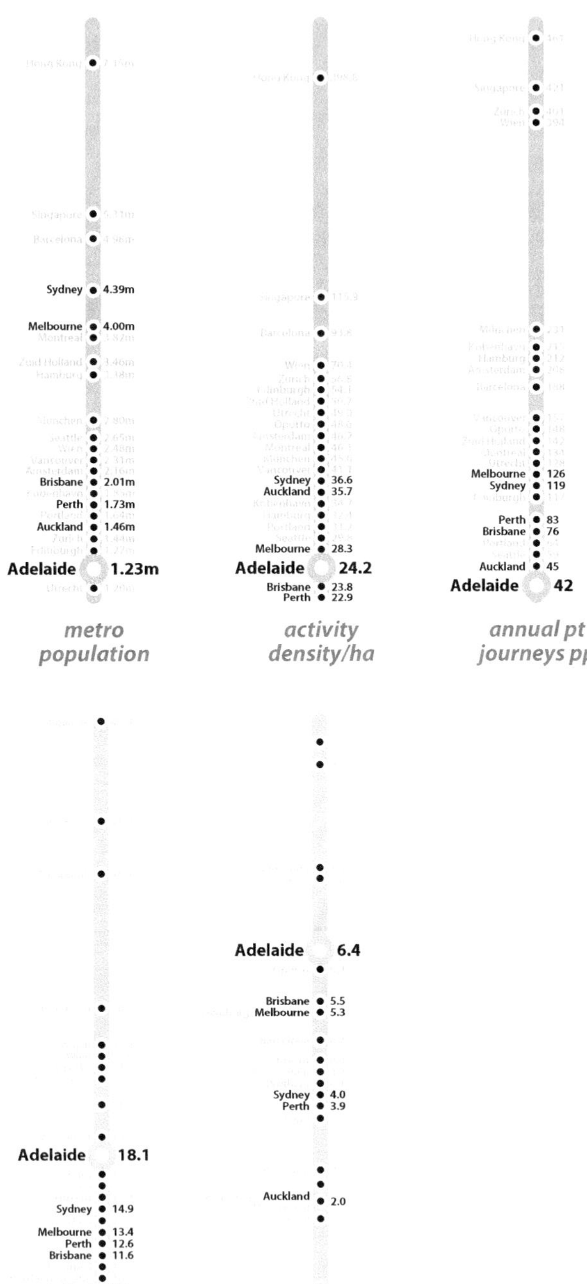

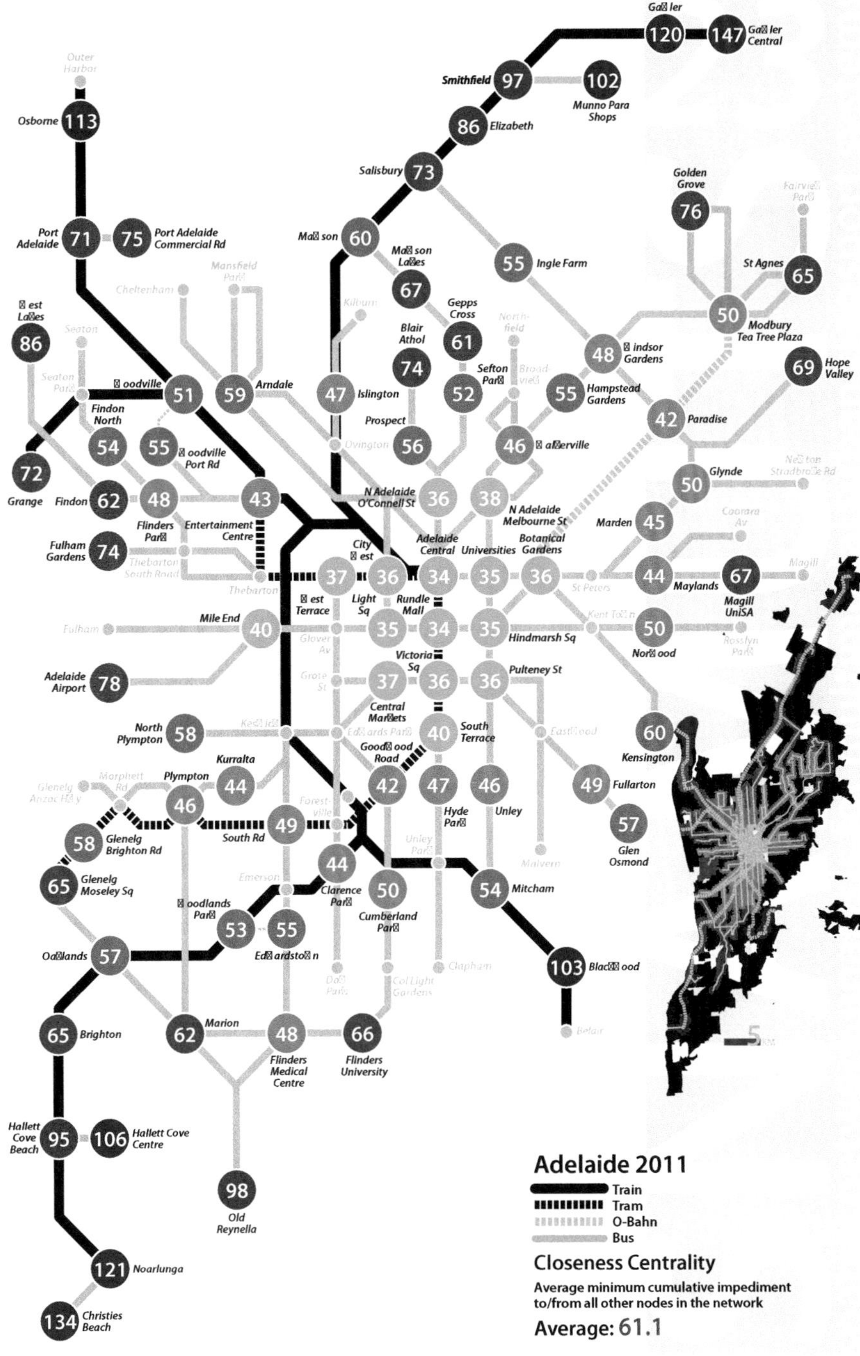

results in a rapid decline in performance towards the end of the radial corridors (Noarlunga, Blackwood, Outer Harbor and Gawler). There are also some middle suburban, bus-based nodes whose poor performance on this index is a reflection of the relative lack of network connectivity outside the central area, particularly in the west and north of the city.

Degree Centrality

This index can be seen as an indicator for the configurational efficiency of the network, providing an insight into whether the city's comparatively high input of operational resources is more due to a genuine quest to maximise the population's access to public transport, or more due to large numbers of congested buses duplicating each other's tasks. There are two 'super-connected' nodes with the lowest degree centrality values at Adelaide Central and Rundle Mall. On the radial lines, buses and trams typically return better degree centrality scores than train lines, given that the surface modes have better penetration of the CBD area than the trains which only touch the terminus at Adelaide Central. There are some classic trunk-and-feeder patterns between rail and bus, or between O-Bahn and street bus, along the rail corridors and in the north-eastern suburbs, which drive up Adelaide's average score on this index to the highest in Australasia by a small margin. Otherwise, most routes connect in the central area and only there, a pattern also apparent in Melbourne and Brisbane. Task-sharing between modes of different performance, especially rail and bus, may have potential for further optimisation in Adelaide.

Network Coverage

The percentage of residents and workers who have access to the network within walking distance is second only

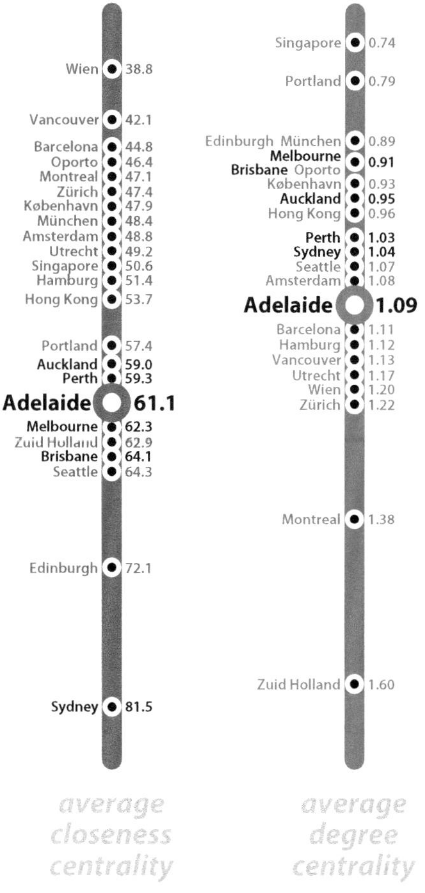

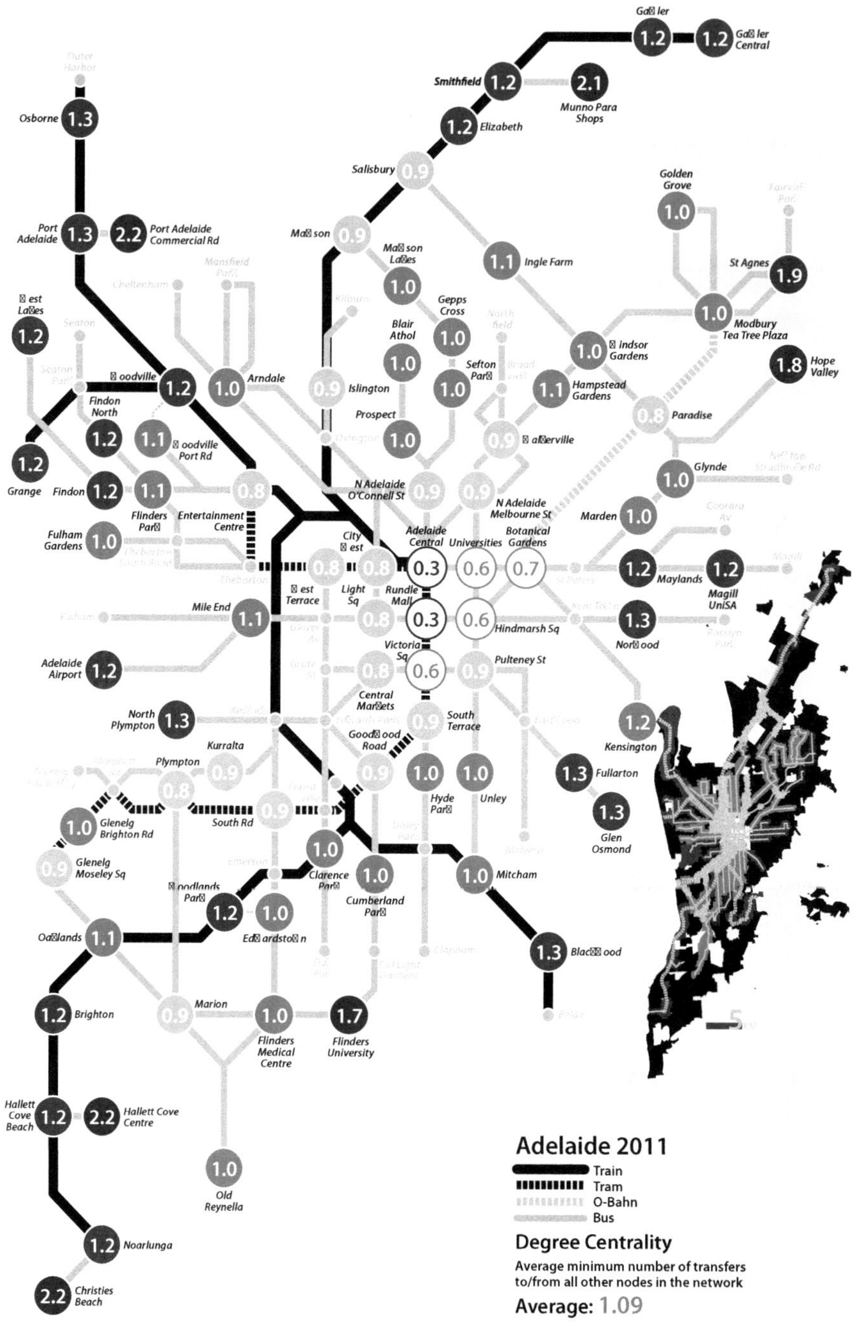

Adelaide 2011

Train
Tram
O-Bahn
Bus

Degree Centrality

Average minimum number of transfers to/from all other nodes in the network

Average: 1.09

to Sydney in the Australasian peer group. The city's successful GO Zone program and the relatively high number of rail stations are key influences here. The GO Zone program generates almost universal area coverage across the inner suburbs. However, most GO Zone corridors are parallel to each other, roughly 800 metres apart, thus offering a spatial endowment with public transport routes but typically restricting movement options to either the inward or outward direction, in a configuration similar to the network structure in Perth's inner suburbs and in Melbourne's inner north.

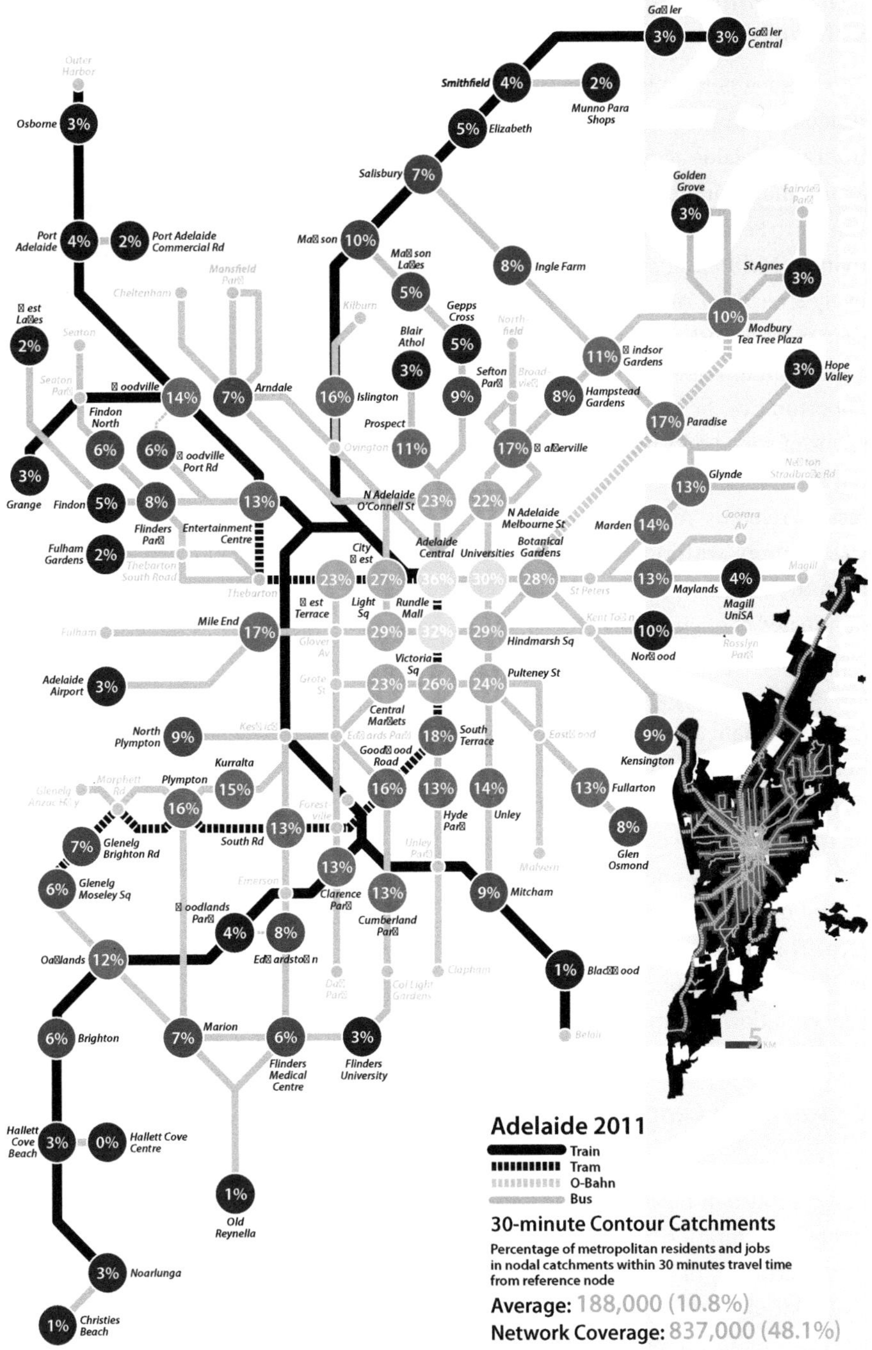

Adelaide 2011

Train
Tram
O-Bahn
Bus

30-minute Contour Catchments

Percentage of metropolitan residents and jobs in nodal catchments within 30 minutes travel time from reference node

Average: 188,000 (10.8%)
Network Coverage: 837,000 (48.1%)

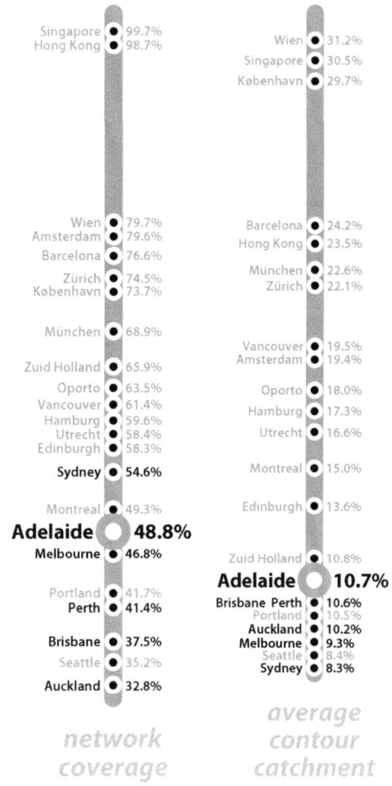

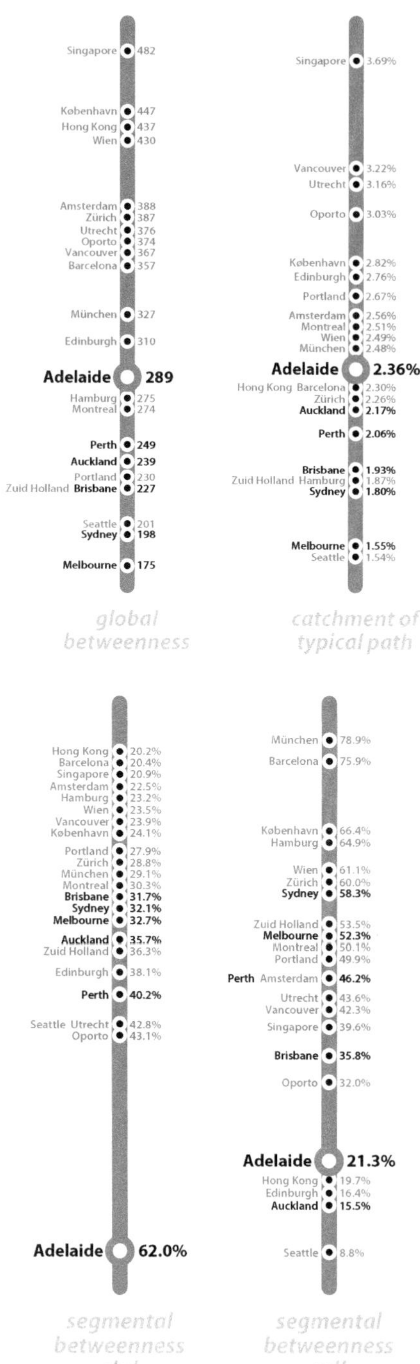

Thirty-Minute Contour Catchments

The average percentage of metropolitan residents and jobs that can be reached from an Adelaide activity node by way of a 30-minute public transport journey is similar to Perth and Brisbane, but higher than in Melbourne and Sydney. This is likely a result of smaller city size rather than of a network configuration offering a substantially greater choice of travel opportunities, or better performance in terms of speed and frequency. The spatial distribution of contour catchments results remains relatively concentric – values drop with increasing distance from the centre, in line with the radially dominated configuration of the network. Notable exceptions are the intermediate nodes of Plympton on the high-frequency tram and bus corridor to Glenelg, and Paradise on the O-Bahn route. Conversely, contour catchment results on the rail lines are depressed by the low service frequency and the relatively low degree of rail penetration into the CBD area. This impact is further exacerbated by the dominance of the CBD in terms of concentration of employment.

Betweenness Centrality

In Adelaide, the relative absence of major suburban business hubs and the radial configuration of the public transport network, in conjunction with a CBD placed at the geographical heart of the city, create a situation where we can

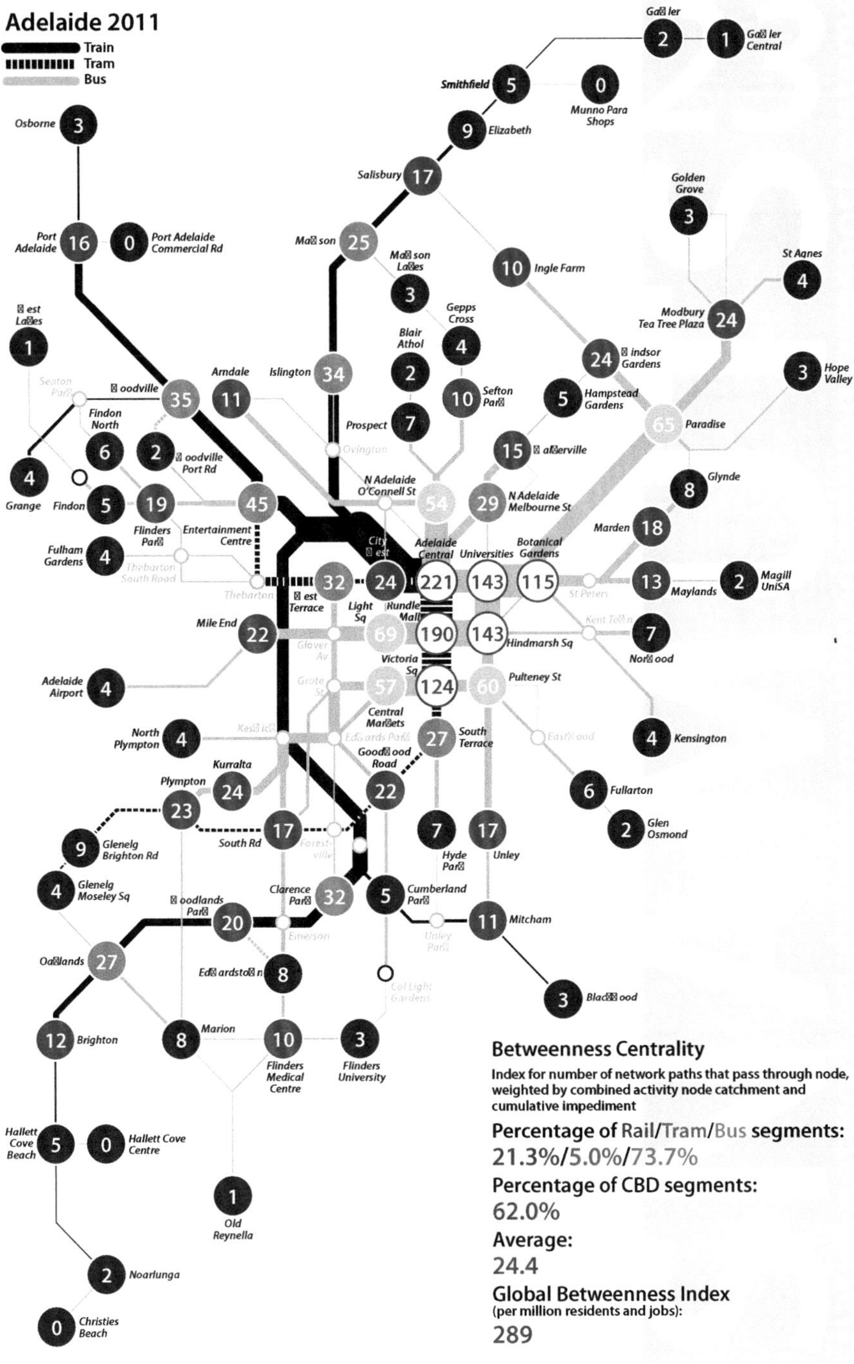

expect pressures in the central area and a relatively low presence of 'movement energy' elsewhere.

The global betweenness index is the highest in the Australasian sample, correlating with Adelaide's comparatively high service input and network coverage. However, it remains significantly below the values typical for European cities, indicating some unmet opportunities for public transport – from a lack of non-radial links as well as from a paucity of major non-CBD destinations.

Adelaide's average typical path length catchment is low in international terms but higher than the Australasian peer cities. The relatively compact settlement area in combination with a radially oriented network often enforcing detours for non-radial journeys inflates the result on this index in an Australasian context, while the low settlement density and the dominance of relatively slow and/or infrequent public transport services depresses it in comparison to most case study cities elsewhere.

From an efficiency perspective, it is desirable to distribute travel opportunities towards higher-performance modes as well as away from the easily congested CBD area. Adelaide currently achieves neither objective: it has the highest share across the sample of travel opportunities concentrated in the CBD, and the second lowest Australasian rail share after Auckland. Current upgrades and extensions to the suburban rail system, if accompanied by speed and frequency improvements, are likely to address the latter shortfall, but a more comprehensive network development and land use decentralisation strategy is required to address the former.

Network Resilience

These pressures are also apparent in the segmental resilience index. While Adelaide's average network resilience figure has a mid-field position within the Australasian and global sample, the mismatch of network significance to actual service levels within the CBD is second only to Sydney in Australia. Adelaide's public transport system, however, attracts only just over half the number

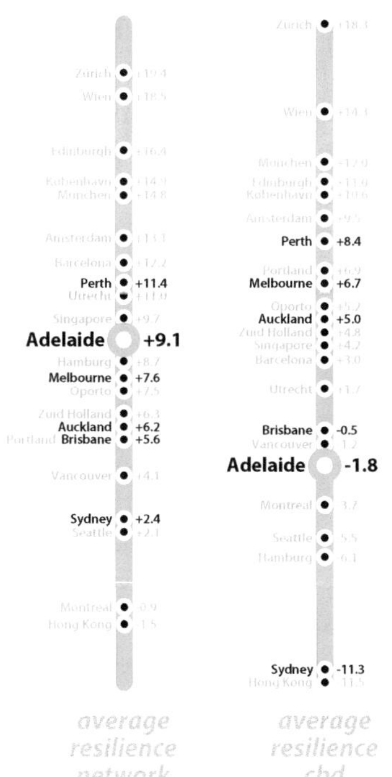

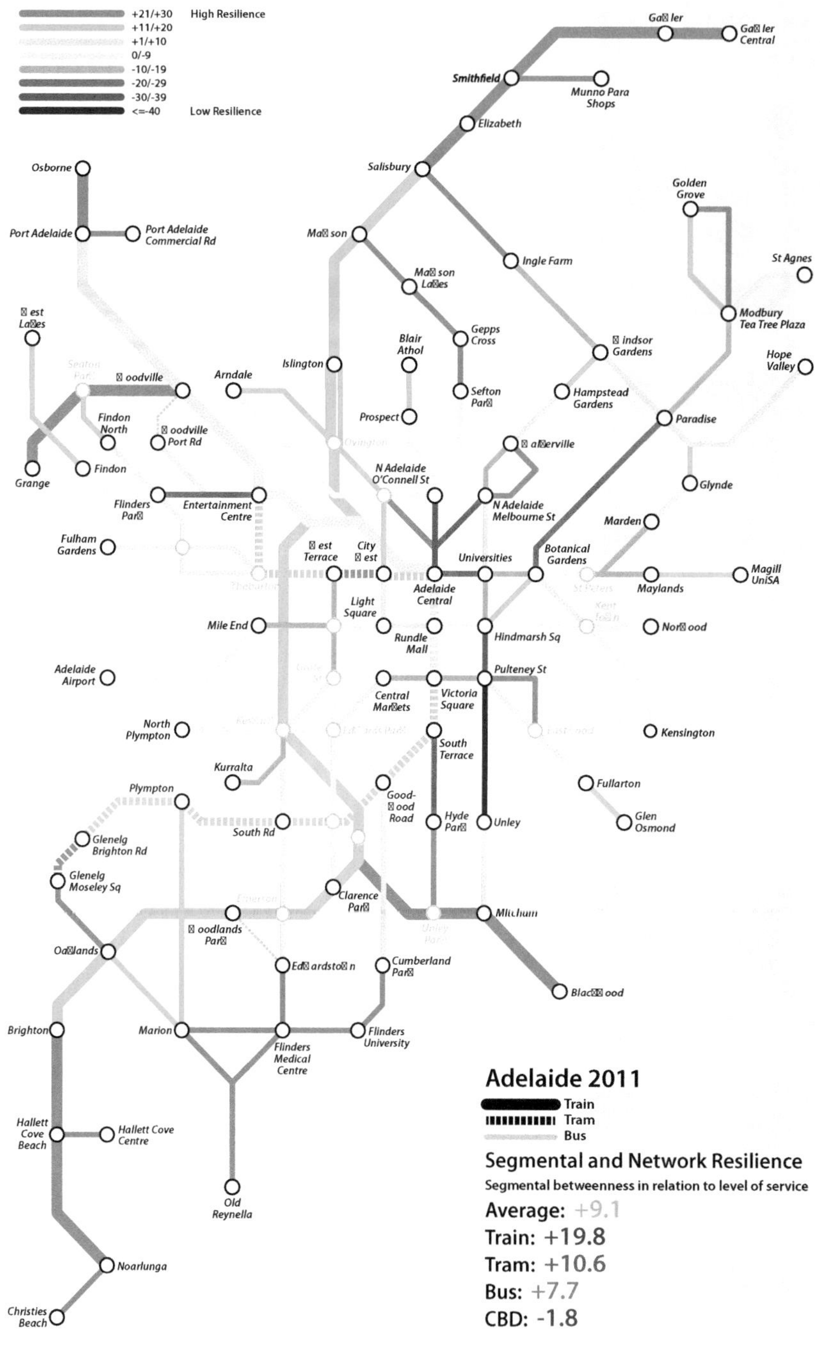

+21/+30 High Resilience
+11/+20
+1/+10
0/-9
-10/-19
-20/-29
-30/-39
<=-40 Low Resilience

Adelaide 2011

Train
Tram
Bus

Segmental and Network Resilience

Segmental betweenness in relation to level of service

Average: +9.1
Train: +19.8
Tram: +10.6
Bus: +7.7
CBD: -1.8

of journeys per capita as Brisbane's or Perth's and one third that of Sydney and Melbourne. It is unlikely that Adelaide would be able to accommodate the patronage levels of its Australian peer cities on its public transport network without a significant expansion of the system's capacity to both radial and orbital network elements.

Nodal Connectivity

Adelaide is characterised by the lowest average result on this index within the sample, and has virtually no nodes outside the CBD prominent as natural contenders for TOD under the current network configuration, levels of service and levels of patronage.

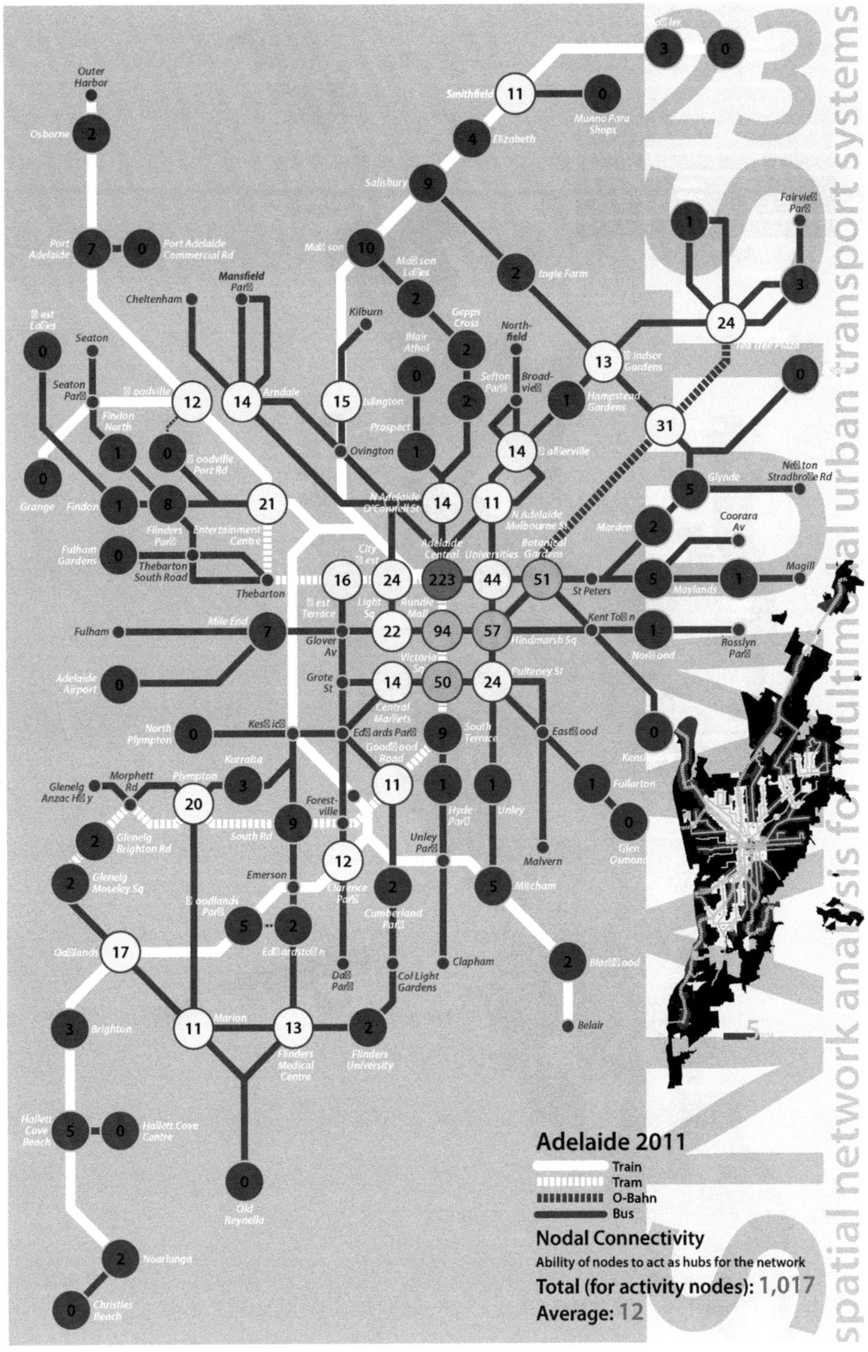

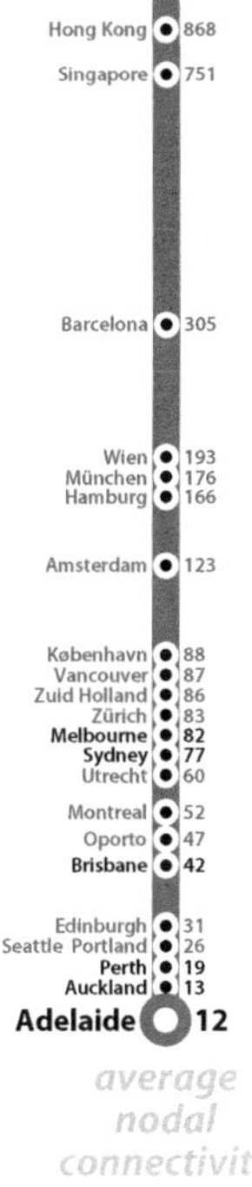

SNAMUTS Composite Accessibility Index and Reflections

The composite index illustrates many of the above findings. In Adelaide's inner suburbs, particularly in the north-west and south, local residents and businesses generally have walking-distance access to some form of full-time, reasonably frequent public transport due to Adelaide's high level of service provision in comparison with its Australasian peers. The resulting network, however, is mostly star-shaped, with the majority of lines and corridors converging in the CBD area but making only a very limited number of connections with each other elsewhere. The near-absence of well- or medium-performing areas on this index (shaded yellow or green) outside the CBD suggests that the land use and public transport system has yet to take up opportunities to form significant suburban sub-centres that could act as accessible hubs of population and employment growth. It is also indicative of a network that is largely configured for the important, but limited pool of journeys to and from the central city, while leaving other journey purposes largely to private transport (Somenahalli et al, 2013). Both constraints depress the potential of Adelaide's public transport to become more competitive in the travel market and to grow its patronage to levels seen in other Australian cities.

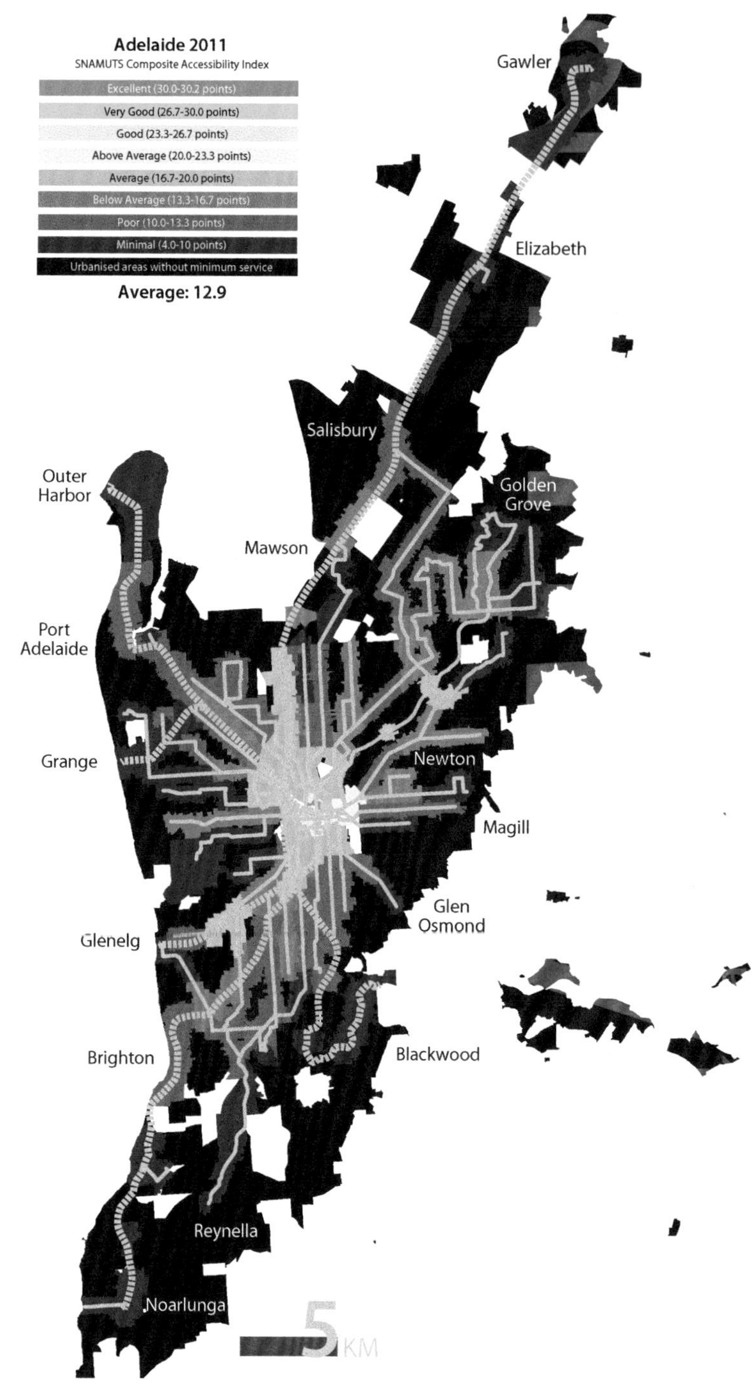

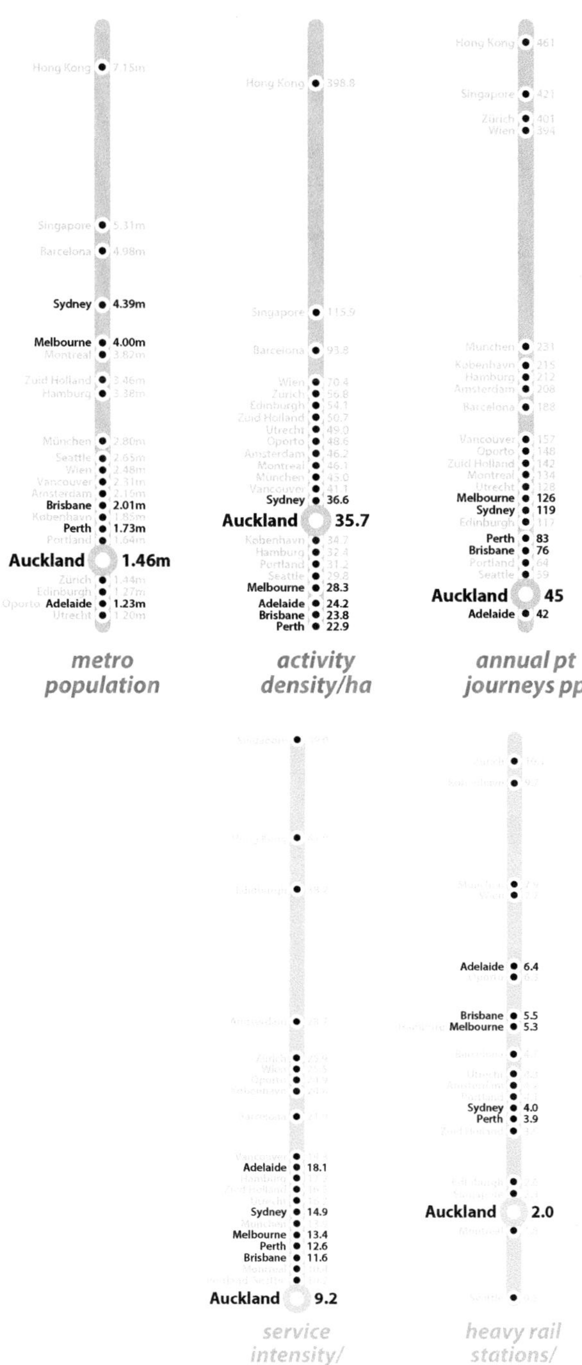

ACCESSIBILITY PROFILE: AUCKLAND

Auckland is New Zealand's largest city and key international gateway. In 2011, the metropolitan region counted 1.46 million inhabitants (approximate annual growth rate since 2006: 30,000) and, uniquely in Australasia, was amalgamated into a single local government area or 'super council'. The heart of the metropolitan area covers a narrow isthmus nestled between two water bodies, Manukau Harbour and the Hauraki Gulf. This limits outward expansion of the urbanised area to a linear corridor each at the northern and southern fringes of the city, as well as necessarily channelling all north–south transport tasks in Auckland and beyond through the central city and its vicinity. The city has attempted to address the resulting bottlenecks by generous road building programs for most of the period since 1945, while largely paying short shrift to public transport (Mees and Dodson, 2007).

Auckland retained a three-line suburban rail network that is currently undergoing an ambitious program of expansion, modernisation and electrification following decades of neglect. A number of ferry routes link the CBD rail terminus at Britomart with Hauraki Gulf islands and peninsulas, but only one of these routes (to Devonport) operates every 30 minutes and meets the SNAMUTS minimum standard. Auckland's bus network, while relatively coherent in terms of layout and numbering, is in the hands of several operators in concessions of groups of lines. As a legacy from the 1980s, Auckland continues to contend with a greater degree of public transport deregulation than any other Australasian city, resulting in the coexistence of a plethora of private operators, each with their own fare system and a continuing relative absence of coordinated service planning (Harris, 2007a, 2007b). Recent attempts at institutional integration and the introduction of a common electronic ticketing system are improving the situation. Some dedicated rail–bus interchanges at certain locations are also emerging.

Owing to its constrained geography, it is not surprising to see Auckland nearly at par with Sydney as Australasia's second most densely urbanised metropolitan area. Public transport usage, however, trails the sample and is second lowest (before Adelaide) among all global SNAMUTS case study cities.

Service Intensity

In 2011, the standard daytime frequency on most rail lines was 30 minutes; however, on the southern suburban corridor between Papakura and Otahuhu two lines overlap and produce relatively even 15-minute frequencies. The bus network at the SNAMUTS minimum standard remains mostly radial and focussed on the CBD, though service frequencies vary between comparable corridors.

A dedicated busway links Albany at the northern fringe along a motorway median across the Harbour Bridge with Britomart; it also serves as a trunk route for many lower-frequency routes fanning out into the northern suburbs from key busway interchanges. In the inner city, a high-frequency circular bus route takes in the CBD and CBD fringe areas; a second, wider circle with similar service standards was introduced after 2011 (post analysis).

Among the global sample of case study cities, Auckland provides the lowest level of public transport services at the minimum SNAMUTS standard relative to population. This is a function of a very frugal extent of infrastructure and service on both rail and bus, as the findings on network coverage and betweenness centrality below demonstrate. Auckland also has the lowest number of heavy rail stations relative to population of all Australasian cities.

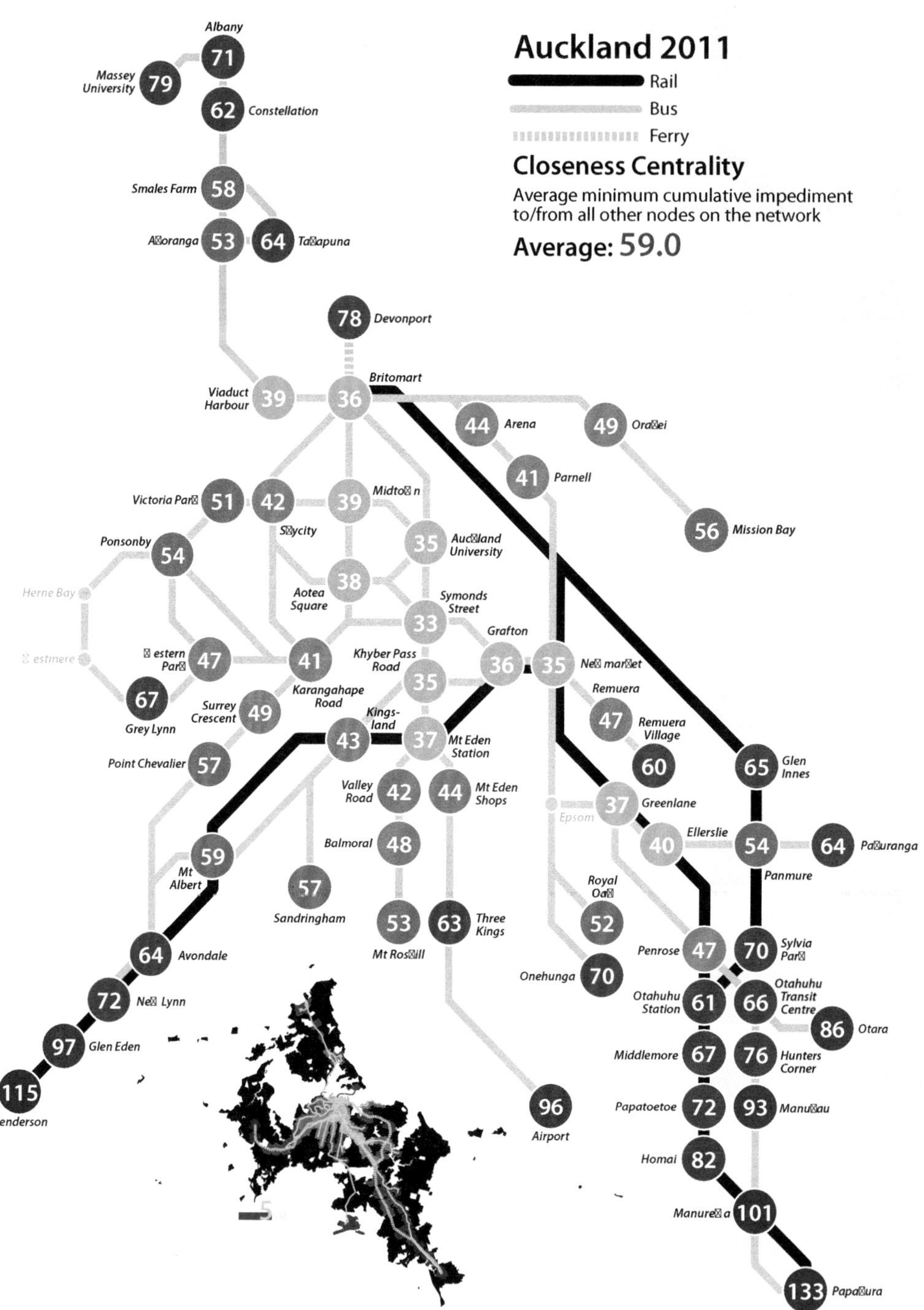

Closeness Centrality

Auckland's average closeness results slightly outperform those of Perth and position Auckland at the top of the Australasian SNAMUTS ranking on this index, despite including a penalty for the additional fares incurred when transferring between different modes and operators. This is mostly owed to the concentration of services at the minimum standard within a relatively compact portion of the urbanised area, while neglecting more dispersed outer

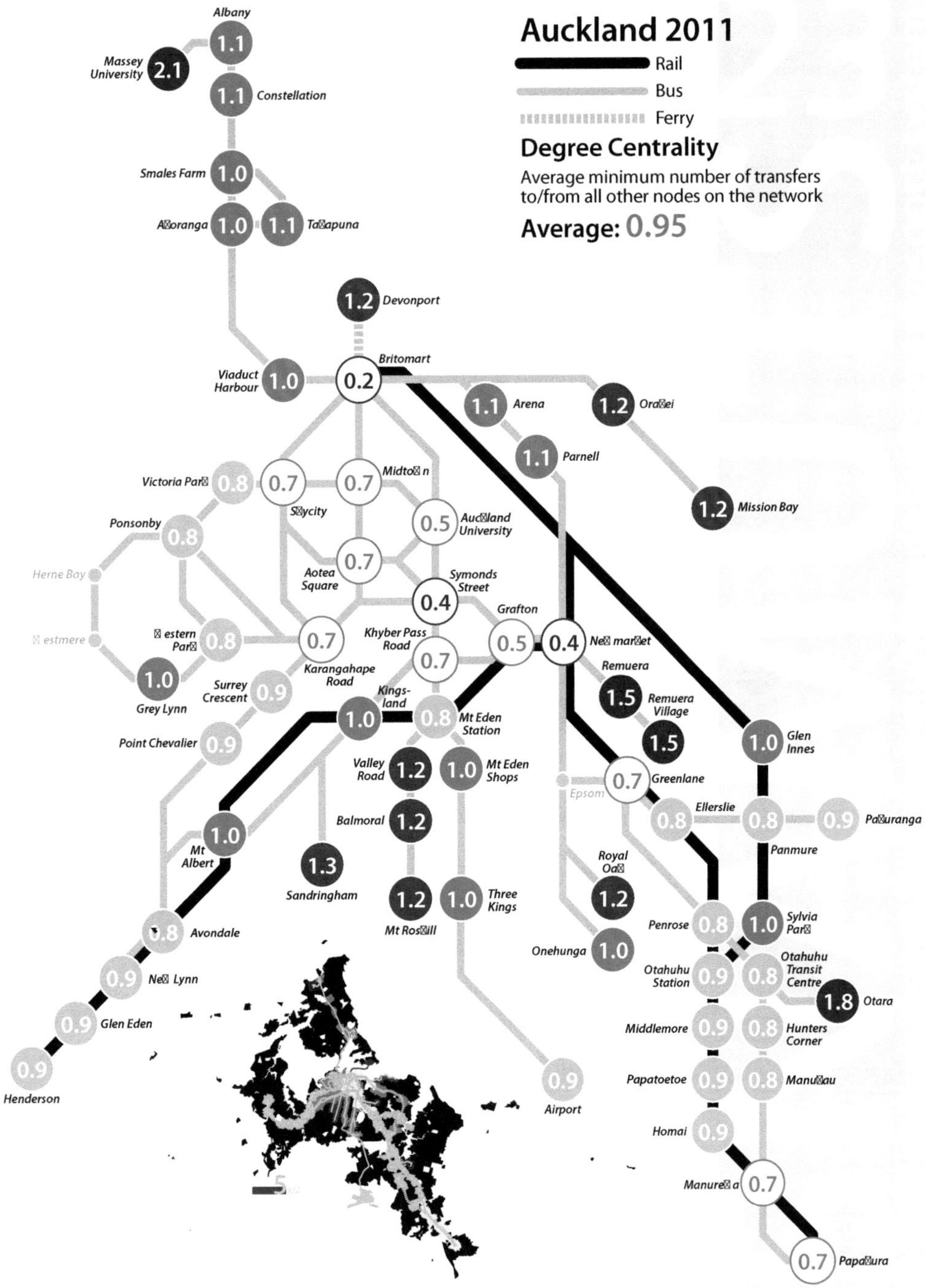

Auckland 2011

Rail
Bus
Ferry

Degree Centrality

Average minimum number of transfers to/from all other nodes on the network

Average: 0.95

suburbs, with a couple of exceptions: the busway corridor to the northern suburbs has high frequencies and short travel times and performs well on the closeness index, while the rail and bus corridor to the south (Manukau and Papakura), at a further distance from the city centre than the North Shore and serviced only every 15 minutes on both modes, delivers the poorest results on the network. Interestingly, the best-performing CBD node in Auckland on the closeness index is not the multi-modal terminus at Britomart, but the intersection at Symonds Street cemetery at the southern CBD edge.

Degree Centrality

The degree centrality index shows remarkable variation between typical

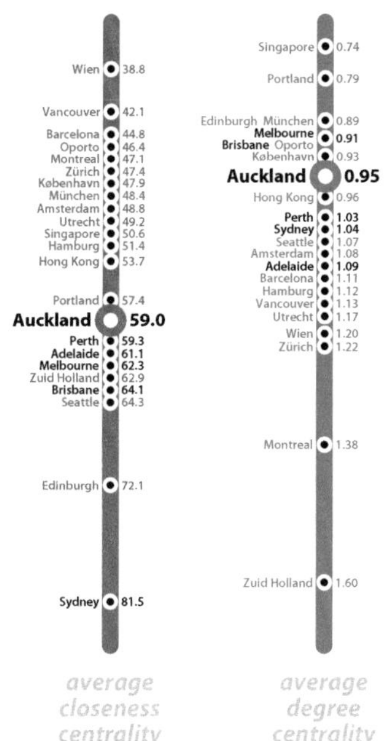

values on different radial bus and rail corridors, for example the parallel inner south main streets of Dominion Road (to Mount Roskill) and Mount Eden Road (to Three Kings). This is indicative of inconsistent (and for passengers, likely poorly legible) connections between bus routes or groups of routes in the CBD area, where there are a multitude of disjointed termini for radial lines besides the relatively recent addition of an integrated, multimodal terminal at Britomart. In an international context, average degree centrality scores for Auckland remain relatively low, at par with Melbourne and Brisbane in Australasia, as there are few suburban activity nodes that fully depend on feeder services to and from a higher-order trunk line.

Network Coverage

Auckland's network coverage is the lowest in the entire global sample. This result, echoing findings by Mavoa et al (2012), is directly correlated to the equally lowest-ranked performance of the city in the service intensity index and underscores the observation, discussed above, that the higher-frequency network largely only covers the key radial corridors of the core city. Moreover, inner suburban on-street bus corridors often act as trunks for several low-frequency lines with the effect that the SNAMUTS minimum standard along these routes only extends as far as the junction, often mid-corridor, where these lines fan out into their separate alignments. Along the western

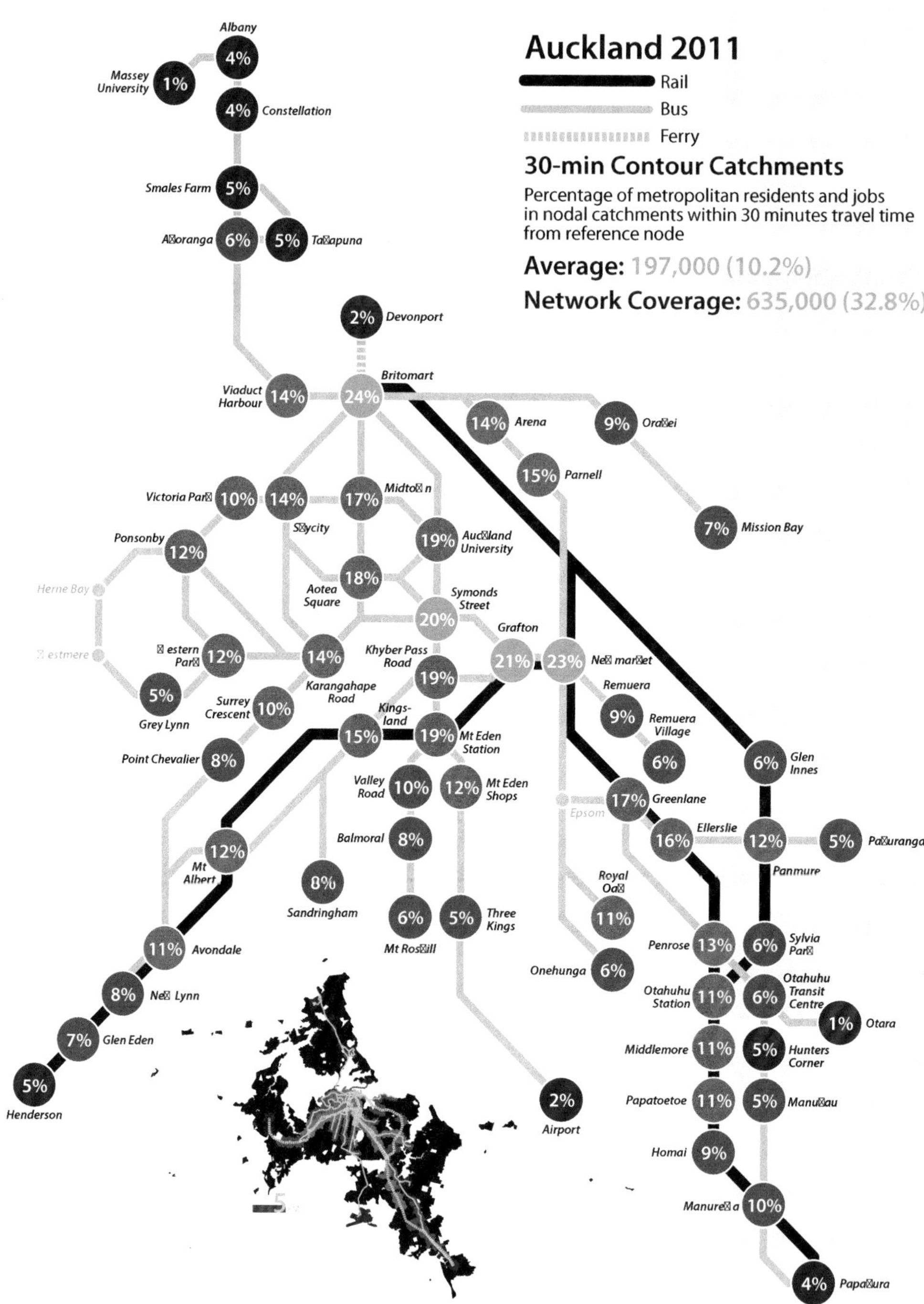

and southern rail lines, high-frequency buses partially duplicate the radial rail service and demonstrate a network integration and task-sharing challenge with scope for reform. In the north, there is only a small number of short links that veer off the busway between central Auckland and Albany and uphold the SNAMUTS minimum standard, accessing nearby centres such as Takapuna and Massey University.

Thirty-Minute Contour Catchments

In the light of a relatively scarce public transport endowment of outer suburban areas, we should find a relatively high average 30-minute contour catchment per node, as the majority of nodes are located within the compact confines of the Auckland isthmus. In percentage terms, Auckland is only marginally behind Perth, Brisbane and Adelaide on this measure, while outperforming Melbourne and Sydney. The largest contour catchment on the network occurs at the multimodal CBD transfer node at Britomart, though it is closely followed by Newmarket station at the eastern CBD fringe, where two rail and several bus corridors intersect in a location that is more geographically central to the Auckland isthmus than the waterfront at Britomart. In suburban areas, the relative speed of the rail system produces contour catchments of 10 per cent or better as far out as Manurewa and Avondale, whereas many centres on inner suburban bus corridors, as well as along the northern busway, remain below this standard.

Betweenness Centrality

Newmarket station, alongside Grafton station and Symonds Street cemetery, also boasts the highest concentration of travel opportunities on the network, significantly ahead of Britomart. Potential movement along the network appears to be strongly dominated by a single bus corridor (along Anzac Avenue, Symonds Street, Khyber Pass Road, Broadway and Great South Road). In comparison, the significance of the rail system is subdued, though a current upgrade and electrification program is likely to change this in the future as travel

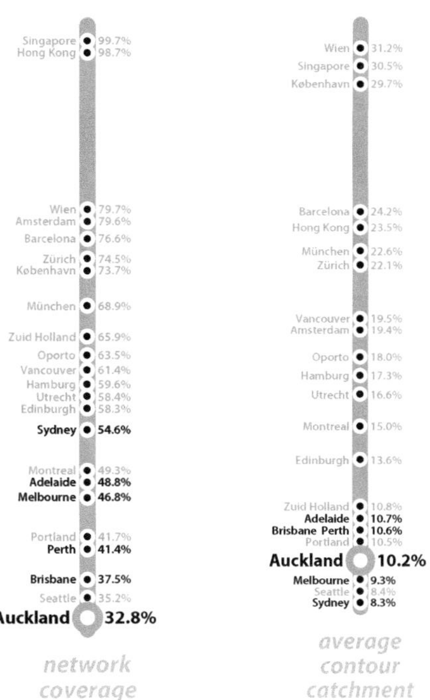

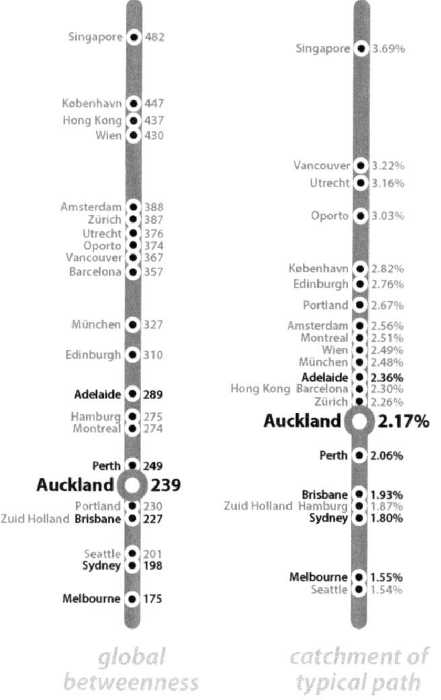

speeds and frequencies are improved. For now, Auckland retains the lowest proportion of travel opportunities on rail in the Australasian sample, and the second lowest (before Seattle) in the global sample. The global betweenness score in relation to population and jobs, and the typical path length catchment measure are in mid-field positions among the New World cities. Auckland's relatively high urban density makes up for the sparse network and service on both indexes: the limited expanse of the network, the relative absence of cross-suburban links and the comparatively high spatial resistance from low travel speeds and frequencies impact negatively on the opportunity value of longer

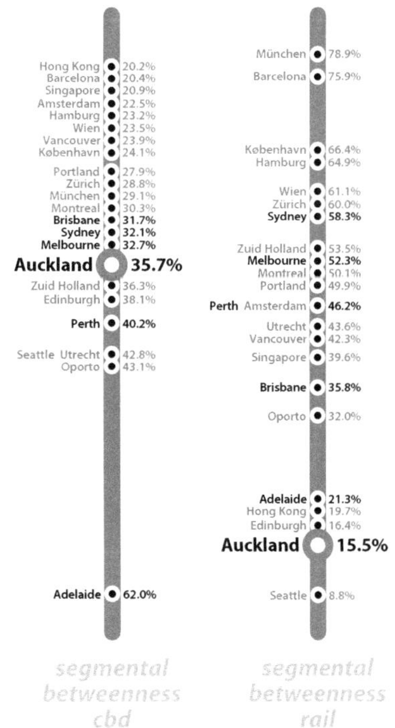

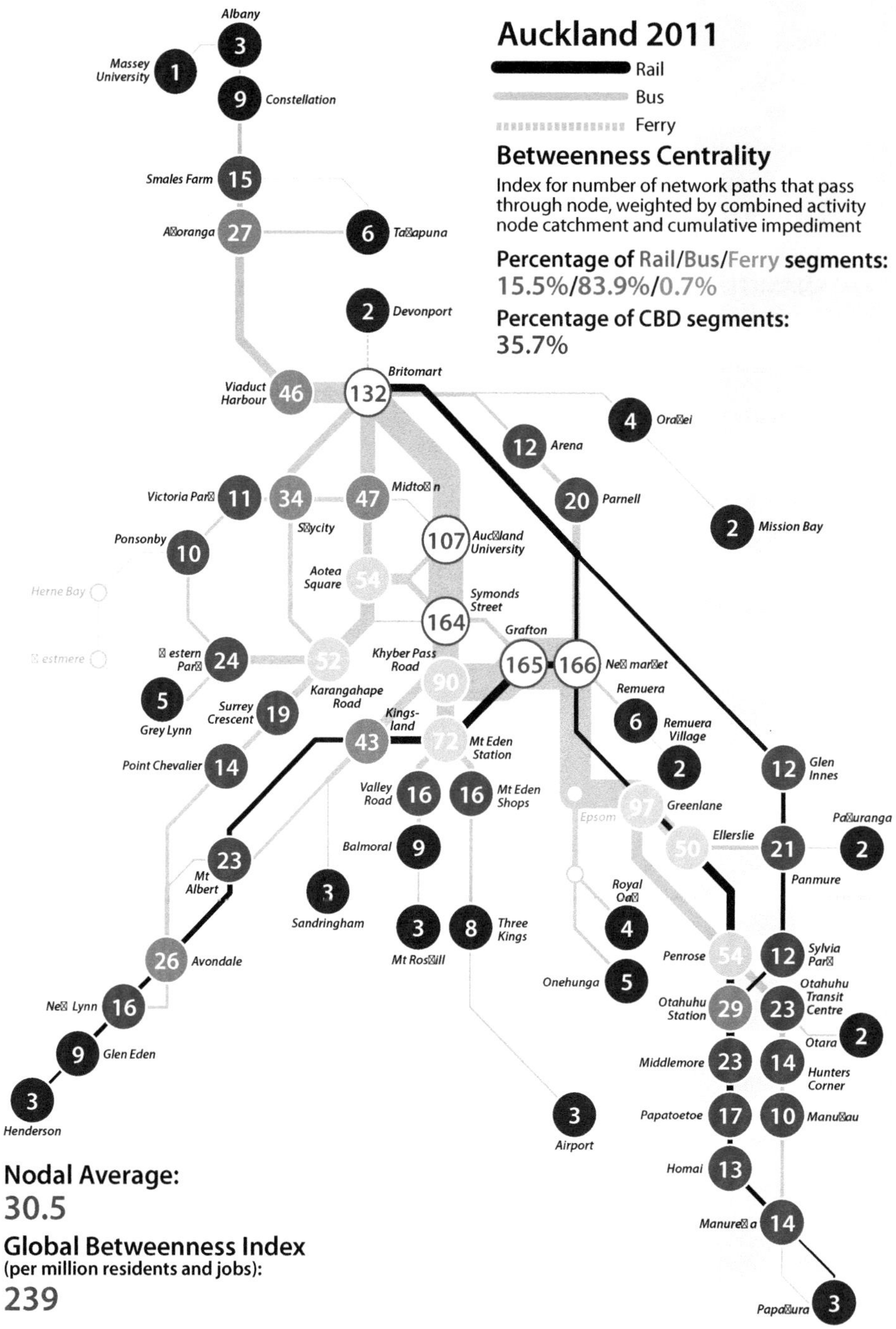

Auckland 2011

Rail
Bus
Ferry

Betweenness Centrality

Index for number of network paths that pass through node, weighted by combined activity node catchment and cumulative impediment

Percentage of Rail/Bus/Ferry segments:
15.5%/83.9%/0.7%

Percentage of CBD segments:
35.7%

Nodal Average:
30.5

Global Betweenness Index
(per million residents and jobs):
239

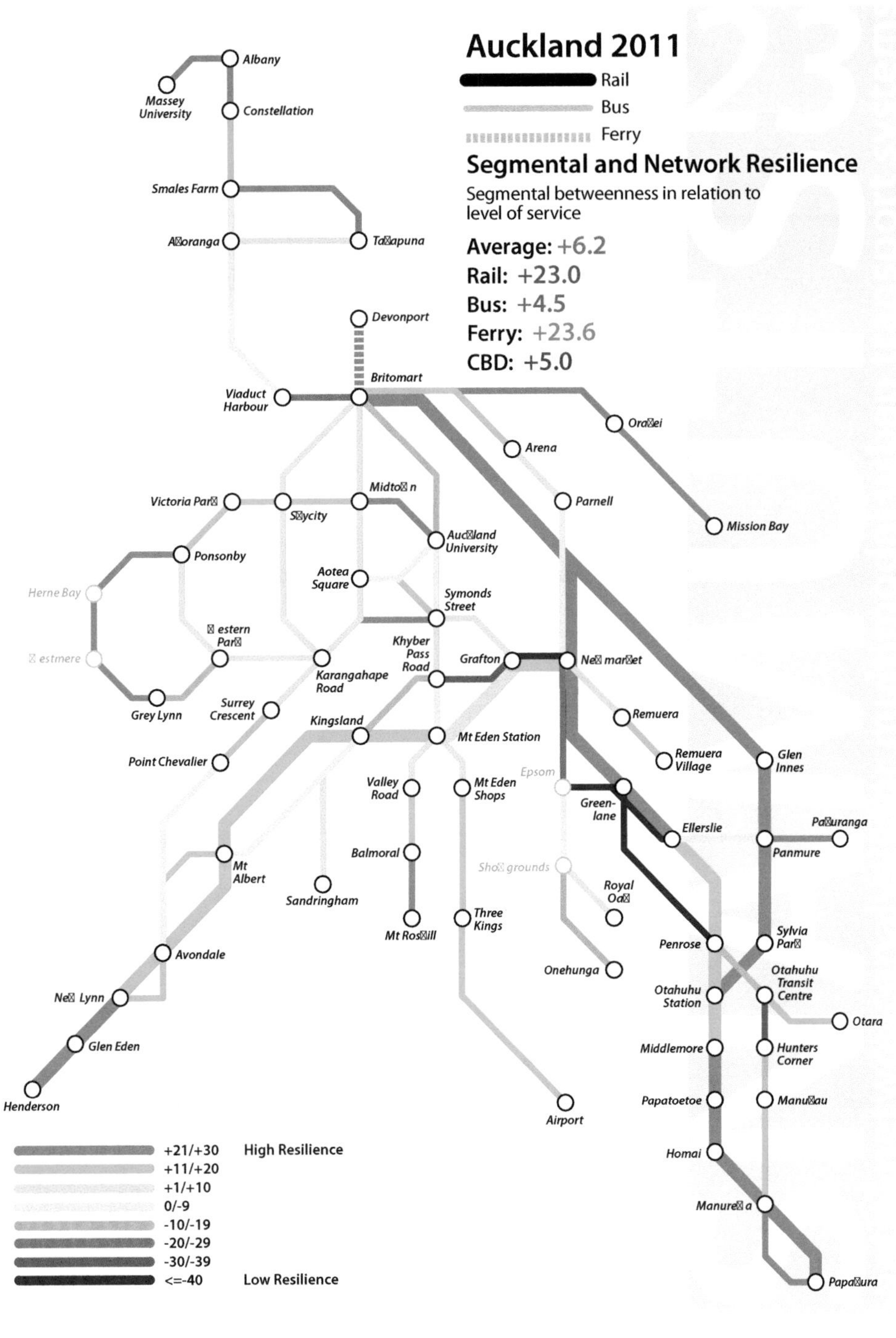

Auckland 2011

Rail
Bus
Ferry

Segmental and Network Resilience

Segmental betweenness in relation to level of service

Average: +6.2
Rail: +23.0
Bus: +4.5
Ferry: +23.6
CBD: +5.0

+21/+30 High Resilience
+11/+20
+1/+10
0/-9
-10/-19
-20/-29
-30/-39
<=-40 Low Resilience

public transport journeys in the Auckland metropolitan area.

Network Resilience

Despite – or perhaps because of – the modest geographical extent of Auckland's public transport network at the SNAMUTS minimum standard, the city records a network resilience figure that is poorer than in Adelaide, Melbourne or Perth and similar to that of Brisbane. Many of the most affected route segments are along bus routes parallel to uncongested rail lines, suggesting underutilised potential for effective task-sharing between modes of different performance. It is also notable, however, that segmental congestion

does not disproportionately occur in the CBD area, where the average resilience value is significantly higher than in Brisbane, Adelaide and Sydney (but slightly lower than in Melbourne and Perth). Better linkages between the many disparate termini of radial bus and rail lines by extending the SNAMUTS minimum standard outward into major suburban interchanges (such as Henderson, New Lynn, Onehunga or Manukau) could alleviate this situation and add much-needed multi-directionality to the network.

Nodal Connectivity

Low levels of patronage and network complexity lead to a very low number of network nodes in Auckland that

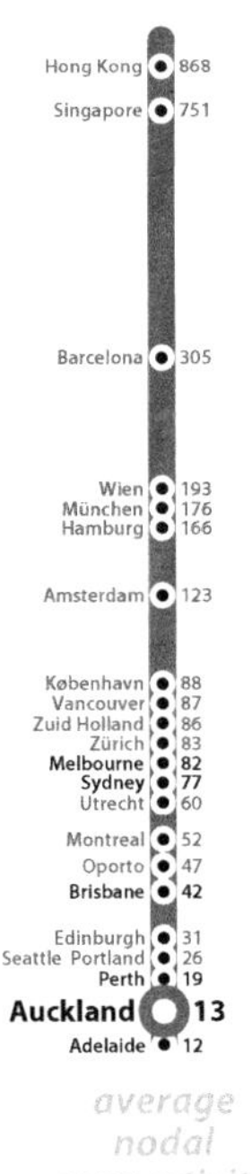

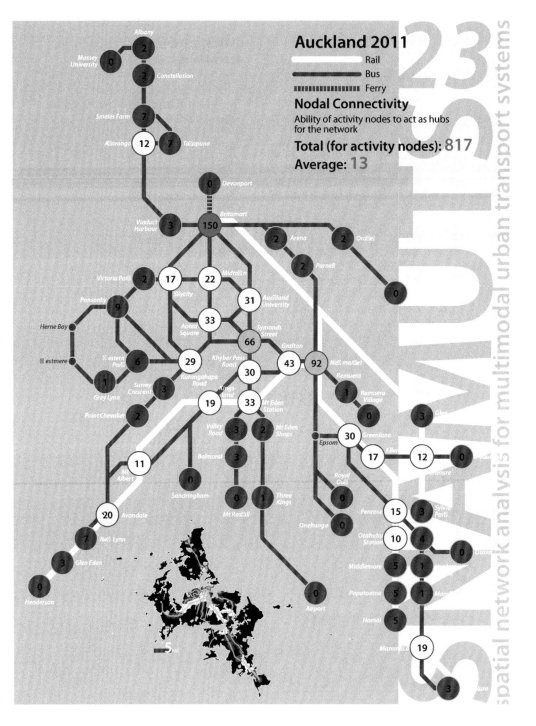

can be categorised as suitable for land use intensification configured around public transport as the primary mode of access – apart from Britomart, this is only somewhat true for the Newmarket-Grafton area but appears already deficient across the remainder of the CBD, and anywhere else in the metropolitan area. On average, Auckland shares the bottom rank in the global SNAMUTS sample on this index with Adelaide.

SNAMUTS Composite Accessibility Index and Reflections

The composite index shows Auckland to have only minor geographical patches of public transport accessibility that could be categorised as above average in international terms. Even the CBD area has several nodal catchments that do not meet this standard. Elsewhere, accessibility performance is markedly better along corridors and in suburban centres where rail and bus services coincide, and calls for measures to further improve their integration in terms of common ticketing and coordinated service frequencies. The geographically compact nature of the Auckland isthmus provides a supportive environment for a more multi-directional network if the service frequency of the existing orbital bus routes could be increased to facilitate transfers to the radial rail and bus routes with minimal waiting times. A template for such a network has been drafted and, at the time of writing, is subject to public consultation (Auckland Transport, 2014). Lastly, a significant boost to public transport accessibility across the network should result from the proposed construction of the CBD rail tunnel linking Britomart and Grafton/Mount Eden as an additional measure to the ongoing modernisation and electrification of the system that is also vigorously pursued by the council.

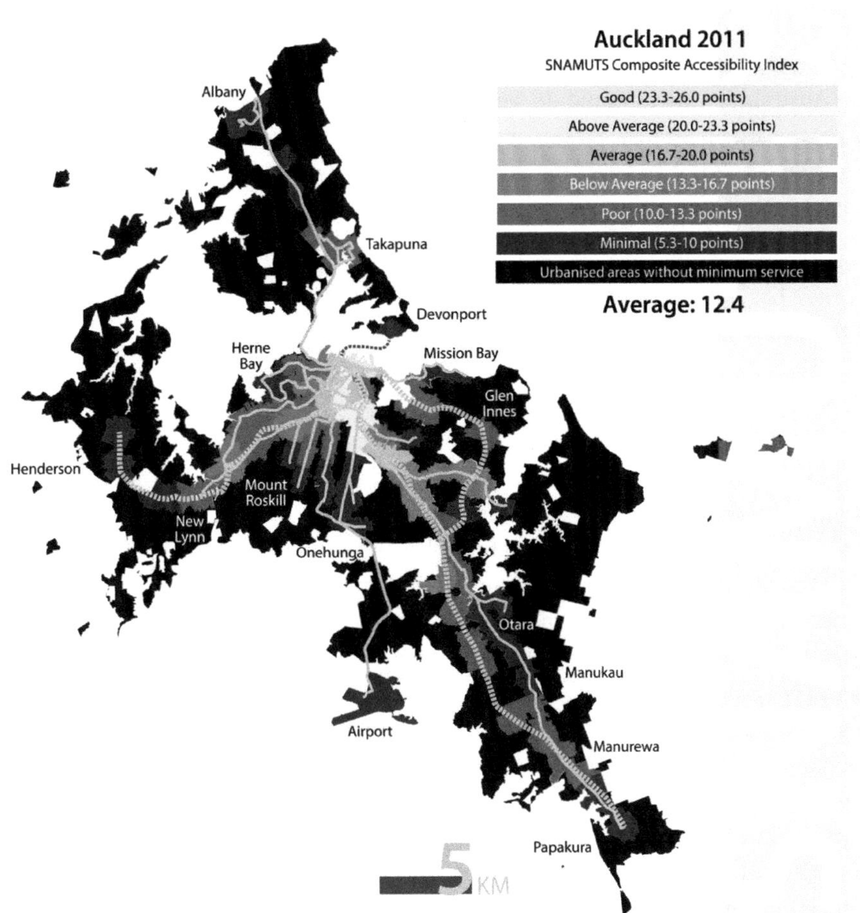

POSITIONING AUSTRALASIAN CITIES IN A GLOBAL CONTEXT

When comparing the data on Australasian cities with that of European and Asian cities (Chapters 5 and 7), it is clear that Australasian cities trail their counterparts on the measures of public transport service intensity, public transport network coverage, average 30-minute contour catchments of public transport journeys, network resilience and the critical resulting measure of public transport journeys per capita per year. Moreover, with few individual-city exceptions, the entire spectrum of performance of Australasian cities is situated below the entire spectrum of performance of European and Asian cities on each index.

The service intensity measure depicts the operational input each city is prepared to supply in order to provide a network at a standard that may allow for both planned and spontaneous public transport journeys for a broad variety of journey purposes. On this measure, Adelaide is prominent as the one Australasian city that exceeds the operational input of the 'frugal' group of European cities (Hamburg, München, Utrecht and Zuid Holland) and in turn, achieves a degree of geographical network coverage that is second only to Sydney among the cohort of Australian cities. This is despite Adelaide being the smallest and slowest-growing major Australasian capital city, and the associated relative absence of significant spatially concentrated clusters of land uses outside the central area in the South Australian capital. It is true that Adelaide has more buses, relative to both population and network size, travelling at low speed through the CBD than its counterparts elsewhere in Australia, marking a degree of operational inefficiency that contributes to the service intensity measure. However, the successful introduction of a minimum service standard (GO Zones at 15-minute frequencies or better on weekdays and 30-minute frequencies weekends and evenings) is a testament to effective planning in the inner suburbs without leaving significant coverage gaps outside walking distance from such corridors. This is a standard that can be found across the contiguously urbanised areas of practically every European city as well as Vancouver, at least within their core jurisdiction, and the remaining Australasian cities would do well to work towards a similar extent of network density (and relative operational input) in the future.

On the network coverage measure, Sydney has the best Australasian performance. This appears to be primarily a result of Australia's largest city's long-standing policy of land use intensification around rail-based activity nodes across the metropolitan area that has been stronger than in other Australian cities (Newman, 2009). In combination with the city's formidable topographical constraints to outer suburban expansion, this strategy has helped to place a larger proportion of metropolitan residents and jobs into walkable catchments of public transport than in its peer cities elsewhere in Australia. This pursuit of urban compactness and transit orientation, while rarely taken to perfection, is also a prevailing theme in the co-evolution of transport and land use systems in European, Canadian and Asian cities. Some cities, such as Barcelona, København, Vancouver and Hong Kong, have comparable or greater topographical constraints to fringe area expansion than Sydney. In other countries, notably the (western) Netherlands and (northern) Switzerland, regional population densities are such that maximising spatial efficiency in urban development has been imperative for generations in order to protect scarce productive agricultural and forestry areas, as well as nature reserves. In these cases, a proactive land policy at a regional scale appears to result in urban growth to cluster around public transport infrastructure (Gallez et al, 2013; Van Wee and Maat, 2003) and thus facilitate the rollout of public transport services to a large proportion of the population without excessive use of operational resources.

On the network resilience measure, Perth and Melbourne are ahead of the Australasian sample. Perth has pursued the most ambitious strategy for public transport network development and investment during the past 25 years (Curtis, 2008a) and, despite maintaining a long list of further worthwhile infrastructure projects yet to be realised, has achieved a relative balance where rail and bus modes are characterised by complementary task-sharing that seeks to maximise the efficiency of both. Most (but not all) European and Canadian cities in the sample follow a similar path and over decades of co-evolution, have optimised their networks to enable a fine-tuned interplay of public transport modes with varying performance and capacity, in many cases using a greater range of transport modes than Perth which currently only has heavy rail and (mostly) street-running buses.

In Melbourne, the relatively good network resilience results are clearly associated with the widespread presence of an intermediate capacity mode in the form of an extensive tram system (Currie and Burke, 2014). Despite Melbourne's trams being relatively short compared to those in most European first-generation operations, their comfortable passenger load is still about twice that of a bus (most of which are also relatively short in Melbourne). This circumstance limits operational input particularly for the CBD surface network compared to Melbourne's peer cities. For instance, according the SNAMUTS database, 22.1 per cent of metro-wide public transport vehicles plying the minimum service standard network can be found in Sydney's CBD at any one time during the weekday inter-peak period, while in Melbourne, this share is only 19.6 per cent. In Sydney, more than 70 buses per hour per direction attempt to travel along George Street and several other CBD corridors even outside peak hours, while in Melbourne, the maximum number of trams along any single route (Swanston Street) is 45. In such circumstances, it is no coincidence that Sydney, Australia's city with the poorest average network resilience results on several measures (network-wide, in the CBD and, jointly with Brisbane, on the bus system) is now pursuing a substantial expansion program for its light rail network to improve operational efficiency, build passenger capacity and free up operational resources currently tied up in CBD bus congestion.

In Europe, the role of intermediate modes, mostly trams and light rail, is not consistent across our 11-city sample, but the majority of cities either look back on long-standing strategies to modernise, prioritise and expand a first-generation tram system (Wien, Zürich, München, Amsterdam, Rotterdam, Den Haag) beside heavy rail/metro and bus operations, or to reintroduce the mode after a long period of absence or relegation to a heritage niche (Utrecht, Barcelona, Oporto, and Edinburgh in 2014). These cities have realised the efficiency dividend that accompanies the differentiation of the mode mix into a greater number of performance categories and with few exceptions, have consequently improved their resilience results to levels not seen in Australasian cities.

This analysis of comparative accessibility performance in Australasian and global cities has shown that the public transport networks of Australasian cities generally have lower operational input, lower geographical coverage and lower levels of resilience against the pressures from increasing patronage than their European and Asian counterparts. To resolve these shortfalls in the manner of the European cities that generally cater for much higher patronage levels than Australasian cities – in some cases three or four times as high – would require the mobilisation of additional resources, over and beyond the rate of population growth, to allow for public transport operations to be allocated to the geographical expansion of the networks. Such geographical expansion would increase the proportion of metropolitan residents and employees that have the opportunity to rely on, and build their daily activities around public transport accessibility. In order to keep the networks functional as passenger numbers grow, however, it will also be necessary to optimise their configuration and to develop them towards a more efficient form of task-sharing between transport modes of different capacities, and to increase the range of transport modes by stepping up investment in the expansion and introduction of higher-capacity modes such as heavy rail, light rail, trams and bus rapid transit. Unfortunately, the prospects for proactive policies of public transport infrastructure investment deteriorated sharply following the change of federal government in 2013 and the subsequent withdrawal of Federal funding for new public transport projects in Australia's major cities. As a consequence, the most prominent proposals for additional urban transport infrastructure have been road projects. In the case of Melbourne's East West Link and Sydney's West Connex projects, they represent some of the costliest infrastructure measures ever undertaken in the country, come with dubious or undisclosed cost – benefit analyses and have attracted fierce opposition from broad sectors of the community as well as local governments (Whitzman et al, 2014). Decision making for transport and accessibility in Australia's major cities has thus returned to a partisan struggle over political hegemony between advocates of road-based mobility planning and those of accessibility planning focussed on the amenity of place. This is in stark contrast to the deliberate consensus-building approaches in this area in some European cities (see Chapters 5 and 6). It is likely that this stand-off will result in a period of stagnation, if not regression, for Australian cities seeking a more public transport–oriented future.

In New Zealand, exemplified by Auckland which is home to a third of the country's population, public transport investment is also far from uncontroversial. However, a mounting traffic congestion crisis in the face of rapid population growth in a geographically constrained region has prompted policy makers and the travelling public to reconsider public transport as a critical component of urban mobility and accessibility after decades of neglect (Mees and Dodson, 2007; Greer and van Campen, 2011). In a country which has not had a precedent for public-transport focussed policy making since the onset of the automobile age and where (particularly in Auckland) prejudice against the mode has been widespread and entrenched in the community (Murray et al, 2010), this is a significant development. Owing to Auckland's political clout in the national context, it has begun to foster growing involvement of national government in urban public transport investment.

4 Stagnation and Aspiration in North American Cities

Overcoming the Totalitarianism of Automobility

In this chapter we move from the New World cities of Australasia to a sample of New World mid-sized cities in Canada and the US – Montreal (QC), Vancouver (BC), Seattle (WA) and Portland (OR). European settlement and urbanisation along the east coast of the continent began significantly earlier than in Australia, but did not reach the Pacific Northwest until the nineteenth century. Hence, the proportion of urban fabric built prior to mass motorisation varies across the sample. A common theme across these and other second-tier North American cities has been the widespread abandonment of rail-based urban transit after 1945. In US cities, private transit operators typically collapsed during this period and were subsequently nationalised at much reduced levels of service (Yago, 1984). In Canada, public operators had been in charge for longer, and the post-war conversion of streetcars to buses (trolleybuses in Vancouver, reusing the streetcar's electricity infrastructure) was less associated with service deterioration. In Montreal, the oldest and densest of the four cities, political pressure for mass transit solutions was already present prior to the era of mass motorisation; in the Pacific Northwest, it emerged during the 1970s and 1980s.

Most North American cities are characterised by a greater legacy of extensive motorway networks developed in the 1950s and 1960s than their Australian and European counterparts. In the US, this was facilitated with massive federal subsidies. However, differences within the sample are apparent. Vancouver saw resistance to motorways and the development of alternative transport strategies since the early 1970s (Punter, 2003; Berelowicz, 2005; Stone, 2013). Portland also experienced an early turnaround from the motorway building movement towards TOD (Arrington, 2009; Schiller et al, 2010). Montreal, in keeping with a modernist paradigm that sought to maximise accessibility by all motorised modes, built complementary motorway and metro networks (Paulhiac and Kaufmann, 2006).

Despite the comprehensive, though temporary, rejection of rail-based urban transit and the facilitation of expansive suburban growth through generous road networks, all four cities retain functional fragments of their pre-1945 structure based on mixed-use streetcar corridors. Their relative significance, however, has declined during many decades of car-oriented planning and spontaneous urbanisation.

Vancouver and Portland were early adopters of governance regimes seeking land use and transport planning integration (LUTI) at the metropolitan scale (Arrington, 2009; Mees, 2007). In Seattle, the Puget Sound Regional Council has more recently grown into a comparable role (Margerum et al, 2013). In Montreal, rivalries over responsibilities and policy directions have impacted on collaboration between the regional planning agency and the regional transit agency (Van Neste and Bherer, 2013; Boudreau et al, 2006; Gauthier, 2005).

Growing numbers of citizens and decision makers in these North American cities share a concern about the car dominance of the twentieth century, and a determination to employ LUTI as a tool to address this. In this sense, the four cities chosen may be considered as pioneers among their regional peers. However, their efforts to strengthen public transit are occurring in starkly different institutional environments, geographical and historical contexts and are yielding different results in terms of accessibility.

ACCESSIBILITY PROFILE: MONTRÉAL, QC

Montreal is the major metropolitan centre of Canada's province of Quebec, located in the east of the country, inland on the Saint-Laurent estuary. At 3.82 million inhabitants in 2011 and an annual growth rate just below 40,000 during the 2000s (Statistics Canada, 2013), it is Canada's second largest city (after Toronto). Geographically, the settlement area is distributed over two major islands (dominated by the municipalities of Montreal and Laval respectively) and adjacent mainland areas. Montreal

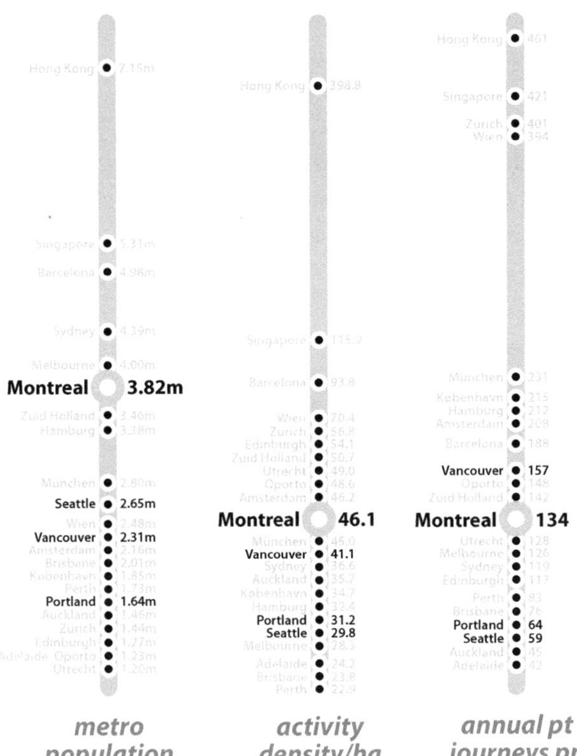

has the highest average urban density of any New World city in the SNAMUTS sample, reflecting an east coast city-building tradition that includes a significant portion of pre-industrial and pre-automobile urban form, and a greater share of apartment living than in the Pacific Northwest case study cities. Montreal also retains a stronger functional dominance of the city centre than most other North American cities and thus has some structural similarities with monocentric European cities (Paulhiac and Kaufmann, 2006; Kenworthy and Townsend, 2009).

A four-line, fully underground metro system, using a rubber-tyred technology first developed in Paris, evolved over several growth and stagnation phases since the 1960s alongside a generous network of urban motorways. There is also a limited suburban rail system (*trains de banlieue*) consisting of five radial lines where passenger service has been restored since the 1980s. However, the most frequent of these rail routes is operated hourly during the day and therefore does not meet the minimum standard required for inclusion in the SNAMUTS analysis.

Within the core city of Montreal, which comprises just under half of the metropolitan population, the bus system is organised as a feeder and distributor network to the metro. There are practically no parallel bus routes at the surface where metro lines run underneath. There is also a relative absence of buses from CBD streets during off-peak hours. The system has a large number of purpose-built metro-bus interchanges facilitating the integration of the two modes. Service planning is overseen by a regional transit agency (*Agence Métropolitaine de Transport* or *AMT*). The AMT operates the suburban rail lines, and bus routes crossing municipal boundaries, while at a local government level there are separate operators in Montreal, Laval and Longueuil on the south bank (*Rive Sud*). Operator-specific and integrated metropolitan fares coexist to an extent. Within the City of Montreal, there is a flat fare (one zone) and a financial incentive towards periodical over single tickets.

There were about 512 million public transit journeys in 2012 (AMT, 2013), translating into 134 annual trips per capita, the second highest among New World SNAMUTS cities after Vancouver.[1]

Service Intensity

At just over 10 vehicles per 100,000 residents in simultaneous revenue operation during the weekday inter-peak period, Montreal follows a lean approach to deploying operational resources compared to the remainder of the global sample. This reflects an efficiency dividend that comes with the division of tasks between metro and buses,

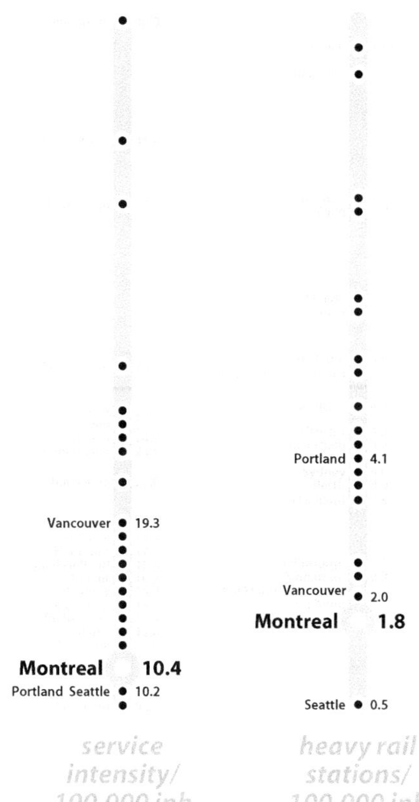

as well as the city's relative compactness. However, in the context of this index it is reasonable to query the scope for significant accessibility improvements should Montreal's operational input be lifted to the level of (for instance) Vancouver, which would represent an increase in excess of 80 per cent.

Montreal's metro network has 68 stations, resulting in a rail station density relative to population towards the bottom end of the global sample. This is partially associated with the limited extent of the network and its slow pace of growth – only three new stations opened during the last 25 years. It is also associated with the low level of service on the suburban rail lines, which excludes their stations from the SNAMUTS analysis.

Closeness Centrality

Average performance on the ease-of-movement index positions Montreal within the field of the European rather than Australasian and US cities. The most likely explanation for this superior score is that the proportion of Montreal's metropolitan area covered by public transit at the minimum standard has characteristics of service levels and urban structure that are comparable to those found in European cities. The metro system, while mostly limited to the core city, is fast, frequent and well-positioned in relation to key movement corridors. It delivers a better-than-average closeness result for every single activity node it serves. Another influencing factor is the lattice shape and resulting multi-directionality that is produced by the combined metro-bus network within the City of Montreal. This offers a choice of routes for most journeys, even though the service frequencies of the bus routes making up the lattice pattern are far from uniform.

The poorest closeness results are at the extremities in the north-east and south-west of Montreal Island, for outlying suburban centres in Laval and Longueuil, and generally along the south-western fringe of the core city between Pierrefonds-Roxboro and Lachine. Here the urbanised area disintegrates into a patchwork of low-density residential, large-scale industrial and transport uses, and the network density of public transit declines in comparison to the more interconnected north-east.

Degree Centrality

The reliance of Montreal's public transit network on transfers is higher than in any other case study city with the exception of the poly-nuclear agglomeration of Zuid Holland. This is partially associated with an efficient organisation of the metro-bus interplay, where transfers help to distribute travel opportunities towards the most appropriate mode for the task. It is also indicative of some disconnections within the network:

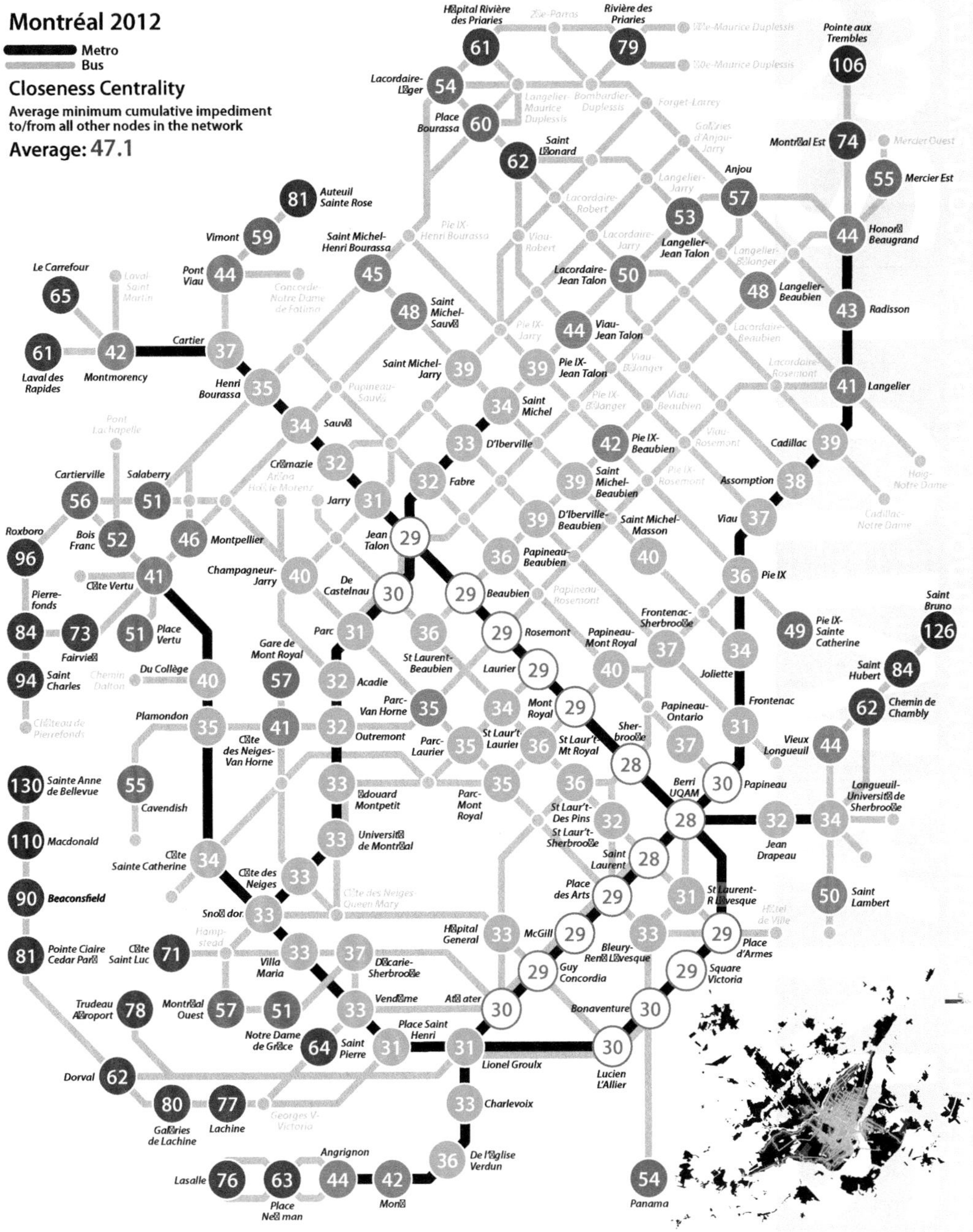

Montréal 2012

Metro
Bus

Closeness Centrality

Average minimum cumulative impediment to/from all other nodes in the network

Average: 47.1

three of the four metro lines (orange, green and yellow) are connected to each other while the fourth (blue) line is only connected to the orange line. Thus some journeys fully within the metro network already require two transfers. The paucity of bus routes in the CBD, where there are barely any opportunities for bus-bus transfers between secondary corridors, also contributes to a high measure of transfer intensity. The functional hierarchy between public transit modes in Montreal is

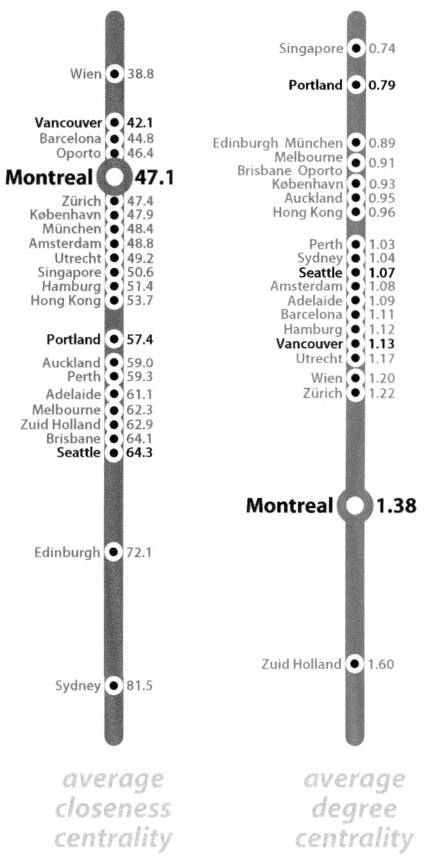

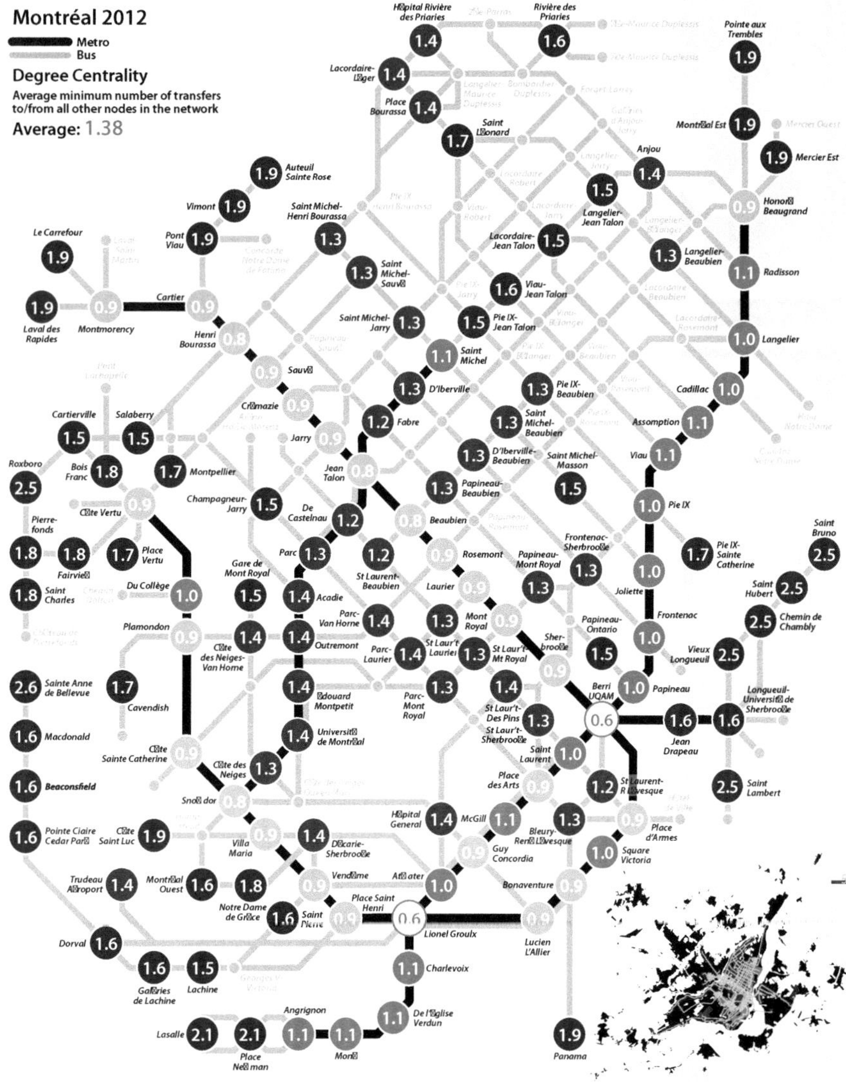

therefore quite pronounced, while the spatial hierarchy of activity nodes along the network is relatively flat: there are only two outstanding performers on the degree centrality index (the metro interchanges of Berri-UQAM and Lionel Groulx). Elsewhere, the network falls short on elevating any particular node into a position of exceptional transfer-free connectivity, an issue returned to in the context of the flexibility of movement index.

Network Coverage

A narrow majority of residents and workplaces in the metropolitan area of Montreal lack walking-distance access to public transit at the SNAMUTS standard. While this is typical for a New World city, it is surprising that Montreal's result on this index is more than 10 per cent below Vancouver. Network coverage reveals a 'tale of two cities' for Montreal that is more pronounced than in most other case study cities. A well-served core city coexists with a suburban belt where public transit access is relatively scarce and limited to a handful of radial feeder lines towards the core city. In comparison to Australian cities, a specific detrimental influence here is the infrequent service on Montreal's suburban rail network, a system that appears to be configured for CBD job commuting alone rather than for a variety of journey purposes.

Thirty-Minute Contour Catchments

The modest extent of network coverage does not necessarily contrast with the finding that the percentage of residents and jobs accessible by an average 30-minute public transit journey is significantly higher in Montreal than in any Australasian or US city in the sample. It equals several European cities which

Montréal 2012

Metro
Bus

30-min Contour Catchments

Percentage of metropolitan residents and jobs in activity node catchments within 30 min travel time from reference node

Average: 835,000 (15.0%)

Network Coverage:
2,745,000 (49.3%)

have more extensive geographical network coverage. The key reason for this can be found in the relative compactness of the core city and its penetration by a limited, but high-performing, metro system along corridors of considerable urban intensity. The best-performing corridor on this index is located along the orange metro line, one of Montreal's first to open in 1966–67, linking the two major transfer stations at Berri-UQAM and Jean Talon through the mixed-use, inner neighbourhoods of Plateau Mont-

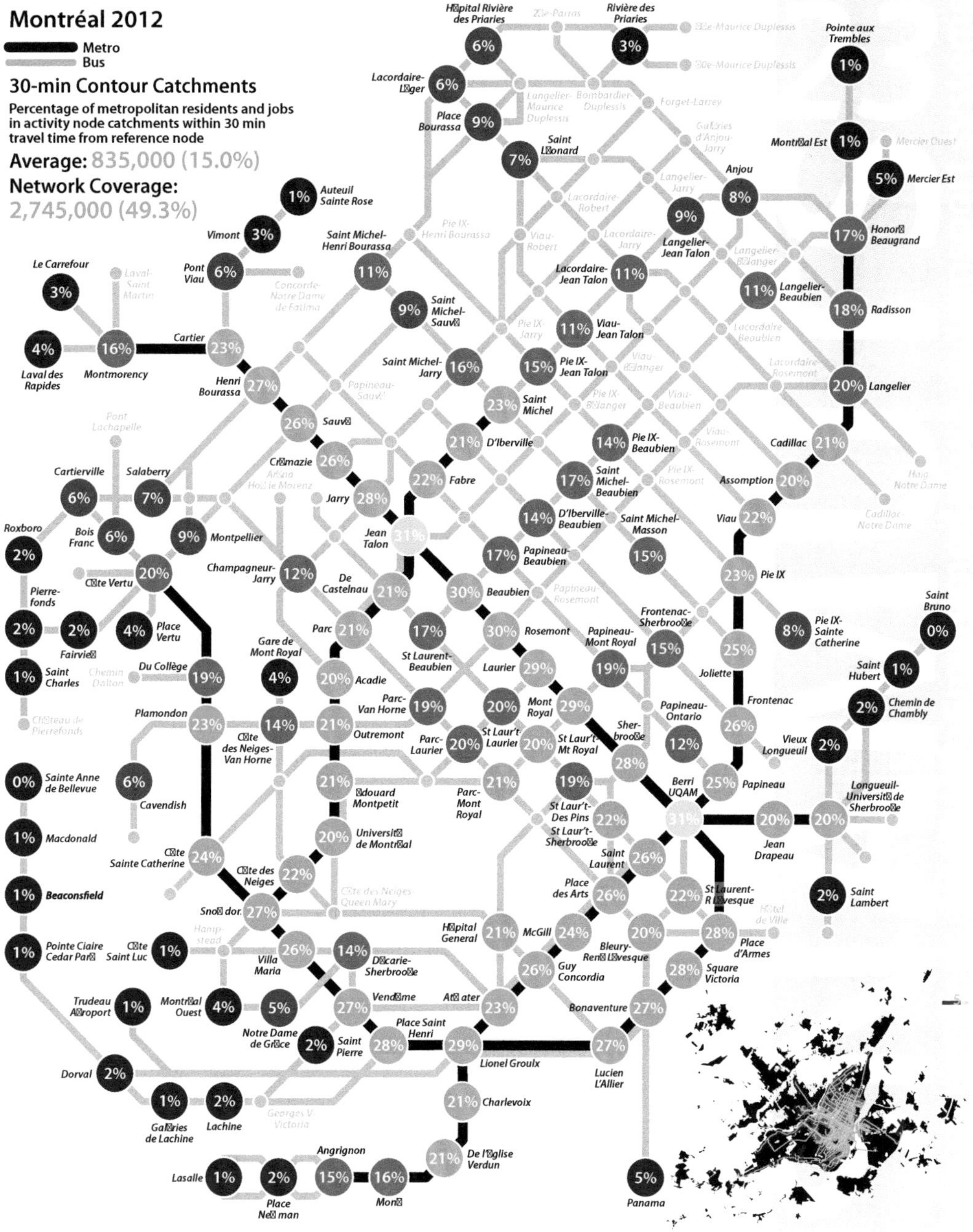

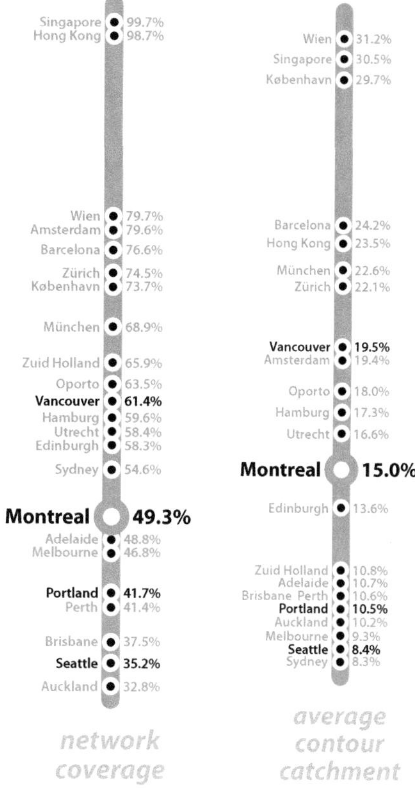

Royal where contour catchment sizes exceed those for the CBD. Conversely, contour catchment results drop very rapidly in suburban locations away from the metro system, with the partial exception of the neighbourhoods in Rosemont-La Petite Patrie, Montréal Nord, Saint Léonard and Anjou which are serviced by a lattice-shaped bus network.

Betweenness Centrality

Montreal's global betweenness score in relation to population and employment is at the higher end of the New World cities in the sample, outperformed only by Adelaide and Vancouver which have far greater service intensity. The effectiveness of the core city metro and bus network in providing accessibility is reflected here. However, the segmental and nodal betweenness figures suggest some imbalances that may limit the potential of public transit in its current form to gain further mode share from the car. The difference in performance between fast, frequent metro trains and slower, usually less frequent bus routes creates a further spatial division, this time within the core city, between super-accessible metro station catchments and more difficult to access bus corridors. As a result, travel opportunities concentrate strongly on the metro network, the smallest heavy rail system of any case study city to achieve a share of the city-wide segmental betweenness score in excess of 50 per cent. This trend is assisted by a modified grid network

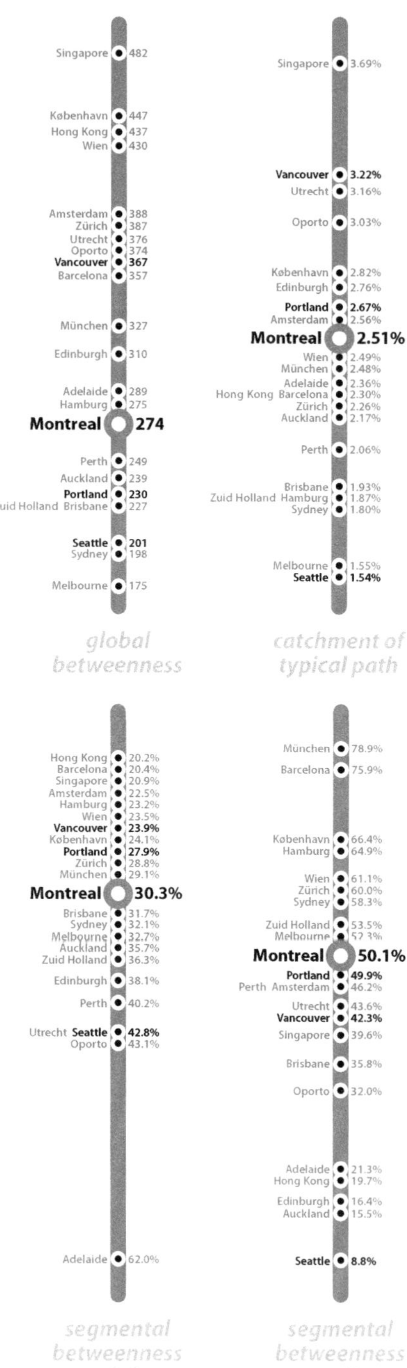

configuration where metro and bus corridors are treated as equal components despite significant variation in capacity and performance. As a consequence, passengers are encouraged to deviate from desire lines in order to make greater use of the metro and residents and workers in metro catchments will experience greater transit availability than users in bus-only catchments. The effect this configuration has on the network's functioning is twofold. Firstly, it generates exceptional ease of movement along the metro system in relation to the network as a whole. This encourages long and sometimes circuitous underground journeys which, in conjunction with the high concentration of land uses along metro corridors, push up the typical path length measure to the second highest level among the larger case study cities (after Singapore). Secondly, it leaves the system vulnerable to congestion and to growth pressures (see following section).

Network Resilience

The average level of network resilience on Montreal's public transit system is the lowest of all case study cities. Despite the low number of services in the CBD, primarily accessed through two metro lines and a handful of terminating bus routes, the specific resilience figure for the central city differs only marginally from the citywide average. The concerning performance of Montreal on this index relates to

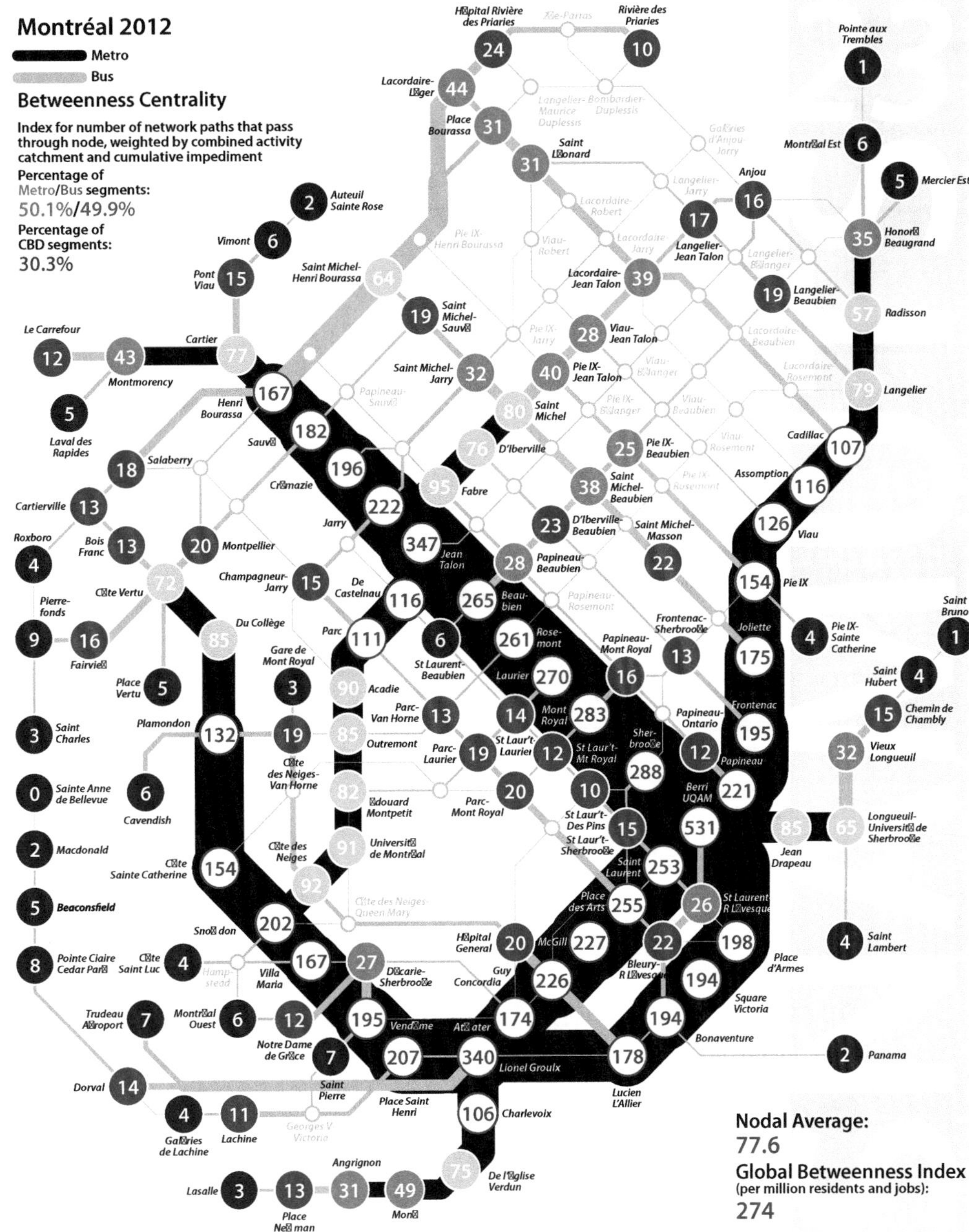

several factors already mentioned. The relatively low service intensity suggests that the frugal approach to allocating operational resources to public transit tasks may be unsustainable. The lattice-shaped network configuration that avoids parallel metro and bus routes, in combination with the sizeable performance gap between metro and bus, results in relatively prescriptive journey paths for passengers who wish to choose the fastest route. The limited extent of the metro system, and the lack of an intermediate mode such as light rail, place significant pressure on certain bus corridors (rue Henri Bourassa; rue Saint Michel; rue Jean Talon and rue Lacordaire in the city's north-east as well as some feeder routes in Laval and Longueuil).

Nodal Connectivity

Montreal shows an average performance among New World cities on this index, trailing Vancouver, Melbourne and Sydney but ranking above the US and smaller Australasian cities. While the four metro interchanges and several other CBD stations predictably return the highest nodal connectivity values, it is notable that above-average results are confined to the metro corridors. For an occasional user there is not a single bus-only node that appears an 'easy place to get to'. Among the metro-connected activity nodes, there is a relatively flat public transit accessibility hierarchy. In this spatial logic, urban intensification programmes would need to focus on entire metro corridors, rather than a smaller number of specific centres. This may explain why dedicated TOD policies have been less successful in Montreal than in Vancouver (Filion and Kramer, 2012).

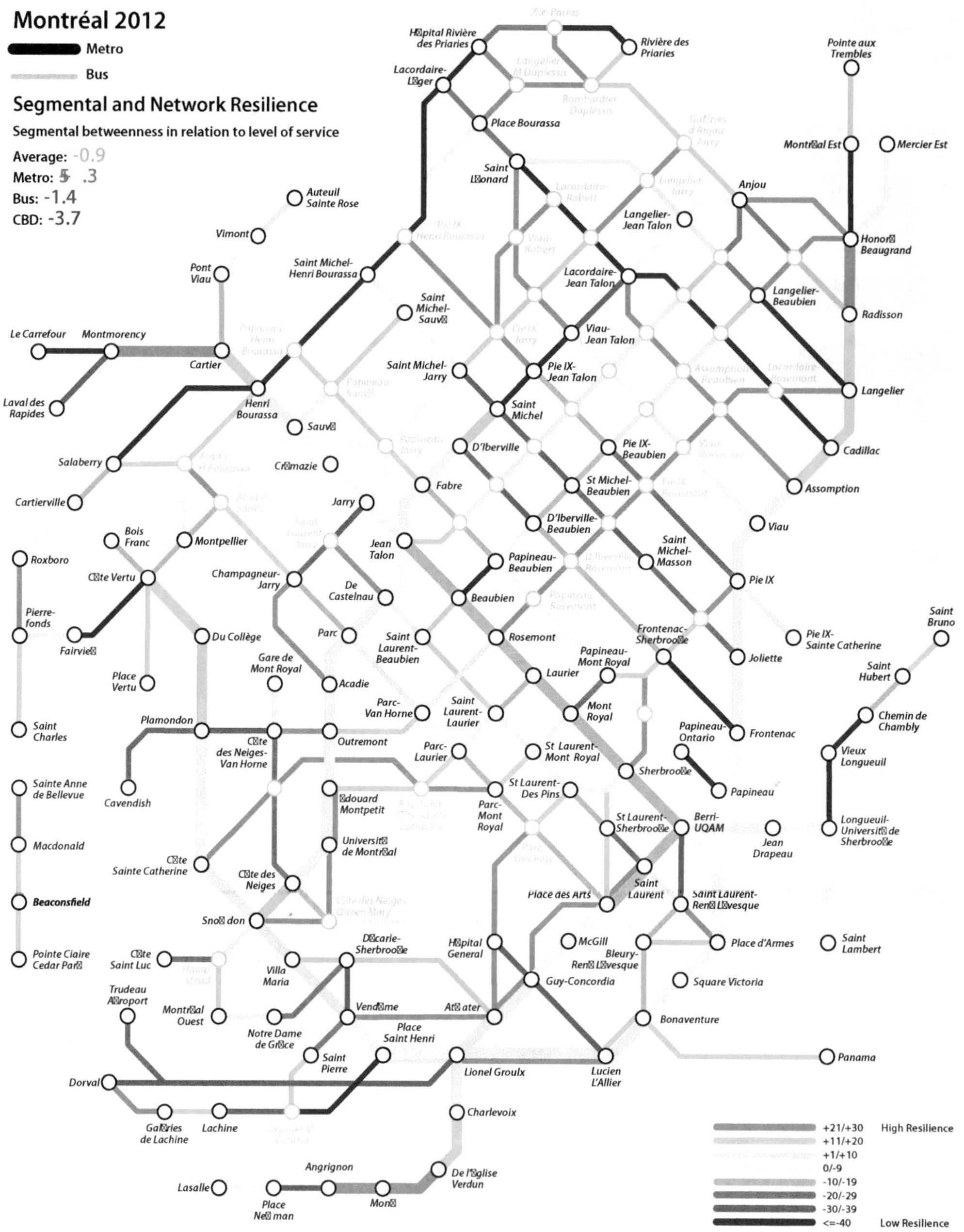

Montréal 2012

Metro

Bus

Segmental and Network Resilience

Segmental betweenness in relation to level of service

Average: -0.9

Metro: -5.3

Bus: -1.4

CBD: -3.7

+21/+30 High Resilience

+11/+20

+1/+10

0/-9

-10/-19

-20/-29

-30/-39

<=-40 Low Resilience

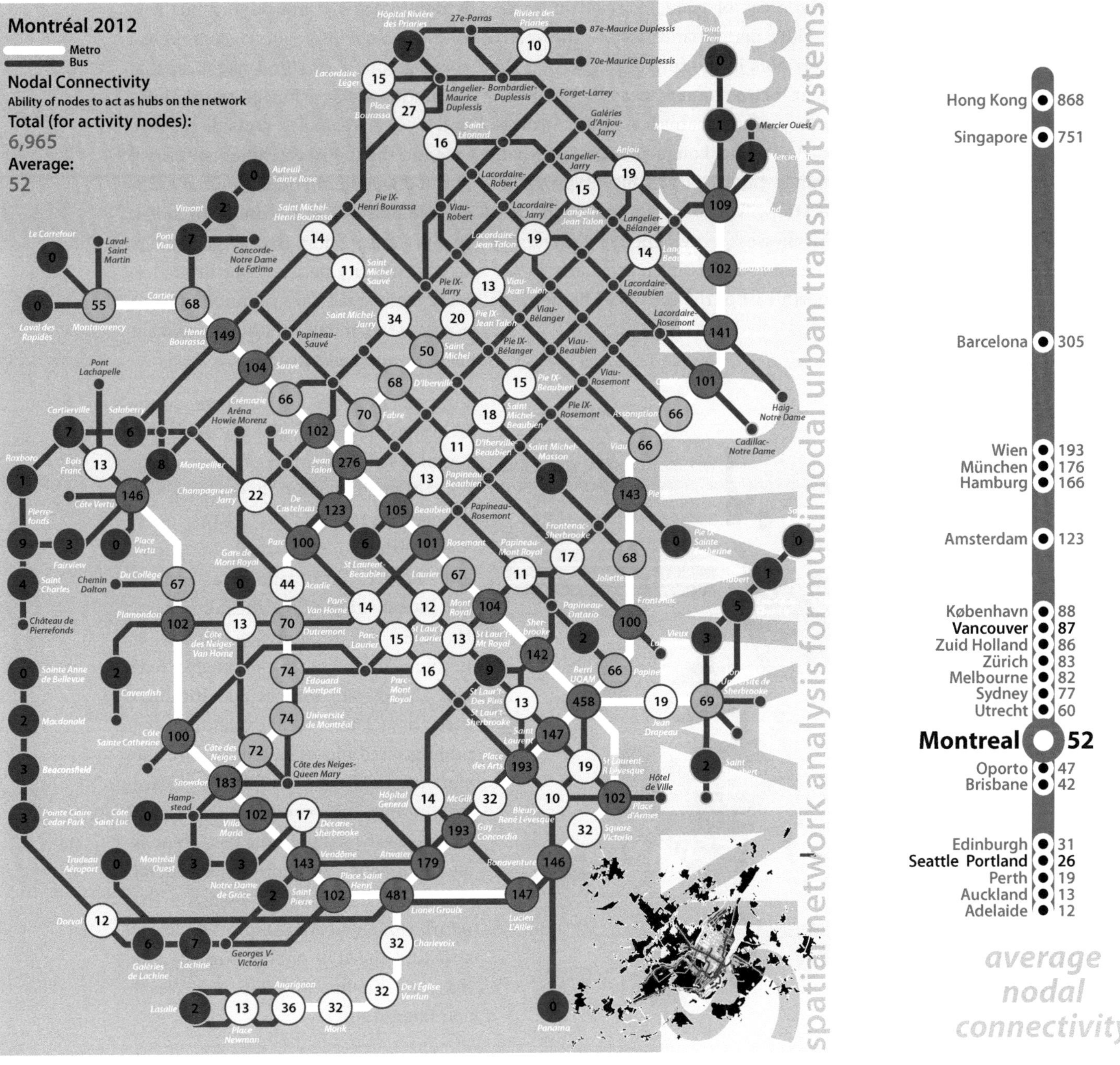
Montréal 2012
Metro
Bus
Nodal Connectivity
Ability of nodes to act as hubs on the network
Total (for activity nodes):
6,965
Average:
52
SNAUTS 23
spatial network analysis for multimodal urban transport systems
Hong Kong 868
Singapore 751
Barcelona 305
Wien 193
München 176
Hamburg 166
Amsterdam 123
København 88
Vancouver 87
Zuid Holland 86
Zürich 83
Melbourne 82
Sydney 77
Utrecht 60
Montreal 52
Oporto 47
Brisbane 42
Edinburgh 31
Seattle Portland 26
Perth 19
Auckland 13
Adelaide 12
average
nodal
connectivity

SNAMUTS Composite Accessibility Index and Reflections

Montreal has the second best average result for a New World city. The difference to best-performing Vancouver is explained by Montreal's lower geographical network coverage, lower network density and more frugal approach to allocating operational resources.

The areas of good to excellent accessibility performance follow the metro corridors in the core city as well as the four metro stations located on the territory of the suburban municipalities of Laval and Longueuil. This is where public transit is capable of providing a strong backbone for residents' and businesses' movement needs. Outside these corridors and particularly in the north-east of the core city, the network is dominated by intersecting bus corridors which offer good geographical coverage but a greater sense of spatial separation due to longer travel times and lower frequencies. Outside the core city and the metro catchments in Laval and Longueuil, frequent public transit, where it exists, is reduced to radial, bus-based corridors that act as feeders to the core city network but little else. Here large areas have no public transit access at the minimum standard and are likely dominated by car use.

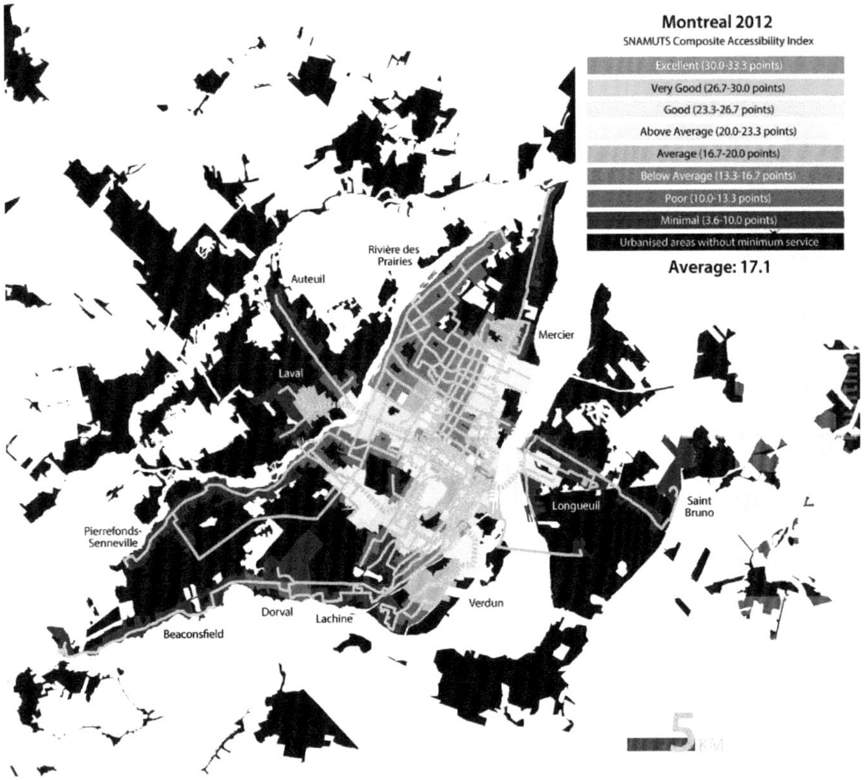

Current projects to improve Montreal's public transit include the opening of a sixth suburban rail line in late 2014, though it offers a similarly low service frequency as the existing ones. Metro extensions in Laval, Longueuil and Montreal are planned, as well as the introduction of a light rail system. However, the difficulty of assembling funding from local, provincial, federal and private sources and the high costs associated with expanding the underground metro system or with the start-up requirements of a new surface system appear to condemn these projects to a slow pace of progress. There is also a tendency in Montreal for Federal transport funding to be spent on the refurbishment of aging motorway infrastructure ahead of public transit (Paulhiac and Kaufmann, 2006; Van Neste and Bherer, 2013).

ACCESSIBILITY PROFILE: VANCOUVER, BC

Vancouver is the heart of an urban agglomeration of 2.31 million nestled between mountains and coastlines in Canada's south-western corner. Despite being a relative newcomer (around 130 years of settlement), Vancouver is considerably denser than many New World and some northern European cities. This is associated with both natural constrains of topography and regulatory constraints on the use of land. For the past four decades, Canada's third largest metropolitan area has been known as a regional and global model city of effective urban planning with strong sustainability overtones (Schiller et al, 2010). Successful metropolitan growth management includes urban intensification, the integration of expanding public transit infrastructure with the urban fabric, people-friendly and environmentally adapted urban design outcomes, and a participatory and inclusive culture of decision making.

A rapid transit system was reintroduced in stages since 1986 in the form of an automated, mostly elevated light metro network (SkyTrain). From the outset this was conceptualised to rely on feeder bus services and land use intensification in station areas in order to build ridership rather than on patronage drawn from park-and-ride access, the solution of many other New World cities. The metro system is fully integrated with buses and trolleybuses which form a grid-shaped network across the core city of Vancouver and to some extent beyond (Punter, 2003; Schiller et al, 2010).

The regional agency (Metro Vancouver) has responsibility for LUTI. Public transit planning and operation, as well as planning for other transport modes, lies with a public body called TransLink. TransLink has a three-zone integrated ticketing system offering single, daily and periodical fares. An electronic ticketing option (Compass card) is being introduced.

As Vancouver's tapestry of public transit network development and urban intensification has consolidated in recent years, accompanied by an annual population growth rate of almost 2 per cent (40,000 residents) in the Vancouver region during the 2000s (Statistics Canada, 2013), public transit has become a more prominent element of the modal mix with 356 million passenger journeys in 2011, a rate of 154 per capita (SCBCTA, 2013), the highest of the sampled New World cities.

Service Intensity

Vancouver's SkyTrain network is based on driverless technology, facilitating high service frequencies throughout the day, generally every 3 to 7 minutes. The core city's trolleybus system, which replaced streetcars in the 1950s, while leaving the interplay of transit infrastructure and activity corridors largely

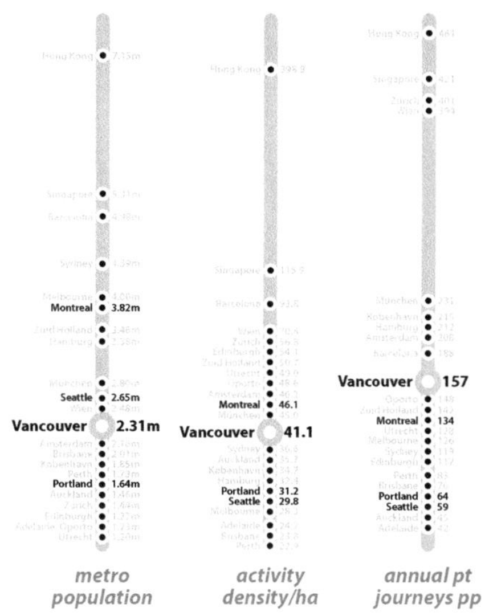

Vancouver 19.3
Montreal 10.4
Portland Seattle 10.2

service intensity/ 100,000 inh

Portland 4.1
Vancouver 2.0
Montreal 1.8
Seattle 0.5

heavy rail stations/ 100,000 inh

intact, also has better service frequencies than many comparison cities. The busiest corridor (Broadway) has 2 to 3 minutes daytime bus frequencies and most suburban routes are serviced every 7.5 to 15 minutes. The traditionally CBD-centred configuration of trolleybus infrastructure has also led to the retention of a significant level of service in the central city as the SkyTrain network expanded, unlike in Montreal which all but eliminated full-service bus routes in the CBD area. Hence, Vancouver has the highest service intensity among the New World sample.

Despite the SkyTrain, Vancouver has a low number of rail stations relative to population compared to most cities outside North America. A commuter service is offered along a mainline railway (West Coast Express); however it only operates during weekday peak hours in the peak direction and thus does not meet the SNAMUTS standard for a full service.

Closeness Centrality

Vancouver records the second best average performance for ease of movement in the worldwide sample after Vienna. This measure is influenced by the spacing of the activity centre network – a proxy for urban compactness – as well as average speeds and service frequencies of the public transit routes that link these centres. Vancouver's exceptional performance is attributed to the operational concept of the SkyTrain system as the network's backbone: its high commercial speeds (due to full grade separation) and high frequencies (facilitated in part by driverless operation, which reduces the marginal cost of additional services) minimise travel impediment along its routes, as the map clearly testifies.

Another contributing factor for Vancouver's relative ease of movement on public transit is the city's grid-shaped surface network, made up of buses and trolleybuses and responsible for the relatively smooth decay of closeness values across most of the core city where the density of the surface network is greatest. Vancouver's constrained geography largely appears to assist rather than obstruct ease of movement by effectively containing a significant part of the urbanised area within the relatively narrow Burrard Peninsula. Only the neighbourhoods of North and West Vancouver, whose share of the metropolitan area is relatively minor, are characterised by closeness results that show the segregation effect of the water.

Degree Centrality

Vancouver's reliance on transfers is lower than in Montreal, but higher than in the other New World cities. There is a hierarchical network design where the limited SkyTrain system takes the role of backbone corridors and the

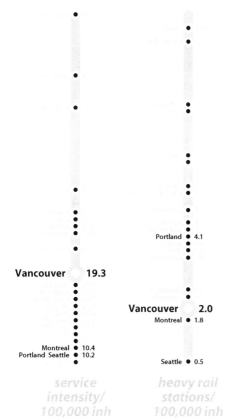

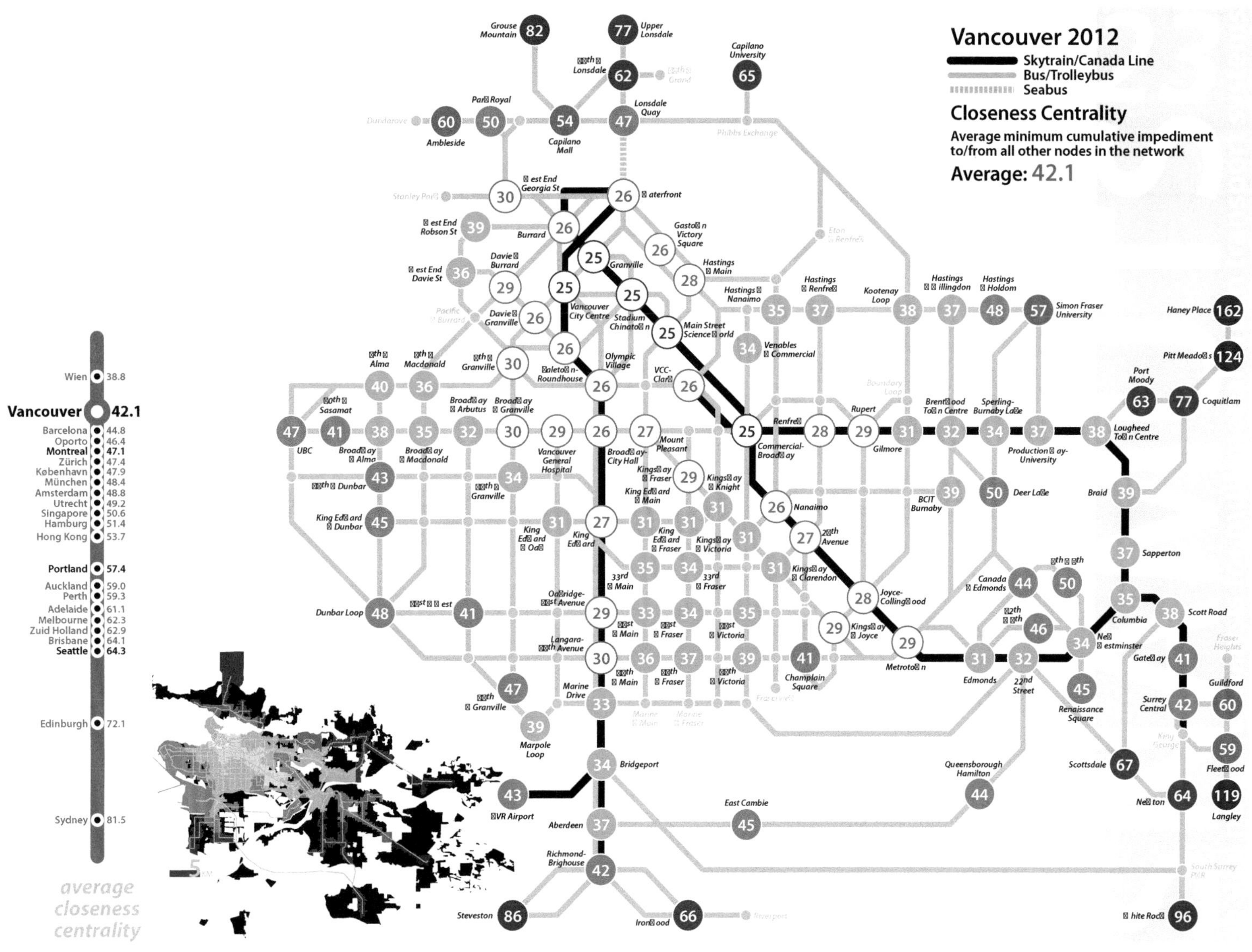

more widespread, grid-shaped network of bus routes that of feeders and distributors. In this task-sharing exercise Vancouver retains a greater role for surface modes in the city centre and thus provides for a greater number of transfer-free connections between CBD and suburban nodes than Montreal. The most transfer-dependent nodes in the Vancouver region are found away from the core city in the adjacent municipalities, where most bus routes act as classic local feeders to rail than as connectors along corridors that extend across several urban sub-regions.

Network Coverage

Vancouver's high network coverage, the best result among the New World sample, is associated with the core city's dense surface network that enables most of its territory to be serviced at the minimum standard within walking distance. In suburban areas, public transit coverage is more corridor-based, though these corridors stretch over the majority of significant centres in the outer metropolitan area. Like all cities in the New World sample, Greater Vancouver has a significant share of low-density, dispersed suburban development that is traditionally difficult to service with high-quality, walking-access public transit. It is notable, however, that the physical constraints of waterfronts and mountain ranges as well as the presence

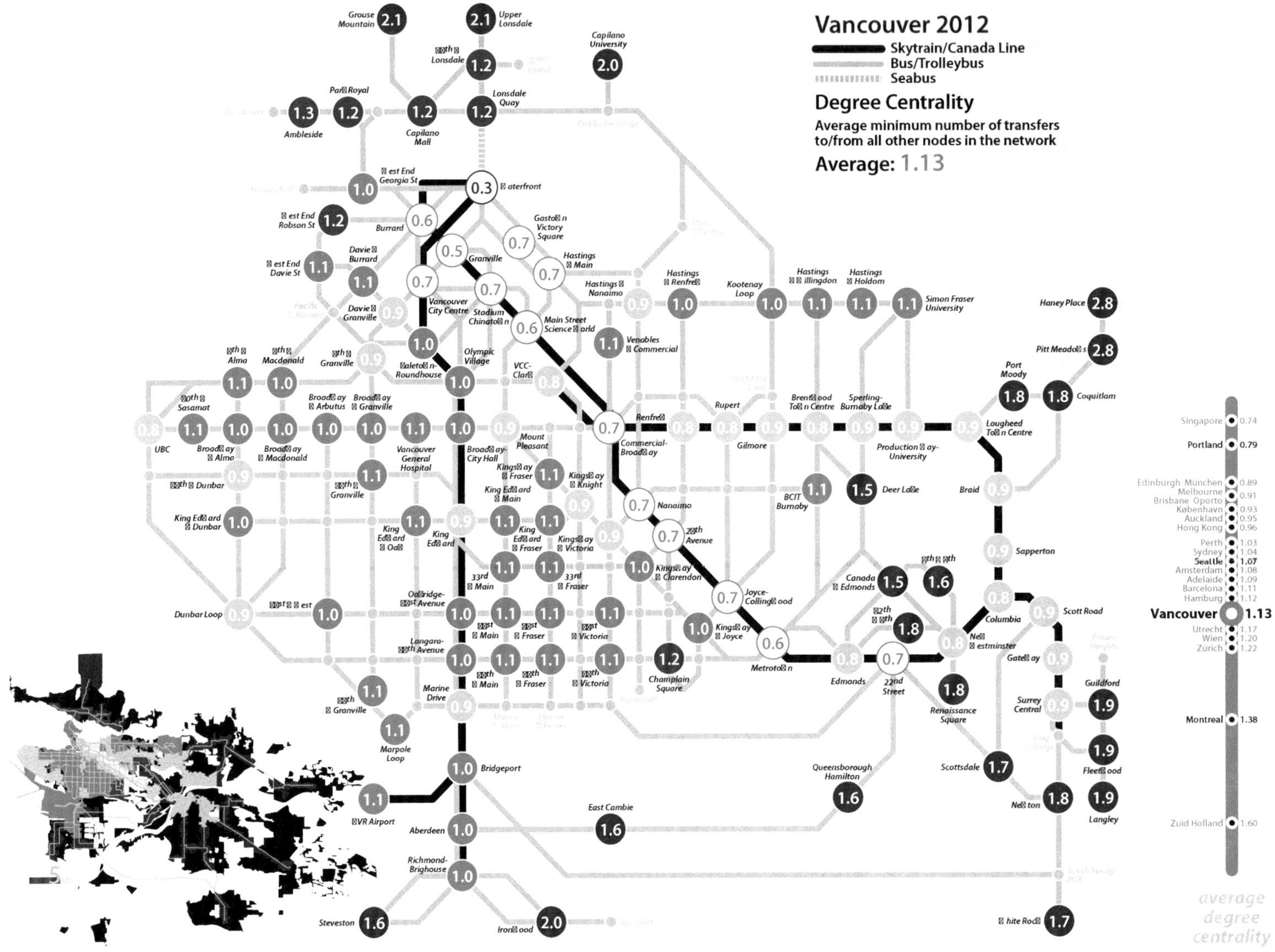

of the Canadian–US border and a significant swathe of protected farmland effectively limit this development pattern to the foothills in North and West Vancouver, and to the eastern fringe of the metropolitan area.

Thirty-Minute Contour Catchments

Vancouver leads the cohort of New World cities and outperforms the majority of European cities on this index, a result associated with several factors that work in favour of LUTI. The speed and frequency of the rail system in conjunction with the relatively dense, grid-shaped expansion of the bus and trolleybus system exerts influence here, expanding the geographical

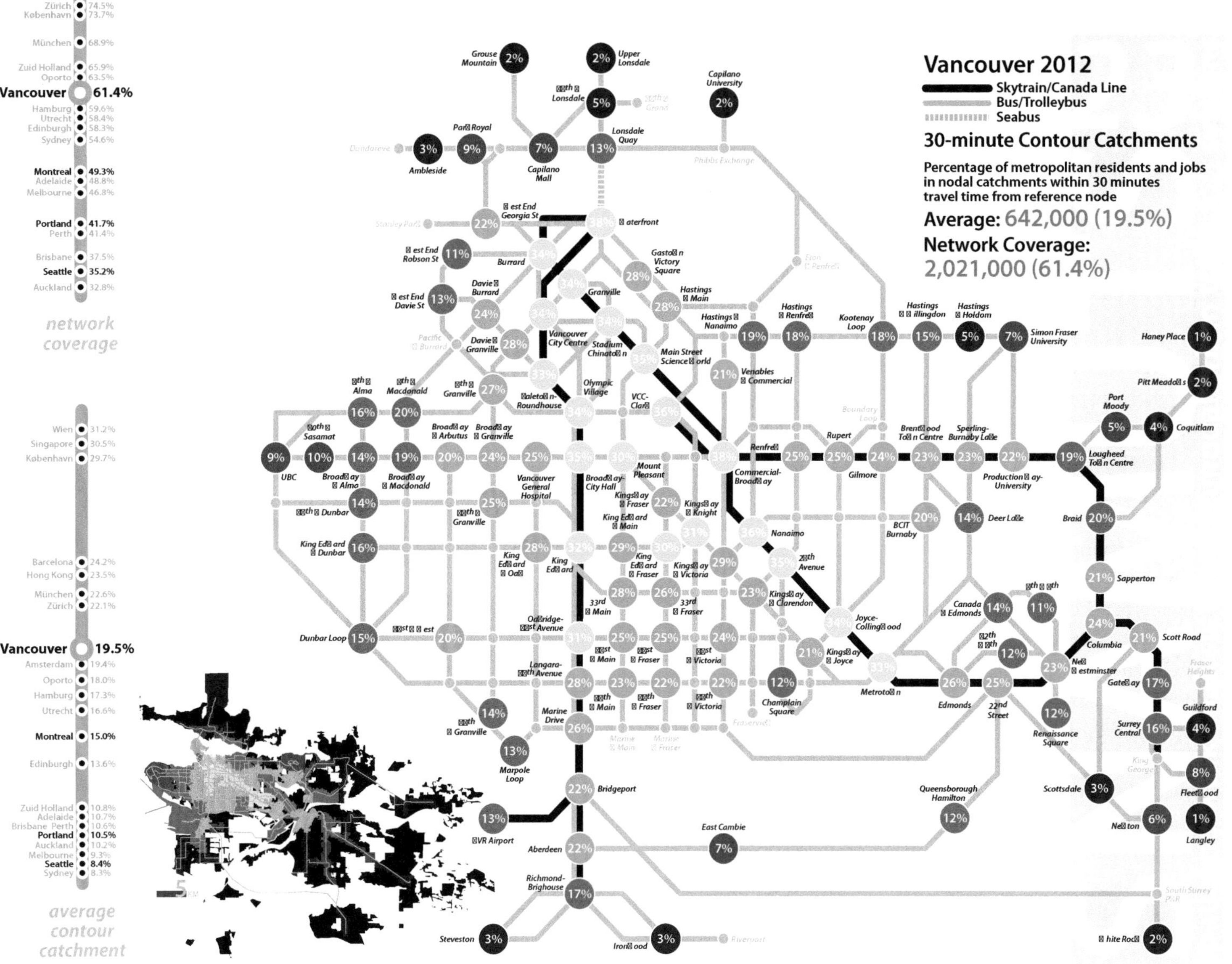

size of contour lines. Additionally, Vancouver's long-standing and effective TOD policy succeeds in agglomerating urban growth around the movement lines of public transit, thus increasing the density of origins and destinations contained within the contour line. Vancouver surpasses Montreal on this measure, which benefits from a larger heritage of older and traditionally denser urban fabric, but arguably has a weaker policy to facilitate further urban intensification around transit (Filion and Kramer, 2012).

Betweenness Centrality

On the global betweenness measure, Vancouver records by far the highest score relative to population and employment among the New World cities studied, a product of urban compactness, good network coverage, high service levels and the resulting richness in travel opportunities. However, Vancouver's high figures also suggest potential problems, manifest in the average nodal betweenness result which is significantly higher than the relatively even field of the Australasian, US and many European cities. The key reason for this can be found in the large performance gap between the two dominant modes operating in Vancouver – SkyTrain and buses. SkyTrain's high service frequencies and fast speed have the effect of minimising travel impediment along its routes – from a user perspective this allows passengers to arrive and go with minimal waiting times and to reach their destinations with minimal delay. On bus routes service frequencies are typically lower, as are travel speeds since buses mostly share the road with general traffic and are subject to congestion and more frequent stops. In combination with the easier legibility of the rail system, these characteristics have the effect of attracting passengers to rail even where more geographically direct connections may be available on the bus network. Such circuitously routed travel opportunities are then counted at every rail station along their path and together drive up average nodal betweenness results. They have a further impact on the average catchment of typical path length measure, which responds to common geographical detours making average journeys longer – and traversing a greater number of intermediate centres – than necessary. While none of these effects may be of concern to the user per se, the concentration of passengers onto a limited number of high-performance routes away from their desire lines may obviously contribute to congestion along such corridors. Despite this 'sponge effect' of high-performance rail lines on the distribution of travel opportunities over the network, Vancouver's overall rail share on this measure remains slightly below that of other New World cities where large investments in rail systems were made during recent decades (Montreal, Portland and Perth), though extensions currently under way or planned (the Evergreen Line to Port Moody and Coquitlam, the proposed Broadway corridor along the 'spine' of the Burrard Peninsula) should narrow this gap.

Vancouver has an unexpectedly low concentration of travel opportunities in the CBD area. This may be attributed to the peripheral location of Vancouver's CBD away from the geographical heart of the regional settlement area, and to a network configuration that succeeds in deflecting travel opportunities away from the city centre via strong orbital

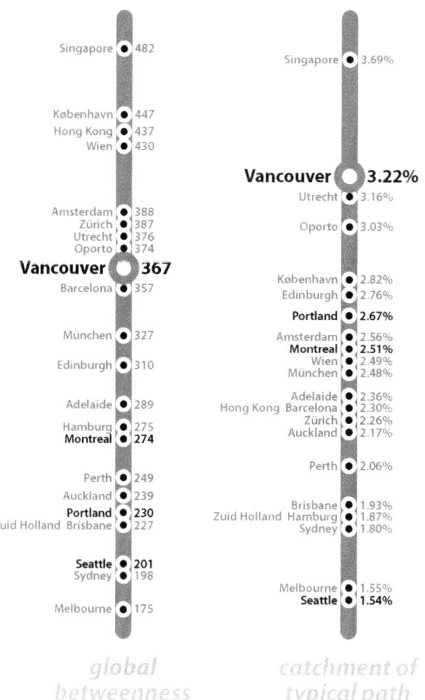

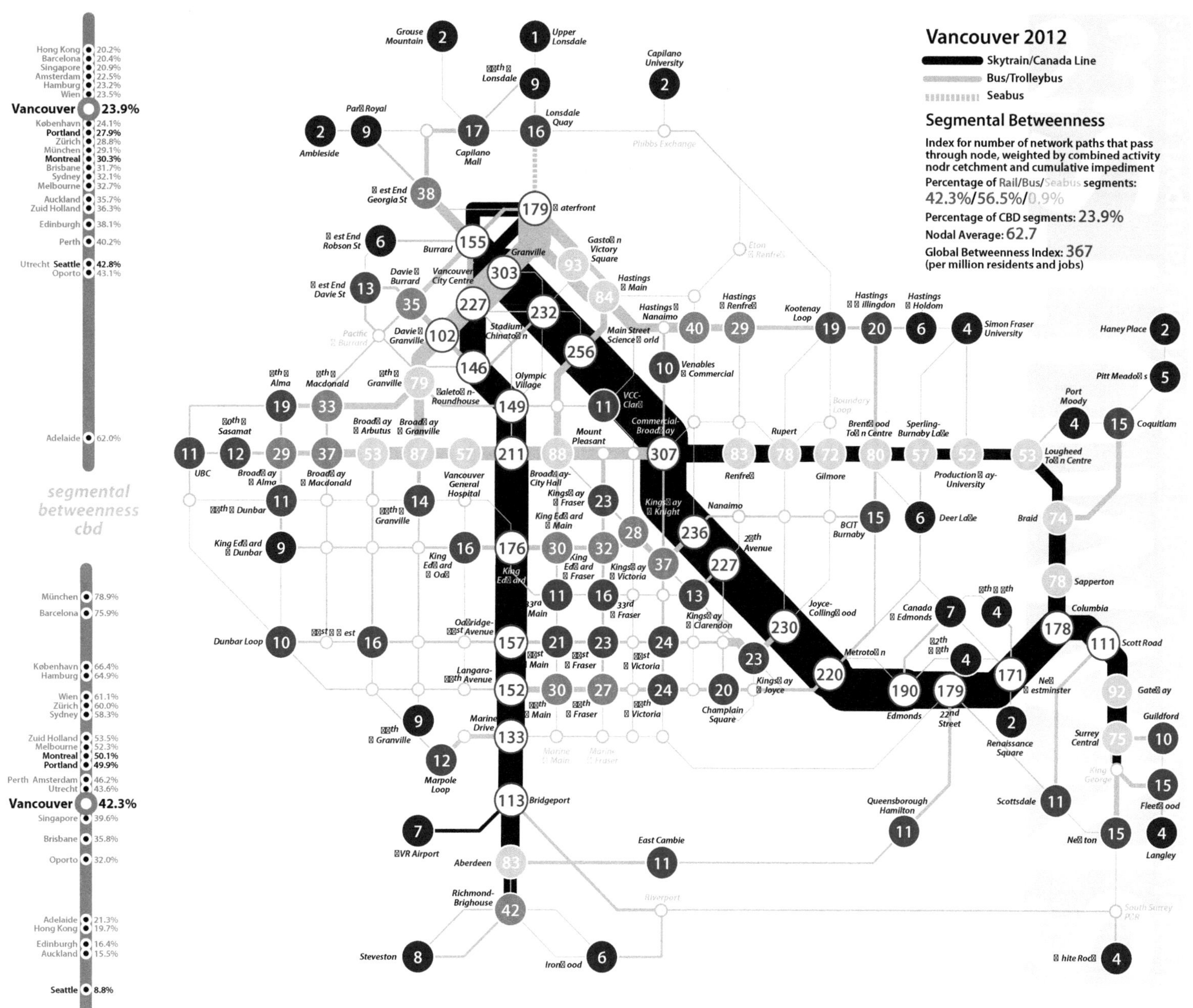

connections. This is more developed in Vancouver than in other sampled New World cities.

Network Resilience

Vancouver's network has a lower average level of resilience than most of the comparison cities; only Sydney, Seattle and Montreal perform worse. In the latter two this can be traced to the

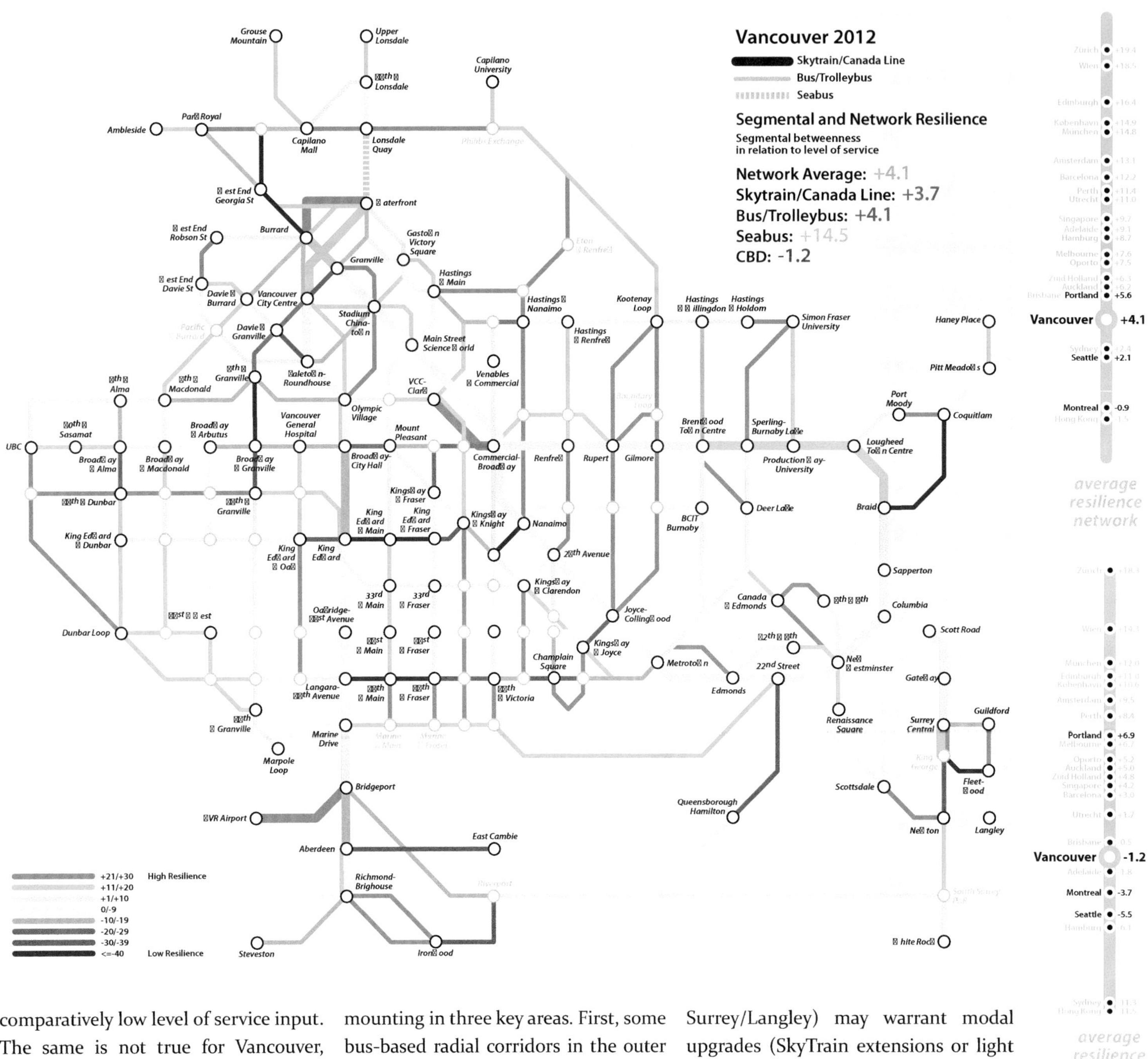

comparatively low level of service input. The same is not true for Vancouver, where potential stress appears to be mounting in three key areas. First, some bus-based radial corridors in the outer suburbs (Port Moody/Coquitlam and Surrey/Langley) may warrant modal upgrades (SkyTrain extensions or light rail) and these are under way or planned.

Second, existing SkyTrain trunk lines experience pressures from the aforementioned 'sponge effect' of travel opportunities and their design for relatively short train and platform lengths, a constraint that affects the recently opened Canada Line along the Cambie corridor. Third, several orbital bus corridors in the core city may not meet the potential for attracting and providing movement opportunities that their position in the land use–transport system would suggest (for example Broadway, King Edward Avenue and 49th Avenue).

Nodal Connectivity

All but two nodes whose count on this index is higher than the metropolitan average are located along the SkyTrain network, highlighting the importance of the Skytrain to facilitate LUTI in

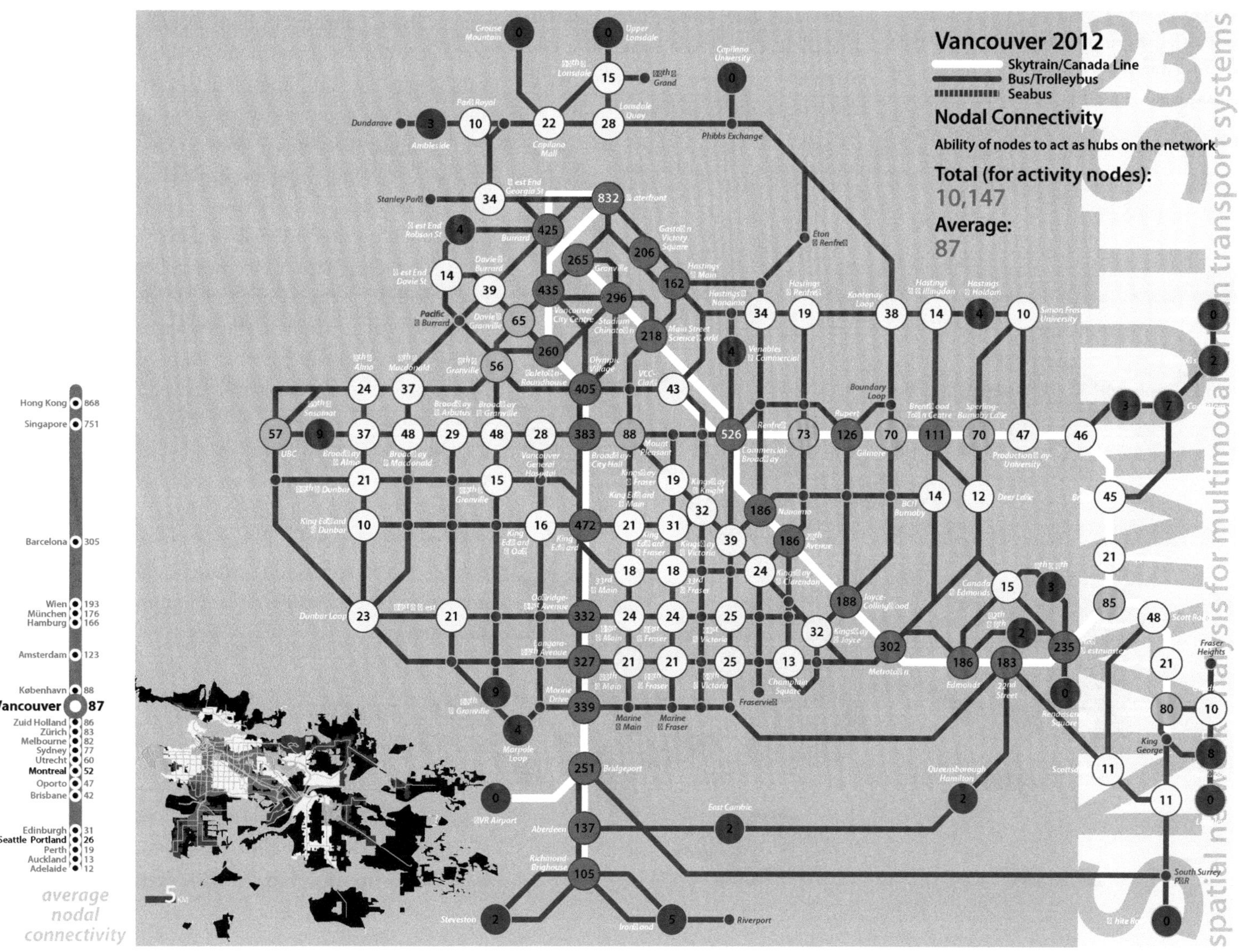

Vancouver. The city leads the New World sample on the average result for this index, underscoring the relative success of TOD strategies in providing users with flexibility of movement between a multitude of centres along key urban corridors. In most other New World cities of Vancouver's population size or smaller, 'red' nodal connectivity scores (100 or above) are confined to the CBD areas.

SNAMUTS Composite Accessibility Index and Reflections

On the average result for this index, Vancouver leads the New World comparison cities by a considerable margin and is more akin to average European performers like Amsterdam, Hamburg or Zurich. This is the result of a comparatively widespread public transit network facilitating relatively fast and frequent movement over a compact urbanised area (achieved by both topographical factors and a long-standing TOD strategy).

These successes are most visible along the SkyTrain corridors where almost all activity centres return composite results above Vancouver's high average. Some core city neighbourhoods located away from the rail lines still return above-average accessibility results due to the multi-directional grid formed by high-frequency bus and trolleybus lines. In contrast, composite accessibility declines towards the edges of the core city. North and West Vancouver suffer in accessibility terms from their separation by water. The outlying suburbs in the south and east are characterised by a public transit accessibility pattern more familiar in other New World cities where corridors with reasonable bus service (but relatively poor accessibility in city-wide terms) alternate with sizeable areas of dispersed suburbia where public transit services, if existent, do not meet the SNAMUTS minimum standard.

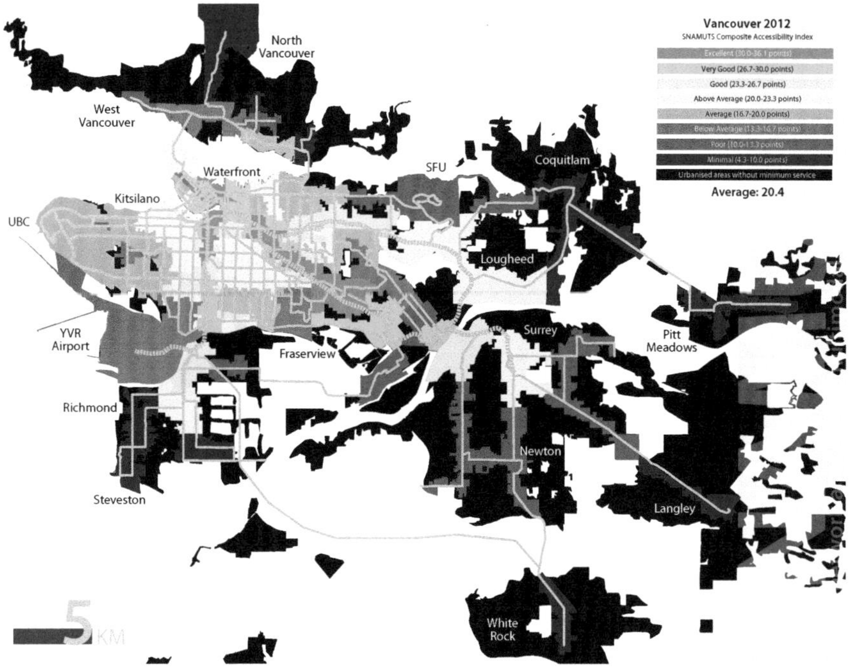

ACCESSIBILITY PROFILE: SEATTLE, WA

Seattle is located at the heart of the Puget Sound Region in the US state of Washington. There are some 3.6 million inhabitants in this region. However,

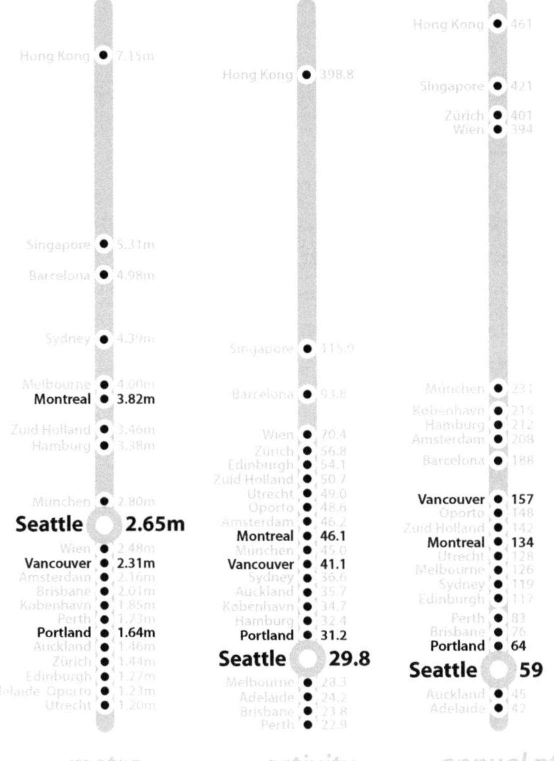

in our analysis the metropolitan area definition includes only two of the four counties that make up the agglomeration (King and Snohomish), as only these two are linked by a coherent public transit network at the minimum standard. Between them, both counties had 2.64 million residents in 2010.

The settlement areas of the Puget Sound Region are built on a topography of peninsulas and isthmuses separated by sizeable water bodies. This channels urban and regional movement along sometimes narrow strips of land and across a limited number of crossing points. The Puget Sound in the west and the foothills of the Cascade Range in the east provide formidable natural growth boundaries, directing urban expansion primarily in a north–south direction. From Everett-Maryville in the north to the King-Pierce county border in the south, the settlement area stretches almost 100 km and varies in width between 15 and 35 km. Average urbanised density is at the lower end of the SNAMUTS sample, comparable to Melbourne but higher than the smaller Australian cities. The region has significant clusters of IT and aviation industries and grew by an average of 30,000 inhabitants per annum between 2000 and 2010.

Seattle abandoned all rail-based urban transit during the early post-war years. With the exception of a short monorail link built for the 1962 World Expo, the region relied on a road-based system until 2009 when a light rail line was opened between central Seattle and SeaTac International Airport. Public transit is managed and operated by county-based public agencies and a regional body (Sound Transit) which operates light rail, regional express buses and a commuter rail line using mainline tracks ('Sounder'). The Sounder, however, only operates during weekday peak hours and therefore does not meet the minimum service standard for the SNAMUTS analysis.

City buses, including some electric trolleybuses, are the responsibility of King County Metro, which also operates a recently built, short streetcar line in a CBD fringe regeneration area (South Lake Union). The City of Seattle has projects under way to expand the streetcar system to further inner city neighbourhoods and to link it with light rail extensions. In the CBD, a five-station transit tunnel was opened in 1990, initially used exclusively by buses but now shared by light rail.

The transit agencies each have their own, relatively simple fare system though they generally accept transfer tickets from other agencies. There is also an electronic ticket (ORCA) that can be used freely across all operators.

Annual transit patronage per capita is modest at only about half the level

Vancouver 19.3
Montreal 10.4
Seattle 10.2
service intensity/ 100,000 inh

Portland 4.1
Vancouver 2.0
Montreal 1.8
Seattle 0.5
heavy rail stations/ 100,000 inh

found in Melbourne, Sydney and the Canadian cities, but higher than the poorest performers in the sample (Adelaide and Auckland).

Service Intensity

Service frequencies on most of Seattle's transit routes are at the lower end of the SNAMUTS minimum standard. During the weekday inter-peak period, 15-minute intervals are most common for individual bus routes, including a set of four specially branded 'Rapid Ride' lines with real-time travel information and some priority measures as well as the streetcar line. The light rail line is operated every 10 minutes.

In Snohomish County, a bus route along the main settlement spine between the Seattle city limit and Everett (Pacific Highway) is branded as Bus Rapid Transit (Swift) and operated every 12 minutes on weekdays. However, this line, like most of the remainder of the bus network in the county, has no Sunday service at all and hence does not meet the SNAMUTS minimum standard.

Many transit agencies in the region depend on sales tax revenue to fund some of their operational costs. During the recession, following the 2008 Global Financial Crisis, drops in sales tax revenue subsequently led to service cuts (lower frequencies and/or more limited service hours). As a consequence, Seattle's service intensity is among the lowest in the sample, despite the network being more reliant on buses than any other and having the lowest number of rail stations relative to population.

Closeness Centrality

With the exception of Edinburgh and Sydney, where a lack of fare integration impedes passengers' ease of movement without financial penalties, Seattle has the poorest average closeness result of all case study cities. This is a function of low average service frequencies and the high degree of spatial separation between activity nodes in the metropolitan region. While there are numerous high-speed express bus services using the motorway network, the long north–south expansion of the settlement area and the barrier effect of Lake Washington have an effect. More than any other city in the sample, Seattle is characterised by a strong 'edge city'-style urbanisation pattern where significant clusters of tertiary employment can be found in suburban locations away from traditional settlement cores. Such clusters are particularly prevalent in the east (Bellevue, Overlake) and the south of the metropolitan area (Tukwila, SeaTac, Renton and Kent). There are currently no full-time, high-frequency direct public transit links between these two sub-regions, other than via a transfer journey through central Seattle.

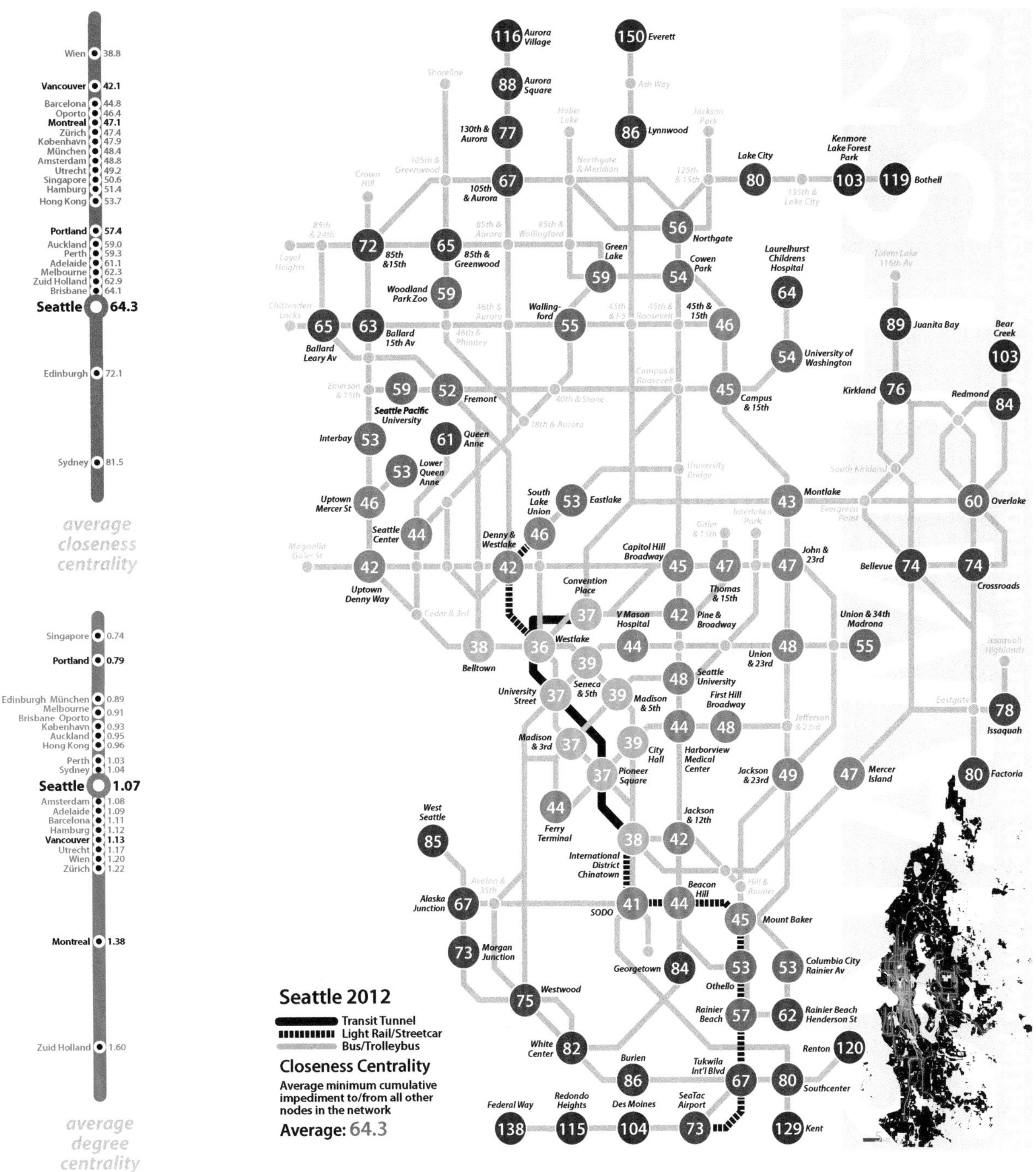

Wien 38.8
Vancouver 42.1
Barcelona 44.8
Oporto 46.4
Montreal 47.1
Zürich 47.4
København 47.9
München 48.4
Amsterdam 48.8
Utrecht 49.2
Singapore 50.6
Hamburg 51.4
Hong Kong 53.7
Portland 57.4
Auckland 59.0
Perth 59.3
Adelaide 61.1
Melbourne 62.3
Zuid Holland 62.9
Brisbane 64.1
Seattle 64.3
Edinburgh 72.1
Sydney 81.5
average closeness centrality
Singapore 0.74
Portland 0.79
Edinburgh München 0.89
Melbourne 0.91
Brisbane Oporto
København 0.93
Auckland 0.95
Hong Kong 0.96
Perth 1.03
Sydney 1.04
Seattle 1.07
Amsterdam 1.08
Adelaide 1.09
Barcelona 1.11
Hamburg 1.12
Vancouver 1.13
Utrecht 1.17
Wien 1.20
Zürich 1.22
Montreal 1.38
Zuid Holland 1.60
average degree centrality
116 Aurora Village
150 Everett
88 Aurora Square
77 130th & Aurora
86 Lynnwood
67 105th & Aurora
80 Lake City
103 Kenmore Lake Forest Park
119 Bothell
56 Northgate
72 85th &15th
65 85th & Greenwood
59 Green Lake
54 Cowen Park
64 Laurelhurst Childrens Hospital
59 Woodland Park Zoo
55 Walling-ford
46 45th & 15th
89 Juanita Bay
103 Bear Creek
65 Ballard Leary Av
63 Ballard 15th Av
54 University of Washington
76 Kirkland
84 Redmond
59 Seattle Pacific University
52 Fremont
45 Campus & 15th
53 Interbay
61 Queen Anne
53 Lower Queen Anne
53 Eastlake
43 Montlake
60 Overlake
46 Uptown Mercer St
44 Seattle Center
46 South Lake Union
42 Denny & Westlake
45 Capitol Hill Broadway
47
47 John & 23rd
74 Bellevue
74 Crossroads
42 Uptown Denny Way
37 Convention Place
42 Thomas & 15th
42 Pine & Broadway
55 Union & 34th Madrona
38 Belltown
36 Westlake
44 V Mason Hospital
48 Union & 23rd
39
37 University Street
39 Seneca & 5th
39 Madison & 5th
48 Seattle University
44
48 First Hill Broadway
78 Issaquah
37 Madison & 3rd
39 City Hall
37 Pioneer Square
49 Jackson & 23rd
47 Mercer Island
80 Factoria
44 Ferry Terminal
38 International District Chinatown
42 Jackson & 12th
85 West Seattle
67 Alaska Junction
41 SODO
44 Beacon Hill
45 Mount Baker
73 Morgan Junction
84 Georgetown
53 Othello
53 Columbia City Rainier Av
75 Westwood
57 Rainier Beach
62 Rainier Beach Henderson St
82 White Center
86 Burien
67 Tukwila Int'l Blvd
80 Southcenter
120 Renton
138 Federal Way
115 Redondo Heights
104 Des Moines
73 SeaTac Airport
129 Kent
Seattle 2012
Transit Tunnel
Light Rail/Streetcar
Bus/Trolleybus
Closeness Centrality
Average minimum cumulative impediment to/from all other nodes in the network
Average: 64.3

Degree Centrality

On this index, Seattle is positioned within a cohort with moderately transfer-dependent public transit networks (Perth, Sydney, Adelaide and Vancouver). Seattle's network consists of a dominant group of radial routes, most of which converge along a single spine (Third Ave) through the CBD (both in the transit tunnel and above ground at street level). There are also orbital routes in the north and east of the core city and in the Bellevue-Redmond area on the eastern side of Lake Washington. In the south, there are some classic feeder bus routes to light rail, linking in the multimodal interchange at Tukwila. Poorer than average degree centrality values are associated with these orbital and feeder routes, while the best performers on this index can be found along Third Avenue in the CBD and in Mount Baker in the inner south, where the light rail line intersects with several bus routes.

Network Coverage

Seattle's extent of public transit network coverage is the second lowest (before Auckland) in percentage terms of metropolitan residents and jobs within the global sample. With the exception of some peninsulas (West Seattle, Magnolia and View Ridge) the core city is reasonably well covered by walking access to public transit at the SNAMUTS standard. In suburban areas to the south and

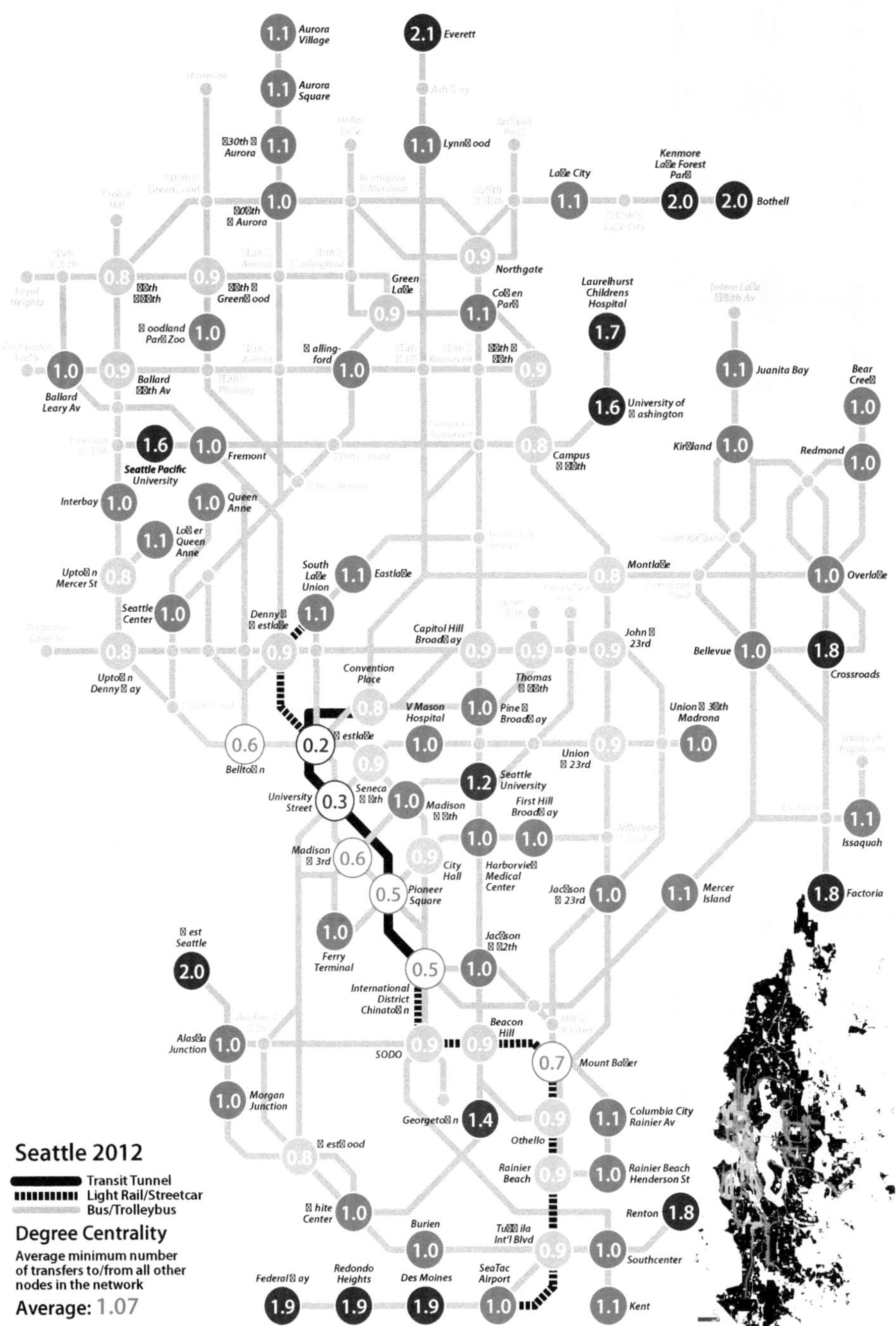

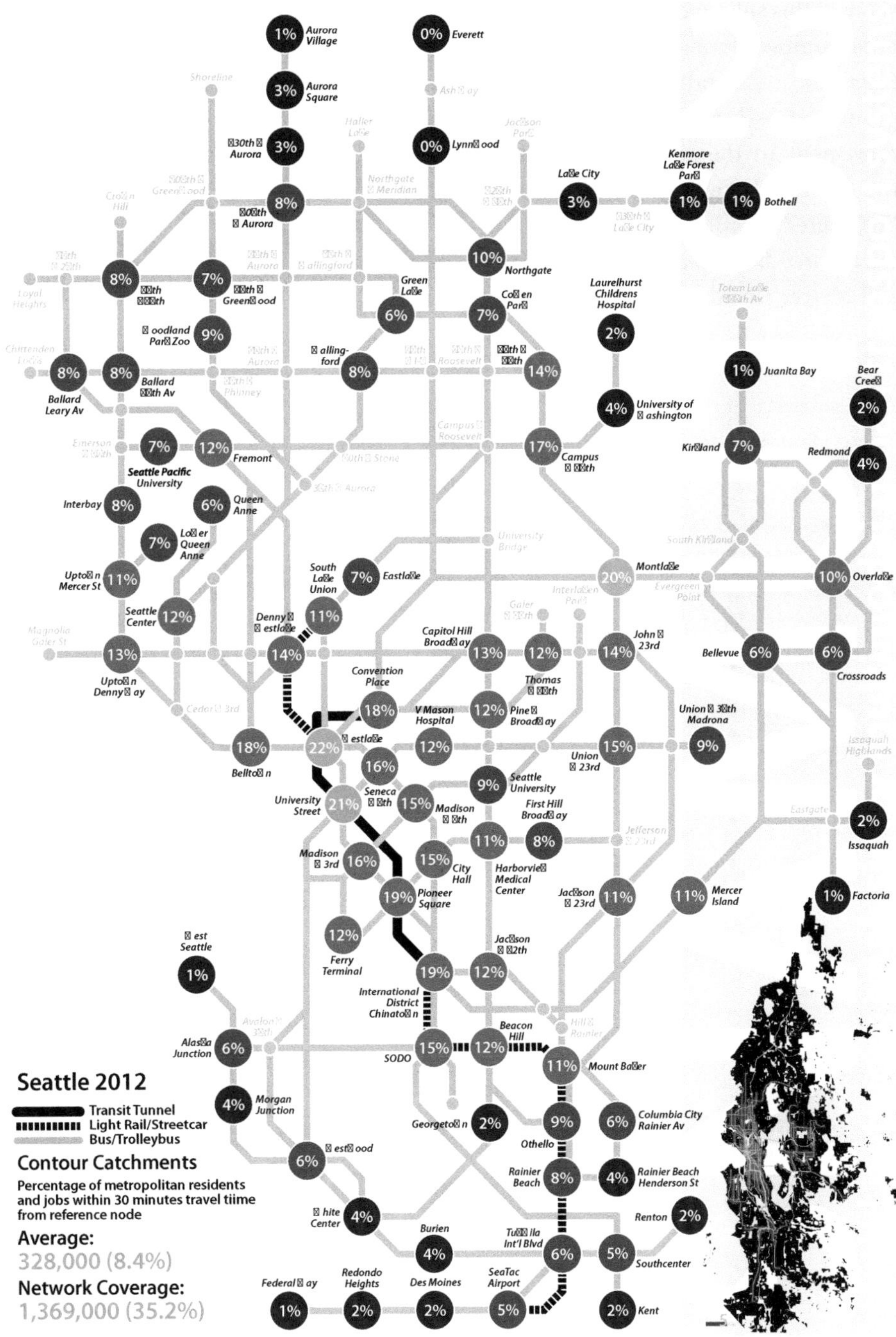

east, a patchwork dominates and settlement areas away from the main urban corridors are generally not serviced at this standard. In Snohomish County in the north, the almost complete absence of public transit service on Sundays eliminates most of the urbanised area from the network coverage count.

Thirty-Minute Contour Catchments

Seattle's average 30-minute travel time contour by public transit enables access to a smaller percentage of the metropolitan population and jobs than in any other case study city except (much larger) Sydney. The low network coverage figure influences this result since it acts as a cap for any nodal 30-minute contour catchment. There are further factors, including the relatively low speed of on-street bus routes and the limited number of stops made by express bus routes along motorways. Within the core city, bus routes form a partial grid and support each other's contour catchments through facilitating transfer journeys. Outside the core city, values on this index drop quite rapidly with the exception of Overlake (served by several express buses) and Tukwila-SeaTac Airport (serviced by light rail). The best-performing node outside the CBD area can be found at Montlake interchange along the I-520 motorway; but the concentration of land uses in this area is limited.

Betweenness Centrality

Seattle's global betweenness result is the lowest among the North American case study cities and internationally, marginally outperforms only Melbourne and Sydney. Geography and the primarily radial configuration of the network channel a relatively high share of this subdued presence of travel opportunities through the central city. Elsewhere, a handful of routes are prominent as key attractors of transit movement in the region, particularly the light rail route and the express bus routes crossing Lake Washington via the two bridges at Evergreen Point and Mercer Island. Strong north–south links in the northern section of the core city can be found along 15th Avenue, Aurora Avenue, the I-5 and around the University District, the terminus of a light rail extension currently under construction.

Owing to the limited extent of the current light rail network, Seattle's share of

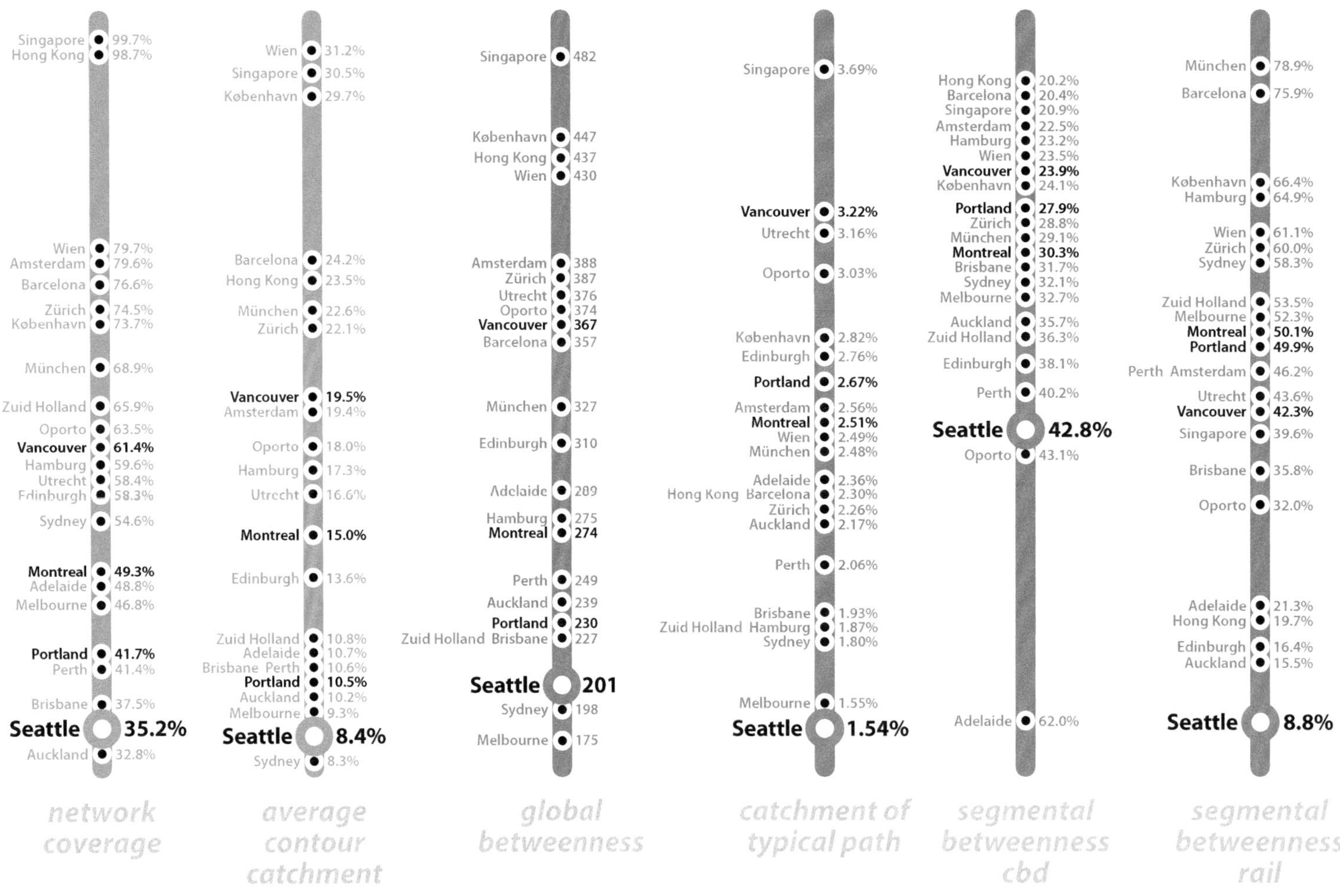

rail modes among travel opportunities is smaller than in any other case study city.

Network Resilience

Seattle is positioned near the bottom end of the ranking table on this index, comparable to Sydney but better than Montreal as a result of low service input and a prescriptive network structure. Remarkably, the high-frequency, two-level CBD spine along Third Avenue as the network's centrepiece records a relatively good resilience value, whereas the greatest weaknesses are apparent along the express bus routes linking the central city to Northgate, Bellevue-Overlake, Westwood and Southcenter. The neighbourhoods of Capitol Hill and First Hill, where the surface network is densest, appear to be the least affected by imbalances between transit supply and potential demand, despite their relatively central location. In practice, Seattle's poor network resilience may be compensated by a low rate of trip making and thus public transit mode share. The current network configuration and service levels may run into severe constraints should the region wish to shift more journeys from car to public transit. The modal upgrades through light rail and streetcar extensions currently under way should help address this problem.

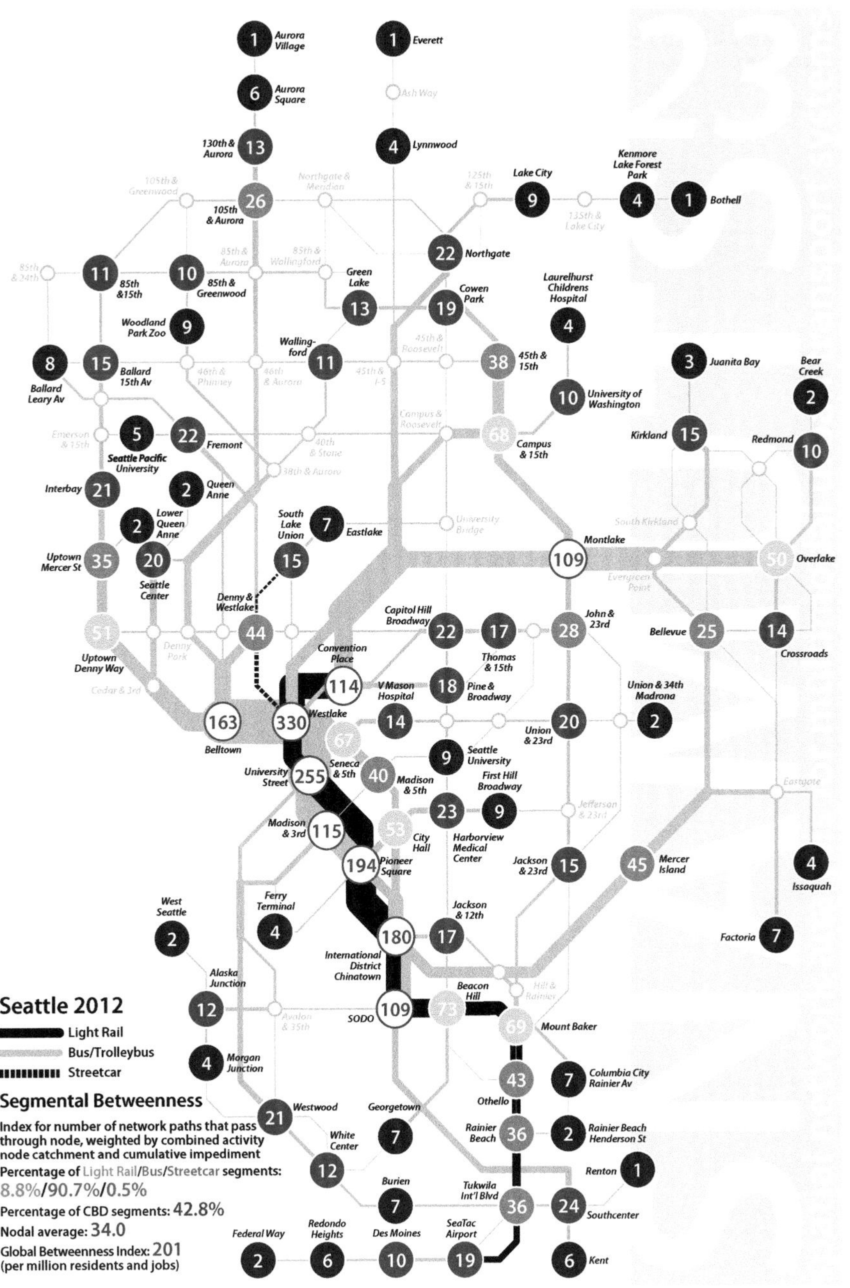

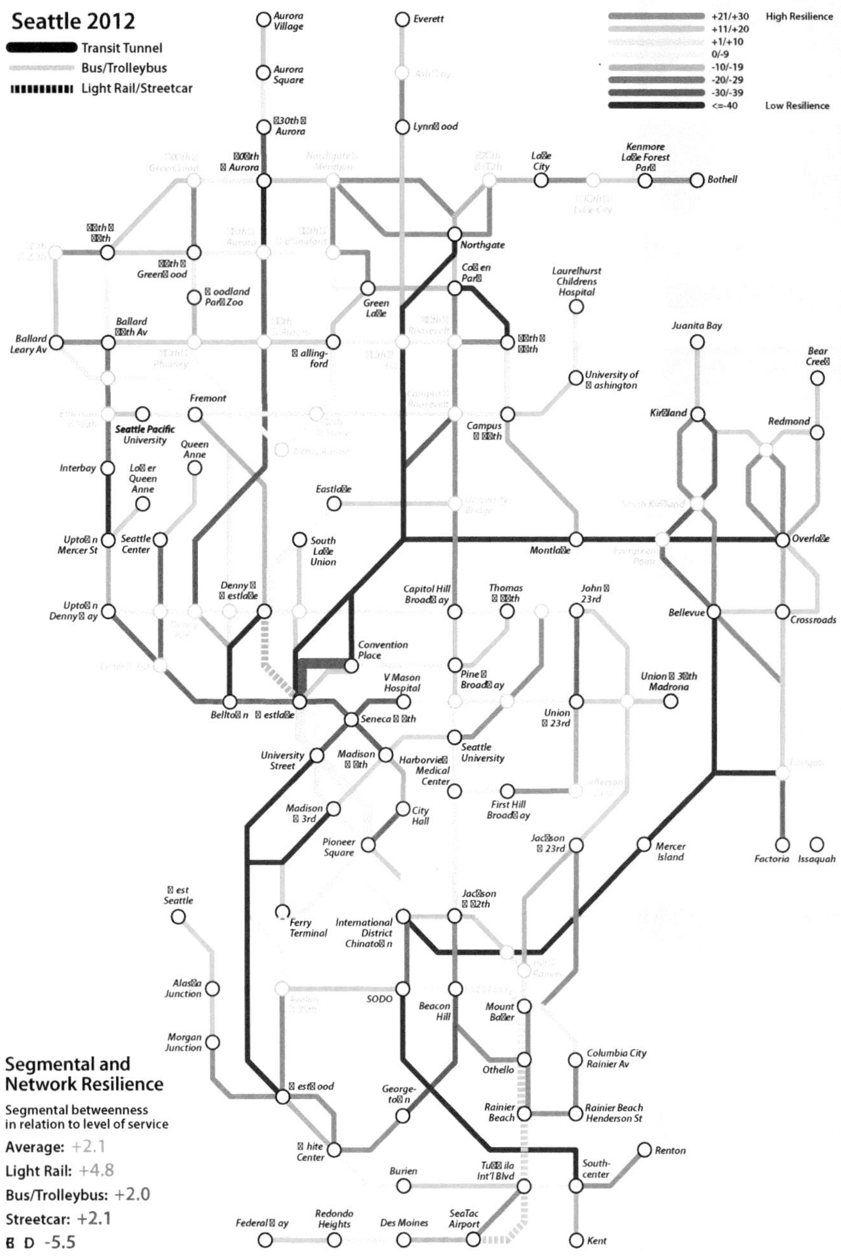

Seattle 2012

Transit Tunnel
Bus/Trolleybus
Light Rail/Streetcar

+21/+30 High Resilience
+11/+20
+1/+10
0/-9
-10/-19
-20/-29
-30/-39
<=-40 Low Resilience

Segmental and Network Resilience

Segmental betweenness in relation to level of service

Average: +2.1
Light Rail: +4.8
Bus/Trolleybus: +2.0
Streetcar: +2.1
CBD -5.5

Nodal Connectivity

The nodes that offer most flexibility for users to access in Seattle are all located along the central CBD spine inside the Transit Tunnel as well as above ground along Third Avenue. In suburban locations, only Mount Baker in the inner south and the University District in the north achieve respectable nodal connectivity results. From a passenger perspective this could be read as a perceived low

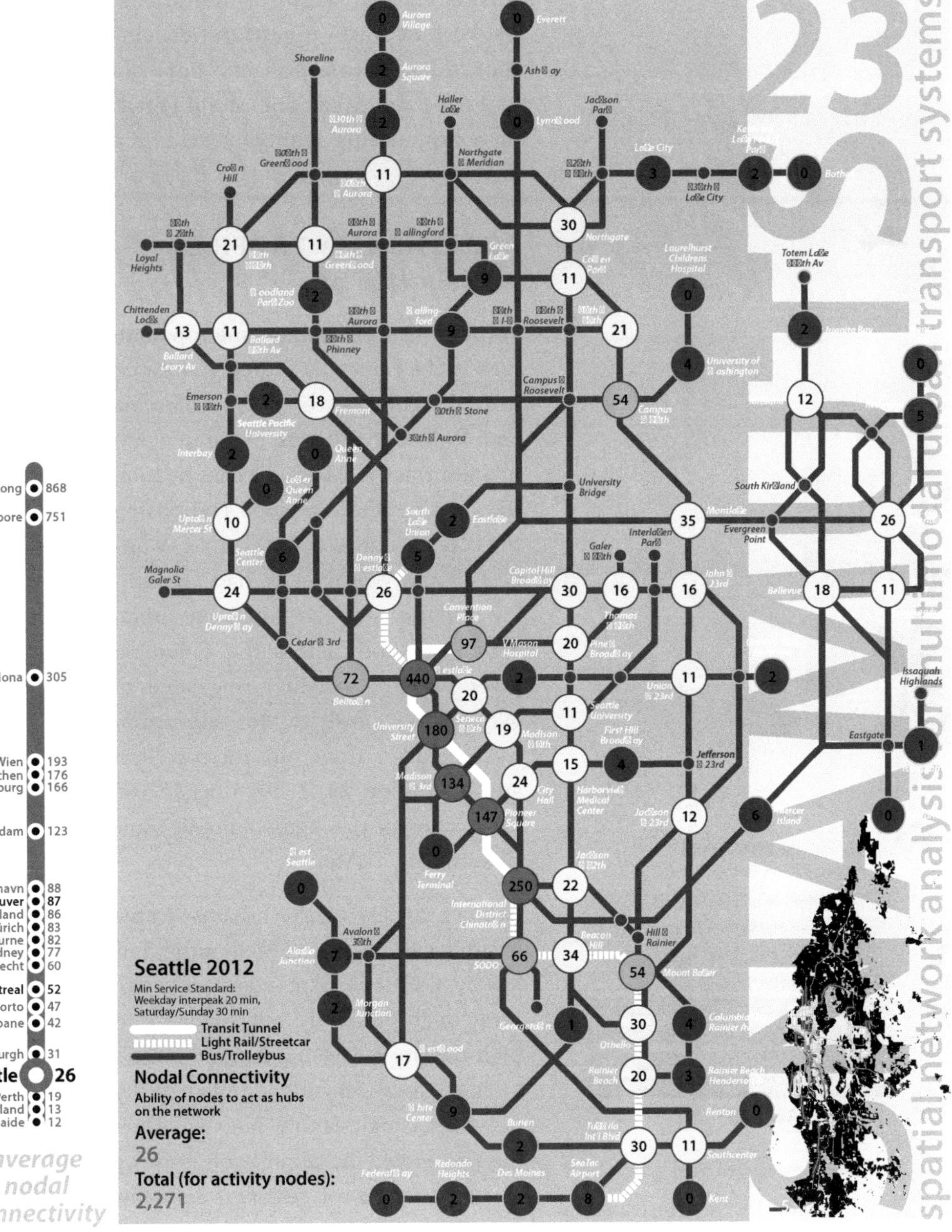

capacity of the network to provide confident, planned or spontaneous access to locations outside these areas, and may help explain why public transit trip making rates in Seattle remain below those of most sampled Canadian and Australian cities. On the other hand, rapid population growth in the metropolitan area has led to numerous urban intensification projects. Some of these are facilitated by recent and future light rail and streetcar routes as transformation agents, while others occur along bus-based corridors and centres.

SNAMUTS Composite Accessibility Index and Reflections

Seattle's average composite accessibility score trails the global sample, a result primarily attributed to the region's low network coverage and density, low typical service frequencies, limited capacity for further increases in patronage in the absence of substantial service and infrastructure upgrades, and an urban geography that imposes barriers to multi-directional movement. Seattle's recent efforts to introduce more light rail, streetcar and high-quality bus lines, as well as foster urban intensification in transit-accessible areas are encouraging trends. However, the region continues to grapple with a legacy of urban growth and infrastructure development designed for car movement.

Seattle's CBD, which accounts for a proportion of metropolitan employment comparable to the CBDs of Vancouver or of Australasian cities, is the only location in the metropolitan region where public transit accessibility could support transit-oriented lifestyles and business operations. If integrated well within a multimodal network of travel opportunities, current infrastructure projects (light rail and streetcar extensions) should gradually expand this quality over the core city.

ACCESSIBILITY PROFILE: PORTLAND, OR

Portland is the largest metropolitan area in the US state of Oregon, located near the confluence of the Columbia and Willamette Rivers about 100 km inland from the Pacific Ocean. In 2010, the metropolitan region, comprising the three counties of Clackamas, Multnomah and Washington, had 1.64 million inhabitants. The functional urban region stretches across the Columbia River into the neighbouring state of Washington; however, this sub-region was excluded from our metropolitan area definition as it lies outside the jurisdiction of the regional public transit authority, TriMet.

Activity density of the urbanised area is similar to Seattle or Melbourne, but low by international standards. Despite some high-profile recent medium to high-density redevelopment, Portland's built-up area remains dominated by detached, single-family housing. During the 2000s, the population grew by an average of 20,000 residents annually, a similar rate to Seattle.

Portland is known for a history of community resistance to road building in

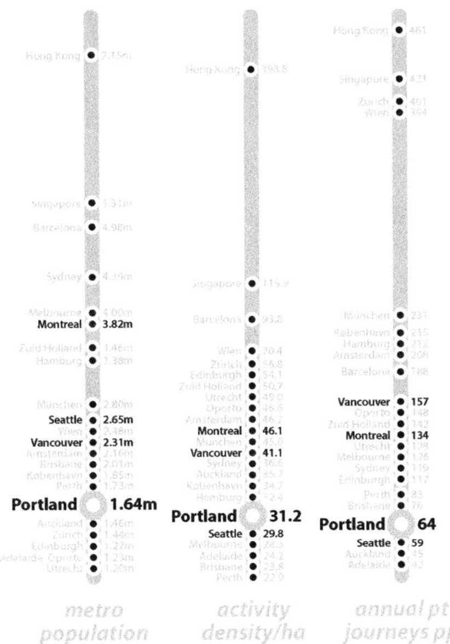

urban areas, though its impact was only felt after a sizeable network of inner-city motorways had been completed in the 1950s and 1960s. A policy turnaround in the 1970s focussed on the revitalisation of the downtown area and emphasised the role of public transit access to it. Since the 1980s, this new set of priorities has led to the gradual implementation of a four-line light rail system servicing the city's main radial corridors. Governance changes have also supported LUTI with the establishment of a metropolitan planning authority seeking to control urban growth at the fringe. A range of locally adapted tools were developed to facilitate TOD. A streetcar network was introduced in the inner city in the 2000s to unlock redevelopment potential and mobilise private investment in brownfield areas, most famously the Pearl District at the northern CBD fringe (Arrington, 2009; Schiller et al, 2010). In absolute figures, public transit use in Portland grew by about a third since the turn of the century and in 2011 was at 101 million passenger boardings (TriMet, 2011). While the rate of growth is encouraging, the relative level of ridership remains similar to that of Seattle and below that of all other case study cities with the exception of Adelaide and Auckland.

Service Intensity

Portland's service intensity figure is at a similar level as that of neighbouring Seattle, translating into typical 15 or 20 minute frequencies on both rail and bus routes. Like Seattle, some frequencies were reduced during the late 2000s recession when public transit funding sources contracted. However, the light rail trunk line between Beaverton and Gateway through downtown Portland, where two or more lines overlap, has a minimum service frequency of eight trains per hour per direction and thus comes closer to the standard in Canadian or European cities.

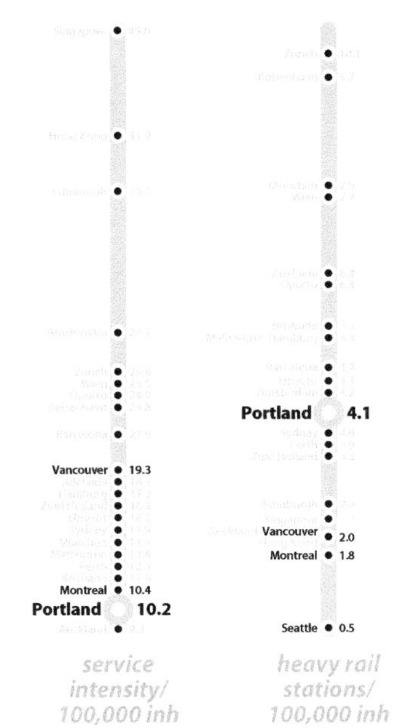

The first line of the light rail system (MAX) opened in 1986. By 2012 there was 84 km of track and this is being extended further, with a branch to Milwaukie in the south of the city under construction. Such rapid pace of growth, in combination with the relative ease of constructing at-grade light rail station facilities, has led to a much higher number of rail stations relative to population in Portland than in Seattle, Vancouver and Montreal. Access to rail in Portland is thus more comparable to Australian cities which, unlike their North American counterparts, generally have commuter rail lines with short station spacings that have been in operation since the pre-car era.

Closeness Centrality

Portland's average ease-of-movement score is the best among the US and Australasian cities in the sample, a result of influences of network shape, modal hierarchy and selective geographical coverage. Portland displays the coexistence of two basic network types. In the CBD and in much of the right bank of the Willamette River (roughly between Broadway in the north and Powell Street in the south and as far east as the Clackamas light rail line) the network is lattice-shaped and capitalises on the varying performance of rail and bus by channelling movement along the east–west light rail trunk line between the CBD

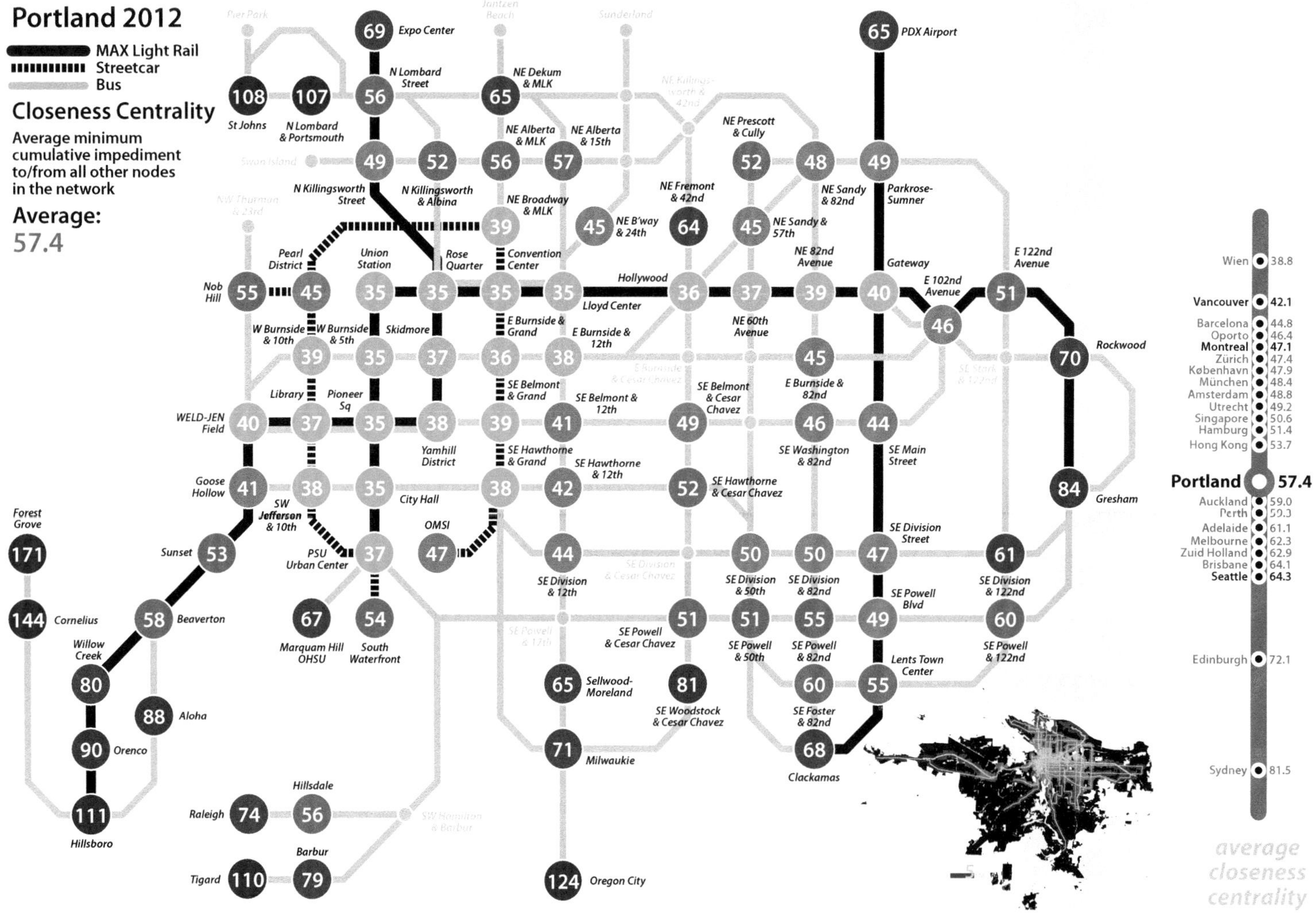

and Gateway. In this sub-region, nodal closeness values deteriorate only gradually with increasing distance from the centre and the high-performing light rail trunk because the bus system allows for movement in a variety of directions. Conversely, in the western suburbs and the fringes of the eastern suburbs the network becomes tree-shaped and more prescriptive in terms of directionality of movement, with the effect that closeness values deteriorate more rapidly with increasing distance from the centre. However, as this pattern is limited to a few selected corridors in these areas and leaves large segments of urbanised land unserved by public transit at the SNAMUTS standard, the impact of these more poorly-performing nodes on the city-wide average results is limited.

Degree Centrality

Portland's public transit network's transfer intensity is the second lowest in the global sample after Singapore. This is the result of a network design that links all radial routes effectively in the CBD, and connects radial and orbital routes in dedicated transfer facilities in suburban areas. Only in the outer west,

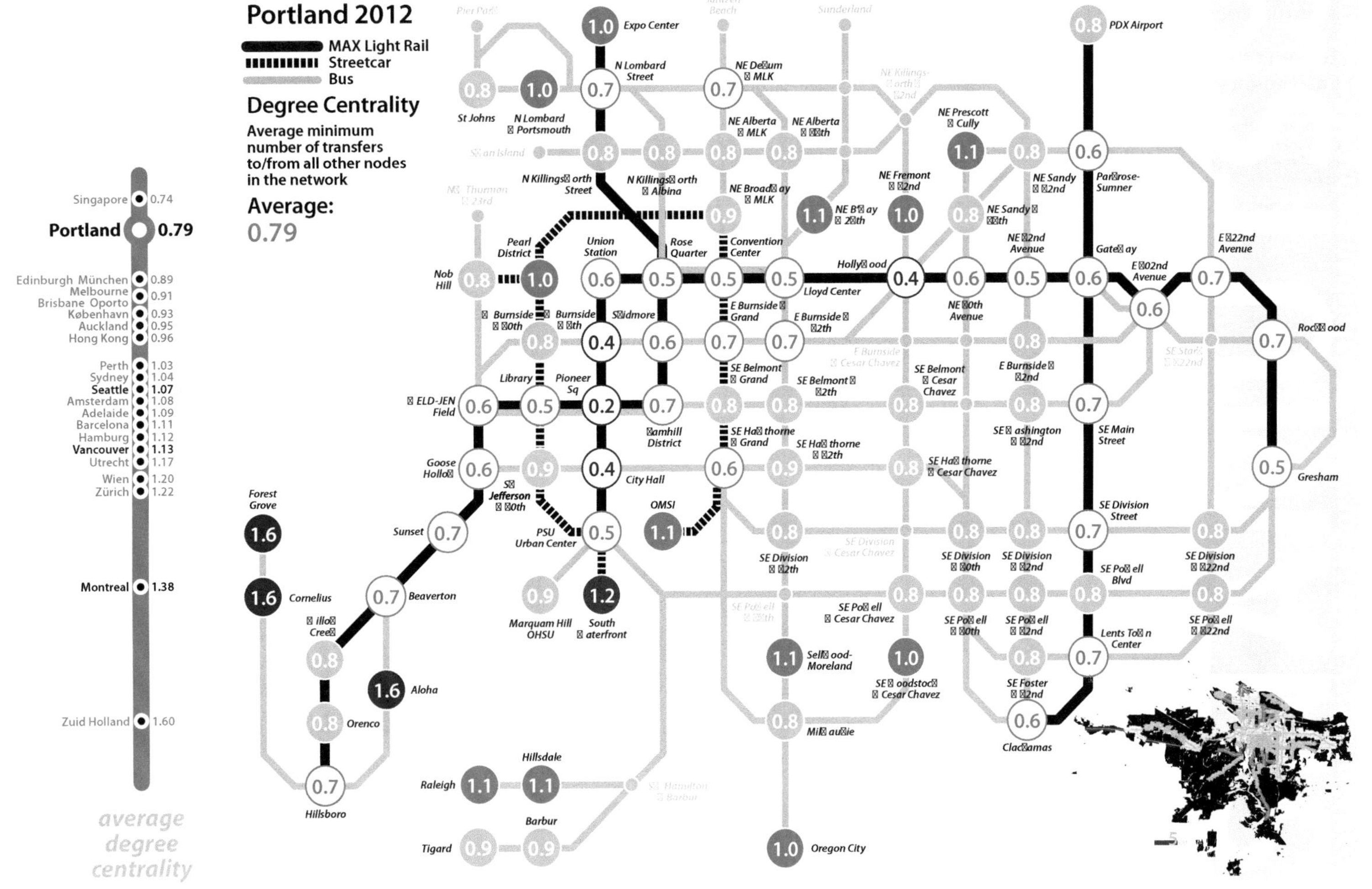

around Beaverton and Hillsboro, are there classic radial bus feeder routes to rail that drive up degree centrality values for the users in their catchments. In the eastern half of the metropolis, it is notable that radial bus routes tend to terminate at outer suburban bus-rail interchanges such as Gresham and Clackamas, rather than at 'cul-de-sacs' that would reduce opportunities for movement and introduce additional transfer needs.

Network Coverage

In terms of network coverage, Portland conveys a 'tale of two cities'. There is a relatively well-covered section in the north and the east of the city with an integrated lattice-shaped, multi-directional bus and rail network. Conversely, there is a large area, mostly to the south and west, where isolated corridors traverse low-density suburbia in a tree-shaped network structure. In combination this produces an average measure of network coverage – higher than some New World's cities

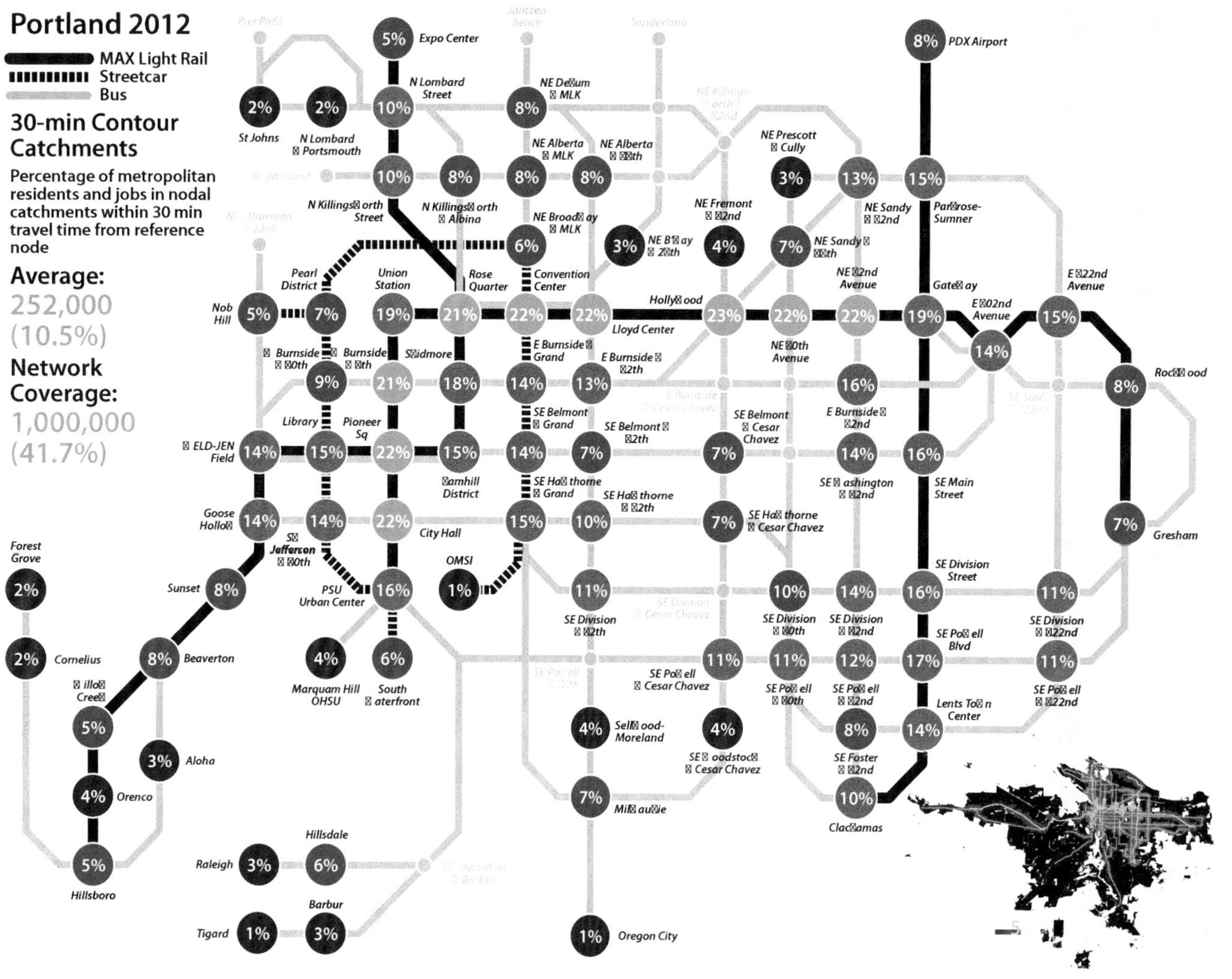

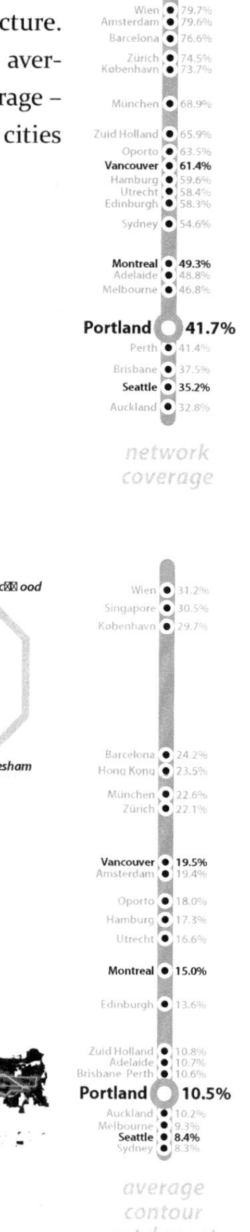

(Auckland, Seattle and Brisbane), but lower than the Canadian and large Australian cities and Adelaide.

Thirty-Minute Contour Catchments

The size of Portland's average 30-minute nodal contour catchment in percentage terms of metropolitan residents and jobs is roughly in line with those found in the smaller Australasian cities (Adelaide, Auckland, Brisbane and Perth). Remarkably, the best nodal results are for the light rail trunk line (mostly following the I-84 motorway in the inner east of the city) rather than downtown. The light rail system has a beneficial influence on Portland's performance on this index. This is achieved by offering travel times competitive with the car and by good integration with the bus system, helping to expand the contour lines further through transfer journeys. On the other hand, the multi-directionality of the network suffers to an extent from the low service frequencies on some bus and streetcar lines (i.e. less than every 15 minutes, the cut-off threshold at which transfer journeys are counted on this index) which explains the poor results in some bus or streetcar nodes that are adjacent to much better performers along the light rail lines.

Betweenness Centrality

Portland's global betweenness level relative to population and jobs is similar to that of the smaller Australasian cities, but trails those of all Canadian, European and Asian cities in the sample. This is due to the small number of high-frequency, high-performance public transit corridors in the network and the relative absence (compared to, for instance, Vancouver) of significant urban intensification on public transit corridors away from downtown and some adjacent dedicated redevelopment areas.

The detailed betweenness analysis of the TriMet network demonstrates the spine character of the light rail system, which caters for half of all travel opportunities generated by the land use – public transit system. The highest segmental betweenness values can be found along the trunk line on the right bank of the Willamette River between Gateway and Rose Quarter. West of Rose Quarter, the light rail trunk line crosses the river and then splits into two CBD thoroughfares. These thoroughfares intersect again at Pioneer Square, the point on the network with the highest nodal betweenness score and also the heart of downtown Portland. Thus there is a good alignment of network significance and perceived centrality in a CBD that was significantly revitalised as part of Portland's efforts, over the past four decades, to create a more people-friendly and accessible city centre (Schiller et al, 2010).

On the bus network, the lattice structure of the CBD and right bank network creates some conspicuously strong corridors, especially at the river crossings as well as along 12th, 82nd and 122nd Avenues (routes 70, 71 and 72) and along Powell Boulevard (route 9). With the exception of route 72, however, this significance is not matched by higher than the typical 15–20 minute service frequencies.

The streetcar system, despite its CBD and CBD fringe focus, does not attract a network significance greater than that of comparable bus routes. The streetcar serves areas where redevelopment is ongoing and where greater land use concentrations in future will lead to

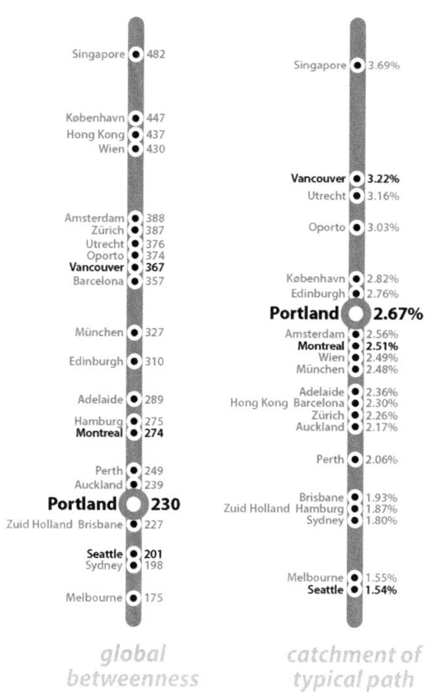

increasing betweenness results. However, it is likely that the original choice for streetcar rather than bus access was based more on its role as a catalyst for development than for its higher performance.

Portland's CBD attracts a relatively low share of travel opportunities for a city its size. This can be explained by the well-developed multi-directional network shape in the eastern suburbs which allow journey paths to be deflected from the central area, as well as the peripheral position of the downtown area between the Willamette River to the north and east, and a hilly nature reserve to the west and south.

Network Resilience

Portland's average network resilience value is better than in the North American peer cities, though in international terms it is poorer than the average. An increase in public transit patronage and mode share would require significant improvements, particularly in

Hong Kong 20.2%
Barcelona 20.4%
Singapore 20.9%
Amsterdam 22.5%
Hamburg 23.2%
Wien 23.5%
Vancouver 23.9%
København 24.1%
Portland 27.9%
Zürich 28.8%
München 29.1%
Montreal 30.3%
Brisbane 31.7%
Sydney 32.1%
Melbourne 32.7%
Auckland 35.7%
Zuid Holland 36.3%
Edinburgh 38.1%
Perth 40.2%
Utrecht Seattle 42.8%
Oporto 43.1%
Adelaide 62.0%
segmental betweenness cbd

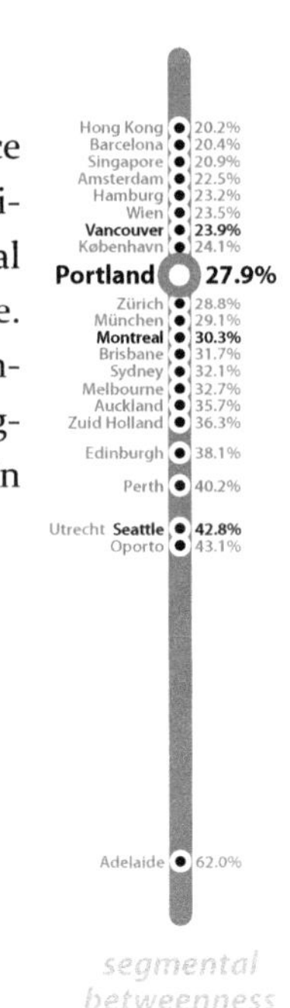

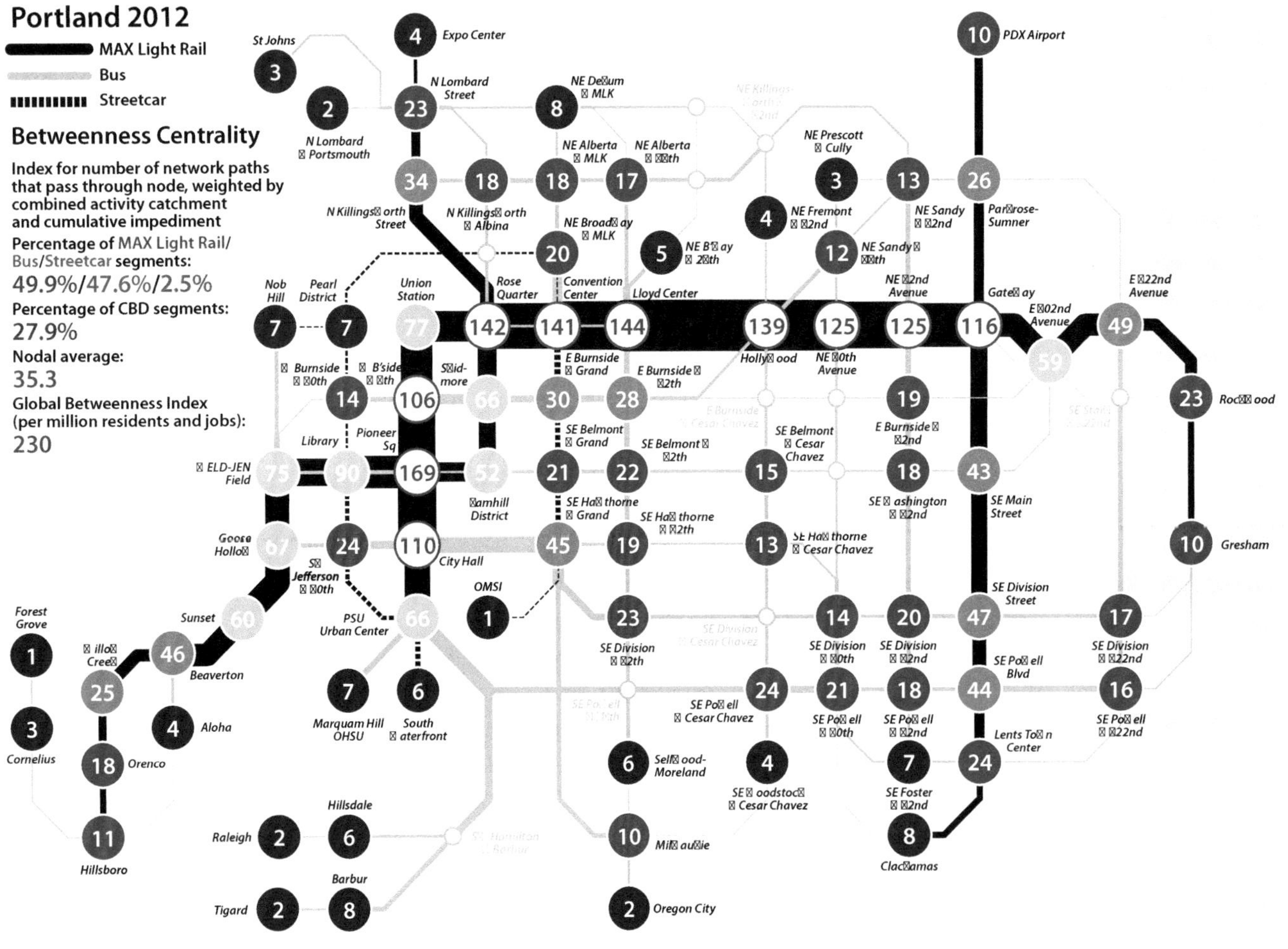

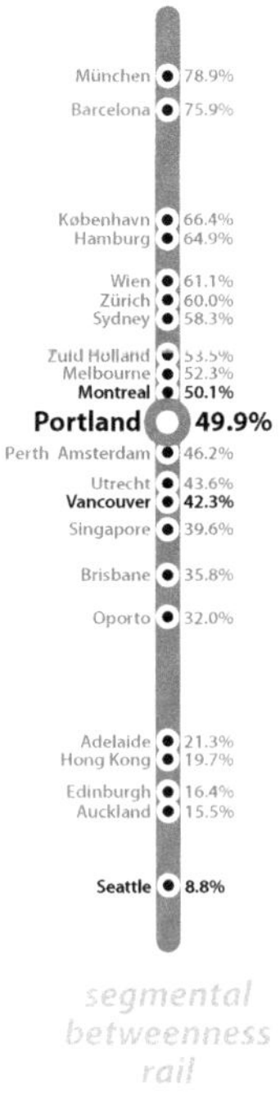

Portland 2012
MAX Light Rail
Bus
Streetcar
Betweenness Centrality
Index for number of network paths that pass through node, weighted by combined activity catchment and cumulative impediment
Percentage of MAX Light Rail/Bus/Streetcar segments:
49.9%/47.6%/2.5%
Percentage of CBD segments:
27.9%
Nodal average:
35.3
Global Betweenness Index (per million residents and jobs):
230
St Johns
Expo Center
N Lombard Street
PDX Airport
Union Station
Rose Quarter
Convention Center
Lloyd Center
Gateway
Gresham
City Hall
OMSI
PSU Urban Center
Marquam Hill OHSU
Hillsdale
Raleigh
Tigard
Barbur
Beaverton
Sunset
Aloha
Orenco
Hillsboro
Cornelius
Forest Grove
Oregon City
Clackamas

München 78.9%
Barcelona 75.9%
København 66.4%
Hamburg 64.9%
Wien 61.1%
Zürich 60.0%
Sydney 58.3%
Zuid Holland 53.5%
Melbourne 52.3%
Montreal 50.1%
Portland 49.9%
Perth Amsterdam 46.2%
Utrecht 43.6%
Vancouver 42.3%
Singapore 39.6%
Brisbane 35.8%
Oporto 32.0%
Adelaide 21.3%
Hong Kong 19.7%
Edinburgh 16.4%
Auckland 15.5%
Seattle 8.8%
segmental betweenness rail

increased service frequencies. In contrast to a fairly robust network structure, low service frequencies appear to be the weakest factor in Portland's current public transit supply. This is visible along the eastern suburbs bus corridors (especially 12th and 122nd Avenues, and Powell Boulevard) where the superior role for the network structure is not reflected in a superior level of service. It is likely, however, that this finding is an indication of latent demand rather than actual overcrowding in an urban fabric where, outside the CBD and CBD fringe, movement remains dominated by the automobile.

Portland's CBD has a better average resilience performance than the network overall, which can be associated with the fine-grained and grid-shaped access provided by the surface routes in this area and that the geographical centre of the TriMet network is located east of the Willamette River.

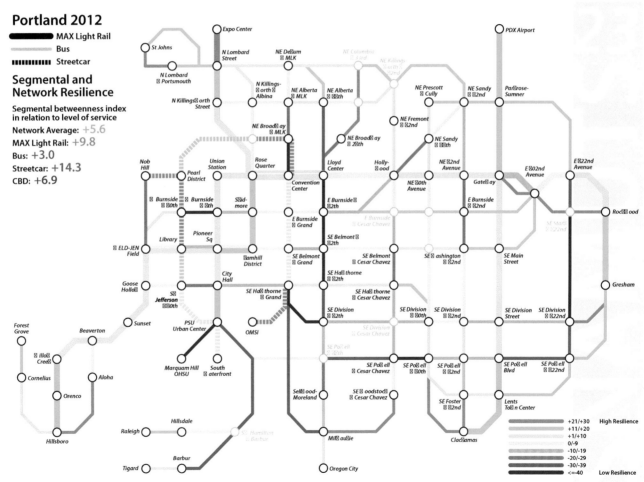

Portland 2012

MAX Light Rail
Bus
Streetcar

Segmental and Network Resilience

Segmental betweenness index in relation to level of service

Network Average: +5.6
MAX Light Rail: +9.8
Bus: +3.0
Streetcar: +14.3
CBD: +6.9

+21/+30 High Resilience
+11/+20
+1/+10
0/-9
-10/-19
-20/-29
-30/-39
<=-40 Low Resilience

Nodal Connectivity

Portland's average nodal connectivity values are modest and indicate that the level of flexibility of movement associated with the ability to perform spontaneous journeys on public transit with ease is confined to destinations within the CBD (particularly Pioneer Square) and along the LRT trunk route to Gateway. This latter corridor follows a motorway and therefore has limited capacity for the degree of land use intensification needed to support such a conspicuous position on this index. Away from the light rail system, low bus frequencies and occupancy rates depress nodal connectivity values, even though many mixed-use, bus-based corridors that were initially urbanised during the first-generation streetcar era survive in Portland's inner and middle suburbs. In these walkable and cyclable neighbourhoods without LRT access, public transit could be improved to offer a better role in the mobility mix.

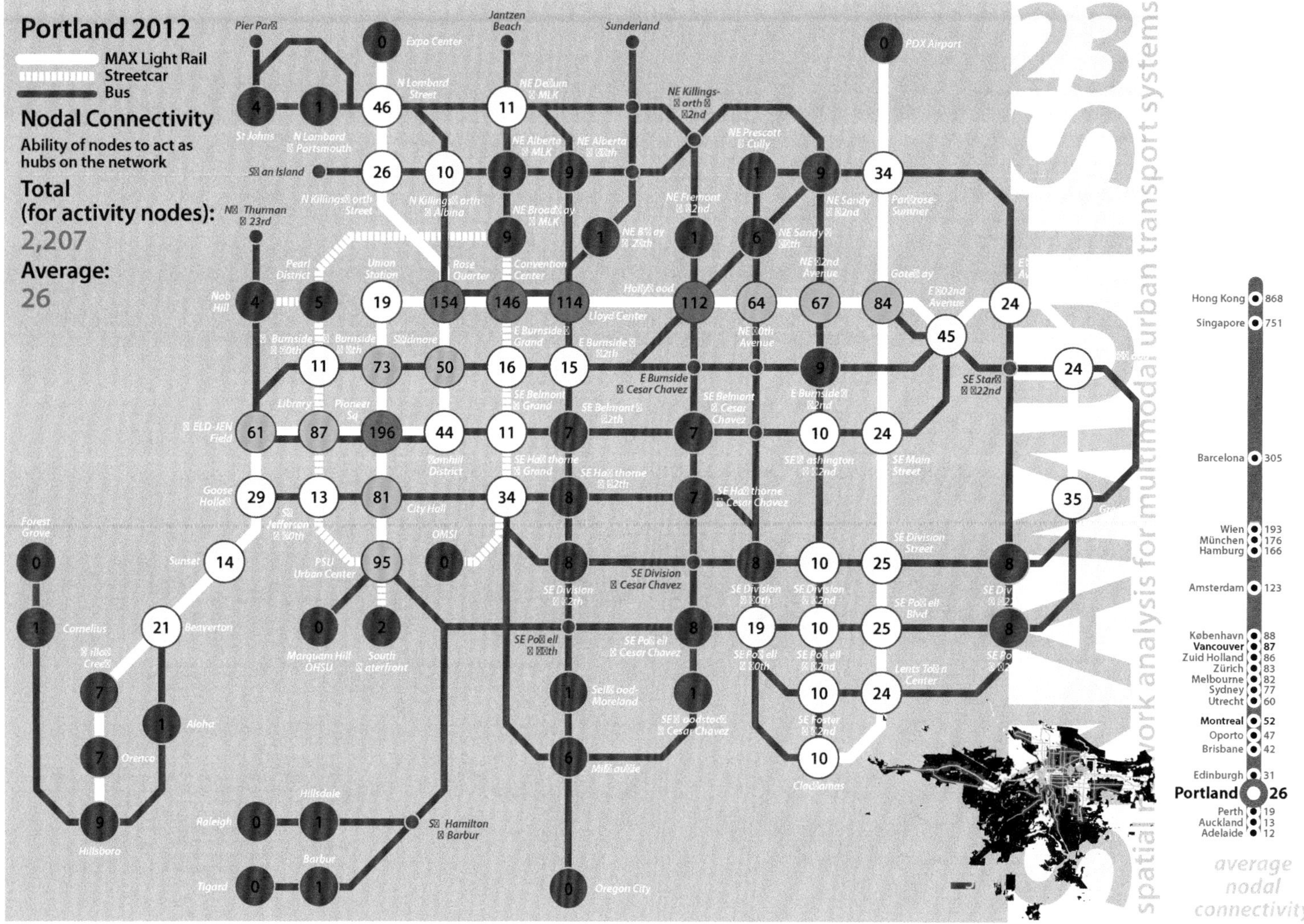

SNAMUTS Composite Accessibility Index and Reflections

The composite map illustrates public transit's lopsided geographical coverage in the Portland metropolitan area. In the suburbs west of the Willamette River, public transit accessibility at the SNAMUTS minimum standard is restricted to a handful of radial corridors with few or no interconnections, and their accessibility standard away from the light rail route is minimal. In the inner and middle suburbs east of the Willamette River, geographical coverage leaves far fewer gaps, while the lattice shape of the network supports a smoother decay gradient of accessibility performance between centre and periphery and between LRT corridors and bus-only areas. Beyond the sub-centres of Milwaukie and Clackamas as well as in the Gresham area, the network thins out considerably and leaves large urbanised areas not served by public transit at the SNAMUTS standard.

This unevenness of access may be based on history and governance: the area where the multimodal network is lattice-shaped conforms with the boundaries of the City of Portland as well as with the geographical expansion

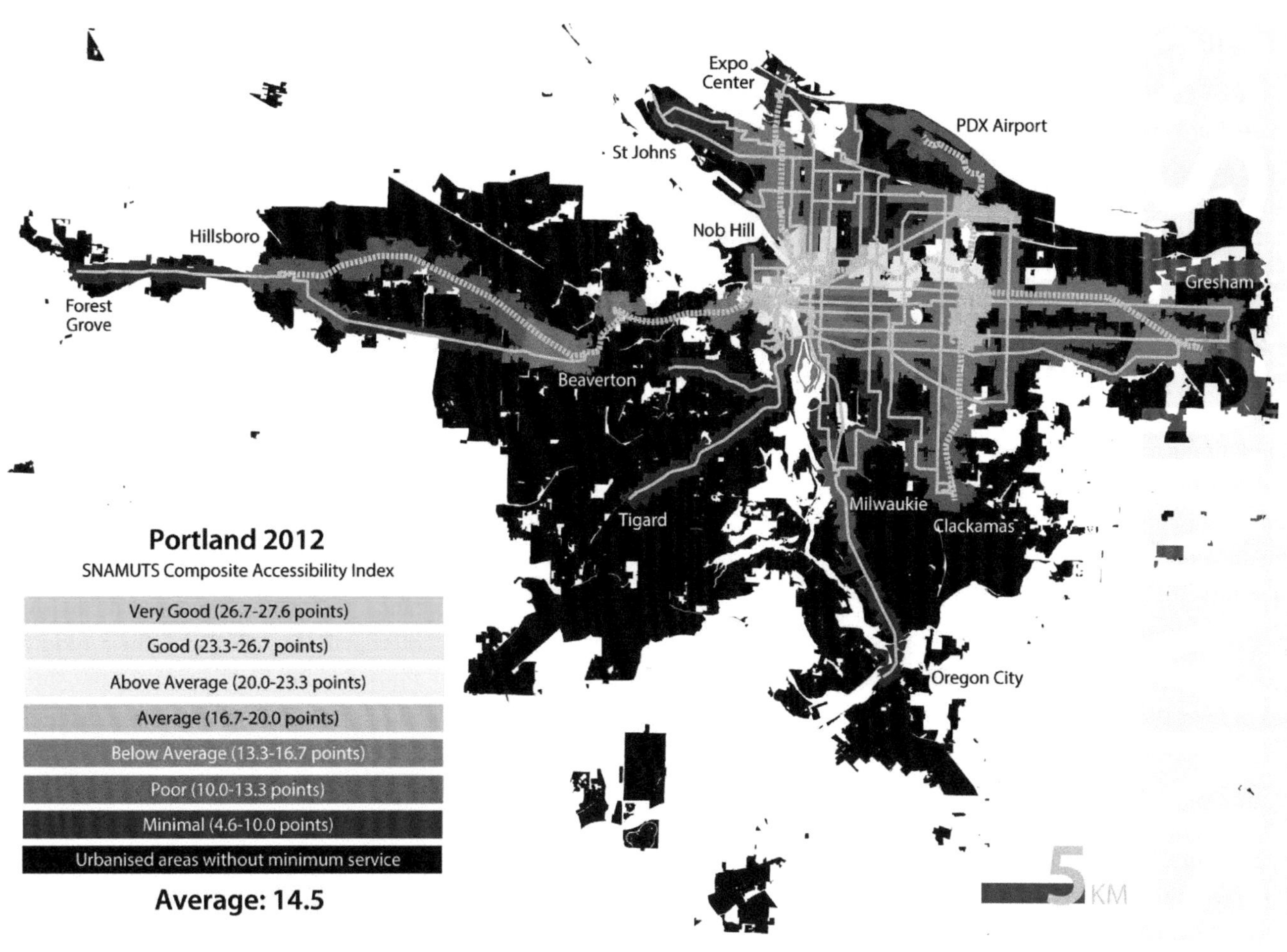

of the first-generation streetcar network prior to its demise in the mid-twentieth century. It is thus largely confined to the pre-WWII settlement area. The challenge for Portland, as well as many other cities within and beyond the SNAMUTS sample, is to expand this level of public transit accessibility across the post-war urban fabric, which dominates the western suburbs.

QUO VADIS, NORTH AMERICA?

In the context of the global sample, the accessibility performance of Montreal and Vancouver can be placed in a leading position among New World cities and an average position compared to their European counterparts. Seattle and Portland are situated roughly at par with the smaller Australasian cities on most indicators – slightly outperformed by Brisbane and Perth while maintaining a small edge over Adelaide and Auckland. This positioning is also reflected in public transit usage according to the annual journeys per capita measure.

The North American case study cities have made ambitious efforts to strengthen the role of public transit in their mobility mix, in the case of Portland, Seattle and to some extent Vancouver starting from a very low base. While transit-supportive policies are no longer uncommon across mid-sized cities in contemporary North America, the evolutionary path taken particularly by Portland and Vancouver is by no means representative for the regional mainstream. This is what motivated us to include these 'aspirational transit metropoles' (Cervero, 1998) in the SNAMUTS sample, alongside Montreal and Seattle where the expansion of transit services and infrastructure has progressed at a much slower pace during the past two or three decades. However, the outstanding narrative of success in LUTI among the North American case study cities is Vancouver. Only here do we find a preparedness to supply operational resources for public transit at par with mainstream practice in European cities. A governance regime has evolved to facilitate a comprehensive transformation of the transport–land use interplay towards greater urban compactness, concentration and transit orientation. Vancouver's leading position among its New World peers on practically every SNAMUTS measure is testimony to the effectiveness of these policies. Yet it also illustrates their limitations and the threat of becoming a victim of their own success: the city's less than favourable results on the resilience index suggest that public transit cannot, and will not continue its expansionary trajectory unless the current pace of network and service improvements is maintained or accelerated. While past experience may convey tentative optimism in this respect, the recurrent emergence of political tension over transit funding between city, regional and provincial tiers of government suggests that such an outcome is far from guaranteed.

The effects of an incremental, 'stop-start' history of public transit expansion are best embodied by Montreal, where the construction of the metro system (mostly during the 1960s to 1980s, when mega-events – World Expo and Olympic Games – provided additional impetus) resulted in a transformative period for urban mobility and the land use–transport interplay. However, during the quarter-century since, public transit improved only marginally. While LUTI is evident in the densely populated inner *arrondissements* of the core city, underscored by good results on nearly every SNAMUTS indicator, this is not the case in suburban areas. Here Montreal displays the hallmarks of a divided city, where a transit-rich, mixed-use core city coexists with an extraordinarily transit-poor periphery: 'Vienna surrounded by Phoenix', a popular phrase describing a similar phenomenon in neighbouring Toronto (Lemon, 1996). As in Seattle and Portland, the partial territorial division of transit agencies and their funding sources along municipal and/or county boundaries, prompting inward-looking perspectives on network and service planning, does not help with overcoming this dilemma at a metropolitan level that has long transcended these individual jurisdictions in functional terms.

The four case study cities chose very different technologies for the rail-based components of their transit systems, with lasting consequences for their contribution to accessibility performance and their prospects for future growth. Montreal imported a then newly developed rubber-tyred metro technology from France in the 1960s and reputedly only discovered post-implementation that the system is unsuitable for operating outdoors in the severe cold of a Quebec winter. As a result, any past or future extension of the network is condemned to expensive tunnelling. The choice of a driverless metro system in Vancouver, easy to operate fast and frequently, has proved a boon to the city's accessibility performance though after the conversion of existing freight rail alignments during the 1980s and 1990s, the expansion of the network along established urban activity corridors also necessitates lengthy underground sections. Furthermore, there are concerns about the relatively low passenger capacity per train, enforced by short platform lengths and producing a detrimental effect on the city's performance on the resilience index. Portland, in contrast, has recorded the fastest pace of rail infrastructure growth during the past three decades, perhaps resulting from the choice of the more adaptable and inexpensive LRT technology, capable of combining on-street running in areas of high activity intensity with fast operation alongside motorways or pre-existing freight rail lines. However, the city lacks the inherited transit-oriented core city fabric of Montreal, or Vancouver's will and resources for large-scale, TOD transformation beyond a laudable suite of incremental urban renewal projects along its growing light rail and streetcar spines. Of the four case study cities, only Seattle represents a geographical pattern where concentrations of employment rivalling those of the CBD have emerged in locations away from fixed public transit during the car age, and which can be found in many large US agglomerations. In an arduous process, the metropolitan region is now playing 'catch-up' to link these areas into a coherent, fixed-track public transit system banking on the notion that their urban environment, never configured to facilitate pedestrian activity, will gradually transform towards a greater sense of spatial integration like in many inner-urban neighbourhoods across this wealthy metropolitan region.

NOTE

1 Varying accounting methods suggest that these figures should be treated with a degree of caution (see Chapter 2).

5 More with Less?

Accessibility and Public Transport Efficiency in European Cities

For a New World observer, the built form and history of public transport provision in European cities suggests a degree of mutually supportive co-evolution of land use and non-car transport rarely observed in North America or Australasia. Many European cities retain expansive urban precincts that predate the arrival of mass motorisation and have preserved, alongside their built form, a culture of walking, cycling and public transport use. Few European cities went through a period of post-war history where the development of public transport was all but abandoned like in the second-tier cities of North America or the South Pacific. Instead, many innovations that led to contemporary understandings of how to design, organise and provide 'best-practice' public transport together with urban growth patterns that enable its delivery are of European origin. European cities were the first to introduce integrated planning and ticketing across disparate operators and jurisdictions from the 1960s onwards. They pioneered and scaled up new public transport technologies such as hybrid metro-light rail systems, hybrid metro-suburban rail systems or bus and tram prioritisation schemes that would eventually spread around the world. They found workable templates for how to integrate public transport infrastructure with highly space-constrained historic environments. They packaged public transport, walking and cycling improvements with strategies to limit the car in urban areas without compromising a city's social or economic vitality. In the light of these success stories, New World practitioners could be forgiven for seeing European cities as an unmitigated source of inspiration when it comes to integrated transport and land use planning.

The growth and evolution of European cities and their transport networks during the last half-century, however, has not only been about the preservation of pre-war heritage in both respects. Simultaneously, most cities have experienced significant outward growth and an ambitious retrofit with high-performance road infrastructure, trends that may have abated somewhat since their peak in the late twentieth century but still continue. The significance of public transport, in most cities, declined in relative terms until about the 1980s, or longer in much of Southern and Eastern Europe where mass motorisation and car-oriented suburbanisation commenced later than in the west and north of the continent. Thus European cities, much like New World cities, added a 'car city' layer to the urban fabric. In many cases this was located at the outer ring of agglomerations or between them, sometimes facilitated during the process of reconstruction of cities devastated in World War II or experiencing profound restructuring effects following post-industrial and post-communist transitions. This urban typology is characterised by lower densities, reduced spatial contiguity, a much coarser grain of land uses and a limited functional mix in comparison to the more 'traditional' ones that co-evolved with public transport in the pre-war era. This poses challenges for the transition to less car-dependence comparable to cities in North America and Australasia – challenges that are being addressed by different European cities in different ways.

FROM A NON-INTEGRATED TO A MULTIMODAL NETWORK: EDINBURGH AND OPORTO

The case study cities in this chapter provide two comparisons. Edinburgh and Oporto are of similar size and, since 2000, have embarked on a fundamental transformation of the public transport–land use interplay towards twenty-first-century needs, after a period of minimal investment in public transport infrastructure during the second half of the twentieth century. Oporto commenced this process earlier than Edinburgh following the opening of a core light rail system since 2002, and by 2009 had a network in a transitional stage. In contrast, Edinburgh's network (in 2011) can be described as 'pre-transition'. Both cities represent a network design approach that the HiTrans project refers to as the 'direct connections – no transfers' principle (Nielsen et al, 2005), guided by the quest to offer as many transfer-free connections between spatially disparate activity centres and corridors as reasonably possible. In Oporto, after new light rail lines were added as spines to the system in the 2000s, this principle evolved towards greater multimodal integration and the strategic development of dedicated transfer facilities while in Edinburgh no such transition has taken place to date.

In the view of the HiTrans project, the 'direct connections-no transfers' network design principle is characterised by some shortfalls. It typically incurs a relatively large number of individual lines providing transfer-free connections between different clusters of origins and destinations, but which are each operated at relatively low frequencies (usually 10–15 minutes as a maximum). On important corridors, several such lines overlap and generate higher combined frequencies, but this limits the legibility of the service for non-regular or new users. There is also an increased vulnerability to operational disruptions, which rapidly reverberate through the network from otherwise localised incidents due to the large number of services affected. Further, it is difficult to achieve regular service intervals between different lines on combined segments, even in smooth operating conditions, due to the complexity of the network. In our sample, many cities are moving away from this network design principle: Barcelona and Auckland are implementing a fundamental surface network redesign; Sydney and Melbourne have recently streamlined tangles of lower-profile services into higher-profile 'MetroBuses' or 'SmartBuses'. These cities undertake such reforms in order to achieve a simpler network layout that offers only one or two bus lines per corridor, but with higher frequencies and the expectation that passengers will transfer to other well-serviced routes if necessary. In Edinburgh (and Singapore and Hong Kong), however, the 'direct connections-no transfers' network structure persists unreformed.

Edinburgh's public transport system is organised under a regime of deregulation that was introduced throughout the UK in the 1980s and differs fundamentally from later attempts to introduce greater private sector involvement through competitive tendering within otherwise centrally planned networks in continental European jurisdictions. In the UK outside London, operators are technically at liberty to compete with each other for passengers within the same service areas or corridors, and allocate their resources according to commercial objectives. Local and regional governments retain the option of ordering (and paying for) additional services that are considered vital from a public interest point of view but are not provided by (and thus do not compete with) commercial operators (Tyson, 1995). The deregulation reforms also constrained efforts by regional agencies (and inter-operator agreements) to retain or introduce integrated or collaborative ticketing, with the result that the benefits of periodical travel cards over single tickets are not as broad or compelling to users as they tend to be in the fare-integrated environments of other cities (White, 1997).

Throughout the UK, the market for public transport operators was subject to a concentration of only a handful of large players with a nationwide (even international) presence, and the emergence of a dominant operator in most urban agglomerations (Cowie and Asenova, 1999). In Edinburgh however, the dominant bus operator (Lothian Buses) remains in public ownership, with the majority of shares in the company held by the City of Edinburgh and the remainder by the surrounding counties.

Our interest in analysing Edinburgh and Oporto is to find out more about the accessibility opportunities and shortcomings associated with the retrofit of a transfer-avoiding, expansive bus network in a medium-size city towards greater multimodal interdependence following the insertion of a high-performance though still limited rail system. Are there savings of operational resources? Does the network become more attractive to users? Does it appear to become more 'future-proof' as patronage and the role of public transport in the urban mobility market improve? The salience of these questions also needs to be seen in the context of Edinburgh having opened its first light rail line in 2014 (after our analysis) and thus embarking on the challenge to create a network with greater coordination between transport modes itself.

TRANSFORMING THE POST-WAR CITY WITH POST-WAR PUBLIC TRANSPORT: THE EXPERIENCES OF HAMBURG AND MUNICH

The second comparison, between the first-tier German cities of Hamburg and Munich, illustrates an approach to public transport network design that is fundamentally different from that of Edinburgh or Oporto, characterised by the HiTrans project as the 'one segment-one line' principle (Nielsen et al, 2005). Here, each urban activity corridor is typically only serviced by a single public transport line, in some cases even with the consequence of surface routes being curtailed where an underground or other off-street route is present. There are many intersections between such routes and in most cases these have been physically optimised to facilitate transfers. It is common to provide a uniform service frequency across the network (10 minutes in both Hamburg and Munich, with some lines running every 5 and some every 20 minutes) in order to generate a 'pulse' that further contributes to facilitating transfers. The number of distinct lines, all other circumstances being equal, tends to be much lower in this network design than under the 'direct connections-no transfers' principle, making the system easier to understand for occasional or new users. There is also an articulated hierarchy of transport modes within the network according to their performance and capacity, though with quite different characteristics in terms of efficiency and accessibility outcomes between Hamburg and Munich.

Both cities suffered widespread destruction during World War II. Reconstruction departed significantly from the pre-war urban form, reducing activity density and functional integration in the badly damaged inner districts and in compensation, adding a middle suburban ring of greenfield housing estates and employment centres – usually spatially segregated – during the early post-war era. In Munich and initially in Hamburg, the tram network was extended to service these new neighbourhoods. Unlike Munich, however, Hamburg already had a rapid transit network. It consisted of two metro systems that had been built by two competing jurisdictions in the 1910s to access suburban corridors popular with wealthy residents seeking to live in scenic waterfront or forested areas. One of these, now the basis of the contemporary U-Bahn system, also contained a circular line designed to connect the city's expansive seaport (Europe's second largest after Rotterdam) with working-class residential neighbourhoods. Following the destruction of many of these precincts in the 1940s, and the demise of the maritime sector as a major industrial employer a few decades later, Hamburg was left with a piece of its public transport system that had been built for an urban structure no longer in existence.

Wartime damage also facilitated the establishment of a generous arterial road network and a can-do spirit about enabling motorised mobility in both cities. However, Hamburg's road-building agenda stopped short of establishing the inner-urban motorway network that was envisioned by early reconstruction plans (Kähler, 2012). Catering for the growing number of cars was further complemented by ambitious investment in metro infrastructure, though the target expansion of the network planned during the post-war reconstruction era was never reached, even though the plans had served as a key rationale for the gradual closure of Hamburg's first-generation tram system in the 1960s and 1970s. As a result,

Hamburg now has a number of strong urban corridors and significant activity centres, particularly in the middle ring suburbs, that rely solely on feeder buses to the metro system, alongside others that have strong rail spines; a 'tale of two cities' theme explored below.

Meanwhile Munich, growing in national significance after taking over from divided Berlin as Germany's leading hub for high-technology industries (Evans and Karecha, 2013), planned an entirely new rapid transit network and opened the first lines in conjunction with hosting the 1972 Olympic Games. This network included the conversion of the city's sizeable suburban rail network into a trunk-and-branches system centred on a new underground link through the CBD and operated under the S-Bahn brand, a metro-style standard with regular frequencies and distinctive diametrical lines already in place in Hamburg, Berlin and Copenhagen. It also included a starter line that, 40 years later, has become a mostly underground urban metro system (U-Bahn) accessing the great majority of post-war residential and employment areas in the middle suburbs and the activity hubs of the inner area.

As Munich's metro system grew, the tram system gradually retreated from corridors newly serviced by U-Bahn lines, a practice tied to the conditions for Federal funding grants towards public transport infrastructure in Germany, which demand that permanent operational savings can be demonstrated on existing surface routes. Like Hamburg, Munich had considered phasing out the mode altogether, but a council decision in 1986 favoured its retention and, eventually, reconfiguration and renewed expansion to focus on secondary and non-radial corridors.

Present-day Hamburg thus has a public transport network that has grown by layers through several historic phases with very distinct and contrasting conditions of urban form and urban life and adapted, more or less, through the transitions. It displays an urban structure that contains high-density post-war suburban hubs around never-built metro extensions and tranquil pre-war garden suburbs around older metro lines with relatively modest patronage, and many types of centres in between those two extremes. It contains some of Europe's busiest bus routes along inner-urban corridors where trams should arguably never have been abandoned. It has a spatially challenging configuration around a large industrial port, gradually vacating some attractive sites for CBD extensions and other high-profile, high-intensity redevelopment very different in style from the post-war modernist urban form.

Where Hamburg's co-evolution of urban form and public transport can be characterised as iterative and discontinuous, land-locked Munich (with only a scenic, non-navigable river as a major geographical constraint dividing the city) had the opportunity to design and almost complete a rapid transit system optimised for the movement needs emerging after 1945. The remaining surface network was adapted and maintained its modal diversity with trams and buses complementing each other. The resulting interplay of urban form and public transport, less the result of a 'grand vision' than a thoughtful coincidence of interlocking steps in infrastructure investment, transport governance and urban planning, nonetheless became a popular exemplar of global best practice (Cervero, 1998).

Our interest in Munich concerns whether, through its more straightforward and targeted investment into coordinated urban and public transport growth, a superior performance is achieved in terms of either spatial accessibility or operational efficiency (or both) than Hamburg. We are also interested in how the trajectory places each city to address the evolving movement and accessibility needs of the current century, beyond the era of post-war modernism.

ACCESSIBILITY PROFILE: EDINBURGH, SCOTLAND (UK)

Edinburgh, the capital of Scotland, is the region's second largest metropolitan area after Glasgow, which is located 90 km to the west and shares some commuter catchments with Edinburgh. For the purposes of the SNAMUTS analysis, however, we refer to an Edinburgh-centred agglomeration consisting of the City of Edinburgh and the five counties of West Lothian, Midlothian, East Lothian, Falkirk and Fife. This region of 3,337 sq km was home to 1.27 million inhabitants in 2001. Of these, approximately half a million lived in the core city, where spatial expansion is constrained by the North Sea coastline and an effective green belt policy (Karou and Hull, 2014). The urbanised area has an average density of 37.1 residents and 17.0 jobs per hectare, similar to the Dutch Randstad, Munich, Zurich and Oporto.

Until recently Edinburgh, uniquely among the European SNAMUTS cities, has seen a relative absence of large-scale, transformative investment in public transport infrastructure for many decades. Thus the network consists of a traditional urban and regional bus system complimented by a handful of commuter rail lines operating along mainline tracks, a structure similar to that found prior to the car age. Simultaneously, Edinburgh successfully resisted inserting large-scale road infrastructure into its UNESCO-listed historic centre and vicinity. In 2011, a light rail starter line between the city centre and the airport was under construction; it opened in 2014 (post analysis). While this project has the potential to act as a 'game changer' for public transport accessibility, at least along its corridor, its implementation has been mired in political and financial controversies which led to decisions to scale back and slow down further extensions to the scheme in the future (Karou and Hull, 2014).

In a deregulated environment of public transport governance, each operator has their own fare system with only minor attempts at integration for some periodical tickets. Generally, single tickets do not allow for transfers, but the larger bus operators offer attractively priced day and periodical tickets. These have the effect of binding users to a particular operator, since using a competitor's service would incur an extra fare. Such financial penalties are likely to influence usage patterns and in our SNAMUTS calculations we have taken this disincentive into account.

Service Intensity

The suburban rail system is operated at variable frequencies, though none exceed 15 minutes during the weekday inter-peak period, making the service more typical of a regional than a metropolitan operation. The bus network, in contrast, is operated at relatively high frequencies particularly in central areas and key radial corridors where several routes overlap. In parts of Princes Street, Edinburgh's busiest bus corridor, we counted a total of 108 inter-peak departures per hour per direction – a

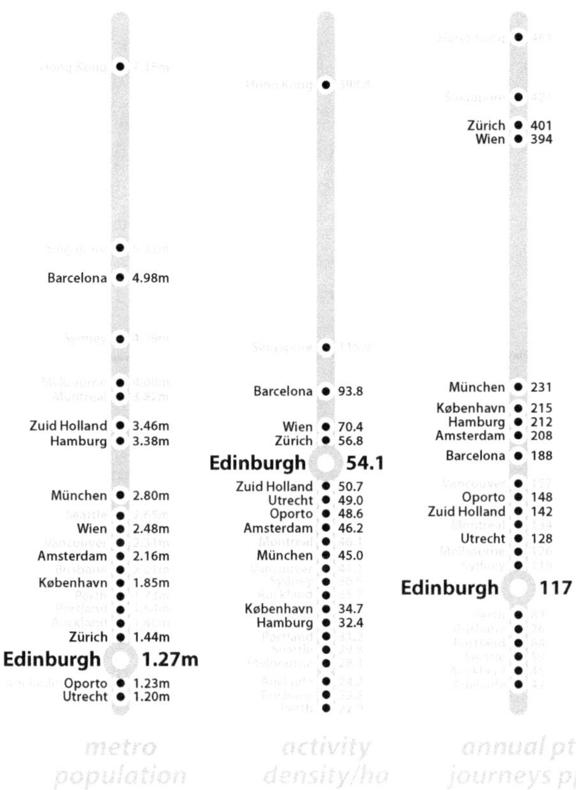

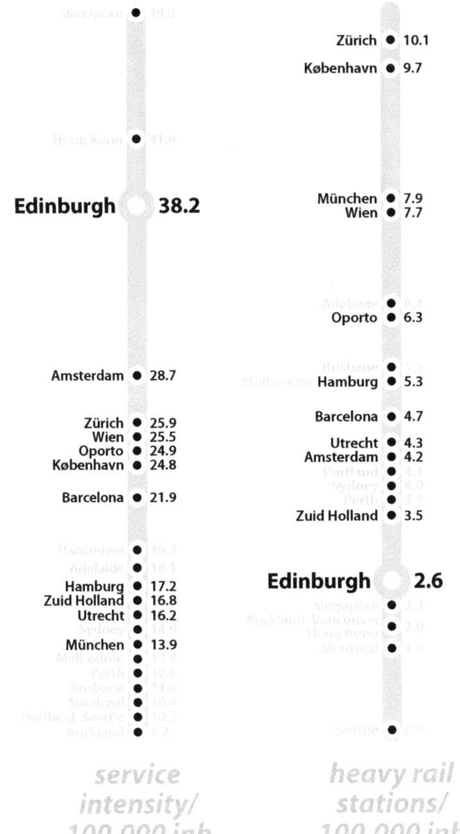

level of service only exceeded in our sample in parts of the Singapore and Hong Kong networks. As a consequence, Edinburgh's service intensity is second only to the Asian cities and 50 per cent higher than that found in its European counterparts with a relatively generous service provision (Amsterdam, Copenhagen, Vienna and Zurich). Conversely, Edinburgh has the lowest rail station density relative to population of all European SNAMUTS cities. The public transport system is heavily dominated by buses and has a flat hierarchy between bus and rail, and even between different types of bus services, thus foregoing many of the network efficiencies known from other European or North American cities.

Closeness Centrality

There are 102 activity nodes accessible to minimum-standard public transport in the Edinburgh region; of these, 63 are in the core city. Edinburgh's central area and surrounding inner suburbs are characterised by the fine-grained, mixed-use, medium-rise, high-density urbanisation pattern typical for the pre-car era. Conversely, in post-war city extensions there is frequently a spatial separation between housing and daily services, more so than in the city's continental counterparts where such housing estates are usually more integrated with neighbourhood retail. Consequently, there is a considerable number of stand-alone shopping centres of various sizes across Edinburgh's middle suburbs. Since the majority of these include dedicated bus interchanges they feature as SNAMUTS activity nodes alongside the housing estates themselves.

Average closeness results in Edinburgh return the poorest performance for a European city, suggesting a public transport system struggling to overcome the spatial separation effects generated by the settlement structure. This is manifest at several levels. The lack of fare integration in Edinburgh's network works as a disincentive for making inter-operator transfers. This leads to some anomalies, such as where the best closeness results occur at nodes along Lothian Road and Leith Walk (served only by the dominant bus operator), rather than at the more central locations along Princes Street or the rail stations at Waverley and Haymarket (where several operators coincide). If full fare integration was available in Edinburgh, average closeness would improve to 64.0, and the best nodal results would be found at the two central rail–bus hubs. Another factor driving up closeness values is the deficient service to/from and within major suburban centres. In Falkirk, for instance, opportunities to configure bus services as effective rail feeders and orbital links to neighbouring regional towns, and thus capitalise on the strengths of both modes, are almost completely foregone. In Dunfermline, bus-rail integration is better but the low frequency of the rail service has a dampening effect on ease of movement.

Degree Centrality

A plausible explanation for offering a service intensity level as elevated as in Edinburgh could be the intent to counter the disincentive to make transfers stemming from the lack of fare integration by configuring a network that minimises the need to make transfers in the first place. In this respect Edinburgh leads a cohort of European cities (alongside Copenhagen, Munich and Oporto) where average degree centrality or transfer intensity is relatively low. In practice, however, the benefit of reaching a large proportion of destinations on the same vehicle is limited to the city centre and a small number of inner urban corridors (Leith Walk, Corstorphine Road and Nicolson Road) where a relatively high number of bus services overlap. Between suburban areas outside the core city, public transport journeys at the minimum standard generally require a transfer trip via central Edinburgh. In Falkirk the (slower) bus corridor into Edinburgh offers transfer-free access between a significantly greater range of origins and

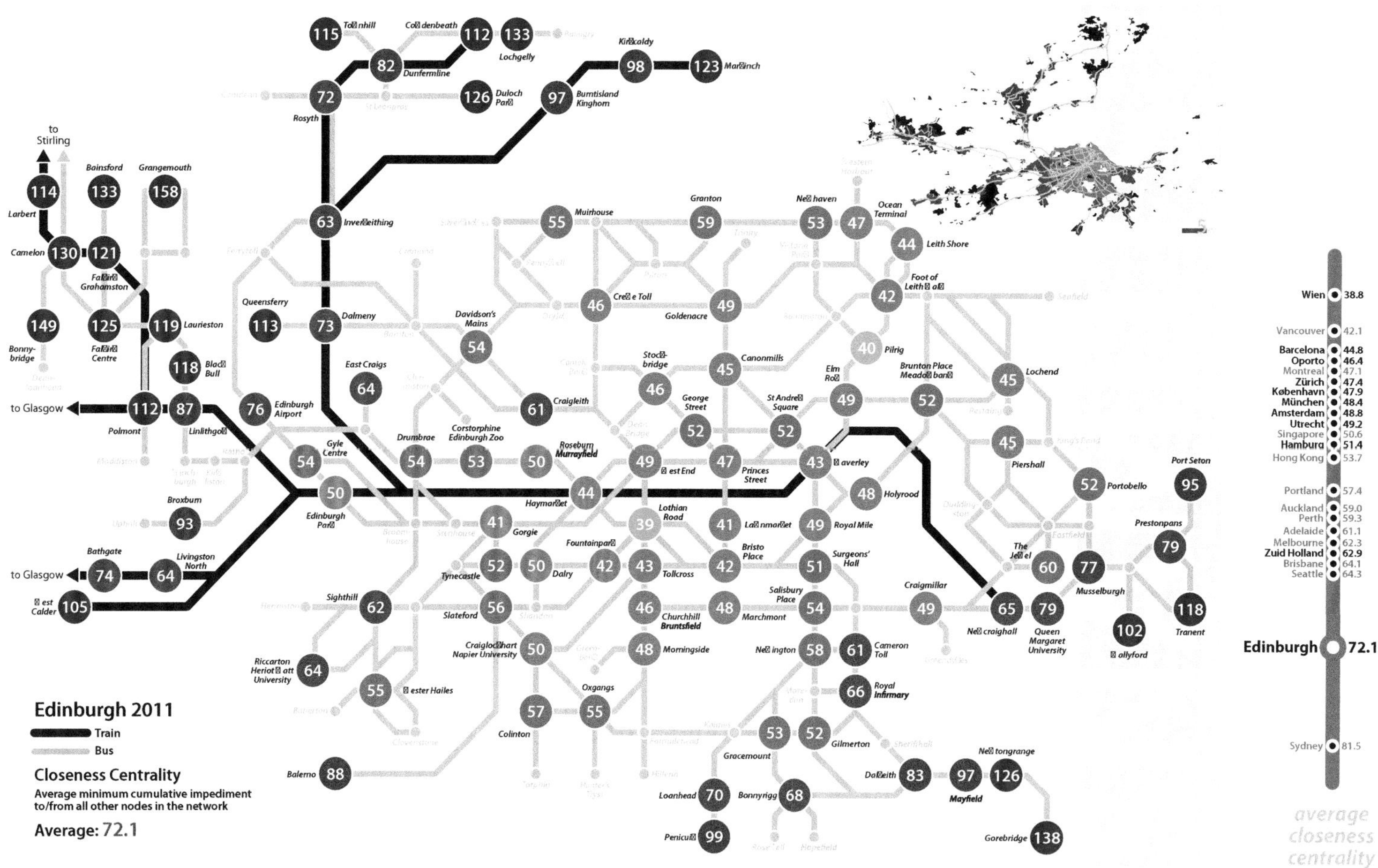

destinations than the (faster) rail corridors. This may be indicative of the inherent conflict between the configuration of the network for competition between operators and the quest to optimise accessibility outcomes to public transport users.

Network Coverage

Geographical network coverage extends to less than 60 per cent of metropolitan Edinburgh's residents and jobs, thus trailing the European cohort of case study cities jointly with Utrecht and Hamburg. While coverage within the core city is nearly universal, it rapidly becomes patchier in suburban areas. This is further accentuated by the peripheral location of some rail stations in neighbouring towns and the lack of bus feeder services at the minimum standard. Livingston is a prime example for this shortfall, but significant coverage gaps are also on record for Falkirk, Kirkcaldy, Glenrothes and North Berwick.

Contour Catchments

There is an accessibility divide between Edinburgh's core city and the surrounding region. Within the City of Edinburgh, where the bus network forms a relatively tightly-woven, interconnected

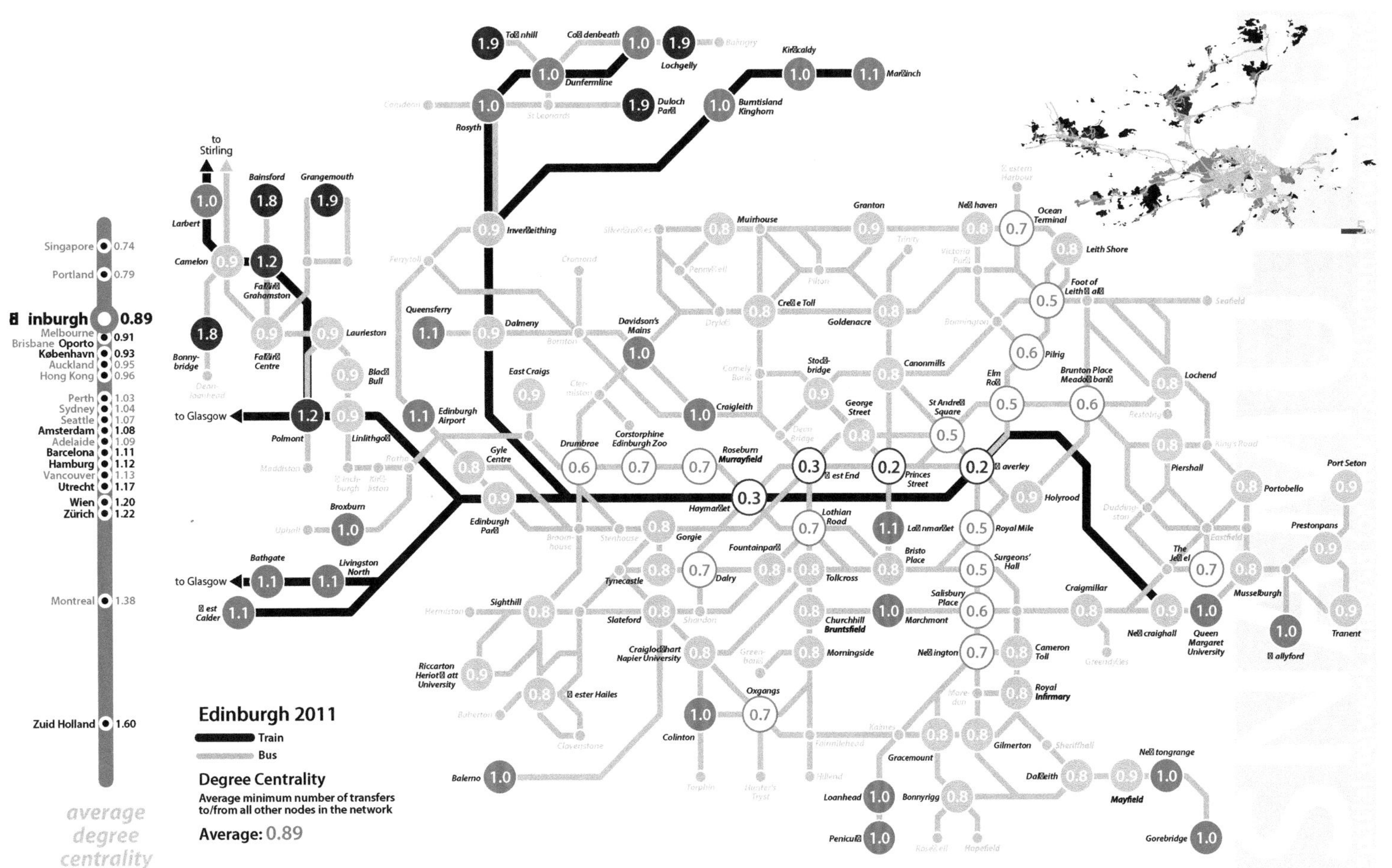

grid, 30-minute contours decline gradually and concentrically from peak values of 36–7 per cent near the two rail stations. Seventeen nodes – one-sixth of the total – offer maximum 30-minute journeys to and from a quarter or more of all metropolitan residents and jobs. While such a proportion is rarely achieved in Australasian cities, in a European context it is an unimpressive result – comparatively-sized Oporto records twice as many nodes that fulfil this criterion, and Edinburgh trails the European SNAMUTS sample in terms of average relative contour catchment size.

Outside the core city, the only nodes achieving contour catchment counts in excess of 10 per cent are located on either side of the Firth of Forth bridge (Dalmeny-Queensferry and Inverkeithing). Elsewhere, the paucity of frequent rail corridors, the low speed of bus services and the lack of public transport links between suburban centres at the minimum standard are apparent. It should be noted, however, that the figures shown for nodes in the west of the metropolitan area – West Lothian and Falkirk – disguise the proximity of this sub-region to destinations in neighbouring Glasgow suburbs, which would add to overall accessibility if they were considered in the analysis (Halden, 2002).

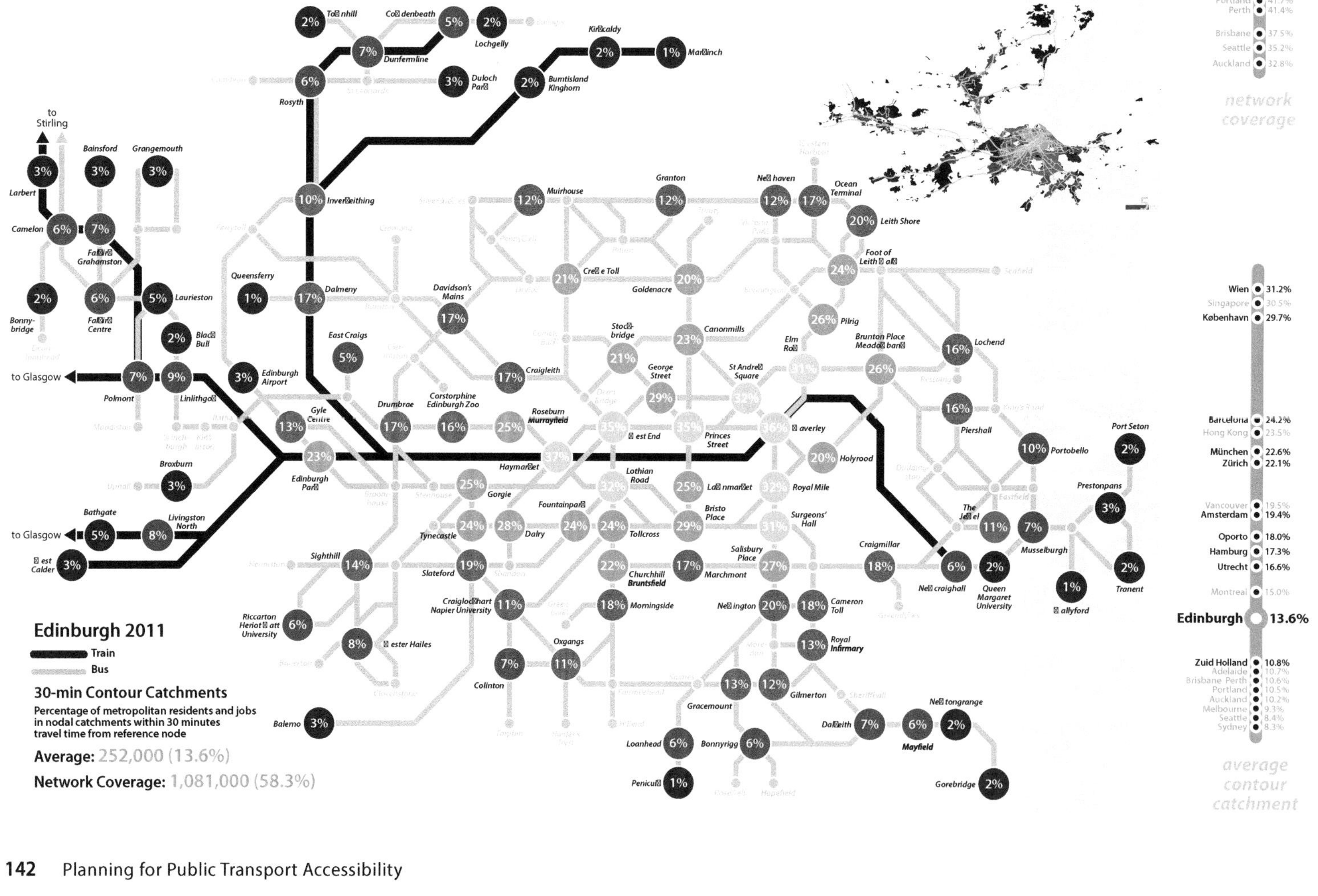

Edinburgh 2011

Train

Bus

30-min Contour Catchments

Percentage of metropolitan residents and jobs in nodal catchments within 30 minutes travel time from reference node

Average: 252,000 (13.6%)

Network Coverage: 1,081,000 (58.3%)

Singapore 482
København 447
Hong Kong 437
Wien 430
Amsterdam 388
Zürich 387
Utrecht 376
Oporto 374
Vancouver 367
Barcelona 357
München 327
Edinburgh 310
Adelaide 289
Hamburg 275
Montreal 274
Perth 249
Auckland 239
Portland 230
Brisbane Zuid Holland 227
Seattle 201
Sydney 198
Melbourne 175

global betweenness

Singapore 3.69%
Vancouver 3.22%
Utrecht 3.16%
Oporto 3.03%
København 2.82%
Edinburgh 2.76%
Portland 2.67%
Amsterdam 2.56%
Montreal 2.51%
Wien 2.49%
München 2.48%
Adelaide 2.36%
Hong Kong Barcelona 2.30%
Zürich 2.26%
Auckland 2.17%
Perth 2.06%
Brisbane 1.93%
Zuid Holland Hamburg 1.87%
Sydney 1.80%
Melbourne 1.55%
Seattle 1.54%

catchment of typical path

Hong Kong 20.2%
Barcelona 20.4%
Singapore 20.9%
Amsterdam 22.5%
Hamburg 23.2%
Wien 23.5%
Vancouver 23.9%
København 24.1%
Portland 27.9%
Zürich 28.8%
München 29.1%
Montreal 30.3%
Brisbane 31.7%
Sydney 32.1%
Melbourne 32.7%
Auckland 35.7%
Zuid Holland 36.3%
Edinburgh 38.1%
Perth 40.2%
Seattle Utrecht 42.8%
Oporto 43.1%
Adelaide 62.0%

segmental betweenness cbd

Betweenness Centrality

The global betweenness score in Edinburgh relative to population and jobs is at the lower end of the European sample, outperforming only Zuid Holland and Hamburg. Edinburgh compares particularly unfavourably with similarly-sized Oporto and Utrecht, not to mention only marginally larger Zurich. The subdued performance on this proxy measure for the overall 'presence' of public transport travel opportunities in an urban agglomeration may be attributed to the underdeveloped capacity of rail and bus networks, and of the networks of different bus operators, to support each other in optimising accessibility outcomes. This index highlights the limitation of the competition-based UK governance model of public transport supply as an opportunity cost to users and as a constraint to effective competition with the car.

Travel opportunities on Edinburgh's public transport network appear to be concentrated on a half-dozen radial bus spines (Leith Walk, London Road, Nicolson Road, Lothian Road, Slateford

München 78.9%
Barcelona 75.9%
København 66.4%
Hamburg 64.9%
Wien 61.1%
Zürich 60.0%
Sydney 58.3%
Zuid Holland 53.5%
Melbourne 52.3%
Montreal 50.1%
Portland 49.9%
Perth Amsterdam 46.2%
Utrecht 43.6%
Vancouver 42.3%
Singapore 39.6%
Brisbane 35.8%
Oporto 32.0%
Adelaide 21.3%
Hong Kong 19.7%
Edinburgh 16.4%
Auckland 15.5%
Seattle 8.8%

segmental betweenness rail

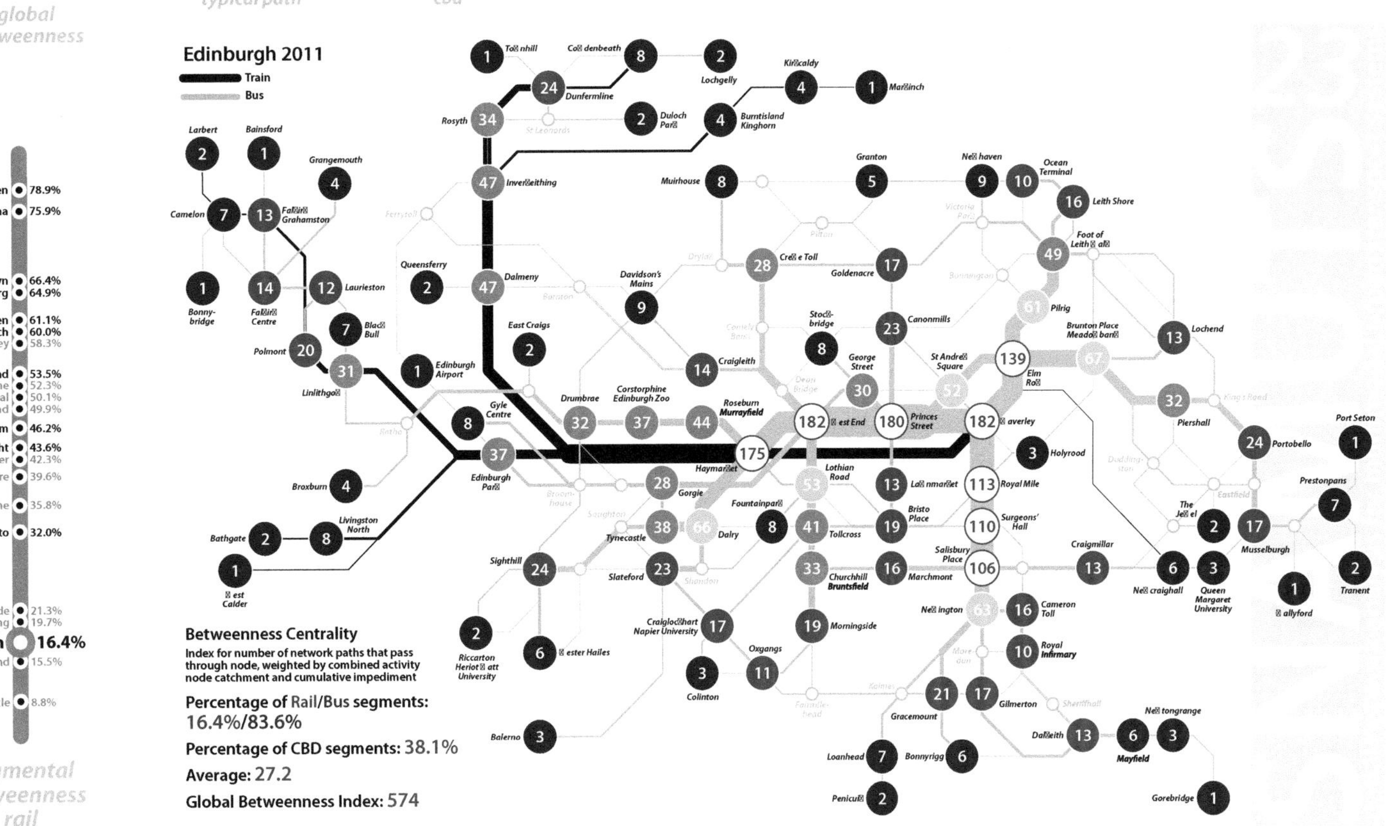

Road, Corstorphine Road) and the rail trunk line between Edinburgh and Inverkeithing, which appears to be the only suburban rail service that displays a modicum of network integration with bus services in its corridor. In practice, this may limit a perception of easy public transport access to users with origins and destinations in the immediate vicinity of these spines, while dropping off rapidly with growing distance. The relative importance of the city centre to facilitate public transport movement throughout the metropolitan region is slightly lower than in Oporto and Utrecht, but higher than in the larger European cities. The importance of rail modes in the same context remains more marginal than in any other European cities and shows room for improvement.

Network Resilience

The high service input present particularly on Edinburgh's bus routes, in combination with the widespread deployment of relatively large (double-deck) buses, produces a high average count of segmental resilience in the network. This suggests that the system, in theory, has sufficient resilience to absorb some future growth in patronage. In practice, however, capacity problems may be of a nature not sufficiently captured by this index. It is difficult to imagine, for instance, that the number of buses plying Princes Street could be further increased without exacerbating

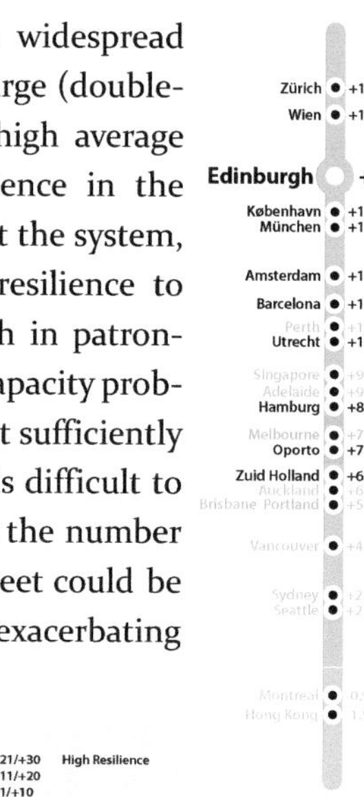

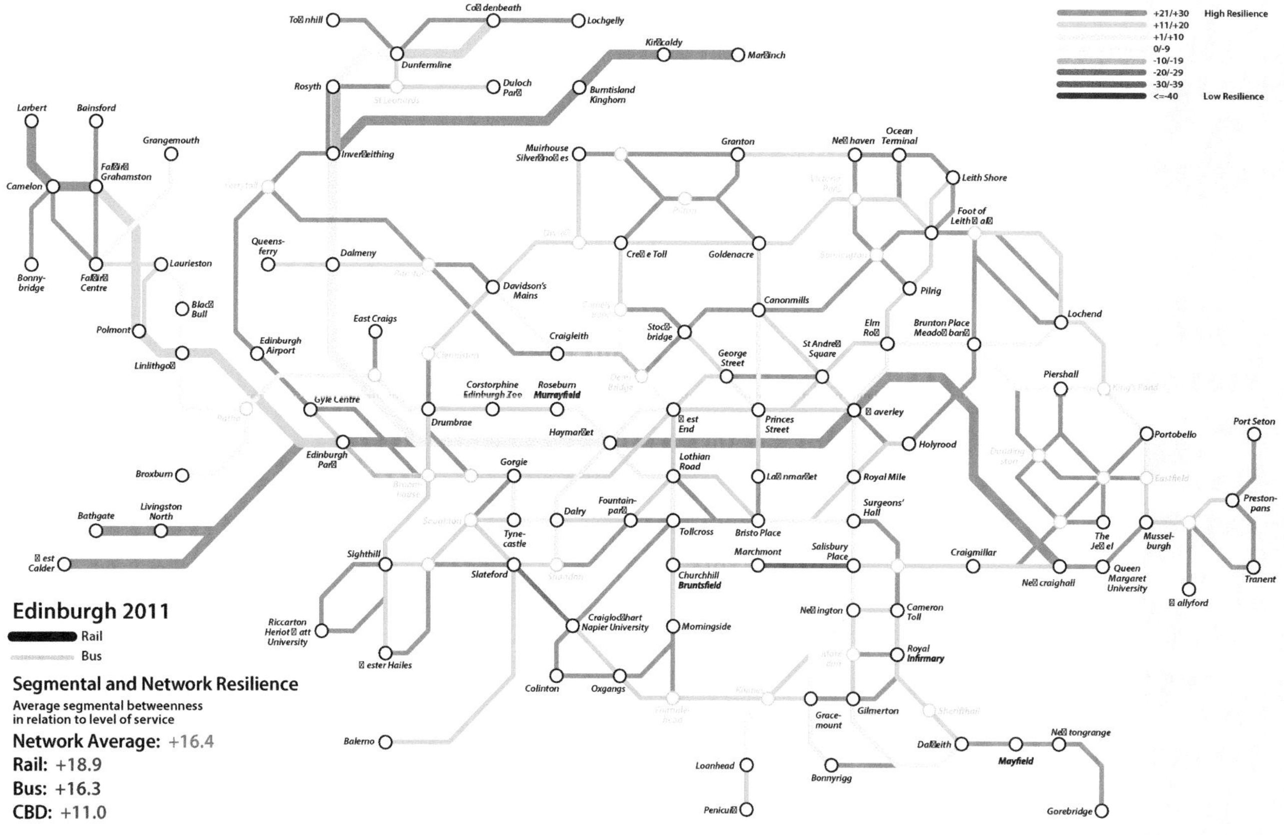

Edinburgh 2011

Rail
Bus

Segmental and Network Resilience

Average segmental betweenness in relation to level of service

Network Average: +16.4
Rail: +18.9
Bus: +16.3
CBD: +11.0

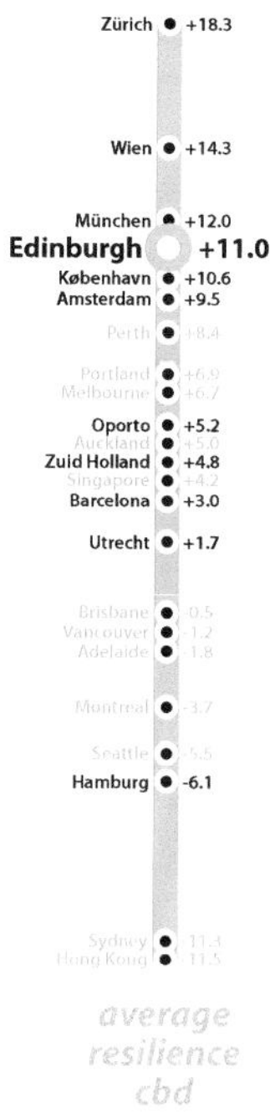

+21/+30 High Resilience
+11/+20
+1/+10
0/-9
-10/-19
-20/-29
-30/-39
<=-40 Low Resilience

Zürich +18.3
Wien +14.3
München +12.0
Edinburgh +11.0
København +10.6
Amsterdam +9.5
Oporto +5.2
Zuid Holland +4.8
Barcelona +3.0
Utrecht +1.7
Hamburg -6.1
average resilience cbd

an already unsatisfactory situation of operational reliability and pedestrian amenity on what is nominally a car-free boulevard. Rather, it appears desirable to reduce the number of bus movements in this and several other corridors without generating detrimental effects to accessibility and the quality of service. As the only tangible example of a network resilience shortfall in the current network configuration, the low service frequency (30 minutes interpeak) of the rail service between Dunfermline and Edinburgh seems to hamper the efficiency of what is perhaps the only relatively functional bus feeder sub-network to rail in the metropolitan area.

Nodal Connectivity

The nodal connectivity average is the lowest in the European SNAMUTS sample reflecting the weak role for high-capacity public transport modes and indicating a fundamental difficulty for public transport users to undertake spatially flexible journeys beyond the city's key corridor (Princes Street) with a sense of ease akin to the car. The suitability of suburban rail nodes as public transport destinations remains severely compromised unless rail frequencies are significantly improved.

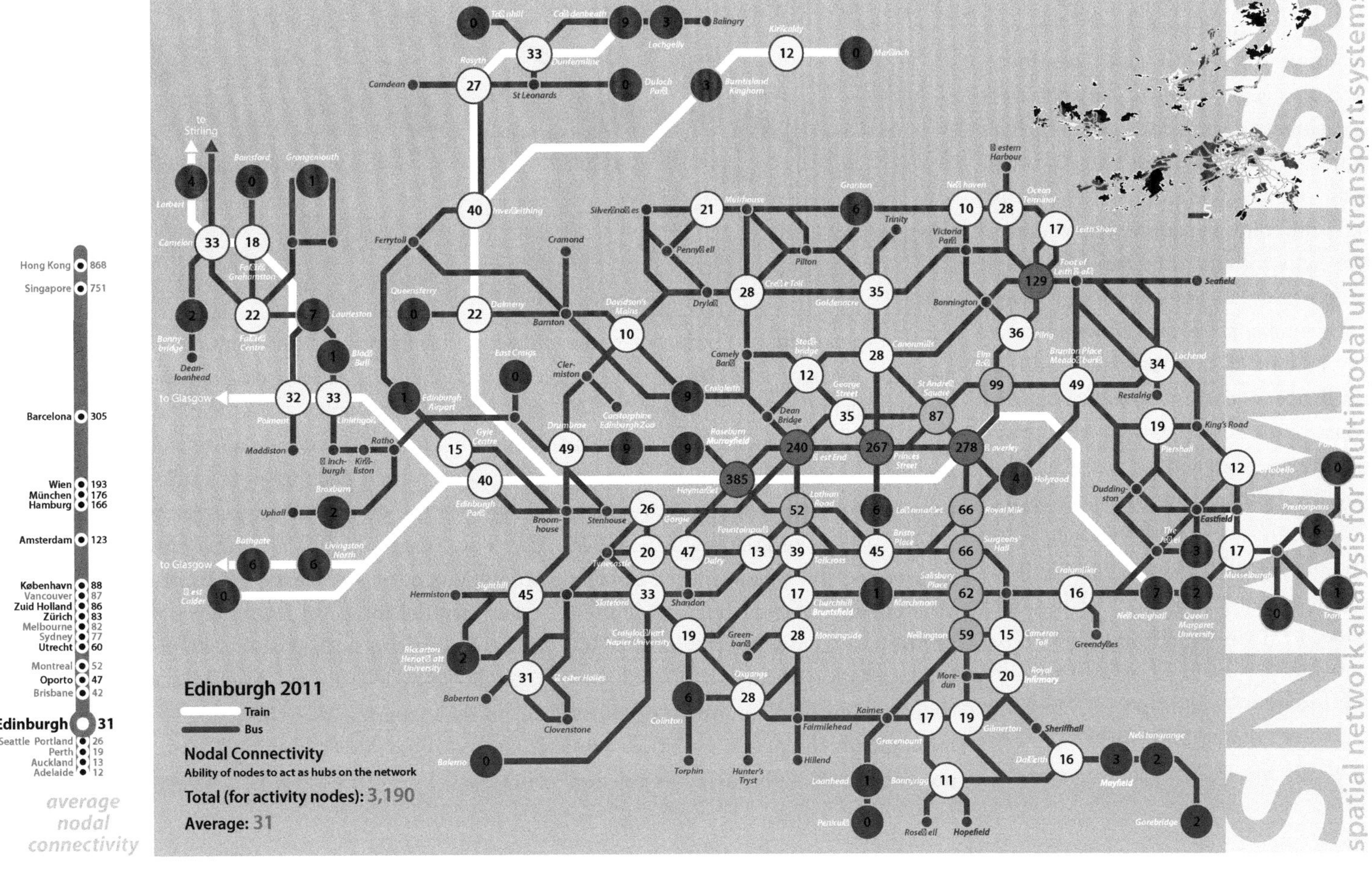

SNAMUTS Composite Accessibility Index and Reflections

Edinburgh's public transport system is representative of a particular approach to network design and service configuration, bearing parallels to that found in the Asian and in some Australasian case study cities, but differing fundamentally from that followed across continental Europe and much of North America. It consists of bus services where individual routes are operated at medium frequencies (every 10 or every 15 minutes is typical) but where overlaps of several routes on key corridors occasionally generate extremely high cumulative frequencies. These overlapping routes are configured to fan out into different corridors elsewhere on the network and thus provide a high proportion of transfer-free linkages between disparate parts of the city. The key benefit of this approach is a high resilience to real and potential capacity constraints as the city's busiest corridors are flooded with services. Simultaneously, however, bus networks such as Edinburgh's are beset by a much higher and more spatially concentrated operational requirement for vehicles compared to the alternative of providing a network consisting of only one or two high-frequency routes per corridor and a greater reliance on transfers (Nielsen et al, 2005).

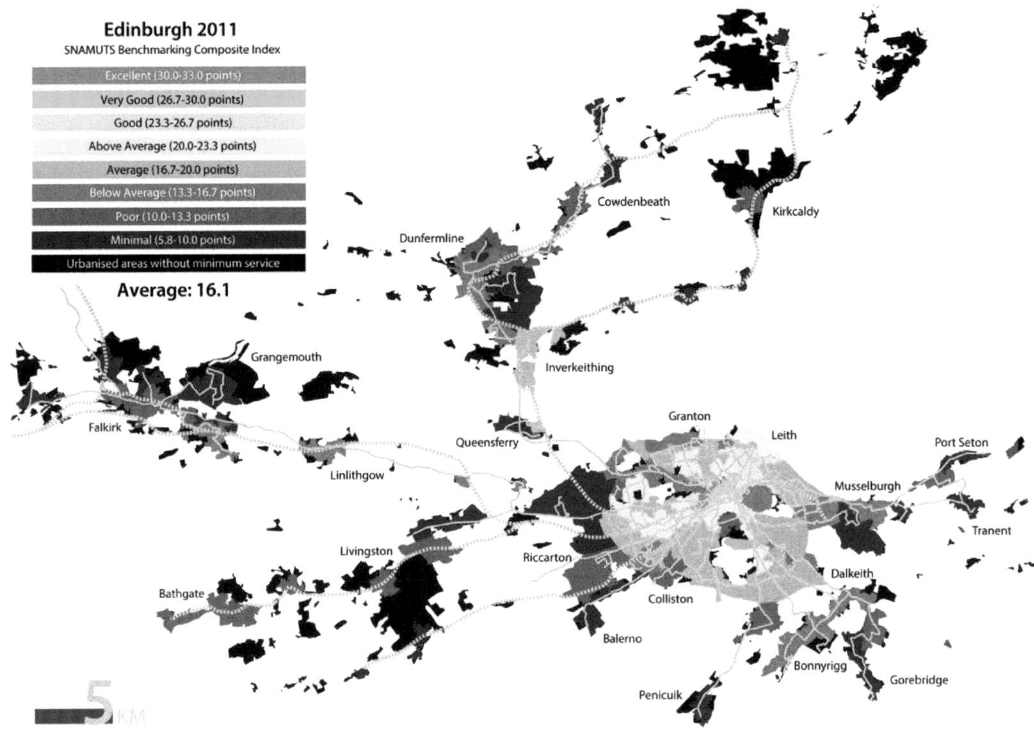

The composite map shows that these network design shortfalls translate into accessibility deficiencies. While the bus network provides for good area coverage of the core city, the range of urban precincts with superior accessibility (yellow or green) where public transport could be considered a viable alternative to the car remains limited to the city centre and a handful of inner urban corridors. Current initiatives to develop a more pronounced hierarchy in the public transport supply, such as the light rail route opened in 2014, may help realise greater operational efficiencies as well as improve accessibility through an enhanced 'network effect'. The roll-out of the new mode, which has integrated ticketing with the dominant bus operator (Lothian Buses), could also enable the redeployment of buses away from corridors parallel to rail in favour of corridors connecting with the rail system, though some statutory constraints currently appear to limit the scope for such coordination (Karou and Hull, 2014).

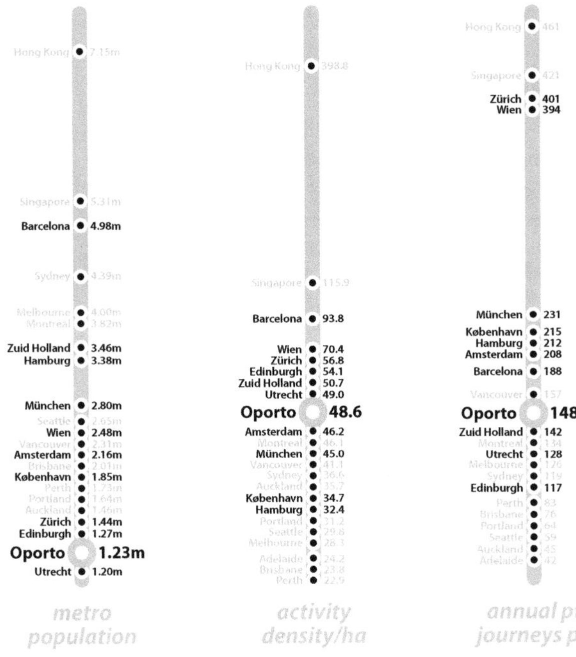

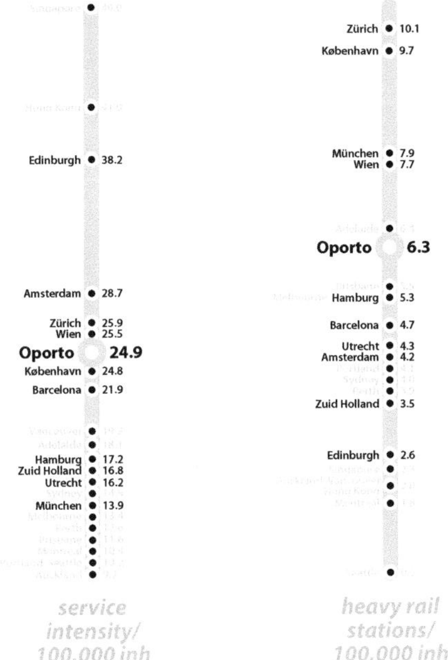

ACCESSIBILITY PROFILE: OPORTO, PORTUGAL

The metropolitan area of Oporto is the country's second largest urban agglomeration. It is located in the north-west of Portugal, stretches over 791 sq km and has a population of approximately 1.23 million residents. Perched around a deep gorge of the river Douro as it meets the Atlantic Ocean, many of the older districts are characterised by a fine-grained, dense urban fabric, often on steep slopes and sometimes only accessible through stairs. The newer districts are generally located on less topographically challenging terrain and significant settlement dispersal has occurred throughout the region in a gradual transition from rural to urban uses (Kasanko et al, 2006; Silva et al, 2014). These factors depress average urbanised density figures to 34.2 residents and 14.4 jobs per hectare (in 2001), similar to the majority of European SNAMUTS cities (except higher-density Vienna and Barcelona and lower-density Copenhagen and Hamburg).

Transport infrastructure for both road and public transport received significant investment during the decade or two prior to the Global Financial Crisis, with transformative effects both to car accessibility around the region and the structure of the public transport network (Silva and Pinho, 2008). A light rail system was opened in 2002 by linking several existing suburban commuter lines with two newly built tunnels in the CBD and several inner urban extensions at street level. The system can be understood as a second-generation light rail system, even though Oporto has also retained several lines of its first-generation tram system, which are operated with heritage vehicles and largely targeted at the recreational and tourist market.

While the light rail (metro) and the city bus system (STCP) have different operators, the opening of the light rail network led to a partial reorganisation of the bus system to integrate the two modes (Silva and Pinho, 2008). There is a common, smartcard-based ticketing system (Andante) which can also be used on the city's limited mainline suburban rail system, of which only two routes (to Ermesinde in the north-east, and to Granja along the southern coast) meet the minimum standard, and on a cable car servicing neighbourhoods at different levels of altitude along the Douro river gorge. Andante fares are based on a zone system with prices calculated per zone travelled through, up to a maximum of 12. There are single tickets, 24-hour tickets, and monthly passes whose price advantage kicks in at less than three weekly return journeys.

Service Intensity

Oporto's entire light rail network, 39 bus routes and the aforementioned two suburban rail trunk lines met the SNAMUTS minimum service standard in 2009. Oporto's service intensity relative to population is roughly equal to Copenhagen, Vienna or Zurich.

Individual metro routes have varying frequencies ranging from every 6 minutes on the north–south route to every 30 minutes on some outlying sections of suburban branches of the east–west route. The trunk section of the east–west route (Senhora da Hora to Campanhã) operated 16 trains per hour per direction in 2009. Most individual bus routes are operated every 10 to 20 minutes, but overlaps of several lines on many inner urban sections increase these frequencies accordingly.

Rail station density relative to population – all light rail stations, on- or off-street, are counted here – is slightly higher than in Hamburg or Barcelona, significantly higher than in the Dutch Randstad (where tram stops are not counted) and Edinburgh, but remains markedly below Copenhagen, Munich, Vienna and Zurich (where on-street tram stops are not counted either).

Closeness Centrality

Average closeness centrality across the network positions Oporto behind Vienna, Vancouver and Barcelona but

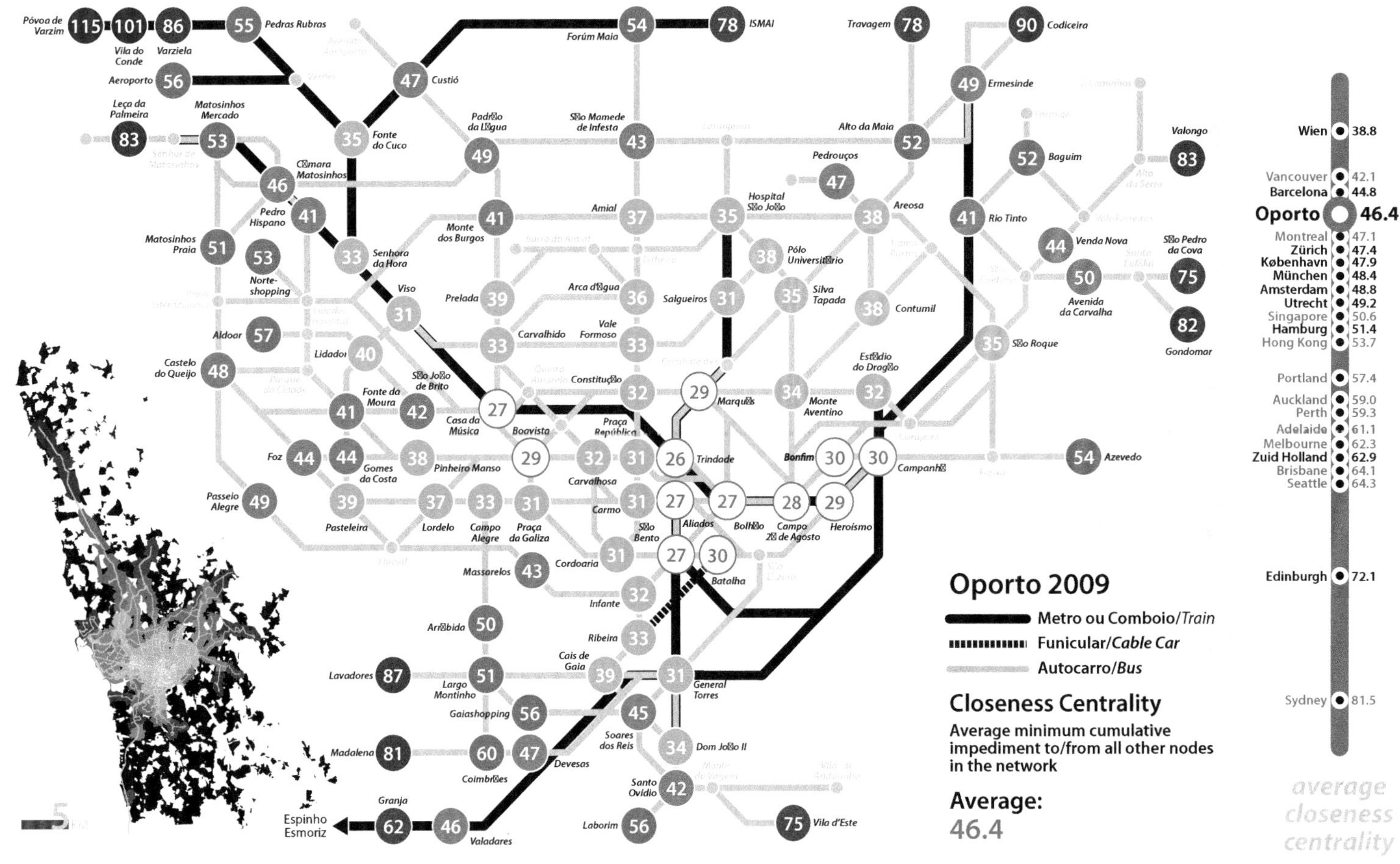

slightly ahead of the remaining European and Canadian cities. This is partially a result of Oporto's comparatively small size. Of Oporto's 96 identified activity nodes, 45 have a closeness score of 40 or less (47 per cent). They are mainly found in the coastal inner western suburbs and throughout the core city (the 240,000-strong municipality of Oporto). The poorest closeness centrality values in Oporto include significant centres in neighbouring municipalities (Valongo, Gondomar and Póvoa de Varzim, the most outlying activity node – 30 km from the central city).

Degree Centrality

Average degree centrality places Oporto in the cohort of 'low-transfer' cities within the European sample alongside Edinburgh, Copenhagen and Munich. Activity nodes with scores at or below this level are found throughout the municipal area of the core city, with the exception of the immediate waterfront (bus route 500), and along the light rail network. This is where the public transport system demonstrates a high degree of interconnectedness: despite the partial transition from a transfer-avoiding to a one route-one line type of network (Nielsen et al, 2005), most bus segments within the municipality of Oporto are still serviced by more than one line. These lines then branch

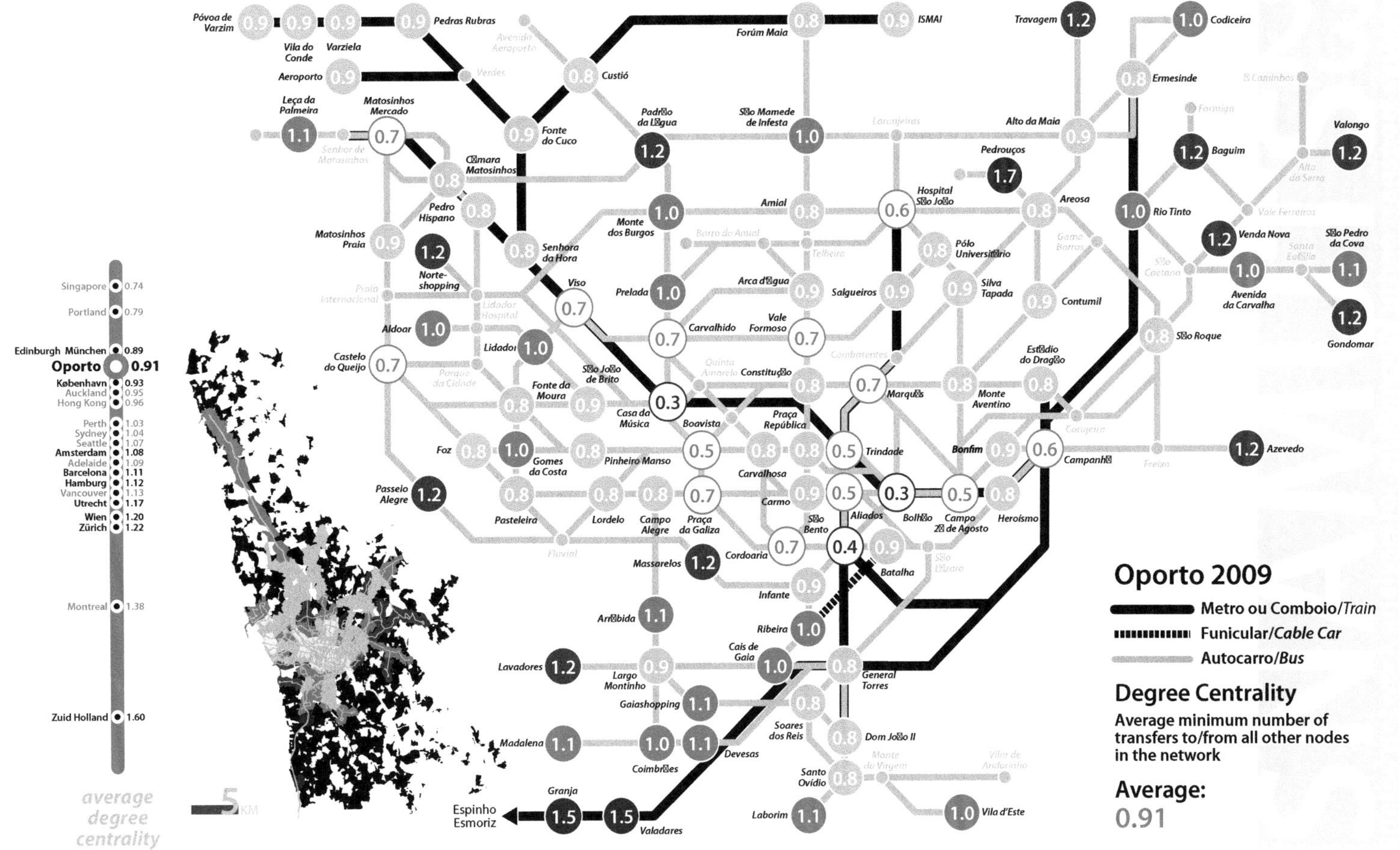

out into different directions at major network hubs and thus offer a greater choice of destinations to transfer-resistant passengers (albeit at lower frequencies than by making transfers). Hence, many bus lines in Oporto do not fit into the neat categories of radial or circumferential: they generate extra connectivity by combining both functions along parts of their routes. This network design is facilitated by a street network pattern in Oporto that has grown organically over a long period than the rigid rectangular street grids common to New World cities. In Oporto's suburbs, however, network density declines and degree centrality values fluctuate, reflecting the dominance of single-route services with a common central city terminus in those areas, and the relatively peripheral location of the main railway station.

Network Coverage

Public transport's geographical coverage places Oporto towards the lower end of the European sample, but slightly above Edinburgh, Hamburg and Utrecht. While the core city and neighbouring Matosinhos and Vila Nova de Gaia are mostly well-endowed with public transport services at the SNAMUTS standard within walking distance, there are sizeable gaps further to the north and

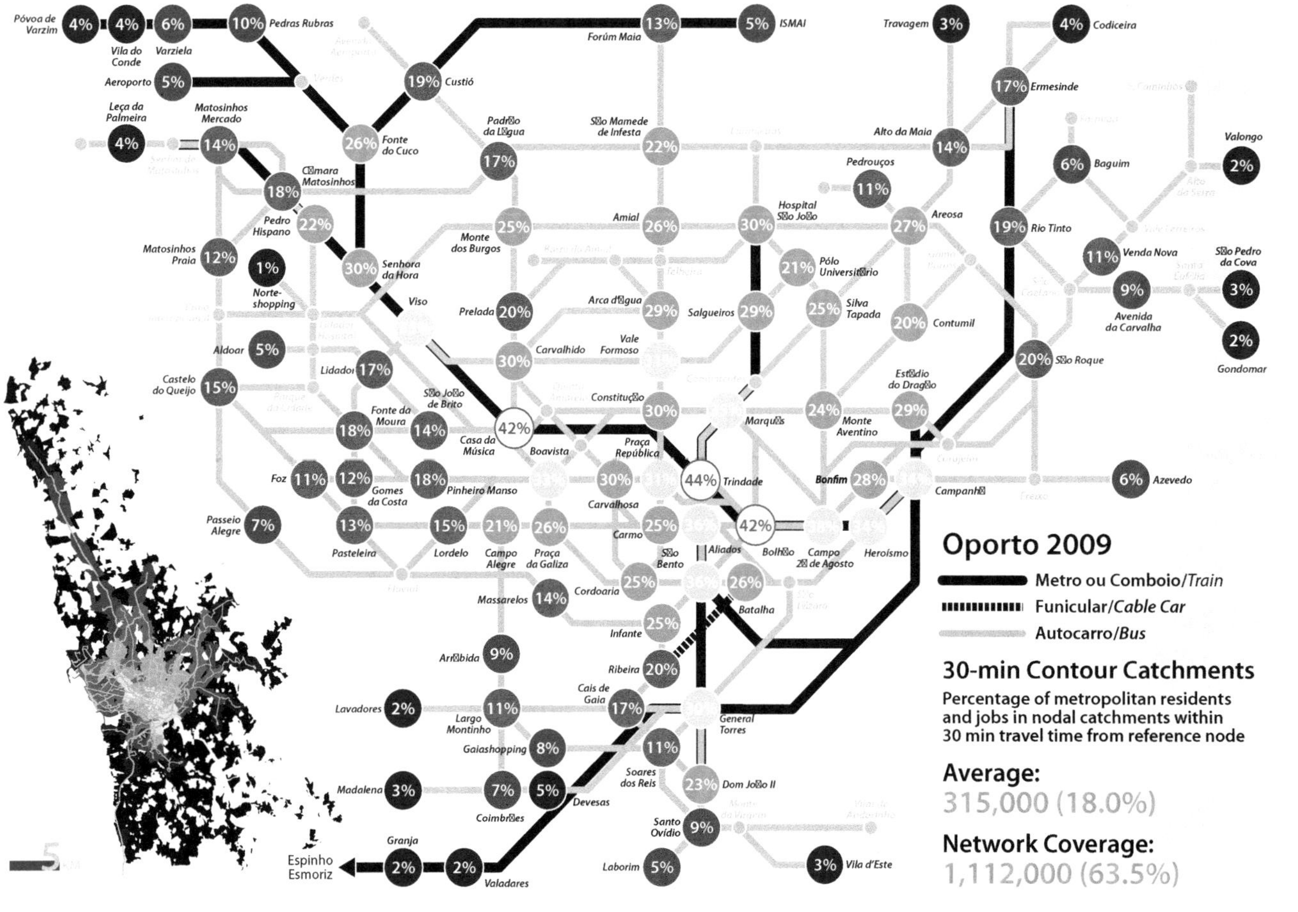

Oporto 2009

Metro ou Comboio/*Train*
Funicular/*Cable Car*
Autocarro/*Bus*

30-min Contour Catchments

Percentage of metropolitan residents and jobs in nodal catchments within 30 min travel time from reference node

Average:
315,000 (18.0%)

Network Coverage:
1,112,000 (63.5%)

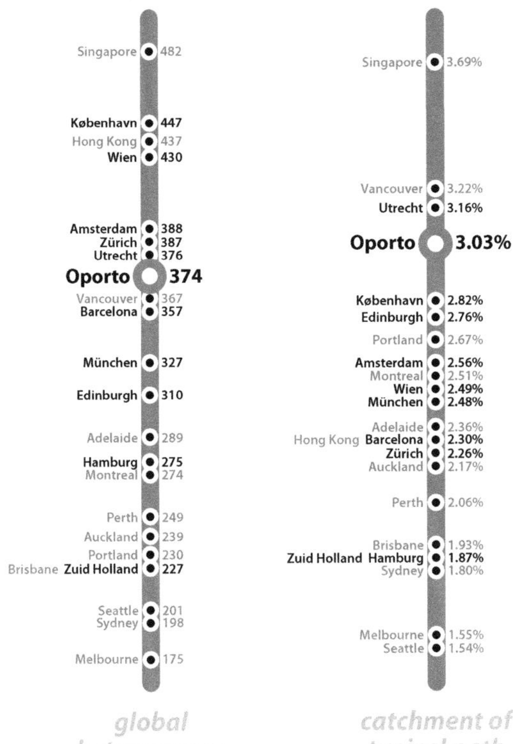

south. These underserviced areas indicate a patchy urbanisation pattern with weakly pronounced centres (Kasanko et al, 2006) and remnants of fragmentation among area-licensed public transport operators and their coordination, or lack thereof.

Contour Catchments

There are 33 nodes in Oporto (more than one third of the total) from where a quarter or more of all metropolitan residents and jobs are accessible by way of a public transport journey of 30 minutes or less. These nodes are aligned along the two metro trunk lines, the city centre and in several neighbourhoods in the north east of the city serviced only by buses. Conversely, only one node south of the river in Gaia (General Torres) offers this standard. The picture among significant suburban centres outside the City of Oporto is mixed: while Maia, Ermesinde and Matosinhos offer 30-minute travel times and 15-minute or better service frequencies to and from the heart of Oporto, one or the other (or both) is absent from Póvoa de Varzim, Valongo, Gondomar or the coastal communities in Gaia. In a European context, Oporto's average contour catchment is larger, in relative terms, than in more bus-dependent Edinburgh and in less compact Utrecht. It is, however, smaller than in Zurich, which is also not compact but counterweighs a dispersed settlement pattern with a dense and fast rail network.

Betweenness Centrality

In a balanced network, the highest-performing route segments on this index should coincide with the highest-performing transport modes; thus in Oporto, light rail and suburban rail segments should on the whole carry greater betweenness weight than bus routes. Both the north–south and the east–west light rail trunk routes perform well on this index, underscoring the significance of these recent additions to the network. Suburban rail routes, however, have low betweenness scores, associated with low service frequency (both routes share their tracks with regional and long-distance services) and deficient intermodal integration with the bus system, especially on the southern route. The bus system is characterised by high, perhaps excessive, betweenness scores along the central section (Boavista/Casa da Música via Carmo and Cordoaria to Bolhão) and further east along the radial route towards São Roque and beyond to Venda Nova and Gondomar – a corridor where light rail was extended in 2011 (post analysis). In 2009, it was notable how the then light rail terminus at Estádio do Dragão was not utilised as an interchange for bus feeders from the north-eastern suburbs, even though this may have facilitated shorter travel times and greater operational efficiency in the area before the opening of the eastern light rail line (which, however, also features only minimal integration with the bus network).

Overall, buses absorb a large majority of network-wide travel opportunities. This mismatch between modal performance and network significance indicates a light rail system still under development and a suburban rail system with significant latent potential if capacity/service frequency and network integration can be improved.

Oporto records the second highest share of segmental betweenness values occurring on CBD segments across the global sample after Adelaide. The central city's location along the Douro gorge with limited crossing points is a factor here, as is the strong radial orientation of the rail lines.

Network Resilience

Occurrences of poor segmental resilience levels in Oporto appear to be limited to the bus network: the eastern corridor to São Roque and Venda Nova (since strengthened by a light rail extension); radial lines along Rua Vale Formoso and Rua Amial; and the orbital corridor along Estrada Circunvalação are the most conspicuous examples. Poor

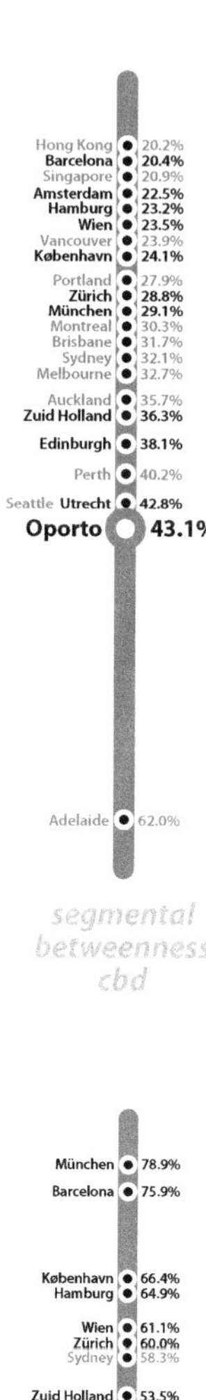

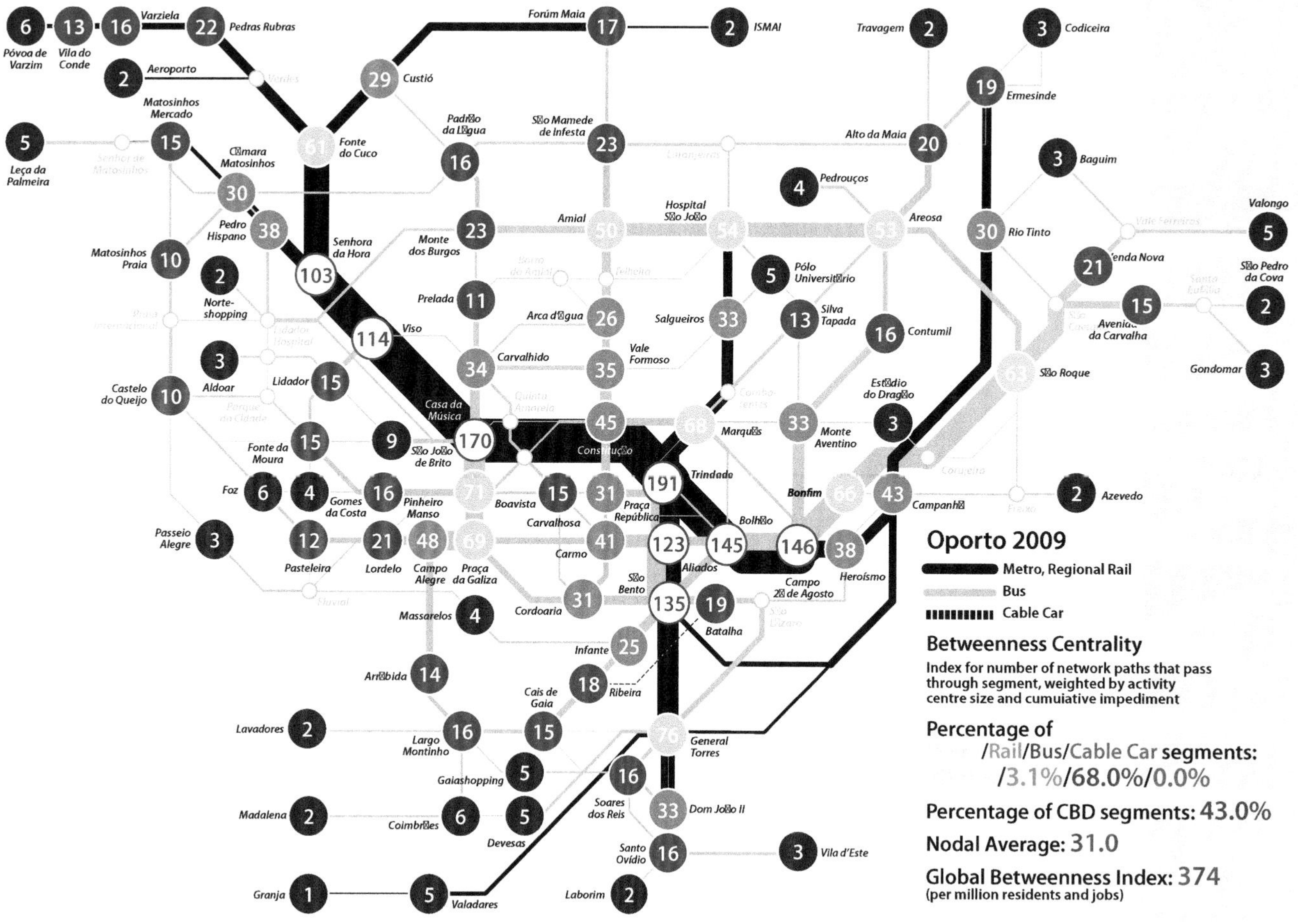

Oporto 2009

Metro, Regional Rail
Bus
Cable Car

Betweenness Centrality

Index for number of network paths that pass through segment, weighted by activity centre size and cumulative impediment

Percentage of /Rail/Bus/Cable Car segments: /3.1%/68.0%/0.0%

Percentage of CBD segments: 43.0%

Nodal Average: 31.0

Global Betweenness Index: 374
(per million residents and jobs)

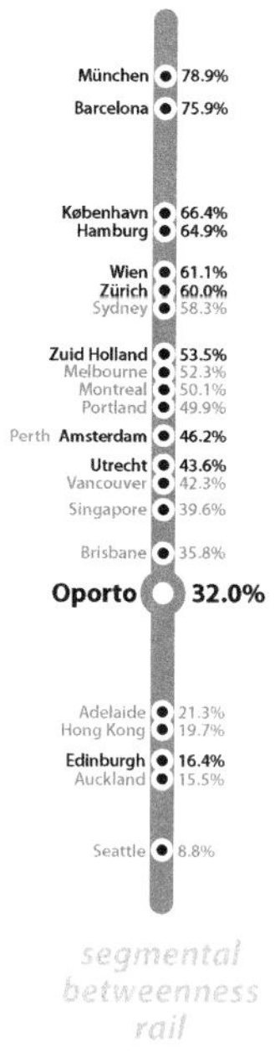

resilience values are also evident at the three river crossings (between Campo Alegre and Arrábida, Ribeira and Cais de Gaia, and São Lázaro and General Torres).

The relatively sluggish resilience performance, particularly on the bus system, is a concern. Within the European sample, Oporto's average network resilience for buses is second worst before Zuid Holland, where buses play a comparatively marginal role in the mix of public transport modes. The combination of this circumstance and the dominance of the network by buses (documented by the segmental betweenness results discussed above) indicates a land use–transport system where rail or tram networks have not yet grown to a size that would allow for a well-balanced sharing of tasks with buses across the metropolitan area. Meanwhile, buses are tasked to serve a range of corridors where public transport remains vulnerable to either overcrowding or to a performance below the potential that the spatial patterns of land use would suggest, or a coincidence of both.

Nodal Connectivity

The connectivity index highlights those activity nodes most suited for clustering land uses to capitalise on the public transport 'movement economy'. Other

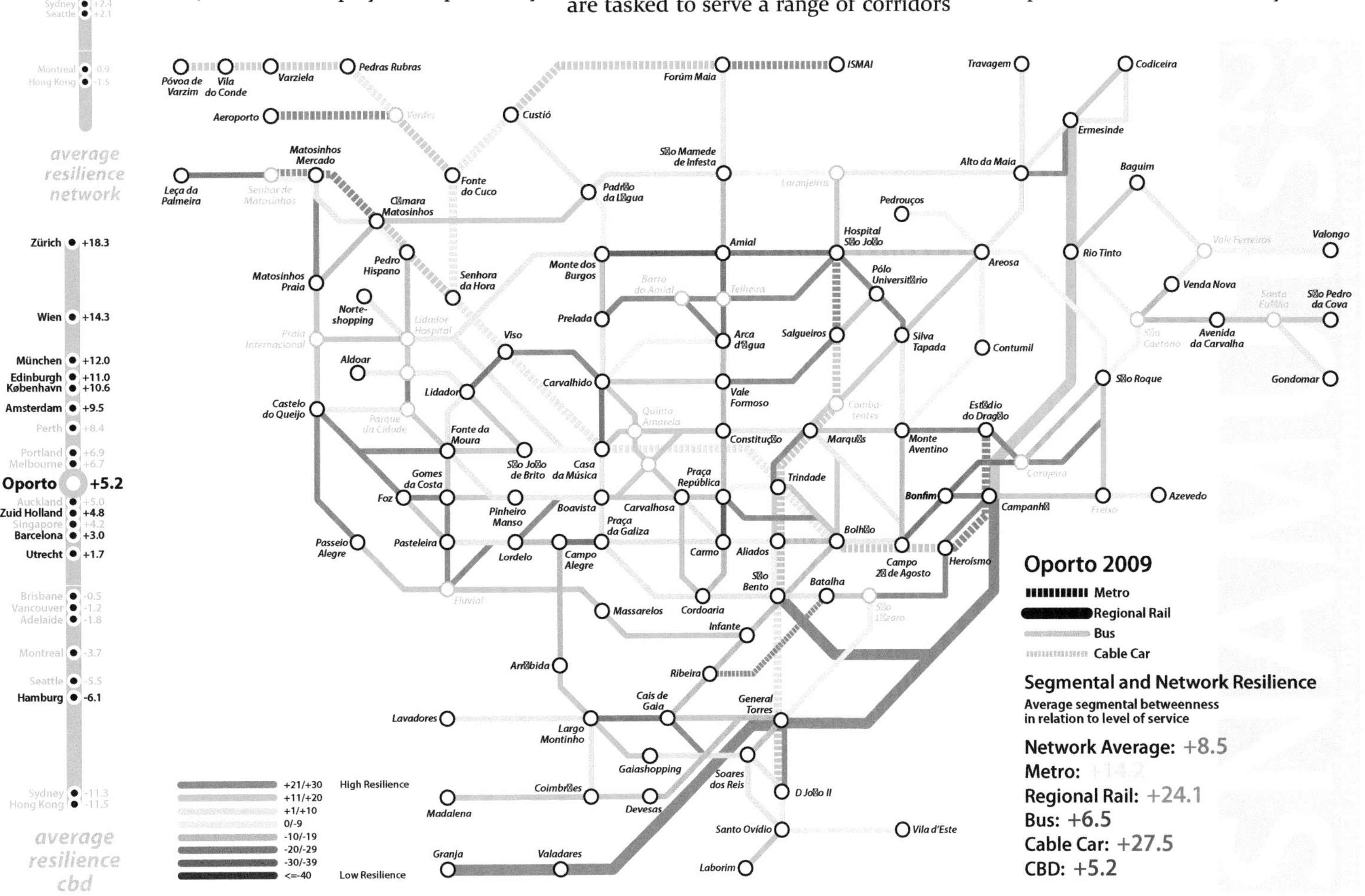

than the nodes around the major light rail stations in the city centre, the high performance of Campanhã (Oporto's main rail terminal) and General Torres is notable. Matosinhos, Hospital São João and Areosa are also significant, while most bus-only nodes perform poorly.

In a European context, Oporto has the second poorest nodal connectivity results of all case study cities before Edinburgh. This can be partially attributed to Oporto's comparatively small size (performance on this index invariably goes up as larger, more complex networks are assessed) and the continued high dependence on buses, whose limited occupancy rate depresses the outcomes on this measure. The best-connected nodes in the network are the two rail-to-rail interchanges at Trindade and Campanhã, though others such as São Bento and General Torres are not far behind.

SNAMUTS Composite Accessibility Index and Reflections

The role of the light rail trunk lines in facilitating superior public transport accessibility is evident from this index. Apart from the heart of the CBD (the Trindade–Bolhão–São Bento area), a second accessibility hotspot is apparent around Boavista and Casa de Música. In contrast, the suburban rail lines

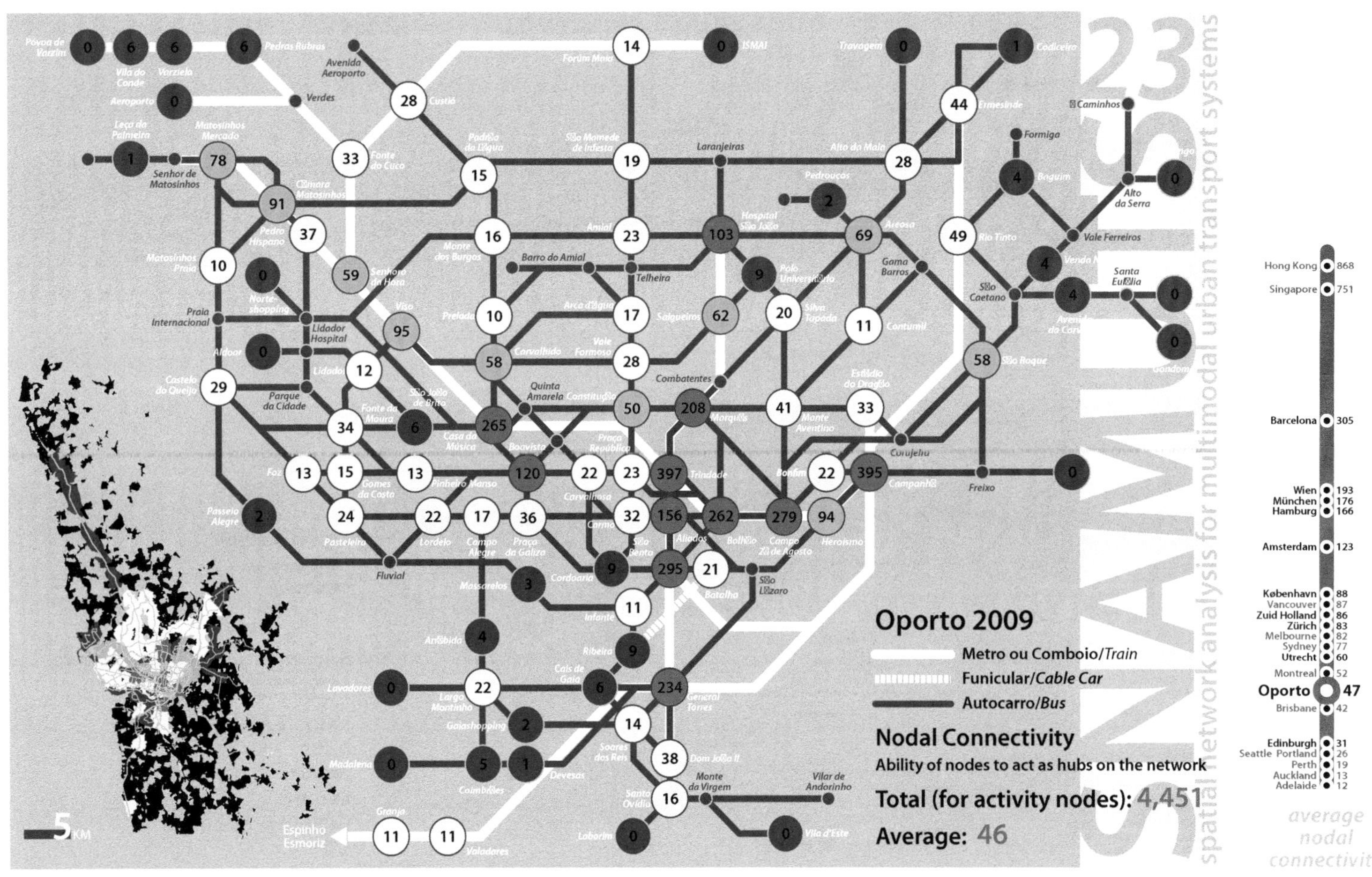

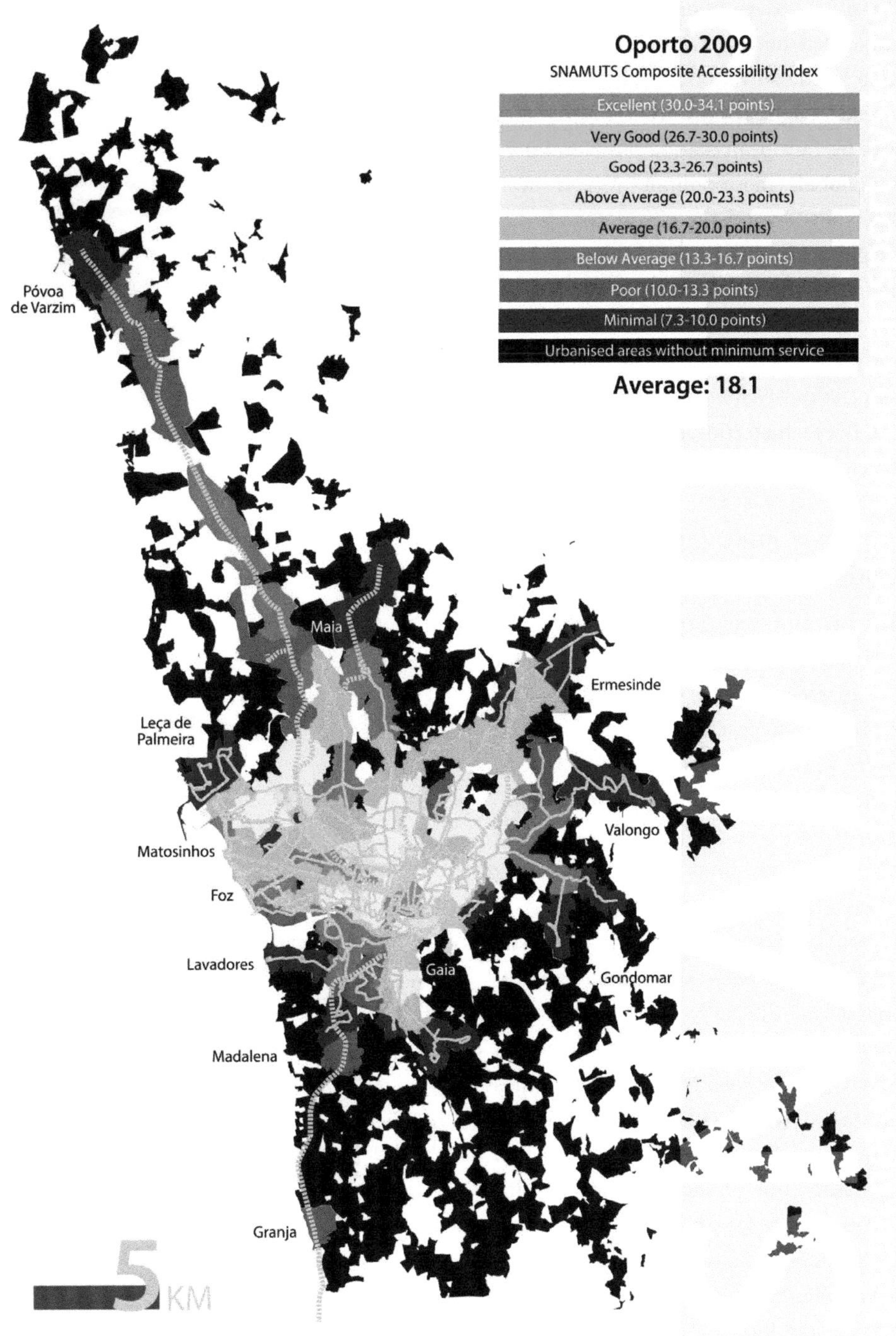

generate a degree of public transport endowment along their corridors, but low frequencies and the peripheral location of the terminus at Campanhã contribute to the lower performance on this index. There are bus-based corridors of above-average performance in the middle north-eastern suburbs (Areosa; São Roque). A rapid decline in accessibility is evident in the coastal western half of the core city around Foz, and across the Douro River in Vila Nova de Gaia (with the exception of the light rail corridor along Avenida da República). In both cases, the geographical effects of constraining water bodies are considered a factor.

Beyond the core city (north of the river), public transport coverage gaps at the SNAMUTS standard are apparent from about 6 km onwards; on the southern side of the Douro, this distance is far smaller. While many suburban centres have a history that predates motorisation and industrialisation (both of which commenced later in Portugal than in other Western countries), the dispersal of urban development in late twentieth-century Oporto appears to have occurred at a faster pace than in many other European cities and was accompanied by population declines in central areas (Kasanko et al, 2006; Oliveira et al, 2013). The establishment of a more hierarchical public transport network with a stronger high-performance element may help reverse this trend.

ACCESSIBILITY PROFILE: HAMBURG (GERMANY)

Hamburg is one of Germany's 16 federal states and one of three city-states, covering an area of around 75,000 hectares with just under 1.8 million inhabitants in 2013. The tradition of political autonomy goes back many centuries and laid the foundations for a partial polycentric structure, following the historic establishment of secondary urban centres in the territory of neighbouring jurisdictions. A series of territorial amalgamations left the city-state at roughly its present geographical expansion by 1937, but prior to that, particularly during the 1910s and 1920s, there was competition between Hamburg and the surrounding state (then Prussia) to lure wealthy aspiring suburbanites into scenic peripheral locations in their respective territory. This competition culminated in the early establishment (1908 and 1912), one by each state, of two urban rapid transit systems to service these new suburbs and which form the basis of today's U-Bahn (Hamburg) and S-Bahn (German Rail) systems.

World War II bombing resulted in major changes to urban structure where neighbourhoods were rebuilt at significantly reduced densities and in adherence to the dominant paradigm of the era, that of functional segregation. Post-war planning objectives aimed to strengthen the polycentric structure of the agglomeration (Kähler, 2012). Contemporary average density – 62.4 residents and jobs per urbanised hectare within the city-state, 20.0 in the surrounding region – shows a recent slight upward trend but remains low by European standards. Hamburg's functional metropolitan region now stretches beyond the city state into the neighbouring states of Schleswig-Holstein (to the north) and Lower Saxony (to the south). Our analysis is based on the service area of the regional transport association (*Hamburger Verkehrsverbund* or *HVV*) which comprises Hamburg and seven neighbouring counties. In 2013 the population was 3.38 million, a modest increase of 16,000 (less than half a per cent) since 2008.

The two aforementioned metro systems now form an integrated system under the auspices of HVV, which was the first regional transport association of its kind in the world when it was founded in 1965 (Pucher and Kurth, 1996; Topp, 1989). The metro systems are supplemented by regional rail lines operated by a mix of privately, federally (German Rail) and regionally owned (AKN) companies. The expansive bus network includes 23 high-frequency, specially branded MetroBus routes (every 10 minutes or better, seven days a week), many local lines and a handful of express routes, and is dominated by two mostly state-owned operators, one of them (VHH) in joint ownership by Hamburg and Schleswig-Holstein. In addition, two ferry routes across the harbour meet the minimum service standard.

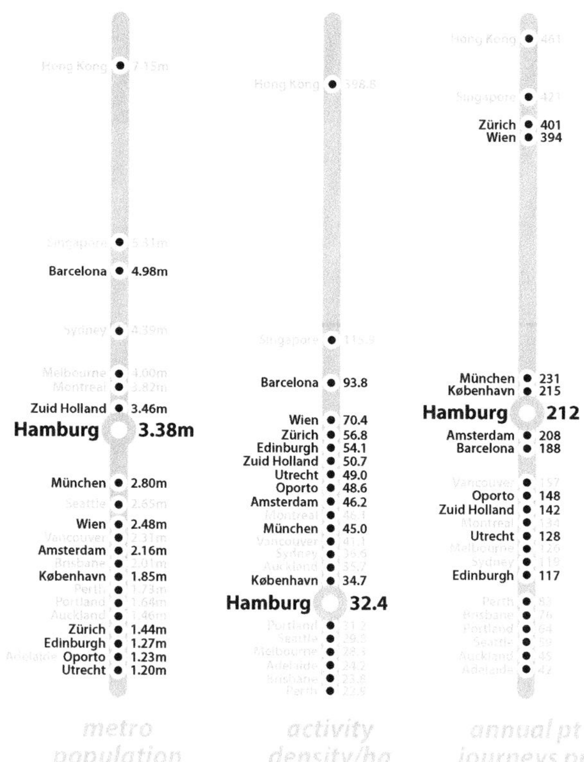

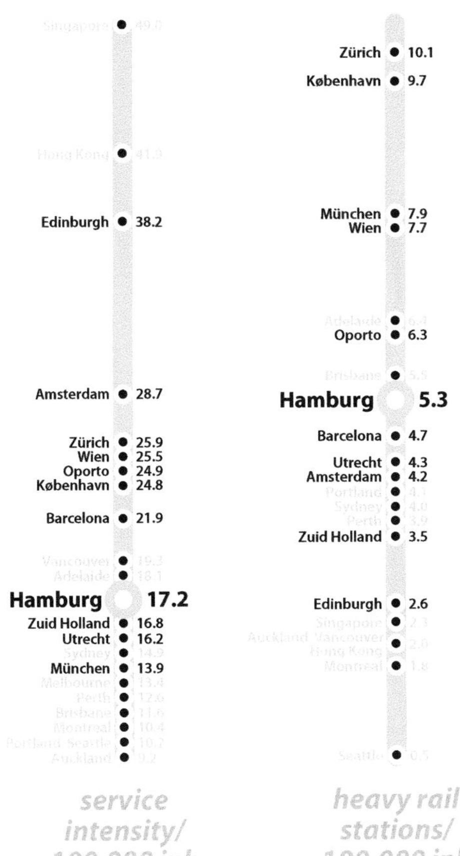

The HVV ticketing system offers strong incentives towards monthly and annual tickets, which are being utilised by nearly three quarters of all passengers (HVV, 2013). About 25 per cent of these periodical passes are salary-packaged through employers, while 10 per cent are heavily discounted off-peak passes. There are also single and daily tickets.

Service Intensity

Hamburg's metro routes, except for some outer suburban sections which run every 20 minutes, are generally operated every 10 minutes all day, seven days a week, with overlaps between lines on the S-Bahn system and short workings on the U-Bahn system creating 5-minute services on Mondays to Saturdays on most inner urban sections. Buses generally conform to the 10/20-minute template, generating a uniform 'pulse' across the network. Regional rail, however, delivers a mixed picture: on the Schleswig-Holstein side, the two AKN routes operate at 20-minute intervals on weekdays, and the DB routes to Elmshorn and Lübeck generally conform to this standard too (by way of a range of overlapping stopping patterns). On the Lower Saxony side, a mix of one local and one semi-express train per hour is common, so the SNAMUTS standard is met only at the major stations where both types of train stop.

Service intensity in Hamburg increased from 15.9 vehicles per 100,000 inhabitants in 2008 to 17.2 in 2013 (8 per cent growth), fostered by, and enabling, an increase in the number of annual public transport journeys per capita from 190 to 212 (12 per cent) during the same period. While the North German city is grouped with European case studies employing a 'frugal' approach to service provision, these figures show that some improvements have taken place in recent years. In a European context, heavy rail station density in Hamburg is higher than in the Dutch Randstad and Edinburgh, similar to the Southern European cities (Barcelona and Oporto) but lower than in Copenhagen, Munich, Vienna and Zurich.

Closeness Centrality

Average closeness centrality in Hamburg represents the third poorest result for average ease-of-movement in a European SNAMUTS city before Edinburgh and Zuid Holland, while outperforming all Australasian and US cities.

As a network largely designed around multimodal transfers, the identification of SNAMUTS activity nodes in Hamburg includes the many rail–bus interchanges; very few rapid rail stations across the core city are not also serviced by connecting bus routes. Post-war reconstruction and expansion created many residential estates (*Großsiedlungen*) in the middle suburbs. These neighbourhoods are usually built around local retail and community facilities but do not feature employment or other regional travel attractors at a significant scale. Nonetheless, the larger examples have been included among Hamburg's 186 activity nodes.

Sixty-nine nodes (37 per cent) have a closeness value of 40 or better, of which 12 are located in the CBD. This standard generally stretches along metro corridors up to a distance of 10 km or more and applies to all but two nodes inside the metro circle route (U3) at a concentric distance of 5–6 km from the centre. Nodal closeness results rapidly deteriorate away from the rail corridors, including in those middle suburbs where post-war planning proposed metro links which were not implemented (the Osdorf-Lurup area in the west, Steilshoop-Bramfeld in the north-east, Jenfeld in the east). A closeness centrality spike at two nodes inside the metro circle (Mühlenkamp and Jarrestraße) demonstrates the limitations of bus-only access in an area that is nominally a dense, mixed-use inner urban neighbourhood.

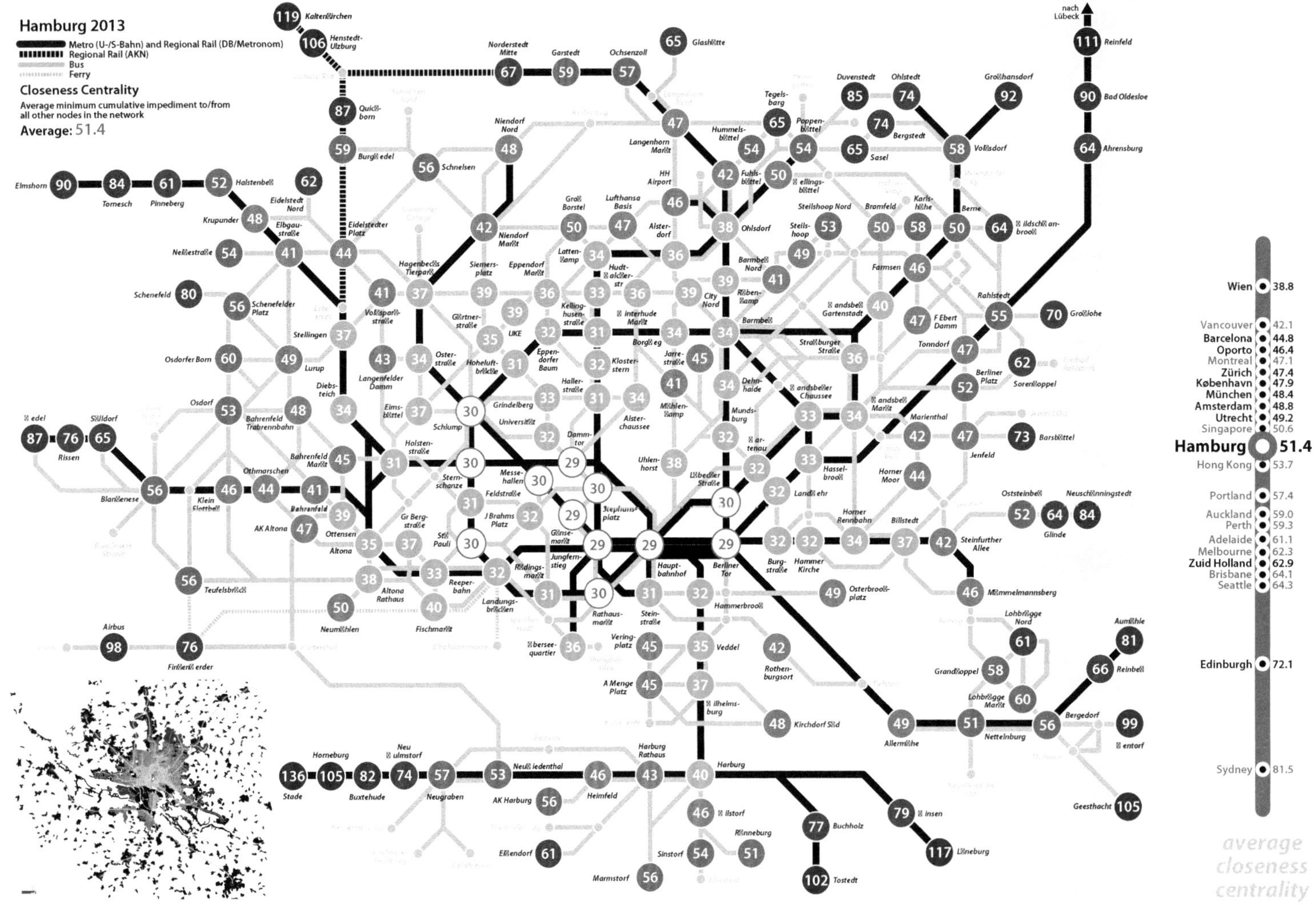

Degree Centrality

On average degree centrality, Hamburg joins the cohort of European cities with greater transfer intensity, alongside Amsterdam, Barcelona, Vienna and Zurich. While Hamburg's network design approach is not radically different from that of Munich, Hamburg's higher transfer intensity results from a more 'organic' pattern of network growth: unfinished post-war rapid rail plans produce a greater number of nodes depending on bus feeders (especially in the eastern and southern suburbs), while network elements from earlier eras, such as the inner metro ring (U3) moderate this effect by offering additional connections. Recent improvements to the bus system have also aimed at strengthening non-radial links. Despite planning inconsistencies Hamburg's network has been optimised – possibly over-optimised, compared to its peers like Copenhagen or Vancouver which, in principle, follow a similar design approach – to eliminate parallel

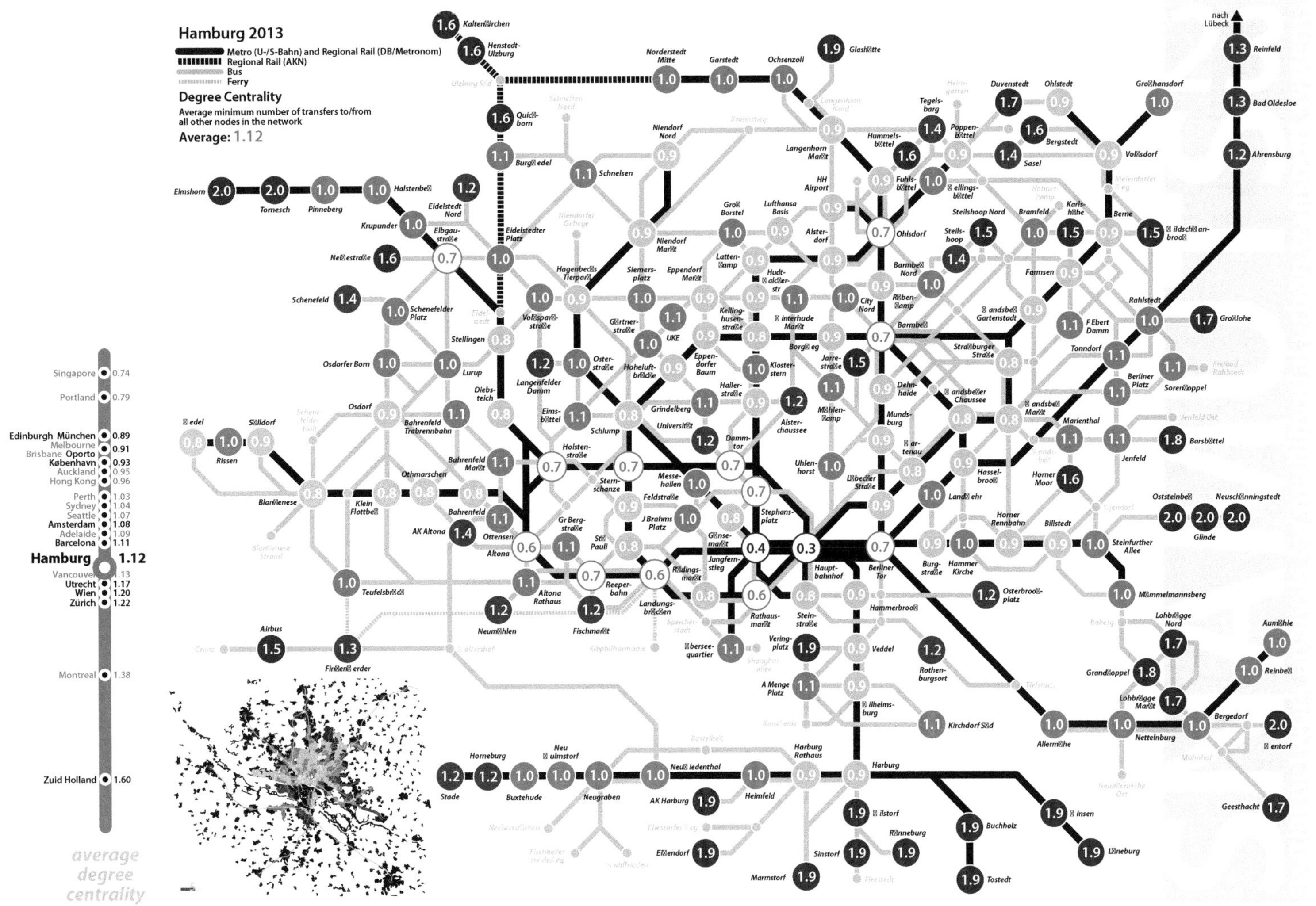

routes of different modes and to rely on transfers for trunk-and-feeder radial links, and for journeys combining segments of orbital and radial corridors.

Transfer intensity in Hamburg is also reduced in practical terms by the existence of no less than six separate stations (Altona and Hauptbahnhof on the S-Bahn system; Barmbek, Kellinghusenstraße, Berliner Tor and Wandsbek-Gartenstadt on the U-Bahn system) where transfers between lines (in one direction) are cross-platform and timetable-coordinated. In the SNAMUTS calculation, such transfers do not incur a time loss for passengers and hence do not enter the transfer count or attract the usual transfer time penalty.

Network Coverage

Hamburg's network coverage value is only slightly better than in Edinburgh and Utrecht; all three cities trail the European sample. Hamburg's

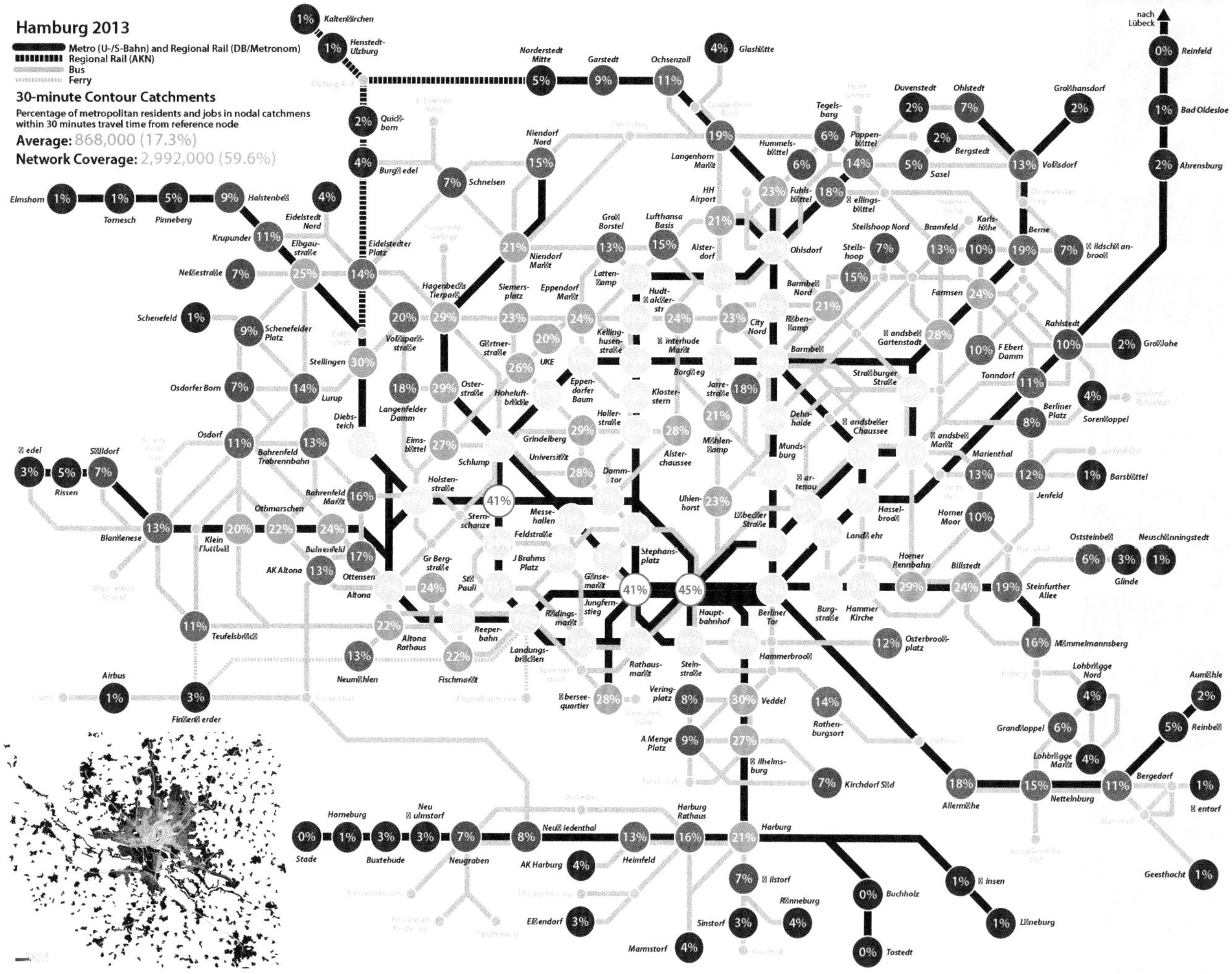

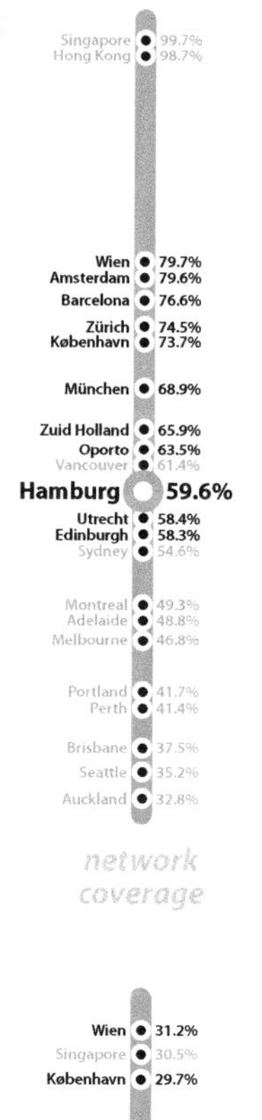

Hamburg 2013
Metro (U-/S-Bahn) and Regional Rail (DB/Metronom)
Regional Rail (AKN)
Bus
Ferry
30-minute Contour Catchments
Percentage of metropolitan residents and jobs in nodal catchments within 30 minutes travel time from reference node
Average: 868,000 (17.3%)
Network Coverage: 2,992,000 (59.6%)

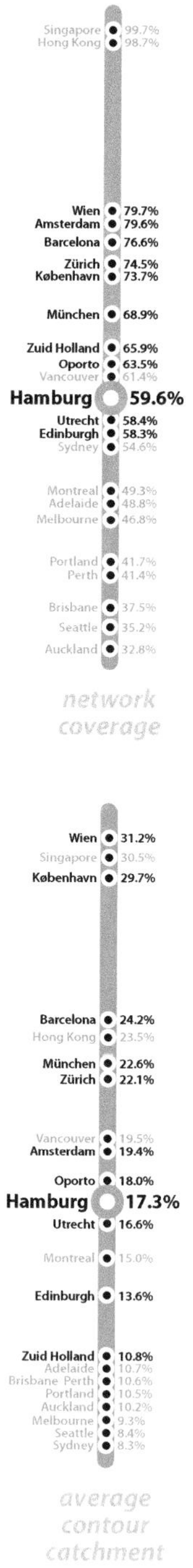

population divides up almost evenly between the core city and a large hinterland of patchy urbanisation in the seven surrounding counties. The core city has good public transport coverage at the minimum standard (with the exception of the expansive semi-rural areas located in the boroughs of Bergedorf and Harburg). The periphery beyond the city-state aggregates mainly around secondary and tertiary centres, most of which are not connected to public transport services at the same standard as the core city. Several significant centres in the surrounding region (Uetersen, Barmstedt, Bargteheide, Schwarzenbek or Jesteburg) have either no rail access at all or none at the minimum standard.

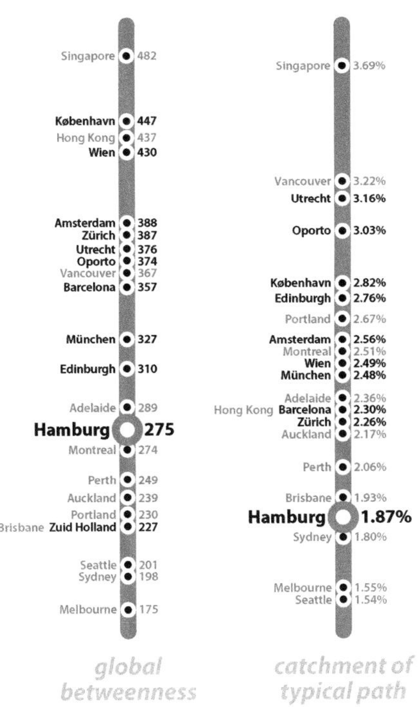

Contour Catchments

Fifty-eight nodes on the Hamburg network (31 per cent of the total) are within 30 minutes public transport travel time of a quarter or more of all residents and jobs in the metropolitan area. This group of nodes are, almost exclusively, along rail corridors and the inner section of the M5 bus route. Average 30-minute contour catchments per node place Hamburg into a mid-field position in comparison to its European and Canadian peers, but well above the public transport travel time contours typically found in Australasian and US cities.

Middle suburban centres along metro lines (Othmarschen, Elbgaustraße, Niendorf Markt, Farmsen or Billstedt) perform much better on this index than neighbouring feeder bus-dependent centres (Lurup, Steilshoop, Bramfeld or Jenfeld) illustrating an inequitable distribution of public transport accessibility across sub-centres that otherwise have comparable levels of significance in the hierarchy of central places.

Betweenness Centrality

Hamburg's global betweenness score relative to population and jobs is the second poorest among its European peers before Zuid Holland; the Hanseatic city is also outperformed by the New World cities of Vancouver and Adelaide on this index. This result indicates a relatively weak presence of public transport travel opportunities in significant parts of the metropolitan region (the mostly poorly serviced outer seven counties) and the core city (the aforementioned bus-dependent major centres).

Almost two thirds of the travel opportunities facilitated by the public transport network concentrate onto rail segments, a share similar to neighbouring Copenhagen and second only to Barcelona and Munich in the global sample. However, in the absence of trams, buses absorb most of the remainder and elevate that mode's significance to a level (34.6 per cent) substantially greater than in the agglomerations with tram-dominated surface networks such as Zuid Holland, Vienna or Zurich.

The concentration of travel opportunities within the CBD area is among the lowest in the global sample. There are several influences: chiefly the existence of strong rail interchanges outside the city centre that allow for convenient 'bypass' journeys (Berliner Tor, Sternschanze, Barmbek) and the relatively large size of the metropolitan area. Conversely, Hamburg's geography, featuring a number of water bodies that create a bottleneck for east–west movement in the CBD, moderates this effect.

The greatest concentration of travel opportunities on individual route segments occurs on the S3/S31 cross-harbour link between the central city and Harburg to the south, followed by the northern S-Bahn trunk line between Hauptbahnhof and Holstenstraße and the eastern U2 branch between Berliner Tor and Billstedt. The inner metro orbital route (U3) between Barmbek and Sternschanze is also a strong performer.

On the bus network, the most significant corridor for facilitating movement across the network is the infamous M5 between central Hamburg and Lokstedt (Siemersplatz) in the north-west, Hamburg's last tram line to be converted to bus operation in 1978. Other bus routes with high betweenness scores are notable (the M20/M25 corridor between Altona and Winterhude; the M10 corridor between Wandsbek and Jenfeld; the 173 corridor between Barmbek and Bramfeld, as well as – perhaps less expectedly – the M22 corridor between Lurup and Eppendorf and the express buses along Wandsbeker Chaussee and Reeperbahn). This may indicate their suitability for a modal upgrade should Hamburg revive its twice-abandoned plans for a second-generation tram system.

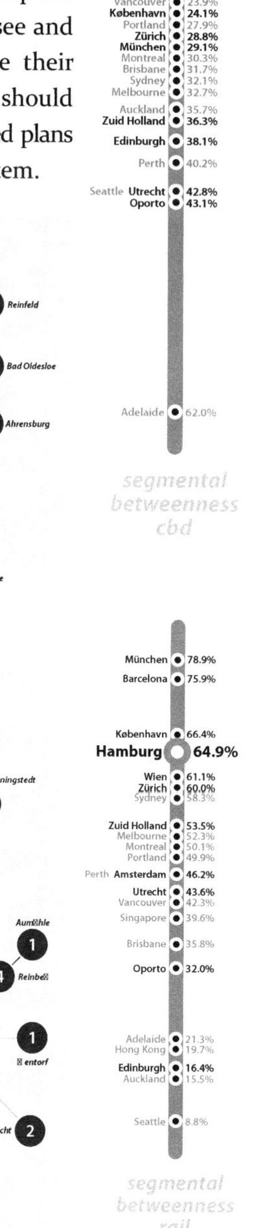

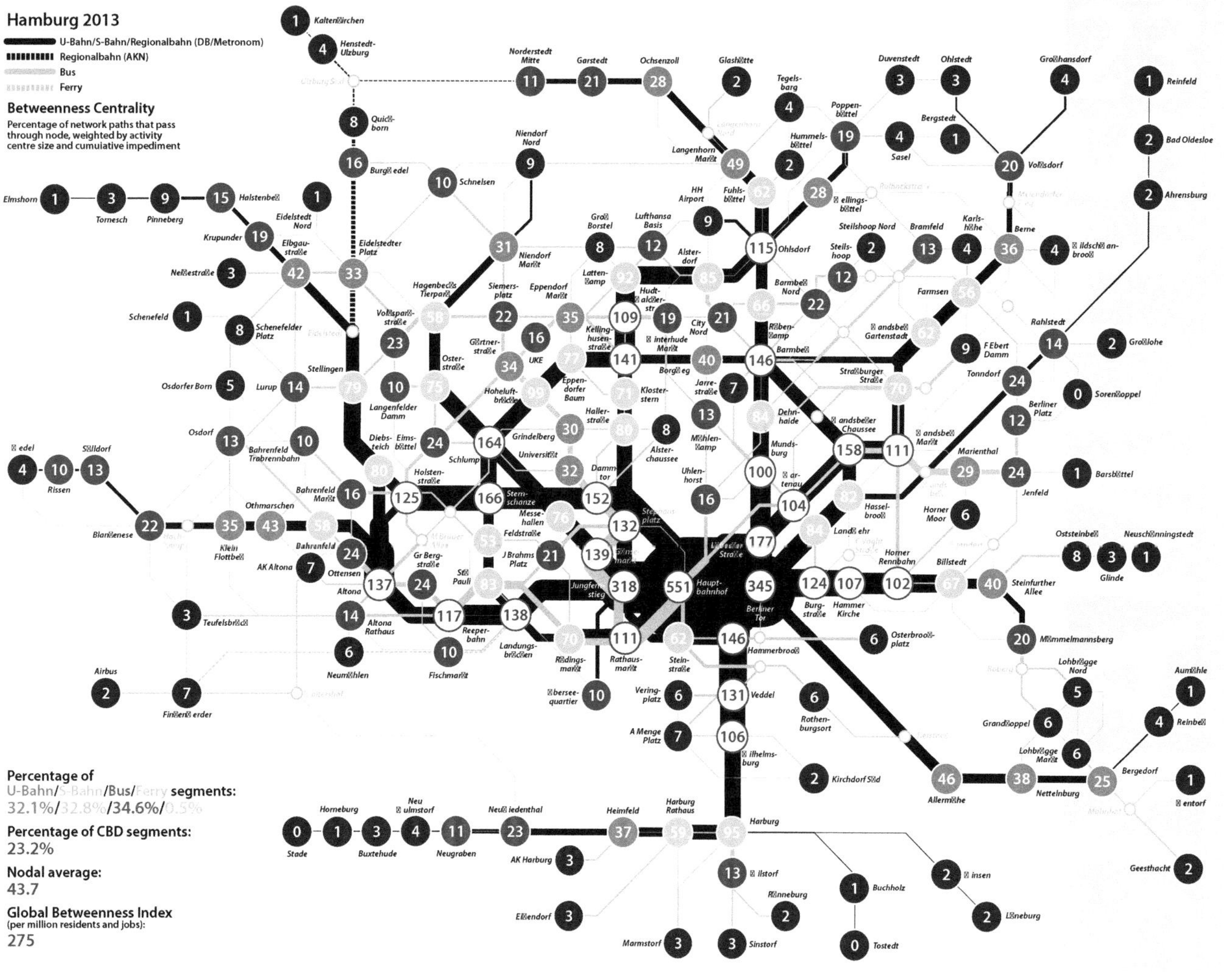

Hamburg 2013

U-Bahn/S-Bahn/Regionalbahn (DB/Metronom)
Regionalbahn (AKN)
Bus
Ferry

Betweenness Centrality
Percentage of network paths that pass through node, weighted by activity centre size and cumulative impediment

Percentage of U-Bahn/S-Bahn/Bus/Ferry segments:
32.1%/32.8%/34.6%/0.5%

Percentage of CBD segments:
23.2%

Nodal average:
43.7

Global Betweenness Index
(per million residents and jobs):
275

Network Resilience

Hamburg's level of segmental resilience in the CBD area is the poorest in the European sample and the third poorest globally after Hong Kong and Sydney. This may be due to the limited surface network in the city centre, where only a single bus trunk line (Dammtor to Hauptbahnhof via Gänsemarkt and Rathausmarkt) with some branches caters for all surface travel opportunities. Compared to Amsterdam, Munich or Vienna where trams ply the city centres, it also indicates the absence of a less congestion-prone intermediate transport mode.

The distribution of low segmental resilience values in detail confirms that it is bus segments, not rail segments, which compromise performance on this index in Hamburg's central city, with below-average scores found on almost every bus segment there and on several approach routes especially towards the east. Most network elements with

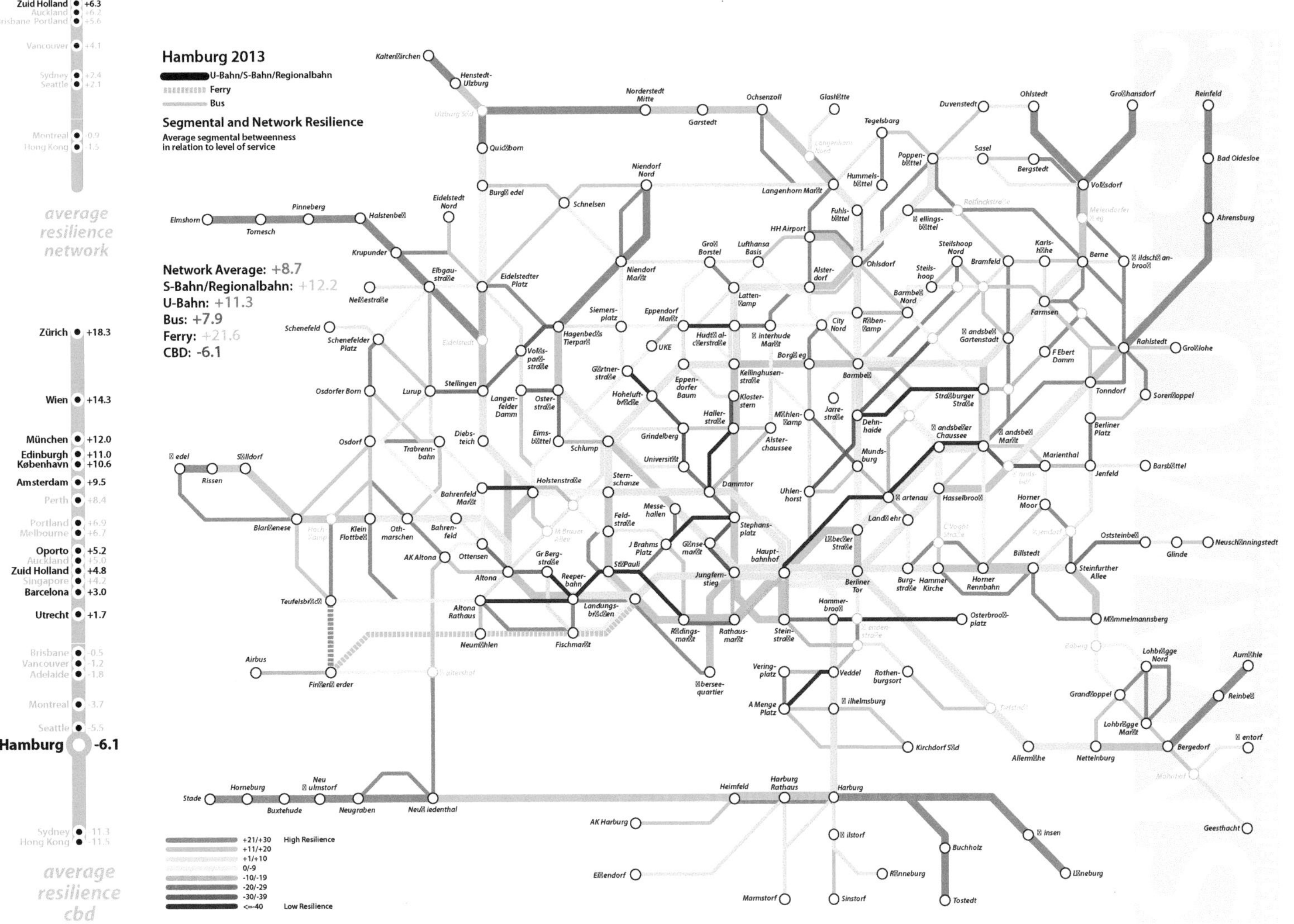

problematic resilience levels outside the CBD correspond to the bus lines mentioned previously in the context of segmental betweenness. Additionally, some segments on express bus routes feature quite prominently on this index, given that these lines provide some transfer-free or otherwise direct links between groups of activity nodes not supplied by regular bus or metro routes.

Nodal Connectivity

Hamburg's average nodal connectivity figure is among the highest in the global sample and can be traced to two key influences. Firstly, as shown by the segmental betweenness index, the role of heavy rail is relatively pronounced and the average occupancy rate for each train is relatively high (and increasing in the face of ongoing patronage growth). Secondly, Hamburg's network, despite some obvious missing links on the rail system, offers a fairly large number of multimodal transfer points, allowing activity nodes to

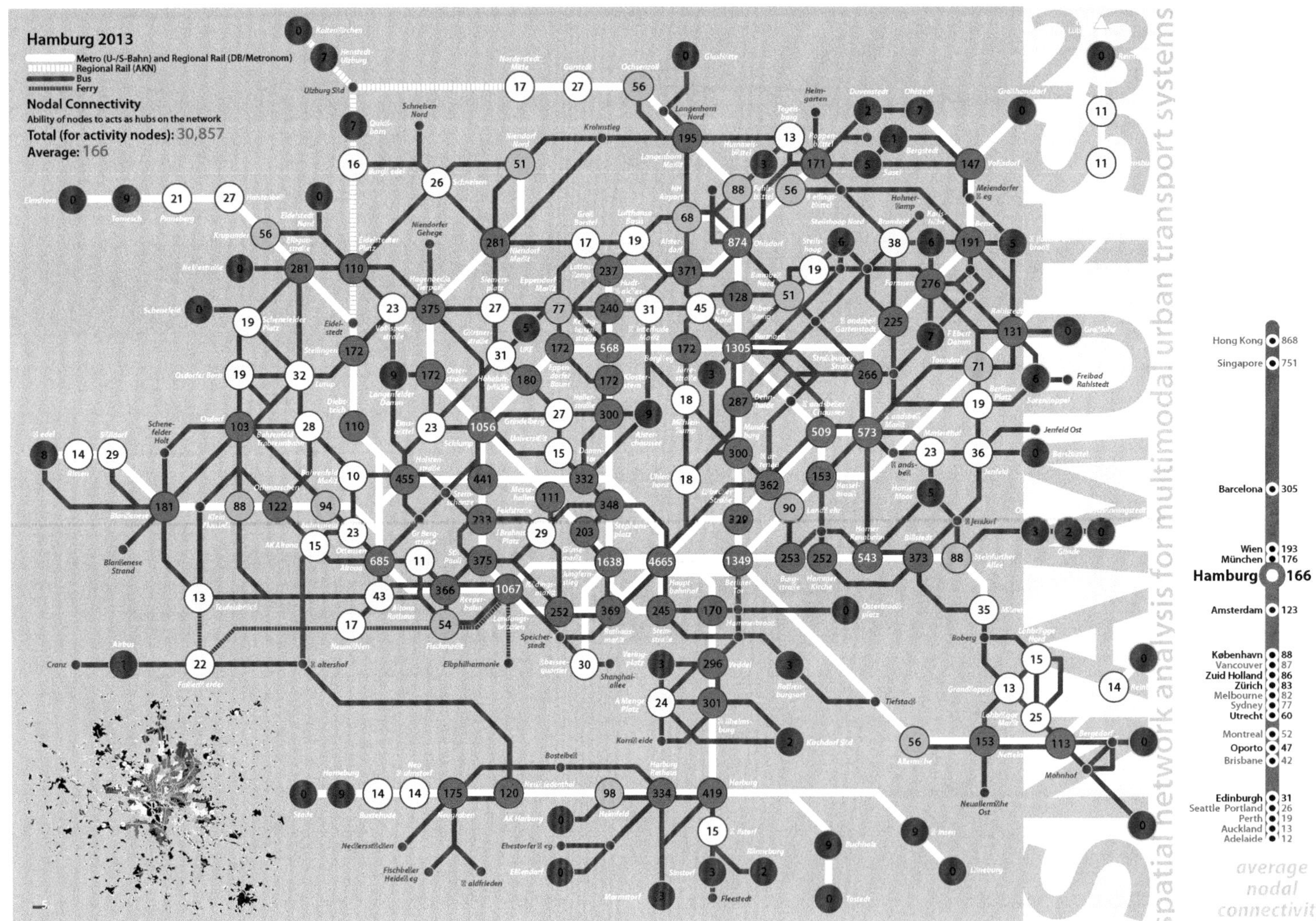

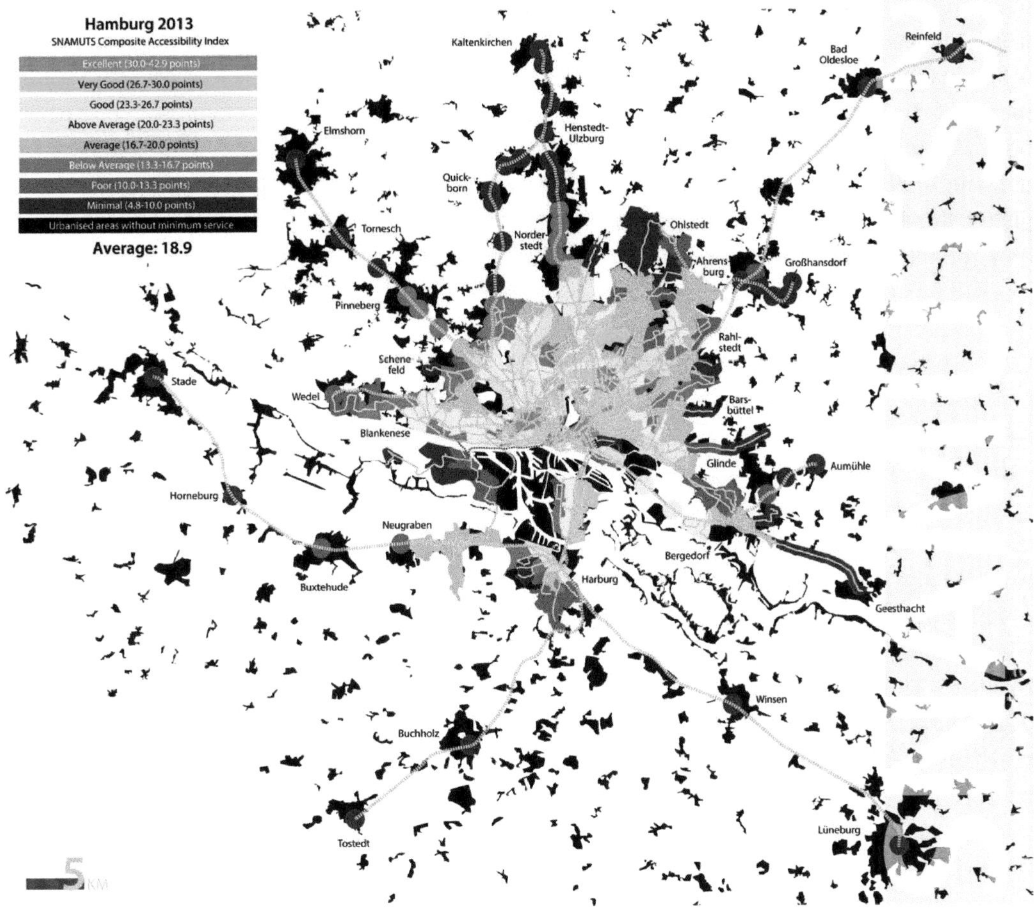

achieve above-average connectivity scores along most metro lines all the way to the city limits. The central station (Hauptbahnhof), already the top performer on all other SNAMUTS indicators, acts as a 'super-node' on this index. Conversely, there is a near-complete absence of network connectivity (i.e. the ability to travel in other than a radial direction at the minimum service standard) in the outer parts of the metropolitan area beyond the limits of the city-state.

SNAMUTS Composite Accessibility Index and Reflections

The composite map illustrates the 'tale of two cities' that derived from a post-war public transport policy short of full implementation, resulting in the lack of an intermediate-capacity mode (trams) and a patchwork of metro and bus corridors accessing suburban centres of comparable importance and geographical location. Along the metro network, good or excellent accessibility (green shades) prevail as far as Elbgaustraße, Niendorf Markt, Fuhlsbüttel, Farmsen, Billstedt and Harburg, roughly the boundary of 5-minute daytime frequencies on rail. Below-average accessibility standards are evident in the bus-dependent corridors towards the mid-western (Lurup and Osdorf), mid-northeastern (Steilshoop and Bramfeld) and particularly mid-eastern suburbs (Rahlstedt, Tonndorf and Jenfeld, where half-hourly regional trains provide a modicum of rail service, but not quite of metro standard). There are also pockets of poor accessibility in inner areas (Winterhude-Uhlenhorst, Hamm Süd and Rothenburgsort) where the absence or peripheral location of rail and a low level of network connectivity combine to create public transport 'accessibility deserts'. In contrast, it is striking how the best-performing locations on this index are scattered not merely around the CBD and its eastern fringe (Berliner Tor, Hammerbrook, Lübecker Straße), but also the inner borough centres at Altona-Holstenstraße-Sternschanze, Kellinghusenstraße, Barmbek and Wandsbeker Chaussee.

The resolution of these spatial inequities through public transport policy has been hampered by partisan agendas and the absence of a long-term consensus on investment priorities. At the time of writing, the only committed infrastructure projects other than bus priority measures include the completion of the HafenCity

U-Bahn branch (whose first stage opened in 2012) to a new interchange with the S-Bahn at Elbbrücken, the upgrade of the Hasselbrook-Bad Oldesloe and Eidelstedt-Kaltenkirchen regional rail lines to full S-Bahn standard, and the insertion of two additional stations along existing (above-ground) metro routes.

ACCESSIBILITY PROFILE: MÜNCHEN, BAYERN (GERMANY)

Munich is the capital of Bavaria, Germany's largest state (by area) and the country's third largest city (by population in the local government area – 1.44 million at the 2011 census). The seat of Bavarian royalty over a number of centuries, the city now forms part of a wider metropolitan region, which for our analysis we defined as the service area of the regional transit association (*Münchner Verkehrsverbund* or *MVV*). This area covers the City of Munich, eight surrounding counties and some adjacent municipalities with a combined population of 2.80 million. Average activity density is comparable to the Dutch Randstad but lower than Barcelona, Vienna or Zurich. There is a strong contrast between the core city activity density (90.4 residents and jobs per urbanised hectare) and the surrounding region (28.4).

Munich was Germany's first city to convert suburban rail lines into a coherent S-Bahn system with diametrical routes, while leaving them fully compatible (in technical terms) with mainline rail operations. This occurred by way of a CBD tunnel acting as a trunk for 12 suburban branch lines (7 to the west, 5 to the east). Simultaneously, Munich also built a new city metro (U-Bahn) system and unlike Hamburg, almost completed the 1960s target network with only minor changes and omissions. The system's three trunk routes meet at three separate transfer stations in the CBD (Hauptbahnhof, Sendlinger Tor, Odeonsplatz) before splitting (in most cases) into two suburban branches at either end, some of which intersect again at suburban transfer stations. There are also a number of suburban interchanges to the S-Bahn system, with three U-Bahn routes terminating at a S-Bahn station (Feldmoching, Moosach and Neuperlach Süd). Thus over a space of four decades, Munich's public transport system transformed from a network dominated by the twin backbones of an expansive tram system that kept pace with post-war urban growth and a radial suburban rail network feeding into city termini. As the metro network grew, the tram system retreated and was anticipated to fully close until a council decision in the mid-1980s confirmed its retention. Today, the remainder of the network has returned to a growth trajectory, usually connected to urban intensification projects and the conversion of overcrowded bus routes.

Like Hamburg, Munich's bus network is branded in two products known as Metrobuses (with guaranteed 10-minute frequencies all day, seven days a week)

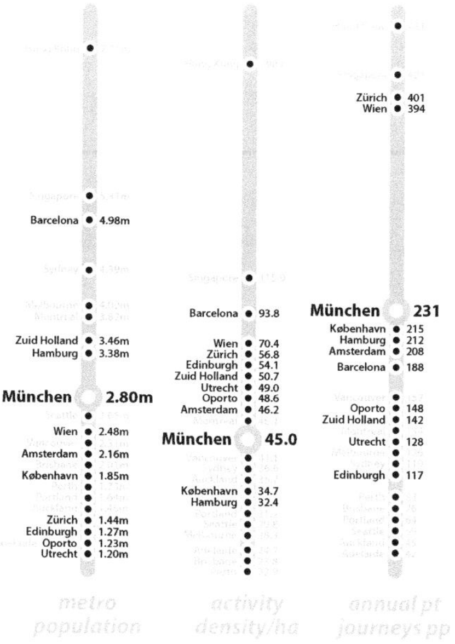

Edinburgh 38.2
Amsterdam 28.7
Zürich 25.9
Wien 25.5
Oporto 24.9
København 24.8
Barcelona 21.9
Hamburg 17.2
Zuid Holland 16.8
Utrecht 16.2
München 13.9

service intensity/ 100,000 inh

Zürich 10.1
København 9.7
München 7.9
Wien 7.7
Oporto 6.3
Hamburg 5.3
Barcelona 4.7
Utrecht 4.3
Amsterdam 4.2
Zuid Holland 3.5
Edinburgh 2.6

heavy rail stations/ 100,000 inh

and standard buses. Jointly with trams, these buses generate a dense, multi-directional surface network across the City of Munich. However, with three minor exceptions the SNAMUTS minimum standard does not extend to surface routes in the surrounding region.

The MVV fare system is fully integrated across all modes and is based on 16 concentric zones. There are periodical tickets, including salary packaging (for large employers) and discounted off-peak options. Generally, periodical passes deliver a financial advantage over single or daily tickets from three to four weekly return journeys onwards. Daily, multi-rider and single tickets are also available.

Service Intensity

Eight of Munich's 12 S-Bahn branch lines also continue to operate regional and long-distance services, in some cases sharing the same tracks. In combination with the need for all branch routes to share the same double track CBD tunnel, this limits the service frequency per branch line to 20 minutes. Since 1972, however, passenger numbers on the S-Bahn system have increased threefold, and this arrangement now acts as a significant constraint on the capacity and attractiveness of the system. U-Bahn operation during the weekday inter-peak period (and on weekends) is generally every 10 minutes per route, generating 5-minute intervals on the common trunks. Most individual tram and Metrobus lines also operate every 10 minutes seven days a week, again with limited instances where two lines overlap. Across the network, however, daytime frequencies better than every 10 minutes are the exception, not the rule.

On the population-weighted service intensity count, Munich is the most frugal provider in the European sample, though Hamburg and the Dutch Randstad component cities other than Amsterdam are not far ahead. This observation is partially the result of a comprehensive efficiency drive accompanying the rapid growth of the metro system since the 1970s, all but eliminating surface routes with saturation-level frequencies across the city. Simultaneously, it indicates average frequencies on the rapid rail network that do not match those common in several other European cities (Barcelona, Copenhagen, Hamburg and Vienna).

Munich's heavy rail station density relative to population, in contrast, is positioned towards the higher end of the spectrum, comparable to that of Vienna and just below Copenhagen and Zurich.

Closeness Centrality

The closeness centrality index records an average result typical for a European SNAMUTS city, almost identical to that of Amsterdam and Copenhagen. There are 87 nodes (48 per cent) with a closeness score of 40 or less (better), the product of a well-connected and tightly spaced activity centre network in the core city and a dependent relationship for the suburban S-Bahn corridors. With the single exception of a joint terminus for two lines at the airport (S1/S8), journeys between nodes on different S-Bahn corridors can only be performed by travelling through the core city, unless bus lines with poor or no weekend service are utilised.

The selection of 179 activity nodes in the Munich metropolitan region was informed by a City of Munich centre strategy that identifies and categorises regional and neighbourhood activity centres within the core city (LMRSB, 2010). Outside the core city, we relied on the existence of rail-bus transfer facilities, even though the buses generally don't meet the minimum service standard, to identify activity nodes. However, usually only one activity node was allocated per local government area.

Degree Centrality

Munich's average degree centrality shares with Edinburgh the position of the least transfer-dependent public transport

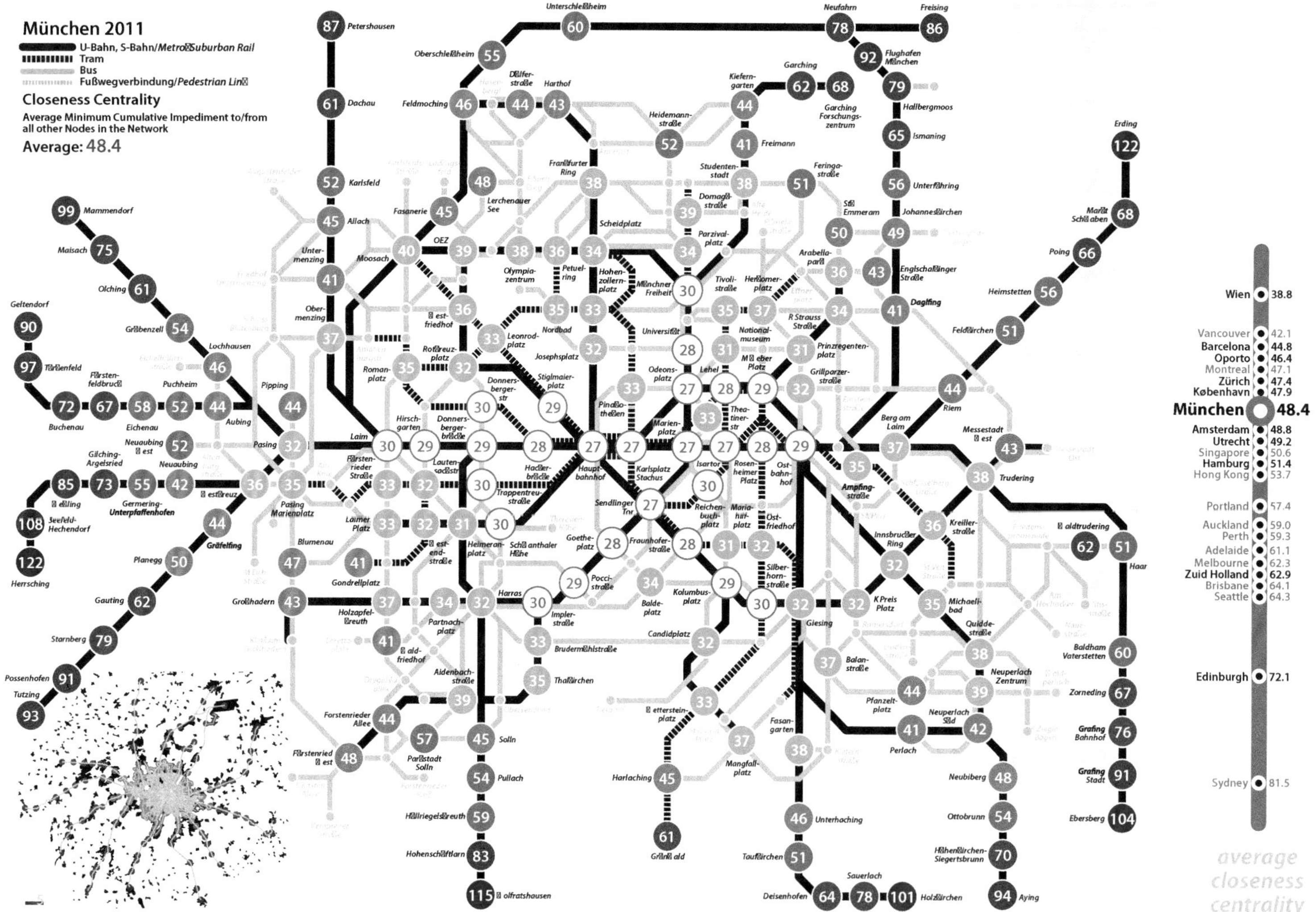

networks in the European sample. This is the result of the mostly completed metro network which minimises the number of nodes that continue to rely on bus or tram feeder routes and further provides timed cross-platform interchanges between suburban branch lines in two locations (Scheidplatz and Innsbrucker Ring), which are not counted as full transfers on this index. The layout of the suburban rail (S-Bahn) system with its pendular lines, most of which link one edge of the metropolitan area to another and converge in a central trunk route whose nodes have the lowest transfer dependency on the network, also contributes to this result. Lastly, the tightly woven surface network with its many orbital and diagonal links ensures that most origins and destinations in the core city are connected with a maximum of one transfer, and that this can usually be done through a choice of several different journey paths.

Network Coverage

Munich's network coverage outperforms Hamburg, Zuid Holland and the

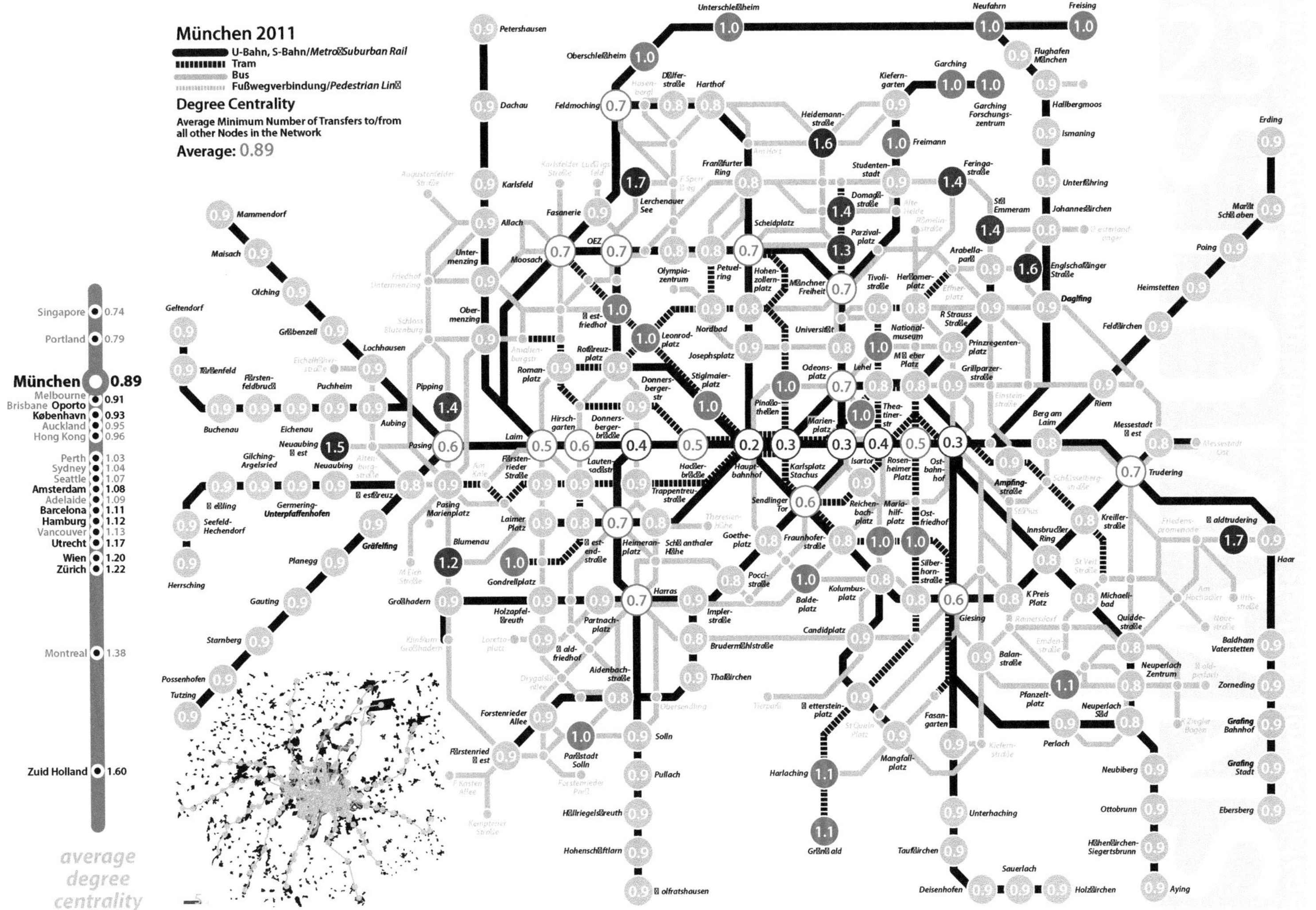

three smallest European case study cities (Edinburgh, Oporto and Utrecht), but trails behind Amsterdam, Barcelona, Copenhagen, Vienna and Zurich. This is the result of the high network density within the core city that places practically the entire urbanised territory within walkable access to public transport, and to the large number and strength of radial settlement corridors around S-Bahn lines in the surrounding region. The shortfall to the higher-performing European cities, however, has its roots in the absence of bus routes at the minimum standard outside the core city, effectively limiting walking access to public transport there to the pedestrian catchments of the rail stations.

Contour Catchments

Munich has 90 nodes, just over half of the total, that offer access to a quarter or more of metropolitan residents and jobs within a 30-minute public transport journey. All of these nodes are located in the core city and outnumber core city nodes that do not achieve this standard by a ratio of three to one. As a result, the City

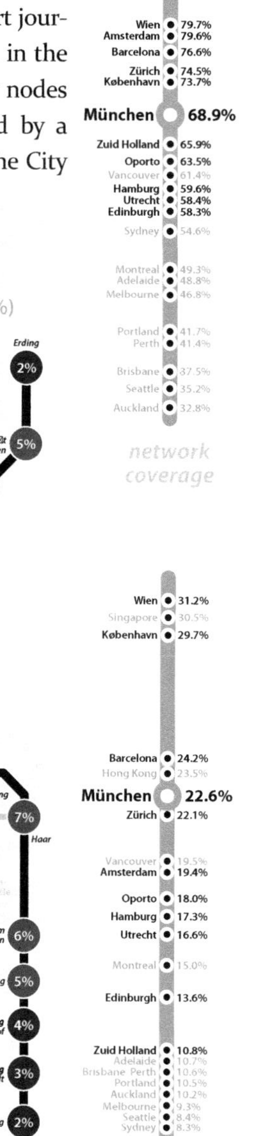

München 2011

U-Bahn, S-Bahn/Metro/Suburban Rail
Tram
Bus
Fußwegverbindung/Pedestrian Link

30-minute Contour Catchments

Percentage of metropolitan residents and jobs in nodal catchments within 30 minutes travel time from reference node

Average: 937,000 (22.6%)

Network Coverage: 2,856,000 (68.9%)

of Munich operates largely as a '30-minute city' for public transport users. The central S-Bahn trunk line between Laim and Ostbahnhof, in recent years subject to Munich's largest-scale urban intensification program along the above-ground section west of Hauptbahnhof (Hale, 2010), consistently achieves contour catchments in excess of 50 per cent of all residents and jobs. This impressive result underscores the transit orientation of the redevelopment, considering that Munich's total network coverage which acts as a cap on this index, is not much higher at 68.9 per cent. However, the values drop quite rapidly along the suburban rail corridors where travel times are inflated by the near-absence semi-express S-Bahn services (in contrast to Copenhagen) and

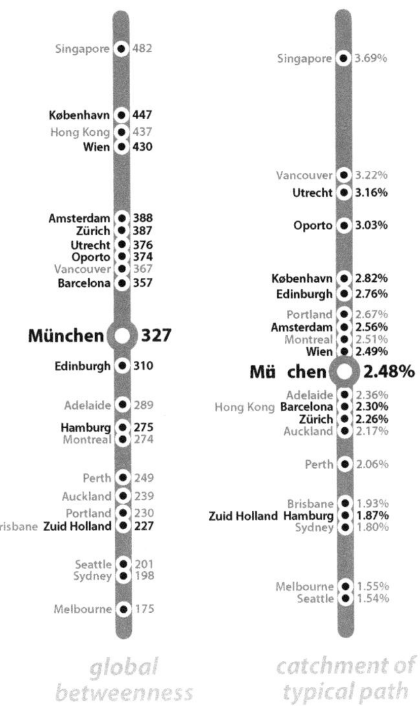

by the relatively low service frequency of 20 minutes (this means that transfer journeys to and from nodes along S-Bahn branch lines are excluded on this index). Consequently, Munich's average 30-minute contour catchment is smaller in percentage terms than in Copenhagen and Vienna and is positioned between those of Barcelona (which makes up for its larger size by greater settlement density) and Zurich (which makes up for its more dispersed settlement structure by faster and more frequent S-Bahn services). It outperforms every other non-Asian city in the SNAMUTS sample though.

Betweenness Centrality

Munich's global betweenness score relative to population and jobs is positioned in the lower mid-field of the European sample, ahead of Hamburg, Zuid Holland and Edinburgh but behind the largest cities (Barcelona, Singapore and Hong Kong) as well as Amsterdam, Copenhagen, Vancouver, Vienna and Zurich. This is a reflection on these smaller cities' success in translating a higher input of service than Munich into a higher overall 'presence' of public transport for users.

Munich has the greatest reliance on heavy rail modes of all case study cities in terms of the distribution of travel opportunities, relegating the surface modes into a marginal position. The relatively high average catchment of typical path length result indicates a network that facilitates longer journeys over shorter ones and should be seen in the context of Munich's numerous and long radial suburban rail corridors. The share of travel opportunities channelled through the CBD area is higher than in the other larger European case study cities, most likely a result of the absence of a high-capacity, high-performance orbital route in Munich's public transport network in contrast with Copenhagen, Hamburg and Vienna. The low ability of orbital surface routes to deflect significant travel opportunities away from the CBD again confirms the relative weakness of buses and trams in Munich's modal mix.

The S-Bahn trunk route between Laim and Ostbahnhof has the highest segmental betweenness result in the network, followed by the common section of metro lines U3 and U6 between Münchner Freiheit and Implerstraße, which at 18 trains per hour per direction in the weekday inter-peak period has the best service level of all metro lines.

Network Resilience

Munich's average level of segmental resilience is similar to Copenhagen and higher than in all other cities in the global sample except Vienna, Zurich and Edinburgh. The distribution of results across modes and geographical areas, however, reveals some resilience problems on several metro segments and along the S-Bahn trunk line, precisely those elements where the performance of the network as a whole is most critically determined. It is unsurprising, then, that there is a high perception among decision makers that relief is needed for the central S-Bahn tunnel, currently operated at capacity, and that frequency boosts should also be facilitated on the U-Bahn system (DB, 2013; MVG, 2014). Despite these constraints, Munich's average CBD network resilience is superior to the entire global sample except for Vienna and Zurich. The city's decision to retain the tram system plays a significant part in this, as trams continue to provide a coherent surface network to move about the central area and a highly visible public transport presence in the public realm (Cervero, 1998). Trams are the mode least affected by network stress according to this index. Low resilience results dominate along the inner sections of some S-Bahn branch lines, particularly the western branches of lines S2 (Petershausen) and S7 (Wolfratshausen), and the eastern branches of lines S3 (Holzkirchen), S7 (Aying) and S8 (Flughafen München). This is where the 20-minute frequency standard imposed by the need for all S-Bahn lines to share the central tunnel

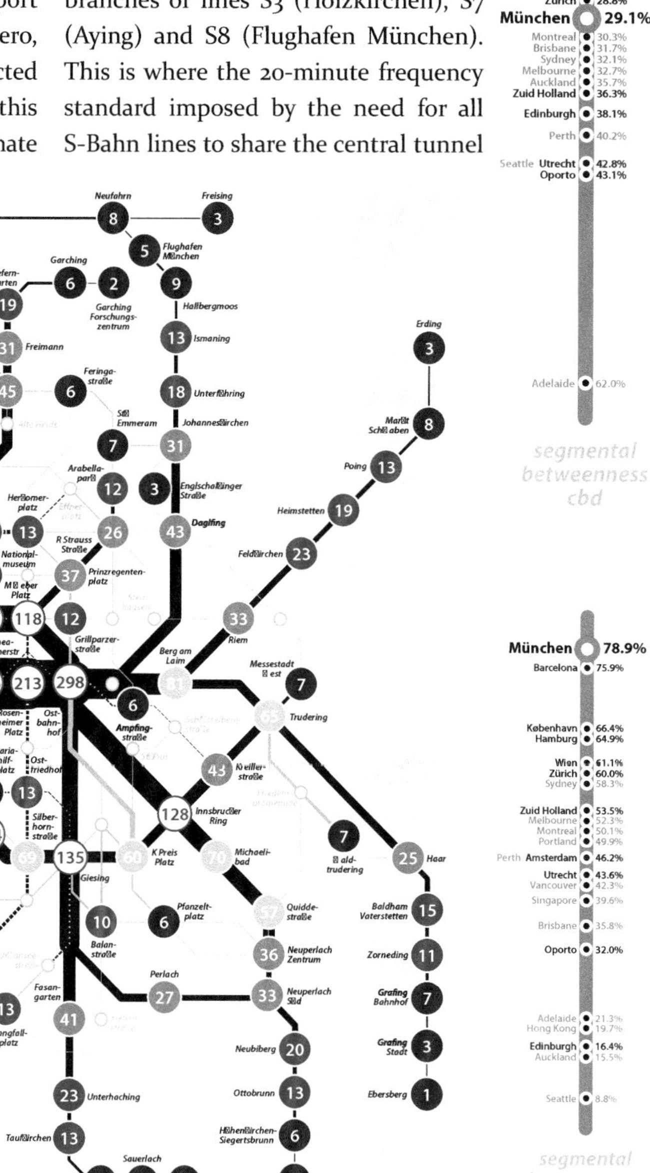

becomes most constraining. In the surface network, the least resilient route appears to be Metrobus line M51 along Fürstenrieder Straße between Laim and Waldfriedhof in the mid-western suburbs. The City of Munich is planning a tram extension (Westtangente) along this corridor (between Romanplatz and Aidenbachstraße) to boost public transport speed and capacity and to service a number of urban redevelopment sites (MVG, 2014).

Nodal Connectivity

The nodal connectivity index in Munich delivers an average result similar to Hamburg and Vienna, and outperformed significantly only by Barcelona and the Asian cities. The network is configured to enable users to move flexibly around most of the core city and is supported by, and further encourages, a transit-friendly urban form. Hauptbahnhof, the crossing point of the S-Bahn

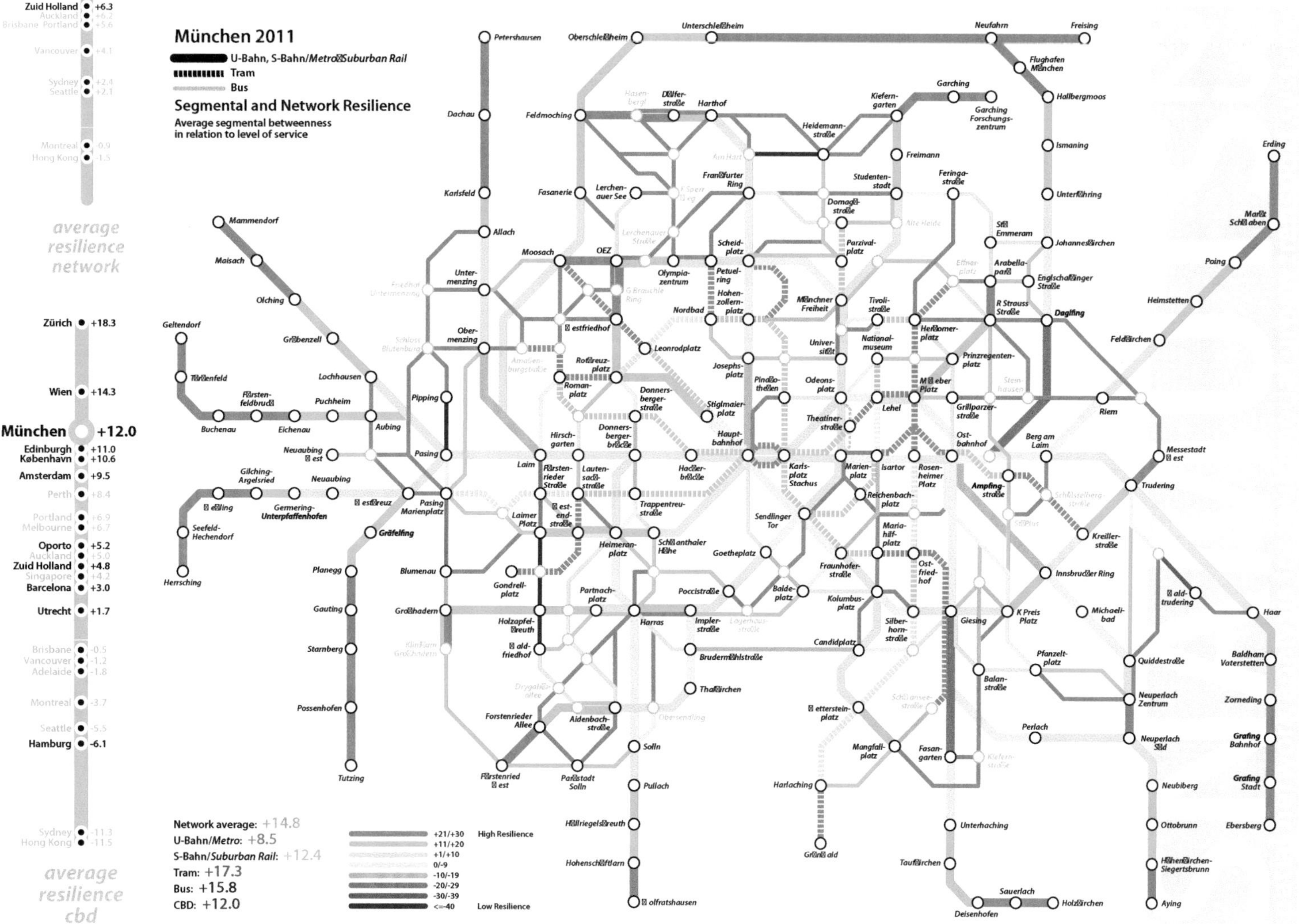

trunk line and two U-Bahn trunk lines, acts as a 'super-node' on this index, followed at some distance by Marienplatz, Sendlinger Tor and (outside the CBD) Ostbahnhof. However, there are also some less well connected pockets away from the rapid rail network even in relatively close proximity to the central city (Baldeplatz, Mariahilfplatz, Pinakotheken, Nationalmuseum, Tivolistraße) where a reliance on surface modes, generally no more frequent than every 10 minutes, generates distinct contrasts in terms of ease of accessibility compared to their metro-connected neighbours. Along the S-Bahn corridors in the surrounding region, the near-complete lack of orbital or feeder bus services at the SNAMUTS minimum standard depresses the results on this index across the board.

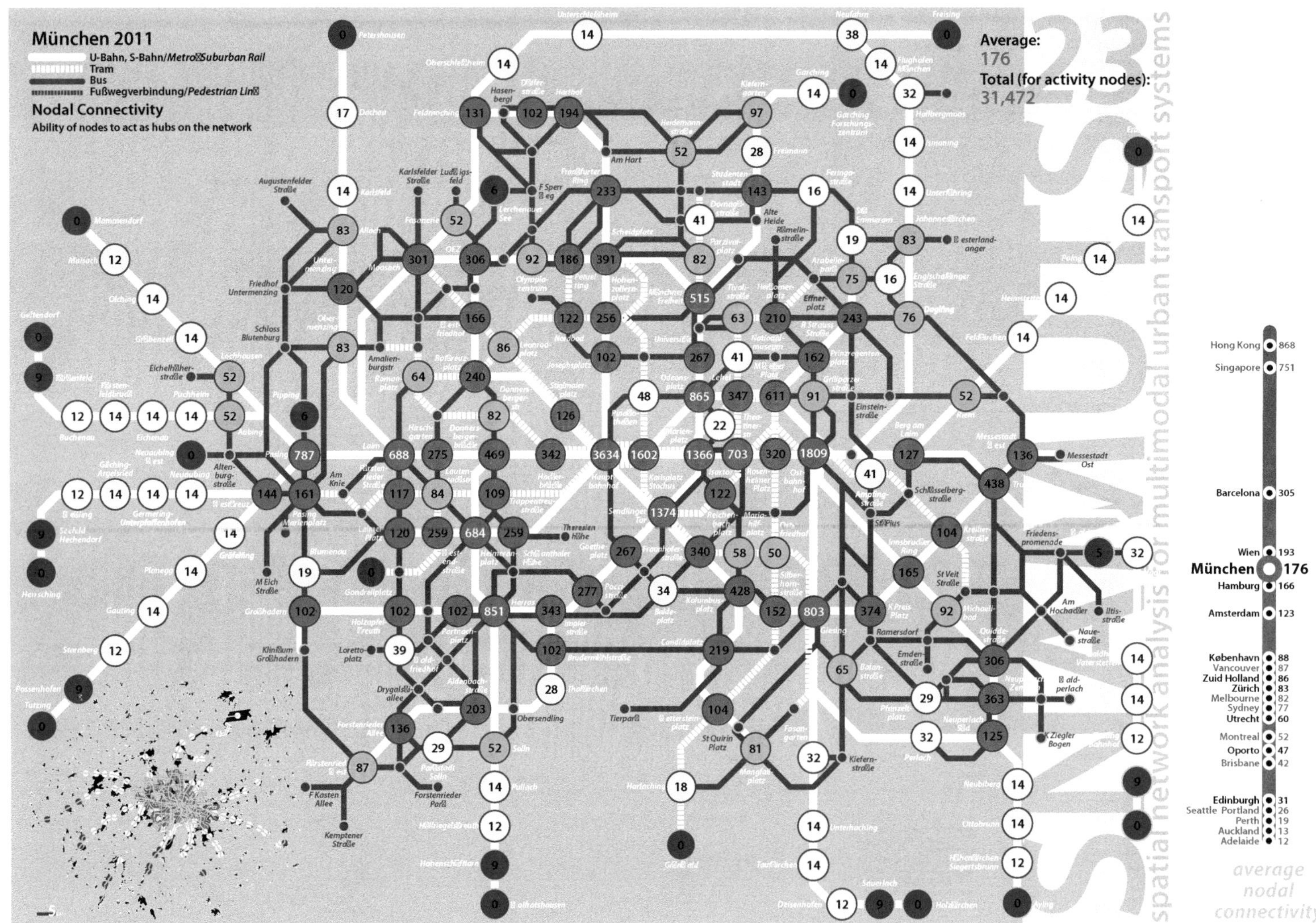

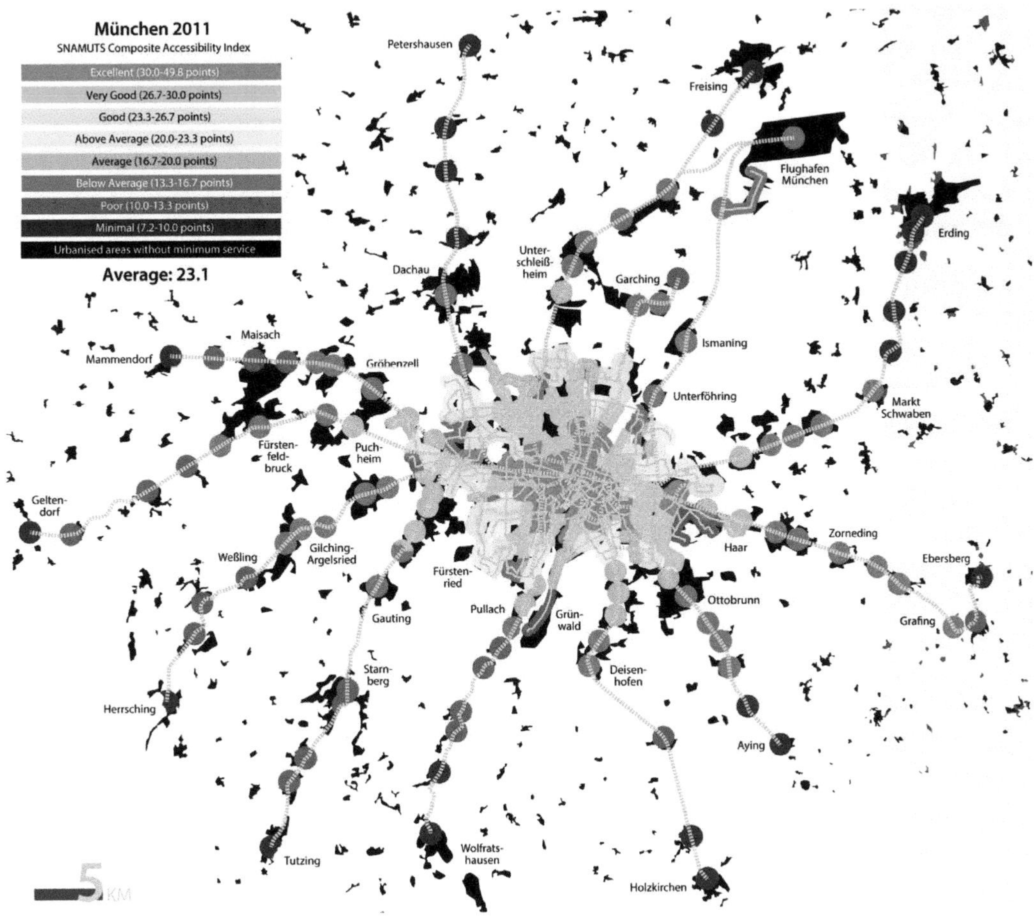

SNAMUTS Composite Accessibility Index and Reflections

There is a uniform picture of good to excellent accessibility performance across the core city, with only minor reductions mostly along the banks of the river Isar, and more substantial reductions for some middle suburban centres that are not on the metro system (Neuaubing, Pipping, Lerchenauer See, St Emmeram, Waldtrudering, Harlaching, Solln, Kleinhadern-Blumenau). Along the suburban S-Bahn branches, accessibility performance declines gradually but usually does not reach the lowest category until close to the outer terminus of each line. Munich has achieved an impressive overall accessibility standard throughout much of the core city despite the frugal approach in terms of allocating operational resources. The city's fast pace of infrastructure growth has enabled careful targeting of resources in order to maximise accessibility outcomes. Some of the most critical network elements are now approaching capacity constraints, however, suggesting the need for investment in additional public transport infrastructure. The flagship project currently being pursued is the duplication of the S-Bahn trunk line by way of an additional east–west tunnel through the CBD. The benefits to network performance that can be achieved with such a project are highly plausible (including much-needed 10-minute frequencies and semi-express services along the S-Bahn branch lines). Simultaneously, the alternative of adding orbital high-capacity network elements has met an unfavourable assessment in the cost – benefit analysis utilised (DB, 2013). Similar existing orbital routes in Hamburg, Copenhagen and Vienna, however, were shown in the SNAMUTS analysis to have a highly beneficial effect for deflecting travel opportunities away from congested central areas. In Munich, their consideration would require a new layer of understanding how the transport network interacts with the urban structure and how an injection of additional infrastructure can sometimes generate substantial flows of travel opportunities where none were thought to exist. It is precisely for such queries of lateral thinking that accessibility tools such as SNAMUTS have been developed.

CONCLUSIONS: EDINBURGH AND OPORTO

The comparison of Edinburgh and Oporto showcases two smaller European cities whose public transport systems, as recently as 15 years ago, bore many similarities. Both were strongly dominated by buses, and in both cases the network was designed to minimise transfers by offering as many direct connections between different corridors and places of activity as possible. Since Oporto's light rail system opened, the roles of rail and bus have been redefined and the 'direct connections-no transfers' network layout partially departed from. The effect has been a lower level of service intensity, more widespread network resilience issues, yet greater ease-of-movement and spatial network coverage than its Scottish counterpart.

Given that the SNAMUTS analysis in both cities only occurred at one point in time we do not know how both cities compared on these indicators prior to Oporto's light rail project which may have reduced service levels on the reconfigured bus network, or prior to bus deregulation in Edinburgh, which across the UK is known to have resulted in increased service levels particularly along busy corridors (White, 1997). Network resilience, too, may have been poorer in both cities prior to these changes. Much of Edinburgh's advantage on the network resilience index is owed to widespread use of higher-capacity double-decker buses; if the system (like Oporto's) was predominantly operated by single-deckers, network resilience would decline accordingly. In the city centre it would record a slightly lower level of resilience than Oporto.

Ease of movement and network coverage can be influenced by the configuration of the urban settlement as much as the design and the organisation of the public transport network. The metropolitan area definition used in the SNAMUTS analysis stretches over more than four times as much territory in Edinburgh than in Oporto, yet the average settlement density (when discounting for non-urbanised land) is relatively similar. Both cities are geographically constrained by coastlines (less convoluted in Oporto than in Edinburgh), yet when comparing the composite index maps Edinburgh's core city appears to have an effective greenbelt policy generating a relatively sharp boundary between urbanised and non-urbanised areas. Thus in Edinburgh urban settlements outside the core city are primarily neighbouring towns and villages that are also relatively contained in spatial terms, whereas in Oporto, a transitional settlement form between rural and urban, as well as commercial/industrial along transport links, has become dominant. It fills much of the space between the core city, which at 135 residents and jobs per hectare remains considerably denser than its Scottish counterpart (72), and its historic neighbours. This is commensurate with findings that Oporto, alongside other southern European cities, experienced urban dispersal only in recent decades, characterised by a growth rate in built-up land that was significantly higher than that of most of its northern and central European counterparts (Kasanko et al, 2006). Nonetheless, Oporto's public transport accessibility, particularly on the ease-of-movement (closeness centrality) and contour catchment indicators, is clearly superior to Edinburgh. An average 30-minute journey provides access to only three quarters as many residents and jobs in Edinburgh as in its Portuguese counterpart. This is an outcome, possibly in equal proportion, of the greater geographical segregation of settlement areas in the Edinburgh region through water bodies and protected greenbelts than in Oporto, and of the speed and attraction of travel opportunities enabled by Oporto's light rail spines that had no equivalent in Edinburgh in 2011.

In the context of recent practice of the majority of European cities, and many New World cities, it appears prudent to make a general recommendation for cities in this size category to subject their public transport networks to modal upgrades, strengthening the role of rail at the expense of buses, in order to improve their accessibility performance. The performance standard achieved in Oporto, however, with two new underground light rail trunk lines intersecting in the city centre, is significantly higher and costlier to construct than Edinburgh's smaller, aboveground light rail system. For several decades no UK city (other than London) has added underground rail infrastructure at the magnitude achieved by Oporto, and the same is true for the majority of New World cities in the sample. Thus the choice of mode upgrade in order facilitate better accessibility performance remains strongly dependent on the resources that can be mobilised locally, regionally, nationally and supra-nationally to bring such projects to fruition.

CONCLUSIONS: HAMBURG AND MUNICH

The comparison of Hamburg and Munich also illustrates the outcomes of distinctly different transport investment programmes over the past half century, despite both cities operating under a common Federal funding regime and a common national body of expertise in this area. However, it is likely that Munich's faster pace of network growth compared to Hamburg is both related to its role as capital of a large, prosperous state with significant political weight at the Federal level (Bavaria's regional conservative party has been a coalition partner in Germany's Federal governments for 45 out of the past 65 years) and a more coherent long-term strategic framework governing integrated land use and transport development. Hamburg not only went through a phase of economic and population contraction during the 1970s and 1980s, but is also constituted as a city-state and thus cannot draw on the tax base of a sizeable regional hinterland for capital investment, or command an equivalent degree of political influence at the Federal level. Hamburg places greater weight on successful inter-state collaboration with neighbours on policy matters, an endeavour that creates added challenge for desirable outcomes compared to acting alone. As a result, the post-war public transport network development plans stalled, leaving a widespread attitude of resignation among decision makers that new infrastructure and (during a low point in the 1980s) even the maintenance of existing service levels were beyond the city's financial reach. This constellation of stagnation and uncertainty in policy terms also eroded the conditions for a broad consensus among stakeholders regarding planning directions and promoted a culture of ad-hoc decisions in transport infrastructure investment and of political partisanship, with incoming new governments liable to start plans afresh rather than capitalise on previous work. Since the turn of the century, Hamburg has seen some public transport and urban development investment, and buoyed as well as pressured by strong growth in ridership since the mid-2000s, renewed interest in resourcing future network growth has emerged.

The divisive potential of transport policy decisions among competing stakeholders has also been of concern in Munich and, in the mid-1990s, led to a concerted effort at consensus-finding as part of a deliberative process known as the Inzell-Initiative (Baumann and White, 2011). This process of collaborative stakeholder dialogue attempts to defuse policy conflicts before they become politically confrontational. It is guided by a charter that contains statements favouring priority for public transport, the imperative of a transit-oriented urban structure and the quest to intelligently manage and control private transport, particularly in central and residential areas (BMW Group, 2013). It thus draws on and consolidates a pro-public transport policy direction that had already evolved over several decades prior to this particular initiative (Cervero, 1998). It is beyond the scope of this work to assess the depth and efficacy of such consensus-building exercises, but it is interesting to see such an effort coincide with exceptional accessibility outcomes (as evidenced by the SNAMUTS analysis), a performance that is achieved with a frugal outlay of operational resources.

This frugal approach to network design and organisation is associated to the HiTrans categorisation of 'one segment-one line' – it attempts to eliminate the spatial duplication of services and, in Munich's case, the wasteful deployment of operational resources that results from operating a route with a mode of inferior performance and capacity to that warranted by the magnitude of travel opportunities generated in the location in question (Nielsen et al, 2005). This last characteristic explains why Munich's service intensity remains below that of Hamburg, which otherwise employs a comparable principle of network design. Munich's denser metro network in a more compact core city, combined with the retention of trams as part of the modal mix, reduces the number of bus routes and particularly of saturated bus routes: there is no equivalent in Munich to the 39 buses per hour per direction that ply Hamburg's Mönckebergstraße during the day on weekdays, even though such a number still appears quite moderate when compared to the 108 buses per hour per direction in Edinburgh's Princes Street.

Both cities have seen healthy patronage growth on public transport in recent years, a trend that is encouraging from a transport sustainability view point yet also highlights the systems' constraints which SNAMUTS attempts to capture, by proxy, in the network resilience index. More broadly, the nexus of patronage growth and system constraints poses the question of what is the most suitable pathway for the networks to expand in the future.

Since the turn of the millennium, successive state governments in Hamburg have twice decided in favour of and later reneged on the reintroduction of light rail as an intermediate mode. At the time of writing, bus prioritisation schemes are pursued in the short term, S-Bahn extensions through capacity upgrades of existing rail lines in the medium term and new underground U-Bahn lines in the longer term, a template that incurs more than cursory reference to the infrastructure plans of the 1960s that ground to a halt during the 1980s downturn. But does the belated revival of these half century-old proposals represent the best use of infrastructure investment to serve the city of the twenty-first century, whose economy has changed from a dominance of trade and manufacturing to one of knowledge and service industries, whose most vibrant growth zones are located in close proximity to the city centre rather than in outlying satellite towns and whose residents' activity patterns have strongly departed from the post-war focus on CBD job commuting and social self-containment in decentralised housing estates?

Similarly, for all its revered consensus culture in transport planning matters, Munich's response to mounting public transport capacity constraints seems to largely revolve around costly duplication of existing infrastructure from the post-war era – apart from the second S-Bahn tunnel, there is also an additional inner-city U-Bahn tunnel in the planning stages that would enable some of the outer branches to no longer having to share a common trunk line. Like Hamburg's proposals, these projects have undeniable merit, yet they also conspire to forego the opportunity for a fundamental rethink of the network structure to respond to the changing mobility and accessibility needs of the current age. They are likely to add to, rather than diminish, both German cities' division into public transport-rich areas in the inner city and along middle suburban rail corridors, and car-dominated outer areas and middle suburban 'accessibility deserts' where public transport remains uncompetitive for the majority of users and trip purposes.

The following chapter introduces another cohort of European cities with exceptional public transport accessibility performance and highlight attempts to overcome such spatial divisions with strategies that depart from the conventional toolbox of 'modernist' infrastructure planning.

6 Eclipsing the Car? Public Transport Designed to Outcompete Private Transport

Here we investigate examples of cities that have addressed the twin challenges of public transport provision and urban growth in unique ways, converting them into European and worldwide pioneers in containing the role of the car in the city and promoting sustainable forms of transport and accessibility. We examine long-term visionary plans of Copenhagen, the deliberate forging of a stakeholder consensus in Barcelona, the impact of popular democracy in the policy history of Zurich and the less conspicuous yet highly successful journey of Vienna to become one of the world's great public transport cities.

COPENHAGEN: A LAND USE-TRANSPORT INTEGRATION HANDPRINT

A discussion of urban form and spatial accessibility in the Danish capital must begin with the 1947 Finger Plan, a blueprint for metropolitan growth that has been repeatedly adapted and survived statutory regime changes over almost 70 years, but remains intact as a guiding vision. The plan identifies five suburban 'fingers' radiating out from the contiguously built-up, pre-1945 'palm' of the coastal core city and ending in five smaller, established towns in approximately 30–40 km distance (Cervero, 1998; Priebs, 2007). Each corridor, designed to absorb the substantial growth pressures experienced in post-war Copenhagen, is anchored by a radial suburban heavy rail line. These lines form a comprehensive rapid transit system already conceived (and partly opened) prior to World War II. New towns, some constructed by government corporations, developed along the railways as predominantly low-rise and garden-oriented suburbs, segregated from industrial and commercial areas but with generous green spaces and exemplary walking and cycling facilities to access the sub-centres lined up like pearls on a string around the rail stations. The green wedges separating the settlement fingers were largely protected from urban development and in some cases re-naturised. Urban renewal projects in the older inner neighbourhoods aimed at improving amenity by 'thinning out' the pre-war urban fabric and encouraging industrial uses to relocate towards the suburban fingers. This planning approach has delivered a city with one of the lowest overall settlement densities among large European cities.

The rail-based settlement structure facilitated job commuting over sizeable distances, strengthened the central city, and achieved decentralisation of employment to sub-centres. Linkages between hubs along different suburban fingers were later added in the form of orbital motorways and bus-based public transport, while the tram network in the core city was abandoned in the 1960s. Expansive pedestrianisation schemes and a restrictive policy towards car access in the inner areas has shifted many short and medium-range journeys to the bicycle, which in Copenhagen's gentle topography is generally speed-competitive with bus-based surface public transport (Gehl et al, 2006).

In the twenty-first century the focus of development has shifted from the suburban fingers to harbour-front sites and reclaimed land in the inner city. A flagship project has been the Ørestad precinct on the island of Amager, facilitated by two major pieces of new public transport infrastructure: a fixed rail link between central Copenhagen, the international airport at Kastrup and the city of Malmö across the Øresund in Sweden, and an automated metro system linking Amager with a new trunk line through the CBD. Designed to attract high-level employment from a global pool of firms and professionals rather than relying on state-directed development, these endeavours mark a shift towards a more entrepreneurial form of co-evolution between urban growth and public transport networks and diversify Copenhagen's urban structure in a more multi-directional and super-regional fashion (Vuk, 2005; Majoor, 2008; Knowles, 2012).

Our analysis examines whether the blueprint for LUTI translates into accessibility outcomes, and whether recent trends to supplement new spatial elements (the aforementioned projects in the inner area and the quest to develop orbital corridors) detract from or further enhance public transport performance.

BARCELONA: INCIDENTAL COMPACTNESS

The co-evolution of land use and public transport development in Barcelona differs from that of its Northern and Western European counterparts. This is linked to different building traditions, cultural preferences, the distribution of wealth in society, and to political, social and economic disruptions during the twentieth century when most of the current interplay of urban form and urban movement was forged.

In the mid-nineteenth century, Barcelona implemented an ambitious urban extension plan under the guidance of city engineer Ildefons Cerdà, for the urban district L'Eixample. The plan, based on an orthogonal grid with chamfered edges at the street corners, anticipated the movement needs (road and rail) of the industrial era, explicitly integrating them with the urban fabric. Barcelona's relatively slow pace of industrialisation, however, translated into a far more modest rate of urban growth in the late nineteenth and early twentieth centuries than in much of Western and Central Europe. As a consequence, L'Eixample was developed more as neighbourhoods for wealthier, 'bourgeois' groups seeking to upgrade their residential amenity than for the working-class (Dura-Guimera, 2003). There was also a greater degree of property speculation than anticipated, resulting in a higher rate of build-out and less open space than originally intended (Ward, 2002). Cerdà's plan thus laid the foundations for a high settlement density and urban compactness throughout Barcelona. The city's elites whose lifestyles and wealth were invested in this urban form generally accepted its implications, and resisted the suburban migration that characterised most English-speaking cities.

The Spanish civil war during the 1930s, followed by four decades of despotic rule under the centralist Franco regime, translated into cultural repression and a period of declining importance at the national scale for Catalan-speaking Barcelona. Economic recovery in the 1960s and 1970s saw a surge in domestic migration, primarily accommodated in a belt of speculative apartment developments at the outskirts of Barcelona (Catalán et al, 2008). Thus the relative urban compactness persisted as the city expanded, while mounting congestion problems (both on the roads and on the rudimentary pre-war metro) sparked a round of major transport infrastructure investment in both systems (Pernau, 2001).

Democratisation in the late 1970s and Barcelona's 1992 Olympic Games nomination saw a gradual shift in the transport and land use policy focus towards urban quality, helping to make Barcelona a pioneer in people-friendly public space design. A full motorway ring around the core city (*ronda del litoral*) was completed for the Olympics, revolutionising private vehicle accessibility in the region. However, growing scepticism among decision makers towards road-based solutions to urban congestion resulted in a moratorium on major inner city road capacity expansion after 1992, and a program to reduce private vehicle capacity in favour of other modes in order to lock in the decongestion effects of the ring road. From 1998 Barcelona also embarked on a deliberative consensus-building initiative (the Barcelona Mobility Pact), an ongoing multi-partisan round table to galvanise these insights into a set of binding policy directives (Ajuntament de Barcelona, 2000).

The expansion of the urban rail network did not occur at the rate envisioned in the 1970s but continued despite numerous changes in conception and planning culture. Public transport now has almost twice the modal share of private vehicles for journeys within the core city and a narrower majority for journeys linking the core city and its suburban hinterland. However, public transport usage has been stagnating since the 2008 financial crisis, with private motorised transport also declining but non-motorised transport increasing (Ajuntament de Barcelona, 2014a).

Meanwhile, urban dispersal gained a foothold in the metropolitan region, though different in character from north-western European or New World cities. For more privileged social groups it is driven by second homes in scenic locations. On a regional scale it is manifest in the strengthening of secondary centres in the outer metropolitan area, moving Catalonia's capital region towards greater polycentricity. Only commercial and industrial development at the urban periphery is at the scale, land consumption and car/truck orientation experienced throughout developed world cities (Dura-Guimera, 2003; Catalán et al, 2008; Garcia-López, 2012).

Despite past disruptive political and economic development and the resulting heterogeneity of its public transport infrastructure, Barcelona retains a high average settlement density and relative spatial containment, closer to Singapore and Hong Kong in these characteristics than to most of its European peers in the sample. This is supported by the topographic constraints of coastlines and mountain ranges. In our analysis we examine to what extent these physical properties and factors of planning history and culture support or detract from good accessibility.

ZURICH: THE BIRTHPLACE OF USER-FRIENDLY PUBLIC TRANSPORT?

Where Barcelona's co-evolution of land use and transport during the twentieth century has been a story of recurrent disruption, Zurich's can be regarded as one of continuity. At a time when Barcelona's decision making processes were still subject to the authoritarian practices of the Franco regime, Switzerland had a unique model of direct democracy. This enabled Zurich's citizens to redefine the modernist paradigms of motorisation, speed and efficiency in a more people-oriented format.

During the early post-war era, Zurich's planning authorities, like their counterparts in other case study cities such as Hamburg, Munich or Montreal, envisioned an urban future where the movement of people was dominated by private motorised vehicles at the surface, and underground public transport below surface in order to enable arterial roads to be freed from tram infrastructure. However, investments of large magnitude require a public referendum in Switzerland, and popular majorities for the associated road and metro projects failed to materialise during the 1960s and 1970s. Instead, an alternative plan to retain a dense surface network of trams, trolleybuses and diesel buses and gradually afford it absolute priority over cars was adopted in 1977 (Ott, 1995). Thus the surface public transport system evolved into a speed-competitive, highly reliable, multimodal and multi-directional turn-up-and-go system, while the capacity of the road system and central city parking facilities were capped. In fact, inner urban road space was routinely reduced whenever a new road was built or upgraded elsewhere in the catchment area (Cervero, 1998).

Zurich is the dominant urban centre of a confederate state, or canton, of the same name, which provides for a large part of its commuter shed. The core city, however, holds less than 30 per cent of the canton's population, and instead the region is characterised by intense functional interdependence and a polynuclear structure. To help public transport cater for these markets and to reduce the traffic congestion effects that resulted from insufficient public transport integration beyond the core city scale, a regional public transport agency (*Züricher Verkehrsverbund* or *ZVV*) was established alongside a region-wide integrated ticketing system in 1990. These steps were accompanied by the conversion of the agglomeration's expansive heavy rail infrastructure into a coherent suburban rail (S-Bahn) system with regular service frequencies and stopping patterns (Mees, 2010a; Bratzel, 1999).

Today, Zurich forms the heart of an extraordinarily successful public transport network, attracting more annual journeys per capita from its metropolitan region than any other within the cohort of SNAMUTS cities outside Asia. Its user-friendliness is also manifest in a planning culture that revolves first and foremost around the needs of the passenger, and that uses desired levels of service and network cohesion (*Verkehrsangebot*) as the starting point for infrastructure and service planning (Stone, 2011). Thus Zurich has established a policy making tradition informed by a type of accessibility thinking. Our interest is in how this favourable policy environment for public transport performance delivers accessibility outcomes.

VIENNA: A QUIET ACHIEVER?

Vienna's annual rate of public transport usage (in terms of journeys per capita) was only marginally behind that of Zurich in 2011, and much higher than any other European SNAMUTS city. While Vienna and Zurich are almost neighbours on a global scale, their settlement structure and history of public transport investment show significant contrast: Zurich's has a relatively small core city and polynuclear urban region; Vienna has a much larger core city and weak surrounding region. During the post-war period when Vienna was located at a geographical extremity of Western Europe, surrounded by the Iron Curtain in three compass directions, the settlement area grew more slowly than in many comparable European city-regions, and the population declined slightly (Kasanko et al, 2006; Faber, 2003). Simultaneously, Vienna's public transport development has centred on the modernisation and expansion of a high-capacity inner urban metro system of the kind that Zurich's voters rejected, while also retaining an extensive surface network of trams and buses. The interplay of mid-capacity modes at both a regional and urban scale, at which Zurich excels, is less prominent in Vienna. Instead the public transport network is organised in a more hierarchical form between modes of different capacity and performance.

Owing to the dominance of the core city and its containment by a large area of protected open space to the west, the Vienna region has a relatively high average settlement density in a European context. There has been a historic emphasis on multi-storey apartment living to a greater extent, and garden-oriented, low-rise housing to a lesser extent than in most of its northern and central European peers. Conversely, the collaboration of the core city and its regional hinterland within the neighbouring state of Lower Austria remains underdeveloped, and comprehensive planning outcomes are sometimes undermined by a degree of competition between Vienna and surrounding municipalities to attract tax-paying residents and businesses.

Within the city-state of Vienna, public transport journeys accounted for 37 per cent of all trips in 2011, compared to 29 per cent of all trips in private cars and 34 per cent by non-motorised modes. Since 1993, this represents a shift of more than 10 per cent of all journeys from cars to public transport and, to a smaller extent, cycling (Wiener Stadtwerke, 2012). Vienna is not only a long-standing European leader in public transport patronage (most other European cities in the sample have mode share figures in the 15–20 per cent range), it has consolidated this position the recent past. Our interest is in whether this success story can be traced to factors that are manifest in accessibility measures.

ACCESSIBILITY PROFILE: KØBENHAVN ⊠DENMARK⊠

Copenhagen is a medium-sized capital of 1.85 million inhabitants in an area of 2,780 sq km (2009). Substantial spatial expansion of the metropolitan area occurred after 1945 and was largely contained within growth corridors (the Finger Plan described above) along radial rail lines, known as the *S-tog* system and comparable to its counterparts from German (*S-Bahn*) and French-speaking countries (*RER*) (Svensson, 1981). Metropolitan planning since the 1970s converted the radial Finger Plan into a more lattice-shaped pattern, aided by the construction of an orbital motorway system alongside the radial rail network. Today, Copenhagen is among the lowest-density metropolitan areas in Europe at 25.2 residents and 9.5 jobs per urbanised hectare (DST, 2010). Fixed bridge and tunnel connections to the Danish mainland and to Malmö in Sweden, opened in the late 1990s and early 2000s, reduced the city's relative geographical isolation and increased functional interdependence particularly with the Swedish province of Skåne, which is now within convenient commuting distance to and from Copenhagen. This analysis, however, has been limited to the Danish side of this wider metropolitan region, even though rail services at the SNAMUTS standard (albeit attracting comparatively high fares) connect the centres of Copenhagen and Malmö.

The first-generation tram system was abandoned in 1972 but a dense, high-frequency, grid-shaped bus system was retained, particularly across the older, inner neighbourhoods. Since 2000 public transport infrastructure development has focussed on upgrading and extending an inner orbital *S-tog* line to take pressure off the central area; the introduction of a new driverless mini-metro system to service a central corridor and to access inner urban redevelopment areas; and the implementation of improved regional rail services, including to Sweden. The bus system, functionally and institutionally integrated with rail, has been restructured to provide three colour-coded types of services: high-frequency inner urban routes (red), cross-city express routes (blue) and suburban feeder routes (yellow). In the outer metropolitan area in particular, there are also a number of non-electrified local rail lines (*lokalbaner*).

Public transport usage per capita is comparable to Amsterdam or Hamburg, and well below the European leaders of Vienna and Zurich. However, Copenhagen is prominent for its very high share of bicycle travel, supported by expansive infrastructure, and for long-standing restrictive policies on car parking in the CBD as well as comparatively high taxes on vehicle sales (Cervero, 1998).

An integrated fare system for all public transport modes is currently being converted from a paper to an electronic ticketing regime (*rejsekort*). Single, multiple, daily and periodical tickets are available, but the fare system seems to offer fewer genuine bargains than other European cities, and promotes relatively prescriptive journey paths through a fine-grained structure of fare zones.

Separate agencies are responsible for the suburban/regional rail lines (*S-tog/R-tog*), metro and bus networks, though each of them is at least partially in public ownership. Service delivery is largely contracted out to private-sector operators.

Service Intensity

In Copenhagen, 20 minutes is the standard pulse of the public transport system: while the suburban rail (*S-tog*) system is generally operated at 10-minute intervals along all routes during business hours, suburban (yellow) and express (blue) buses vary between 10-minute and 20-minute intervals. Most inner urban (red) bus routes and the metro have intervals of less than 10 minutes – 3 minutes in the case of the metro trunk route. Conversely, the regional rail lines (*R-tog*) connecting Copenhagen with destinations outside the metropolitan area in Western Sjælland, and the majority of outer suburban *lokalbaner* and the inner

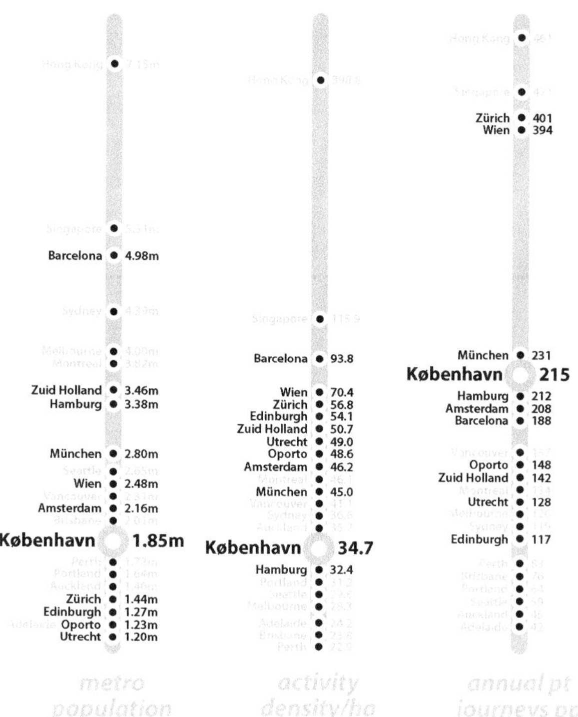

Edinburgh 38.2
Amsterdam 28.7
Zürich 25.9
Wien 25.5
Oporto 24.9
København 24.8
Barcelona 21.9
Hamburg 17.2
Zuid Holland 16.8
Utrecht 16.2
München 13.9

service intensity/ 100,000 inh

Zürich 10.1
København 9.7
München 7.9
Wien 7.7
Oporto 6.3
Hamburg 5.3
Barcelona 4.7
Utrecht 4.3
Amsterdam 4.2
Zuid Holland 3.5
Edinburgh 2.6

heavy rail stations/ 100,000 inh

urban ferry line are operated every 30 minutes.

In a European context, Copenhagen has a relatively generous provision of operational resources, alongside Amsterdam, Vienna, Zurich and Oporto and in contrast to the more frugal remaining Dutch and German cities. Relative to population, Copenhagen's service intensity is roughly 50 per cent higher than, for instance, that of neighbouring Hamburg.

Copenhagen has the second highest numbers of heavy rail stations relative to population after Zurich. This position can be explained in part by the presence of the expansive network of non-electrified regional rail lines in the outskirts of Copenhagen's metropolitan region (*lokalbaner*). Even if these are discounted, Copenhagen again outsupplies its southern neighbour of Hamburg by more than 50 per cent.

Closeness Centrality

There are 140 SNAMUTS activity nodes in the metropolitan area, mostly drawn from the large pool of dedicated rail-bus interchanges, transit-oriented suburban centres on the *S-tog* and *R-tog* network, and some intersections of surface routes in inner urban areas. Linked to Copenhagen's low overall settlement density, there are extensive built-up areas with a relatively low intensity of activities, or dedicated to a single land use where the identification of SNAMUTS activity nodes was subject to a higher threshold than in the denser case study cities in Europe.

The average closeness centrality value lies within a relatively small band shared with most other European and Canadian case study cities. In the inner area the structure of the network, particularly within the area circumscribed by the inner orbital rail line (*S-tog* line F), is akin to a tightly-knit grid, offering a multitude of route choices for any node-to-node journey and a similar abundance of potential transfer points. Passengers thus have the option to travel along geographical desire lines, including for chain journeys involving multiple destinations. For this reason, closeness results within most of the inner area (Cities of Copenhagen and Frederiksberg and in some cases beyond) are consistently within a narrow spectrum at the higher end of the scale, though it is notable that rail nodes perform slightly better than bus-only nodes in their vicinity. In the outskirts of the metropolis the network is sparser and, as a result, closeness values there rise (deteriorate) at a faster rate with growing distance from the central area. This is especially true for activity nodes along the relatively slow and low-frequency local rail lines along the urban fringe in Copenhagen (Fredensborg, Gilleleje, Herfølge) or Hundested, which has the highest closeness centrality value in the European sample.

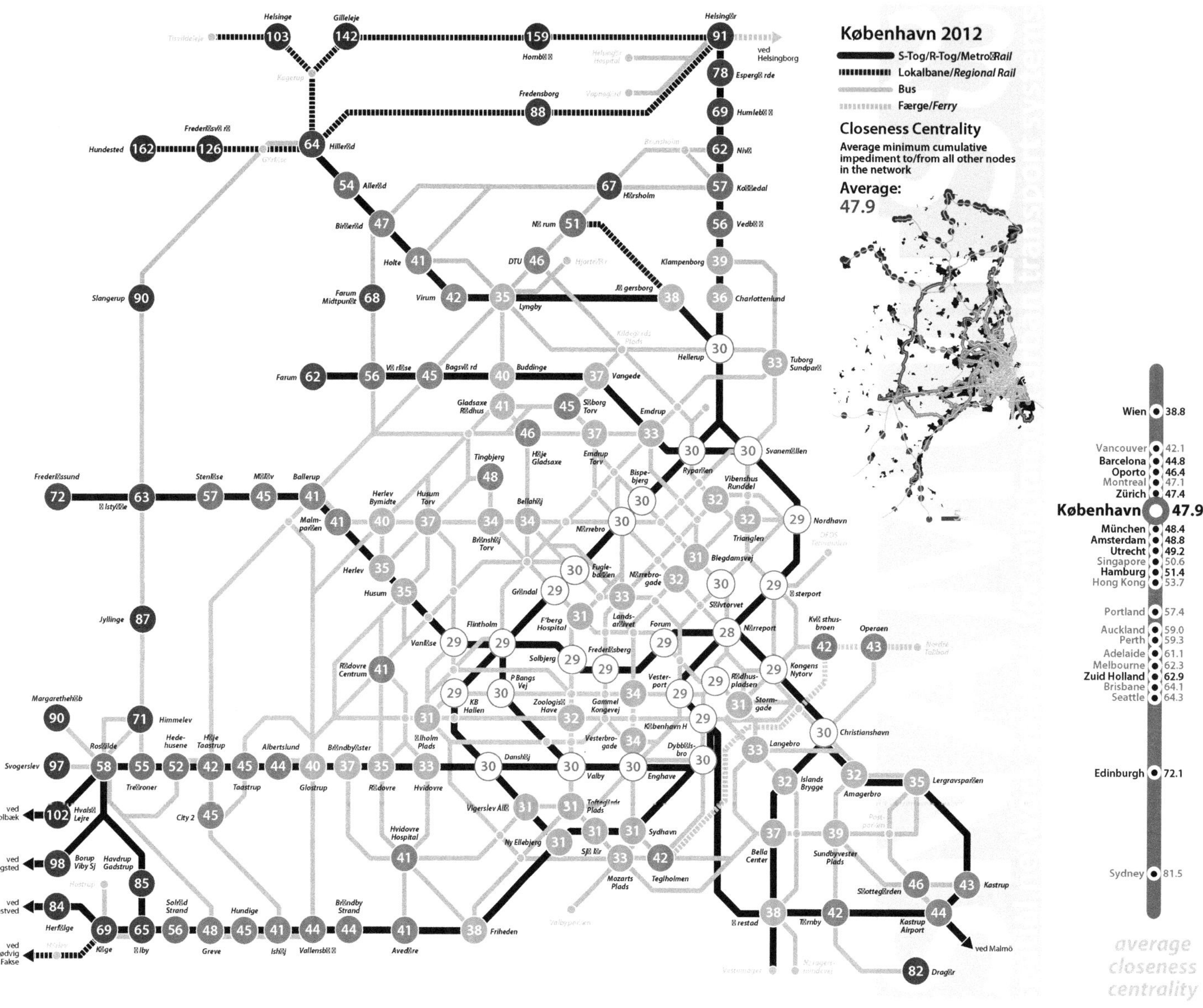

Degree Centrality

On the degree centrality index, European cities split into two distinct groups: those with an average below one transfer and those with an average above one transfer. Copenhagen belongs to the former, less transfer-intensive group, even though the network is predominantly organised around a functional hierarchy between modes of varying performance (buses, metro and suburban rail). The key reason for a superior performance on this index is linked to the substantial number of radial, orbital and diagonal routes traversing the city from settlement edge to settlement edge. These connections offer transfer-free travel opportunities between nodes that in other cities would require one or more transfers. As a consequence, the bus network at minimum service standards provides a geographically congruent movement system in its own right, dedicated to frequent service along second-order urban corridors linking a multitude of transfer points with rail and with each other.

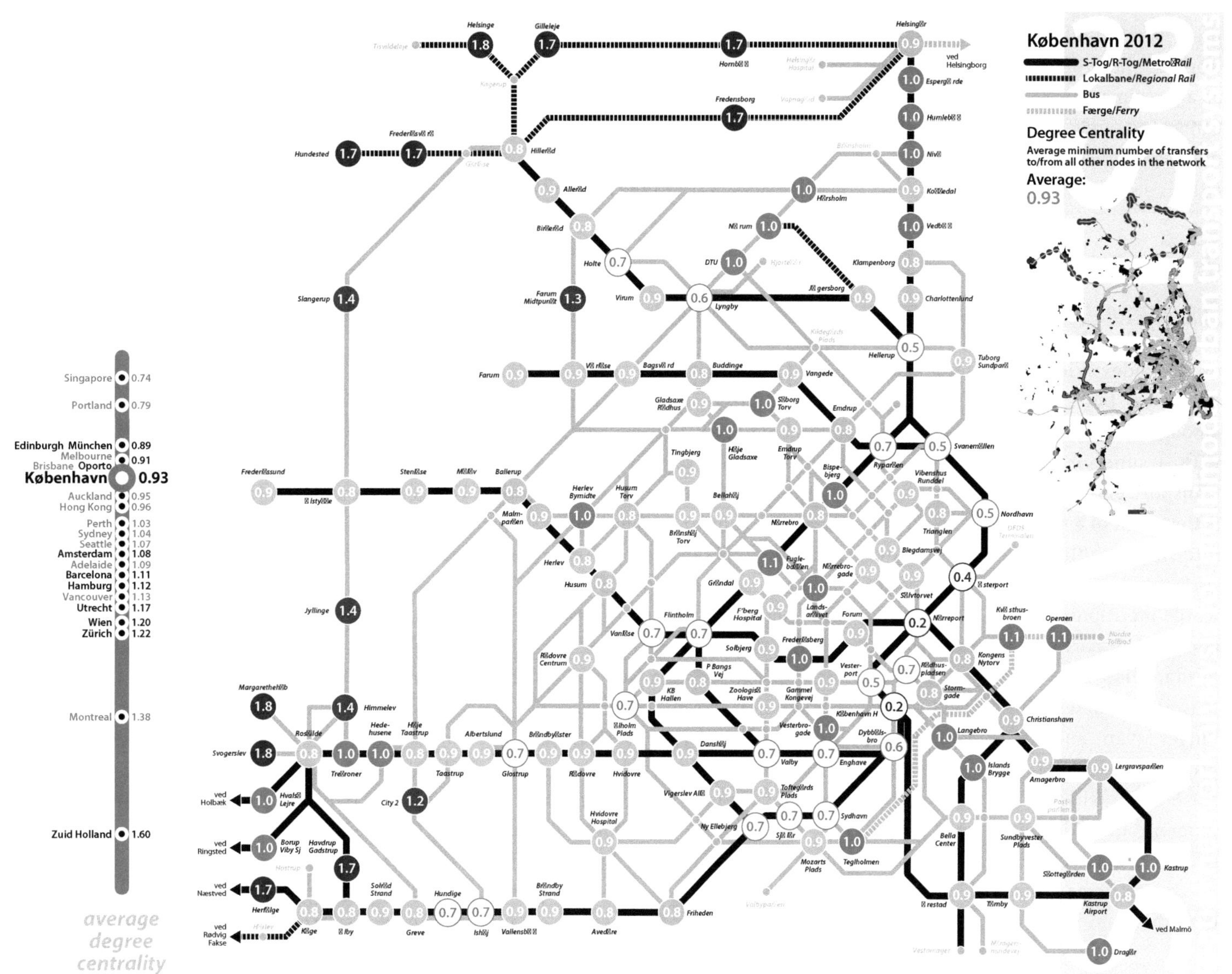

Unlike more transfer-dependent Hamburg, Copenhagen largely retained the surface network density inherited from the former tram system when it was converted to buses in the 1960s and 1970s. Copenhagen's location on an island also facilitated the establishment of a comprehensive suburban orbital bus network, as the orbital links only traverse an approximate 135-degree segment of a concentric circle (between coastlines), not 360 degrees as in most landlocked cities.

Network Coverage

Copenhagen falls a few percentage points short of Europe's best performers on this index (Vienna, Amsterdam and Barcelona), but is still clearly positioned among the group of European cities with a superior geographical public transport endowment. This outcome is the result of a relatively high service intensity, enabling a comprehensive surface network designed to cover the whole metropolitan area, rather than confined to particular administrative borders like in Vienna and Munich. It is also linked to the impact of the Finger Plan and its long-standing protection of green wedges between the *S-tog* corridors from urban development, in addition to the natural southern and eastern containment of the settlement area through the coastline.

Contour Catchments

Copenhagen records the second largest average relative catchments in the global sample after Vienna. This outcome is an indication that, despite the city's low average settlement density in comparison with most of its European peers, the public transport system offers excellent travel time standards and levels of integration with the land use pattern.

From the two most important rail hubs (Nørreport and København H), 60 per cent of metropolitan residents and jobs can be reached within 30 minutes which, alongside Vienna, are the equal highest such scores found in any SNAMUTS city. Along both the diametrical *S-tog* trunk line and the inner orbital between Hellerup and Ny Ellebjerg, there are 22 activity nodes with contour catchment values consistently at 50 per cent or higher. For activity nodes within the area circumscribed by these two lines that are based on bus-only access, the figures drop, owing to lower travel speeds. Even key middle suburban centres (such as Lyngby, Herlev or Glostrup) are accessible to a greater proportion of metropolitan residents and jobs by way of a 30-minute public transport journey than the central cities of several of its European peers. Only beyond the outer termini of the high-frequency *S-tog* system (Køge, Høge Taastrup, Frederikssund, Farum, Hillerød and Klampenborg) is there a prevalence of activity nodes that do not provide access to a significant proportion of the metropolitan area within this time bracket.

Betweenness Centrality

According to the global betweenness index relative to metropolitan population and jobs, Copenhagen has the highest concentration of public transport travel opportunities in the global sample outside Asia. High frequencies and speeds on the *S-tog* system, the compactness and close spacing of activity nodes in the core city (Copenhagen and Frederiksberg), and the relatively small number of significant suburban activity nodes away from the rail system, owing to six decades of mostly effective finger planning, all contribute to this result.

The catchment of typical path length measure is a proxy for the number of residents and jobs travelled past on an average journey. On this index, Copenhagen is a relatively strong performer, likely related to the city's hand-shaped settlement form and rail network which have the effect of encouraging longer journeys along the radial corridors, passing a relatively large number of activity nodes aligned along the way. On the other hand, the functional interplay of radial, circumferential and diagonal lines in Copenhagen's public transport system facilitates multi-directional movement without deviating excessively from geographical desire lines.

Copenhagen's reliance on heavy rail modes to generate travel opportunities across the city is inferior only to Barcelona and Munich and very close to that of Hamburg, the only other large tram-free city in the European sample.

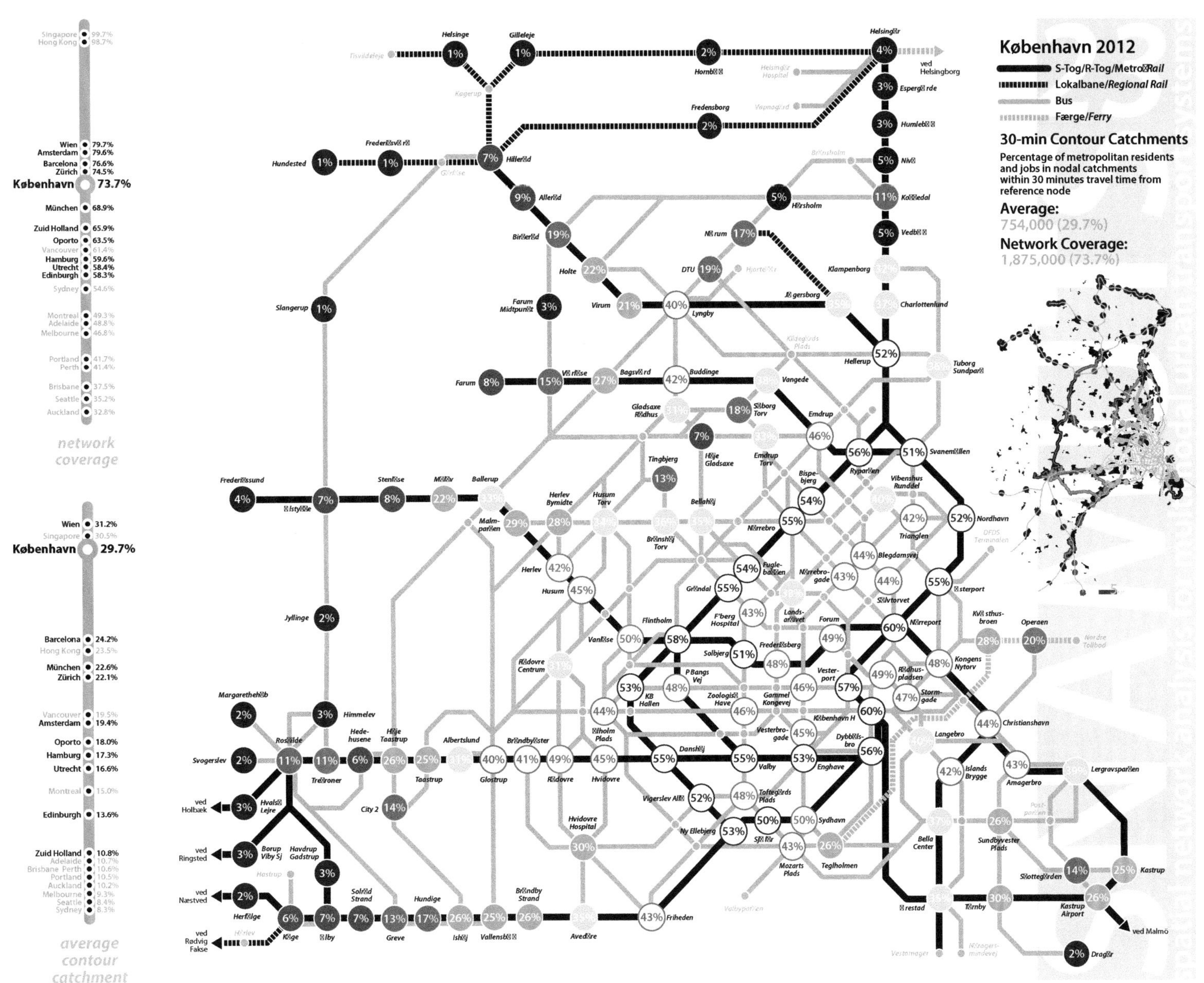

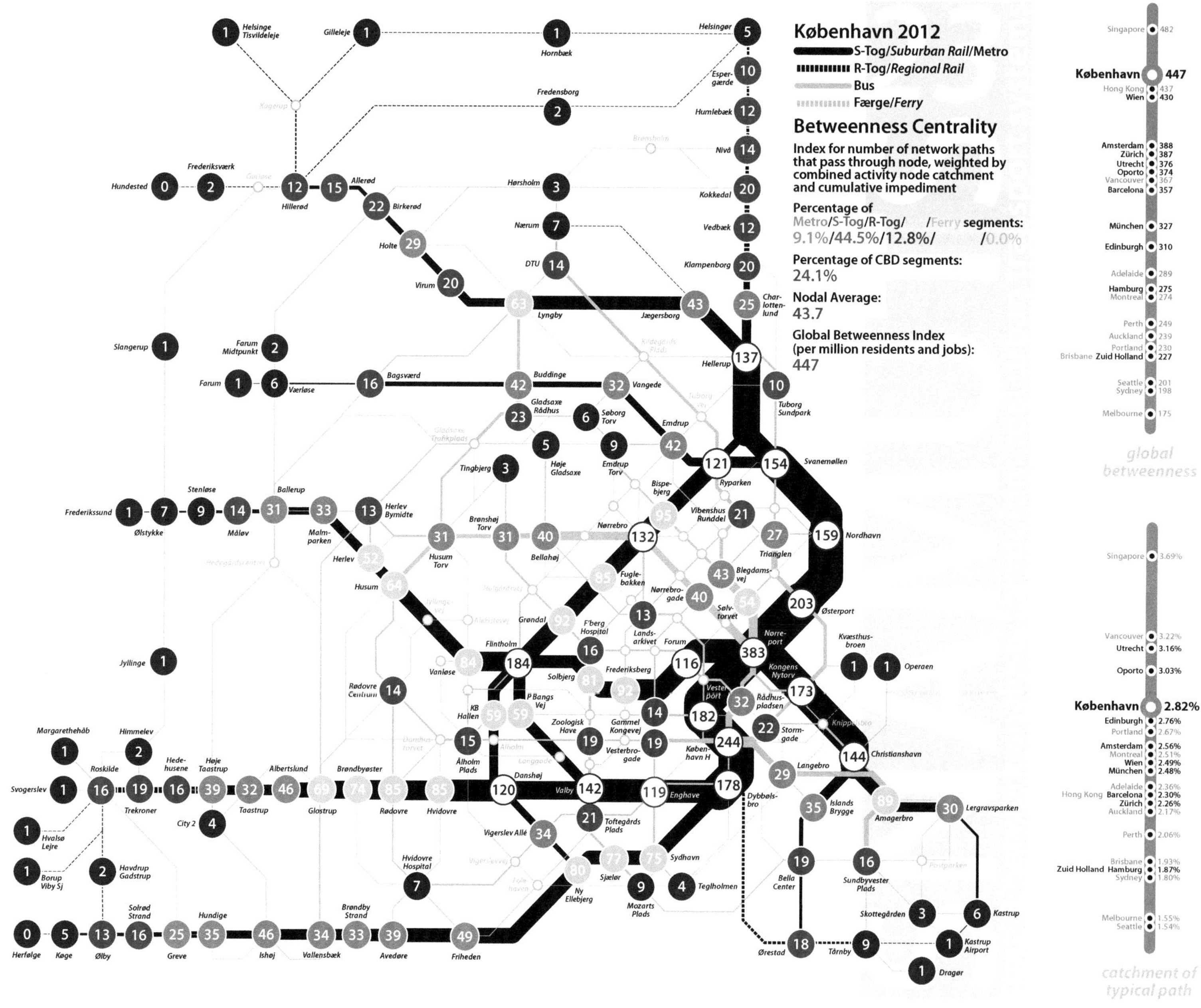

København 2012
S-Tog/Suburban Rail/Metro
R-Tog/Regional Rail
Bus
Færge/Ferry
Betweenness Centrality
Index for number of network paths that pass through node, weighted by combined activity node catchment and cumulative impediment
Percentage of Metro/S-Tog/R-Tog/ /Ferry segments:
9.1%/44.5%/12.8%/ /0.0%
Percentage of CBD segments:
24.1%
Nodal Average:
43.7
Global Betweenness Index (per million residents and jobs):
447
Singapore 482
København 447
Hong Kong 437
Wien 430
Amsterdam 388
Zürich 387
Utrecht 376
Oporto 374
Vancouver 367
Barcelona 357
München 327
Edinburgh 310
Adelaide 289
Hamburg 275
Montreal 274
Perth 249
Auckland 239
Portland 230
Brisbane Zuid Holland 227
Seattle 201
Sydney 198
Melbourne 175
global betweenness
Singapore 3.69%
Vancouver 3.22%
Utrecht 3.16%
Oporto 3.03%
København 2.82%
Edinburgh 2.76%
Portland 2.67%
Amsterdam 2.56%
Montreal 2.51%
Wien 2.49%
München 2.48%
Adelaide 2.36%
Hong Kong Barcelona 2.30%
Zürich 2.26%
Auckland 2.17%
Perth 2.06%
Brisbane 1.93%
Zuid Holland Hamburg 1.87%
Sydney 1.80%
Melbourne 1.55%
Seattle 1.54%
catchment of typical path
Helsinge Tisvildeleje 1
Gilleleje 1
Hornbæk 1
Helsingør 5
Espergærde 10
Fredensborg 2
Humlebæk 12
Nivå 14
Hundested 0
Frederiksværk 2
Hillerød 12
Allerød 15
Birkerød 22
Hørsholm 3
Kokkedal 20
Nærum 7
Vedbæk 12
Holte 29
DTU 14
Klampenborg 20
Virum 20
Lyngby 63
Jægersborg 43
Charlottenlund 25
Slangerup 1
Farum Midtpunkt 2
Hellerup 137
Farum 1
Værløse 6
Bagsværd 16
Buddinge 42
Vangede 32
Tuborg Sundpark 10
Gladsaxe Rådhus 23
Søborg Torv 6
Emdrup 42
Høje Gladsaxe 5
Emdrup Torv 9
Ryparken 121
Svanemøllen 154
Tingbjerg 3
Bispebjerg 95
Stenløse 9
Ballerup 31
Frederikssund 1
Ølstykke 7
Måløv 14
Malmparken 33
Herlev Bymidte 13
Vibenshus Runddel 21
Brønshøj Torv 31
Husum Torv 31
Bellahøj 40
Nørrebro 132
Trianglen 27
Nordhavn 159
Herlev 52
Fuglebakken 85
Blegdamsvej 43
Husum 64
Nørrebrogade 40
Sølvtorvet 64
Østerport 203
Grøndal 92
F'berg Hospital
Landsarkivet 13
Flintholm 184
Forum 116
Nørreport 383
Kvæsthusbroen
Jyllinge 1
Vanløse 84
Solbjerg 81
Frederiksberg 92
Vesterport 182
Kongens Nytorv 173
Operaen 1
Rødovre Centrum 14
KB Hallen 59
P Bangs Vej 59
Zoologisk Have
Gammel Kongevej 14
Rådhuspladsen 32
Stormgade 22
Christianshavn 144
Margarethehåb 1
Himmelev 2
Ålholm Plads 15
Vesterbrogade 19
København H 244
Langebro 29
Svogerslev 1
Roskilde 16
Trekroner 19
Hedehusene 16
Høje Taastrup 39
Taastrup 32
Albertslund 46
Glostrup 69
Brøndbyøster 74
Rødovre 85
Hvidovre 85
Danshøj 120
Valby 142
Enghave 119
Dybbølsbro 178
Islands Brygge 35
Amagerbro 89
Lergravsparken 30
City 2 4
Vigerslev Allé 34
Toftegårds Plads 21
Hvalsø Lejre 1
Borup Viby Sj 1
Havdrup Gadstrup 2
Hvidovre Hospital 7
Sjælør 77
Sydhavn 75
Ny Ellebjerg 80
Mozarts Plads 9
Teglholmen 4
Bella Center 19
Sundbyvester Plads 16
Skottegården 3
Kastrup 6
Solrød Strand 16
Hundige 35
Brøndby Strand 33
Herfølge 0
Køge 5
Ølby 13
Greve 25
Ishøj 46
Vallensbæk 34
Avedøre 39
Friheden 49
Ørestad 18
Tårnby 9
Kastrup Airport 1
Dragør 1

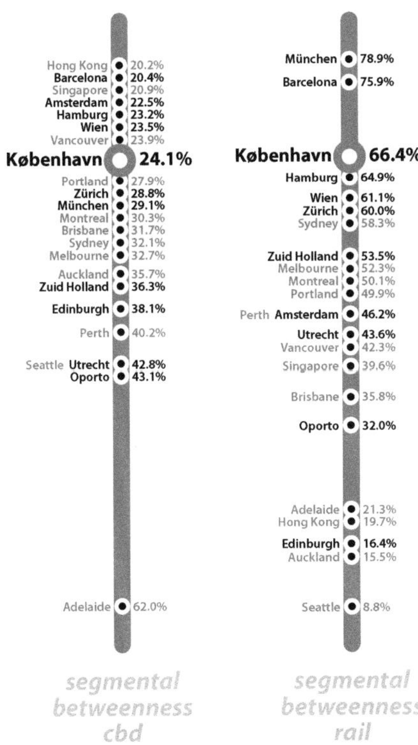

The degree of reliance on traversing the CBD for public transport journeys is at par with other larger European cities such as Amsterdam, Hamburg or Vienna, but significantly lower than in Munich or in the smaller cities. This may be owed to the effectiveness of the inner orbital rail link (*S-tog* line F) in deflecting non-CBD related movement paths away from the central area.

Network Resilience

Average segmental resilience results are superior to those of most European peer cities. This suggests that the system is able to accommodate some future growth in travel opportunities from land use intensification and increased public transport mode share, provided such growth is distributed well over the network. The multidirectional network facilitates this more readily than the more prescriptive ones in places such as Hamburg or the New World cities. In Copenhagen, however, the predominant picture of balanced network performance conceals some local weaknesses. A radial bus corridor along Lyngbyvejen, connecting the outlying main campus of DTU directly with central Copenhagen, accommodates the poorest resilience values on the network and reveals deficiencies in the provision of Copenhagen's usually high standard of multimodal integration in its catchment. Further challenges are apparent around some centres away from the rail network in the dense inner urban neighbourhoods of Nørrebro and Østerbro, where a new circular metro line currently under construction may provide some relief in years to come. No committed modal conversion plans are in place for the two radial bus corridors experiencing the lowest resilience levels in the core city, namely between Husum and Nørreport in the inner north-west, and between Langebro and Sundbyvester Plads on Amager. The resilience levels of the regional rail line between København H and the airport are likely overstated, and its network significance understated, since this route continues on to Malmö on the Swedish side which was omitted from this network analysis exercise.

Nodal Connectivity

Among the European SNAMUTS cities, Copenhagen is outperformed on the nodal connectivity index by Amsterdam, Hamburg, Munich, Vienna and Barcelona. Metropolitan area size influences this index to an extent, as travel opportunities and patronage in a constrained area (such as a group of central city nodes) tend to grow exponentially with network size for reasons of geometry. However, it is also true that Copenhagen's average occupancy of public transport services, and thus average levels of actual congestion, remain lower than in most of its European peer cities.

The highest nodal connectivity results can be found along the *S-tog* trunk line between Danshøj/Sjælør and Hellerup, and the northern section of the inner orbital line between Flintholm and Hellerup. Some suburban centres such as Ishøj, Glostrup, Ballerup, Lyngby and Roskilde also score well on this index. With the exception of the two 'super nodes' at København H and Nørreport, the performance gradient is quite smooth from centre to periphery, leaving only a small number of relative 'connectivity deserts' in the urban fabric of inner and middle suburban Copenhagen.

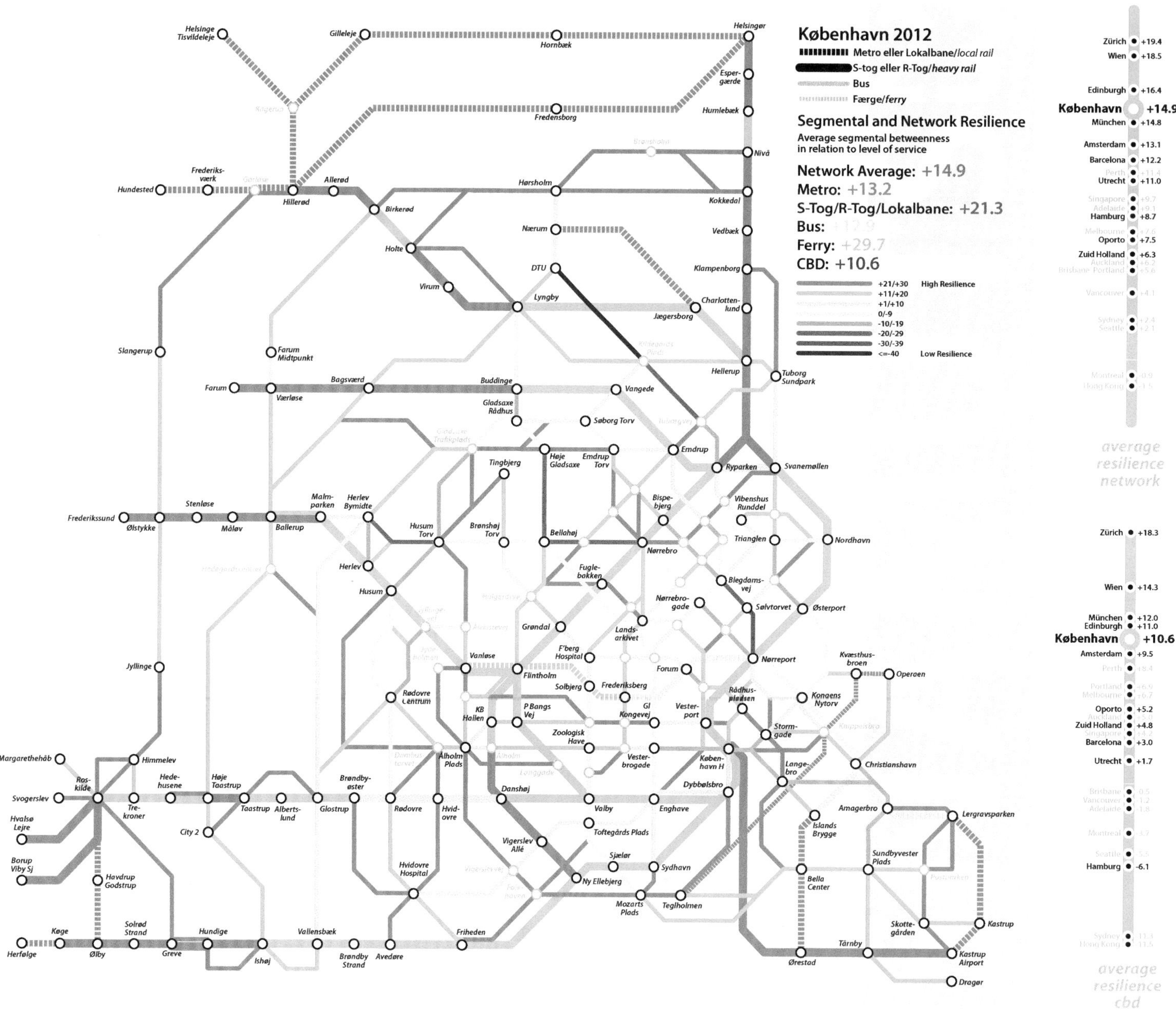
København 2012
Metro eller Lokalbane/local rail
S-tog eller R-Tog/heavy rail
Bus
Færge/ferry
Segmental and Network Resilience
Average segmental betweenness
in relation to level of service
Network Average: +14.9
Metro: +13.2
S-Tog/R-Tog/Lokalbane: +21.3
Bus: +12.9
Ferry: +29.7
CBD: +10.6
+21/+30
High Resilience
+11/+20
+1/+10
0/-9
-10/-19
-20/-29
-30/-39
<=-40
Low Resilience
Zürich +19.4
Wien +18.5
Edinburgh +16.4
København +14.9
München +14.8
Amsterdam +13.1
Barcelona +12.2
Utrecht +11.0
Hamburg +8.7
Oporto +7.5
Zuid Holland +6.3
average resilience network
Zürich +18.3
Wien +14.3
München +12.0
Edinburgh +11.0
København +10.6
Amsterdam +9.5
Oporto +5.2
Zuid Holland +4.8
Barcelona +3.0
Utrecht +1.7
Hamburg -6.1
average resilience cbd
Helsinge Tisvildeleje
Gilleleje
Hornbæk
Helsingør
Esper-gærde
Humlebæk
Fredensborg
Nivå
Frederiks-værk
Hundested
Hillerød
Allerød
Birkerød
Hørsholm
Kokkedal
Vedbæk
Nærum
Holte
Virum
DTU
Lyngby
Klampenborg
Charlotten-lund
Jægersborg
Slangerup
Farum Midtpunkt
Hellerup
Tuborg Sundpark
Farum
Værløse
Bagsværd
Buddinge
Gladsaxe Rådhus
Vangede
Søborg Torv
Emdrup
Høje Gladsaxe
Emdrup Torv
Ryparken
Svanemøllen
Tingbjerg
Frederikssund
Ølstykke
Stenløse
Måløv
Ballerup
Malm-parken
Herlev Bymidte
Husum Torv
Brønshøj Torv
Bellahøj
Bispe-bjerg
Vibenshus Runddel
Trianglen
Nordhavn
Nørrebro
Herlev
Husum
Fugle-bokken
Blegdams-vej
Nørrebro-gade
Sølvtorvet
Østerport
Grøndal
Lands-arkivet
Jyllinge
Vanløse
Flintholm
F'berg Hospital
Nørreport
Forum
Kvæsthus-broen
Operaen
Solbjerg
Frederiksberg
Rødovre Centrum
KB Hallen
P Bangs Vej
Gl Kongevej
Vester-port
Rådhus-pladsen
Kongens Nytorv
Storm-gade
Zoologisk Have
Margarethehåb
Himmelev
Ålholm Plads
Vester-brogade
Køben-havn H
Lange-bro
Christianshavn
Ros-kilde
Svogerslev
Hede-husene
Høje Taastrup
Brøndby-øster
Danshøj
Dybbølsbro
Tre-kroner
Taastrup
Alberts-lund
Glostrup
Rødovre
Hvid-ovre
Valby
Enghave
Amagerbro
Lergravsparken
Hvalsø Lejre
City 2
Toftegårds Plads
Islands Brygge
Vigerslev Allé
Borup Viby Sj
Havdrup Godstrup
Hvidovre Hospital
Sjælør
Sydhavn
Sundbyvester Plads
Ny Ellebjerg
Bella Center
Mozarts Plads
Teglholmen
Skotte-gården
Kastrup
Køge
Solrød Strand
Hundige
Vallensbæk
Friheden
Tårnby
Herfølge
Ølby
Greve
Ishøj
Brøndby Strand
Avedøre
Ørestad
Kastrup Airport
Dragør

SNAMUTS Composite Accessibility Index and Reflections

Copenhagen's overall performance is positioned in third place among the European SNAMUTS cities, behind Barcelona and Vienna and marginally ahead of Munich. In the context of the low settlement density, comparable only to Hamburg in the European sample, this is a remarkable achievement and can be traced to the visionary Finger Plan and rail orientation of Copenhagen's post war city expansion (Cervero, 1998). Copenhagen's suburban rail (*S-tog*) system is the finest among all SNAMUTS cities, adapted to

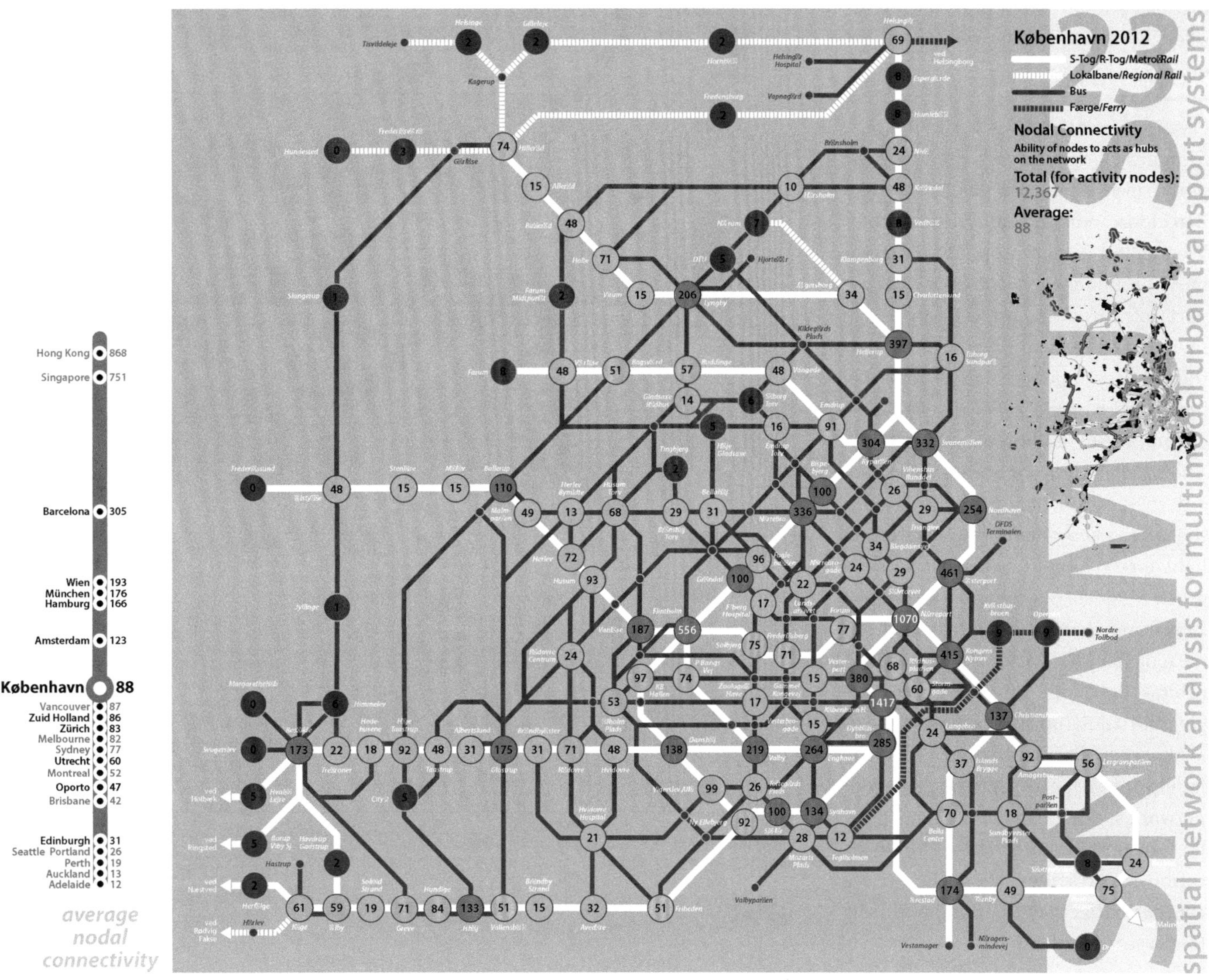

the urban form as much as the urban form evolved around it, operated at metro service levels yet facilitating travel speeds that exceed those in most of its peer cities. The multi-directional and dense surface network unimpeded by arbitrary boundaries of agency jurisdictions and although operated exclusively by buses, further reinforces this quality.

Despite exceptional accessibility performance, Copenhagen's public transport trip-making rate per capita, like Barcelona, remains much lower than Vienna and Zurich. Copenhagen's two most prominent current public transport infrastructure projects are likely to narrow this gap when completed, though they appear to pursue contrasting goals in terms of mode shift and generation of additional accessibility. The circular metro line around the core city, to be completed in 2018, aims to fill the relative accessibility gaps there (the light green patches between the dark green *S-tog* corridors) and may draw a significant share of its patronage from current bicycle users. The proposed orbital light rail line between Lyngby and Glostrup, in contrast, weaves a perpendicular sixth finger into the handprint shape of Copenhagen's rail network, aiming to facilitate more public transport–oriented urban intensification in a corridor where the private car currently plays a dominant role (Østergaard et al, 2013).

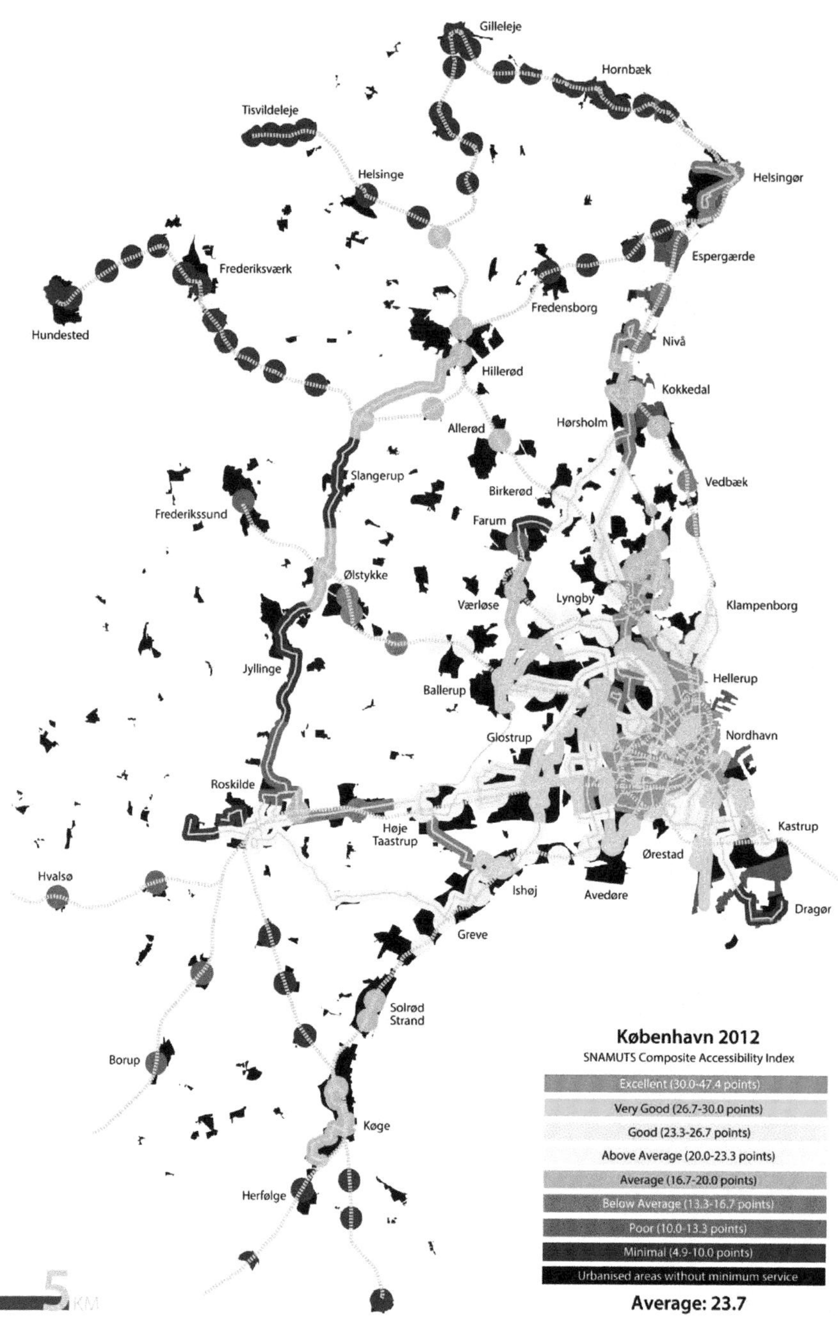

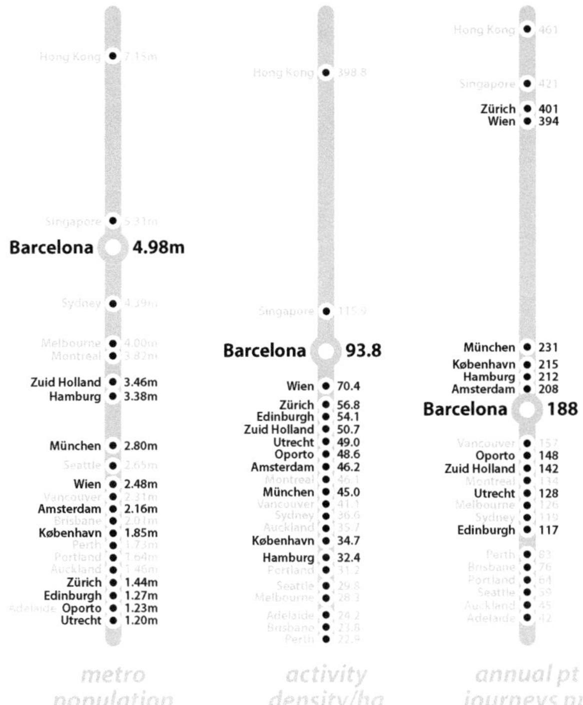

ACCESSIBILITY PROFILE: BARCELONA, CATALUNYA (SPAIN)

Barcelona is Spain's second largest city and the capital of the north-eastern autonomous region of Catalunya, culturally and linguistically distinct from the remainder of the country and traditionally one of its wealthiest and most industrialised parts. At nearly five million inhabitants in the metropolitan region, Barcelona is the largest case study city in the sample outside Asia. It is also the densest, with a scale of activity intensity more reminiscent of Asian cities than of its European counterparts. However, the core city and adjacent, similarly urbanised municipalities in Besòs and L'Hospitalet de Llobregat (average density of 293 residents and jobs per hectare) differ starkly from the surrounding region (59 per hectare).

Barcelona's core city, Baix Llobregat and Besòs sit in a six to seven kilometre wide linear corridor between the Mediterranean coast line and a parallel mountain range (Serra de Collserola). The wider metropolitan area then continues in either direction along the coast (counties of Maresme and Garraf) over a length of nearly 100 km. It also spills beyond the Collserola range into the counties of Alt Penedès, Vallès Occidental and Vallès Oriental, including suburban centres such as Terrassa, Sabadell and Granollers, which are major regional cities in their own right and operate their own local public transport networks.

Barcelona's first underground railways emerged in the 1920s, though a coherent network was only formed following an expansionary push during the 1960s and 1970s. To this day, there is a coexistence of a city metro system (*Transports Metropolitans de Barcelona*, or *TMB*), several lines operated by a regional government agency (*Ferrocarrils de la Generalitat de Catalunya*, or *FGC*) and the suburban network of the national rail operator RENFE (*Rodalies de Catalunya*). With the exception of a short heritage line, the first-generation tram system was abandoned during the Franco era. A second-generation tram system opened in two disconnected parts since 2004, accessing suburban communities in Baix Llobregat to the west, and post-industrial urban redevelopment areas in the north-east of the city.

Besides the metro, TMB is also a large bus operator and runs an extensive network of bus routes in the core city of Barcelona. The bus system is currently being comprehensively reorganised from a historically grown layout with many inefficiencies into a more legible grid of north–south and east–west lines (Ajuntament de Barcelona, 2014b). There are further separate bus operations in most suburban municipalities. In the mountainous terrain that covers much of the Barcelona region, there are also several incline railways (cable cars) that form part of the TMB and FGC system and, in some cases, operate at metro or suburban rail-style frequencies.

The integrated fare system is overseen by an agency known as ATM (*Autoritat del Transport Metropolità*). It is based on 35 fare zones, though a flat fare is charged across the core city, Baix Llobregat and Besòs. Integrated fares only apply to periodical and multi-trip tickets, while single-trip tickets remain operator-specific (and vary in cost between operators).

In 2011, 935 million public transport journeys were recorded on Barcelona's network, a rate of 188 per capita, slightly fewer than in Amsterdam, Copenhagen or Hamburg but significantly more than in any New World city.

Service Intensity

Relative to population, Barcelona's service intensity is lower than in Copenhagen, Vienna and Zurich, but higher than in the more 'frugal' cities such as Hamburg or Munich. A critical reason for this intermediate position can be found in Barcelona's extraordinary concentration of land uses (which should provide for shorter journey paths and thus travel times between greater numbers of activities, all other factors being equal). Another reason lies in the relative absence of attempts to reduce the surface network as the rapid transit system grew, in contrast to the practice of Hamburg or Munich where metro extensions were routinely accompanied by closures of bus or tram routes.

Three heavy rail networks overlap in Barcelona. The TMB metro network (almost exclusively underground) has five conventional and three shorter, driverless lines with service frequencies generally five minutes or better, all day, every day. The FGC has three high-frequency urban routes and, sharing the same tracks, a number of suburban ones linking Barcelona with Terrassa, Sabadell, Martorell and places beyond, though in some cases service frequencies drop to 30 minutes or even less. RENFE operates six main suburban branch lines at service intervals ranging from 2 to 6 trains per hour per direction.

Barcelona's supply of heavy rail stations relative to population is lower than in Vienna, Zurich, Munich and Copenhagen, but comparable to Hamburg and slightly higher than in the Dutch Randstad. To some extent, this effect may be a result of higher activity density, as each rail station is typically associated with a higher catchment of residents and jobs than those in more sparsely built up cities. On the other hand, the outer metropolitan area of the Catalan capital retains a number of high-intensity urban corridors or nodes that lack rail access.

Closeness Centrality

SNAMUTS identified 235 public transport–connected activity nodes in the Barcelona metropolitan area. Within the core city, Besòs, Baix Llobregat and the larger regional centres of Sabadell, Terrassa and Granollers, the settlement structure is dominated by dense apartment buildings with non-residential ground floor uses, bestowing activity centre characteristics on much of these cities' built up area, and SNAMUTS activity node status on all but

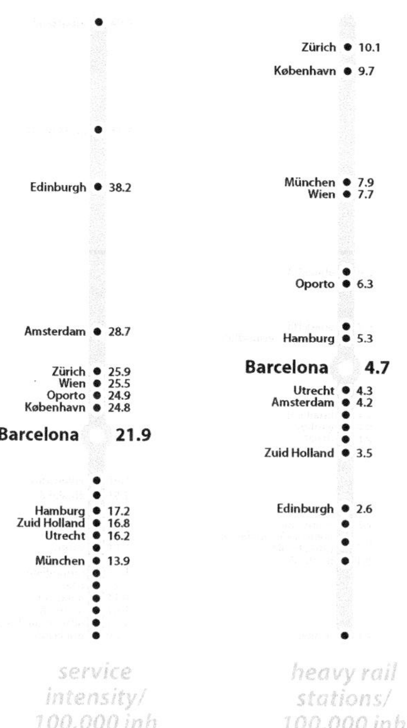

a handful of metro stations and rail–bus intersections. In more suburban areas which are less compactly urbanised, only rail stations of larger municipalities were selected for the activity node matrix.

Average closeness performance is among the best in the global sample, outperformed only by Vienna and Vancouver. Barcelona's high settlement density, which nominally helps with ease of movement, may be partially offset here by a less favourable geography that involves long linear corridors following coastlines and inland valleys towards Calella, Sant Celoni, Vilafranca del Penedès and Vilanova i la Geltrú, where closeness results spike at the extremities.

In the centre, Barcelona has 70 nodes, almost 30 per cent of the total, with a closeness score of 30 or less. There is a flat hierarchy and a relatively uniform standard of superior ease of movement around the inner area of the core city. Remarkably though, the affected area extends further towards (and in a couple of cases, into) neighbouring

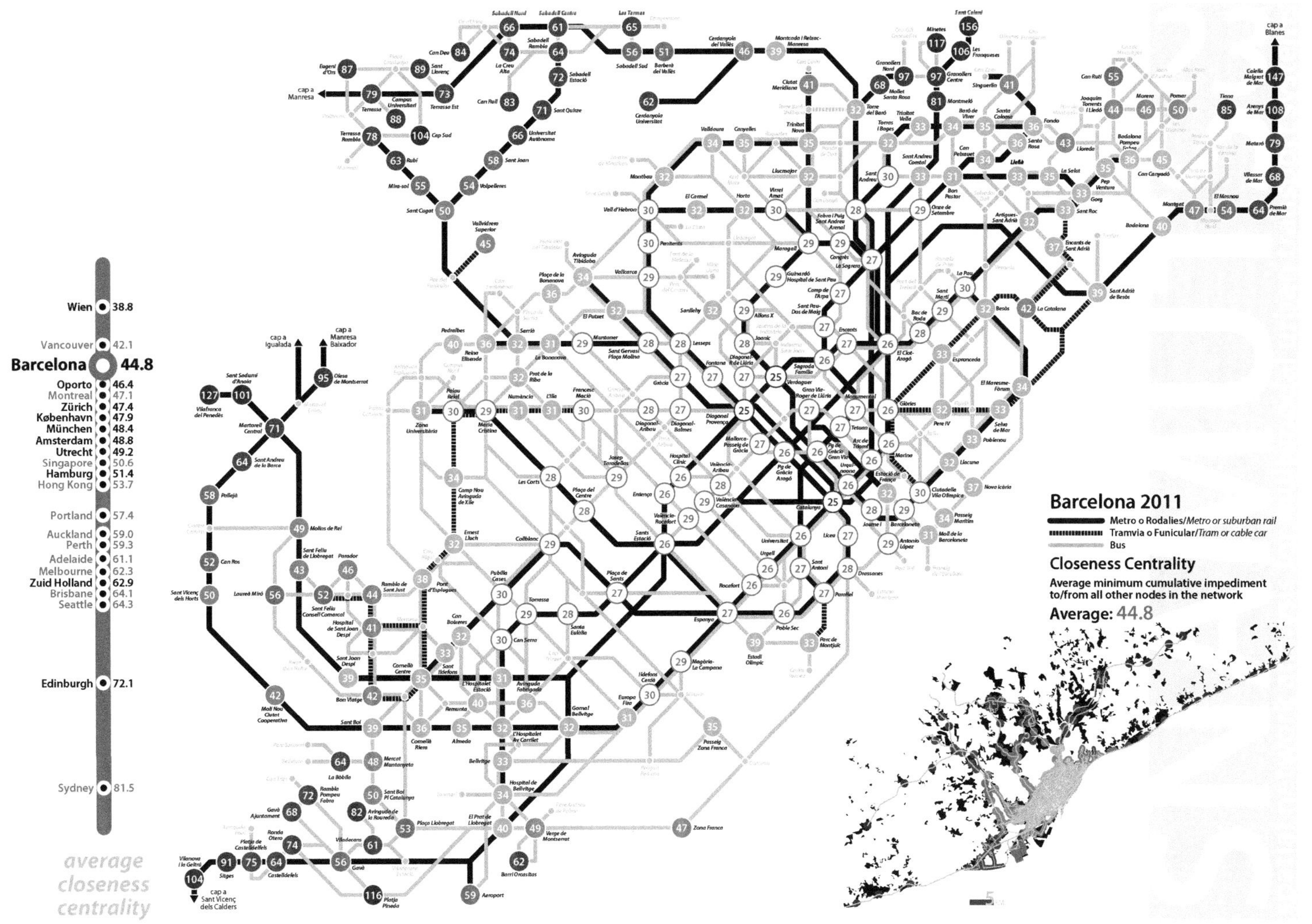

L'Hospitalet in the south-west than the north-eastern city limit, and further along metro L3 (Vall d'Hebron) than parallel L7 (Avinguda Tibidabo). Coastal neighbourhoods around Poblenou and, more plausibly, the mountainous Montjuïc area are conspicuously exempt.

Degree Centrality

Average degree centrality is positioned within the slightly more transfer-dependent cohort of European cities, alongside Amsterdam, Hamburg, Vienna and Zurich. There is a relatively flat hierarchy of bus and rail services in the core city that generates numerous transfer-free links, and there are only a small number of nodes depending on classic feeder buses to rail, mostly in suburban municipalities. Conversely, the iterative historic growth of Barcelona's rail network from three separate systems, and the incomplete nature of the most recent additions (the driverless

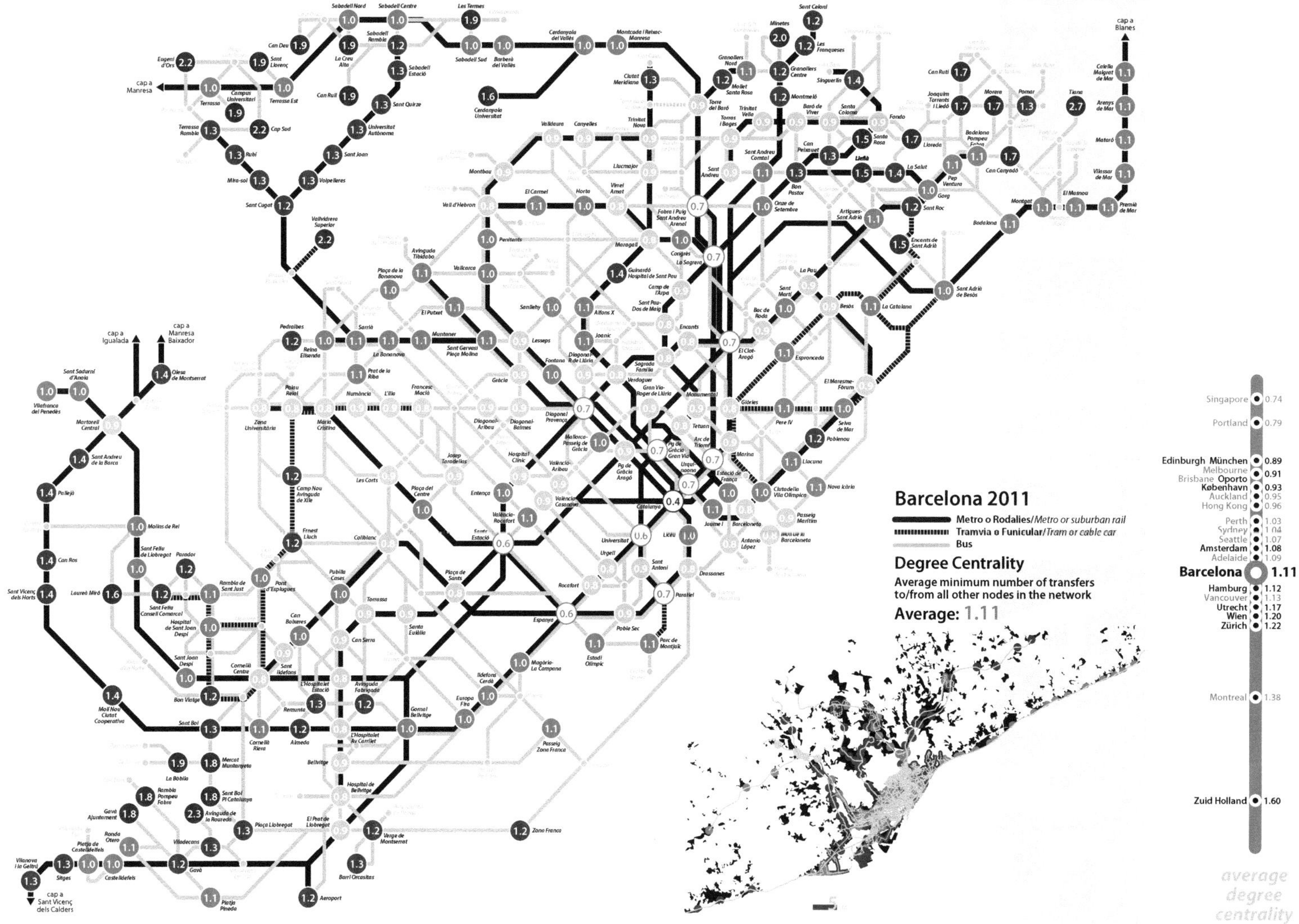

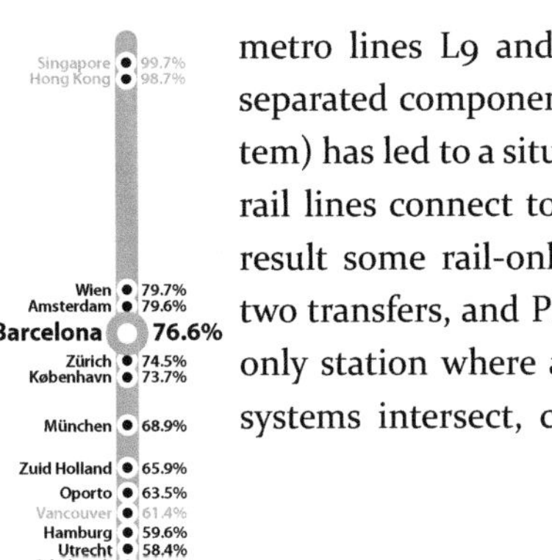

metro lines L9 and L10, and the two separated components of the tram system) has led to a situation where not all rail lines connect to one another. As a result some rail-only journeys require two transfers, and Plaça Catalunya, the only station where all three heavy rail systems intersect, can be regarded as the system's sole 'super node' on this index. There are some missing links, such as the spatial separation of the FGC and RENFE lines in Sabadell and Terrassa and the associated high transfer dependence of the local bus networks. FGC line extensions currently under way (though temporarily stalled as a result of the global financial crisis), will resolve this shortfall.

Network Coverage

Barcelona's network coverage draws almost even in percentage terms with the top-performing European cities of

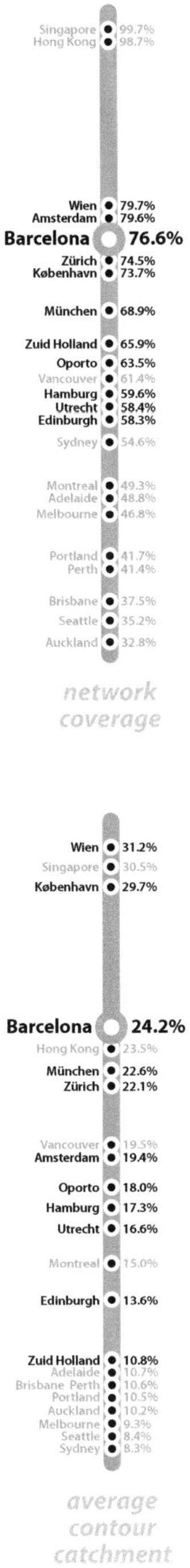

Singapore 99.7%
Hong Kong 98.7%
Wien 79.7%
Amsterdam 79.6%
Barcelona 76.6%
Zürich 74.5%
København 73.7%
München 68.9%
Zuid Holland 65.9%
Oporto 63.5%
Vancouver 61.4%
Hamburg 59.6%
Utrecht 58.4%
Edinburgh 58.3%
Sydney 54.6%
Montreal 49.3%
Adelaide 48.8%
Melbourne 46.8%
Portland 41.7%
Perth 41.4%
Brisbane 37.5%
Seattle 35.2%
Auckland 32.8%
network coverage
Wien 31.2%
Singapore 30.5%
København 29.7%
Barcelona 24.2%
Hong Kong 23.5%
München 22.6%
Zürich 22.1%
Vancouver 19.5%
Amsterdam 19.4%
Oporto 18.0%
Hamburg 17.3%
Utrecht 16.6%
Montreal 15.0%
Edinburgh 13.6%
Zuid Holland 10.8%
Adelaide 10.7%
Brisbane Perth 10.6%
Portland 10.5%
Auckland 10.2%
Melbourne 9.3%
Seattle 8.4%
Sydney 8.3%
average contour catchment

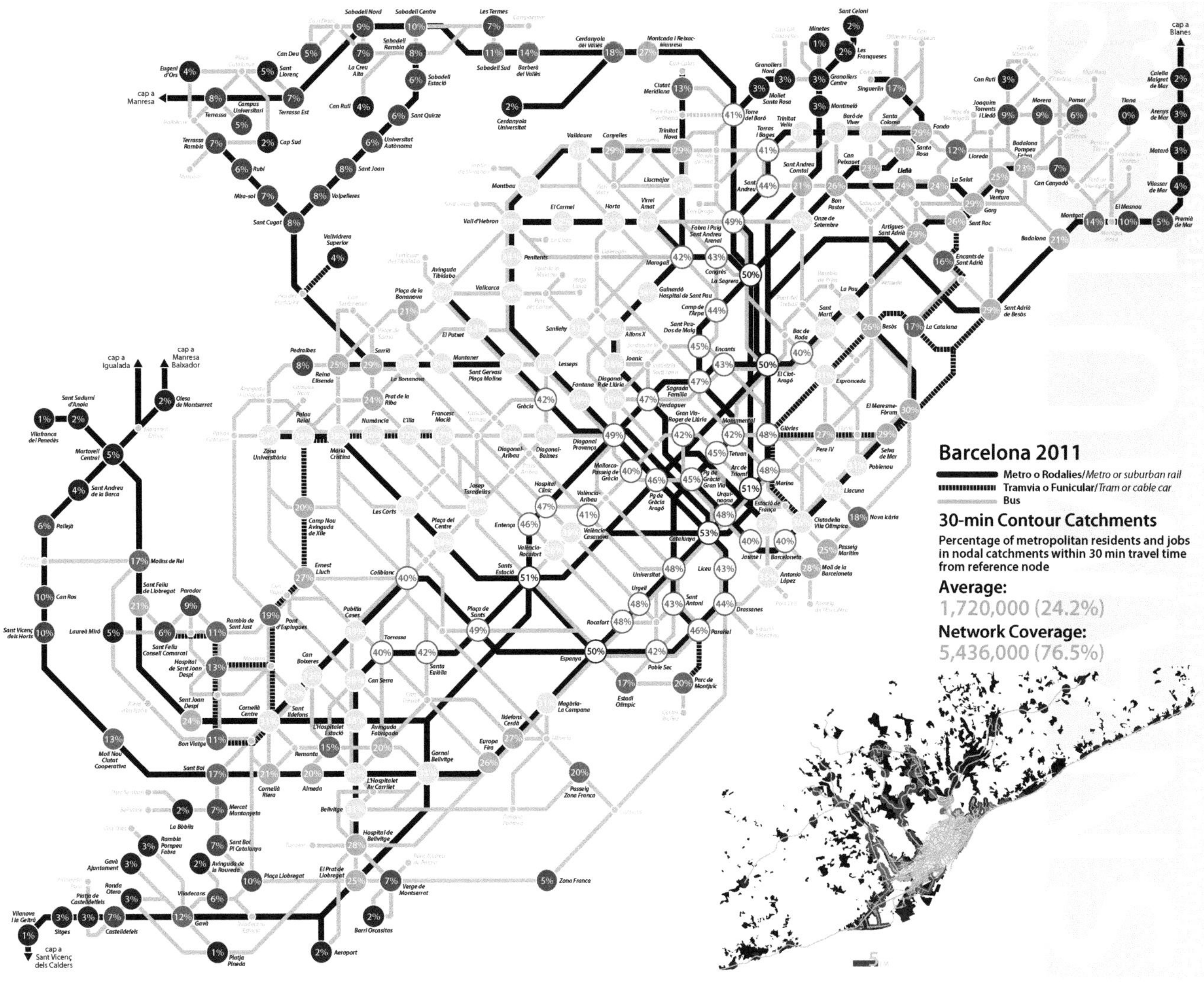

Barcelona 2011
Metro o Rodalies/Metro or suburban rail
Tramvia o Funicular/Tram or cable car
Bus
30-min Contour Catchments
Percentage of metropolitan residents and jobs in nodal catchments within 30 min travel time from reference node
Average:
1,720,000 (24.2%)
Network Coverage:
5,436,000 (76.5%)
cap a Manresa
cap a Igualada
cap a Manresa Baixador
cap a Blanes
cap a Sant Vicenç dels Calders

Amsterdam and Vienna, and is closely followed by Copenhagen and Zurich. This high percentage of public transport endowment is facilitated by a dense core city and core city fringe (Besòs, Baix Llobregat), leaving only marginal gaps in terms of walkable access to public transport services. It is also facilitated by a regional topography that focusses settlement areas into valleys and along coastlines. The Maresme suburban rail line in the north-east is a case in point: while its immediate waterfront alignment places half of the stations' theoretical walkable catchments in the Mediterranean Sea, it responds well to the maritime orientation of the landside development with its high share of second homes and holiday apartments.

Contour Catchments

The average 30-minute contour catchment, expected to decline in relative terms with increasing city size, gives Barcelona one of the European sample's best results, trailing only Vienna and Copenhagen in percentage terms and scoring highest of all in absolute figures (1.7 million residents and jobs can be reached within half an hour from an average Barcelona activity node). The interplay of an extraordinarily compact settlement form and the superior performance of fast and frequent public transport links throughout the inner region are responsible for these effects.

Six Barcelona nodes rise above the 50 per cent mark on this index, each serviced by at least two of the three heavy rail systems. Unlike in the closeness index, the geographical spread of best-performing nodes shifts north-east towards the boroughs of Sant Andreu and Barris Nous, most likely because several RENFE lines to and from the populous suburban centres in the Vallès region pass through this area. Conversely, once arrived in the Vallès region itself, contour catchments drop quite rapidly – below 10 per cent along the entire length of the FGC lines from Terrassa and Sabadell through Sant Cugat, and down to just a few percentage points in Granollers, where relatively low service frequencies do not allow for transfer connections to be counted according to the definitions of this index.

Betweenness Centrality

Global betweenness, measuring the aggregate 'presence' of public transport travel opportunities in a metropolitan region, positions Barcelona in a cohort of cities which includes Amsterdam, Oporto, Utrecht, Vancouver and Zurich. Among the global sample, only Copenhagen, Vienna and the Asian cities outperform this group.

The high intensity of land use in Barcelona translates into extraordinary channelling effects of travel opportunities through central areas, even though the CBD share of the total segmental betweenness score remains below the range of comparable cities. On the heavy rail network, the lines with the greatest concentration of travel opportunities are metro L1 and metro L5, which run parallel to coast, mountains and each other between L'Hospitalet and La Sagrera/ Sant Andreu. The highest concentration

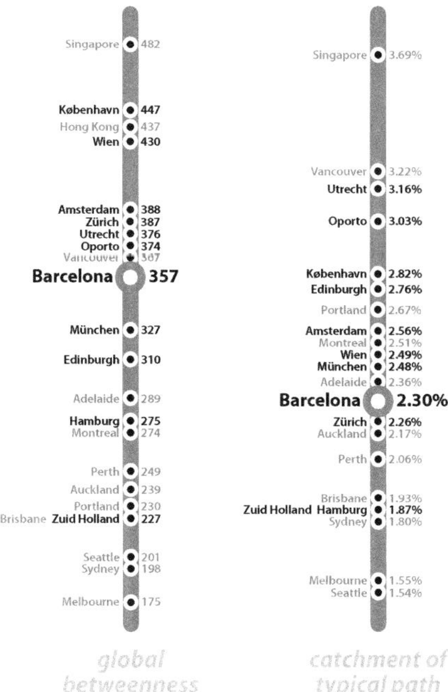

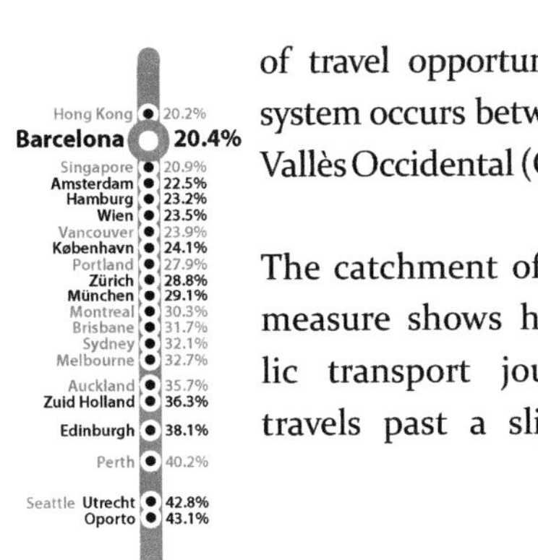

of travel opportunities on the RENFE system occurs between Sant Andreu and Vallès Occidental (Cerdanyola, Sabadell).

The catchment of typical path length measure shows how an average public transport journey in Barcelona travels past a slightly below-average percentage of residents and jobs among the SNAMUTS cities. This is not an unexpected outcome for a large metropolitan area – Hong Kong, the largest city in the sample, records a similar result. It is likely that this index would be lower if it were not for Barcelona's high land use density that generates more populous average activity node catchments than in most of its peer cities, and for a public transport network configured to encourage longer over shorter journeys, manifest especially in a relatively underdeveloped surface network compared to the more highly-powered rail systems.

Hong Kong 20.2%
Barcelona 20.4%
Singapore 20.9%
Amsterdam 22.5%
Hamburg 23.2%
Wien 23.5%
Vancouver 23.9%
København 24.1%
Portland 27.9%
Zürich 28.8%
München 29.1%
Montreal 30.3%
Brisbane 31.7%
Sydney 32.1%
Melbourne 32.7%
Auckland 35.7%
Zuid Holland 36.3%
Edinburgh 38.1%
Perth 40.2%
Seattle Utrecht 42.8%
Oporto 43.1%
Adelaide 62.0%

segmental betweenness cbd

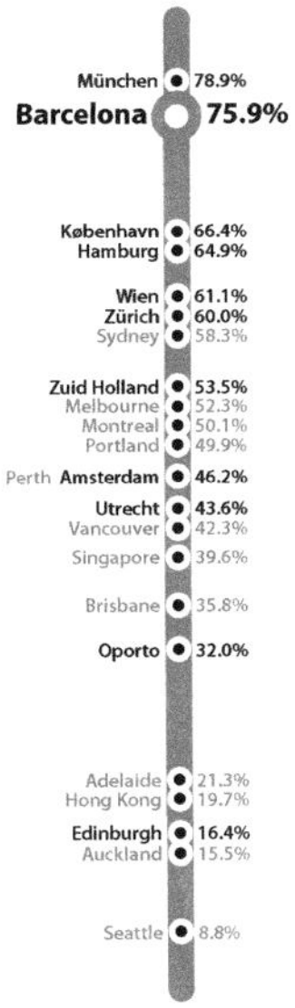

München 78.9%
Barcelona 75.9%
København 66.4%
Hamburg 64.9%
Wien 61.1%
Zürich 60.0%
Sydney 58.3%
Zuid Holland 53.5%
Melbourne 52.3%
Montreal 50.1%
Portland 49.9%
Perth Amsterdam 46.2%
Utrecht 43.6%
Vancouver 42.3%
Singapore 39.6%
Brisbane 35.8%
Oporto 32.0%
Adelaide 21.3%
Hong Kong 19.7%
Edinburgh 16.4%
Auckland 15.5%
Seattle 8.8%

segmental betweenness rail

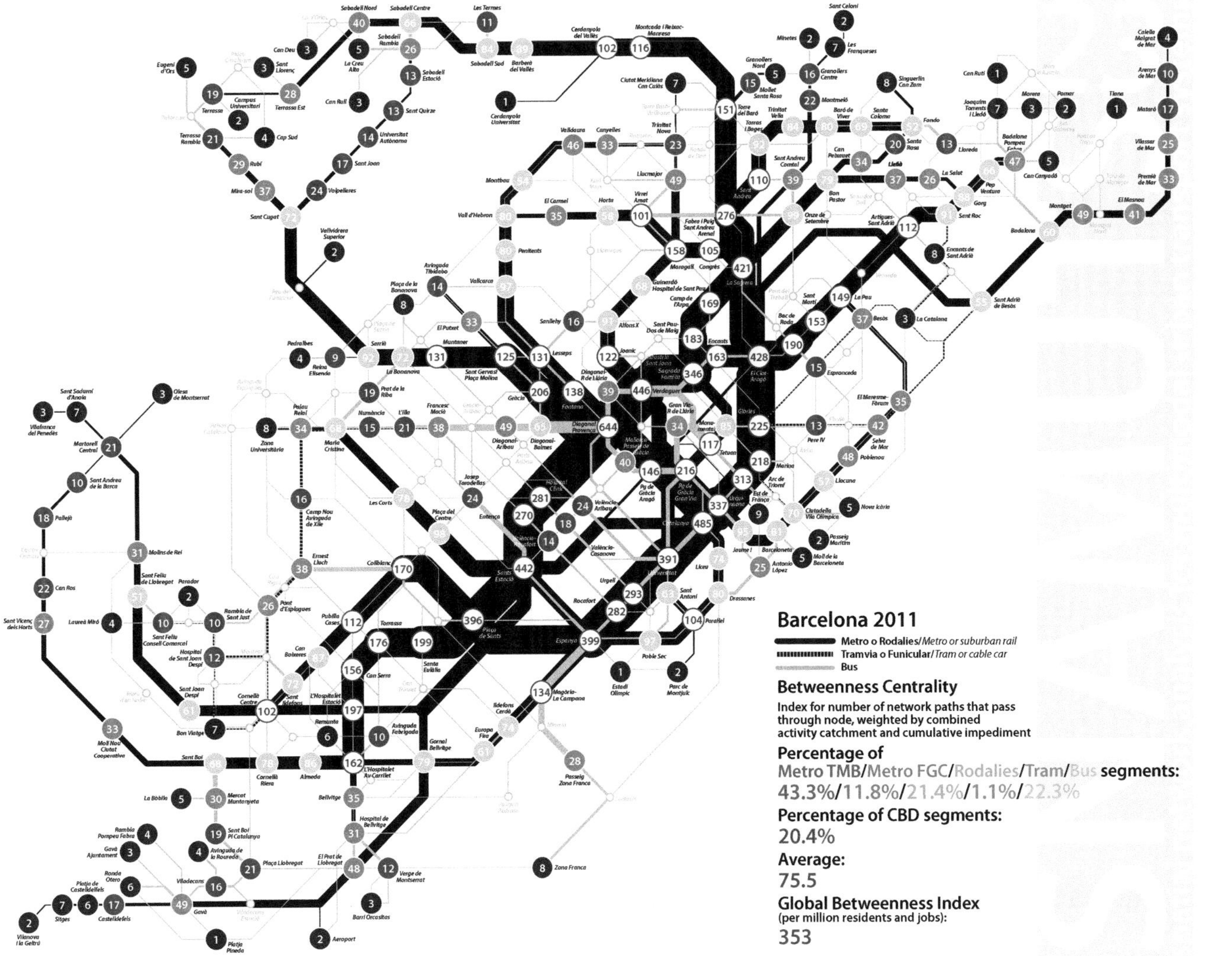

Barcelona 2011
Metro o Rodalies/Metro or suburban rail
Tramvia o Funicular/Tram or cable car
Bus
Betweenness Centrality
Index for number of network paths that pass through node, weighted by combined activity catchment and cumulative impediment
Percentage of
Metro TMB/Metro FGC/Rodalies/Tram/Bus segments:
43.3%/11.8%/21.4%/1.1%/22.3%
Percentage of CBD segments:
20.4%
Average:
75.5
Global Betweenness Index
(per million residents and jobs):
353

Network Resilience

The network-wide level of segmental resilience in Barcelona claims the middle ground across the European sample. There is a lower resilience level on average on Barcelona's higher-performing rail modes than on the surface modes, indicative of some success in placing the pressure from the land use system's movement needs onto those modes that are best equipped to absorb it. Among the heavy rail modes, the more regionally oriented RENFE and FGC lines carry a greater burden of pressure than the TMB metro servicing the core city and some adjacent areas similar in urban form. This discrepancy is most obvious on the RENFE Vallès Occidental line linking Terrassa and Sabadell with central Barcelona. This daytime quarter-hourly service may experience some relief when the extensions of the FGC lines to connect with RENFE in both cities are completed, though the FGC trunk line between Sant

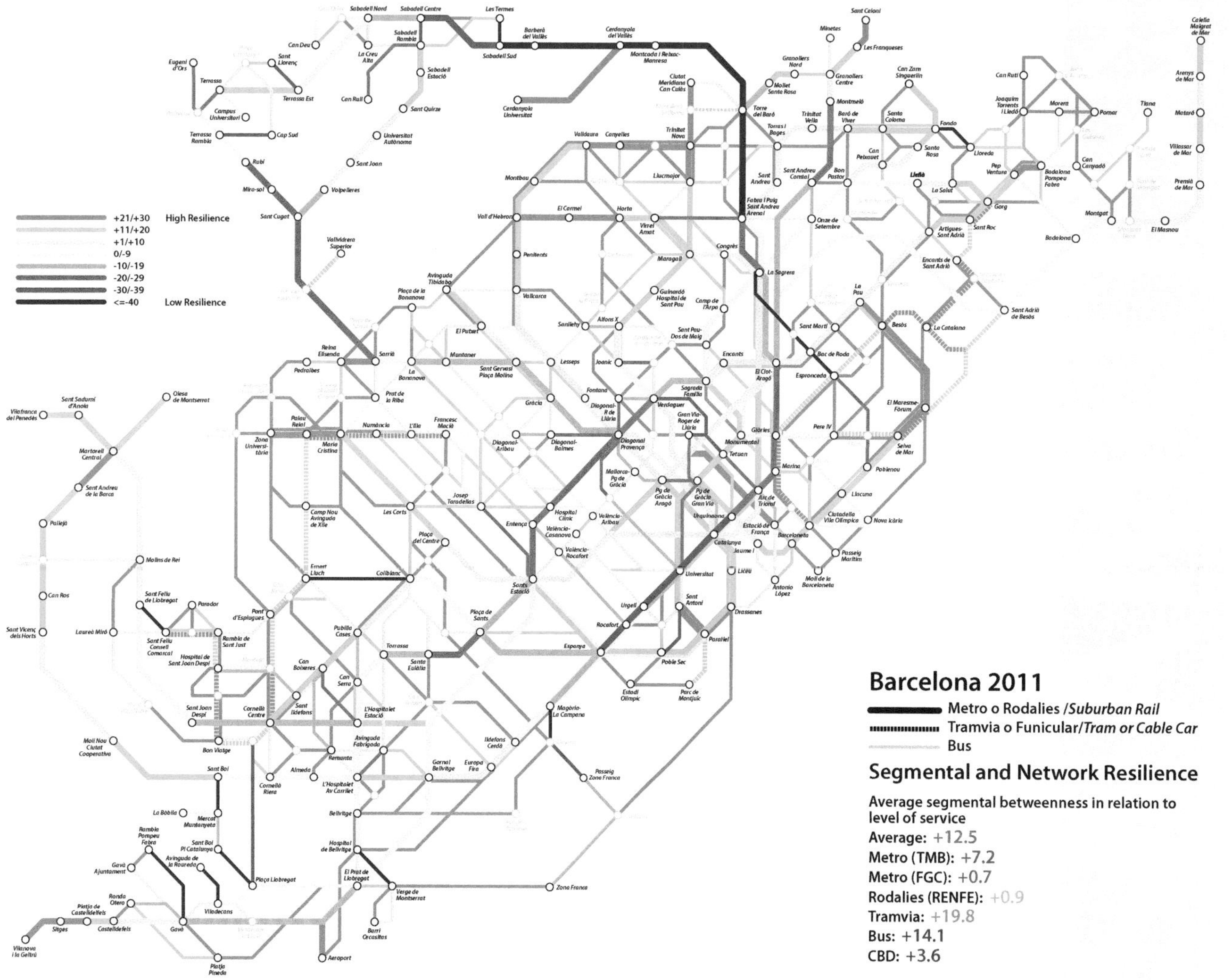

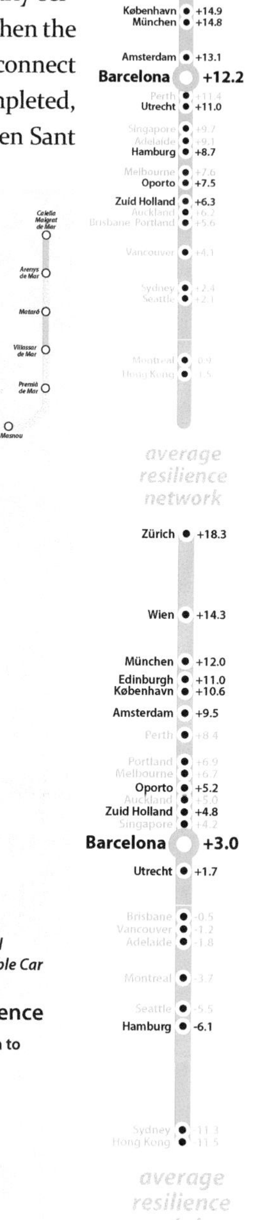

+21/+30 High Resilience
+11/+20
+1/+10
0/-9
-10/-19
-20/-29
-30/-39
<=-40 Low Resilience

Barcelona 2011

Metro o Rodalies /*Suburban Rail*
Tramvia o Funicular/*Tram or Cable Car*
Bus

Segmental and Network Resilience

Average segmental betweenness in relation to level of service
Average: +12.5
Metro (TMB): +7.2
Metro (FGC): +0.7
Rodalies (RENFE): +0.9
Tramvia: +19.8
Bus: +14.1
CBD: +3.6

Cugat and central Barcelona already shows a relatively high level of network stress in its current state.

While TMB's metro lines have a higher resilience level on average than the other two heavy rail systems, there remain some segments that deliver extraordinary low values on this index, in particular routes L1 and L5 between their two common interchanges at Plaça de Sants and La Sagrera, and in the case of route L1 even beyond. The extension of routes L9 and L10 south-west from La Sagrera to form a third parallel metro link will relieve this situation, but progress stalled after the 2008 financial crisis and its completion date remains uncertain.

Nodal Connectivity

Barcelona has by far the highest average nodal connectivity result in the sample outside Asia. To some extent, this is related to network size and the

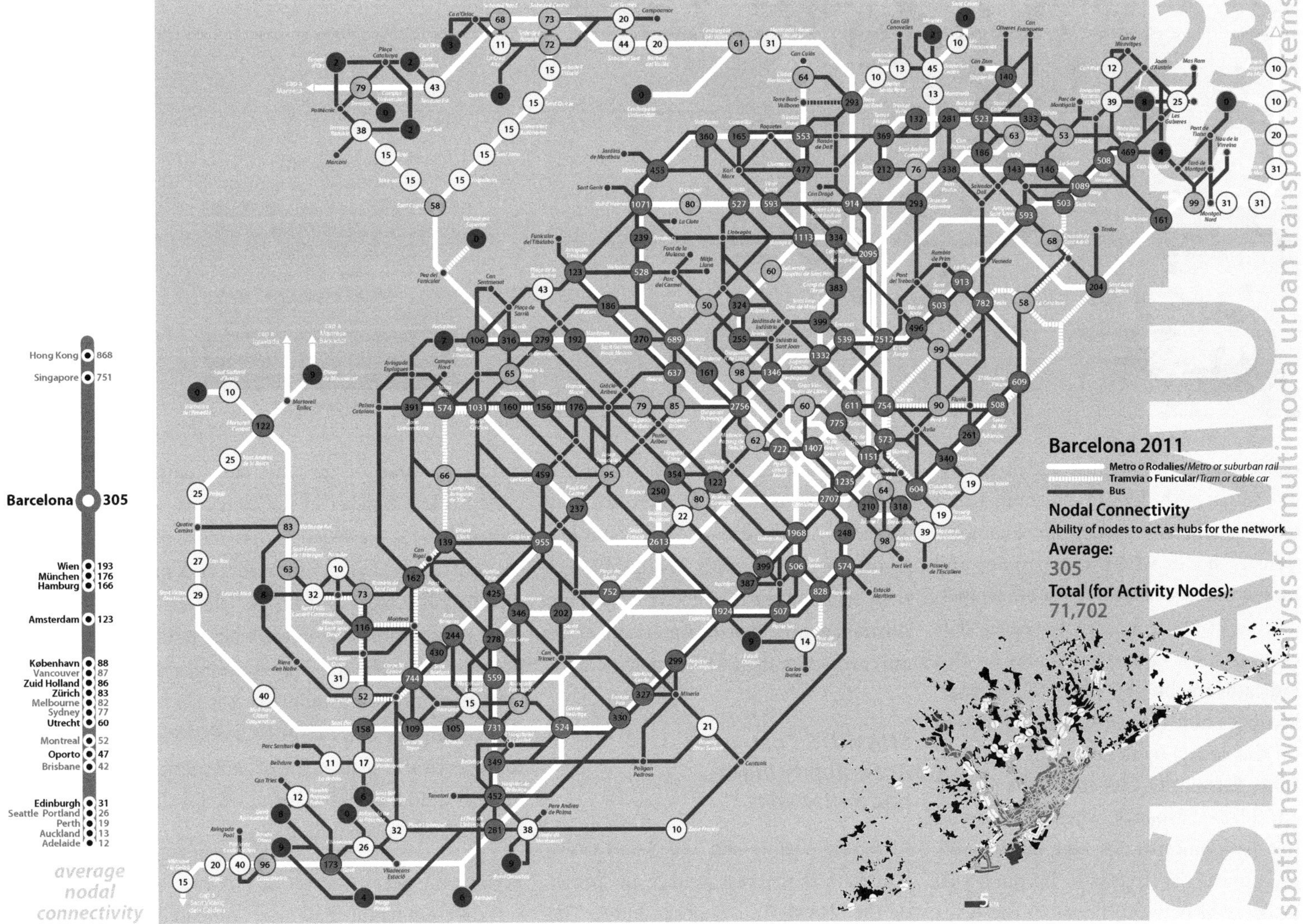

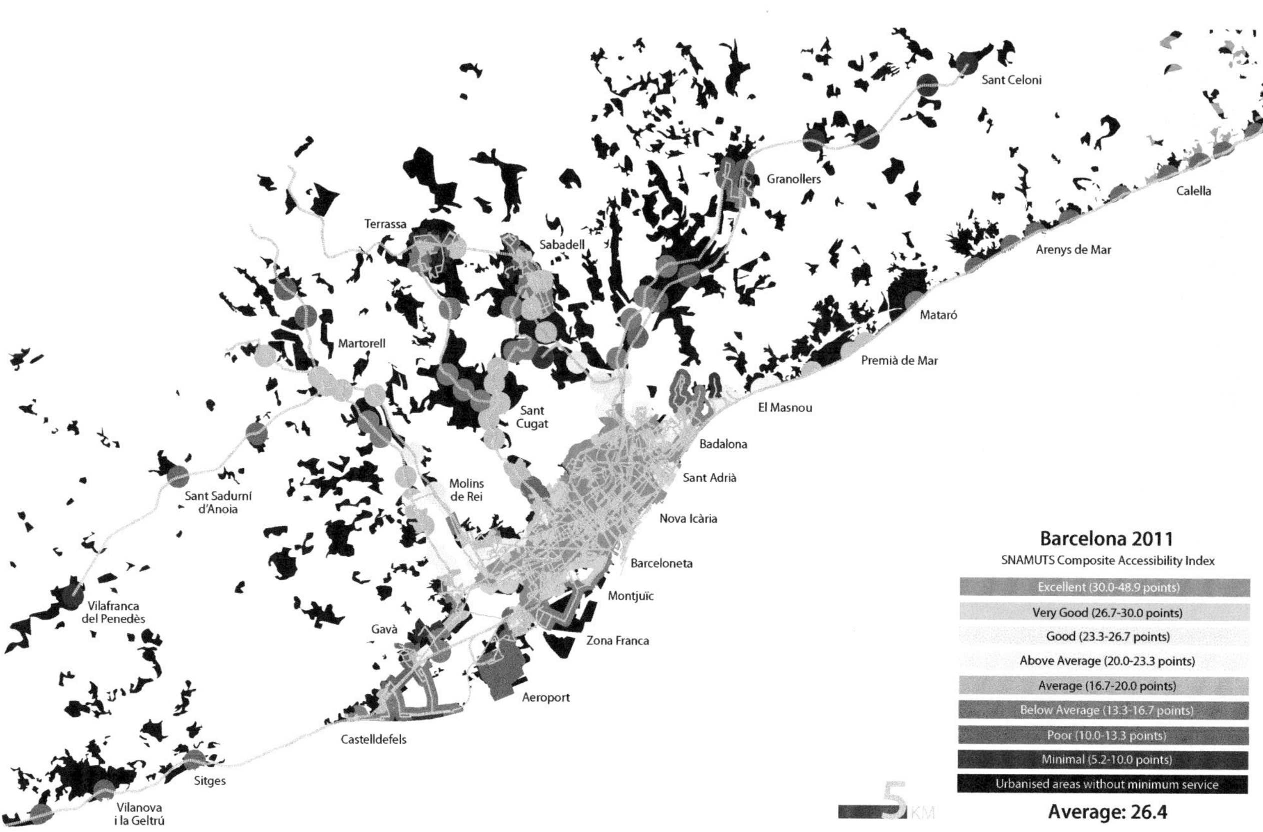

concentration of land use activities relative to network density – a context that tends to generate typically more complex transfer nodes where more routes and modes intersect than in most other cities, driving up the connectivity scores. Barcelona's most connected nodes on this indicator are the CBD nodes of Diagonal-Provença and Plaça Catalunya, followed (in this order) by the non-CBD nodes of Sants-Estació, El Clot-Aragó, La Sagrera and Plaça d'Espanya, whose position on this list demonstrates how the benefits of connectivity appear to be quite well distributed between nodes in the heart of the city and in other locations. In this context, it is notable that there are only a very small number of metro stations across the core city with a nodal connectivity score of less than 100, a level some Australian and North American cities only exceed for their CBD 'super-nodes'.

SNAMUTS Composite Accessibility Index and Reflections

Alongside Vienna and the Asian cities, Barcelona is the best average performer on the SNAMUTS composite index. The threshold value of 30, the best (dark green) colour bracket in the comparison undertaken, is exceeded across most of the core city and along the metro corridors into Baix Llobregat and Besòs. This suggests an accessibility standard where public transport can be considered the default choice for motorised mobility. It is likely that current projects for further additions to the network, such as the orbital metro routes L9 and L10 when completed, will help to close the remaining gaps.

Beyond the Serra Collserola, however, a very different picture emerges. Compared to the situation in other polycentric agglomerations in the sample (see Zurich and the Dutch Randstad), the public transport links between suburban centres such as Terrassa, Sabadell, Granollers and the core city (and among each other) can be regarded as underdeveloped, configured for a greater level of local self-containment than what is likely, or viable in the longer term, within a dynamic metropolitan region expected to grow beyond five million people in the near future. This is also where the most formidable barriers become visible for Barcelona to follow the path of Vienna, the European top performer on this index which records more than twice the annual per-capita rate of trip making on public transport. Should Barcelona desire to increase public transport usage towards Vienna levels, it will need to address a plethora of resilience weak spots, especially outside the core city where the potential for greater functional interdependence of settlement clusters and hence increased public transport usage appears highest.

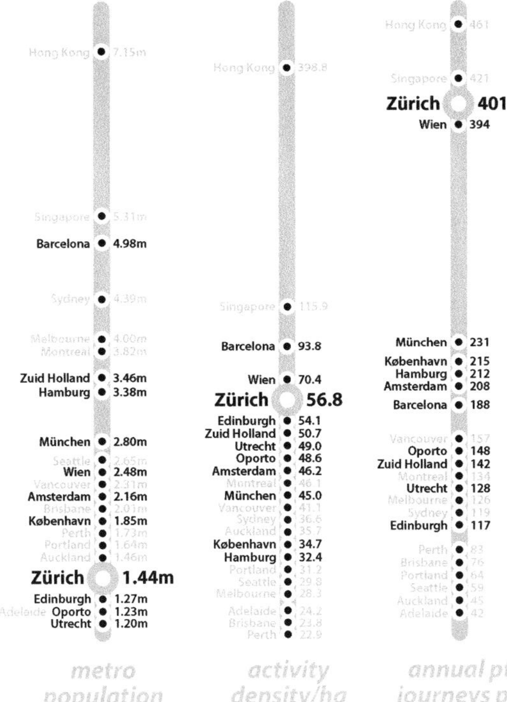

ACCESSIBILITY PROFILE: ZÜRICH (SWITZERLAND)

Switzerland's largest city is located in the north-east of the country. It is the population, economic and administrative centre of the canton (confederate state) of the same name. Less than 30 per cent (390,000) of the canton's population reside in the core city of Zurich while the remainder disperses across the canton, where mountainous topography interspersed by lakes generates a multitude of natural separators between urban settlements. There is a historic pattern of strong local autonomy with over 170 separate local government areas within the canton of Zurich.

The urbanisation pattern of the Zurich region is considerably less contiguous and centralised than any of the other European case study cities, with the partial exception of the Dutch Randstad. It also extends considerably beyond the canton borders and the service area of the regional transport agency (*Züricher Verkehrsverbund* or *ZVV*). Specifically, the Zurich region appears to accommodate a far greater number of jobs than its population base would require, suggesting a substantial amount of regular commuting by residents from outside this area. The practicalities of data collection and the quest to focus our investigation on the specific public transport policy legacy of Zurich and the ZVV, however, prompted us to use the cantonal definition, give or take a small number of adjacent municipalities, of the metropolitan area. In 2009, it covered some 1.44 million inhabitants in a land area of 1,802 sq km.

Since its inception in 1990, the ZVV has optimised the efficiency and integration of regional rail, trams and buses in the region, and overseen an ambitious program of network expansion. As a result the number of region-wide public transport passenger trips reached 590 million in 2011, or 401 annual trips per capita.

On the heavy rail system, there is a mixed operation of intercity, regional and suburban (S-Bahn) services. Most of these lines are the responsibility of national rail operator SBB, except for routes S4 and S10 which are operated by a rail company in joint federal, regional and local ownership (SZU).

Operated by a city subsidiary (*Verkehrsbetriebe Zürich* or *VBZ*) also bearing responsibility for buses, the tram network is renowned for one of the world's most advanced traffic priority schemes and a corresponding restrictive approach to private motor vehicle access in central areas (Cervero, 1998; Mees, 2010a). During the 2000s, the network was extended along faster, segregated routes to cover the Glattal region in Zurich's north, an area characterised by post-war patchwork urbanisation, home to the international airport and much associated employment. Tram infrastructure is also shared by an older regional light rail line (Forchbahn) on its city section.

Within the City of Zurich, trams in conjunction with buses and trolleybuses form a tightly woven, grid-shaped network facilitating multi-directional movement and constrained only by the Uetliberg and Dolder mountain ranges to the north and south of the core city. Transfer points are clearly identified on ubiquitous, high-quality mapping material, and real-time information about connecting services is displayed on board many vehicles. Well-timed transfers are also a feature of many hubs in the surrounding region, with a pulse timetable system applied between trains and buses particularly where frequencies on both modes drop to 30 minutes.

The ZVV fare structure is based on 45 zones and a strong financial incentive towards monthly and annual tickets, which generally offer a cost advantage from two weekly return journeys onwards. Single and daily tickets are also available, and considerable discounts apply to off-peak tickets.

Service Intensity

Relative to population, Zurich sits in the upper band of the European sample for service intensity: the figures are similar to those of Vienna, Oporto and Copenhagen.

Zurich's S-Bahn system is organised by numbered and colour-coded lines with fixed stopping patterns, the majority of which are operated every 30 minutes, seven days a week, with overlapping lines on major routes generating 15-minute or better intervals. However, the coexistence of all-stop and semi-express lines across the system has the result that some intermediate stations even on the busier routes receive only half-hourly services.

Zurich's trams and inner city bus lines have typical 7½-minute intervals during the day – less where two or more of the 15 full-time tram lines overlap. These service standards generate a very tangible presence for surface public transport in Zurich's activity centres and corridors. Alongside Copenhagen, Zurich has the highest number of heavy rail stations per capita in the SNAMUTS sample, though the region's sizeable segregated light rail infrastructure does not enter the count.

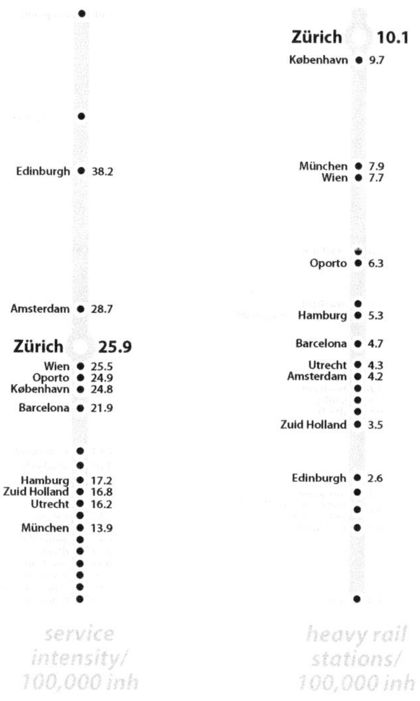

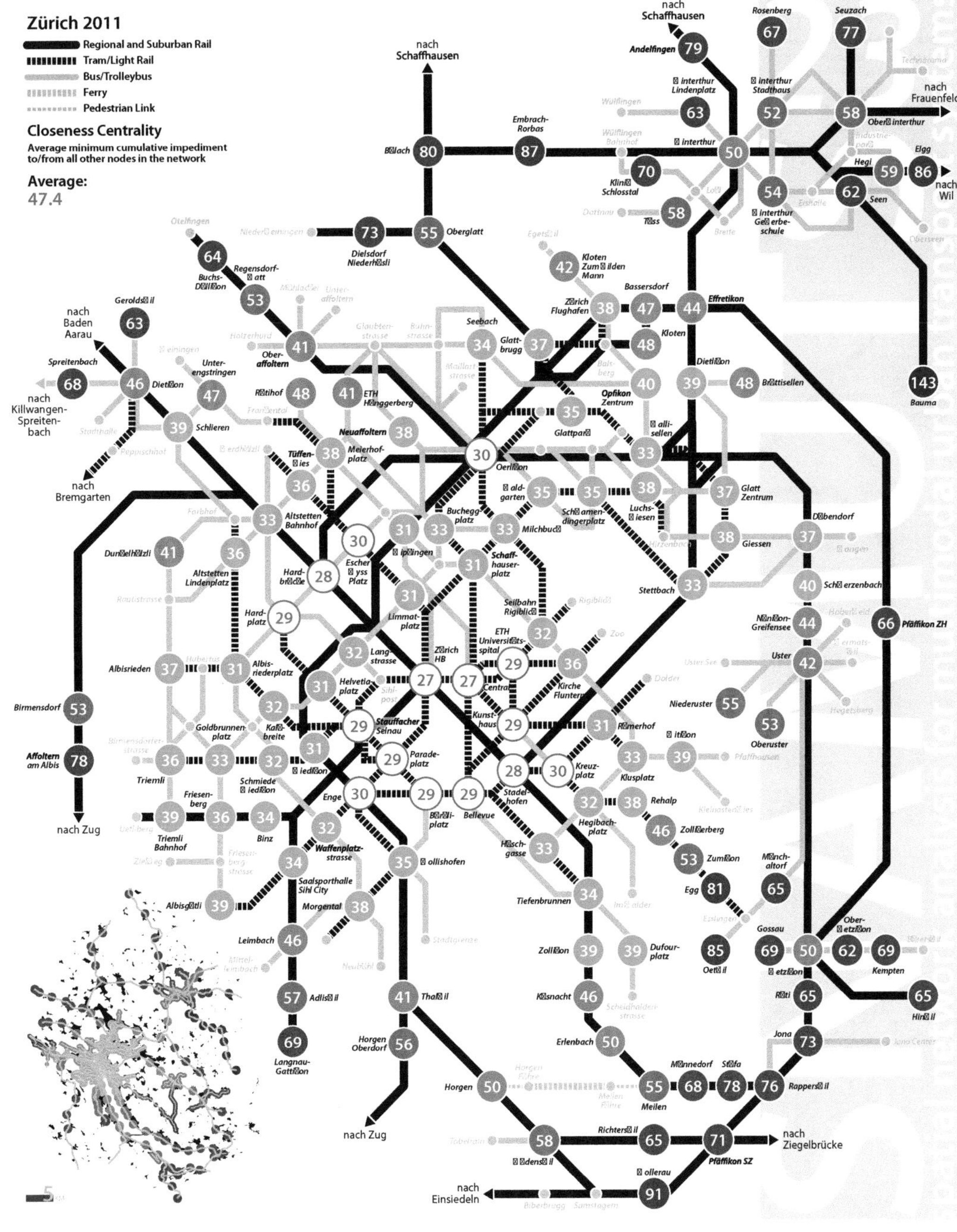

Closeness Centrality

Zurich's relatively high number of 137 SNAMUTS activity nodes for an agglomeration of its size reflects the many medium and smaller-sized settlement cores in this polycentric region. Despite this urbanisation pattern (more dispersed than in any of its peers with the exception of Zuid Holland) Zurich remains well within the relatively narrow average ease-of-movement bandwidth shared by eight out of 11 European and the Canadian SNAMUTS cities. More remarkably, Zurich has a quite narrow spread between lowest (best) and highest (poorest) nodal closeness score, if the result of 143 for remotely located Bauma is considered an outlier (the next highest figure – 91 – is found at Wollerau). This may be indicative of a service approach that attempts to harmonise and provide equity in public transport accessibility across a settlement area whose non-contiguous character nominally presents formidable challenges for penetration by attractive public transport services. Conversely, for the lowest closeness scores on the network, the less polycentric peer cities in this chapter have an edge over Zurich, where only 13 nodes (9 per cent) fall below the threshold value of 30. Along the faster, relatively high-frequency rail network, good closeness values extend further away from central Zurich than along surface modes and in turn influence the performance of some bus or tram nodes in their vicinity, an effect that is most obvious at Hardplatz and Escher Wyss Platz, either side of the CBD fringe rail–bus transfer station of Hardbrücke.

Degree Centrality

The transfer intensity of Zurich's network is higher than in any case study city except Montreal and Zuid Holland. The key reason is the existence of a number of localised sub-networks in the Zurich metropolitan region, most prominently in Winterthur but also, at a smaller scale, in centres such as Uster, Wetzikon and Dietikon. Additionally, the configuration of Zurich's S-Bahn network sometimes enforces transfers in terms of how SNAMUTS counts them. For example, every

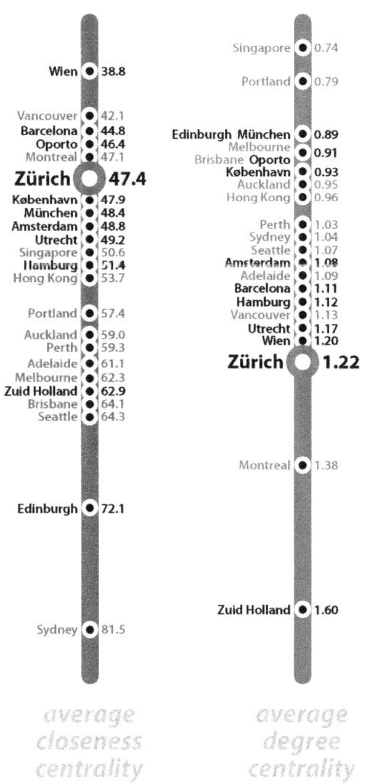

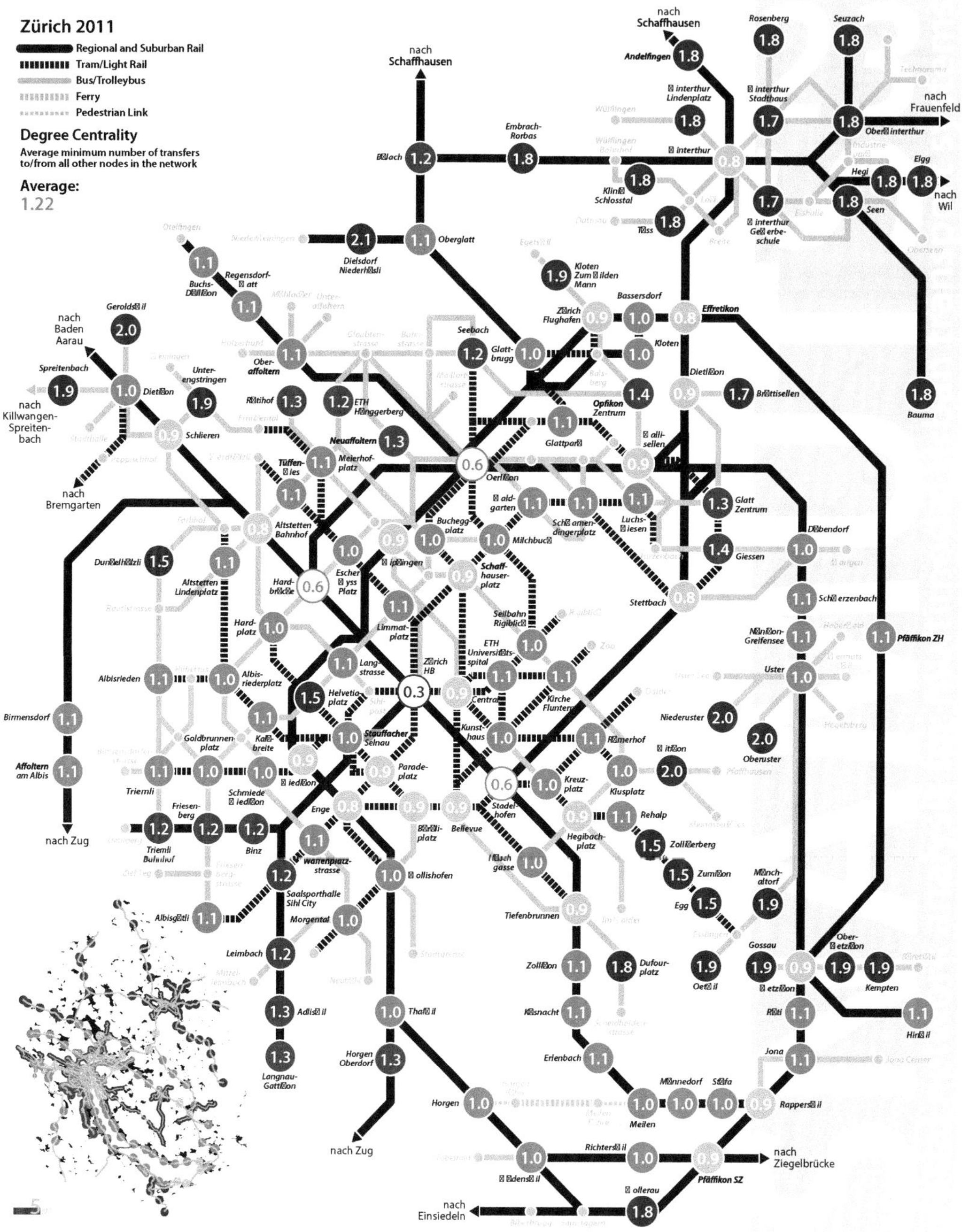

Zürich 2011
Regional and Suburban Rail
Tram/Light Rail
Bus/Trolleybus
Ferry
Pedestrian Link
Degree Centrality
Average minimum number of transfers to/from all other nodes in the network
Average:
1.22

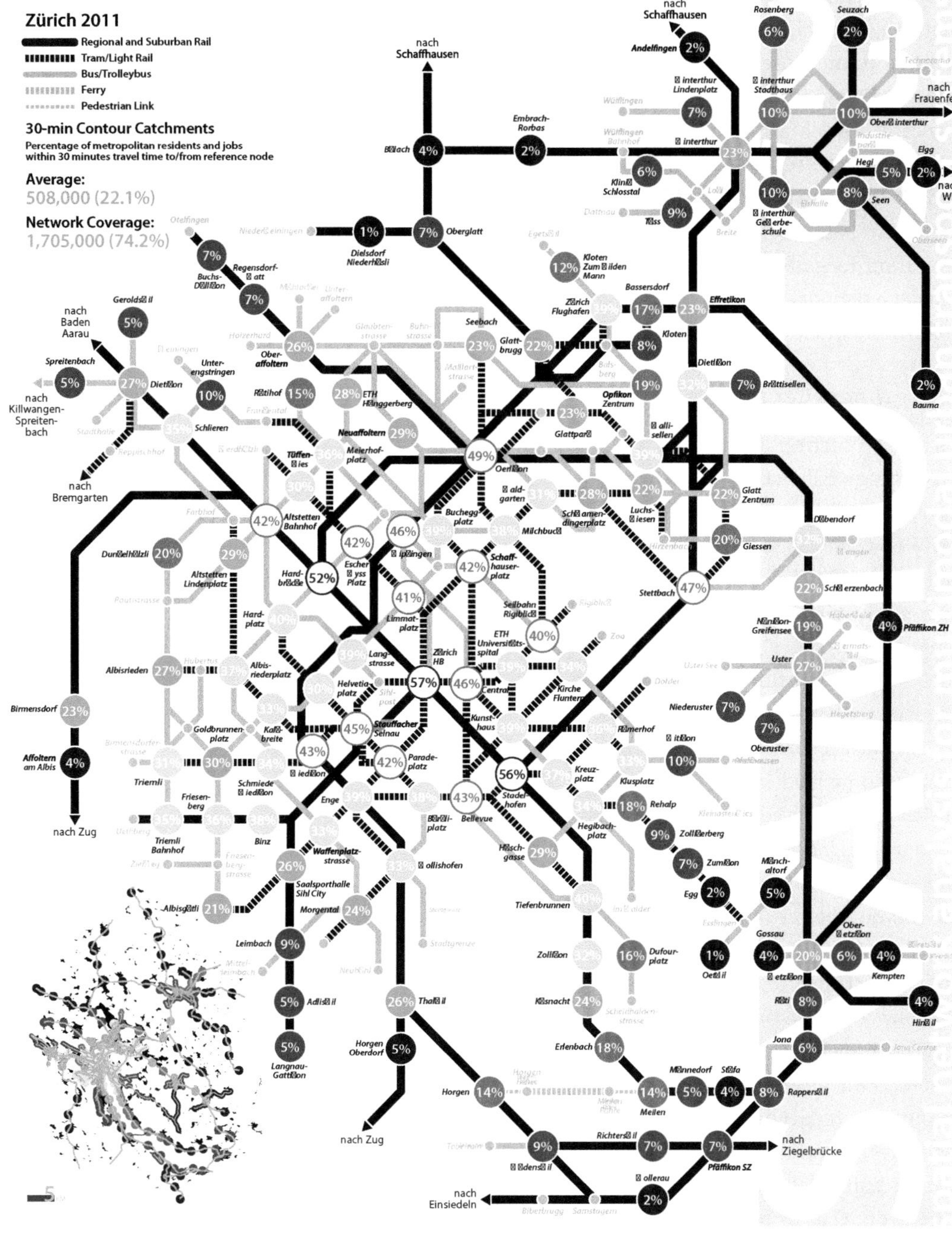

other train on the half-hourly section between Niederweningen and Oberglatt (S5) terminates at Oberglatt rather than continuing into central Zurich, necessitating a transfer to a connecting train that originated in Bülach, which reduces the Niederweningen to Oberglatt section to a transfer-dependent shuttle service (as no half-hourly through trains are provided) and inflates the degree centrality score for the activity node at Dielsdorf accordingly.

At the other end of the scale, Zürich HB has by far the lowest (best) degree centrality result, followed by its neighbouring rail-surface hubs at Oerlikon, Hardbrücke and Stadelhofen. There is a relatively narrow band of better-than-average transfer intensity scores within most of the tram and light rail network, with the exception of those nodes that are not directly connected to the central city or an SBB station (Helvetiaplatz, Glattal and Forch).

Network Coverage

Zurich's network coverage in percentage of metropolitan residents and jobs is similar to that of Copenhagen, and remains slightly below that of Vienna, Amsterdam and Barcelona. It is still positioned within the group of SNAMUTS cities with the highest geographical public transport endowment in the global sample outside Asia. Zurich achieves this remarkable result though an extraordinary rail network and station density relative to its population, effectively accommodating topographical constraints. Network coverage also benefits from a 1988 cantonal ordinance that all new residential development must be located within walking distance from public transport services of a minimum standard, precisely the quality that this index seeks to reflect (Ott, 1995).

Contour Catchments

Average 30-minute contour catchments in Zurich relative to metropolitan population and jobs are similar to those in Munich, smaller than in Vienna, Copenhagen and Barcelona but larger than elsewhere in the global sample outside Asia. Greater compactness of the settlement area may explain the edge of the Austrian, Danish and Catalan capitals on this index, while Zurich benefits from a smaller metropolitan area size (average percentage contour catchments tend to be smaller in larger agglomerations) and from the high prevalence of fast rail services in Zurich's network, as elaborated earlier.

Zurich's peak-performing nodes on this index, and the only three that provide access to more than half of the metropolitan area's residents and jobs within a half-hour public transport journey, are the three CBD or CBD fringe rail stations of Zürich HB, Stadelhofen and Hardbrücke, followed closely by Oerlikon and Stettbach in the north of the core city. Within the City of Zurich, only nine out of 61 activity nodes are accessible to and from less than 25 per cent of all residents and jobs within the ZVV area. Important regional centres such as Dietikon, Thalwil, Effretikon, Uster and Winterthur are close to the 25 per cent mark on this index. Overall, the performance of Zurich as a highly dispersed and polycentric region on this index is remarkable, illustrating the efficacy of a settlement pattern of decentralised concentration for public transport accessibility at a regional scale (Flückinger and Koll-Schretzenmayr, 2000; Bose, 2001).

Betweenness Centrality

Relative to metropolitan residents and jobs, the global betweenness result is similar to that of Amsterdam, below those of Copenhagen and Vienna, but higher than those of all other non-Asian case study cities. This comparatively generous 'presence' of public transport travel opportunities, however, is matched with a fairly low catchment of typical path length figure. This observation can be read in two ways. Firstly, Zurich has achieved great efficiencies in moving passengers between origins and destinations while minimising the number of intermediate places traversed en route, by way of offering a multi-directional regional rail network allowing for more direct journey paths and by providing a large number of semi-express services (which this index counts at a reduced rate at intermediate nodes). Secondly, the ratio of settlement density and network density may differ from that in most other cities in the sample: in Zurich, a larger network

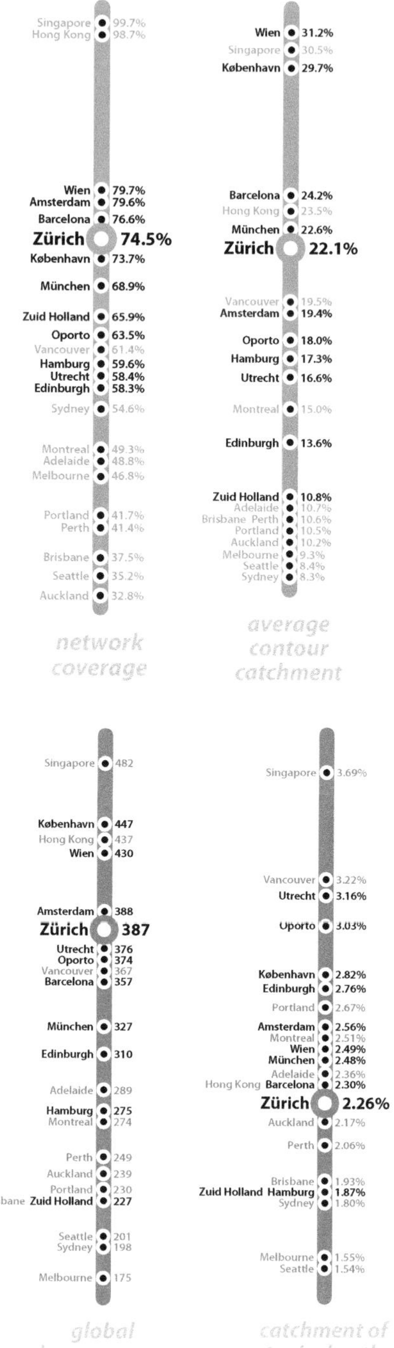

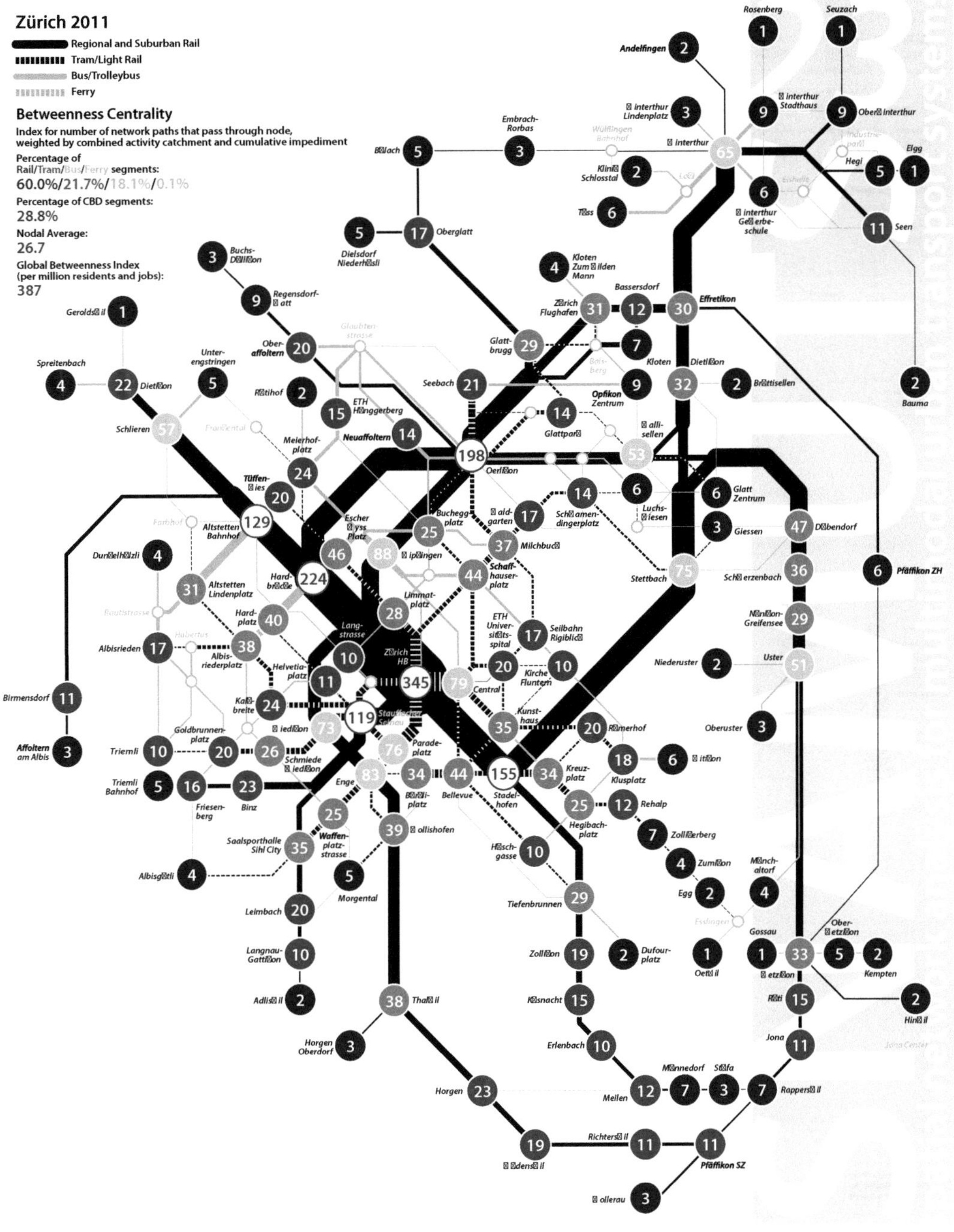

Zürich 2011

Regional and Suburban Rail
Tram/Light Rail
Bus/Trolleybus
Ferry

Betweenness Centrality

Index for number of network paths that pass through node, weighted by combined activity catchment and cumulative impediment

Percentage of Rail/Tram/Bus/Ferry segments:
60.0%/21.7%/18.1%/0.1%

Percentage of CBD segments:
28.8%

Nodal Average:
26.7

Global Betweenness Index (per million residents and jobs):
387

with a greater proportion of high-performance modes is provided for a sparser urban settlement. This may be linked to the high level of public transport usage, which leads the European sample in terms of number of annual journeys per capita and thus appears to squeeze greater levels of patronage out of a smaller pool of potential users.

According to the segmental betweenness index, Zurich's reliance on heavy rail for facilitating movement across its public transport network is of similar magnitude to Vienna's and inferior only to Barcelona, Copenhagen, Hamburg and Munich, all larger than Zurich (some significantly) and moreover, with no or more marginal tram or light rail systems.

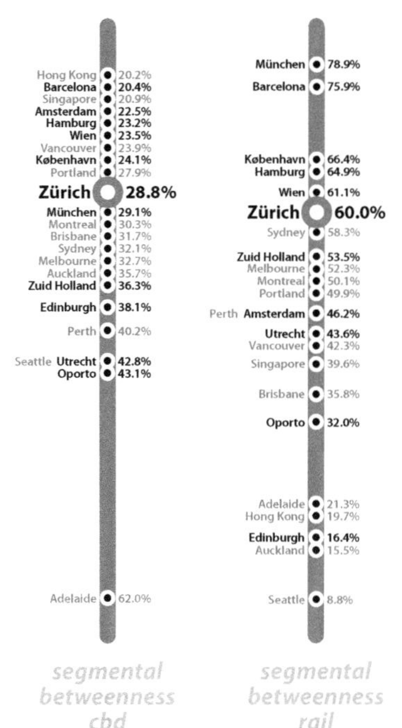

Despite the region's – and the network's – polycentric structure, there is a greater relative importance of the CBD for the facilitation of public transport movement in Zurich than in the larger European cities, with the exception of Munich. However, among the smaller European and all New World cities except Portland and Vancouver (where the CBD is located excentrically), Zurich's central city reliance on this index remains comparatively low.

The nodal betweenness count confirms the existence of a dominant 'super node' at Zürich HB where a particularly high number of metropolitan travel opportunities converge. The centripetal rate of decay of betweenness figures in Zurich generally seems to be well balanced, following the dense grid structure of the surface network and its good integration with heavy rail in the core city. On the north-western approach route, however (the Altstetten–Dietikon corridor), betweenness results appear to be higher than on comparable corridors elsewhere. The strong concentration of travel opportunities here has a flow-on effect on connecting orbital bus routes at Altstetten and Hardbrücke, producing the highest segmental betweenness scores on the bus network across the metropolitan area and the highest scores on any surface route outside the immediate CBD area.

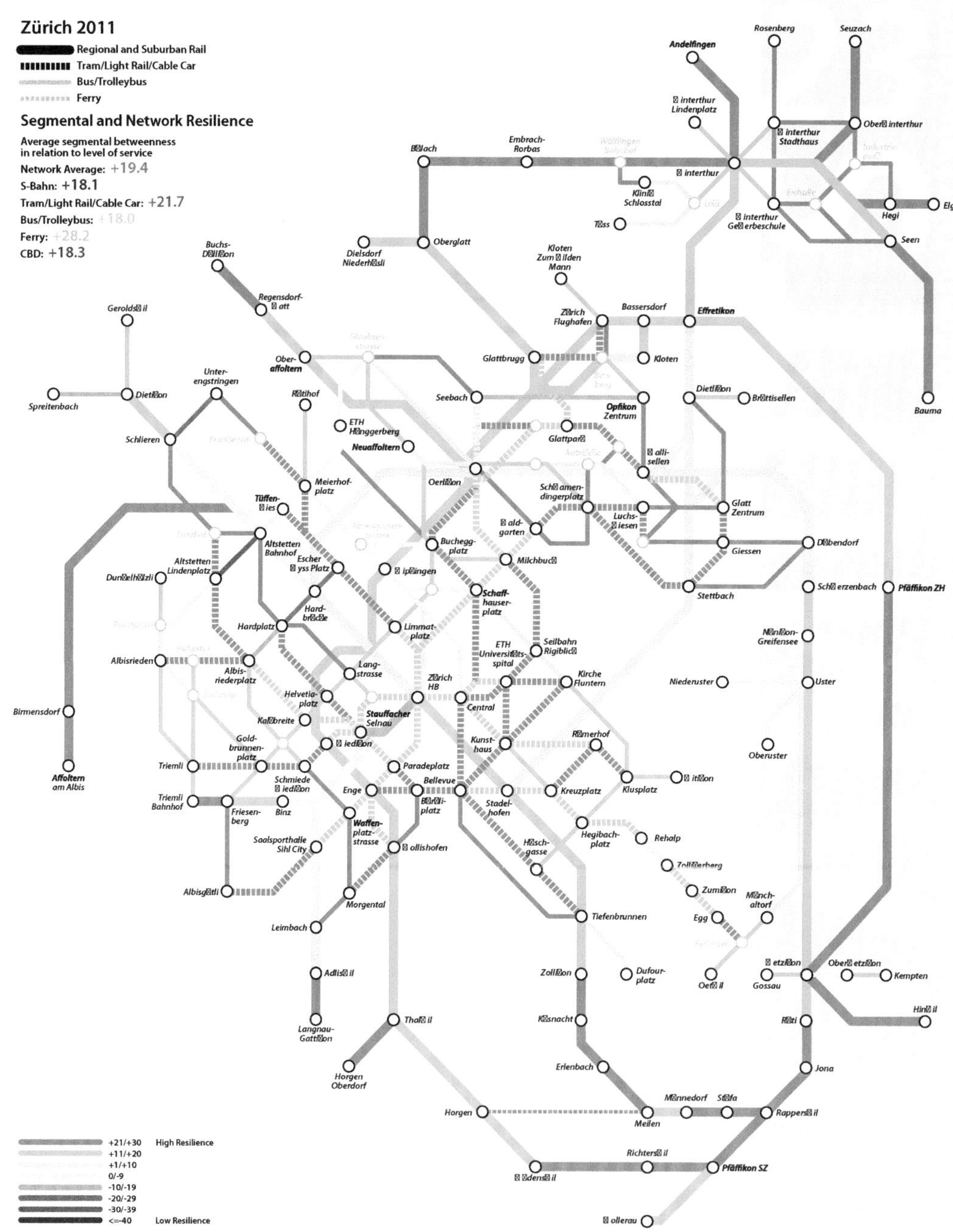

Network Resilience

Zurich's average levels of network resilience are the highest in the global

sample. This finding neatly supports the assumption made previously that Zurich's provision of public transport services in relation to its land use pattern is relatively generous – not merely in number of vehicles or train sets (as discussed in the service intensity index), but also in terms of carrying capacity due to the greater weight of higher-performance modes. This has a dual effect on the network resilience index: it subdues segmental betweenness scores (the negative numerator of the index) by enabling much of the transport task to be done at the relatively modest frequencies of the rail system, while lifting the average passenger capacity of each service (the denominator of the index) through greater reliance on high-capacity rail.

Some variation in network resilience remains across the network. The trunk route of the SZU lines (S4 and S10) in the city centre appears as the most pressured segment on the rail system, while most bus segments with potential congestion intersect with the Altstetten–Dietikon rail corridor, itself characterised by the highest segmental congestion results on the SBB rail network. Conversely, there is a notable absence of poor network resilience across the entire tram and light rail system, perhaps indicating that its mature network extension, high service frequencies and mid-range speeds appear to be a near-ideal fit for the accessibility needs of the core city.

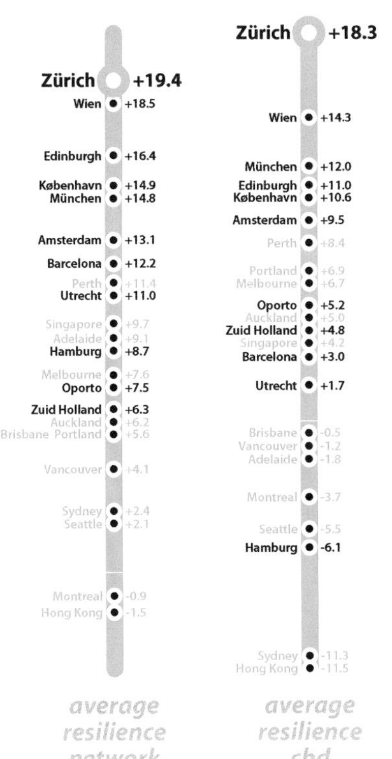

Nodal Connectivity

Zurich's average nodal connectivity result is positioned in the vicinity of those of Copenhagen and Vancouver, the polycentric region of Zuid Holland and the much larger Australian cities of Melbourne and Sydney. While the complexity of Zurich's rail network generates some good performers even at a formidable distance from the core city (Winterthur, Uster), the absence of very high, metro-like frequencies on the suburban rail system like in some of the larger cities (Amsterdam, Hamburg, Munich, Vienna) depresses the figures on this index.

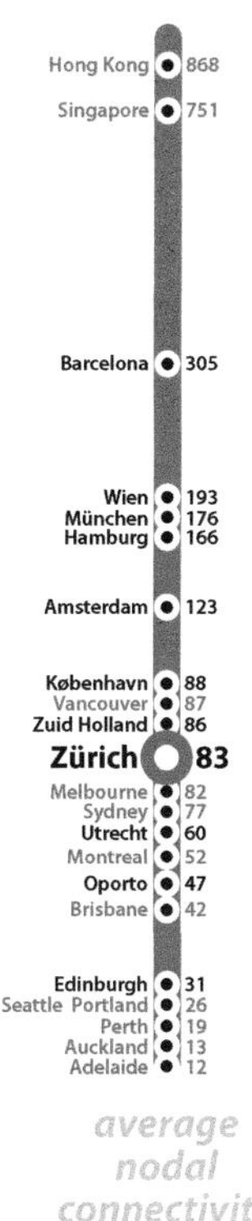

As expected, Zürich HB and Oerlikon show as the nodes with by far the highest nodal connectivity score. However, the dense tram network in inner Zurich, like Vienna's largely organised in a triangular rather than a rectangular grid, clearly has the effect of distributing the benefits associated with this index across the central city and in some cases beyond.

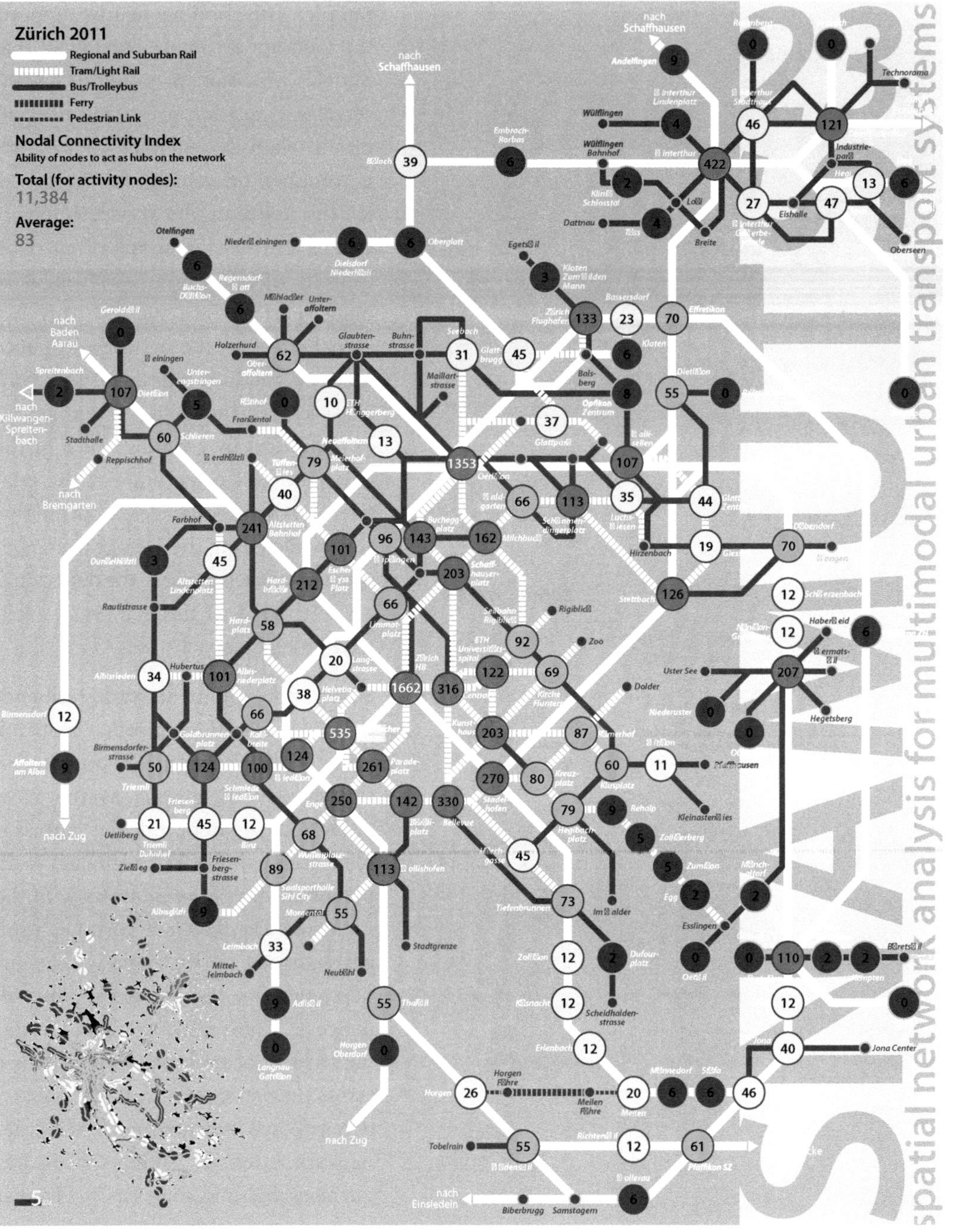

SNAMUTS Composite Accessibility Index and Reflections

Zurich's moderate average performance on the composite index – ranked fifth among 11 European case study cities – may raise questions as to why the city is held up as a model for a successful public transport system (Cervero, 1998; Newman and Kenworthy, 1999). However, the assessment needs to take into account that the Zurich agglomeration is dominated by settlement areas outside, and in some cases at considerable distance from the relatively small core city, yet still manages to cover a proportion of this region with public transport access at the SNAMUTS standard that is near-equal to or greater than that of more large-core, monocentric cities such as Vienna, Munich and Copenhagen. The seamless integration of the suburban and regional rail network, the densest in relation to population across the global sample, with some of the best laid out and operated local surface networks in the world is a particular success

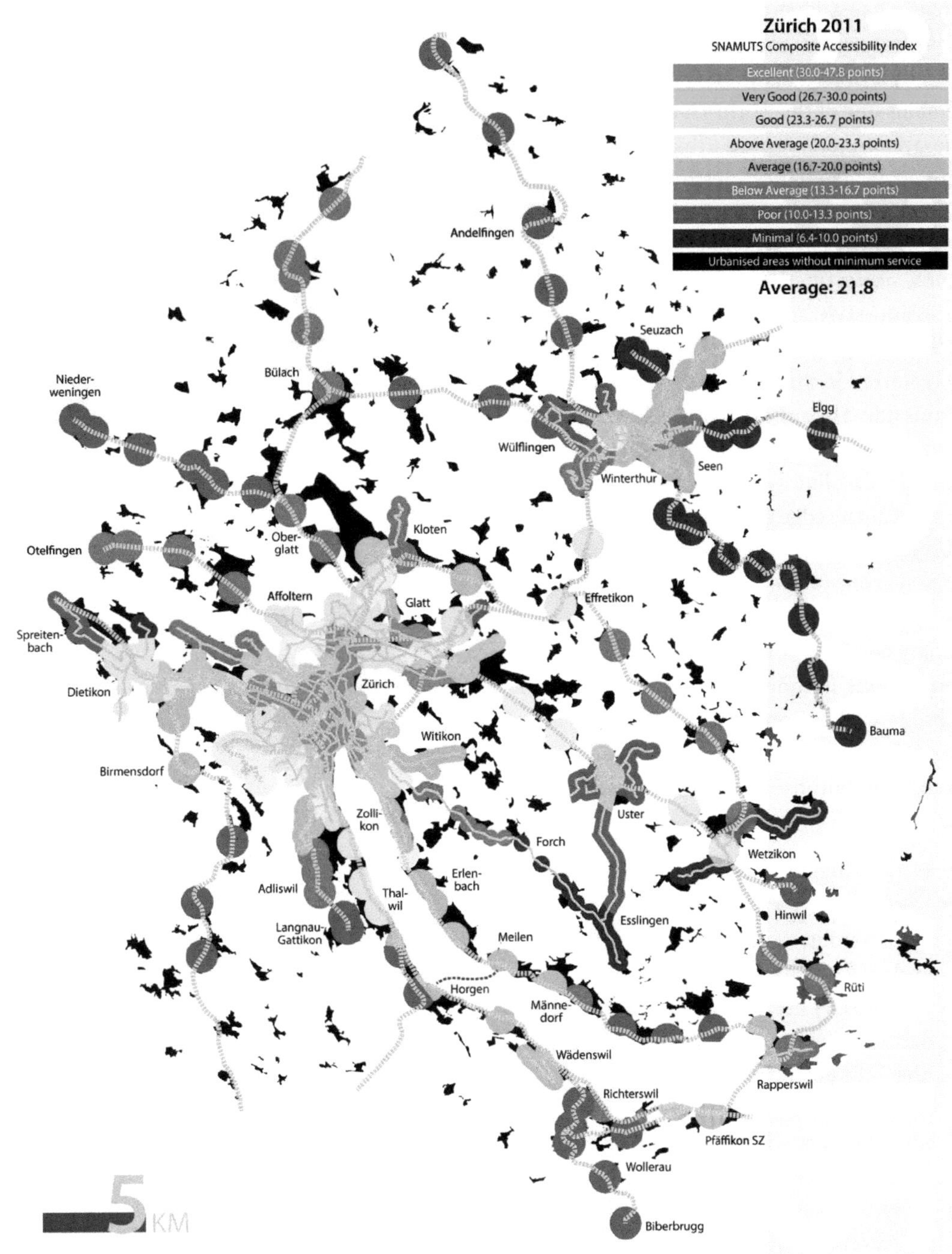

factor. These efforts are rewarded with the highest public transport trip-making rate outside Asia within the global sample. The prevalence of yellow and orange shades on the composite map also needs to be seen in the context of public transport's competitiveness with the private car which faces the same topographical constraints in the form of lakes, mountain ranges and other spaces segregating disparate settlement clusters.

Zurich has ambitious plans to further enhance the performance of its regional rail system, guided by a desired future timetable which serves as a blueprint for infrastructure investment that will enable more direct services at 15-minute or better frequencies across the metropolitan region, and less interference between regional and intercity trains (ZVV, 2014).

ACCESSIBILITY PROFILE: WIEN (AUSTRIA)

Vienna is the capital of Austria and by far the country's largest metropolitan region, located in the east of the country and not far from the borders with Czech Republic, Slovakia and Hungary. Within Austria's federal system of governance, the capital city forms a federal state in its own right. It is surrounded by a geographically much larger state called Lower Austria, and further to the south the metropolitan area stretches into the state of Burgenland. The jurisdiction of the regional transport agency (*Verkehrsverbund Ost-Region* or *VOR*), however, only covers part of these two larger states and has been used as the metropolitan area definition in this analysis: it extends to 2.48 million residents and 1.18 million jobs over an area of 6,650 sq km. Of this residential population, almost 70 per cent – 1.73 million – are concentrated within the 415 sq km that make up the city-state of Vienna. Such dominance of the core city, greater than in Barcelona, Hamburg or Munich where the respective core city only makes up about 50 per cent of the metropolitan area, translates into the second highest average urban density recorded across the European sample (after Barcelona).

Vienna is bisected by the river Danube, though most of the urbanised area, and 155 out of 187 SNAMUTS activity nodes, are located on the right bank (south-west). To the west, the Wienerwald range provides an effective natural urban growth boundary of protected open spaces, permeated only by a single transport corridor linking Vienna to St Pölten and Linz. The southern corridor towards Baden and Wiener Neustadt, serviced by reasonably frequent trains and light rail, is the traditional industrial heartland of the metropolitan region. Recent growth at the periphery is thus confined to the south east and particularly the north east, on the left bank of the Danube ('*Transdanubien*').

Vienna has a long tradition of public transport expansion (and preservation – the city's first-generation tram system remains one of the world's largest) and the accommodation of urban growth around it. The city's metro (*U-Bahn*) system, in parts, dates back to the era of city architect Otto Wagner in the early 1900s, as testified by some stunning secession-style stations and viaducts. A major expansionary push, however, only started in the 1970s and continues to this day. The suburban rail (*S-Bahn*) system feeds suburban branches into a central trunk line as well as into several termini at the edge of the inner city. As the metro network grew, Vienna's tram system transformed to focus away from the main trunks and more on secondary corridors, orbital and diagonal connections in inner and middle suburbs, as well as some outer suburban feeder lines to the metro, usually connected in purpose-designed transfer facilities.

Buses take another step down in the very pronounced modal hierarchy of Vienna's public transport and serve lower-density areas and many secondary and tertiary corridors in areas that are not contiguously urbanised (such as the aforementioned *Transdanubien*). However, the high frequencies, coverage and network density of public transport service typical for the core city tends to end abruptly at the boundary separating Vienna and Lower Austria. The local transport operator,

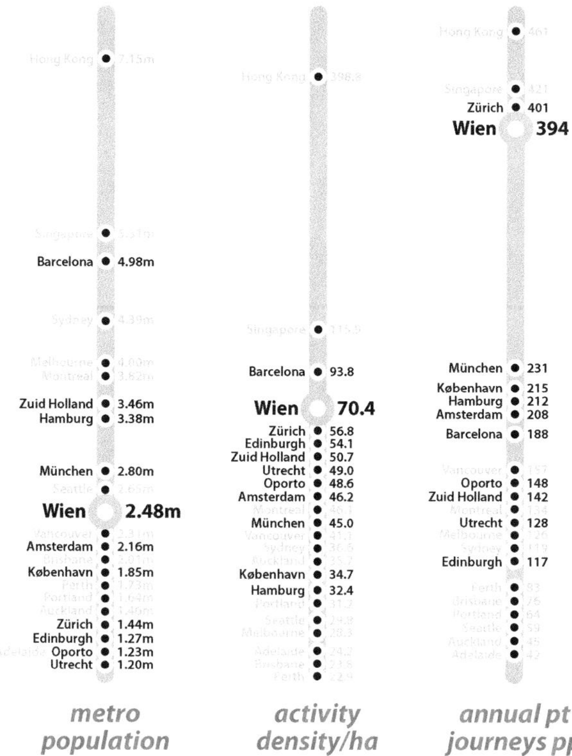

Edinburgh 38.2
Amsterdam 28.7
Zürich 25.9
Wien 25.5
Oporto 24.9
København 24.8
Barcelona 21.9
Hamburg 17.2
Zuid Holland 16.8
Utrecht 16.2
München 13.9

service intensity/ 100,000 inh

Zürich 10.1
København 9.7
München 7.9
Wien 7.7
Oporto 6.3
Hamburg 5.3
Barcelona 4.7
Utrecht 4.3
Amsterdam 4.2
Zuid Holland 3.5
Edinburgh 2.6

heavy rail stations/ 100,000 inh

Wiener Linien, remains a city subsidiary, with a traditional responsibility for servicing only the city-state of Vienna and no incentive to expand beyond the border.

Public transport fares, collected and distributed by VOR, are configured to offer strong incentives towards periodical tickets, with which the regional transport agency achieved more than three quarters of its fare income in 2010 (VOR, 2012). Within the city-state of Vienna, flat fares apply, whereas for journeys to, from and within the surrounding region there is a zonal structure.

Service Intensity

Vienna's provision of operational resources relative to population trails that of Amsterdam, Edinburgh and the Asian cities, draws roughly even with Copenhagen, Oporto and Zurich, and is significantly higher than in Barcelona, Hamburg, Munich or the Dutch Randstad cities outside Amsterdam.

All five metro lines are operated at least every five minutes, all day, every day, from terminus to terminus. The same standard also applies to the central trunk of the *S-Bahn* system between Meidling-Philadelphiabrücke and Floridsdorf, effectively adding a sixth high-frequency rapid transit line to the network. Further out, however, frequencies on the *S-Bahn* peter out quite rapidly, with some branch lines only operating every 30 minutes and/or sharing their tracks with express services. Typical daytime frequencies on *Wiener Linien* trams – there are 27 full-time lines, one of the world's largest tram operations – range between every 6 and every 10 minutes. Similar service levels can be found on inner-city bus lines, though in more suburban areas there are also 15- and 20-minute intervals.

The density of rail stations, including a regional light rail route (WLB) outside the inner city where it operates on a segregated alignment, is lower than in Zurich and Copenhagen, comparable to Munich and higher than any in other case study city.

Closeness Centrality

The closeness results for Vienna's 187 SNAMUTS activity nodes deliver the lowest (best) average in the global sample. Compared to its European peers, this exceptional result is facilitated by a monocentric form and core city dominance, greater network density and higher (or more consistently high) service frequencies. In addition, Vienna's relatively high average urban density reflects closer typical geographical spacings between network hubs, which in turn (provided the speed and frequency of the public transport routes linking them are not inferior to those in other cities)

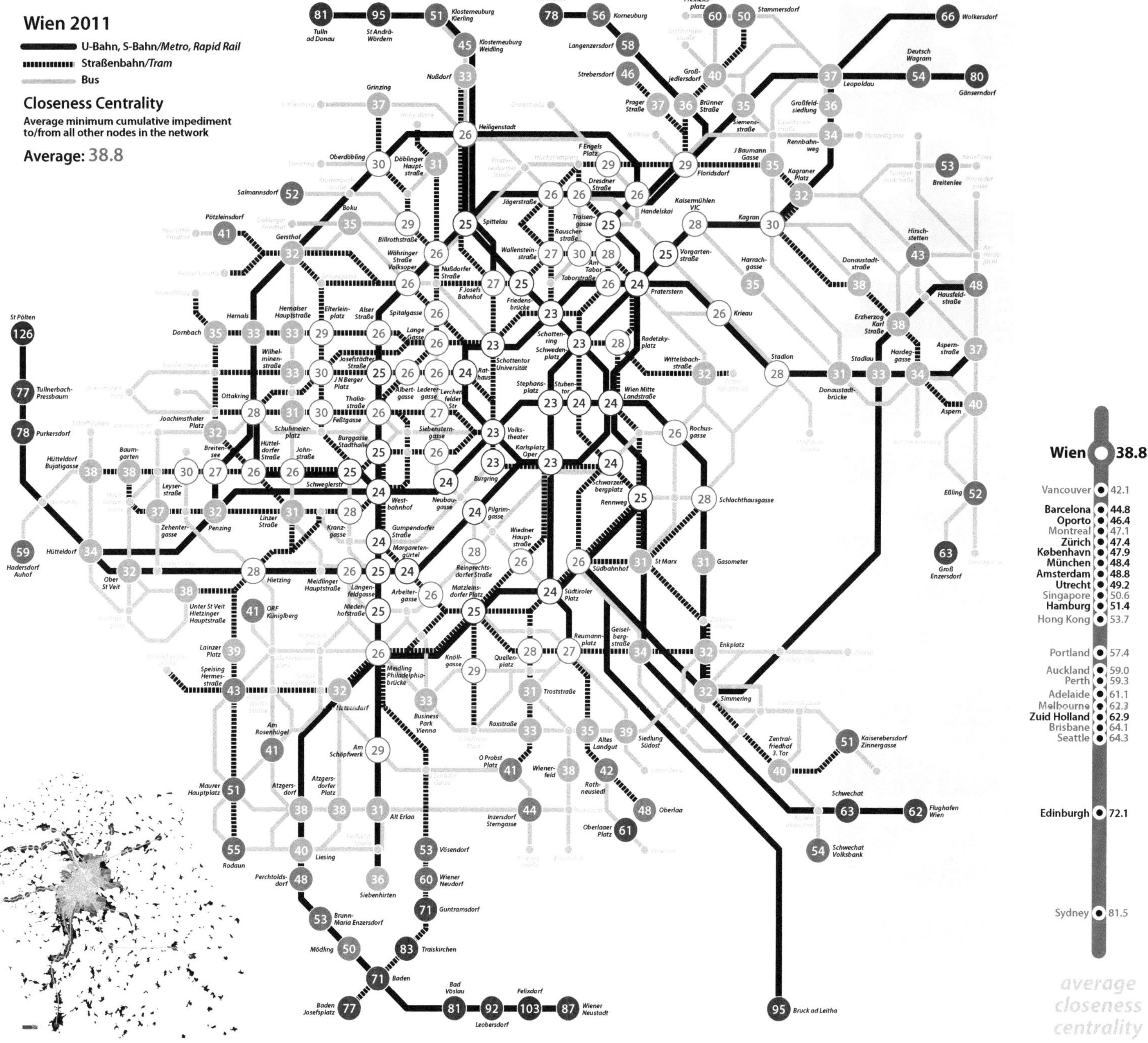

Wien 2011
U-Bahn, S-Bahn/Metro, Rapid Rail
Straßenbahn/Tram
Bus
Closeness Centrality
Average minimum cumulative impediment to/from all other nodes in the network
Average: 38.8
Wien 38.8
Vancouver 42.1
Barcelona 44.8
Oporto 46.4
Montreal 47.1
Zürich 47.4
København 47.9
München 48.4
Amsterdam 48.8
Utrecht 49.2
Singapore 50.6
Hamburg 51.4
Hong Kong 53.7
Portland 57.4
Auckland 59.0
Perth 59.3
Adelaide 61.1
Melbourne 62.3
Zuid Holland 62.9
Brisbane 64.1
Seattle 64.3
Edinburgh 72.1
Sydney 81.5
average closeness centrality

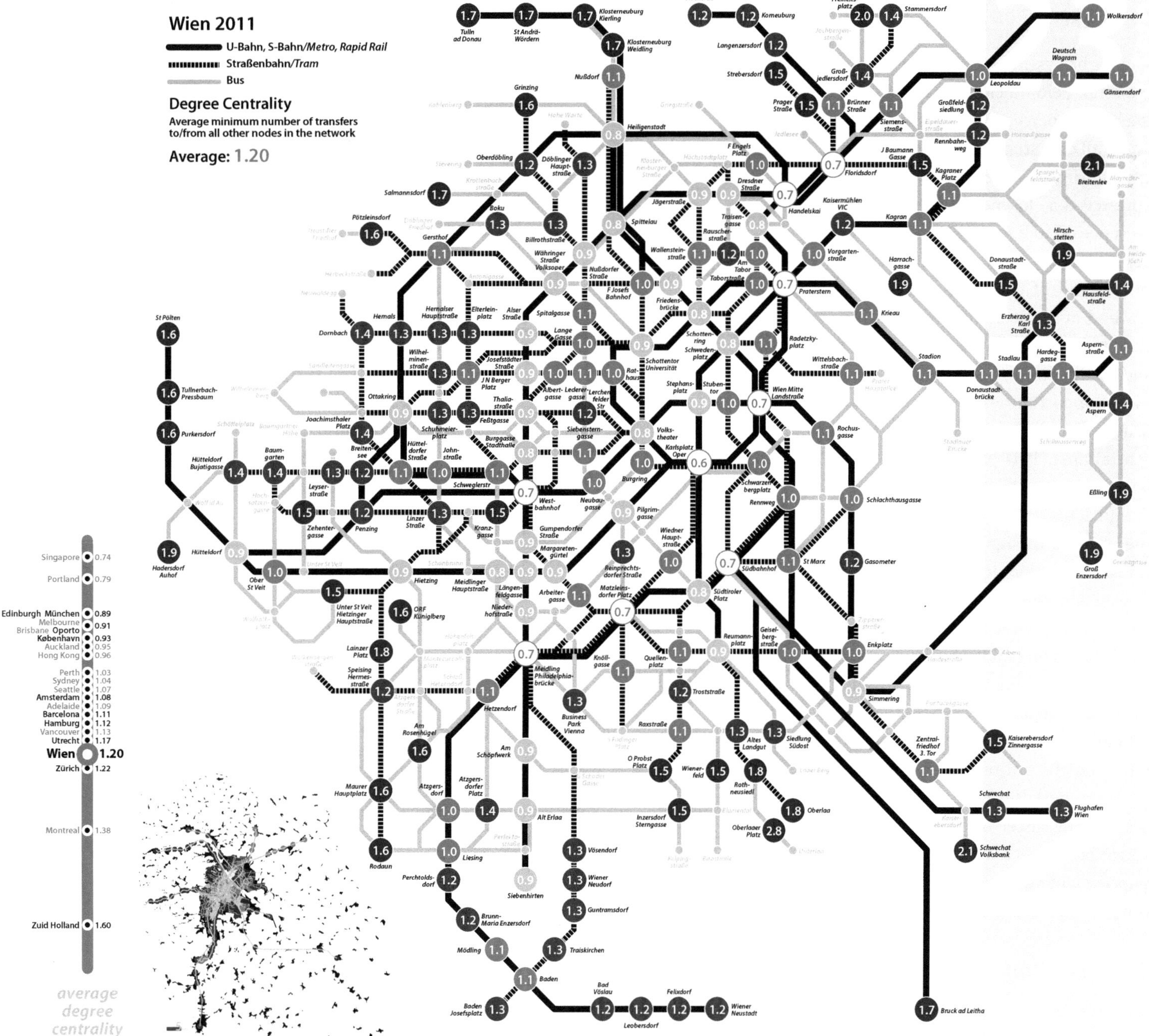

Wien 2011
U-Bahn, S-Bahn/*Metro, Rapid Rail*
Straßenbahn/*Tram*
Bus
Degree Centrality
Average minimum number of transfers to/from all other nodes in the network
Average: 1.20
Singapore 0.74
Portland 0.79
Edinburgh München 0.89
Melbourne
Brisbane Oporto 0.91
København 0.93
Auckland 0.95
Hong Kong 0.96
Perth 1.03
Sydney 1.04
Seattle 1.07
Amsterdam 1.08
Adelaide 1.09
Barcelona 1.11
Hamburg 1.12
Vancouver 1.13
Utrecht 1.17
Wien 1.20
Zürich 1.22
Montreal 1.38
Zuid Holland 1.60
average degree centrality
Tulln ad Donau
St Andrä-Wördern
Klosterneuburg Kierling
Klosterneuburg Weidling
Nußdorf
Heiligenstadt
Stockerau
Korneuburg
Langenzersdorf
Strebersdorf
Prager Straße
Freiheitsplatz
Stammersdorf
Groß-Jedlersdorf
Brünner Straße
Siemensstraße
Floridsdorf
Wolkersdorf
Deutsch Wagram
Leopoldau
Gänserndorf
Großfeldsiedlung
Rennbahnweg
Kagraner Platz
Kagran
Kaisermühlen VIC
Breitenlee
Grinzing
Oberdöbling
Döblinger Hauptstraße
Salmannsdorf
Pötzleinsdorf
Gersthof
Boku
Billrothstraße
Währinger Straße Volksoper
Spittelau
Jägerstraße
Dresdner Straße
Handelskai
Traisengasse
Rauscherstraße
Wallensteinstraße
Am Tabor
Taborstraße
Praterstern
Vorgartenstraße
Harrachgasse
Donaustadtstraße
Hirschstetten
Erzherzog Karl Straße
Hausfeldstraße
Aspernstraße
Aspern
Eßling
Groß Enzersdorf
Stadlau
Hardeggasse
Donaustadtbrücke
Stadion
Krieau
Nußdorfer Straße
F Josefs Bahnhof
Friedensbrücke
Spitalgasse
Alser Straße
Lange Gasse
Schottenring
Schwedenplatz
Schottentor Universität
Radetzkyplatz
Wittelsbachstraße
Rathaus
Stephansplatz
Stubentor
Wien Mitte Landstraße
Rochusgasse
Volkstheater
Karlsplatz Oper
Burgring
Schwarzenbergplatz
Rennweg
Schlachthausgasse
St Pölten
Tullnerbach-Pressbaum
Purkersdorf
Hütteldorf Bujatigasse
Hütteldorf
Hadersdorf Auhof
Dornbach
Hernals
Hernalser Hauptstraße
Elterleinplatz
Wilhelminenstraße
Josefstädter Straße
J N Berger Platz
Ottakring
Joachimsthaler Platz
Schuhmeierplatz
Thaliastraße
Feßtgasse
Albertgasse
Lederergasse
Lerchenfelder Str
Siebensterngasse
Burggasse Stadthalle
Hütteldorfer Straße
Johnstraße
Breitensee
Baumgarten
Leyserstraße
Zehentergasse
Penzing
Linzer Straße
Schweglerstr
Westbahnhof
Kranzgasse
Neubaugasse
Pilgrimgasse
Gumpendorfer Straße
Margaretengürtel
Reinprechtsdorfer Straße
Wiedner Hauptstraße
Südbahnhof
St Marx
Gasometer
Ober St Veit
Unter St Veit Hietzinger Hauptstraße
Hietzing
Meidlinger Hauptstraße
Längenfeldgasse
Arbeitergasse
Matzleinsdorfer Platz
Südtiroler Platz
Niederhofstraße
ORF Küniglberg
Lainzer Platz
Speising Hermesstraße
Meidling Philadelphiabrücke
Knöllgasse
Quellenplatz
Reumannplatz
Geiselbergstraße
Enkplatz
Simmering
Hetzendorf
Business Park Vienna
Troststraße
Raxstraße
Altes Landgut
Siedlung Südost
Am Rosenhügel
Am Schöpfwerk
O Probst Platz
Wienerfeld
Rothneusiedl
Oberlaa
Zentralfriedhof 3. Tor
Kaiserebersdorf Zinnergasse
Maurer Hauptplatz
Atzgersdorf
Atzgersdorfer Platz
Alt Erlaa
Inzersdorf Sterngasse
Oberlaaer Platz
Schwechat
Flughafen Wien
Schwechat Volksbank
Rodaun
Liesing
Vösendorf
Perchtoldsdorf
Siebenhirten
Wiener Neudorf
Guntramsdorf
Brunn-Maria Enzersdorf
Mödling
Traiskirchen
Baden
Baden Josefsplatz
Bad Vöslau
Leobersdorf
Felixdorf
Wiener Neustadt
Bruck ad Leitha

are associated with greater ease of movement.

Vienna has 75 nodes, or 40 per cent of the total, below a closeness score of 30, the highest percentage and absolute figure of all case study cities. Nodes on the city's entire five-line metro network do not exceed a closeness value of 37. The presence of no less than 24 nodes at the heart of the network within a relatively small band of closeness values at the low end of the scale (between 22.6 and 25.0) indicates a relatively flat hierarchy and an effective spatial distribution of travel opportunities between a multitude of activity nodes that serve the central area. This pattern is facilitated by a highly multi-directional network design across most of the core city, and the absence of significant topographical barriers except for the river Danube. Conversely, outside the city-state the network becomes more tree-shaped and is based on radial corridors with few or no connections other than through the central area. This is where the highest closeness values are found, often at intermediate stations of *S-Bahn* lines since the outer termini are usually also serviced by faster semi-express trains, which bring down the cumulative travel impediment by way of reduced travel times and greater frequency.

Degree Centrality

Vienna's average degree centrality returns the third highest network-wide level of transfer dependence among the European SNAMUTS sample, after Zuid Holland and Zurich. The network layout is designed for transfers and facilitates this with a high level of legibility, convenience and widespread information about transfer opportunities. This approach is in the interest of optimising network performance by assigning the right mode to the right purpose, although the structure particularly of the rapid transit network does not work entirely in Vienna's favour on this index. Out of the five metro lines, four connect to all other routes while the fifth (U6 between Siebenhirten and Floridsdorf) only connects to two others, necessitating two-transfer trips between some origins and destinations even within the metro system. Another influencing factor is the disjointed nature of the S-Bahn network, where not all routes feed into the central trunk line but instead into terminus stations away from the remainder of the network (Westbahnhof, Franz Josef Bahnhof and Südbahnhof). Despite these configurational and geographical gaps it is remarkable how both components of the rapid transit network deliver an effective mix of radial and orbital routes. Perhaps this structure can be traced to the foresight of Otto Wagner and his contemporaries, who built much of the inner orbital U6 and the outer orbital S45 between Handelskai and Hütteldorf.

Network Coverage

Vienna shares the top spot in the global SNAMUTS ranking on this index (outside Asia) with Amsterdam, followed relatively closely by Zurich, Copenhagen and Barcelona. This achievement is made possible by Vienna's strong domination by the core city, an area almost universally endowed with public transport services in walking distance which are in turn facilitated by a generous approach to allocating operational resources (shown in the service intensity index). The spatial containment of the core city is also associated with a large area of protected forest in the hills to the west of the city (Wienerwald), within the distance band from the city centre where in many peer cities, a car-oriented dispersed settlement pattern dominates.

Contour Catchments

Vienna's average 30-minute public transport catchment is the largest in the global sample in percentage terms of metropolitan residents and jobs. Thus in comparison to its peers, Vienna's public transport has maximised both its geographical range and its ability to link centres of activity within limited time windows. Thirty-four out of 187 nodes (18 per cent) are accessible to and from at least half of all metropolitan residents and jobs within half an hour – a ratio otherwise only found in Copenhagen. For tram

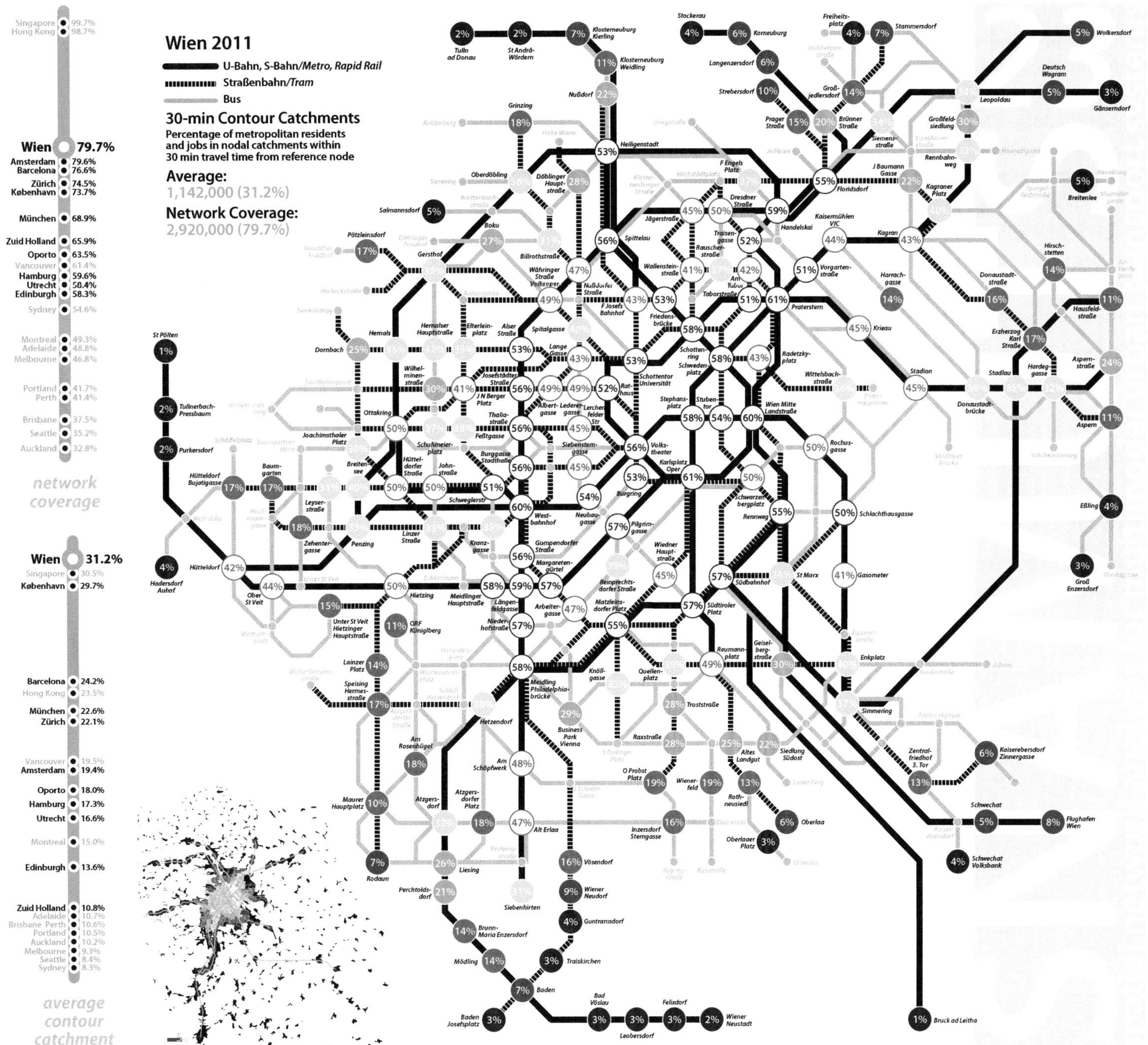
Wien 2011
U-Bahn, S-Bahn/Metro, Rapid Rail
Straßenbahn/Tram
Bus
30-min Contour Catchments
Percentage of metropolitan residents and jobs in nodal catchments within 30 min travel time from reference node
Average:
1,142,000 (31.2%)
Network Coverage:
2,920,000 (79.7%)
Singapore 99.7%
Hong Kong 98.7%
Wien 79.7%
Amsterdam 79.6%
Barcelona 76.6%
Zürich 74.5%
København 73.7%
München 68.9%
Zuid Holland 65.9%
Oporto 63.5%
Vancouver 61.4%
Hamburg 59.6%
Utrecht 50.4%
Edinburgh 58.3%
Sydney 54.6%
Montreal 49.3%
Adelaide 48.8%
Melbourne 46.8%
Portland 41.7%
Perth 41.4%
Brisbane 37.5%
Seattle 35.2%
Auckland 32.8%
network coverage
Wien 31.2%
Singapore 30.5%
København 29.7%
Barcelona 24.2%
Hong Kong 23.5%
München 22.6%
Zürich 22.1%
Vancouver 19.5%
Amsterdam 19.4%
Oporto 18.0%
Hamburg 17.3%
Utrecht 16.6%
Montreal 15.0%
Edinburgh 13.6%
Zuid Holland 10.8%
Adelaide 10.7%
Brisbane Perth 10.6%
Portland 10.5%
Auckland 10.2%
Melbourne 9.3%
Seattle 8.4%
Sydney 8.3%
average contour catchment

and bus-only nodes within the inner ring of neighbourhoods, however, the figures consistently drop to below 50 per cent owing to the lower speed of these modes. The smallest contour catchment on the five-line metro network (at Aspernstraße) is 24 per cent, roughly equivalent to the highest such scores at the CBD rail hubs of Melbourne or Sydney. Along the suburban rail branches and some feeder bus lines in the outskirts of the core city, however, contour catchments tend to drop to very low values, partially as a result of the low service frequencies there that do not allow for transfer connections to be counted on this index.

Betweenness Centrality

Global betweenness, or the overall 'presence' of public transport travel opportunities relative to population and employment in the Vienna metropolitan region, is second only to Copenhagen in the global sample outside Asia. High settlement density, contiguity and service intensity all assist this result. The catchment of typical path length measure places Vienna in the midfield among European and global case study cities. The influence of relatively high settlement density (inflating this index) is counterbalanced here with the tightly-knit network structure which enables users to minimise detours from geographical desire lines (moderating this index and simultaneously enhancing public transport's competitiveness to individual transport modes).

Vienna's reliance on surface modes to capture travel opportunities is comparable to that of Zurich, but slightly greater than that of tram-free Hamburg and Copenhagen, and significantly greater than that of heavily rail-dominated Barcelona and Munich. It is lower than in any other European or non-European SNAMUTS city though.

The significance of CBD network elements for the distribution of travel opportunities in Vienna appears relatively low for a monocentric, strong-core city whose functional centre is positioned at its geographical heart. However, Vienna's trams do not penetrate the CBD (they encircle the CBD instead) and the presence of several orbital and diagonal heavy rail lines has the effect of redistributing travel opportunities away from the city centre.

A notable detail in Vienna's betweenness performance is the relatively even distribution of travel opportunities across multiple routes and transfer nodes in the central area. The highest betweenness scores are in the 260–280 range (Westbahnhof, Karlsplatz-Oper, Wien Mitte-Landstraße and Praterstern). In many other cities there is a tendency for a single 'super-node' to dominate all others on this index. Since extremely high nodal betweenness

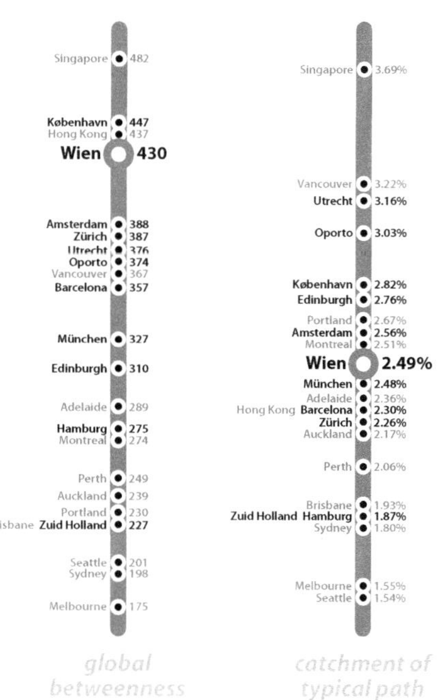

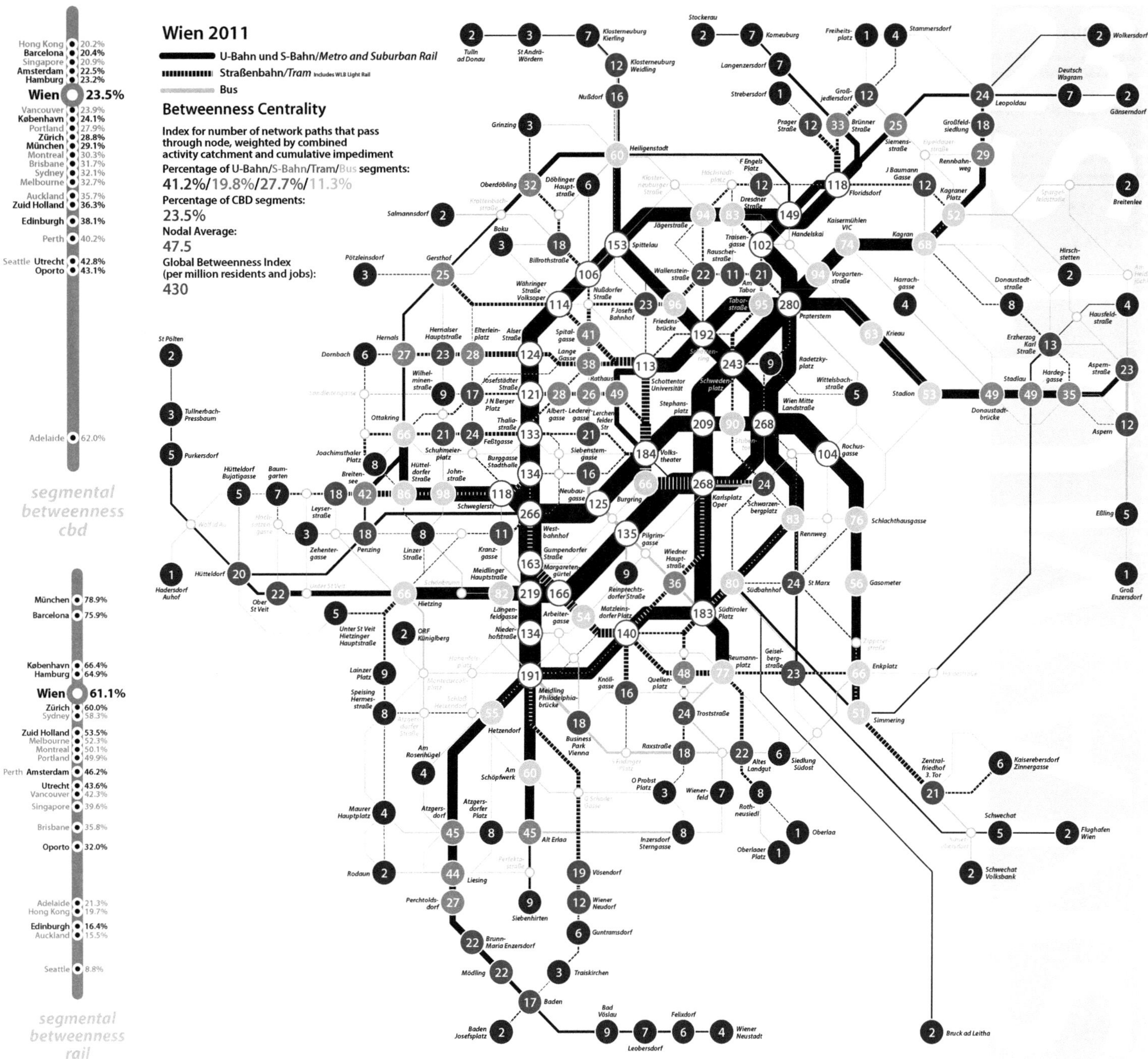

Wien 2011
U-Bahn und S-Bahn/Metro and Suburban Rail
Straßenbahn/Tram Includes WLB Light Rail
Bus
Betweenness Centrality
Index for number of network paths that pass through node, weighted by combined activity catchment and cumulative impediment
Percentage of U-Bahn/S-Bahn/Tram/Bus segments:
41.2%/19.8%/27.7%/11.3%
Percentage of CBD segments:
23.5%
Nodal Average:
47.5
Global Betweenness Index (per million residents and jobs):
430
Hong Kong 20.2%
Barcelona 20.4%
Singapore 20.9%
Amsterdam 22.5%
Hamburg 23.2%
Wien 23.5%
Vancouver 23.9%
København 24.1%
Portland 27.9%
Zürich 28.8%
München 29.1%
Montreal 30.3%
Brisbane 31.7%
Sydney 32.1%
Melbourne 32.7%
Auckland 35.7%
Zuid Holland 36.3%
Edinburgh 38.1%
Perth 40.2%
Seattle Utrecht 42.8%
Oporto 43.1%
Adelaide 62.0%
segmental betweenness cbd
München 78.9%
Barcelona 75.9%
København 66.4%
Hamburg 64.9%
Wien 61.1%
Zürich 60.0%
Sydney 58.3%
Zuid Holland 53.5%
Melbourne 52.3%
Montreal 50.1%
Portland 49.9%
Perth Amsterdam 46.2%
Utrecht 43.6%
Vancouver 42.3%
Singapore 39.6%
Brisbane 35.8%
Oporto 32.0%
Adelaide 21.3%
Hong Kong 19.7%
Edinburgh 16.4%
Auckland 15.5%
Seattle 8.8%
segmental betweenness rail

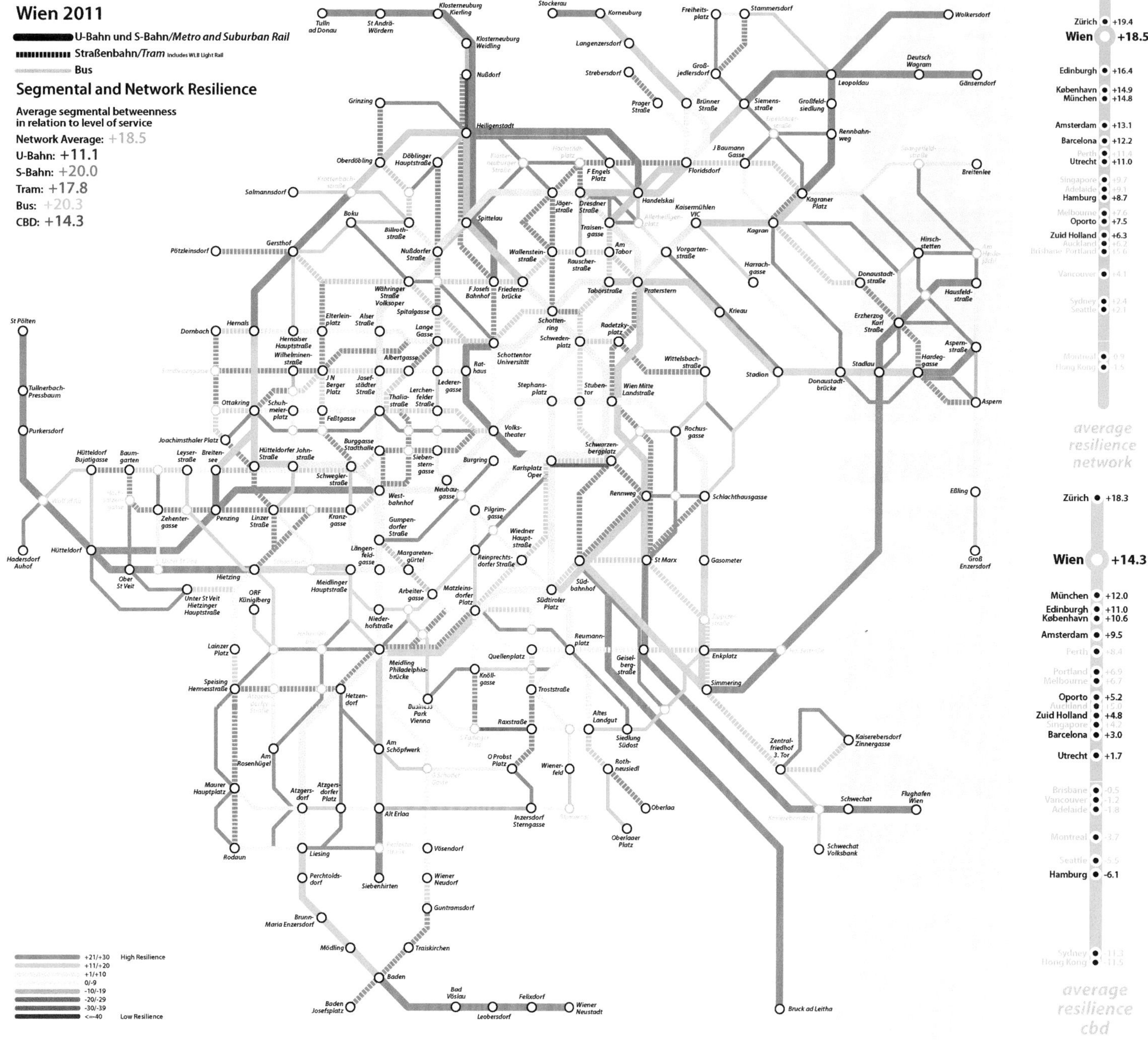

Wien 2011
U-Bahn und S-Bahn/Metro and Suburban Rail
Straßenbahn/Tram includes WLB Light Rail
Bus
Segmental and Network Resilience
Average segmental betweenness in relation to level of service
Network Average: +18.5
U-Bahn: +11.1
S-Bahn: +20.0
Tram: +17.8
Bus: +20.3
CBD: +14.3
Tulln ad Donau
St Andrä-Wördern
Klosterneuburg Kierling
Klosterneuburg Weidling
Nußdorf
Stockerau
Korneuburg
Langenzersdorf
Strebersdorf
Prager Straße
Freiheitsplatz
Stammersdorf
Groß-jedlersdorf
Brünner Straße
Siemensstraße
Großfeldsiedlung
Leopoldau
Deutsch Wagram
Gänserndorf
Wolkersdorf
Grinzing
Heiligenstadt
Oberdöbling
Döblinger Hauptstraße
Salmannsdorf
Boku
Billrothstraße
Spittelau
Jägerstraße
Dresdner Straße
F Engels Platz
Floridsdorf
J Baumann Gasse
Rennbahnweg
Breitenlee
Kagraner Platz
Handelskai
Kaisermühlen VIC
Traisengasse
Kagran
Pötzleinsdorf
Gersthof
Nußdorfer Straße
Wallensteinstraße
Rauscherstraße
Am Tabor
Vorgartenstraße
Harrachgasse
Hirschstetten
Währinger Straße Volksoper
F Josefs Bahnhof
Friedensbrücke
Taborstraße
Praterstern
Donaustadtstraße
Hausfeldstraße
St Pölten
Dornbach
Hernals
Elterleinplatz
Alser Straße
Spitalgasse
Schottenring
Krieau
Erzherzog Karl Straße
Hernalser Hauptstraße
Lange Gasse
Schottentor Universität
Schwedenplatz
Radetzkyplatz
Aspernstraße
Wilhelminenstraße
Albertgasse
Rathaus
Wittelsbachstraße
Stadion
Stadlau
Hardeggasse
Tullnerbach-Pressbaum
J N Berger Platz
Josefstädter Straße
Lerchenfelder Straße
Lederergasse
Stephansplatz
Stubentor
Wien Mitte Landstraße
Donaustadtbrücke
Aspern
Ottakring
Schuhmeierplatz
Thaliastraße
Feßtgasse
Purkersdorf
Volkstheater
Rochusgasse
Joachimsthaler Platz
Burggasse Stadthalle
Schwarzenbergplatz
Hütteldorf Bujatigasse
Baumgarten
Leyserstraße
Breitensee
Hütteldorfer Straße
Johnstraße
Siebensterngasse
Burgring
Karlsplatz Oper
Schweglerstraße
Neubaugasse
Westbahnhof
Rennweg
Schlachthausgasse
Eßling
Zehentergasse
Penzing
Linzer Straße
Kranzgasse
Pilgramgasse
Gumpendorfer Straße
Wiedner Hauptstraße
Hadersdorf Auhof
Hütteldorf
Längenfeldgasse
Margaretengürtel
Reinprechtsdorfer Straße
St Marx
Gasometer
Groß Enzersdorf
Ober St Veit
Hietzing
Unter St Veit Hietzinger Hauptstraße
ORF Küniglberg
Meidlinger Hauptstraße
Arbeitergasse
Matzleinsdorfer Platz
Südtiroler Platz
Südbahnhof
Niederhofstraße
Reumannplatz
Lainzer Platz
Meidling Philadelphiabrücke
Quellenplatz
Knöllgasse
Geiselbergstraße
Enkplatz
Speising Hermesstraße
Hetzendorf
Troststraße
Simmering
Business Park Vienna
Raxstraße
Altes Landgut
Siedlung Südost
Zentralfriedhof 3. Tor
Kaiserebersdorf Zinnergasse
Am Rosenhügel
Am Schöpfwerk
O Probst Platz
Wienerfeld
Rothneusiedl
Maurer Hauptplatz
Atzgersdorf
Atzgersdorfer Platz
Alt Erlaa
Inzersdorf Sterngasse
Oberlaa
Schwechat
Flughafen Wien
Rodaun
Liesing
Vösendorf
Oberlaaer Platz
Schwechat Volksbank
Perchtoldsdorf
Siebenhirten
Wiener Neudorf
Guntramsdorf
Brunn-Maria Enzersdorf
Mödling
Traiskirchen
Baden
Baden Josefsplatz
Bad Vöslau
Leobersdorf
Felixdorf
Wiener Neustadt
Bruck ad Leitha
+21/+30 High Resilience
+11/+20
+1/+10
0/-9
-10/-19
-20/-29
-30/-39
<=-40 Low Resilience
Zürich +19.4
Wien +18.5
Edinburgh +16.4
København +14.9
München +14.8
Amsterdam +13.1
Barcelona +12.2
Perth +11.4
Utrecht +11.0
Singapore +9.7
Adelaide +9.1
Hamburg +8.7
Melbourne +7.6
Oporto +7.5
Zuid Holland +6.3
Auckland +6.2
Brisbane Portland +5.6
Vancouver +4.1
Sydney +2.4
Seattle +2.1
Montreal -0.9
Hong Kong -1.5
average resilience network
Zürich +18.3
Wien +14.3
München +12.0
Edinburgh +11.0
København +10.6
Amsterdam +9.5
Perth +8.4
Portland +6.9
Melbourne +6.7
Oporto +5.2
Auckland +5.0
Zuid Holland +4.8
Singapore +4.2
Barcelona +3.0
Utrecht +1.7
Brisbane -0.5
Vancouver -1.2
Adelaide -1.8
Montreal -3.7
Seattle -5.5
Hamburg -6.1
Sydney -11.3
Hong Kong -11.5
average resilience cbd

values may be associated with nodal congestion (Bertolini, 2005), this finding may suggest that Vienna's network configuration makes a critical contribution to defusing pressures from the spatial concentration of travel opportunities, as discussed presently.

Network Resilience

Vienna's network resilience performance joins Zurich at the top of the global city comparison. There is a correlation here with the higher levels of service intensity and greater network density prevalent across the Vienna network compared to many other cities, as elaborated above. However, lower congestion pressures on this index also suggest a land use–transport system that distributes travel opportunities more evenly across the network and the urban geography.

Of further importance in this context is the distribution of resilience values across the different modes. In Vienna, with the exception of the *S-Bahn* (which has a dominant role in servicing outer suburban areas), average modal resilience appears to be in proportion to mode performance: the lowest values are present on the *U-Bahn* system and the highest ones on the bus system. This is a significant factor in the operation of an efficient network, where each mode is employed for the tasks that most suit its characteristics.

On a local level, Vienna's network resilience map is remarkable for the near-absence of network elements with critically low segmental results, with the two bus segments returning the poorest values probably a result of statistical anomalies rather than as indicative of an imbalance between supply and network significance. Next worst is the southern orbital bus corridor along Wienerbergstraße and Raxstraße in the Favoriten district, taking in Vienna's largest employment node without rail access (Business Park Vienna). The network significance of this corridor is likely to increase further when a metro interchange is opened along the U1 extension at Altes Landgut in 2017, and a planned conversion of the corridor to tram operation comes to fruition.

Nodal Connectivity

Vienna has the second highest average nodal connectivity score among the European SNAMUTS cities after Barcelona. Compared to other large cities such as Munich or Hamburg (which are not far behind on this index), Vienna clearly draws an edge from its large tram system, a mid-capacity mode that brings up the nodal connectivity scores compared to buses due to its greater occupancy rate. Furthermore, Vienna's dense network structure offers a particularly high number of options for multi-directional movement, an observation that is manifest in a large number of nodes with more than four routes converging in them, as would be the case in a rigid rectangular grid. Instead, Vienna's network, particularly in the central area, has a greater prevalence of triangular grid fragments with an augmenting effect on multi-directionality.

Vienna's best-performing node on this index, interestingly, is Praterstern at the CBD fringe where the *S-Bahn* trunk line and two *U-Bahn* lines and several surface routes intersect. Praterstern is followed (in this order) by Karlsplatz-Oper, Wien Mitte-Landstraße, Volkstheater, Meidling-Philadelphiabrücke, Spittelau and Westbahnhof.

SNAMUTS Composite Accessibility Index and Reflections

It is difficult to find significant fault in Vienna's interplay of public transport and land use, and the results of the composite index support this notion.

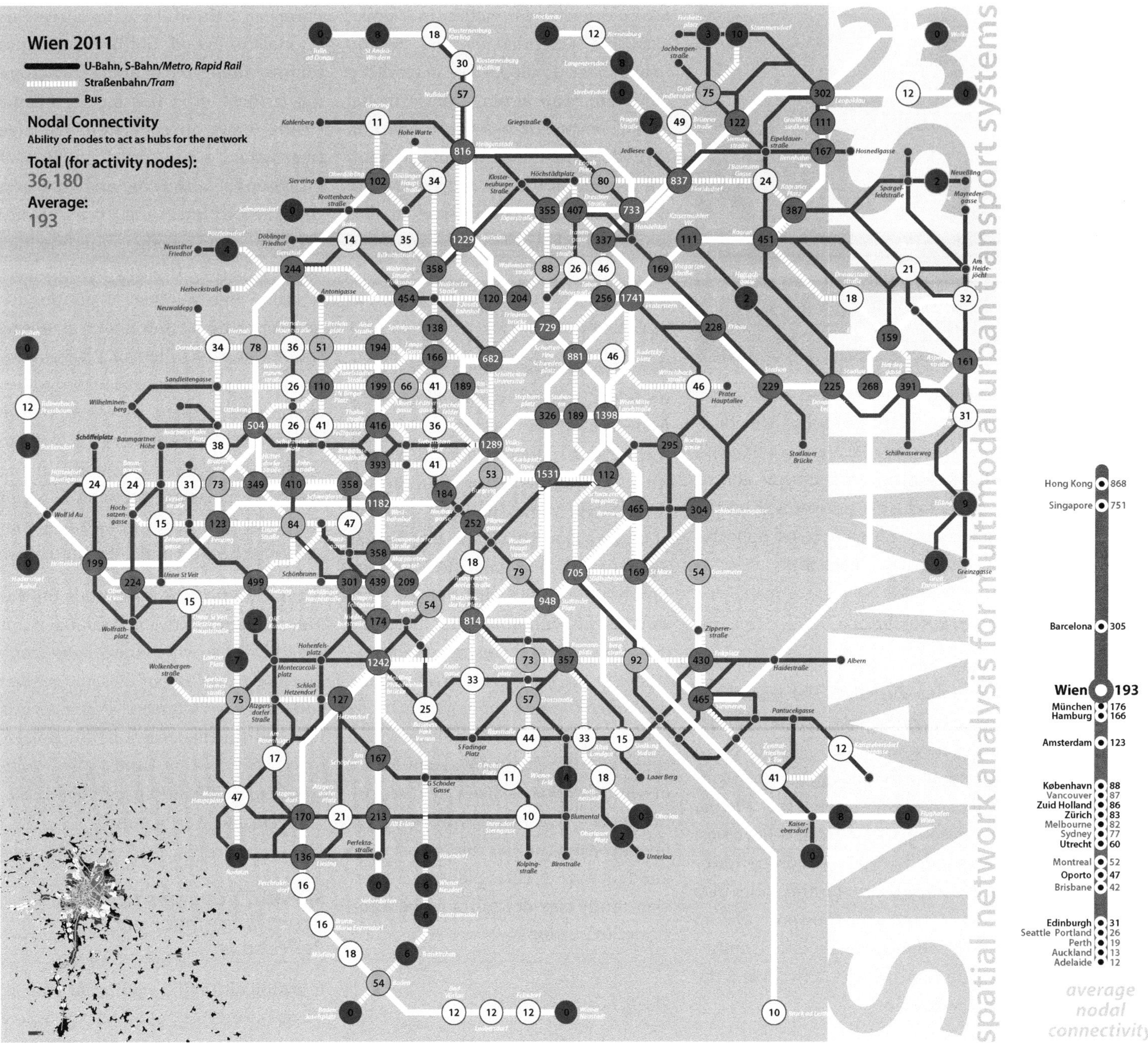
Wien 2011
U-Bahn, S-Bahn/Metro, Rapid Rail
Straßenbahn/Tram
Bus
Nodal Connectivity
Ability of nodes to act as hubs for the network
Total (for activity nodes):
36,180
Average:
193
spatial network analysis for multimodal urban transport systems
Hong Kong 868
Singapore 751
Barcelona 305
Wien 193
München 176
Hamburg 166
Amsterdam 123
København 88
Vancouver 87
Zuid Holland 86
Zürich 83
Melbourne 82
Sydney 77
Utrecht 60
Montreal 52
Oporto 47
Brisbane 42
Edinburgh 31
Seattle Portland 26
Perth 19
Auckland 13
Adelaide 12
average nodal connectivity

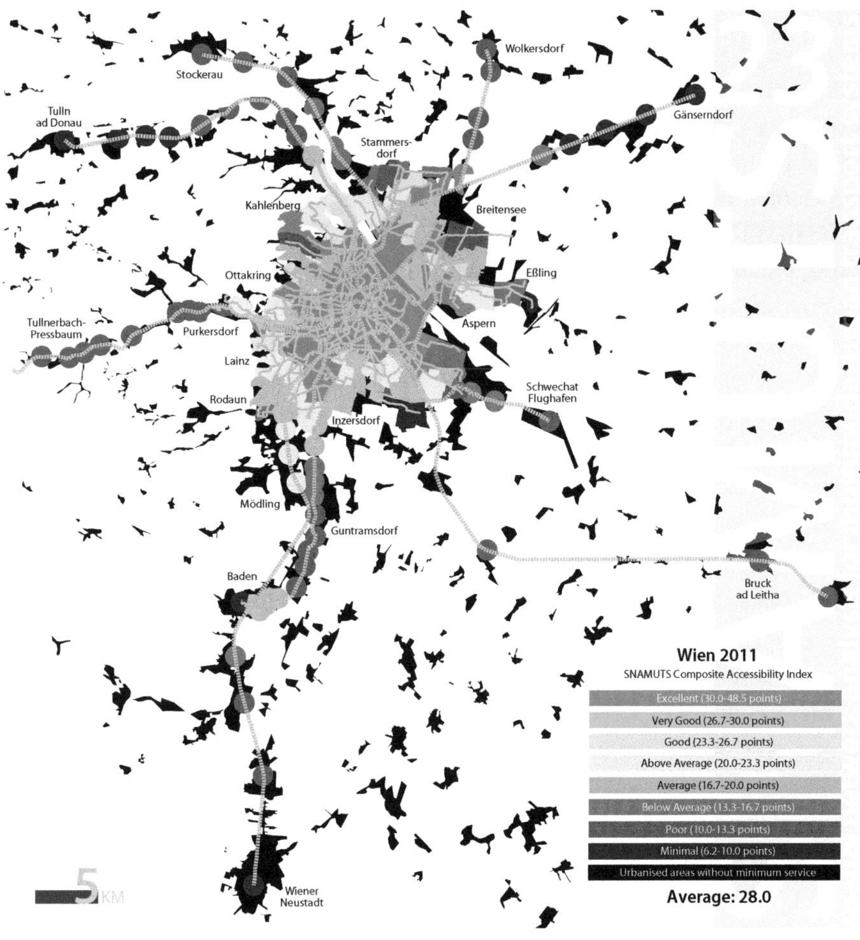

An accessibility standard in the highest category utilised in this comparison (exceeding 30) applies to practically the entire pre-1945 settlement area and in some cases beyond. Vienna leads the global sample on ease of movement, public transport endowment (outside Asia), average contour catchments and (jointly with Zurich) on network resilience. Most significantly, among the non-Asian SNAMUTS cities, Vienna also shares the top spot with Zurich in public transport usage, eclipsing its closest European followers almost by a factor of two in terms of annual trips per capita. This suggests that Vienna is a global model for successful public transport planning, organisation and accessibility. The question is, is it likely to remain in this position?

Vienna appears to have managed to stem suburban dispersal to a much greater extent than its peers, with 70 per cent of the metropolitan population contained within the core city. This may be the outcome of a location at the edge of the Western world, surrounded by the Iron Curtain during the four decades of the twentieth century when suburban sprawl was a prevalent force elsewhere. Today, with open European borders, Vienna's commuter shed is edging towards overlap with those of the Slovakian capital, Bratislava (65 km), and the Czech Republic's second city, Brno (135 km). Future upgrades of cross-border rail links with these cities towards higher speed and greater frequency are likely to deepen an emerging functional interdependence and convert a traditionally monocentric capital region into the dominant urban centre within an increasingly polycentric, transnational urban network. In the process, the accessibility of the interstitial spaces between urban centres will also be enhanced and present the region with new challenges to maintain, and redefine, the role of public transport at a much broader spatial scale than what is covered by the exemplary accessibility performance of the present-day core city.

CONCLUSION AND REFLECTION

The four cities profiled in this chapter have each made unique and location-specific contributions to furthering the interplay of public transport network development and the evolution of urban form. Historically, this occurred both by design or deliberation in the form of visionary planning strategies or democratic processes that allowed for a departure from the policy mainstream, and by circumstance, including constraints to urban dispersal through topographic or geopolitical factors. Today, all four cities have reined in the dominance of the private car with greater ambition and success than any of the other case study cities discussed in this volume up to here. Yet the role of public transport to provide the necessary travel and accessibility alternatives varies greatly and is most conspicuously manifest in the statistic of annual trip making rates. Here, Vienna and Zurich outperform Barcelona and Copenhagen by a ratio of around two to one.

This observation raises several questions. First, does it actually represent a problem in either sustainability terms (from the vantage point of enhancing urban transport's environmental performance, contribution to social equity and facilitation of economic opportunity), or in accessibility terms when the full spectrum of non-car modes is considered? Of the four cities examined, Copenhagen has by far the highest (and still growing) mode share for bicycles at 29 per cent of all intra-urban journeys (Københavns Kommune, 2014). The SNAMUTS analysis has shown that Copenhagen's public transport system behaves somewhat complementary to the characteristics of bicycle mobility: its strengths are most prevalent beyond the normal distance and speed range of cycling. Can the Danish capital thus 'afford' to sustain a relatively modest trip making rate on public transport as long as the balance is dominated by bicycle rather than car journeys – particularly given the finding that the network in its current state is among the most resilient in the SNAMUTS sample? As mentioned previously, Copenhagen's future public transport investment program does not seem to have made up its mind about these priorities: it includes measures that add rail infrastructure both in bicycle-rich inner areas and in more car-oriented suburban corridors.

In Barcelona, a similar though perhaps less conspicuous effect to that of Copenhagen's bicycle culture can be detected in the prevalence of walking, which at 47 per cent of all intra-urban journeys dominates the modal split (Ajuntament de Barcelona, 2014a). In conjunction with the core city's extraordinarily high urban density, which places a significant number and diversity of destinations within the range of a typical walking trip, this circumstance may contribute to the suppression of public transport trip making rates. In both cities, it is also likely that the lower emphasis on and/or higher cost of periodical fares in the ticketing system works as a disincentive against discretionary journeys on public transport in comparison to Vienna and Zurich.

Second, if Copenhagen and Barcelona were to increase public transport trip-making rates towards the level of Vienna and Zurich, how would their public transport systems be prepared, or in need to be adapted, for the onslaught of additional patronage? It is here where the differences between the two cities become most obvious: in Copenhagen with its long-standing history of carefully planned co-evolution of urban growth and transport infrastructure, a largely resilient public transport system emerged whose utilisation rates in the present appear to offer some room for ridership increases in the future. In Barcelona, many key elements particularly of the rail system seem to be close to capacity and not in a position to absorb significant numbers of additional passengers. Moreover, there is limited scope for substantial capacity increases through modal upgrades on the surface network, with the exception of the desirable (though highly controversial) connection of the two halves of the tram system through the heart of the city along Avinguda Diagonal. To make a tangible difference to resilience performance across the network, Barcelona would have to add further high-capacity underground rail lines through the core city, as well as boost the connections to and between its regional 'satellites' – in terms of increased frequencies, reduced travel times and where needed, additional links. These tasks obviously incur infrastructures with high investment costs and relatively long time spans for implementation: infrastructures, however, that have formed a part of the region's transport planning framework for some time (ATM, 2014). Their construction is thus less of a political challenge in Barcelona's relatively consensus-driven planning culture (Pernau, 2001), but more one of funding in a period of economic crisis that has slowed government capital expenditure across much of southern Europe.

Third, Vienna's and Zurich's exceptionally high public transport usage rates are also a reflection of a particular approach to public transport service planning and network optimisation. In both cities, the dominant user experience is one of seamless trip-making along geographical desire lines, largely regardless of the number or location of transfers between vehicles or modes this incurs. In Vienna, this quality of maximum user flexibility or 'autonomous mobility' (Dowling and Kent, 2013) is achieved by the provision of a high network density across the core city, a maximisation of the number of transfer points allowing for multi-directional trip making, and standards of network-wide service frequencies across practically the entire day and week that do not require the consultation of timetables in order to optimise one's travel time. In Zurich, a similar effect is achieved by coordinating all modes of public transport on a 'pulse-timetable' principle. This incurs that even at lower frequencies such as every 30 minutes, the network layout and service patterns have been continuously optimised to allow for simultaneous arrivals of vehicles from all directions in as high a number of transfer points as possible, in a painstaking planning process stretching over several decades (Mees, 2010a). Furthermore, the network structure in the central areas of Vienna and Zurich assumes a geometrical pattern of triangles between nodes and links. Compared to the rectangular grids prevalent in Barcelona's or Copenhagen's nineteenth-century city extensions (and in practically all New World cities), triangular grids lead to a greater number of links converging in the most significant nodes and order them in a more nuanced hierarchy, which can usefully inform their categorisation as strategic land use centres as well.

In both Alpine cities, the desired service offer (*Verkehrsangebot*) to the user does in fact provide the template for planning the network, informing decisions about infrastructure upgrades and writing timetables (Stone, 2011). This process is facilitated further by the more widespread presence of a greater range of public transport modes than in Copenhagen or Barcelona, where a relatively large performance and capacity gap exists between (heavy) rail and bus operations. Compared to buses, Zurich and Vienna's tram and light rail systems offer the advantages of higher passenger capacity per vehicle, greater propensity for effective prioritisation over private vehicle traffic and a more legible and durable presence in the cityscape, helping with transit-oriented land use consolidation and intensification (Newman and Scheurer, 2010). It is arguable that Zurich and Vienna have made the most of the performance niche offered by this intermediate mode as they gradually concentrated its deployment on the inner urban corridors of the core city in Zurich (a hierarchical step below the regional corridors across the agglomeration serviced by heavy rail) and on secondary radial and orbital corridors in Vienna.

Lastly, there remains a formidable performance gap between Vienna and Zurich in the SNAMUTS accessibility profiles, contrasting with the comparable levels of trip-making the public transport systems in both cities attract. On most indicators, this discrepancy in Vienna's favour can be traced directly or indirectly to a more compact and centralised settlement structure in the Austrian capital than in its Swiss neighbour. This observation raises an obvious question: do monocentric, core-city dominated metropolitan regions inherently offer better conditions for public transport accessibility than polycentric, dispersed ones, even where such settlement dispersal is concentrated around public transport routes (as it is in the Zurich region)? Would this notion suggest that cities that seek to boost the role of public transport in their mobility mix were well advised to devise a complementary land use strategy that aims at intensifying the core city at the expense of the outer metropolitan area?

7 Public Transport Dominance in Wealthy Asian Cities

This chapter examines the accessibility conditions in two developed Asian cities experiencing a greater public transport mode share and trip-making rate than Europe's top performers, Vienna and Zurich. Hong Kong, and particularly Singapore, are recent additions to the ranks of wealthy global cities and have been subject to rapid urban growth – in population terms, they are the two largest cities in the SNAMUTS sample. Both cities have the development of a strong public transport system and the pursuit of a transit-oriented settlement pattern as central goals to address the twin challenges of urban mobility and growth management against a background of increasing general prosperity. In most Western cities, this circumstance was accompanied by explosive growth in car ownership and usage. Singapore and Hong Kong, however, are characterised by spatial and regulatory regimes that resisted this trend, and private vehicle numbers are at a fraction of the level typical elsewhere. Both cities also face unique territorial constraints to their expansion: Singapore is a sovereign state located on an island with a fully controlled international border to neighbouring Malaysia; in functional terms, it can be characterised as a 'city without outer suburbs'. Hong Kong is a Special Administrative Region separated from mainland China by similar restrictions regarding border crossings and functional integration. Its land surface is larger than that of Singapore; however, it is also more topographically constrained by mountainous areas and islands unsuitable for urban settlement, separated from each other by water bodies and/or listed as protected open space. As a result, Hong Kong is known as one of the most densely urbanised metropolitan areas globally.

Our interest in assessing the accessibility performance of Singapore and Hong Kong's public transport systems lies in an exploration of these extremes: the high public transport usage rates achieved at least in part by suppressing car mobility; the significant concentration of land uses and their effect on the potential loading and resilience of the networks; the transformation under way from bus-based public transport systems to an expanding network of high-capacity rail lines; and the pioneer character of Singapore and Hong Kong's packages of transport and land use policies for other large cities in the Asian region that are experiencing fast growth in both population and wealth.

ACCESSIBILITY PROFILE: SINGAPORE (SINGAPORE)

Singapore is a sovereign city state located at the tip of the Malaysian peninsula, on an island with a surface area of 716 sq km inhabited by 5.31 million people in 2012 (LTA, 2013). Following independence from Britain in 1963 and from Malaysia in 1965, Singapore evolved into one of Asia's leading commercial

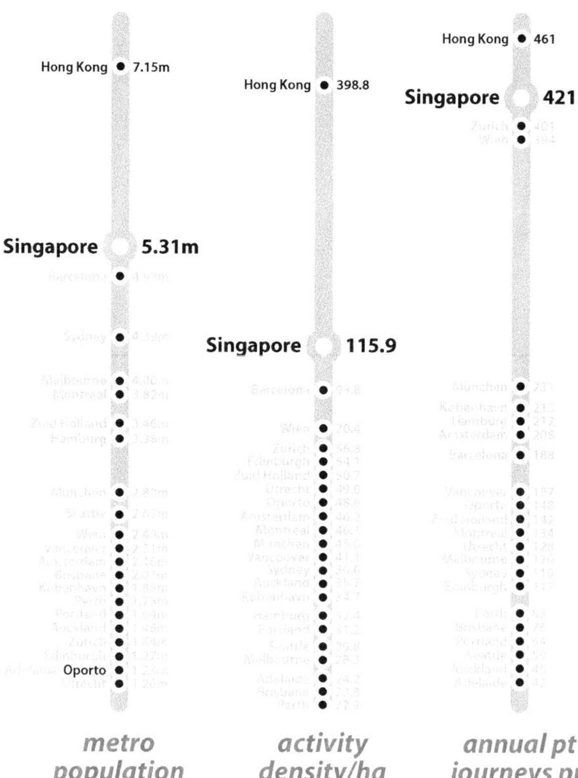

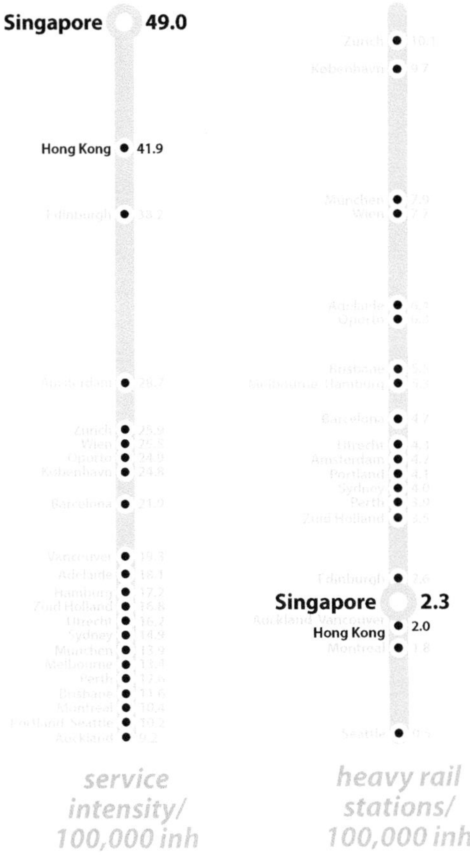

centres and had reached a level of wealth comparable to Western countries before the end of the century. The city's rapid pace of industrialisation and population growth – roughly three-fold in half a century – was accompanied by a large-scale urban modernisation agenda, especially the establishment of master-planned New Towns now covering the majority of the island's territory and built to average densities significantly higher than in the non-Asian case study cities discussed in this volume (only Barcelona comes close). By the late 1970s, pressures had mounted to service the spatial reorganisation of the city with a state-of-the-art public transport system. Competing teams of Western advisors, backed respectively by the United Nations Development Programme (UNDP) and the World Bank, debated the merits of a combined rail–bus versus a bus-only system. The Singapore government, whose party held all seats in the national parliament at the time, decided in favour of rail on a narrative of control, order and progress in contrast with the chaos, disorder and obsolescence that was attributed to a fully road-based transport system. Importantly, it also supplied the capital cost for its implementation (Richmond, 2008).

The construction of the Mass Rapid Transit (MRT) system commenced in 1982, and by 1990 a 67-km initial network was operational. By 2012, it had grown to 149 km and further extensions are under construction. Physical integration of the early stages of the MRT network with surrounding land uses and road-based public transport was not consistently of a high standard, partially as a result of uncoordinated planning institutions (May, 2004). This situation changed with the consolidation of all land transport planning tasks in a single agency in 1995 (*Land Transport Authority* or *LTA*) which also forged closer ties to the land use planning authority (*Urban Redevelopment Agency* or *URA*). As a result, subsequent MRT extensions were better co-designed with land use development, though the recessions of the late 1990s and 2000s and their effects on real estate markets and the construction industry had a disruptive impact on the synchronicity of infrastructure and housing completion in some cases (May, 2004; Richmond, 2008).

The promotion of public transport instigated in the 1970s went hand in hand with a unique regime to control private motorisation in Singapore, even though a high-performance urban road network was built alongside the public transport infrastructure during the same period. Growth rates for private vehicles were limited to 3 per cent per year by the government, only slightly higher than the annual rate of population growth, and have recently been reduced further (Barter, 2013). Licences for the limited pool of additional cars are auctioned to allow a market-based price to form (*Vehicle Quota System* or *VQS*). Effectively this licensing regime, in combination with various import and sales taxes, more than doubles the purchasing cost for prospective vehicle owners. Singapore also pioneered a road pricing system to control private vehicle access to the central area, which has been in place since 1975 (Willoughby, 2001; May, 2004).

The combination of these policies within a regime of top-down governance put Singapore in a unique position in relation to actual patterns of LUTI and transport usage. The city-state records the second-highest annual public transport trip-making rate in the SNAMUTS sample after Hong Kong.

Service Intensity

In 2013, Singapore's public transport network (at the SNAMUTS minimum standard) consisted of four MRT lines (plus two short branches), three light rail (LRT) lines and 198 bus lines. The two older (red and green) MRT lines have drivers and relatively long trains (six carriages). The two newer lines (purple and orange) are driverless and, in the latter case, operated by shorter trains. Daytime service frequencies vary between 3.5 minutes and 12 minutes. LRT in Singapore is an elevated, driverless rail system with small (bus-sized) vehicles, not dissimilar to the people movers used between terminals in many large airports. It circulates the housing estates around Choa Chu Kang-Bukit Panjang, Sengkang and Punggol as a feeder service to MRT. The infrastructure provided by both rail systems in combination still leaves Singapore near the lower end of the global sample in terms of rail station density relative to population, though the results for other cities with recently instigated heavy rail systems (Vancouver, Montreal and Hong Kong) are comparable.

Singapore's bus network is organised around the 'direct connections-no transfers' principle (Nielsen et al, 2005), where individual bus lines link many of the city's corridors and hubs in different combinations. This results in large numbers of different bus lines converging along most corridors and in dedicated interchanges with high combined frequencies, but this has a detrimental effect on the legibility of the network especially for non-regular users. As a result, Singapore's service intensity (relative to population) is the highest in the global sample.

Two privately owned operators share the bus and MRT network (both companies operate lines of either mode). The LTA, however, has authority over the network structure, fare and service levels while maintaining the profitability of the operation, so avoiding the need for public operating subsidies (May, 2004). However, Richmond (2008) argues that the expansion of the MRT network has placed bus operations under commercial pressures by supplanting previously profitable bus corridors, leading to a culture of rampant cost cutting and discouraging innovative approaches to network and service planning on behalf of the operators.

Singapore has an electronic fare system (ez-link) which can be used across all modes and operators. Fares are per trip and calculated based on distance (passengers must tag on and off each time they enter or leave a vehicle or station area), with transfer journeys between bus and rail or between bus and bus usually incurring a higher cost than direct journeys. A periodical (weekly or monthly) ez-link pass existed in 2013, but was discontinued in late 2014.

Closeness Centrality

Singapore's average ease-of-movement results are placed towards the lower end of the spectrum of European and Canadian cities, but are superior to those of all Australasian and US cities in the sample. Good nodal closeness values are conspicuous along the central sections of the MRT lines, and more so in the north-eastern parts of the city than in the western parts. Bus-based nodes in between the MRT corridors, even in relatively central areas, record spikes in closeness values; this takes into account that the fare system penalises transfer journeys between buses or between bus and rail. It is thus assumed that passengers with origins or destinations

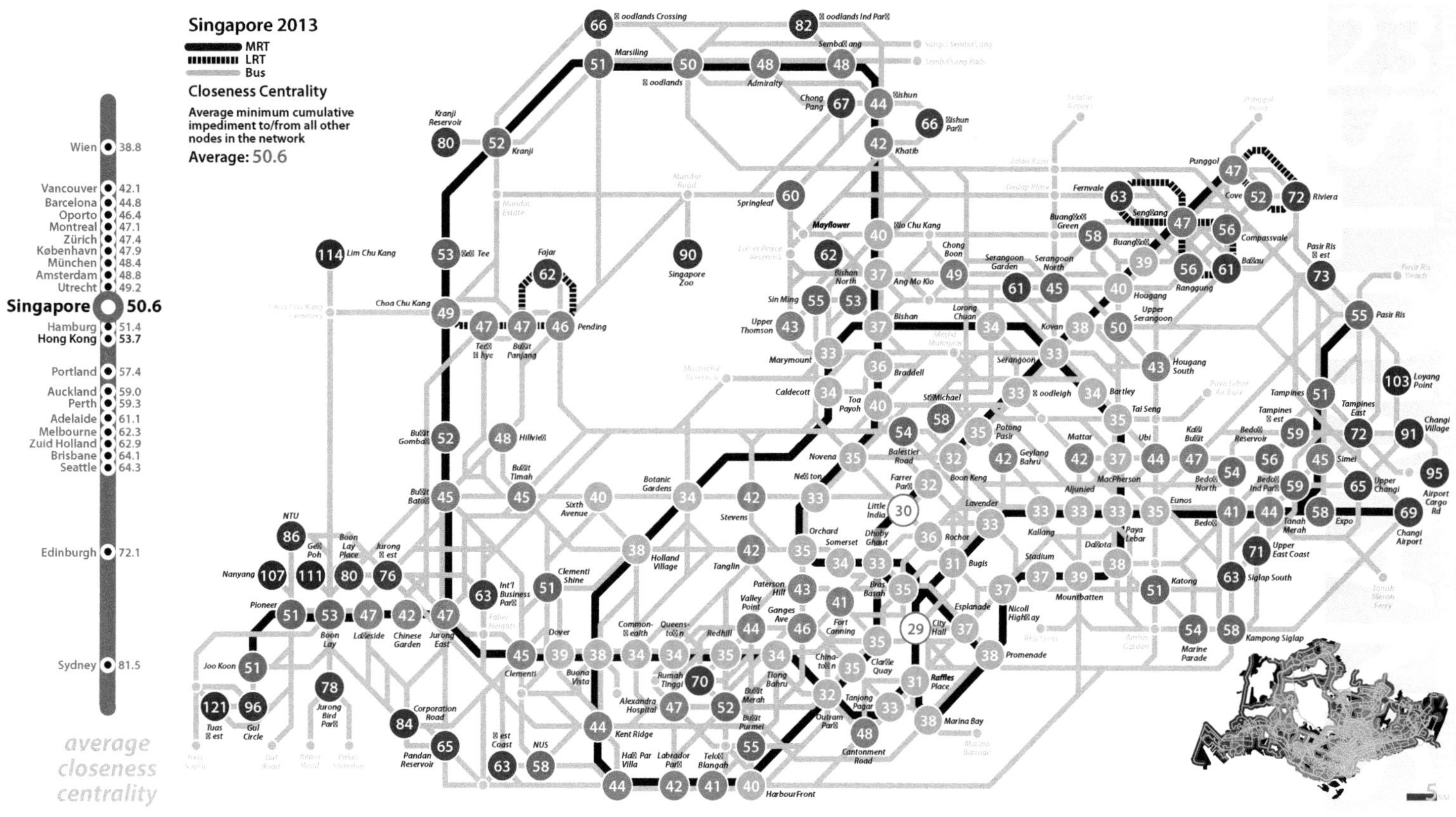

away from the MRT system will prefer transfer-free bus connections where available. Lau (2011) has shown from empirical work that this is an accurate reflection of behaviour at least for price-sensitive, low-income users.

Degree Centrality

Partially as a result of the transfer-avoiding bus network design, Singapore records the lowest average figure for transfer intensity across the global sample. Yet the best nodal values are generally found where rail and bus services coincide. Only a handful of nodes, most of them in predominantly industrial areas at the western extremity of the island, can be considered as significantly transfer-dependent in their accessibility to and from the rest of the city. It should be noted, however, that this impressive result for Singapore does not necessarily conform to the everyday experience of the majority of users: in reality, many transfer journeys between bus and rail offer travel time and/or frequency advantages over direct journeys on individual bus routes, whose service frequency is often quite modest. This may be why Richmond (2008) laments the detrimental effect on the public transport systems' competitiveness to the car due to the inconvenience and time loss associated with frequent transfers.

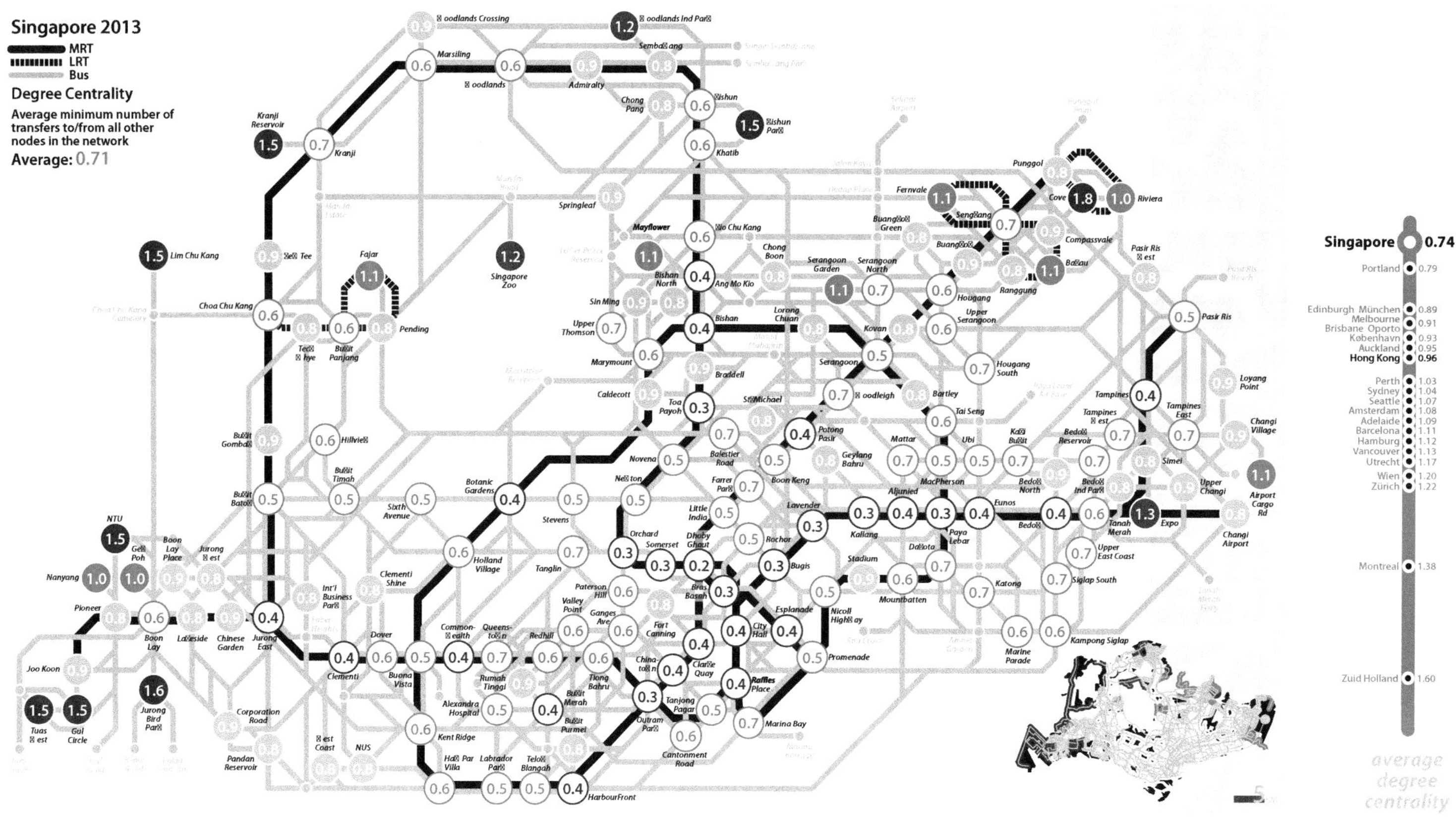

Network Coverage

Of all SNAMUTS case study cities, Singapore records the highest and almost universal network coverage figure. A result aided by the absence of a dispersed suburban hinterland within the city-state's jurisdiction. It is also helped by a regulatory requirement where all urban development must be located within 400 metres of a bus stop with a service standard not far below the minimum used in the SNAMUTS analysis (Richmond, 2008).

Contour Catchments[1]

The relative compactness of Singapore's settlement area also contributes to the city-state achieving the second largest 30-minute contour catchment in the sample (in percentage of metropolitan residents and jobs), after Vienna. Interestingly, the best nodal result is for Bishan, in the mid-north of the city and located close to the geographical centre of the island, followed by the suburban MRT interchanges at Serangoon and Paya Lebar rather than any of the CBD nodes. However, most MRT stations are located within a half-hour journey from at least a quarter of Singapore's population and jobs (with the exception of the Changi Airport branch line and the western terminus of the green line at Joo Koon). This is an indication of the tight integration of the rail network with the most significant concentrations of land use. In contrast, nodes dependent on slower bus access (and often characterised by smaller local activity catchments) are at a disadvantage on this index.

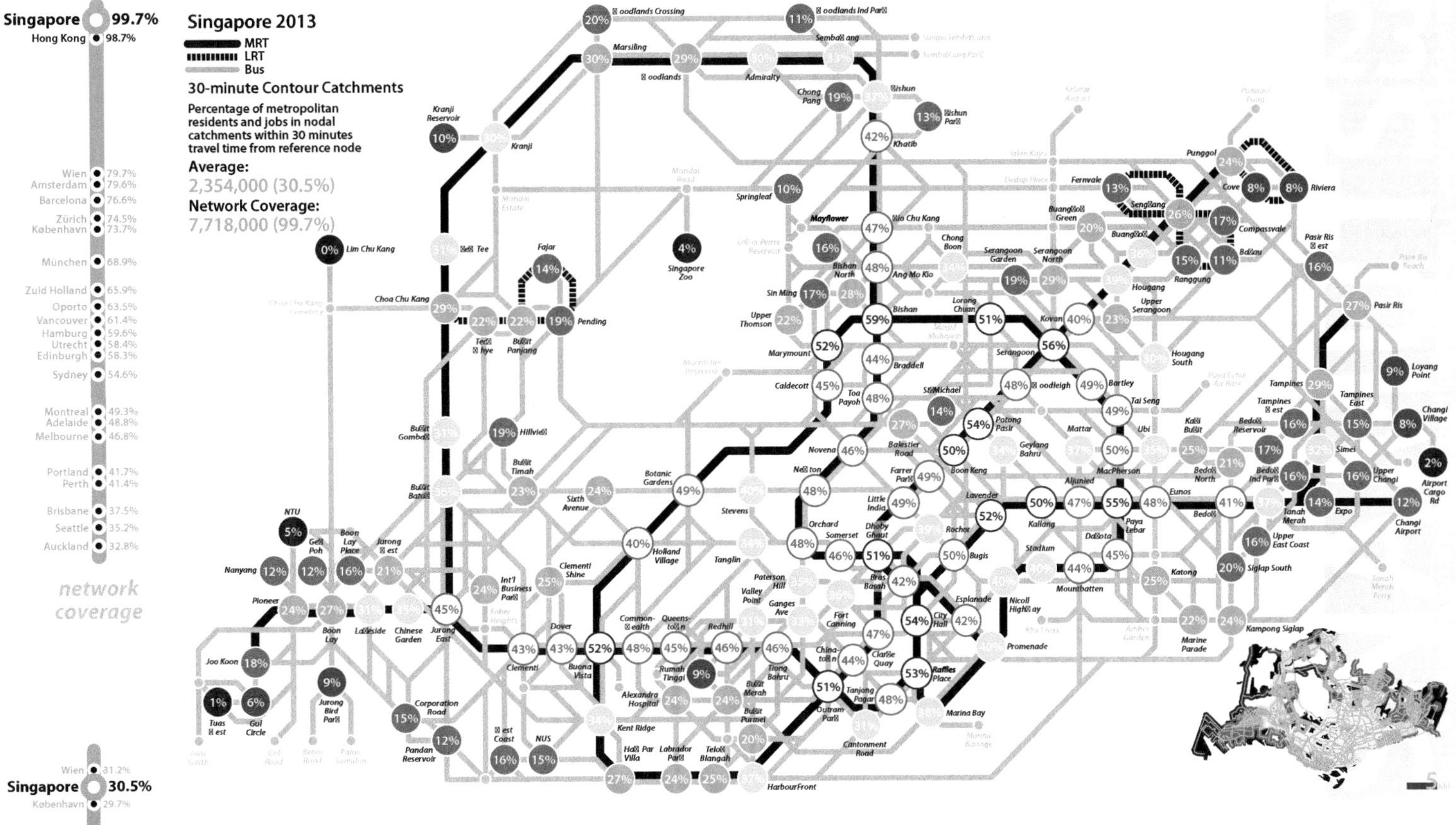

Wien 31.2%
Singapore 30.5%
København 29.7%
Barcelona 24.2%
Hong Kong 23.5%
München 22.6%
Zürich 22.1%
Vancouver 19.5%
Amsterdam 19.4%
Oporto 18.0%
Hamburg 17.3%
Utrecht 16.6%
Montreal 15.0%
Edinburgh 13.6%
Zuid Holland 10.8%
Adelaide 10.7%
Brisbane Perth 10.6%
Portland 10.5%
Auckland 10.2%
Melbourne 9.3%
Seattle 8.4%
Sydney 8.3%
average contour catchment

Betweenness Centrality

Singapore's global betweenness result is the highest in the global sample, indicating a widespread and significant 'presence' of public transport movement opportunities across the city. Singapore also records the highest result on the catchment of typical path length index. This is indicative of a network with a significant concentration of land uses around public transport facilities, as well as a network design that facilitates longer journeys over shorter ones. This may be related to the observation that the degree of employment decentralisation envisioned in strategic planning failed to materialise in reality (Lau, 2011) and that the ensuing job-housing imbalances in many parts of Singapore necessitate relatively long commuting journeys, although we note that decentralisation policies are still actively in process and it may be too early to draw this conclusion.

The highest nodal betweenness results are found along the intersections between the radial MRT lines and the orbital (orange) line in the city's north-east (Paya Lebar, Bishan and Serangoon) – mirroring the contour catchment result – highlighting the importance of this recent addition to the network to the facilitation of movement in the wider area. The CBD, in contrast, records the third lowest concentration of travel opportunities in the global sample, only marginally greater than Hong Kong and Barcelona.

The distribution of betweenness values across public transport modes still shows buses in a dominating position and this is also born out in terms of patronage levels. In 1999, Singapore's buses carried

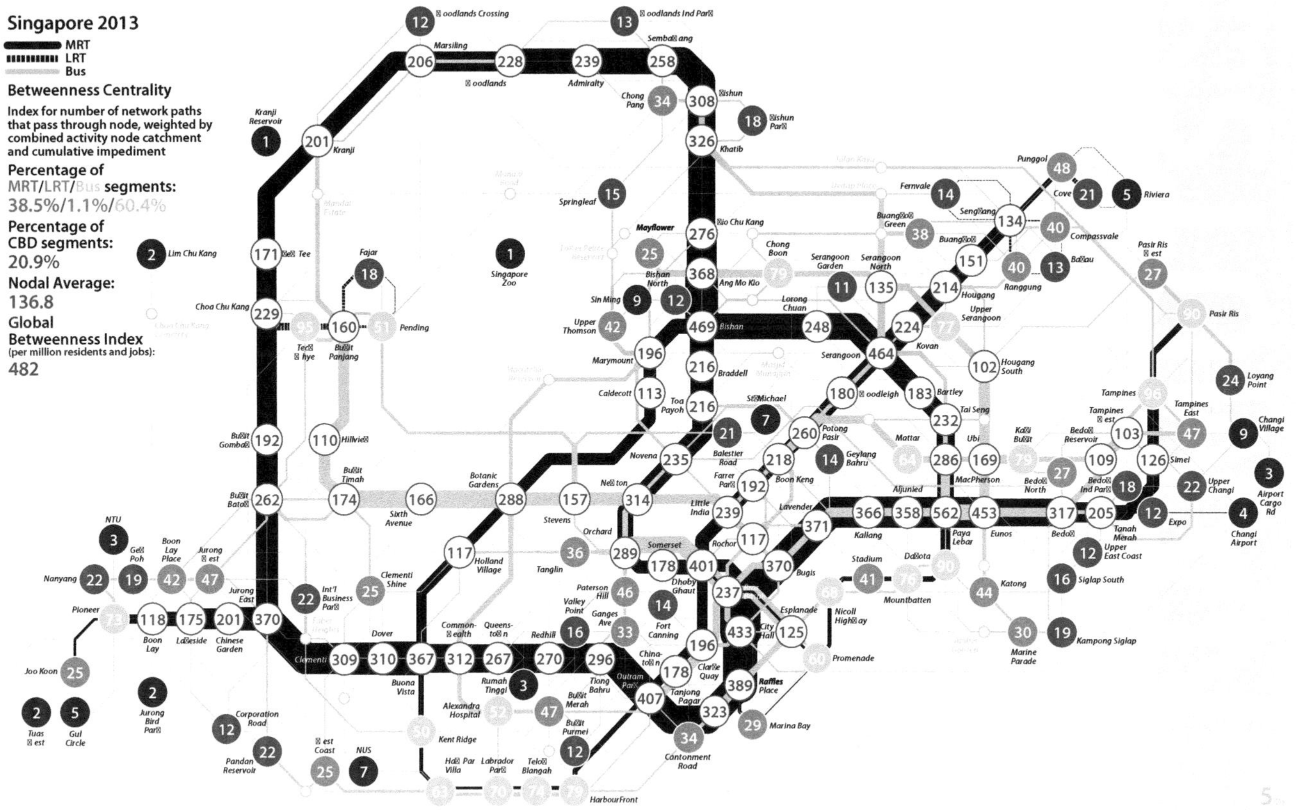

Singapore 2013

MRT
LRT
Bus

Betweenness Centrality

Index for number of network paths that pass through node, weighted by combined activity node catchment and cumulative impediment

Percentage of MRT/LRT/Bus segments:
38.5%/1.1%/60.4%

Percentage of CBD segments:
20.9%

Nodal Average:
136.8

Global Betweenness Index
(per million residents and jobs):
482

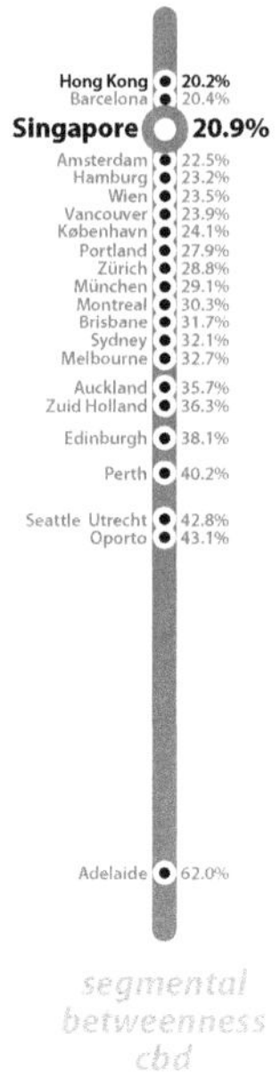

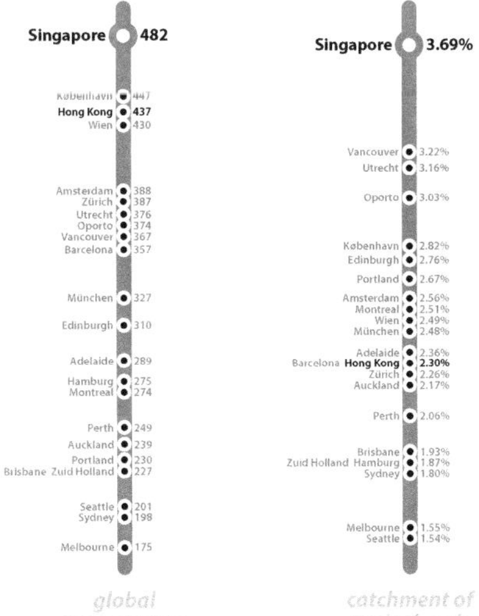

three times as many passengers as rail. By 2006, this had reduced to two times, and the gap has closed further since as the rail systems continues to expand (May, 2004; Richmond, 2008; LTA, 2013).

Network Resilience

The continued dominance of buses in the facilitation of travel opportunities may also be explicable in the context of the network resilience index. Singapore's MRT records the poorest average result for any heavy rail system across the global SNAMUTS sample: significant segments of the network appear to be overwhelmed by the potential movement pressures placed onto them through the land use system. From this vantage point, it is no surprise that the LTA is now developing additional radial MRT lines roughly parallel to the most notorious existing corridors towards Bukit Panjang, Woodlands and Tampines. This places the bus system in a precarious position since the bus network, on the whole, currently appears to be better placed to absorb additional patronage than the MRT network, despite numerous individual bus route segments with poor resilience

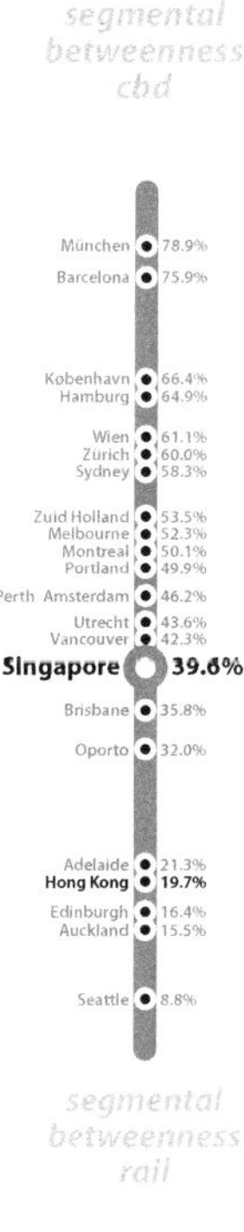

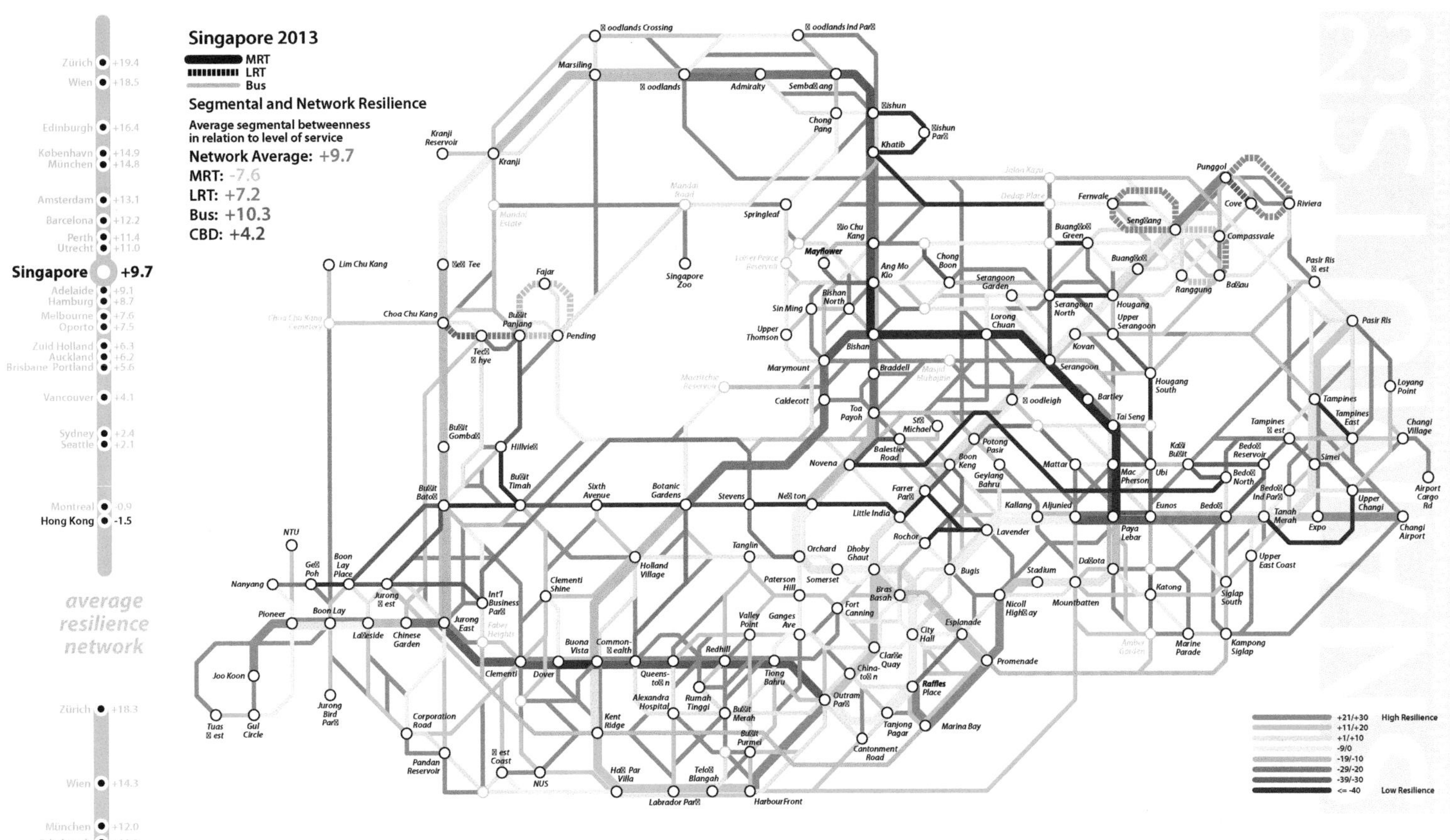

results. This situation, however, could reverse should ridership increase dramatically beyond the rate of population growth, in which case buses would hit a congestion ceiling much faster than the higher-capacity rail system.

Notably, the most pressured MRT segments can be found outside the CBD area, which as a whole has an average resilience performance among its peer cities within our global sample. Poor resilience on the MRT is particularly apparent on the Bishan to Paya Lebar section of the orange (circular) line, which is operated with shorter trains and, like much of the remainder of the network, at 7-minute daytime frequencies that seem to offer room for improvement.

Nodal Connectivity

Singapore's average nodal connectivity results are the second highest in the sample after Hong Kong, which is commensurate with its position in terms of population size. The figures show that good flexibility of movement for users, and a suitability of public transport hubs and corridors for TOD, are almost universal characteristics across the city with only some minor exceptions around the fringes of the island. The best value can be found at the CBD node of Outram Park, followed by suburban Serangoon and Sengkang on the purple MRT line in the north-east.

SNAMUTS Composite Accessibility Index and Reflections

On average, Singapore is the best performer in the world-wide sample on the composite index. The highest (excellent)

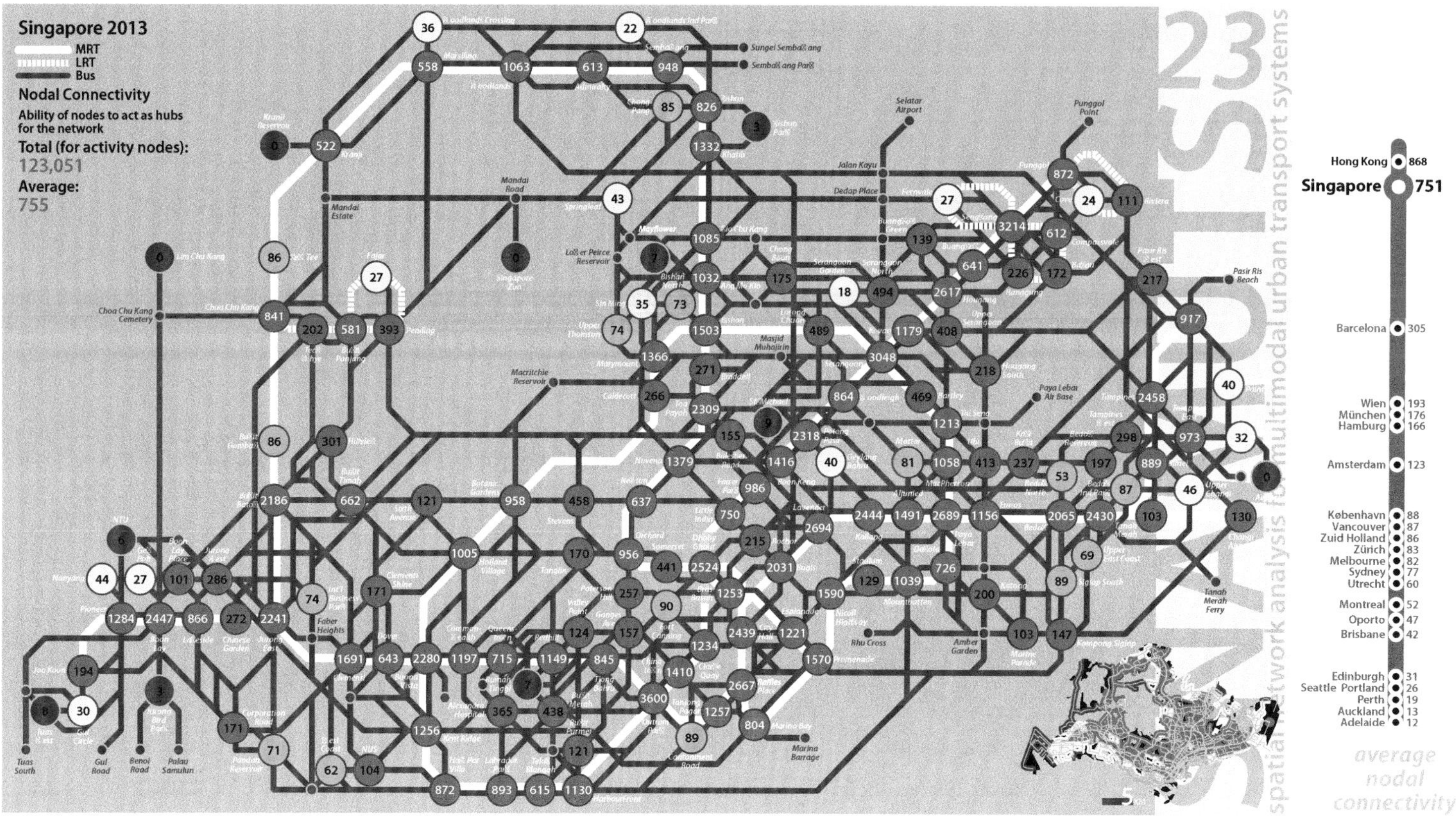

colour bracket covers, with few exceptions, not only the central city and adjacent neighbourhoods, but large portions of suburban corridors around Woodlands-Sembawang, Jurong-Bukit Batok, Yio Chu Kang, Hougang-Sengkang and Pasir Ris. MRT extensions currently under construction are likely to fill the remaining gaps of less-than-excellent performance in the inner areas. Pockets of poor or minimal public transport accessibility are largely confined to industrial and semi-rural areas in the west of the island (Tuas and Lim Chu Kang), the non-urbanised Central Catchment Nature Reserve (Singapore Zoo) and the airport service area in Changi.

Do these findings thus elevate Singapore as the undisputed global leader of a public transport-oriented metropolis? The combination of public transport investment, particularly in rail, in combination with a tightly managed individual motorisation process has clearly produced impressive results in terms of transport mode splits, with (scheduled) public transport trips making up 56 per cent of all motorised trips (2008), and in terms of car ownership which at around 100 per 1,000 inhabitants is at a level typically found in cities of less than half Singapore's per-capita wealth (Willoughby, 2001; Barter, 2013). However, Singapore's unique policy package regarding motorisation has, perhaps inadvertently, produced some potent side effects. Barter (2013) argues that due to their cost and scarcity, cars enjoy a high status among the Singapore public and that there is a widespread expectation, supported by government rhetoric, that the managed

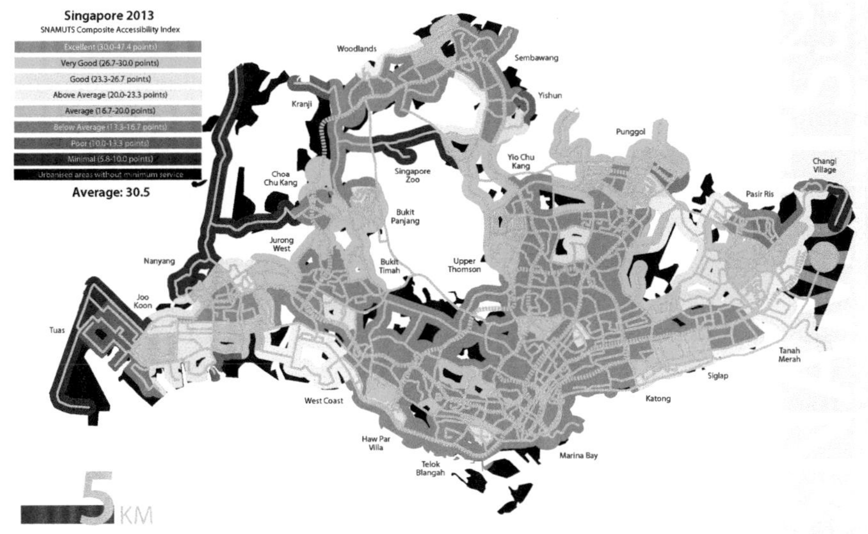

motorisation process will eventually culminate in car ownership levels comparable to other developed cities. For those households owning cars – 38 per cent of the total in 2008 (ibid.) – there is a tendency to regard a high standard of car infrastructure as an entitlement, a fair public return for the substantial personal investment made to attain car ownership under the VQS (May, 2004). Political responses to such attitudes include the provision of a generous, high-capacity expressway system across the island, more expansive than in most European or Australian cities described in this volume. They also include traffic management measures that generally focus on maximising speed and minimising congestion, even in the mixed environments of the remaining pre-car neighbourhoods where this works to the detriment of the needs of pedestrians, cyclists and place functions. In combination with the electronic road pricing system, motorists in Singapore are thus offered a movement network that is generally speed-competitive with the MRT even for peak-hour radial CBD journeys, and the tools available to planners are sufficient and effective to maintain this status. User responses to these favourable conditions are apparent in a rate of car use among the minority of car owners that despite the limited geographical range of movement in a city-state, is comparable to that in the more inherently car-dependent cities of North America or Australasia. Barter (2013) suggests that Singapore's transport narrative is more one of 'suppressed automobility' than a public transport success story in its own right. Other commentators have noted that Singapore already has all the spatial form and transport system ingredients in place that would allow it to wind back, rather than expand, the proliferation of the private car if this was desired politically (Gehl, 2014).

ACCESSIBILITY PROFILE: HONG KONG (CHINA)

Hong Kong is a Special Administrative Region within the People's Republic of China, located in the south of the country across an archipelago of peninsulas and islands on the South China Sea coast. Forming part of the Pearl River Delta region, one of the most heavily urbanised areas in the world, Hong Kong's unique history as a British colonial possession (until 1997) continues to set it apart from mainland China in economic and political terms. Among other markers of autonomy, this is manifest in continuing border controls between Hong Kong and mainland China, bestowing the city with a comparable status to Singapore when it comes to functional integration with its regional hinterland and neighbouring urban centres. In 2012, Hong Kong was home to 7.15 million inhabitants. Its territory of 1,107 sq km is approximately 50 per cent larger than that of Singapore, but due to mountainous terrain and offshore islands its proportion of urbanisable land is much smaller, resulting in the highest settlement density of all cities in the SNAMUTS sample.

The urbanised area consists of the three main segments. Hong Kong Island and (peninsular) Kowloon are located at opposite shores of Victoria Harbour. The much larger area known as New Territories surrounds central Kowloon to the west, north and east and extends north to the mainland Chinese border. The CBD stretches over parts of both Hong Kong Island and Kowloon, which are linked by a total of six rail and road tunnels.

Traditionally, Hong Kong Island has been served by a first-generation tram system (still in operation) and buses, while Kowloon had a bus network and a heavy rail line linking it to mainland China (*Kowloon and Canton Railway* or *KCR*). Ferries connected the opposite shores of Victoria Harbour prior to the construction of the tunnels, and some continue operating today. A modern mass transit railway (MTR) system has been added since the 1970s and eventually integrated the KCR. This facilitated the growth of new towns along its route. During the 1980s, the emerging mixed rail–bus network was organised in a hierarchical fashion with a focus on efficiency: regulatory restrictions limited bus operations parallel to the new rail lines and privileged franchised bus operators over the plethora of minibus and other non-franchised services. During the 1990s, similar to the deregulation agenda pursued in the British homeland at the time (see Chapter 5 in the context of Edinburgh), this regime was relaxed considerably in order to enable greater competition between different bus operators as well as between bus and rail. In the 2000s, strategic objectives favoured strengthening the role of rail at the expense of buses due to its higher performance and capacity. In practice, the deregulation regime introduced in the previous decade remained in place and offered few incentives for operators or politicians to intervene in the interest of a modified division of transport tasks among modes (Tang and Lo, 2008).

At around 90 per cent, Hong Kong has one of the highest public transport mode shares among motorised trips of any city world-wide and records the highest annual number of public transport journeys per capita in the global SNAMUTS sample. Car ownership remains at a level of around 50 vehicles per 1,000 inhabitants, half that of more tightly regulated Singapore (Cervero and Murakami, 2009; Lam, 2003). While Hong Kong does not control car ownership through direct regulations, it has a long-standing policy of high vehicle sales taxes comparable to Singapore, and its high settlement density leads to a very low provision of and high user costs for parking. Hong Kong does not have an area-based road pricing system, but user tolls apply to all major bridges and tunnels linking the disparate components of the archipelago. Disincentives to car ownership are thus strongly related to incidental costs as well as scarcity of space (Cullinane, 2003).

Hong Kong's fare system is based on an electronic stored-value card (Octopus) that can be used on all modes of transport, including non-franchised minibuses. Rail fares are based on distance, while bus fares are flat and vary from route to route (as advertised in the front of the vehicle). This means that the same journey can incur a different price depending on which bus line is being used. With few exceptions, transfers between buses or between bus and rail or trams attract an additional fare, translating into a clear financial incentive towards selecting direct services over transfer connections.

Service Intensity

Hong Kong's MTR system has been developed since 1979 and now extends to 175 km of heavy rail lines, including the KCR which was merged with the public-private Mass Transit Railway Corporation (MTRC) in 2007. Additionally, there is a 36-km light rail (LRT) network in the north-western new towns of Tuen Mun-Tin Shui Wai-Yuen Long developed since 1988. Unlike in Singapore, LRT in this corridor stands for a conventional modern tram system. An older, first-generation tram system serves the narrow linear settlement corridor along the Victoria Harbour side of Hong Kong Island, and a number of ferry lines connect the Kowloon and Hong Kong Island shores as well as other destinations in the archipelago. In the count of rail stations, we included the MRT and LRT facilities (since the LRT

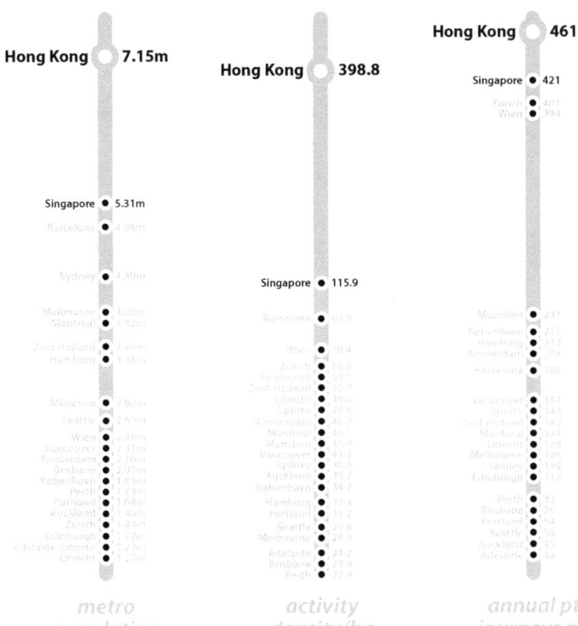

is fitted with controlled-access station areas) but not the tram stops on Hong Kong Island. Hong Kong's rail station density per capita is at the low end of the global cohort, but roughly similar to Singapore and the Canadian cities.

There are 375 bus lines in Hong Kong meeting the SNAMUTS minimum service standard, divided across five franchised, private-sector bus operators and operated predominantly by double-deckers. In addition, there are several non-franchised operators as well as a comprehensive network of minibuses (16-seaters) serving point-to-point connections with no fixed timetables (but with regulated fares). In the SNAMUTS analysis, these minibus routes were disregarded as beyond the manageable scope of our inquiry, despite their undeniable contribution to spatial accessibility in Hong Kong.

The bus network, like in Singapore, is largely organised around the 'direct connections-no transfers' principle (Nielsen et al, 2005), and it appears that this characteristic has become more pronounced since the deregulation measures of the 1990s, which enabled bus operators to increase services on profitable lines and expand onto corridors serviced by competitors, including the MTR and LRT lines. As a result, bus service levels across Hong Kong grew approximately four times faster than the increase in population, and did so in an 'indiscriminate' fashion in the view of Tang and Lo (2008). Consequently, ridership increases fell behind the pace of service expansion, leading to declining bus occupancy rates across all franchised operators and lower than projected patronage on new rail lines in whose corridors bus networks were not adapted to assume a

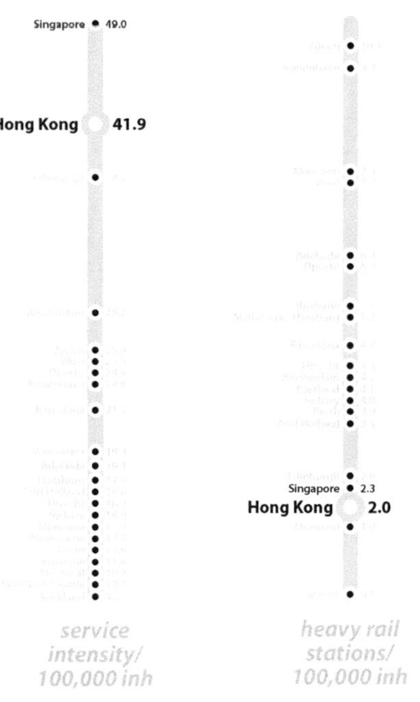

feeder and distributor function (ibid.). Tang and Lo (2008) lament that this regime amounts to a form of 'wasteful competition', resulting in underutilisation of infrastructures and operational resources and undermining the long-term viability and sustainability of the public transport system as a whole.

In SNAMUTS terms, the network organisation as found in 2013 delivers the second highest service intensity figure relative to population in the global sample after Singapore.

Closeness Centrality

Average ease-of-movement in Hong Kong is poorer than in Singapore and the majority of case study cities in Europe and Canada, but better than in the US and Australasian cities. Despite the high service input, Hong Kong's poor performance on this index can be traced partly to its convoluted geography, which introduces numerous separators between settlement areas in the form of mountains and water bodies and places a relatively large number of housing estates into 'cul-de-sac' locations halfway up hillsides. It is further related to the ticketing system which penalises transfer journeys where buses or trams are involved and led to an assumption in the calculation of preferred journey paths that passengers will generally choose direct surface connections over transfer journeys wherever available. Lau (1997) found that in terms

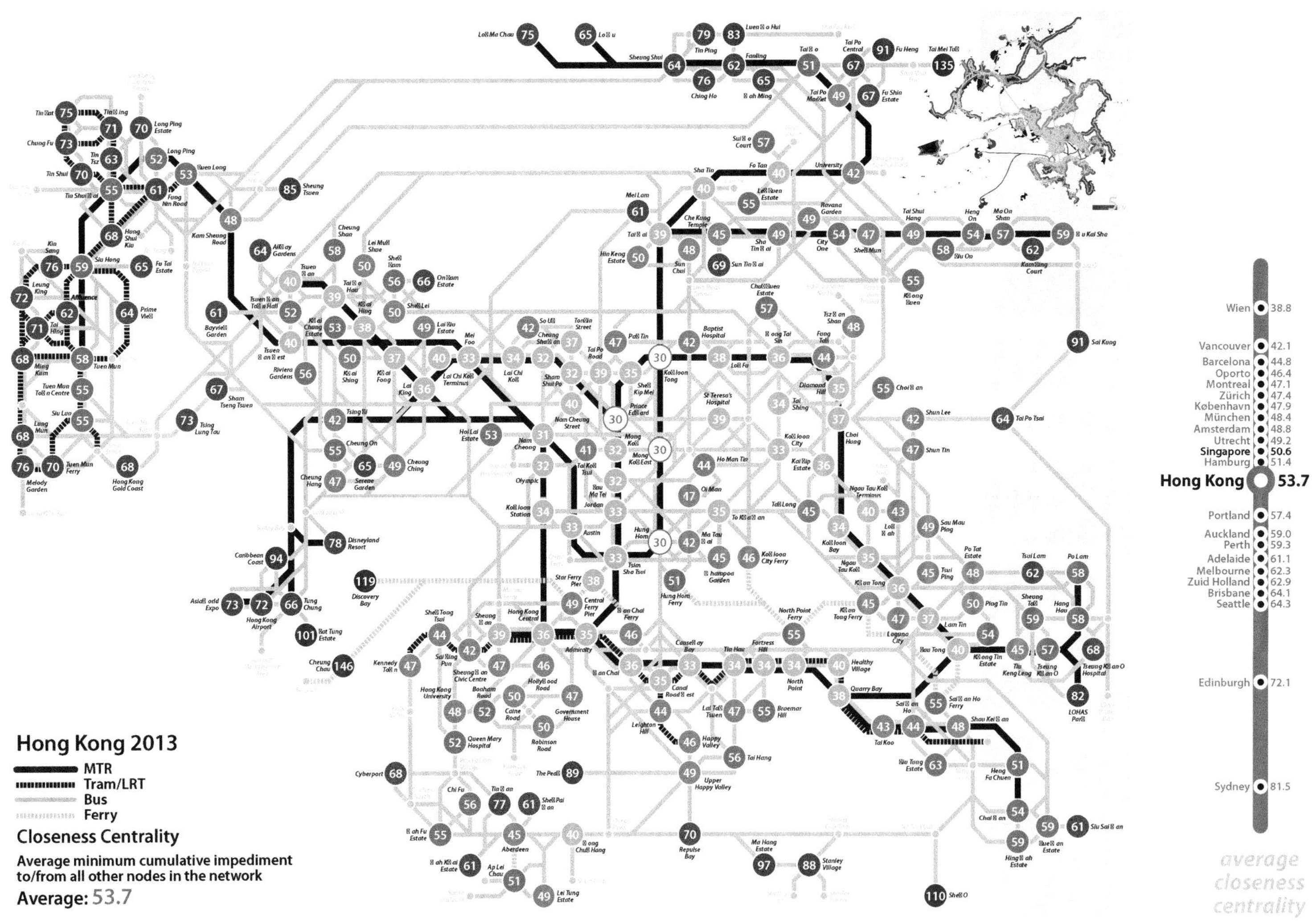

of actual behaviour, lower-income users tend to avoid, as much as possible, transfer journeys from bus to rail or the use of cross-harbour bus lines which carry a fare premium. Conversely, Tang and Lo (2008) assert that the majority of passengers are more time-conscious than price-conscious and will generally board the first bus arriving at their stop, rather than wait for a cheaper alternative.

The best nodal closeness values are found along rail–bus interchange stations in Kowloon, and otherwise follow the MTR lines including the original KCR line (now East Rail) as far as Sha Tin in the New Territories. Away from the MTR system, closeness performance drops off quite rapidly in many cases, including for some fairly centrally located nodes such as the ferry terminals lining Victoria Harbour and bus-based housing estates in the foothills of the mountain ranges.

Degree Centrality

Despite Hong Kong's transfer-minimising bus network, average transfer intensity across the system does not stand out as particularly low among its peer cities, though it is lower than in the deliberately

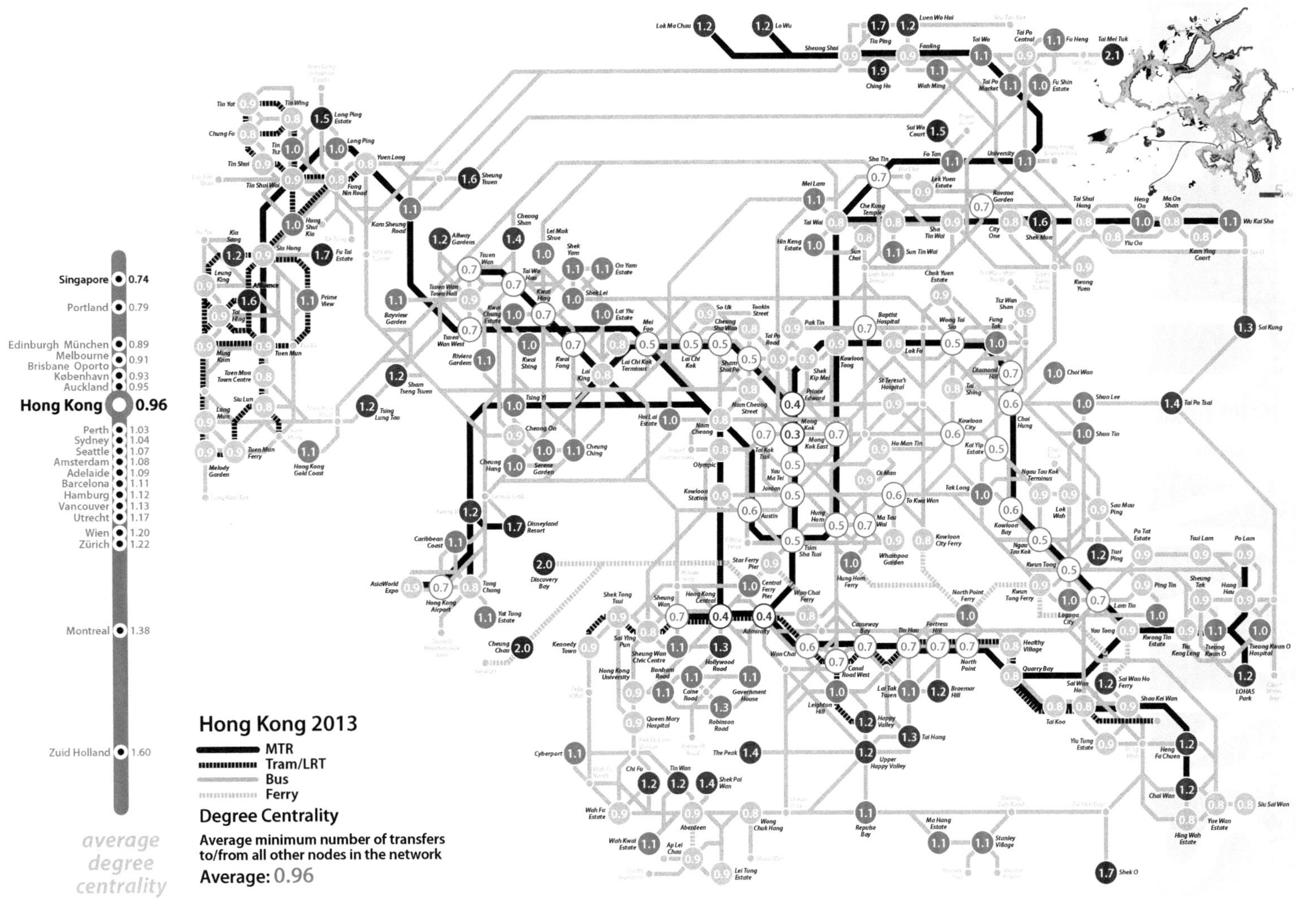

transfer-dependent networks such as Vienna or Zurich. Average results on this index are inflated by the existence of several regional sub-networks that are connected to each other only by a small number of MTR or express bus links, such as the LRT system in the Tuen Mun-Tin Shui Wai area. They are further inflated by the fact that not all MTR lines connect to one another – for example, the green line and the ex-KCR West Rail and East Rail lines only operate on the Kowloon side of Victoria Harbour, while the blue line only services Hong Kong Island, and journeys between the two require a minimum of two transfers.

Network Coverage

Like Singapore, Hong Kong is characterised by a public transport network that reaches into almost every corner of the settlement areas at the SNAMUTS standard with only minor exceptions for some offshore islands and the

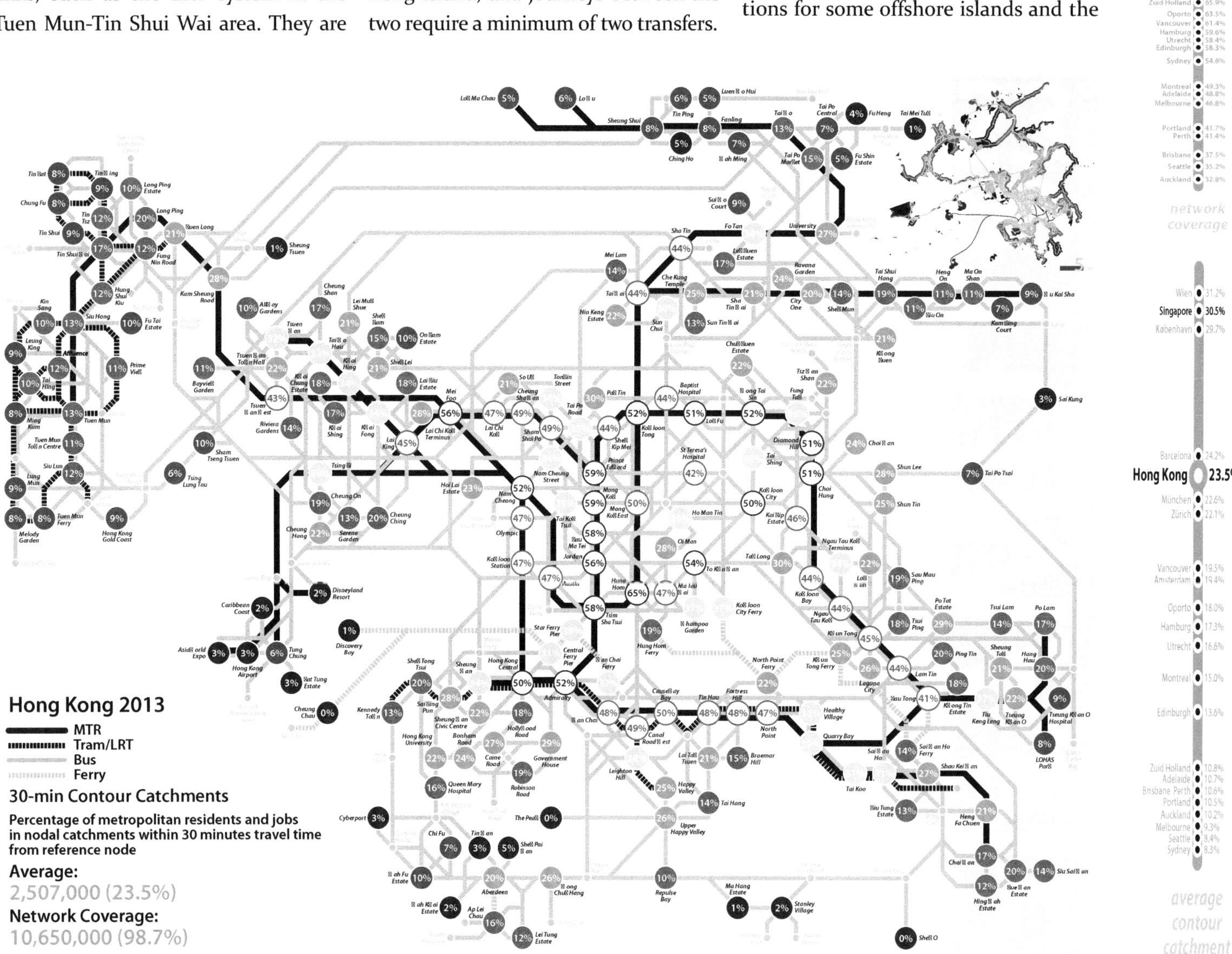

semi-rural outskirts of the New Territories. The high dependence of the Hong Kong population on public transport for their everyday mobility is likely to be the prevailing factor here, as only a small minority can draw on the use of a private car as an alternative.

Contour Catchments

The average 30-minute contour catchment as a percentage of metropolitan residents and jobs for a Hong Kong node is smaller than that of the top performers in global sample (Vienna, Singapore and Copenhagen), but in line with the remaining better performers in Europe and significantly higher than that of any New World contender. The topographical separators between settlement areas work to reduce this result, while the high concentration of land use activities around public transport infrastructures enhances it.

Hung Hom has a stand-out nodal performance, serving as the terminus of the West Rail and East Rail lines and also an interchange for the bus routes traversing the cross-harbour tunnel. The next highest values are found along Nathan Road, the principal artery of Kowloon, and Mei Foo in the North West. Results then drop consistently towards the edges of the settlement areas, particularly where they are contained by waterfronts or mountain ranges. Outside the major centres around Tsuen Wan, Tsing Yi, Sha Tin and Tseung Kwan O, the New Territories are consistently characterised by below-average performances on this index.

Betweenness Centrality

Hong Kong's global betweenness result relative to metropolitan population and jobs is positioned towards the higher end of the global sample confirming the strong presence of public transport movement opportunities across the city. Compared to the other leaders on this index (Singapore, Vienna and Copenhagen), however, the catchment of typical path length measure is lower. This is an expression of a network that, despite the high concentration of land uses around public transport, is largely configured to facilitate shorter over longer journeys.

The strong dominance of buses in the modal distribution of segmental betweenness values, or travel opportunities, is remarkable. The network form and the effects of deregulation discussed above have privileged accessibility by bus to a greater extent than the expanding MTR network has improved accessibility by rail. While the percentage values of segmental betweenness per mode are not representative of their actual mode share in the overall public transport market, it has been noted that the growth of rail at the expense of bus that was intended by the initial construction of the MTR network as well as by contemporary strategic directions, has stalled since the late 1990s and in some years, reversed (Cullinane, 2003; Cervero and Murakami, 2009). The betweenness map shows that the competition between bus and rail appears particularly cannibalistic on the key corridors of Hong Kong Island and Kowloon, with the cross-harbour tunnel and its hourly throughput of more than 100 buses per direction perhaps recording the highest concentration of travel opportunities in any case study city. Conversely, rail appears to capitalise on its strength over buses along the West Rail and East Rail lines, as well as the Tseung Kwan O line servicing the New Territories where its lower travel times into central areas put it at a clear advantage.

Network Resilience

As a consequence of this modal imbalance in generating travel opportunities, Hong Kong records the poorest average network resilience in the global sample both across the network and for the CBD areas on Hong Kong Island and Kowloon. Unlike Singapore, the majority of this shortfall can be traced to the bus system while the MTR, with the exception of the West Rail line, seems to be less affected. In practice however, and despite the competition issues discussed previously, MTR patronage is higher compared to buses than what the SNAMUTS betweenness figures, which determine the outcome of this index, would suggest. Thus the

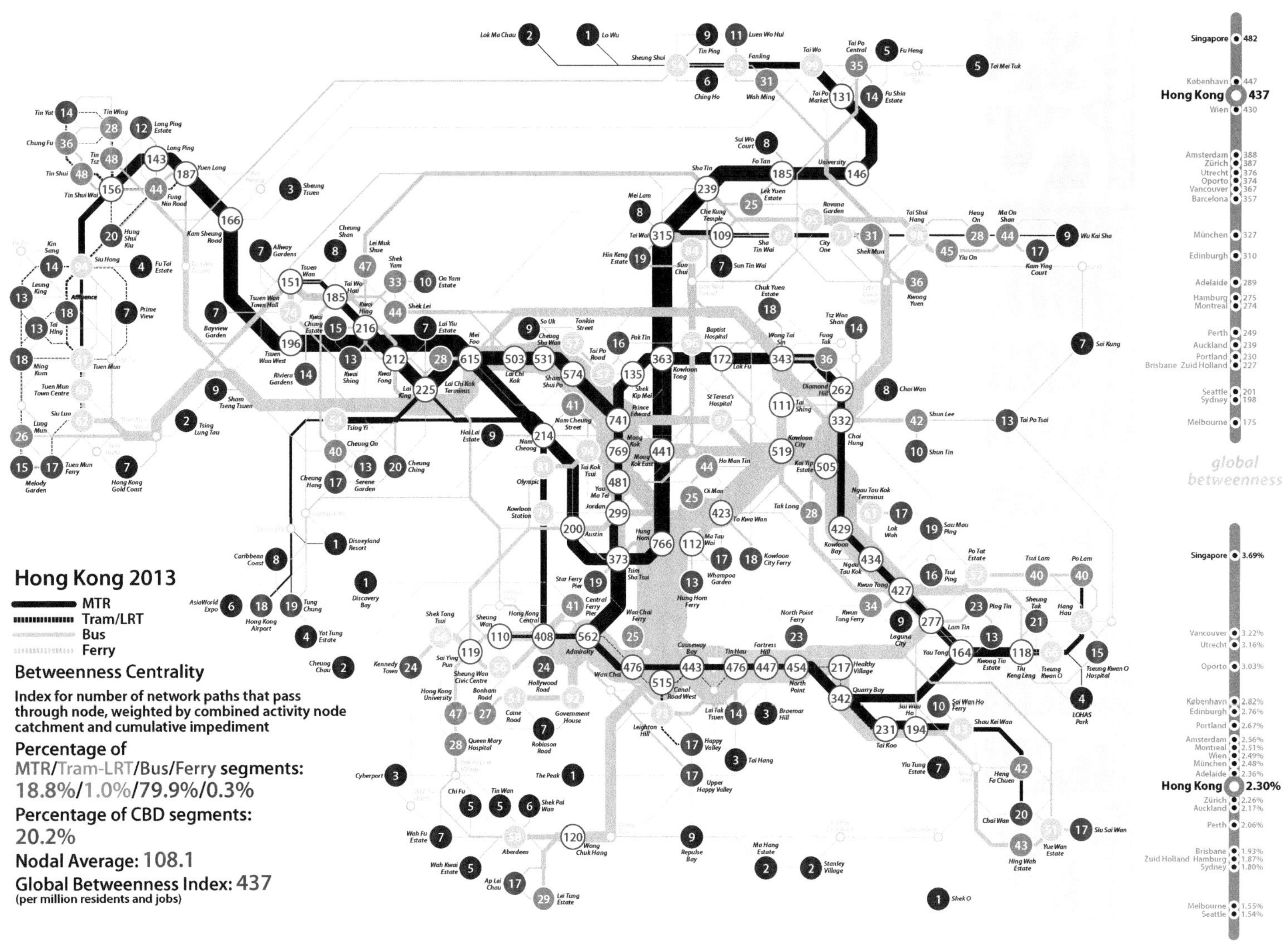

Hong Kong 2013
MTR
Tram/LRT
Bus
Ferry
Betweenness Centrality
Index for number of network paths that pass through node, weighted by combined activity node catchment and cumulative impediment
Percentage of MTR/Tram-LRT/Bus/Ferry segments:
18.8%/1.0%/79.9%/0.3%
Percentage of CBD segments:
20.2%
Nodal Average: 108.1
Global Betweenness Index: 437
(per million residents and jobs)
Singapore 482
København 447
Hong Kong 437
Wien 430
Amsterdam 388
Zürich 387
Utrecht 376
Oporto 374
Vancouver 367
Barcelona 357
München 327
Edinburgh 310
Adelaide 289
Hamburg 275
Montreal 274
Perth 249
Auckland 239
Portland 230
Brisbane Zuid Holland 227
Seattle 201
Sydney 198
Melbourne 175
global betweenness
Singapore 3.69%
Vancouver 3.22%
Utrecht 3.16%
Oporto 3.03%
København 2.82%
Edinburgh 2.76%
Portland 2.67%
Amsterdam 2.56%
Montreal 2.51%
Wien 2.49%
München 2.48%
Adelaide 2.36%
Hong Kong 2.30%
Zürich 2.26%
Auckland 2.17%
Perth 2.06%
Brisbane 1.93%
Zuid Holland Hamburg 1.87%
Sydney 1.80%
Melbourne 1.55%
Seattle 1.54%
catchment of typical path

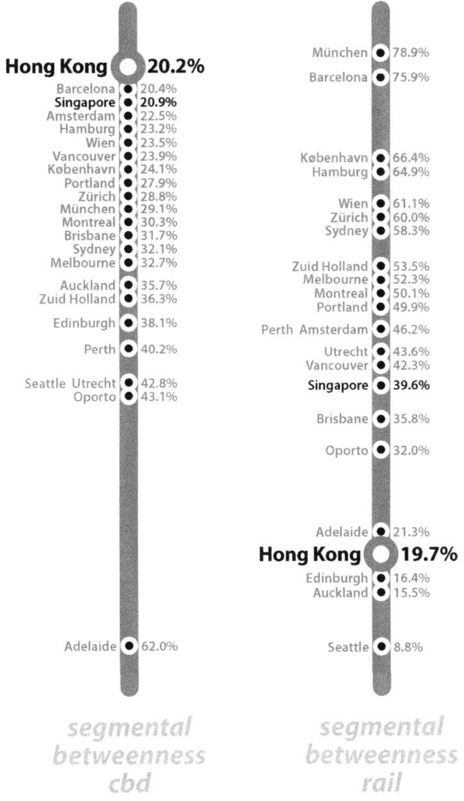

resilience gap between bus and rail is likely to be narrower in actual experience. Greater numbers of buses particularly on already high-performing lines have led to increasing bus congestion in central areas, resulting in declining travel times that negated the effect of improved service frequencies on waiting times. On the other hand, the expansion of road capacity across Hong Kong since the 1990s has improved travel times and reliability particularly of express bus services, improving their competitive position to rail (Tang and Lo, 2008).

Nodal Connectivity

In line with its position as the largest city in the global sample, Hong Kong records the highest average nodal connectivity result, though Singapore is not far behind. Flexibility of movement for users and an attraction for public transport–oriented land use activities are maintained across practically the entire densely built-up parts of Hong Kong and only drop off for some housing estates located in foothill or waterfront locations away from the busier areas. The highest nodal values can be found at Hong Kong Central and Admiralty on Hong Kong Island and Mei Foo in Kowloon, followed by Hung Hom (Kowloon), Sha Tin (New Territories) and Mong Kok (Kowloon).

SNAMUTS Composite Accessibility Index and Reflections

Hong Kong's average composite index places the city into fourth place for overall public transport accessibility among the global sample, after Singapore, Vienna and Barcelona. The highest colour bracket (excellent) applies to the central corridor along the Hong Kong Island northern shore as well as the majority of the territory of Kowloon. In the New Territories, it extends into Tsuen Wan, Tsing Yi and Sha Tin. In the latter case, it is apparent that bus-based access appears to deliver slightly better composite results along the corridor of the Ma On Shan branch MTR line than rail-based nodes, providing a prime example for the effects of a non-hierarchical, competitive spatial and functional relationship between the two modes as discussed earlier.

Minimal composite accessibility results are restricted to the offshore island of Cheung Chau, the ferry-based node of Discovery Bay on Lantau Island, as well as some nodes on the south shore of Hong Kong Island and in the north-eastern New Territories.

More than the performance of the network as such, Hong Kong holds a significant narrative about the co-evolution of public transport and urban form. The relative scarcity of urbanisable

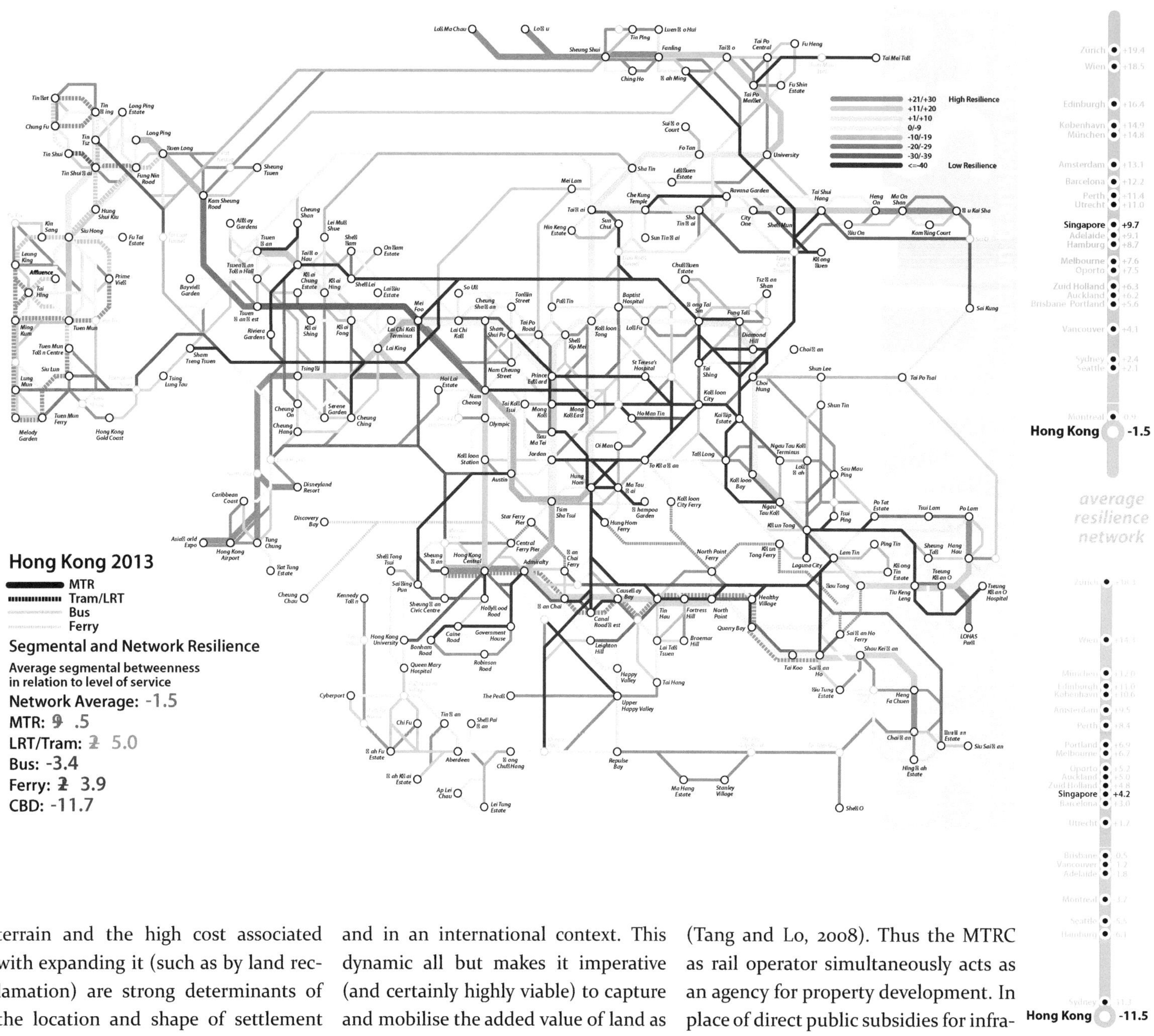

terrain and the high cost associated with expanding it (such as by land reclamation) are strong determinants of the location and shape of settlement areas, and lead to formidable spikes in property prices both at a local scale and in an international context. This dynamic all but makes it imperative (and certainly highly viable) to capture and mobilise the added value of land as a result of accessibility improvements to finance public trnsport infrastructure (Tang and Lo, 2008). Thus the MTRC as rail operator simultaneously acts as an agency for property development. In place of direct public subsidies for infrastructure investment like in most other cities, the MTRC is granted exclusive

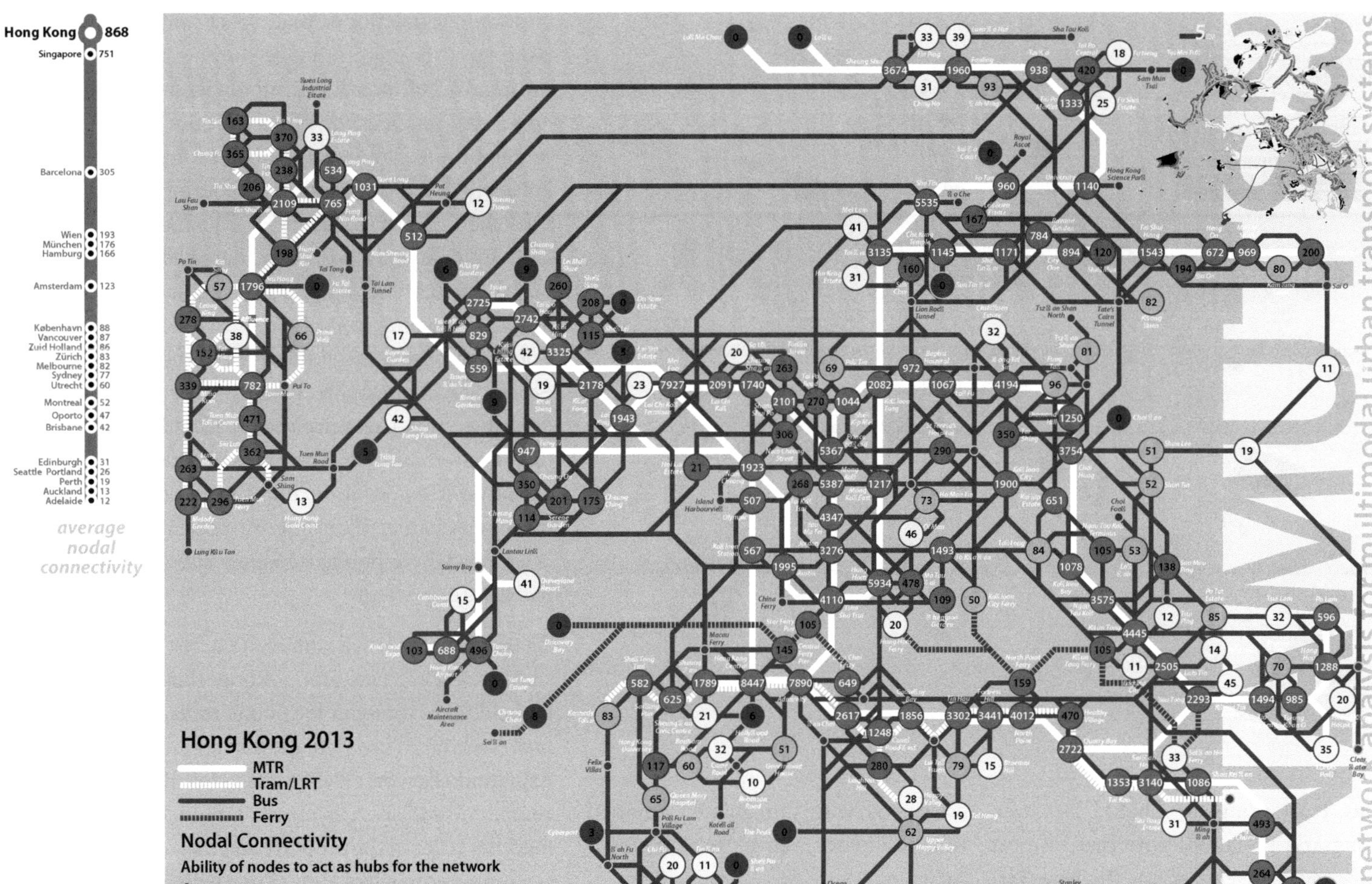

development rights for station area land by the Hong Kong government as a major land owner (Cullinane, 2003) which it can on-sell once rail projects are under way and land value gains have materialised. This integration of infrastructure and property development is not only a powerful planning instrument, it also ensures the profitability of the MTRC which received twice as much revenue from its property activities than from the farebox during the 2001–05 period (Cervero and Murakami, 2009). A trend towards comprehensive station area master planning in recent rail extension projects has sought to maximise this return by improving design standards along

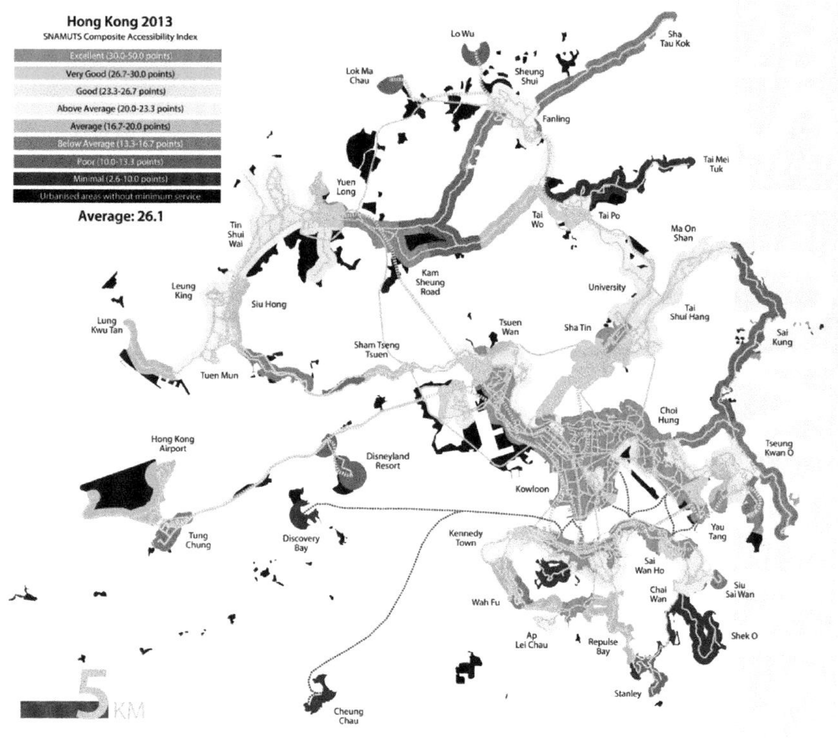

the TOD template (ibid.). However, Tang and Lo (2008) note that in most new town projects across the New Territories, rail infrastructure only followed land use development with a 10–20 year time lag, since it was considered imperative to build up a critical mass of potential passengers before a railway would be viable. The negative consequence of this approach was that opportunities to implement an integrated public transport network (with a division of tasks between rail and bus according to their performance and capacity characteristics) and to avoid the shortfalls associated with unregulated competition (discussed above) were generally foregone.

Cullinane (2003) identifies the potential for closer functional integration between Hong Kong and the Pearl Delta region and a relaxation of border crossing procedures as a possible driver for increasing car ownership in Hong Kong in the future. Presently, and confined to the territory of the Special Administrative Region, there are simply not many places to go to in a car without significant inconvenience in terms of the cost and availability of road space and parking. This might change, however, in the wake of increasing interdependency, and associated flows of commuter, business and recreational traffic, between Hong Kong and neighbouring Shenzhen or places beyond. Cullinane and Cullinane (2003) also detected behaviour patterns among the minority of car-owning households in Hong Kong that bore some similarities to the experience in Singapore, discussed earlier, suggesting that once the threshold to car ownership has been passed, the car often becomes a default choice of movement rather than one for special occasions where public transport alternatives are deficient.

Given the impressive composite accessibility results, can Hong Kong thus be held up as a model for public transport and land use integration across Asia (and elsewhere)? The answer is of course mixed! There is clearly a model for other cities in the property and infrastructure approach of Hong Kong which is of considerable value to other global cities struggling to deliver public transport. On the other hand, the dilemma between competition policy and strategic rail priority requires resolution if the 'cannibalistic coexistence' of the two is to be avoided. From an amenity perspective, the city appears traffic-saturated due to its very limited road space, despite the small number of cars. Buses, with up to 200 inter-peak departures per hour per direction along some main arteries, contribute to this problem. There is a need to deliver greater pedestrian amenity and stronger place functions, but this will be challenging given these conditions.

CONCLUSION

Both cities show impressive results for public transport accessibility, in Singapore brought about by a strong planning regime where not only land use and transport were to be integrated, but also strategies for modal integration were critical – the relationship between high investment in public transport *and* constraints to car ownership and use. Hong Kong also has constrained car use, but not by regulation, more by situation. The contrasts between strong public control over the public transport network and supply in Singapore and the private competition in Hong Kong are of interest, and while the overall outcome by our measures is that both cities deliver impressive public transport accessibility, in Hong Kong there are inefficiencies reported as a result of this regime. Both cities are spatially constrained, leading to a more compact structure and helping to promote a TOD approach, and this has clearly assisted in the impressive public transport accessibility. As to resilience, in is clear that both cities are planning ahead in switching from bus-based to rail-based systems, but concerns over the future role of the car may mar progress.

NOTE

1 The remainder of the SNAMUTS indicators in this section rely on derived data from the MATSim Singapore jobs quantification process which itself has various assumptions and is based on estimates of land use. These are estimated figures by an independent party, and not provided by the Singapore government. We acknowledge the assistance of Alexander Erath of the Future Cities Laboratory, ETH Zurich, and previous work which details their methodology in Ordóñez M., Arturo, S., Erath, A. (2013) Estimating Dynamic Workplace Capacities by Means of Public Transport Smart Card Data and Household Travel Survey in Singapore. *Transportation Research Record: Journal of the Transportation Research Board 2344*: 20–30. doi:10.3141/2344-03.

8 Polycentric and Multimodal Interfaces in the Dutch Randstad

The Dutch Randstad is a polynuclear metropolitan region comprising the four major urban centres of Amsterdam, Den Haag, Rotterdam and Utrecht and many smaller centres. Shaped as a roughly circular urbanised perimeter surrounding a 'green heart' of predominantly rural uses (the term 'randstad' translates as 'ring city'), the Randstad has no clear geographical centre of settlement and no one component city that eclipses the others in terms of population size or political and economic significance. The country's capital city functions are also distributed between Den Haag and Amsterdam.

The Netherlands are one of the most densely populated countries in the world and one of the most low-lying. The scarcity of arable as well as developable land and the need to reconcile human settlements and the ever-present influence of water has, over centuries, forged a strong national tradition of regional planning. Careful management of multiple pressures towards the efficient utilisation of land required collective and coordinated action. Contemporary planning dilemmas experienced in many developed cities were manifest earlier and with greater urgency in the Netherlands. The search for solutions elevated the country as a global pioneer. Since the 2000s this is particularly true for the nexus of integrated transport and land use planning, and the emerging field of accessibility research can trace a significant part of its origins to a network of Dutch practitioners, consultants and academics.

Strong rates of post-war growth and the proliferation of the car led Dutch decision makers towards a nationwide strategy of guided decentralisation during the 1960s and 1970s, to address the interrelated challenges of growing housing needs, mounting traffic congestion and the threat of uncontrolled suburban dispersal. The key solution to these problems was the establishment of planned new towns in the vicinity of, but physically separate from established population centres (Van der Burg and Dieleman, 2004). They were originally conceived as self-sufficient in employment relative to their population base. In reality it has been difficult to attract significant economic activity besides housing, or to achieve the level of economic or demographic diversity associated with the established cities. As a result, commuting patterns had a tendency to exacerbate rather than relieve the growing trends of car dependence and increasing distances between home and work (Priemus, 1999).

Emerging sustainability concerns in the 1980s fostered a new national spatial planning directive advocating for the compact city. The aim was to encourage growth within existing settlement areas (and where that was insufficient, on greenfield land adjacent to existing settlement areas) as 'seamless' city extensions with good public transport, walking and cycling links. Greenbelts and urban growth boundaries were instigated to protect non-urban open space. This is how the 1990s and early 2000s legacy of the 'VINEX neighbourhoods' was initiated, a specific style of low-rise, medium-density greenfield urban design whose closest New World equivalent is found in the New Urbanism movement of North America and Australasia, such as Perth's Liveable Neighbourhoods initiative (Curtis and Punter, 2004). New spatial priorities for residential growth in cities were complemented by a policy that guided the location choices of businesses according to mobility needs. Businesses attracting large numbers of employees or customers but little freight traffic were encouraged into public transport-oriented *A-locations* with restrictions on road access and parking, whereas businesses with low numbers of employees or customers but large volumes of freight traffic were encouraged to road-oriented *C-locations* away from fine-grained urban uses. Businesses characterised by significant levels of people as well as freight flows were encouraged to locate at the interfaces of public transport and road infrastructure (*B-locations*). The ABC-location policy thus attempted to steer urban development towards integrated land use and transport outcomes (Van der Burg and Dieleman, 2004).

The compact city model and the ABC-location policy soon ran into severe constraints. Residents in VINEX neighbourhoods did not establish below-average rates of car ownership or use, or above-average public transport use. Located at the edge of urban settlement areas, they are often 'at the end of the line' in terms of public transport access, yet close to the well-developed motorway network. For non-radial journeys by VINEX residents (in this polycentric agglomeration the majority of attractive destinations are found in a non-radial direction) the private car had an accessibility advantage over public transport. Meanwhile the ABC-location policy, applied predominantly to large firms, saw poor demand for A-locations – both because of the restrictive regulatory framework towards car access and parking and because most designated A-locations were in densely developed, historic city centres with limited scope to accommodate additional large office or retail facilities, or to do so cost-effectively. Instead, demand was buoyant for the more permissive B-locations but since the number of well-serviced interfaces between road and public transport infrastructure was limited, the definition of what constituted good public transport access for a B-location was interpreted ever more leniently. A significant share of new office development occurred in the vicinity of motorway exits at the urban periphery, where public transport accessibility was no better and some cases poorer than in the VINEX residential neighbourhoods (Van den Boomen and Venhoeven, 2012).

Thus the compact city policy, which aimed to reduce car dependence, had almost the opposite effect. However, despite the unconducive trajectory of market forces during the compact city era, a conglomerate of emerging social and economic trends was working in favour of reduced automobility. The compact city and ABC location policies were superseded in the mid-2000s by a new guiding vision (Van der Burg and Dieleman, 2004; Van Oort et al, 2010). This vision draws on a different understanding of the interdependence between land use dynamics and transport networks – on complementarity and intermodality, rather than competition, between public and private transport. Urban growth is viewed through the lens of its position on movement networks and draws on the distinction of the node and place properties of locations (see Chapter 2). By accepting the coexistence of a car-dominated domain (in regional areas and urban peripheries) and a public transport, walking and cycling domain (within and between core cities), this new thinking, in an almost ironic reversal of the more antagonistic ABC location policy, aims at strengthening the interfaces between private motorised and public/non-motorised transport modes to mutual advantage, and to configure urban growth around these interfaces to capitalise on their multimodal accessibility (Bertolini and Le Clerq, 2003; Bertolini, 2005; Van der Bijl and Hendriks, 2010).

The 2008 global financial crisis saw a downturn for the property sector and revealed a degree of overinvestment in office development during the preceding two decades. Widespread vacancies of office space predominantly affect the watered-down B-locations along motorways, while the traditional city centres (the former A-locations) weathered the crisis in better shape. These latter areas offer a fertile environment for small business and entrepreneurial initiatives in the knowledge industries, a sector that thrives on face-to-face contact and proximity to urban amenities. This corresponds to the growing attraction of urban over suburban living among broadening demographic groups, and to changing employment practices that increasingly blur the lines between home and workplace. Instead the city's open spaces, cultural facilities and hospitality industry become informal venues for business-related communication and productive work. Accordingly, these trends place increasing demands on the quality as well as accessibility of such spaces for interaction (Van den Boomen and Venhoeven, 2012).

In the 2010s the Dutch Randstad may be in an emerging new phase of accessibility planning informed by a new compact for the interplay of transport and land use in the twenty-first century, with implications relevant for other world cities. Our interest is in illuminating this context through accessibility analysis and in understanding how its application may differ when performed on a multi-nuclear agglomeration with fluid edges rather than a traditional, monocentric metropolis. Testing the SNAMUTS methodology and the calibration of its indicators in a polynuclear agglomeration is related to a significant local policy debate about the appropriate spatial level(s) or governmental tier(s) of decision making in integrated land use and transport planning. This in turn is related to the behaviour of transport users in accessing the opportunities provided in a polynuclear urban system, and the question whether the Randstad is functionally or merely morphologically polycentric (Burger et al, 2014). How is the Randstad equipped in terms of settlement structure and public transport service levels to maximise the role of public transport in supporting a 'daily urban system' from the perspective of the user? In particular, to what extent can the system provide for differences in individual spatial reach – contained within core cities, within sub-regions, or across the Randstad as a whole?

THE STRUCTURE OF THE DUTCH RANDSTAD

In administrative terms, the simplest definition of the Randstad metropolitan region would include the four Dutch provinces of Noord Holland, Flevoland, Zuid Holland and Utrecht (approximately 7.8 million inhabitants on 8,272 sq km in 2010). While the inclusion of the entire provinces of Zuid Holland (Den Haag-Rotterdam) and Utrecht is uncontroversial, the provinces of Noord Holland (Amsterdam) and Flevoland (Almere) contain large, comparatively sparsely populated areas beyond easy reach of the metropolitan centres such as the Frisian island of Texel and the Noordoostpolder region in Flevoland. Discounting for these two areas reduces the Randstad land area definition to 7,637 sq km and its population to 7.7 million.

The SNAMUTS analysis refers both to this definition of the entire Randstad as well as separately to three component regions, namely the provinces of Zuid Holland and Utrecht and the Amsterdam metropolitan area, encompassing the province of Noord Holland with the exception of the Alkmaar region and the rural expanses in the north (Kop van Noord Holland), as well as the city of Almere, the largest urban centre in Flevoland. These three separate agglomerations of Amsterdam, Utrecht and Zuid Holland differ quite significantly in settlement size and characteristics as well as historical and contemporary approaches to the policy context of land use and public transport.

Metropolitan Amsterdam is a medium-sized European city, about halfway between Copenhagen and Vienna in terms of population size. It contains a dominant core city surrounded by secondary centres (prominently Haarlem, Almere and Hilversum) that have maintained a greater degree of spatial and functional separateness and autonomy from the centre than their Danish or Austrian counterparts. Of the Randstad urban centres, Amsterdam attracts the greatest number of international visitors and contains the country's largest airport, providing a strong gateway function for the Netherlands in terms of movement of people.

Utrecht is a smaller urban centre, comparable in size to Edinburgh, Oporto or Adelaide. It is concentrated around a relatively compact core city, but like Amsterdam contains significant secondary centres with a substantial degree of functional self-sufficiency, particularly Amersfoort. The boundary between the Amsterdam and Utrecht regions, while traceable along the provincial border, is fluid in spatial terms: the sub-region of Hilversum/het Gooi, for example, could arguably be counted towards either metropolitan area definition, and the central stations of both core cities are within a 28-minute commute of each other.

Zuid Holland, in contrast, compares in population size with Melbourne, Hamburg, Munich or Montreal. Unlike each of these monocentrically dominated cities, Zuid Holland consists of two primary urban centres of equal weight within easy commuting distance of each other. Den Haag is the country's main public service centre with the majority of national government institutions and associated employment. Rotterdam encompasses Europe's largest seaport and forms a gateway for significant freight movement. The city is the only major Randstad centre severely destroyed during World War II, necessitating a post-war reconstruction process that departed significantly from the historic city-building template. More recently, the diversification of the city's employment base away from the traditional dominance of maritime industries during the 1980s and 1990s led to a period of structural adjustments accompanied by high local unemployment and temporary population losses. Apart from Den Haag and Rotterdam, there are a number of secondary urban centres in Zuid Holland (Leiden, Delft, Dordrecht, Zoetermeer, Gouda) occupying positions in the city hierarchy comparable to Haarlem, Alkmaar, Almere, Hilversum and Amersfoort in the Randstad north wing.

PUBLIC TRANSPORT SUPPLY IN THE RANDSTAD SUB-REGIONS

Public transport across the Netherlands is generally distinguished by the national rail system, mostly operated by state-owned rail company *Nederlands Spoorwegen* (NS), and urban and regional public transport (*openbaar vervoer* or OV). Urban and regional public transport is organised into area-based licences and contracted to private operators, with the exception of the three largest cities where city subsidiaries act as intermodal operators of all metro, tram and bus lines (GVB in Amsterdam, HTM in Den Haag and RET in Rotterdam). In Utrecht, there are separate private operators for the urban bus network and the two-line *sneltram* (light rail) system.

All urban and regional public transport across the Netherlands has been fare-integrated since 1980. Until around 2010 this was based on a nation-wide zonal system and a multiple-ride paper ticket known as *nationale strippenkaart* (with single-ride and periodical tickets also available). By 2011 this was converted to an electronic system (*OV-chipkaart*), which calculates fares by distance as passengers tag on and off at the beginning and end of each trip leg, and adds this per-kilometre fare to a base fare per journey. However, the ticketing systems for the national rail network (NS) and urban/regional public transport (OV) remain separated, with NS tickets subject to a different fare calculation than OV tickets. While a transfer between OV lines will attract a discount, this does not apply for transfer trips between OV and NS lines. For such multimodal journeys, the *OV-chipkaart* thus assumes the character of

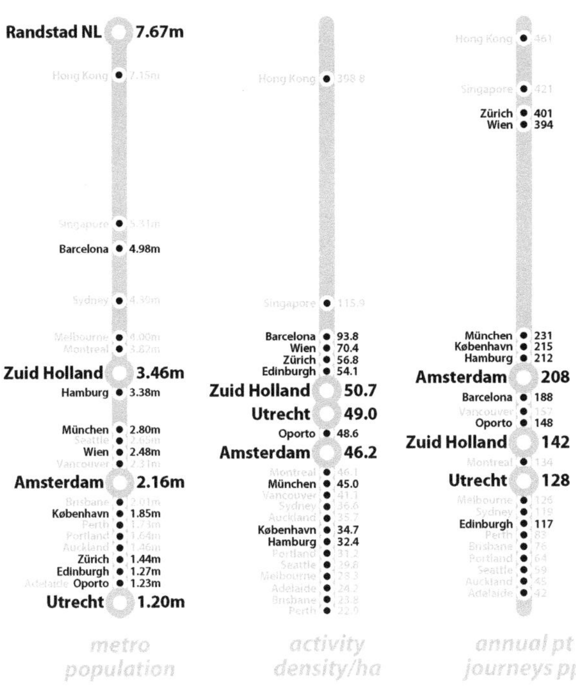

a universal payment option rather than a truly integrated ticket.

The national rail network is operated at regular frequencies (mostly every 30 minutes all day, every day) across the Netherlands, with overlapping lines in urban areas such as the Randstad generally producing 15-minute or better intervals. There is, however, usually a coexistence of services with different speeds and stopping patterns, meaning that a significant number of smaller stations along some of the key rail routes in the Randstad receive only half-hourly services. Generally, a greater priority is afforded to the ability to operate some fast services between major centres than to maximise the service frequency along the entire route. As such, the Randstad heavy rail system resembles a mixed regional rail network akin to Zurich or Sydney rather than a metro-like S-Bahn or S-Tog system in say, Copenhagen or Hamburg.

There are metro networks in Amsterdam and Rotterdam, developed in the 1960s and 1970s. Both systems combine segments of fully grade-separated underground or elevated metro routes and segments of street-level (but physically segregated) light rail. Rotterdam's metro was recently extended over several former NS branch lines and now connects the city with neighbouring Den Haag, as well as Den Haag with the post-war new town of Zoetermeer in a light rail network branded as RandstadRail. Some RandstadRail lines continue through a dedicated tram tunnel underneath Den Haag's CBD and further along conventional tram routes.

There are first-generation tram systems in Amsterdam, Den Haag and Rotterdam. While these networks suffered some post-war shrinkage, when most regional lines connecting the major cities with neighbouring centres such as Haarlem or Leiden were lost, the core city tram systems have generally kept pace with urban growth and continue to be expanded. In Utrecht the first-generation tram system was closed in 1949. A second-generation light rail network (*sneltram*), introduced in 1983, connects central Utrecht with the post-war suburban centres of Kanaleneiland, Nieuwegein and IJsselstein. There are ambitious plans to expand this system to cover most key corridors in the city-region.

Almere, the largest post-war new town in the Netherlands, is oriented around a rail spine while local public transport comprises a fully segregated, high-frequency bus rapid transit (BRT) network. BRT lines also exist in the southern and western suburbs of Amsterdam, linking Haarlem with Schiphol airport, Amstelveen and the employment hubs at Amsterdam Zuid and Bijlmer ArenA. Buses also have a prominent role in accessing the suburban centres in the Waterland region north of Amsterdam, which has only a low-frequency, indirect rail service and, until completion of Amsterdam's north–south metro line later this decade, no rail harbour crossing into the centre of Amsterdam. The urban networks of Utrecht, Amersfoort, Haarlem, Leiden and Dordrecht are bus-dominated, whereas in Den Haag and Rotterdam buses complement the metro and tram network servicing the key corridors.

Service Intensity

Service intensity figures relative to population are much higher in the Amsterdam region than in the provinces of Utrecht or Zuid Holland. While Amsterdam's averages, within the European sample, are second only to Edinburgh, those of Utrecht and Zuid Holland form a ranking cluster with the German cities (Hamburg and Munich) at the bottom end of the European table. Since high service intensity figures can reflect both largesse on behalf of the relevant agencies to put resources into public transport supply, as well as the inefficiencies of a system excessively dependent on slow modes and small vehicles, it is useful to examine this context in more detail.

Amsterdam's high service intensity figure can be traced across all modes. Alongside Utrecht, Amsterdam has a more developed heavy rail and metro system than neighbouring Zuid Holland, with almost 40 per cent more services and 20 per cent more stations relative to population. Service intensity for Amsterdam's trams is about 30 per cent higher than in Zuid Holland, even though the tram networks of Den Haag and Rotterdam put together are more expansive relative to population size than that of Amsterdam. This is the result of average service frequencies on tram lines being some 50 per cent higher in Amsterdam than Zuid Holland, as well as – to a smaller extent and as a moderating factor – a lower average operational speed of Amsterdam trams, likely related to a greater proportion of alignments along very constrained streetscapes with high activity intensity in comparison to their counterparts in Den Haag and Rotterdam.

Service intensity for buses is more than 60 per cent higher in Amsterdam than in Zuid Holland and 15 per cent higher than in Utrecht, and this figure does not even consider the highly developed, high-frequency BRT systems in Almere and in Amsterdam's south-west (which have no equivalent in Zuid Holland). Like with trams, better average service frequencies, which are about 20 per cent higher in both Amsterdam and Utrecht than in Zuid Holland, explain part of this difference. However, a more significant factor is the much greater geographical expansion of metropolitan Amsterdam's bus network in conjunction with the rail-based modes compared to Zuid Holland and Utrecht, a finding we will discuss in more detail in the section on network coverage.

The service intensity comparison of the Randstad sub-regions raises some important policy issues. How are the additional services found in the Amsterdam region funded? To the extent that national government agencies are involved, why is such a difference in public transport service levels and coverage between adjacent cities deemed acceptable? In the subsequent analysis, we are interested in testing whether Amsterdam's edge in service intensity translates into superior accessibility performance compared to its neighbours.

Closeness and Degree Centrality

The inner areas of Amsterdam and to a lesser extent Den Haag, Rotterdam and Utrecht are characterised by concentrations of mixed land uses and thus transport origins and destinations along most public transport corridors and their intersections, which have generally been included in the SNAMUTS list of activity nodes. In suburban areas, where land use segregation is more prevalent and where densities drop, significant concentrations of mid- or high-rise residential uses are often grouped around local retail and service facilities as their sole non-residential uses. These focal points were also generally included as activity node centre points in the analysis, even where they are unlikely to draw much destination travel from outside the neighbourhood.

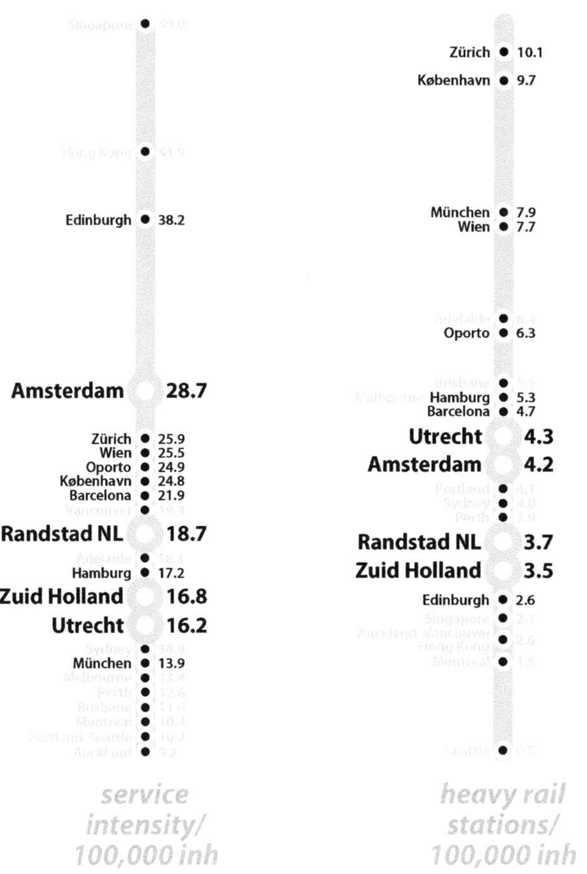

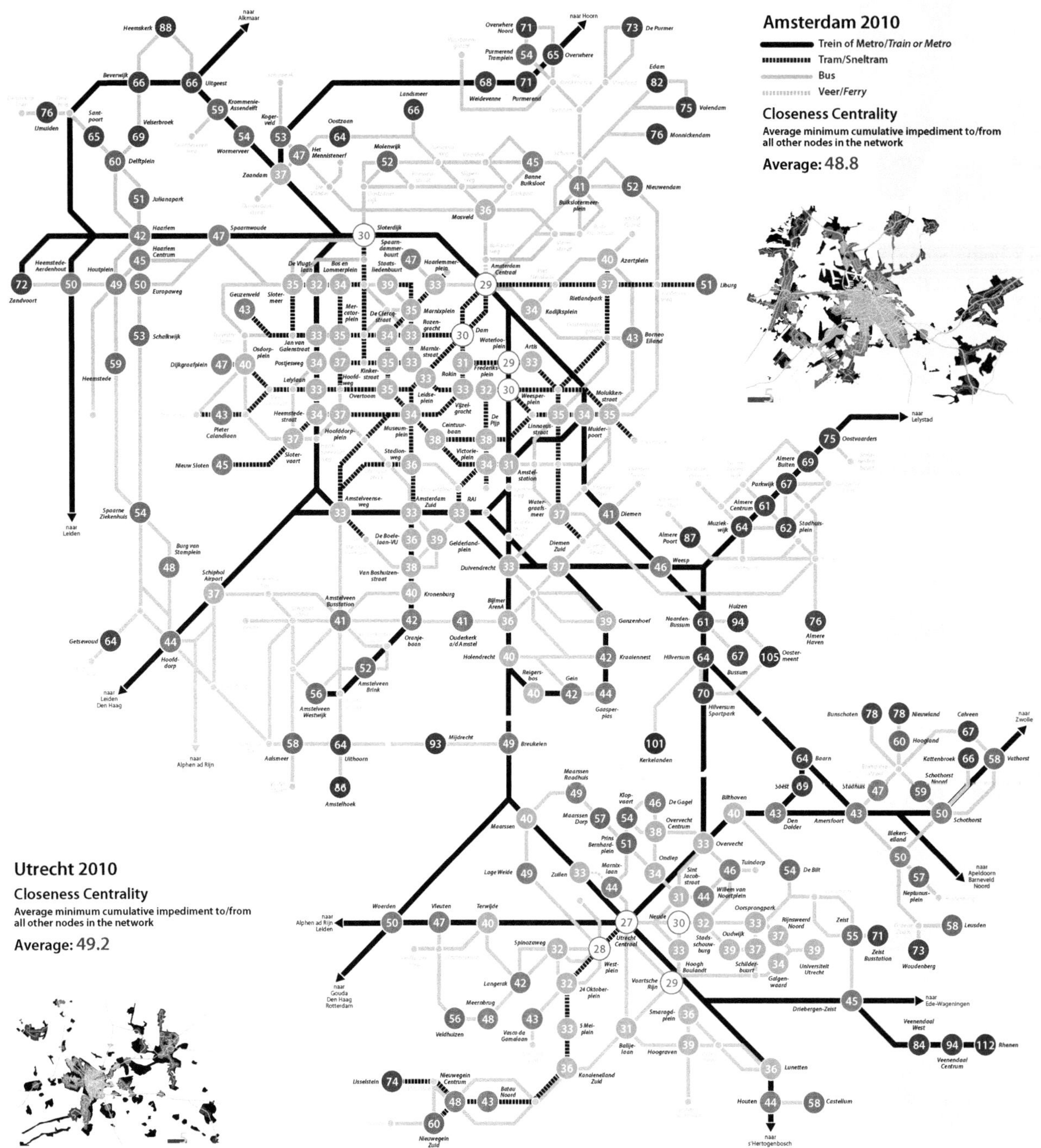
Amsterdam 2010
Trein of Metro/Train or Metro
Tram/Sneltram
Bus
Veer/Ferry
Closeness Centrality
Average minimum cumulative impediment to/from all other nodes in the network
Average: 48.8
Utrecht 2010
Closeness Centrality
Average minimum cumulative impediment to/from all other nodes in the network
Average: 49.2

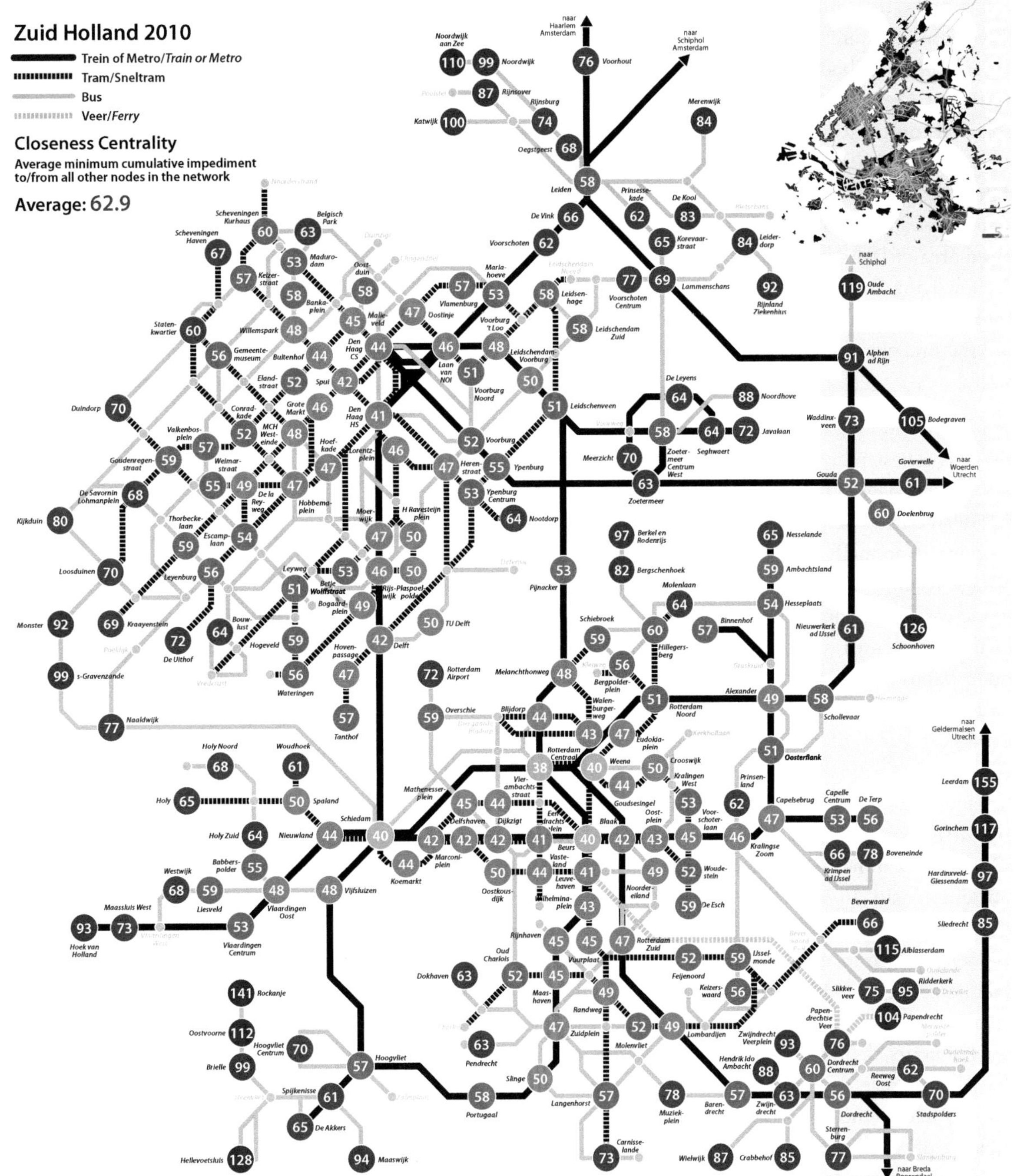

Zuid Holland 2010
Trein of Metro/Train or Metro
Tram/Sneltram
Bus
Veer/Ferry
Closeness Centrality
Average minimum cumulative impediment to/from all other nodes in the network
Average: 62.9
naar Haarlem Amsterdam
naar Schiphol Amsterdam
Noordwijk aan Zee 110
99 Noordwijk
87 Rijnsover
Katwijk 100
74 Rijnsburg
76 Voorhout
Oegstgeest 68
Merenwijk 84
58 Leiden
Prinsessekade 62
De Kooi 83
De Vink 66
65 Korevaarstraat
84 Leiderdorp
Voorschoten 62
69 Lammenschans
92 Rijnland Ziekenhuis
77 Voorschoten Centrum
naar Schiphol
119 Oude Ambacht
Scheveningen Kurhaus 60
63 Belgisch Park
Scheveningen Haven 67
53 Madurodam
57 Keizerstraat
58 Bankaplein
58 Oostduin
57 Mariahoeve 53
47 Oostinje
Vlamenburg
58 Leidsenhage
58 Leidschendam Zuid
Statenkwartier 60
Willemspark 48
45 Malieveld
56 Gemeentemuseum
Buitenhof 44
44 Den Haag CS
46 Laan van NOI
48 Voorburg 't Loo
51
Leidschendam-Voorburg
91 Alphen ad Rijn
Elandstraat 52
Spui 42
50 Voorburg Noord
Grote Markt 46
41 Den Haag HS
51 Leidschenveen
De Leyens 64
88 Noordhove
Duindorp 70
Conradkade 52
MCH Westeinde 48
52 Voorburg
58 Zoetermeer Centrum West
64 Seghwaert
72 Javalaan
Waddinxveen 73
105 Bodegraven
Valkenbosplein 57
Hoefkade 47
46 Lorentzplein
Meerzicht 70
Goudenregenstraat 59
Weimarstraat 55
49
47 Herenstraat
55 Ypenburg
63 Zoetermeer
Gouda 52
Goverwelle 61
naar Woerden Utrecht
De Savornin Lohmanplein 68
De la Reyweg
Hobbemaplein
53 Ypenburg Centrum
64 Nootdorp
60 Doelenbrug
Kijkduin 80
Thorbeckelaan 59
Escamplaan 54
Moerwijk 47
H Ravesteijn plein 50
97 Berkel en Rodenrijs
65 Nesselande
Loosduinen 70
Leyenburg 56
Leyweg 53
Betje Wolffstraat 51
46
50
Rijs-Plaspoelpolder
53 Pijnacker
82 Bergschenhoek
59 Ambachtsland
Bogaardplein 49
Molenlaan 64
54 Hesseplaats
Monster 92
69 Kraayenstein
64 Bouwlust
50 TU Delft
Schiebroek 59
60 Hillegersberg
57 Binnenhof
Nieuwerkerk ad IJssel 61
126 Schoonhoven
72 De Uithof
Hogeveld 59
Hovenpassage 42 Delft
s-Gravenzande 99
56 Wateringen
47
72 Rotterdam Airport
Melanchthonweg 48
56 Bergpolderplein
Alexander 49
58 Schollevaar
77 Naaldwijk
57 Tanthof
59 Overschie
Blijdorp 44
Walenburgerweg 43
47 Eudokiaplein
51 Rotterdam Noord
51 Oosterflank
Holy Noord 68
Woudhoek 61
38 Rotterdam Centraal
40 Weena
50 Crooswijk
44 Kralingen West
naar Geldermalsen Utrecht
Leerdam 155
Holy 65
50 Spaland
Mathenesserplein 45
44 Vierambachtsstraat
53 Goudsesingel
Prinsenland 62
47 Capelsebrug
Capelle Centrum 53
De Terp 56
Holy Zuid 64
44 Nieuwland
40 Schiedam
42 Delfshaven 42
42 Dijkzigt
41 Eendrachtsplein
40 Beurs
Blaak 42
43 Oostplein
45 Voorschoterlaan
46 Kralingse Zoom
66 Krimpen ad IJssel
78 Boveneinde
Gorinchem 117
Babberspolder 55
44 Koemarkt
Marconiplein
50 Oostkousdijk
44 Vasteland
41 Leuvehaven
49 Noordereiland
52 Woudestein
Hardinxveld-Giessendam 97
Westwijk 68
59 Liesveld
48 Vlaardingen Oost
48 Vijfsluizen
Wilhelminaplein 43
59 De Esch
Maassluis West
Beverwaard 66
Hoek van Holland 93
73
53 Vlaardingen Centrum
Rijnhaven 45
45
47 Rotterdam Zuid
52 Feijenoord
59 IJsselmonde
115 Alblasserdam
Sliedrecht 85
Dokhaven 63
Oud Charlois 52
45 Vuurplaat
Maashaven
49 Randweg
Keizerswaard 56
Slikkerveer 75
95 Ridderkerk
141 Rockanje
104 Papendrecht
Papendrechtse Veer 76
Oostvoorne 112
Hoogvliet Centrum 70
47 Zuidplein
52 Molenvliet
49 Lombardijen
Zwijndrecht Veerplein 93
Brielle 99
57 Hoogvliet
63 Pendrecht
Hendrik Ido Ambacht 88
60 Dordrecht Centrum
Reeweg Oost 62
Spijkenisse 61
Slinge 50
58 Portugaal
Langenhorst 57
78 Muziekplein
57 Barendrecht
63 Zwijndrecht
56 Dordrecht
70 Stadspolders
65 De Akkers
Sterrenburg
Carnisselande
Hellevoetsluis 128
94 Maaswijk
73
Wielwijk 87
Crabbehof 85
77
naar Breda Roosendaal

Topographical constraints that influence network performance are all related to the presence of water bodies, in particular the IJ and Nieuwe Maas rivers with associated port facilities in central Amsterdam and Rotterdam respectively, and the North Sea coastline which provides a north-western boundary to the urbanised area of Den Haag. Conversely, in the low-lying flat plains of the Randstad changes in elevation do not play a role as structural elements in the urban geography.

Of the three Randstad sub-regions, Amsterdam achieves the best network averages on closeness and degree centrality, while Zuid Holland trails behind both northern regions. Nominally we would expect average results on these two indicators to increase (deteriorate) with growing metropolitan area size. This explains Zuid Holland's poorer performance as the largest sub-region while suggesting that (larger) Amsterdam's performance compared to (smaller) Utrecht relates to a much greater outlay of operational resources (see previous section), enhancing ease of movement and reducing transfer intensity. In Zuid Holland the high degree of fragmentation of the settlement area into geographically distinct parcels, driven by a more pronounced polynuclear structure than its northern neighbours, depresses performance. The poor average degree centrality score is also due to the relative self-containment of the surface networks in Zuid Holland's component cities; with the exception of a bus line each between Den Haag and Leiden and between Den Haag and Schiedam (Rotterdam), the core cities have no public transport linkages with each other at the SNAMUTS standard except through the (limited) heavy rail network.

Amsterdam's results also illustrate the effect of a tightly-knit, web-shaped network of surface routes surrounded by a ring of high-frequency metro and heavy rail routes: only one activity node within this area returns a closeness centrality score higher than 40 while all others are nestled within a relatively close band. These are the hallmarks of a network that integrates well with the activity centre structure. In fact, the network shaped the activity centre structure by way of late nineteenth-century inner urban tram corridors and by a heavy rail ring built more recently along an orbital corridor that has attracted some of the highest concentrations of office employment in the Netherlands. Further out, the core city of Amsterdam has a pronounced settlement boundary, naturally enforced by the IJsselmeer's water body (IJburg) and also as a result of planning policies (the northern edge around Buikslotermeer, the western edge around Sloten and Osdorp and the south-eastern edge around Bijlmer). A deterioration in closeness performance beyond the metropolitan average only occurs for places beyond this boundary, though it is uneven: central Haarlem and the Schiphol airport-Hoofddorp area, with good rail links to central Amsterdam and the orbital BRT system to connect them with each other, return scores comparable to nodes at the periphery of the core city. The more distant regional centres of Almere and Hilversum, expectedly, perform more poorly, but their results are comparable to those found in the Waterland corridor (Purmerend, Edam, Volendam) and the IJmuiden-Beverwijk area, which are both located closer geographically to central Amsterdam. This last group of centres, however, rely on access by bus and/or relatively slow and infrequent rail services, unlike Almere and Hilversum which are each connected to several parts of Amsterdam by fast and frequent trains.

Amsterdam's degree centrality map highlights the existence of a dominant 'super-node' at Amsterdam Centraal, with a substantially higher degree of network integration (lower transfer intensity) than any of its peers. However, the secondary rail stations at Sloterdijk, RAI, Amsterdam Zuid, Schiphol airport and Hoofddorp also score well on this index. Nodes with relatively high transfer intensity scores can primarily be found away from rail stations in the cities of Haarlem, Almere and Hilversum, where buses act as rail feeders for journeys to and from outside each of these secondary centres.

Zuid Holland's network shape differs from Amsterdam's by the presence of

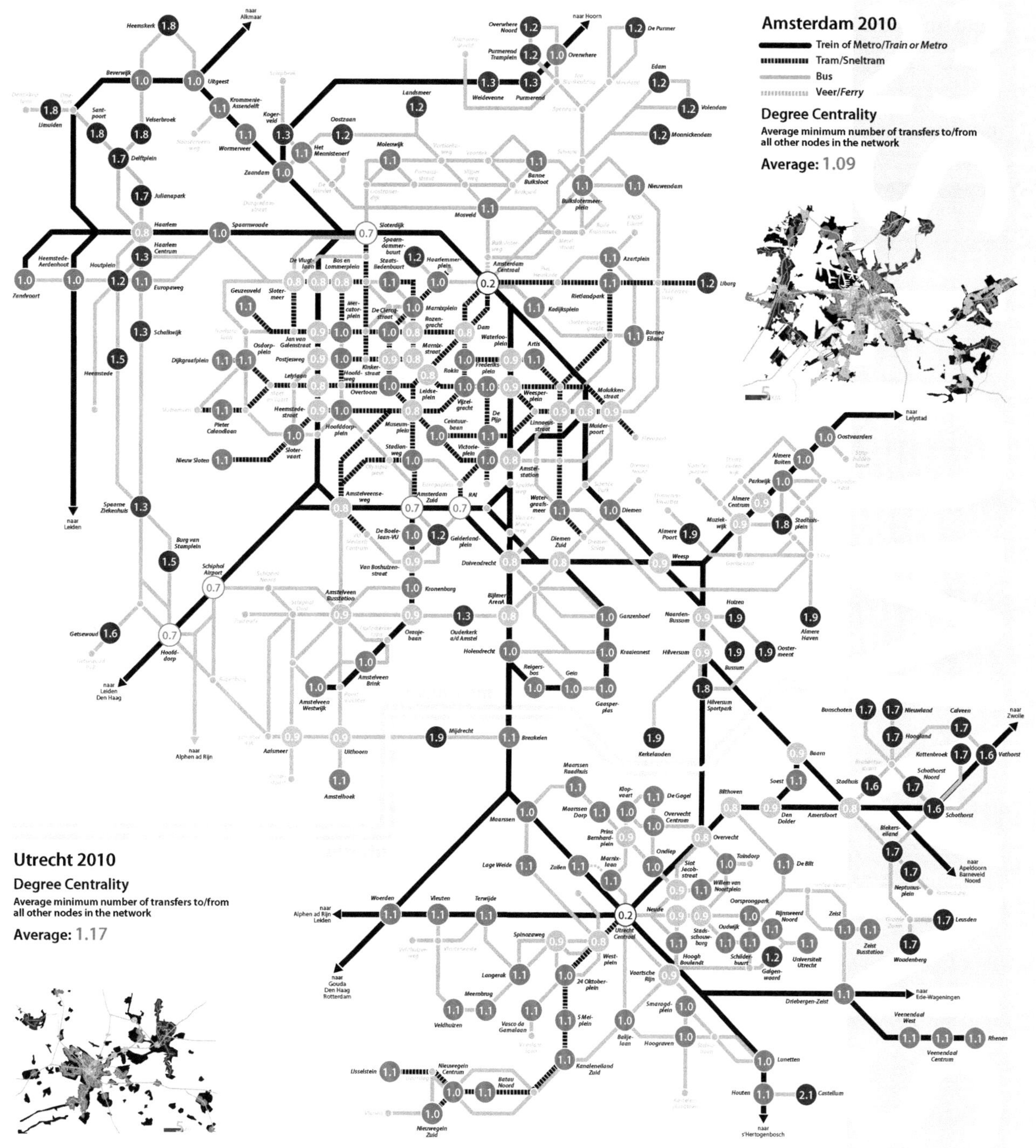

Amsterdam 2010
Trein of Metro/Train or Metro
Tram/Sneltram
Bus
Veer/Ferry
Degree Centrality
Average minimum number of transfers to/from all other nodes in the network
Average: 1.09
Utrecht 2010
Degree Centrality
Average minimum number of transfers to/from all other nodes in the network
Average: 1.17
naar Alkmaar
naar Hoorn
naar Lelystad
naar Leiden
naar Leiden Den Haag
naar Alphen ad Rijn
naar Zwolle
naar Apeldoorn Barneveld Noord
naar Alphen ad Rijn Leiden
naar Gouda Den Haag Rotterdam
naar Ede-Wageningen
naar s'Hertogenbosch
Heemskerk
Beverwijk
Uitgeest
IJmuiden
Zandvoort
Haarlem
Spaarnwoude
Sloterdijk
Amsterdam Centraal
Zaandam
Purmerend
Edam
Volendam
Monnickendam
Landsmeer
Oostzaan
Nieuwendam
IJburg
Diemen
Weesp
Duivendrecht
Holendrecht
Bijlmer ArenA
Amstelveen Busstation
Schiphol Airport
Hoofddorp
Aalsmeer
Uithoorn
Amstelhoek
Mijdrecht
Breukelen
Hilversum
Bussum
Naarden-Bussum
Almere Poort
Almere Haven
Almere Centrum
Oostvaarders
Kerkelanden
Baarn
Soest
Den Dolder
Bilthoven
Amersfoort
Schothorst
Vathorst
Leusden
Woudenberg
Maarssen
Woerden
Vleuten
Terwijde
Utrecht Centraal
Overvecht
De Bilt
Zeist
Driebergen-Zeist
Veenendaal West
Veenendaal Centrum
Rhenen
Lunetten
Houten
Castellum
IJsselstein
Nieuwegein Zuid

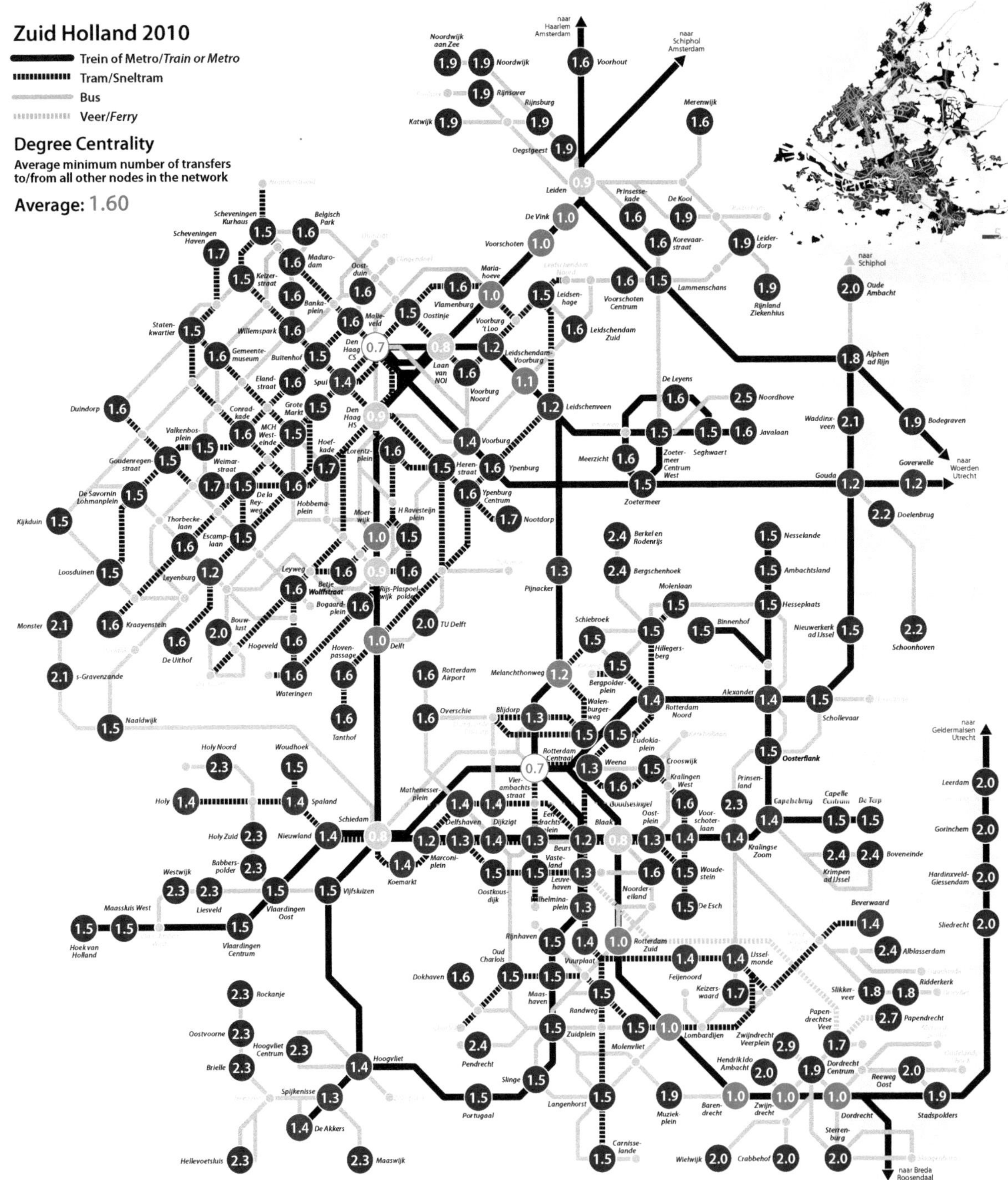

Zuid Holland 2010
Trein of Metro/Train or Metro
Tram/Sneltram
Bus
Veer/Ferry
Degree Centrality
Average minimum number of transfers to/from all other nodes in the network
Average: 1.60
naar Haarlem Amsterdam
naar Schiphol Amsterdam
Noordwijk aan Zee 1.9
1.9 Noordwijk
1.9 Rijnsover
Rijnsburg 1.9
Katwijk 1.9
1.6 Voorhout
Oegstgeest 1.9
Merenwijk 1.6
Leiden 0.9
De Vink 1.0
Voorschoten 1.0
Prinsessekade 1.6
De Kooi 1.9
1.6 Korevaarstraat
1.9 Leiderdorp
1.5 Lammenschans
1.9 Rijnland Ziekenhuis
naar Schiphol
2.0 Oude Ambacht
1.8 Alphen ad Rijn
Waddinxveen 2.1
1.9 Bodegraven
naar Woerden Utrecht
Goverwelle 1.2
Gouda 1.2
2.2 Doelenbrug
2.2 Schoonhoven
Nieuwerkerk ad IJssel 1.5
Mariahoeve 1.0
1.5 Leidsenhage
1.6 Voorschoten Centrum
1.6 Leidschendam Zuid
Vlamenburg 1.6
1.5 Oostinje
Voorburg 't Loo 1.2
Leidschendam-Voorburg 1.1
Laan van NOI 0.8
Voorburg Noord 1.6
Den Haag CS 0.7
Den Haag HS 0.9
1.2 Leidschenveen
De Leyens 1.6
2.5 Noordhove
1.6 Javalaan
Seghwaert 1.5
Zoetermeer Centrum West 1.5
Meerzicht 1.6
Zoetermeer 1.5
1.4 Voorburg
Herenstraat 1.5
1.6 Ypenburg
Ypenburg Centrum 1.6
1.7 Nootdorp
Scheveningen Kurhaus 1.5
Belgisch Park 1.6
Scheveningen Haven 1.7
Keizerstraat 1.5
Madurodam 1.6
Oostduin 1.6
Bankaplein 1.6
Malieveld 1.6
Statenkwartier 1.5
Willemspark 1.6
Gemeentemuseum 1.6
Buitenhof 1.5
Elandstraat 1.6
Spui 1.4
Grote Markt 1.5
Duindorp 1.6
Conradkade 1.6
MCH Westeinde 1.5
Valkenbosplein 1.5
Goudenregenstraat 1.5
Weimarstraat 1.7
Hoefkade 1.7
Lorentzplein 1.6
De la Reyweg 1.5
Hobbemaplein 1.6
De Savornin Lohmanplein 1.5
Kijkduin 1.5
Thorbeckelaan 1.6
Escamplaan 1.5
Moerwijk 1.0
H Ravesteijnplein 1.5
Loosduinen 1.5
Leyenburg 1.2
Leyweg 1.6
Betje Wolffstraat
Rijs-Plaspoelpolder 0.9 1.6
Bogaardplein 1.6
Monster 2.1
1.6 Kraayenstein
De Uithof 1.6
Bouwlust 2.0
Hogeveld 1.6
Wateringen 1.6
Hovenpassage 1.6
Delft 1.0
2.0 TU Delft
Tanthof 1.6
2.1 s-Gravenzande
1.5 Naaldwijk
1.3 Pijnacker
2.4 Berkel en Rodenrijs
2.4 Bergschenhoek
Molenlaan 1.5
Schiebroek 1.5
Hillegersberg 1.5
1.5 Binnenhof
1.5 Nesselande
1.5 Ambachtsland
1.5 Hesseplaats
Melanchthonweg 1.2
Bergpolderplein 1.5
Walenburgerweg
1.6 Rotterdam Airport
1.6 Overschie
Blijdorp 1.3
1.4 Rotterdam Noord
Alexander 1.4
1.5 Schollevaar
1.5 Oosterflank
Rotterdam Centraal 0.7
Weena 1.3
Ludokiaplein
Crooswijk 1.5
Kralingen West 1.6
Prinsenland 2.3
Capelsebrug 1.4
Capelle Centrum 1.5
De Terp 1.5
naar Geldermalsen Utrecht
Leerdam 2.0
Gorinchem 2.0
Hardinxveld-Giessendam 2.0
Sliedrecht 2.0
Holy Noord 2.3
Woudhoek 1.5
Holy 1.4
1.4 Spaland
Holy Zuid 2.3
Schiedam 0.8
Nieuwland 1.4
Babberspolder 2.3
Westwijk 2.3
Liesveld 2.3
Vlaardingen Oost 1.5
1.5 Vijfsluizen
Maassluis West 1.5
Hoek van Holland 1.5
Vlaardingen Centrum 1.5
Mathenesserplein 1.4
Vierambachtsstraat 1.4
Delfshaven 1.3
Dijkzigt 1.4
Eendrachtsplein 1.3
Blaak 1.2
0.8
Goudsesingel
Oostplein 1.3
Voorschoterlaan 1.4
Kralingse Zoom 1.4
2.4 Krimpen ad IJssel
2.4 Boveneinde
Marconiplein 1.2
Koemarkt 1.4
Oostkousdijk 1.5
Beurs
Vasteland 1.5
Leuvehaven 1.3
Wilhelminaplein 1.3
Noordereiland 1.6
Woudestein 1.5
1.5 De Esch
Rijnhaven 1.5
1.4
Rotterdam Zuid 1.0
Feijenoord 1.4
IJsselmonde 1.4
Beverwaard 1.4
2.4 Alblasserdam
Oud Charlois 1.5
Dokhaven 1.6
Vuurplaat 1.5
Maashaven
Keizerswaard 1.7
Slikkerveer 1.8
Ridderkerk 1.8
2.7 Papendrecht
Randweg 1.5
1.5
Lombardijen 1.0
Rockanje 2.3
Oostvoorne 2.3
Hoogvliet Centrum 2.3
Brielle 2.3
Hoogvliet 1.4
Zuidplein 1.5
2.4 Pendrecht
Molenvliet
Zwijndrecht Veerplein 2.9
Papendrechtse Veer 1.7
Hendrik Ido Ambacht 2.0
1.9 Dordrecht Centrum
Reeweg Oost 2.0
Slinge 1.5
Spijkenisse 1.3
1.5 Portugaal
Langenhorst 1.5
1.9 Muziekplein
Barendrecht 1.0
Zwijndrecht 1.0
Dordrecht 1.0
1.9 Stadspolders
1.4 De Akkers
Carnisselande 1.5
Sterrenburg 2.0
Hellevoetsluis 2.3
2.3 Maaswijk
Wielwijk 2.0
Crabbehof 2.0
naar Breda Roosendaal

two rather than one primary urban centre, and also with regard to the network structure of these centres. In Den Haag, a lattice-shaped network made up of tram and bus routes covers most of the urbanised area of the core city. The highest performing node on the closeness index is Hollandsche Spoor (HS) station, one of the city's two intercity rail stations, though not the one closest to the CBD. From here, the decay of closeness values towards the city's periphery is roughly diamond-shaped and of greater magnitude than in Amsterdam, likely associated with lower average service frequencies and greater spacing between activity nodes through lower urban density. The one exception from this pattern is the rail trunk line that connects Den Haag with Rotterdam to the south and which has consistently low (good) closeness values at its intermediate stops in Moerwijk, Rijswijk and Delft, as well as influencing activity nodes in their vicinity.

In Rotterdam, the shape of the network is distinct from Den Haag. The lowest (best) closeness results are along the two metro trunk lines (Schiedam to Capelsebrug; Rotterdam Centraal to Slinge) again surrounded by some nearby activity nodes away from the metro lines but within their spatial influence. Beyond this cross-shaped spine, Rotterdam's network displays prominent tree-shaped elements where there is only a small number of orbital or diagonal connections and where radial lines or feeders end in 'cul-de-sacs' at the edge of the area served at the minimum standard: there are 24 such termini in Rotterdam compared to only 12 each in Den Haag and Amsterdam. In such cases, closeness results deteriorate quite rapidly and movement across the network becomes more route-prescriptive. Part of this is an outcome of Rotterdam's geography: the city has developed around Europe's largest seaport – large areas of waterfront land create formidable barriers in the urban structure with only a limited number of crossing points. In addition the post-war reconstruction of Rotterdam's central city saw a decrease in urban density, an enlargement of the urban grain and a 'thinning out' of the surface public transport network (similar to Hamburg and Munich).

Zuid Holland's degree centrality performance trails behind that of any other case study area due to the limited number of activity nodes along the rail spine connecting the key centres (Leiden, Den Haag, Delft, Rotterdam and Dordrecht) and the relative self-containment of the urban networks in each core city. In both Den Haag and Rotterdam, the CBD rail terminals have the lowest average transfer intensity (Rotterdam Centraal also scores best on the closeness centrality index).

Utrecht's distribution of closeness and degree results reveals a 'super-node' at Utrecht Centraal, more prominent than in Amsterdam, and generally sports clusters of better-performing nodes on the closeness index in the south and east of the city than in the north and west. This result may be assisted by the presence of the light rail route in the south and a high-frequency, partially segregated bus corridor in the east. The secondary centre of Amersfoort has a good rail connection to Utrecht, but its internal bus and rail network can only be reached by transfers which drive up the degree centrality results across that city. For a relatively small metropolitan

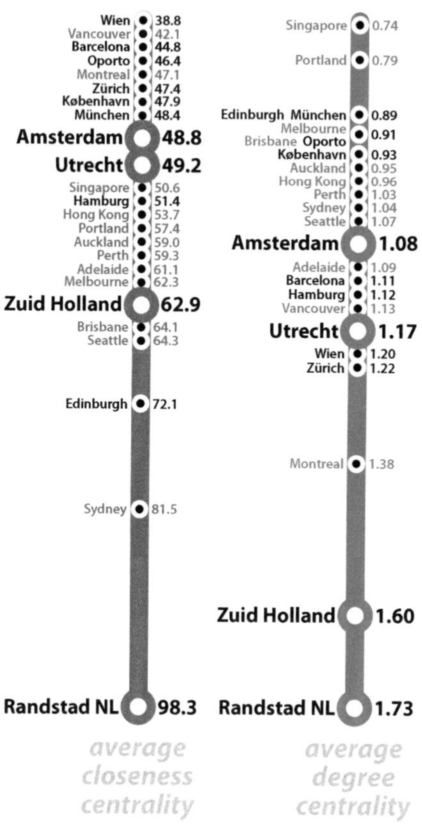

region, it is remarkable that the highest (poorest) closeness result (in Rhenen, accessible from Utrecht by a half-hourly train service) eclipses that of any node in neighbouring Amsterdam.

For the Randstad Holland, average closeness and degree values climb to a higher (poorer) level than in any singular case study city in our sample. In this context, we need to understand the agglomeration as a hybrid between a coherent metropolitan area and a loose collection of component cities that retain a significant degree of functional autonomy. Nevertheless, it is conspicuous that the NS rail network is the key provider of ease of movement at a regional scale, manifest in the lowest (best) closeness and degree centrality values found along its corridors. Den Haag and Utrecht have a small edge over Amsterdam and Rotterdam on the closeness count, while Amsterdam Centraal is the node with the lowest transfer intensity result across the Randstad.

Network Coverage

There is a significant difference in network coverage between the three Randstad sub-regions. Almost four in five residents and employees in metropolitan Amsterdam can find minimum-service public transport in walking distance from their homes and workplaces, a result near the top of the European sample alongside Vienna, Copenhagen, Zurich and Barcelona. In Zuid Holland this figure drops to less than two thirds. In Utrecht it drops further, aligning the smallest Randstad sub-region with the bottom end of the European sample on this index, alongside Edinburgh and Hamburg. On average across the Randstad, public transport at the SNAMUTS standard is provided within walking distance of 65 per cent of all residents and jobs. This finding strongly supports the hypothesis that Amsterdam's higher input of operational resources is manifest in greater network coverage, rather than wasted in less efficient network operation. The comparative figures do not yet explain, however, why Zuid Holland and Utrecht perform so differently on this index despite having a comparable level of overall service intensity. One reason may be Utrecht's greater reliance on buses and their higher average frequency compared to Zuid Holland (see above). The deployment of buses, all other things being equal, arguably has a smaller impact on network coverage than the deployment of rail, metro or tram services due to their typically lower speed, greater number of vehicles required to achieve a similar passenger capacity, and as a longer-term effect, their lower ability to attract or justify land use intensification around their routes.

Contour Catchments

Average 30-minute contour catchments in Amsterdam and Utrecht behave more or less proportionally to network coverage and in a European context, are

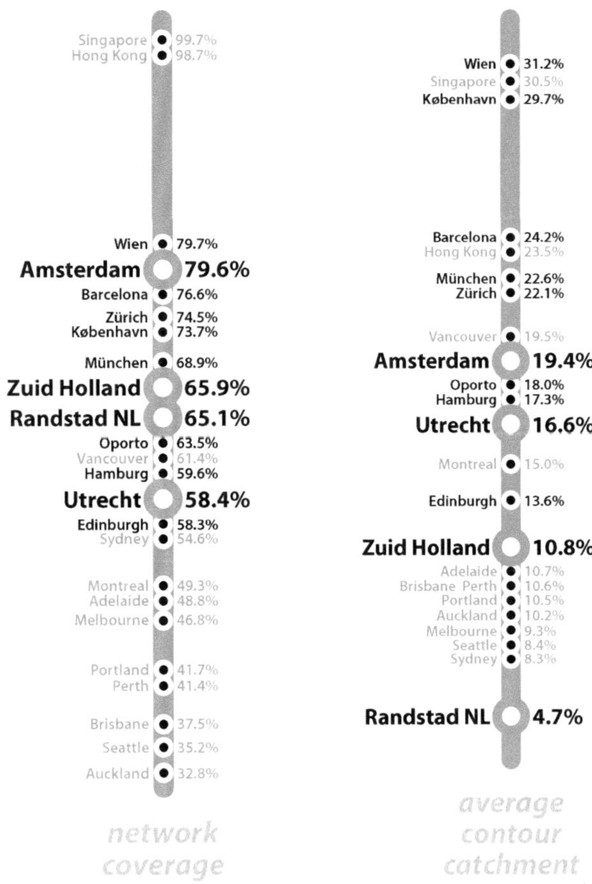

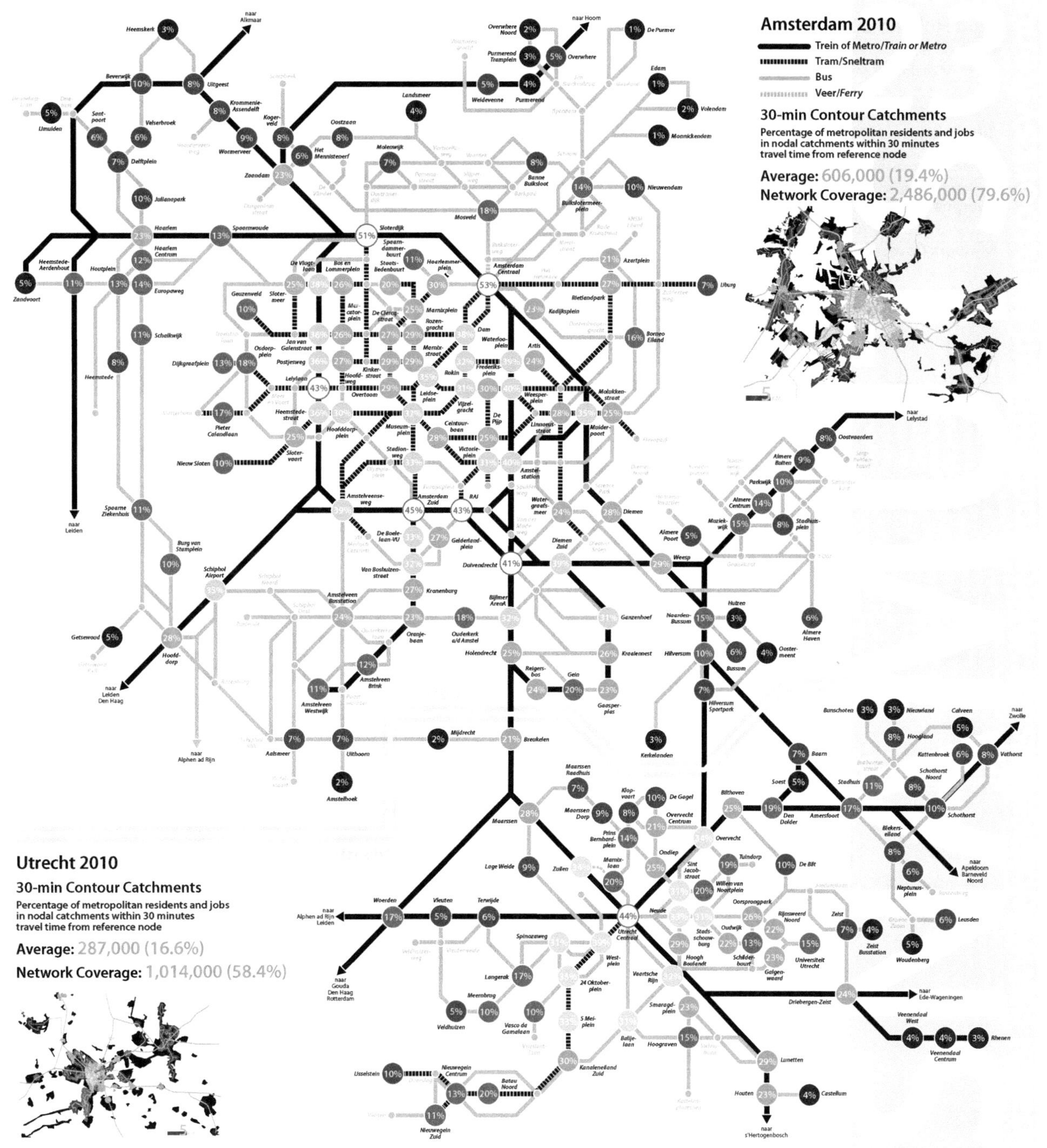
Amsterdam 2010
Trein of Metro/Train or Metro
Tram/Sneltram
Bus
Veer/Ferry
30-min Contour Catchments
Percentage of metropolitan residents and jobs in nodal catchments within 30 minutes travel time from reference node
Average: 606,000 (19.4%)
Network Coverage: 2,486,000 (79.6%)
Utrecht 2010
30-min Contour Catchments
Percentage of metropolitan residents and jobs in nodal catchments within 30 minutes travel time from reference node
Average: 287,000 (16.6%)
Network Coverage: 1,014,000 (58.4%)

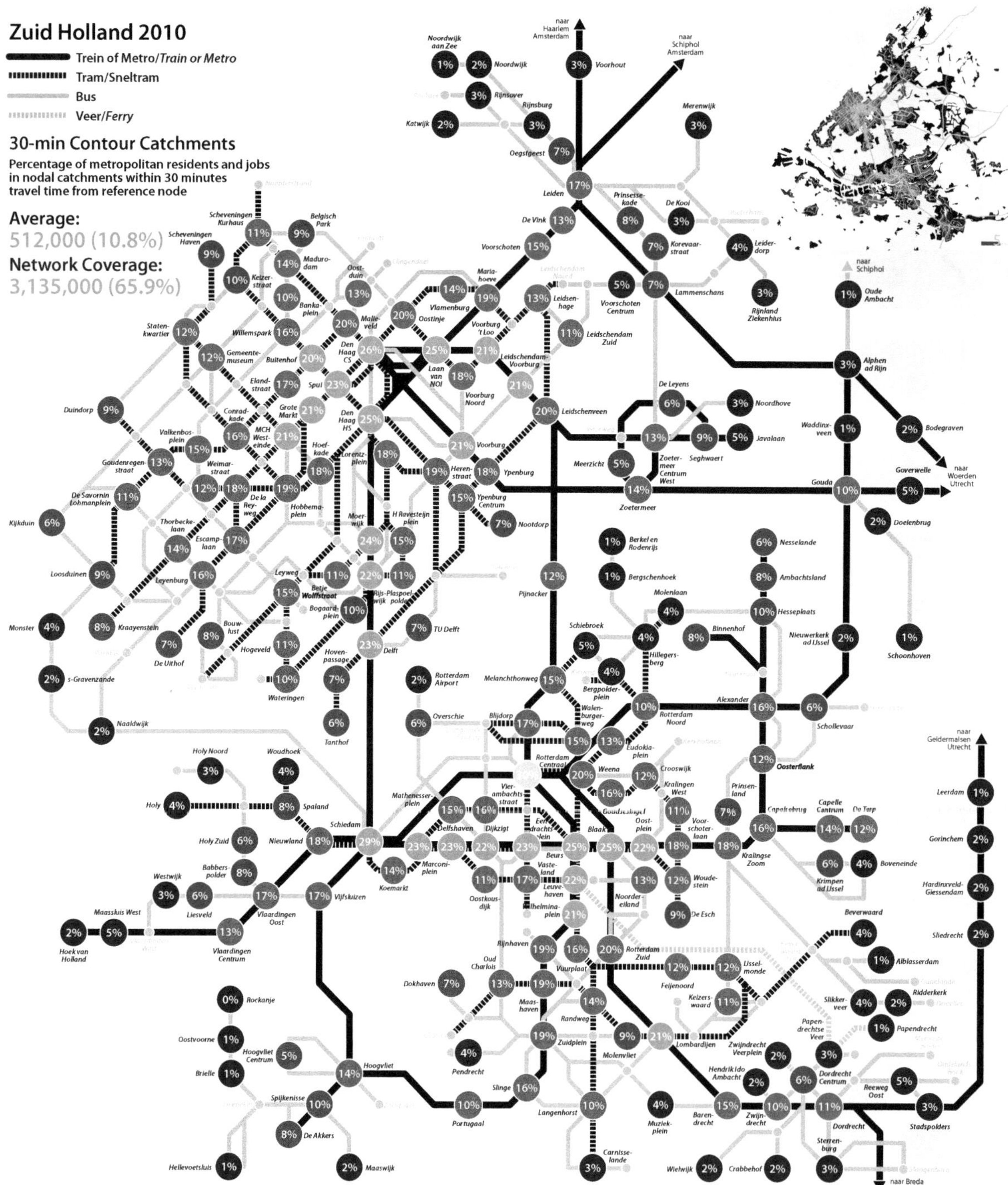

Zuid Holland 2010
Trein of Metro/Train or Metro
Tram/Sneltram
Bus
Veer/Ferry
30-min Contour Catchments
Percentage of metropolitan residents and jobs in nodal catchments within 30 minutes travel time from reference node
Average:
512,000 (10.8%)
Network Coverage:
3,135,000 (65.9%)
naar Haarlem Amsterdam
naar Schiphol Amsterdam
naar Schiphol
naar Woerden Utrecht
naar Geldermalsen Utrecht
naar Breda Roosendaal
Noordwijk aan Zee 1%
Noordwijk 2%
Voorhout 3%
Rijnsover 3%
Katwijk 2%
Rijnsburg 3%
Oegstgeest 7%
Merenwijk 3%
Leiden 17%
Prinsessekade 8%
De Kooi 3%
De Vink 13%
Voorschoten 15%
Korevaarstraat 7%
Leiderdorp 4%
Lammenschans 7%
Rijnland Ziekenhuis 3%
Voorschoten Centrum 5%
Oude Ambacht 1%
Alphen ad Rijn 3%
Waddinxveen 1%
Bodegraven 2%
Goverwelle 5%
Gouda 10%
Doelenbrug 2%
Schoonhoven 1%
Nieuwerkerk ad IJssel 2%
Scheveningen Kurhaus 11%
Belgisch Park 9%
Scheveningen Haven 9%
Madurodam 14%
Keizerstraat 10%
Bankaplein 10%
Oostduin 13%
Statenkwartier 12%
Willemspark 16%
Malieveld 20%
Oostinje 20%
Mariahoeve 19%
Vlamenburg 14%
Leidsenhage 13%
Leidschendam Zuid 11%
Gemeentemuseum 12%
Buitenhof 20%
Den Haag CS 26%
Laan van NOI 25%
Voorburg 't Loo 21%
Leidschendam-Voorburg 21%
Elandstraat 17%
Spui 23%
Voorburg Noord 18%
Grote Markt 21%
Den Haag HS 25%
Leidschenveen 20%
Duindorp 9%
Conradkade 16%
MCH Westeinde 21%
Valkenbosplein 15%
Voorburg 21%
Goudenregenstraat 13%
Weimarstraat 12%
Hoefkade 18%
Lorentzplein 18%
Herenstraat 19%
Ypenburg 18%
De Savornin Lohmanplein 11%
De la Reyweg 18%
Hobbemaplein 19%
Ypenburg Centrum 15%
Nootdorp 7%
Kijkduin 6%
Thorbeckelaan 14%
Escamplaan 17%
Moerwijk 24%
H Ravesteijn plein 15%
Loosduinen 9%
Leyenburg 16%
Leyweg 15%
Betje Wolffstraat 11%
Rijs-Plaspoelpolder 22%
11%
Bogaardplein 10%
Monster 4%
Kraayenstein 8%
De Uithof 7%
Bouwlust 8%
Hogeveld 11%
Hovenpassage 7%
Delft 23%
TU Delft 7%
's-Gravenzande 2%
Wateringen 10%
Tanthof 6%
Naaldwijk 2%
Zoetermeer 14%
Meerzicht 5%
Zoetermeer Centrum West 13%
De Leyens 6%
Seghwaert 9%
Noordhove 3%
Javalaan 5%
Pijnacker 12%
Berkel en Rodenrijs 1%
Bergschenhoek 1%
Nesselande 6%
Ambachtsland 8%
Hesseplaats 10%
Molenlaan 4%
Schiebroek 5%
Hillegersberg 4%
Binnenhof 8%
Melanchthonweg 15%
Bergpolderplein 4%
Rotterdam Airport 2%
Rotterdam Noord 10%
Alexander 16%
Schollevaar 6%
Overschie 6%
Blijdorp 17%
Walenburgerweg 15%
Eudokiaplein 13%
Rotterdam Centraal
Weena 20%
Crooswijk 12%
Oosterflank 12%
Holy Noord 3%
Woudhoek 4%
Holy 4%
Spaland 8%
Holy Zuid 6%
Mathenesserplein 15%
Vierambachtsstraat 16%
Kralingen West 11%
Prinsenland 7%
Capelsebrug 16%
Capelle Centrum 14%
De Terp 12%
Leerdam 1%
Nieuwland 18%
Schiedam 29%
Delfshaven 23%
Dijkzigt 22%
Eendrachtsplein 23%
Beurs 25%
Blaak 25%
Oostplein 22%
Voorschoterlaan 18%
Kralingse Zoom 18%
Gorinchem 2%
Babberspolder 8%
Koemarkt 14%
Marconiplein 23%
Vasteland 17%
Leuvehaven 22%
Noordereiland 13%
Woudestein 12%
Krimpen ad IJssel 6%
Boveneinde 4%
Hardinxveld-Giessendam 2%
Westwijk 3%
Liesveld 6%
Vlaardingen Oost 17%
Vijfsluizen 17%
Oostkousdijk 11%
Wilhelminaplein 21%
De Esch 9%
Sliedrecht 2%
Maassluis West 5%
Hoek van Holland 2%
Vlaardingen Centrum 13%
Rijnhaven 19%
Rotterdam Zuid 20%
Beverwaard 4%
Alblasserdam 1%
Oud Charlois 13%
Dokhaven 7%
16%
Feijenoord 12%
IJsselmonde 12%
Vuurplaat 19%
Rockanje 0%
Maashaven 14%
Keizerswaard 11%
Slikkerveer 4%
Ridderkerk 2%
Papendrecht 1%
Oostvoorne 1%
Hoogvliet Centrum 5%
Randweg 9%
Zuidplein 19%
Lombardijen 21%
Papendrechtse Veer 3%
Zwijndrecht Veerplein 2%
Brielle 1%
Pendrecht 4%
Molenvliet
Hendrik Ido Ambacht 2%
Dordrecht Centrum 6%
Reeweg Oost 5%
Hoogvliet 14%
Slinge 16%
Spijkenisse 10%
De Akkers 8%
Portugaal 10%
Langenhorst 10%
Muziekplein 4%
Barendrecht 15%
Zwijndrecht 10%
Dordrecht 11%
Stadspolders 3%
Sterrenburg 3%
Hellevoetsluis 1%
Maaswijk 2%
Carnisselande 3%
Wielwijk 2%
Crabbehof 2%

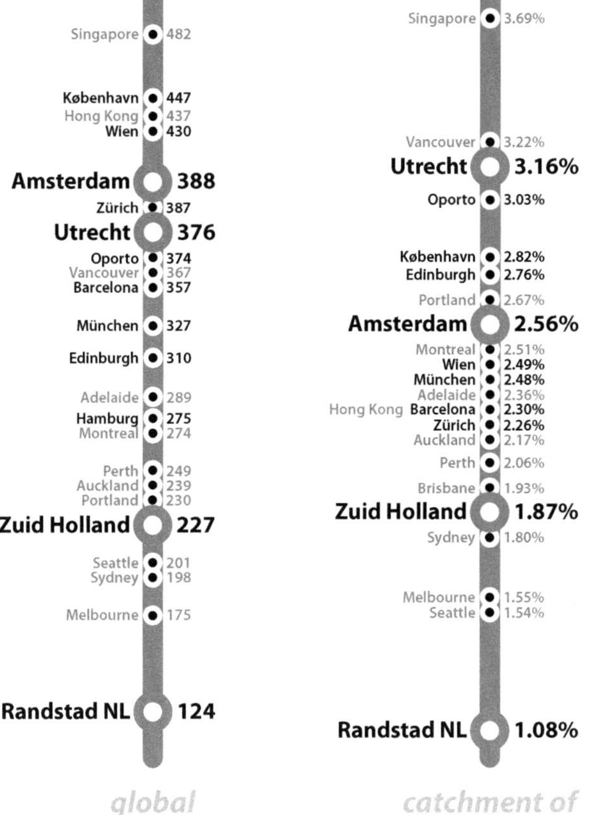

in a performance band with Edinburgh, Hamburg and Oporto while trailing Copenhagen, Vienna, Munich, Zurich and Barcelona. Zuid Holland has the lowest average 30-minute contour catchments in the European sample, a likely result of the agglomeration's polynuclear structure that puts only the principal rail stations of the component cities within reach of each other during the 30-minute window. It should be noted, however, that Zuid Holland still outperforms its size-comparable, more monocentric Australian counterparts (Melbourne and Sydney) on this index.

In Amsterdam, the nodal results again confirm the significance of the orbital rail corridor, with all stations served by both NS rail and metro (Amsterdam Centraal, Sloterdijk, Lelylaan, Amsterdam Zuid, RAI, Duivendrecht) being accessible to and from more than 40 per cent of all metropolitan residents and jobs within 30 minutes. Contour catchment figures drop off significantly for nodes inside the rail ring, reflecting the slower speeds and hence shorter reach of the tram services that dominate this area, yet they mostly remain above 25 per cent. The poorest-performing cluster can be found in the Waterland region north of the core city where none of the nine activity nodes score higher than 5 per cent.

In Zuid Holland, the largest contour catchments are at Rotterdam Centraal, followed by Schiedam, underscoring the critical location of this node as a transfer point for several regional rail and metro corridors, trams and buses. Otherwise, the decay in contour catchment sizes in Rotterdam is predominantly in line with the previously described tree-shaped hierarchy, with the highest values present along rail and metro spines but then dropping off rapidly along tram and bus feeder services. In Den Haag's lattice-shaped network, the familiar diamond shape of value decay is traceable again, though in the (inland) south-east of the city, the prominence of the rail spines is also obvious. Overall, there are many more poorly performing nodes at the periphery of the province as a whole as well as in the spaces between the core cities in Zuid Holland than there are in Amsterdam.

In Utrecht, larger contour catchments are present in the south and east of the central city than in the north and west, facilitated, as with superior closeness performance, by light rail and high-performance bus routes in these areas. Other than along the Veenendaal-Rhenen rail corridor and some nodes at the periphery of Amersfoort, there are very few low performers on this index in this relatively compact agglomeration.

At the Randstad scale, average 30-minute contour catchments drop below 5 per cent, a poorer result by far than any of the 23 singular case study cities and once more illustrating the effect of the spatial segregation of the agglomeration's settlement cores compared to the relative contiguity of most other cities in the sample. The best performers on this index are Amsterdam Centraal and Sloterdijk, accessible to and from more than 15 per cent of all Randstad residents and jobs within 30 minutes. It appears that it is the interplay of regional and urban network integration that maximises these two nodes' contours, compared to their more regionally oriented counterparts such as Schiphol or Amsterdam Zuid, or to nodes in central Amsterdam that are away from the rail network.

Betweenness Centrality

On the global betweenness index relative to population and employment, Amsterdam and Utrecht return a far higher result than Zuid Holland, another expression of the pattern of a greater 'presence' of public transport in Amsterdam already indicated above. But why does Utrecht with its poorer results on other indicators perform as strongly as Amsterdam on this index? A connection may be drawn here with the catchment of typical path length measure, which has Utrecht at the highest level of the three Randstad sub-regions (and the third-highest in the global sample). Since the concentration of land use activities around public transport as a template for urban settlement does not differ much between Utrecht and Zuid Holland, it follows that Utrecht's network is configured to facilitate longer journeys (relative to the size of the network) to a greater extent than its larger neighbouring province whose component cities retain strongly self-contained local networks and whose region-wide rail network, as discussed above, remains limited. Amsterdam achieves a higher catchment of typical path length result than Zuid Holland, partially because of higher activity densities in the core city and partially because the regional rail links are better developed.

For the Randstad as a whole, average results on both measures are below the spectrum of the global sample. In an exacerbation of the trends discussed in the context of Zuid Holland, this is indicative of the relative weakness of region-wide public transport opportunities in comparison to the more evolved local ones in the core cities, and by extension a continuing dominance of functional integration at the individual city scale over the regional scale for public transport accessibility.

The interpretation of betweenness (as well as network resilience) results in the Randstad must distinguish carefully between the findings for each sub-region and those for the agglomeration as a whole. This is because the separate assessment of Amsterdam, Utrecht and Zuid Holland only relates to travel opportunities internal to each region, while discounting for the substantial number of travel opportunities generated between these regions at the scale of the Randstad (such as for journeys between Amsterdam and Utrecht or between Haarlem and Den Haag). The omission of inter-regional trip relations results in a measure of understatement for all betweenness and resilience scores when considered from the perspective of Randstad-wide movement. For this reason, we present both scales in this section and highlight how the results describe different understandings of how the agglomeration functions as a 'daily urban system' (Schwanen et al, 2004).

For travel opportunities within each region, Zuid Holland is the most rail-dominated of the three Randstad cases, with the highest relative share of regional rail (NS), metro/light rail and tram segments for the functioning of the network as a whole. Buses, in contrast, fulfil a comparatively marginal role. In comparison to Amsterdam, it is easy to understand why: there is no equivalent in Zuid Holland to the prominent BRT system in the south and west of Amsterdam (*Zuidtangent*), or to the bus-based radial commuter network in the Waterland area. Even the two largest post-war new towns of both regions differ in the role of rail and bus modes for access: Almere (Amsterdam) has a BRT network around a heavy rail spine, while Zoetermeer (Zuid Holland) is linked to Den Haag as well as internally by a light rail system. In an international context, Zuid Holland's distribution of

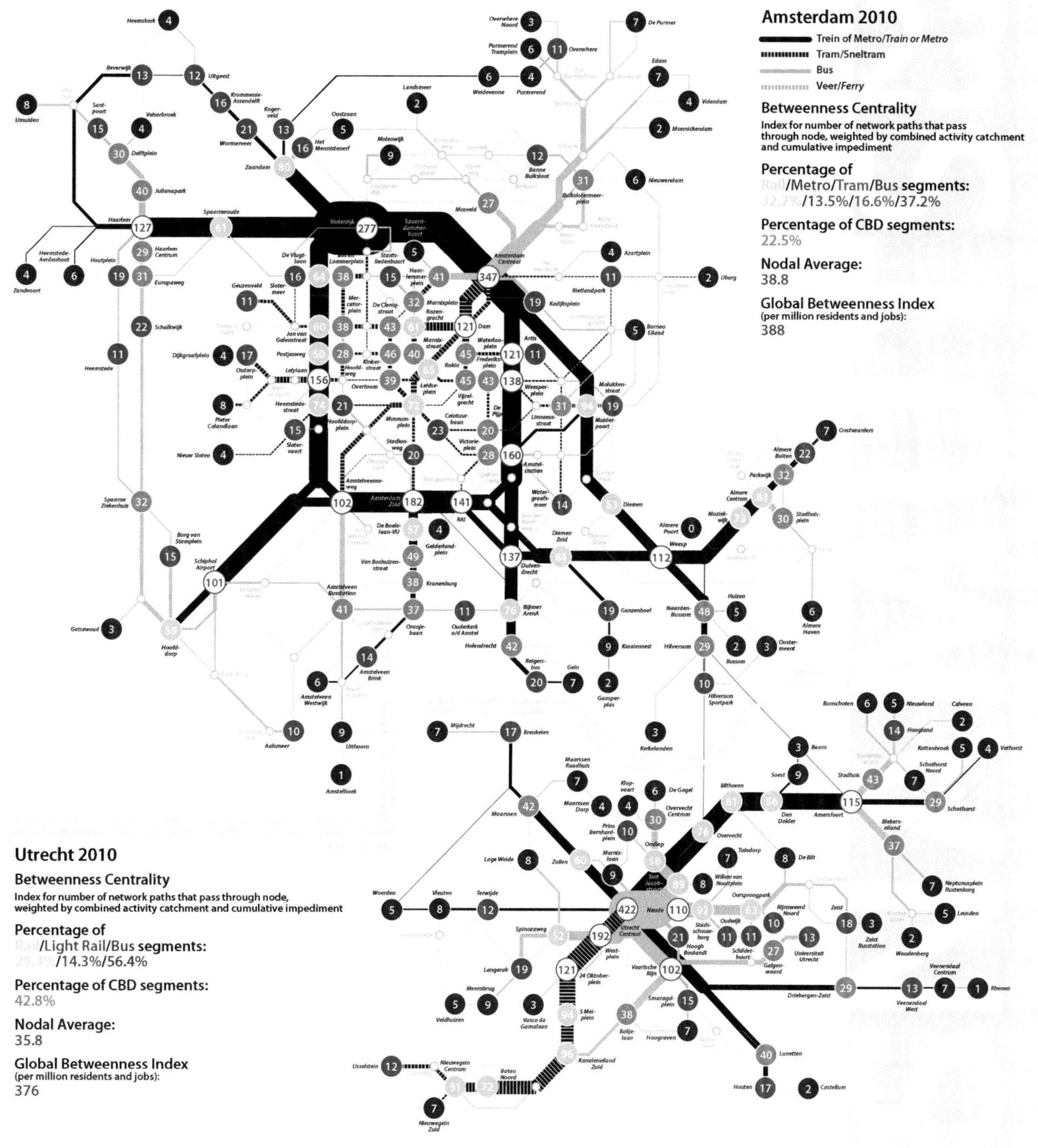

Amsterdam 2010
Trein of Metro/Train or Metro
Tram/Sneltram
Bus
Veer/Ferry
Betweenness Centrality
Index for number of network paths that pass through node, weighted by combined activity catchment and cumulative impediment
Percentage of Rail/Metro/Tram/Bus segments:
32.7%/13.5%/16.6%/37.2%
Percentage of CBD segments:
22.5%
Nodal Average:
38.8
Global Betweenness Index
(per million residents and jobs):
388
Utrecht 2010
Betweenness Centrality
Index for number of network paths that pass through node, weighted by combined activity catchment and cumulative impediment
Percentage of Rail/Light Rail/Bus segments:
29.3%/14.3%/56.4%
Percentage of CBD segments:
42.8%
Nodal Average:
35.8
Global Betweenness Index
(per million residents and jobs):
376

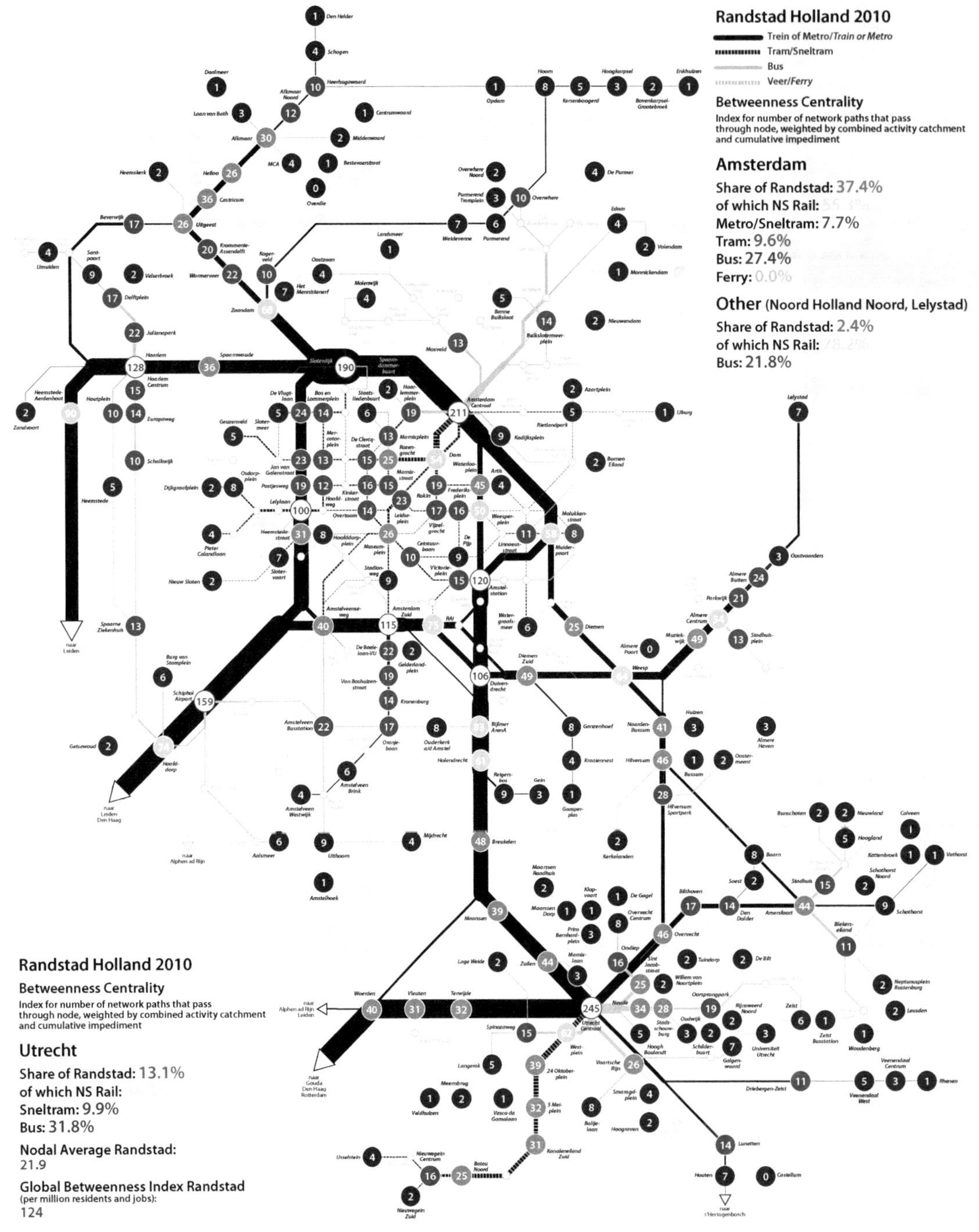

Randstad Holland 2010
Trein of Metro/Train or Metro
Tram/Sneltram
Bus
Veer/Ferry
Betweenness Centrality
Index for number of network paths that pass through node, weighted by combined activity catchment and cumulative impediment
Amsterdam
Share of Randstad: 37.4%
of which NS Rail:
Metro/Sneltram: 7.7%
Tram: 9.6%
Bus: 27.4%
Ferry: 0.0%
Other (Noord Holland Noord, Lelystad)
Share of Randstad: 2.4%
of which NS Rail:
Bus: 21.8%
Randstad Holland 2010
Betweenness Centrality
Index for number of network paths that pass through node, weighted by combined activity catchment and cumulative impediment
Utrecht
Share of Randstad: 13.1%
of which NS Rail:
Sneltram: 9.9%
Bus: 31.8%
Nodal Average Randstad:
21.9
Global Betweenness Index Randstad
(per million residents and jobs):
124

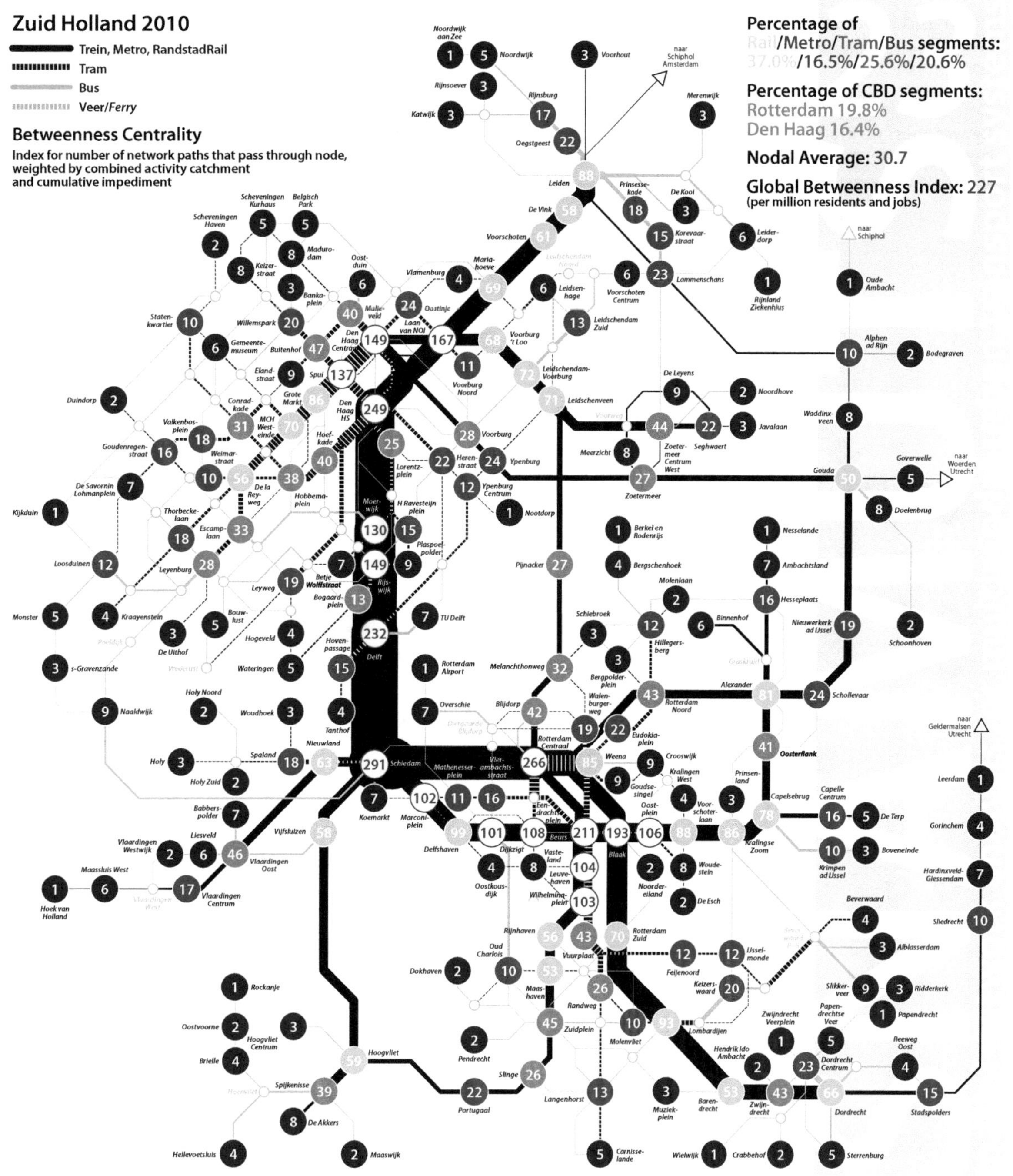

Zuid Holland 2010
Trein, Metro, RandstadRail
Tram
Bus
Veer/Ferry
Betweenness Centrality
Index for number of network paths that pass through node, weighted by combined activity catchment and cumulative impediment
Percentage of Rail/Metro/Tram/Bus segments: 37.0%/16.5%/25.6%/20.6%
Percentage of CBD segments:
Rotterdam 19.8%
Den Haag 16.4%
Nodal Average: 30.7
Global Betweenness Index: 227
(per million residents and jobs)
naar Schiphol Amsterdam
naar Schiphol
naar Woerden Utrecht
naar Geldermalsen Utrecht
Leiden
Den Haag Centraal
Den Haag HS
Delft
Schiedam
Rotterdam Centraal
Blaak
Beurs
Gouda
Alphen ad Rijn
Zoetermeer
Dordrecht

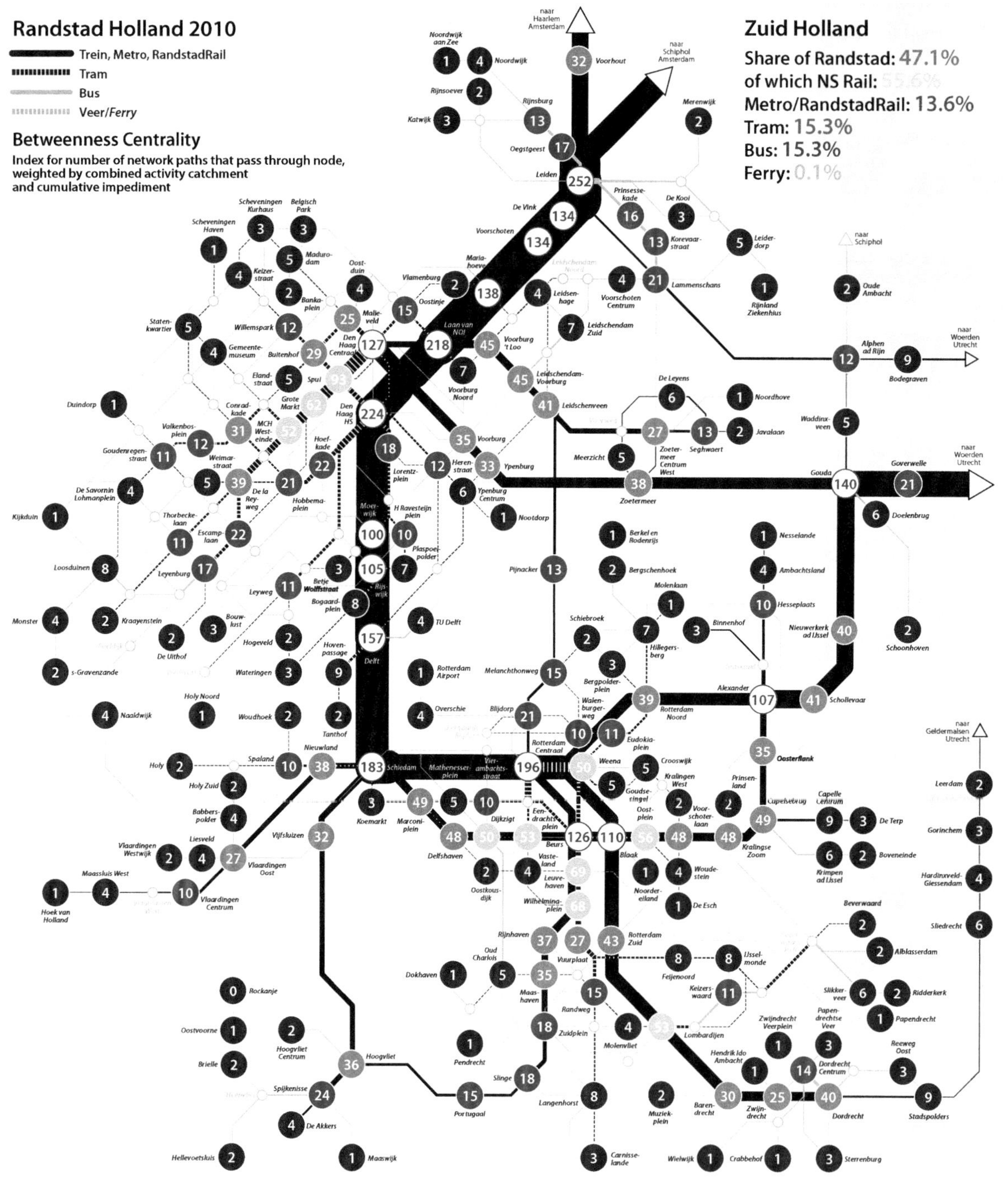

Randstad Holland 2010
Trein, Metro, RandstadRail
Tram
Bus
Veer/Ferry
Betweenness Centrality
Index for number of network paths that pass through node, weighted by combined activity catchment and cumulative impediment
Zuid Holland
Share of Randstad: 47.1%
of which NS Rail: 55.6%
Metro/RandstadRail: 13.6%
Tram: 15.3%
Bus: 15.3%
Ferry: 0.1%
naar Haarlem Amsterdam
naar Schiphol Amsterdam
naar Schiphol
naar Woerden Utrecht
naar Geldermalsen Utrecht
Noordwijk aan Zee
Noordwijk
Voorhout
Rijnsoever
Katwijk
Rijnsburg
Merenwijk
Oegstgeest
Leiden
De Vink
Voorschoten
Prinsessekade
De Kooi
Korevaarstraat
Leiderdorp
Lammenschans
Rijnland Ziekenhuis
Oude Ambacht
Alphen ad Rijn
Bodegraven
Mariahoeve
Vlamenburg
Oostinje
Laan van NOI
Leidsenhage
Voorschoten Centrum
Leidschendam Zuid
Voorburg 't Loo
Voorburg Noord
Leidschendam-Voorburg
Leidschenveen
De Leyens
Noordhove
Javalaan
Seghwaert
Waddinxveen
Meerzicht
Zoetermeer Centrum West
Zoetermeer
Gouda
Goverwelle
Doelenbrug
Voorburg
Ypenburg
Ypenburg Centrum
Herenstraat
Nootdorp
Scheveningen Haven
Scheveningen Kurhaus
Belgisch Park
Madurodam
Keizerstraat
Oostduin
Bankaplein
Statenkwartier
Willemspark
Malieveld
Den Haag Centraal
Gemeentemuseum
Buitenhof
Elandstraat
Spui
Grote Markt
Conradkade
Den Haag HS
Duindorp
Valkenbosplein
MCH Westeinde
Hoefkade
Goudenregenstraat
Weimarstraat
De la Reyweg
Hobbemaplein
De Savornin Lohmanplein
Lorentzplein
Kijkduin
Thorbeckelaan
Escamplaan
Moerwijk
H Ravesteijnplein
Plaspoelpolder
Loosduinen
Leyenburg
Leyweg
Betje Wolffstraat
Rijswijk
Bogaardplein
Monster
Kraayenstein
Bouwlust
TU Delft
De Uithof
Hogeveld
Hovenpassage
Delft
's-Gravenzande
Wateringen
Rotterdam Airport
Holy Noord
Naaldwijk
Woudhoek
Tanthof
Overschie
Holy
Spaland
Nieuwland
Schiedam
Holy Zuid
Babberspolder
Vlaardingen Westwijk
Liesveld
Vijfsluizen
Vlaardingen Oost
Maassluis West
Hoek van Holland
Vlaardingen Centrum
Koemarkt
Marconiplein
Mathenesserplein
Vierambachtsstraat
Delfshaven
Dijkzigt
Eendrachtsplein
Rotterdam Centraal
Blijdorp
Melanchthonweg
Pijnacker
Schiebroek
Berkel en Rodenrijs
Bergschenhoek
Molenlaan
Hillegersberg
Binnenhof
Bergpolderplein
Walenburgerweg
Rotterdam Noord
Alexander
Schollevaar
Nesselande
Ambachtsland
Hesseplaats
Nieuwerkerk ad IJssel
Schoonhoven
Eudokiaplein
Weena
Crooswijk
Kralingen West
Goudsesingel
Oostplein
Voorschoterlaan
Prinsenland
Capelsebrug
Capelle Centrum
De Terp
Oosterflank
Beurs
Blaak
Kralingse Zoom
Krimpen ad IJssel
Boveneinde
Leerdam
Gorinchem
Hardinxveld-Giessendam
Sliedrecht
Oostkousdijk
Vasteland
Leuvehaven
Wilhelminaplein
Woudestein
Noordereiland
De Esch
Rijnhaven
Rotterdam Zuid
Beverwaard
Alblasserdam
Oud Charlois
Dokhaven
Vuurplaat
Maashaven
Feijenoord
IJsselmonde
Keizerswaard
Slikkerveer
Ridderkerk
Papendrecht
Rockanje
Randweg
Zuidplein
Molenvliet
Lombardijen
Zwijndrecht Veerplein
Papendrechtse Veer
Oostvoorne
Hoogvliet Centrum
Pendrecht
Brielle
Hoogvliet
Slinge
Hendrik Ido Ambacht
Dordrecht Centrum
Reeweg Oost
Spijkenisse
Portugaal
Langenhorst
Muziekplein
Barendrecht
Zwijndrecht
Dordrecht
Stadspolders
De Akkers
Hellevoetsluis
Maaswijk
Carnisselande
Wielwijk
Crabbehof
Sterrenburg

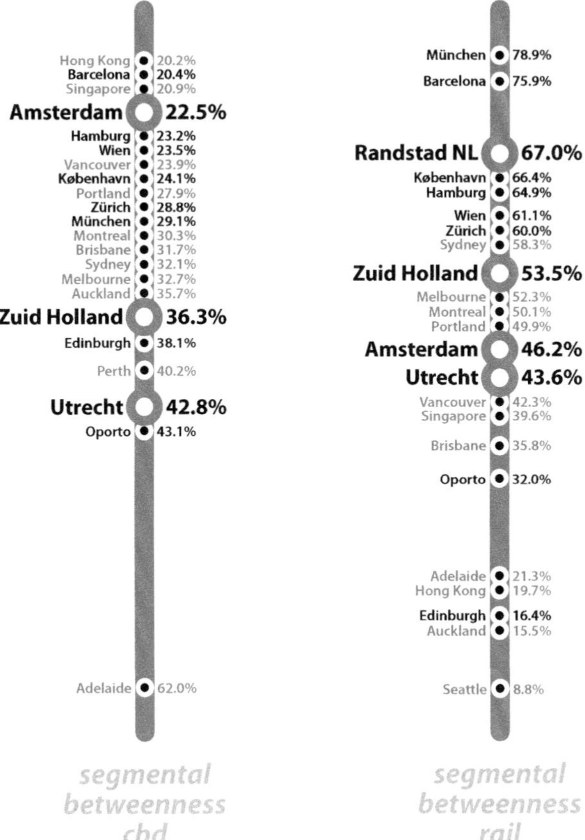

segmental betweenness over heavy rail, trams and buses is similar to that of Melbourne, while Amsterdam's share of bus segments is higher than in tramless Hamburg and Copenhagen. Both northern cities have a much greater role for heavy rail than Amsterdam, largely due to their metro-like S-Bahn/S-Tog operations on or alongside national rail tracks which is of a standard generally not achieved on the NS network in the Dutch Randstad.

In Utrecht, there is a very similar role for the city centre to channel travel opportunities as in Oporto. Utrecht Centraal, however, is prominent for its second highest nodal betweenness score in the Randstad, after Leiden which is situated at the crossroads of travel opportunities linking the metropolitan regions of Amsterdam and Zuid Holland. Amsterdam Centraal, though returning the highest nodal betweenness figure for its host metropolitan region, sits below two nodes in Den Haag on this index. There is a decentralisation effect at play here, with Sloterdijk, Schiphol and to a lesser extent Amsterdam Zuid and Amstel also offering intercity rail connections and taking pressure off the peak node. In Zuid Holland, the city centre stations of Den Haag and Rotterdam (in this order) are closely followed by suburban Schiedam in nodal betweenness terms. This hub, located along the rail line that links the two core cities, also has a prominent role as a rail–metro interchange and serves to connect Rotterdam's inner-city metro spine as well as its south-western suburbs around Hoogvliet and Spijkenisse into a network of regional travel opportunities. The metro link (RandstadRail) between Rotterdam and Den Haag, in contrast, appears to be reduced to a relatively marginal role for the functioning of both the Randstad-wide and the Zuid Holland network. This may have improved since the analysis in 2010 as this line's frequency was boosted from 15 to 10 minutes and a through service to Rotterdam's inner south introduced.

To investigate the position of each component region within the Randstad it is useful to highlight the context between their respective shares of population and employment (relative size of each agglomeration within the Randstad), service intensity (relative input in terms of public transport operation) and segmental betweenness (generation of public transport travel opportunities). In Table 8.1 we find our hypothesis confirmed that Amsterdam's disproportionately high outlay of operational resources results in a concentration of travel opportunities to its component region that is significantly higher than its population and employment share would suggest. Zuid Holland, too, attracts a greater share of travel opportunities than population and employment in relation to the Randstad, albeit at a smaller margin. The 'losers' in accessibility terms appear to be Utrecht and particularly the non-allocated areas in Noord Holland Noord and Lelystad (listed in the table as 'other'), whose proportion of travel opportunities is below that of its share of the Randstad's population. Since a similar ratio is apparent in terms of operational input (service intensity), this suggests that public transport provision and accessibility has a significantly more marginal role in these smaller sub-regions than in the larger agglomerations of Amsterdam and Zuid Holland. While not surprising in a predominantly rural region outside the three major agglomerations, it might indicate some shortfalls in Utrecht (see below).

Table 8.1: Proportions of population and employment, public transport operational input (service intensity) and public transport travel opportunities (segmental betweenness) of four Randstad sub-regions in relation to the entire Randstad

Randstad Sub-Region	Population and Jobs	Service Intensity	Segmental Betweenness
Amsterdam	29.1%	43.1%	37.4%
Utrecht	16.2%	13.5%	13.1%
Zuid Holland	44.4%	40.4%	47.1%
Other	10.1%	2.9%	2.4%

Network Resilience

Like the betweenness index, the network resilience index is strongly affected by the impact of Randstad-wide travel opportunities in addition to the ones internal to the sub-regions, particularly for the NS rail figures as most cross-boundary links occur by this mode. This effect may be felt most significantly in Utrecht, where some of the sub-region's most critical rail links (Amersfoort and Utrecht to Amsterdam, Utrecht to Rotterdam and Den Haag) are omitted from the internal calculation. The sub-regional segmental resilience figures for rail in Utrecht and, to a lesser extent, in Amsterdam and Zuid Holland can thus be expected to be overstated.

Average network resilience levels vary quite strongly between the three sub-regions and this appears to be correlated with findings from earlier indicators. Zuid Holland's average resilience results are poorest, not just within the Randstad but also across the cohort of European case study cities. The centrepiece of Zuid Holland's public transport network, the sole NS rail line connecting Den Haag and Rotterdam via Delft and Schiedam, is one of the rail lines with the lowest level of segmental resilience found within the European sample (only a few stretches of track in Barcelona reach similar levels). The relative underperformance of parallel metro/ RandstadRail line E (discussed above), and the small number of rail corridors available in Zuid Holland, in comparison with similar-sized metropolitan areas elsewhere, may explain this finding. Poor resilience figures in Zuid Holland are also found in the Leiden area, where a bus-based local network connects to the regional rail network in only one dominant location, and on bus routes in some suburban or ex-urban areas of Den Haag and Rotterdam, usually where these act solely as radial feeders to rail, metro or tram services (see Krimpen a/d IJssel, Hellevoetsluis, TU Delft and Ridderkerk – the latter two have tram extensions planned).

In Amsterdam the greatest pressures on the rail network on this index are for the link between Amsterdam and Haarlem. On the bus system the most problematic routes are located on the Haarlem urban network (along the Zuidtangent between Haarlem and Schiphol – in discussion for conversion to light rail in the medium term) and in the Waterland area. In Utrecht the bus system appears to be less affected by resilience shortfalls compared to its larger neighbours. The exception here is the CBD area where many bus routes converge on the dominant multimodal interchange at Utrecht Centraal, resulting in the second poorest CBD resilience figure in the European sample after Hamburg. Utrecht has plans for expanding its light rail network along critical corridors in order to relieve this situation.

In Table 8.2 we have compiled a comparison of network and mode-specific resilience figures for each component city by contrasting the results from our analysis of each sub-region on its own (internal travel opportunities) and for the entire Randstad, adding the travel opportunities generated between the sub-regions. In all cases, network resilience drops, as would be expected, but it does so at different degrees and towards different levels. Across the Randstad, travel opportunities internal to each sub-region generate only one third to one fifth of the potential stress on the NS rail system, highlighting this mode's critical role in facilitating journeys between component cities as well as its comparatively subdued importance for local journeys. In Zuid Holland, the aforementioned relative scarcity of rail infrastructure produces a rail resilience figure of concern. Conversely, the urban rail modes (metro and tram) in Amsterdam and Zuid Holland accommodate only a modest number of additional travel opportunities when the Randstad-wide perspective is considered alongside the internal one and retain the best average mode-specific resilience results across the agglomeration. The same is not true for Utrecht's Sneltram or for buses in Amsterdam and Utrecht. A possible explanation for this finding is that the urban network of Utrecht, as well as those of some smaller centres in neighbouring sub-regions (Leiden, Haarlem or the Waterland corridor north of Amsterdam) retains a predominantly radial, tree-shaped structure towards the major rail–bus interchange. This pattern struggles to allow for a spatial distribution of pressures from the flow of travel opportunities and in turn deteriorates the network resilience results. It also places greater emphasis on the role of these routes as feeders to the regional network relative to other, more local accessibility functions. In this regard, the lattice or web-shaped urban networks in Den Haag and Amsterdam can be considered as more robust, providing for a greater choice of journey paths than their more prescriptive counterparts in Utrecht and the smaller centres.

Table 8.2: Comparison of sub-regional and mode-specific average network resilience results considering internal travel opportunities only, and internal and Randstad-wide travel opportunities in conjunction

Randstad Holland	Mode	Internal Travel Opportunities	Internal and Randstad-wide Travel Opportunities
Amsterdam	**Total**	**+13.1**	**–0.3**
	Rail	+15.0	–19.4
	Metro/Sneltram	+14.1	+9.1
	Tram	+18.1	+13.9
	Bus/BRT	+11.0	–4.2
Utrecht	**Total**	**+11.0**	**–6.2**
	Rail	+20.3	–15.7
	Sneltram	+8.6	–14.4
	Bus	+10.0	–3.6
Zuid Holland	**Total**	**+6.3**	**–3.9**
	Rail	+2.4	–46.5
	Metro/RandstadRail	+5.4	+1.7
	Tram	+11.8	+7.6
	Bus	+3.1	–5.2

Can the Randstad's network resilience results, the poorest across the SNAMUTS sample on average, be interpreted as a severe level of accessibility crisis? Ambiguity over such an interpretation could derive from the notion that we only examine the *potential* for trip-making here, not *actual* trip-making with its concomitant instances of overcrowding were network resilience results to translate into occupancy rates in a linear fashion. In the real world, however, Randstad residents and employees may simply not travel to the same magnitude as the accessibility analysis suggests they could. There is a methodological caveat here, as well as a functional one. The configuration of the SNAMUTS tool calculates travel impediment and hence allocates travel opportunities for this index based solely on travel time and service frequency while disregarding other factors that could influence travel behaviour, including monetary cost. There are two different fare systems governing public transport in the Randstad, even though they can be paid for with the same card. As a result, a half-hour journey on NS rail will generally attract a far higher fare than a half-hour journey on urban public transport. The ticketing system thus includes a potent disincentive

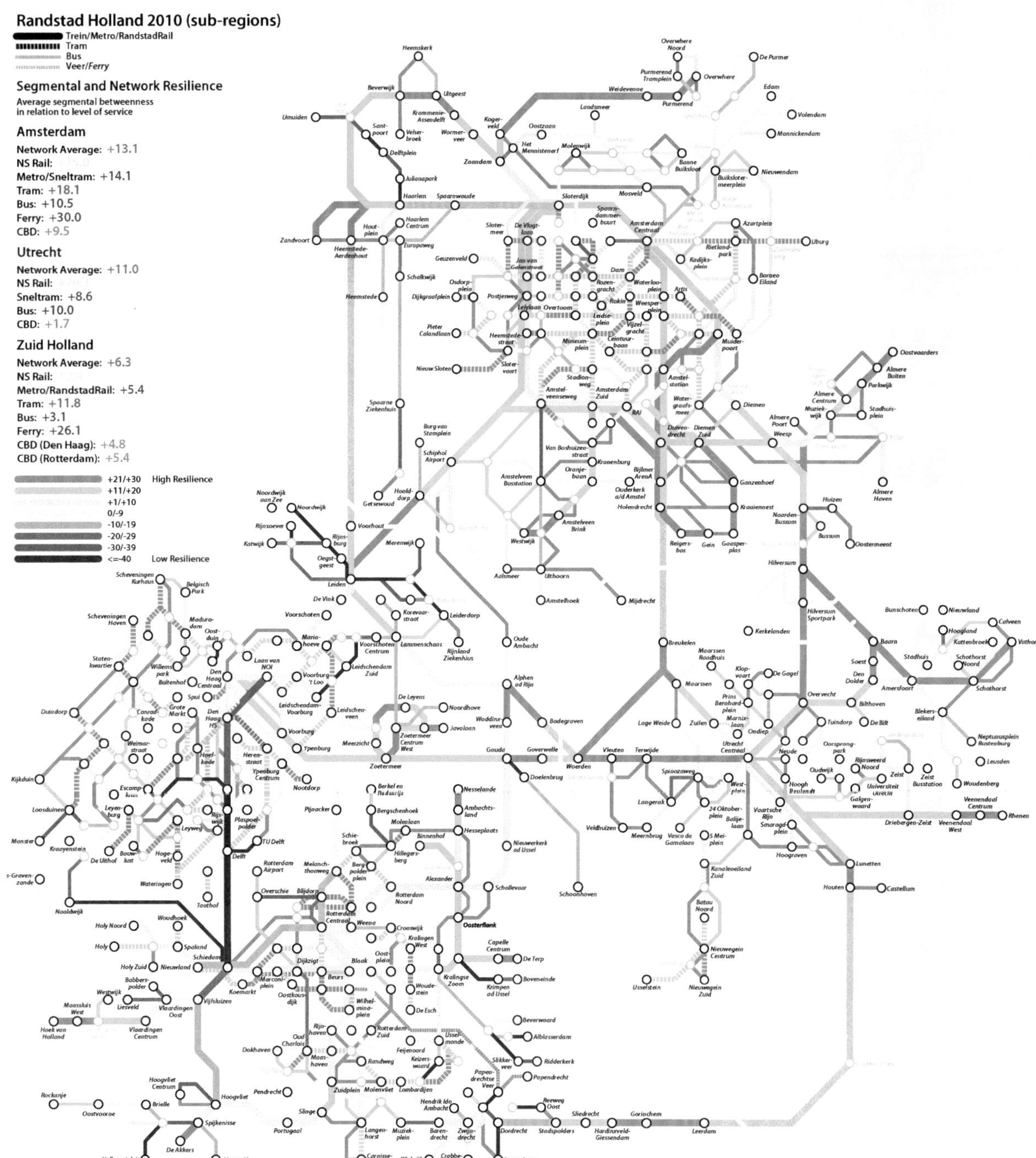

Randstad Holland 2010 (sub-regions)
Trein/Metro/RandstadRail
Tram
Bus
Veer/Ferry
Segmental and Network Resilience
Average segmental betweenness in relation to level of service
Amsterdam
Network Average: +13.1
NS Rail:
Metro/Sneltram: +14.1
Tram: +18.1
Bus: +10.5
Ferry: +30.0
CBD: +9.5
Utrecht
Network Average: +11.0
NS Rail:
Sneltram: +8.6
Bus: +10.0
CBD: +1.7
Zuid Holland
Network Average: +6.3
NS Rail:
Metro/RandstadRail: +5.4
Tram: +11.8
Bus: +3.1
Ferry: +26.1
CBD (Den Haag): +4.8
CBD (Rotterdam): +5.4
+21/+30 High Resilience
+11/+20
+1/+10
0/-9
-10/-19
-20/-29
-30/-39
<=-40 Low Resilience

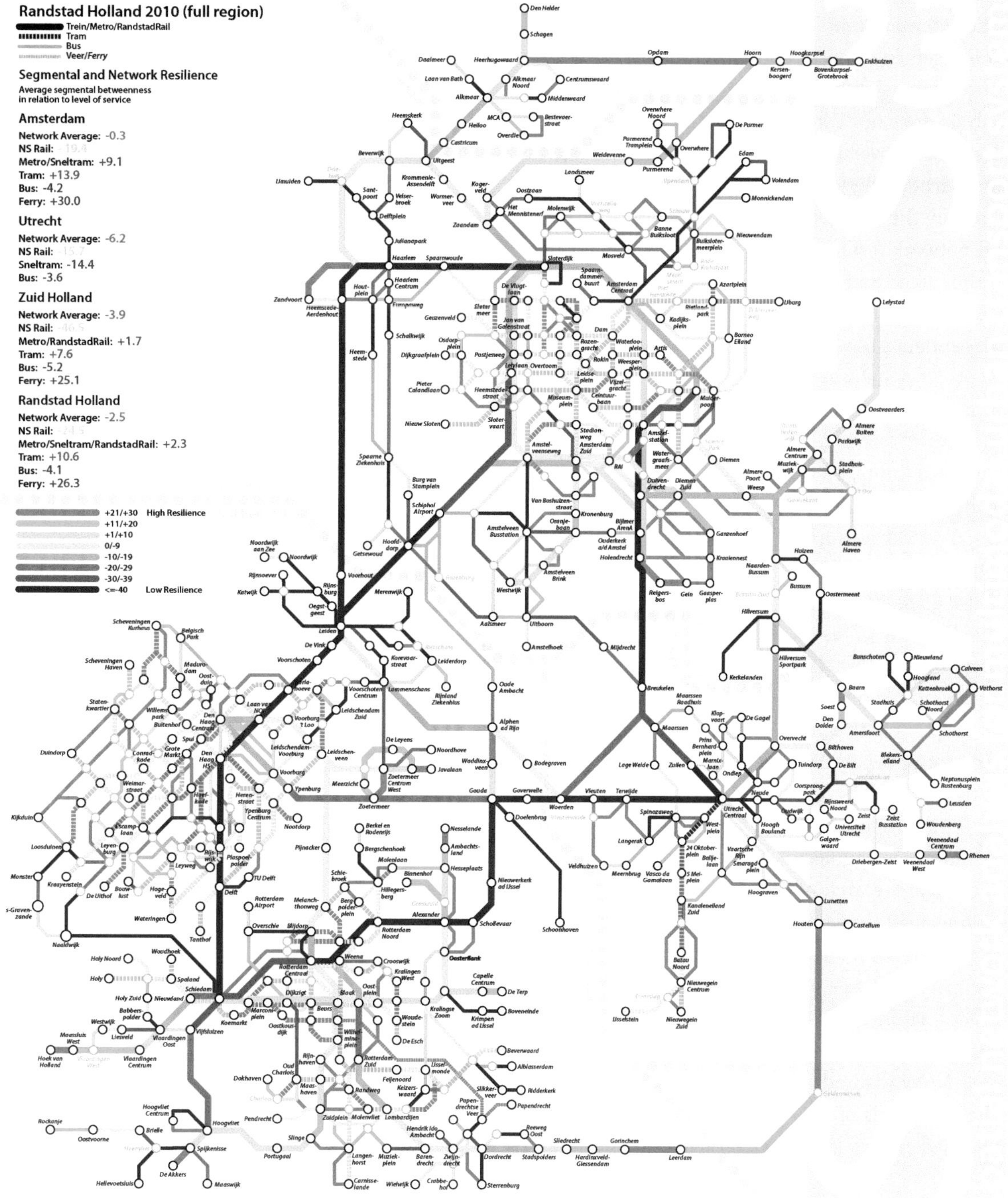

Randstad Holland 2010 (full region)
Trein/Metro/RandstadRail
Tram
Bus
Veer/Ferry
Segmental and Network Resilience
Average segmental betweenness
in relation to level of service
Amsterdam
Network Average: -0.3
NS Rail: -19.4
Metro/Sneltram: +9.1
Tram: +13.9
Bus: -4.2
Ferry: +30.0
Utrecht
Network Average: -6.2
NS Rail: -15.7
Sneltram: -14.4
Bus: -3.6
Zuid Holland
Network Average: -3.9
NS Rail: -46.5
Metro/RandstadRail: +1.7
Tram: +7.6
Bus: -5.2
Ferry: +25.1
Randstad Holland
Network Average: -2.5
NS Rail: -24.5
Metro/Sneltram/RandstadRail: +2.3
Tram: +10.6
Bus: -4.1
Ferry: +26.3
+21/+30 High Resilience
+11/+20
+1/+10
0/-9
-10/-19
-20/-29
-30/-39
<=-40 Low Resilience

against journeys between Randstad component cities when viewed from the perspective of fixed budgets in terms of either travel time or financial means. The SNAMUTS analysis does not cater for this effect and so likely overstates the significance of journeys between Randstad sub-regions in the segmental betweenness and network resilience indexes. Further, the Randstad has unique patterns of urbanisation as well as functional interdependence between its various components. It is helpful to consider this region as a hybrid between a coherent large city and a network of smaller, autonomous urban units, a status also confirmed by a large body of empirical research on travel patterns and business relations (Limtanakool et al, 2009; Van Oort et al, 2010). In consequence, the inclination of users to organise their activities within the confines of a component region may be lower than in a group of cities characterised by greater spatial separation and less developed transport links, but it also likely remains far higher than in a similar-sized, more contiguously urbanised city with a single overarching centre. These phenomena are fluid and subject to future change, for which reason accessibility exercises that assume varying levels of functional integration are useful for assessing trends and possible future pressures. Notwithstanding this, we concede that the levels of network resilience identified in this index are unlikely to be an accurate representation of the circumstances that prevail in the Randstad in the 2010s.

Nodal Connectivity

Individual results for the nodal connectivity index do not change with the size of the network segment under investigation; the maps for the Randstad sub-regions thus assemble neatly into an agglomeration-wide picture. Increasing network complexity, more likely to be found in larger centres, will drive up the total as well as average results, so it is unsurprising that Utrecht, the smallest of the three sub-regions, has the lowest average nodal connectivity score (though the total is all but identical to similar-sized Oporto). Between Amsterdam and Zuid Holland, however, average nodal connectivity performance is contrary to agglomeration size: Amsterdam once again benefits from its higher average levels of service and the greater presence of heavy rail infrastructure relative to population compared to Zuid Holland.

Among individual nodes, Amsterdam Centraal has the highest nodal connectivity score in the Randstad, owing to its role as the principal hub both for the national rail system and the urban tram system. Utrecht Centraal, the southern agglomeration's 'super-node' occupies second place before Zuid Holland's Rotterdam Centraal, Rotterdam Beurs and Den Haag Centraal.

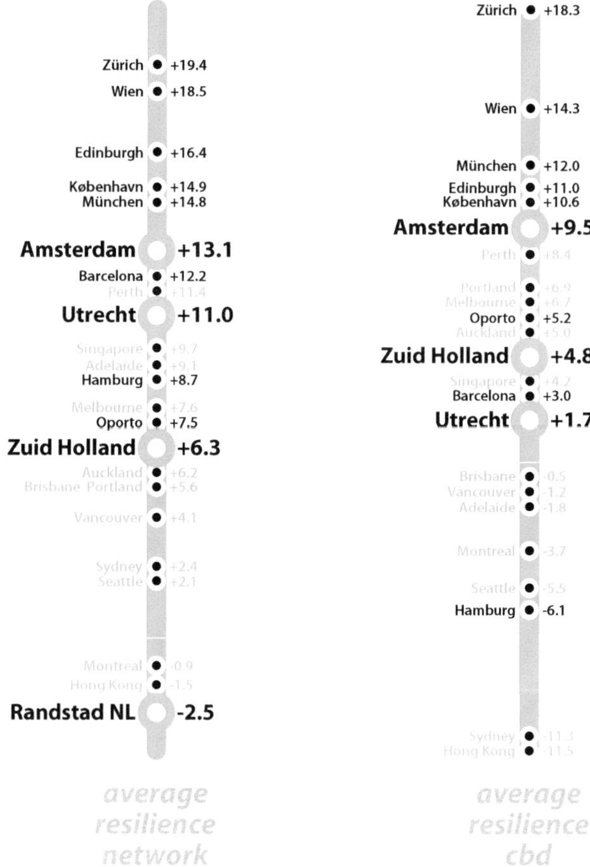

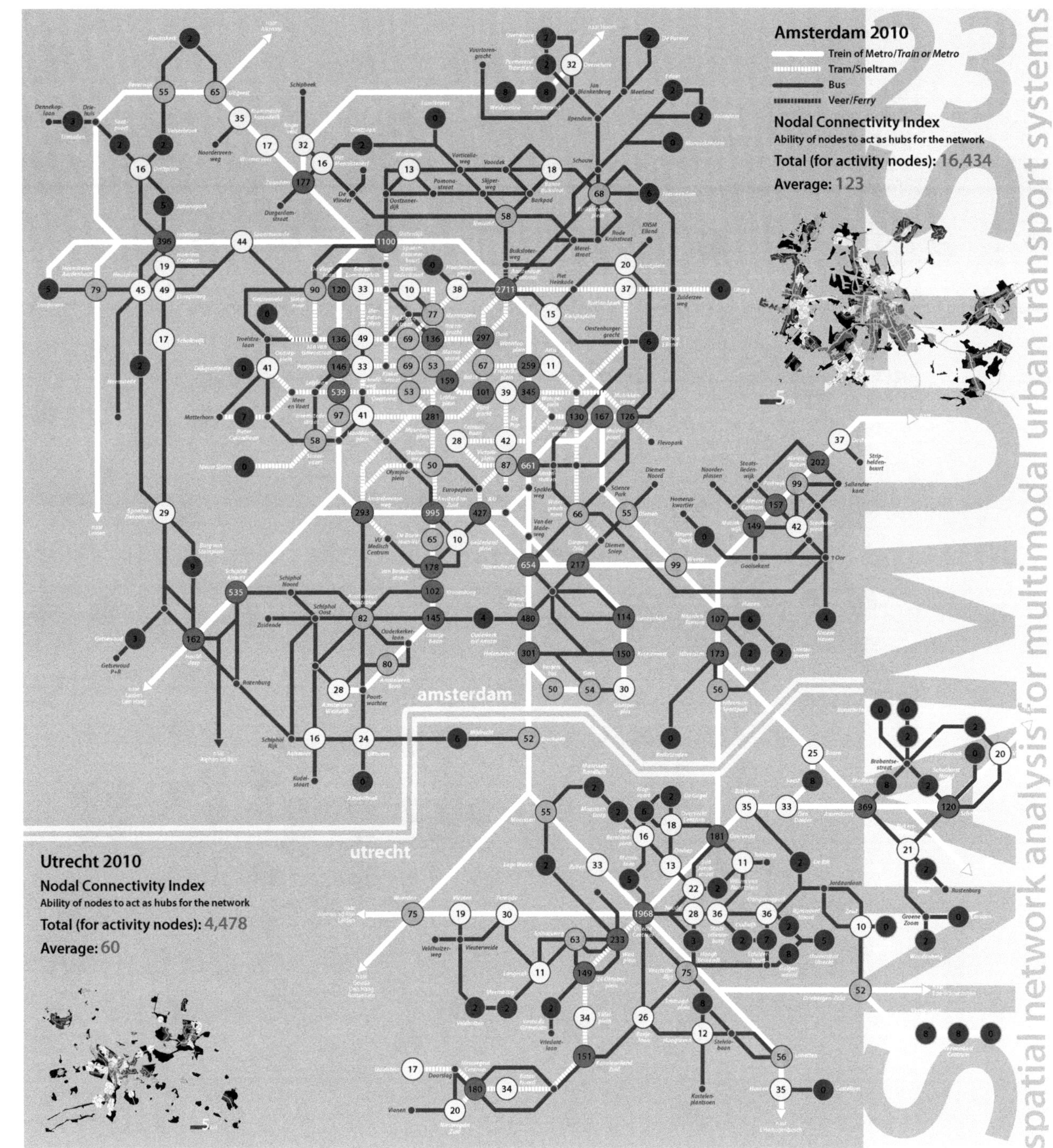

City	Average nodal connectivity
Hong Kong	868
Singapore	751
Barcelona	305
Wien	193
München	176
Hamburg	166
Amsterdam	**123**
Randstad NL	**90**
København	88
Vancouver	87
Zuid Holland	**86**
Zürich	83
Melbourne	82
Sydney	77
Utrecht	**60**
Montreal	52
Oporto	47
Brisbane	42
Edinburgh	31
Seattle Portland	26
Perth	19
Auckland	13
Adelaide	12

average nodal connectivity

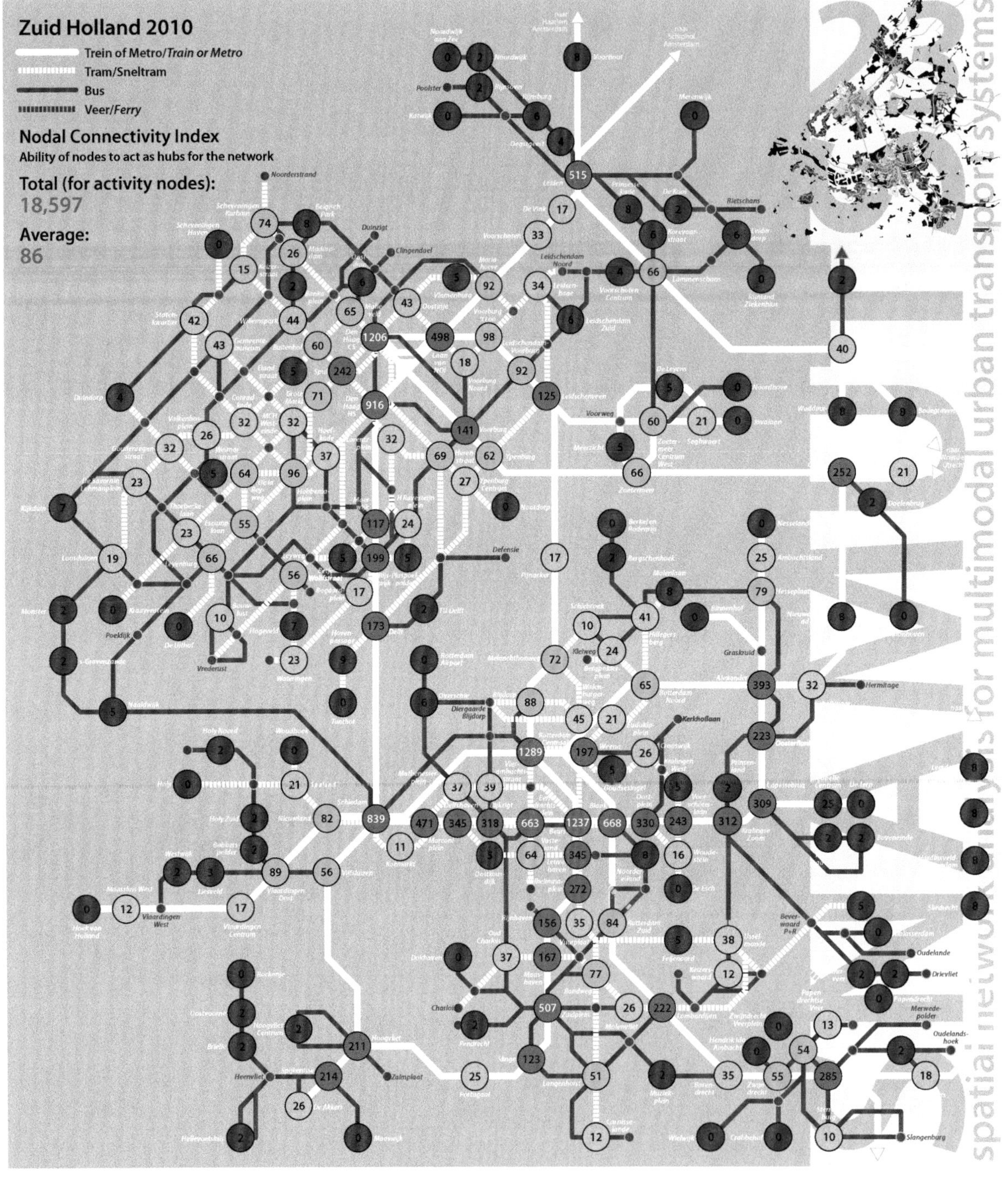
Zuid Holland 2010
Trein of Metro/Train or Metro
Tram/Sneltram
Bus
Veer/Ferry
Nodal Connectivity Index
Ability of nodes to act as hubs for the network
Total (for activity nodes):
18,597
Average:
86
spatial network analysis for multimodal urban transport systems

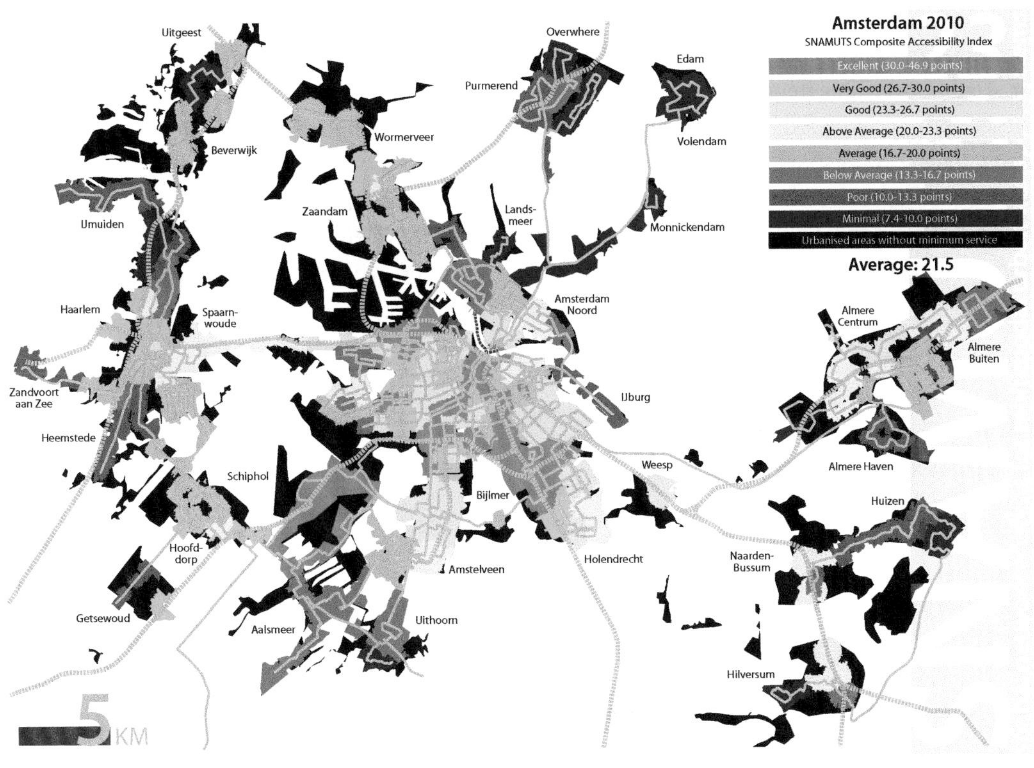

SNAMUTS Composite Accessibility Index and Reflections

Greater service intensity, geographical coverage and a multi-directional surface network structure in the core city can be regarded as the key influences that elevate Amsterdam's average performance on the composite index beyond that of its neighbours in Utrecht and Zuid Holland. In all three subregions, the best accessibility results are achieved at the interchanges between regional rail and urban public transport modes. This confirms the relevance of contemporary policy regimes seeking to strengthen such multimodal hubs, intensify the surrounding land use and improve their urban amenity. However, only in Amsterdam (and to a lesser extent, the east–west metro trunk line in Rotterdam) does a similar accessibility standard extend to sizeable parts of the core city away from such regional rail stations. Across the Randstad, despite a usually quite clear demarcation between urbanised and non-urbanised land, there are numerous centres at the peripheries of settlement areas where public transport accessibility is below average or poor. This concerns the 1960/70s new towns (Purmerend, Almere or Zoetermeer) and many of the later VINEX neighbourhoods (Nieuw Sloten or IJburg in Amsterdam; Leidsche Rijn or IJsselstein in Utrecht; Wateringen or Ypenburg in Den Haag; Nesselande or Carnisselande in Rotterdam) and illustrates the shortfalls (discussed above) associated with both spatial policy eras in reducing car dependence and devising a strong role for public transport in the mobility mix of Randstad users.

Amsterdam's performance in this accessibility analysis stands out from its neighbours, but there remains room for improvement. The city's extensive role for buses in the modal mix, despite also having a mature tram network and some metro lines, is traceable along several conspicuous network elements. There is the highly efficient and well-suited BRT system catering for local movement and accessibility within the new town of Almere. There is another BRT system in the south and west of the core city, which is likely to be closer to its inherent capacity limits and may require upgrades to light rail in the future. The Waterland radial commuter bus network north of the core city is plying a corridor that would be better suited to a high frequency rail spine in both efficiency and accessibility terms. The north–south metro line currently under construction will only partially fulfil this role, given that its northern terminus lies within Amsterdam's city limits rather than at Purmerend.

Elsewhere in the Randstad, there are numerous missing links, or links only served by half-hourly bus routes that do not meet the standard for inclusion in our analysis – the standard reasonably expected by users who wish to rely on them to facilitate their everyday activities. In Zuid Holland, for instance, there are no full-time, medium or high-frequency direct links between Rotterdam and Zoetermeer or between Gouda and Dordrecht. Further east the same is true for the centres of Almere and Amersfoort. Utrecht's Sneltram corridor ends in Nieuwegein and IJsselstein without offering minimum-standard connections from there into other directions. At a smaller scale a similar pattern can be observed in many locations around the edge of Rotterdam's settlement area. In an international context, the Randstad's endowment with high-capacity public transport infrastructure, particularly heavy rail lines and stations with frequent service, remains comparatively sparse in relation to population size. While the NS regional rail network is generally of a high engineering standard and with ongoing upgrades, is arguably beset with less severe capacity constraints than its counterparts in Sydney, Melbourne, Munich or Barcelona, it is clear that historically, it evolved primarily as an intercity system. There is no equivalent in the Randstad to the dedicated suburban rail lines that facilitated transit-oriented peripheral growth in cities such as Copenhagen or Hamburg and now (at 5- or 10-minute daytime frequencies) generate exceptional standards of accessibility along their corridors. Instead, numerous smaller rail stations in the Randstad have trains stopping only half-hourly, as non-stop intercity services are prioritised.

Of interest to urban planners is whether the trend of many metropolitan regions to develop a more polycentric structure is a beneficial influence when it comes to serving daily activity needs by public transport. This is not an easy question to answer post-analysis, particularly given the changing roles of networks in the Randstad region, where new or modified public transport modes such as hybrid heavy and light rail (e.g. the RandstadRail project in Zuid Holland) or Bus Rapid Transit (the Zuidtangent in Amsterdam) have emerged in recent years. In addition, there is a growing focus on developing TOD around public transport infrastructures. From our analysis, however, it appears that the Randstad land use–transport system shows various layers of maturity at present. Dense, multi-directional surface networks are present in Amsterdam and

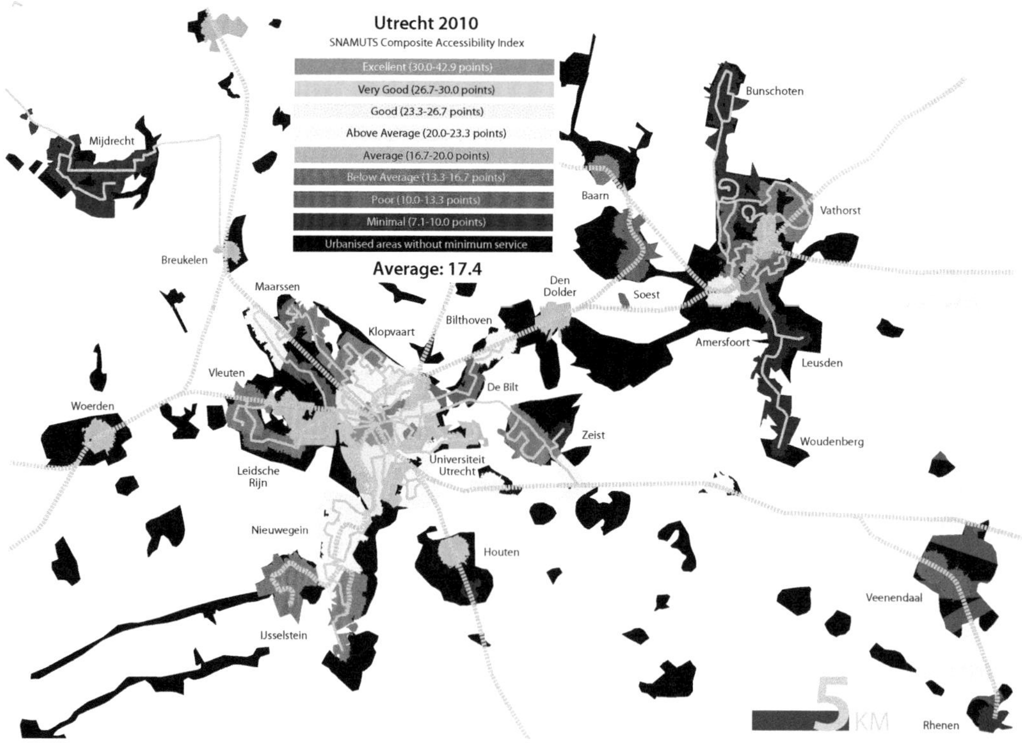

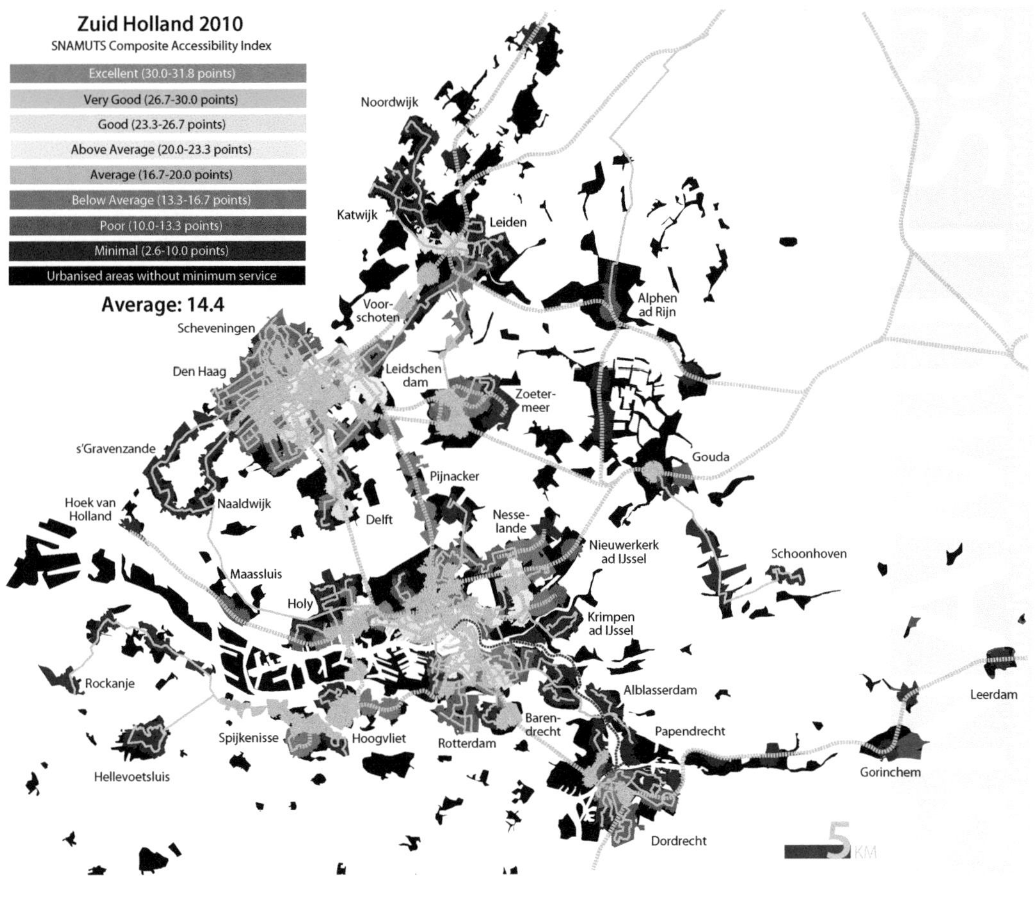

to a lesser extent Den Haag, perhaps also supported by the high number of tourists and other outside visitors there. In Rotterdam, Utrecht and the smaller cities, public transport networks are patchier, and their performance is compromised both 'within city' (due to poor service and/or connectivity) or 'within region' (due to the ring-shaped settlement structure which creates many more peripheral locations than a monocentric, contiguous one).

Are the Randstad's public transport networks a sufficient organising principle for the future of transport and land use integration in the region? Following the experience of a failing ABC location policy in the 1990s and early 2000s, Van der Burg and Dieleman (2004) respond in the negative. They point to the dominant role of the private car in providing mobility across the Netherlands. However, during the decade since, it has become clearer that the dichotomy of public transport versus car does not need to be regarded in competition. Instead, it can be viewed as an opportunity to work towards intelligent solutions of task-sharing and mutual support between these modes, and for walking and cycling and the growing range of hybrid forms of transport that do not neatly fit the traditional categories of collective and individual, such as shared cars and bicycles, online ride-sharing or user-responsive public transport services. This type of thinking around multimodal accessibility, rather than single-mode market shares, can be understood as the most significant contribution to global practice in integrated transport and land use planning to emerge from the Randstad and its unique interplay of settlement patterns and transport networks.

9 Conclusion

Accessibility and Best-Practice Land Use–Transport Integration

At the outset of this book we highlighted the lack of strategic overview of public transport accessibility at the city or metropolitan level. We noted that this left a challenge for planners concerned with planning for better integration of land use development and public transport as cities embraced the goal of sustainable mobility. We have demonstrated in the preceding chapters how the new generation accessibility tools can assist in addressing this gap.

In our analysis of selected cities across four continents we have shown how it is possible to measure accessibility from a number of perspectives. The perspective, of course, will depend upon your policy question (below). At the base of any policy question, however, the analysis of accessibility should occur from the perspective of the individual traveller. This requires that both the transport network and its relationship to land use are measured if a person's daily activity needs are to be served by public transport. With the SNAMUTS indicators we are able to measure, separately, specific aspects of the public transport network, such as journey speed, service frequencies, transfers between services and the service input (number of public transport vehicles in simultaneous service). We are also able to measure the land use dimension, considering the extent to which residents and employees are served by the transport system within the context of urban places and urban structure.

The SNAMUTS accessibility indicators link to a range of policy questions that planners and community members may ask. Closeness centrality is the indicator that responds to the question – 'how quickly (on average) can I navigate my city by public transport'? – taking into account both the speed of the journey (as travel time) and the ease of the journey (as frequency of services). Degree centrality enables interrogation of – 'how many transfers (on average) do I have to make in order to access my city' – taking into account the legibility of the network (its hierarchy) and the convenience. Other indicators respond to such questions as 'who gets access to public transport' – measured both for the proportion of inhabitants in the city as a whole and also in relation to each activity centre; 'does public transport provide a viable alternative to the car'; 'what opportunities are there for land use development' – taking into account the extent of public transport accessibility and the extent of development informed by the 'balanced/unbalanced node' concept; and importantly for the future – 'where might the public transport system become constrained' – taking into account the supply of service across the network relative to capacity.

We have demonstrated how it is possible to compare accessibility *within* a city and also *between* cities. In this way there is a clear strategic overview. The SNAMUTS tool provides a powerful visualisation of the city for each indicator. In this way planners, and the wider community, are able to view their city it its entirety and to quickly see where there are accessibility shortfalls and where good transport accessibility could be capitalised on with more intensive urban development. This is what Bertolini (2005) highlights when he refers to unbalanced nodes and places – the ideal would be to balance these, and while Bertolini asserts that there is an inherent tendency that place and node functions will evolve towards equilibrium, it is our view that planners can and should intervene to accelerate this process and capitalise on locations with good public transport accessibility by facilitating supportive land use activity and vice versa. Town planners can interrogate the outputs of accessibility tools to consider how to optimise future development within the urban structure so that residents and employees can have public transport accessibility that is competitive to the car in terms of spatial reach and convenience. Public transport planners can interrogate the outputs to consider how to optimise the network and service. Where town planners and transport planners collaborate it is possible to weigh both dimensions and consider how best to integrate land use and transport for future development and investment decisions.

The SNAMUTS tool can be used (and has been – see Curtis and Scheurer, 2010; Curtis et al, 2013; te Brömmelstroet et al, 2014) to facilitate dialogue among stakeholders about future scenarios for city development and investment. The ability to compare between cities assists this thinking: which peer cities can be held up as exemplars in the context of a given city and what can planners learn from the different approaches? Indeed this was our starting point for the research. We set out to develop a benchmark for public transport accessibility for Australian cities by learning from elsewhere. With this in mind we selected a range of cities from different perspectives: those known as exemplars for public transport accessibility; New World cities that developed during a similar period to Australian cities; cities with different mixes of public transport modes – bus-dominant/rail dominant; cities with different governance frameworks and so on.

The idea of a benchmark can be seen from two dimensions: as a reference against which things can be compared – so how do public transport systems of international cities compare; and as a standard of excellence – so which cities can be seen as best practice as regards public transport accessibility. Having completed the reading of the analysis of our global sample of cities, it should be clear to the reader that it is not possible to place any one city on a pedestal as the exemplar. There is no one-size-fits-all approach, as is clearly demonstrated throughout the book. The point of reference depends upon the cities context – for example topography impacts (see in Sydney and Vancouver), city size impacts (compare a large dispersed city like Perth to one that is more compact like Vienna); the life-stage of the city impacts (compare New World cities built in the car era to older cities). It is not possible to suggest the most suitable urban form (polycentric/monocentric, contiguous/dispersed, concentrated/spread out) to optimise public transport accessibility. Similar topographical constraints appear to have contrasting effects – in Sydney and Auckland water bodies work to the detriment of accessibility performance, while supporting strong performance in Vancouver and Copenhagen. Monocentric cities may have more spatially coherent and hierarchical patterns of internal movement compared to polycentric cities where region-wide and city orientations compete. That said, there are clearly cities that deliver world-class public transport accessibility. If we take just the metric of *network coverage,* which measures the proportion of residents that get access to a standard of public transport competitive with the car[1], some of the cities do very well. Vienna, Amsterdam, Barcelona, Zurich and Copenhagen have systems that place over 70 per cent of their residents and employees within walking distance to this standard of service – for Singapore and Hong Kong the figure rises to 99 per cent. Vancouver, a New World city, exceeds 60 per cent. But there are many cities falling well short of this standard.

We do not suggest that city planners should follow the same complete model from any of these cities; this may be inappropriate given that the particular context of the city impacts the outcome. Rather, we suggest that there are particular accessibility attributes that can be linked to success (evidenced with high per capita patronage).

Network density and multi-directionality are critical. The whole city should aspire to a network comprising a mix of radial, orbital and diagonal elements to create lattice or spiderweb network shapes. These networks provide for easy multi-directional movement by public transport. For network density, it is specifically the intersection or transfer point density that is critical. For example, inner Adelaide and inner Vienna both have 100 per cent network coverage, but Vienna offers multiple public transport choices in walking distance, while Adelaide generally only offers one.

The **network must be well integrated, physically, functionally and institutionally**. By this we mean that public transport needs to be integrated with land use at centres of activity such that these are within walking distance of the stop/station. The integration must function properly – so be legible to users of the place and system, make transfers between services easy, ensure walkability between modes and land uses, and so on. Integration of governance assists these tasks – structures that ensure land use planners, transport planners and public transport planners work together to create the system; structures that integrate between different levels of government too. Strong integration of public transport and land use – transit oriented development – improves network coverage by placing a greater number of residents and employees in accessible locations.

Minimum service frequencies are critical. The 'backbone' services should operate at 10 minute frequencies or better during off-peak periods, seven days a week and into the evening. This standard seems to mark a turning point for accessibility performance according to SNAMUTS, a threshold below which frequencies do not seem to weigh negatively on ease of movement or contour catchments due to minimised waiting times and the convenience of transfers. The aim must be to create a public transport system that can offer a real alternative to the car, such that the individual can go anywhere and whenever. Achieving this level of service dispenses the idea of a transfer being a 'penalty'. Vienna maximises transfer points between high frequency services that serve a fine grained network and centres of activity in order to strike the right balance between network legibility and ease/convenience of movement. This provides for 'seamless' travel – here the transfer is actually a 'positive', rather than 'penalty', since it improves accessibility.

An **optimised multimodal public transport network is critical**, especially in the face of an uncertain future where cities must develop resilient solutions. Cities where planners draw on the broadest range of modes[2], and allocate each mode to a role that plays to its inherent strengths (speed, spatial reach, carrying capacity), succeed in offering high levels of accessibility. Planners who misunderstand these relationships waste precious resources where they compete or oversupply in some places and undersupply in others. There is a tendency by some to save money by cutting corners – for example planners asserting that a high-speed bus will suffice where in fact rail is warranted on accessibility and capacity grounds. This is a short term 'saving' if the outcome experienced is one of sub-optimal network performance. The bigger issue here is the question of 'solutionism' versus 'incremental optimisation' – do city decision-makers focus on the single big-ticket project solutions with the expectation that this will somehow solve all problems, or do they address each accessibility shortfall in a purpose-designed, best-fit fashion? All too often it is the big-ticket project that is seen as politically attractive.

Our research has shown how city decision-makers have organised and prioritised public transport infrastructure and so enabled insights into the extent that they offer a user-friendly public transport service. From the analysis of the global cities sample we detect four key network types. First, the **high surface network density with transfer minimisation** type, of which Edinburgh, Singapore and Hong Kong are the strongest examples. This network type offers many low-frequency bus lines with the aim to offer many transfer-free connections between places of activity. There are corridors where several lines overlap and have high (but not necessarily regular) frequencies. As a network with many individual lines, the user will find it challenging to comprehend, and this problem is compounded because there is often no or limited fare integration. This is an approach that capitalises on the low infrastructure costs of bus systems and which results in a high operational input, but, as seen in earlier chapters, the accessibility outcome can be sub-optimal for ease and flexibility of movement and in terms of geographical coverage (there is of course variation – for Edinburgh this holds true but not for Singapore and Hong Kong).

The second type, defined by its **low surface network density and transfer reliance**, is opposite to type one. Hamburg, Munich, Utrecht, Zuid Holland, Montreal and Perth are all examples of this type. Here there is a pronounced hierarchy between rail and surface modes, and avoidance of geographical duplication. Frequencies across the network are moderate to high and standardised. Multimodal integration is offered in dedicated, purpose-designed transfer facilities. The network is simplified and legible with a limited number of individual routes. In contrast to type one, operational input is low but there is only average geographical coverage and ease of movement. These cities achieve large operational economies without destroying accessibility performance. Thus in relation to operational input, accessibility is generally good, but within the context of all four network types it is only average and accessibility is quite varied.

Type three, defined as **medium surface network density networks with complementary integrated rapid transit**, sees a higher level of sophistication on the overall design. There is provision of a 'complete', multi-directional surface network as well as a complementary rapid transit network. Modes are integrated in dedicated transfer facilities. There are moderate to high standardised frequencies across the network. This type provides choices of movement for different journey lengths and purposes. The accessibility outcome is good with high ease of movement and geographical coverage, while transfer intensity varies. There is a high presence of public transport opportunities. The key differences of type three to the previous type can be seen in Copenhagen and Vancouver. There is confidence in allocating operational resources into a spatially comprehensive surface network (as in type one but more legibly organised) while still coordinating it well with the rapid transit lines. Bus and rail thus perform different tasks (speed, capacity, comfort) in the same spatial context and create genuine choices, whereas type two forces passengers into multimodal journeys and prescribes journey paths more rigidly, even where this is far from convenient to the user. This underscores the need to optimise the role of each mode.

The final type, defined by **medium surface network density and seamless multimodal integration**, can be seen as the final natural progression from the earlier three in design choice for decision-makers. Vienna and Zurich are examples of this type. There is high geographical network density, high or pulsed frequencies throughout the network and a large number of dedicated transfer points, enabling movement along geographical desire lines. The modal hierarchy and distribution of task is differentiated and generally includes a large range of transport modes. This design type offers outstanding accessibility outcomes. Vienna and Zurich achieved this type of network following several decades of many small and large incremental interventions to optimise network design and performance.

We suggest this categorisation represents a natural progression in public transport network design. It can act as a guide to the direction that city planners and citizens may wish to pursue where the objective is to achieve public transport accessibility as a genuine alternative to the car. Our Asian cities may well sit outside this typology and thus represent a fifth category, where cities have a much higher transport task to serve. While their bus networks follow similar lines to those found in type one (high surface network density with transfer minimisation), their rail networks are more similar to type three (medium surface network density networks with complementary integrated rapid transit), although their dense but legible networks appear insufficient for these strongly public transport dominated mega-cities. Instead their 'spaghetti-like' bus network design offers particular niches for regular public transport users, while rail offers a more legible network to casual public transport users.

At the outset we also asked about the prospects of implementing the recommendations from our study in cities that do want to improve public transport accessibility. In some ways this question offers a segue to a new piece of research and we set the agenda here to complete the book. The critical question is: why do some cities succeed in providing world class accessibility where others fall short? Our findings above give insights into what is needed. Planners may not be cognisant of these insights to the extent that there has not been a global comparative study of public transport accessibility like this one. For us the answers to these questions will also lie in a focus on the governance issues that arise. They are likely to be found in an analysis of the institutional structures (agency structure, rules, regulations) and the mental models of players within these agencies (Curtis and Low, 2012). Traditionally, road planners have held the upper hand, based in strong consolidated institutions and able to draw plans with long term funding assured. Public transport planners have been based in a multiplicity of different agencies, suffering endless fragmentation and change with resultant difficulties in long term planning and the financing of their infrastructure projects. Where public transport institutions have achieved success, it appears to be where public transport agencies and city planners have mobilised together and also with the road agencies to deliver a different transport outcome for their city (Vancouver offers a case in point). It becomes clear that planners and decision-makers do have a choice and can choose to deliver a city strong on public transport accessibility. There is also an important role for citizens in advocating for public transport accessibility.

Our final comment, in positioning this international sourcebook, concerns knowledge of good practices in public transport accessibility. Some of our cities are held up as exemplars – for land use–transport integration and in particular, transit oriented development. For many readers it would come as no surprise to see Zurich, Vancouver and Portland included in this book on that basis. Yet post-analysis it would appear that the boosterism of the Portland case has been more about demonstrating that new styles of transit oriented development can be carved into North American cities that have been dominated by designs to facilitate private car travel. Our analysis suggests that in international terms, Portland's public transport accessibility performance is modest at best. Contrast this with Vienna, where there has been relative silence in publications, yet this is a city with most of the attributes of global best practice in public transport accessibility – until now a well-kept secret (unlike its sachertorte!).

NOTES

1 Specifically measuring frequency of service and operational span in a way that assesses whether public transport users can rely on the service for both planned and spontaneous journeys.

2 Bus, trolleybus, bus rapid transit, tram, light rail, metro, suburban rail, ferries, cable cars as appropriate to context.

Bibliography

[AMT] Agence Métropolitaine de Transport (2013) *Rapport Annuel 2012*. Montréal: ATM.

Ajuntament de Barcelona (2000) *Pacte per la Mobilitat*. Available online at www.bcn.cat/pacteperlamobilitat.

Ajuntament de Barcelona (2014a) *Dades Bàsiques de Mobilitat 2013*. Available online at www.bcn.cat.

Ajuntament de Barcelona (2014b) *Nova Xarxa de Bus*. Available online at www.novaxarxabus.bcn.cat.

Alexander, I., McManus, P. (1992) A new direction for Perth transport? *Urban Policy and Research*, Vol 10, No 4, pp 6–13.

Arrington, G. B. (2009) Portland's TOD Evolution: From Planning to Lifestyle. Chapter 9 in Curtis, C., Renne, J. L., Bertolini, L. (eds) *Transit Oriented Development. Making it Happen*. Farnham, UK: Ashgate.

Auckland Transport (2014) *New Public Transport Network*. Available online at www.at.govt.nz/projects-roadworks/new-public-transport-network.

[ABS] Australian Bureau of Statistics (2012) *Census 2011*. Available online at www.abs.gov.au/census.

[ATM] Autoritat del Transport Metropolità (2014) *Pla Director d'Infraestructures (PDI)*. Available online at www.atm.cat.

Barter, P. A. (2013) Singapore's Mobility Model: Time for an Update? Chapter 12 in Institute for Mobility Research (IFMO, ed) *Megacity Mobility Culture. How Cities Move on in a Diverse World.* Heidelberg: Springer.

Baumann, C., White, S. (2011) Pathways to Sustainable Urban Transport Development. Investigating the transferability of Munich best practice in collaborative stakeholder dialogue to the context of Sydney. *5th State of Australian Cities Congress (SOAC)*, Melbourne (VIC), Australia, November/December.

Berelowitz, L. (2005) *Dream City. Vancouver and the Global Imagination*. Vancouver (BC): Douglas & McIntyre.

Bertolini, L. (1999) Spatial development patterns and public transport: The application of an analytical model in the Netherlands. *Planning Practice and Research*, Vol 14, No 2, pp 199–210.

Bertolini, L. (2005) Cities and Transport: Exploring the Need for New Planning Approaches. Chapter 5 in Albrechts, L., Mandelbaum, S. J. (eds) *The Network Society. A New Context for Planning*. Oxford: Routledge.

Bertolini, L., Le Clercq, F. (2003) Urban development without more mobility by car? Learning from Amsterdam, a multimodal urban region. *Environment and Planning A*, Vol 35, No 4, pp 575–89.

[BITRE] Bureau of Infrastructure, Transport and Regional Economics (2013) *Cities: Population Growth, Jobs Growth and Commuting Flows – A Comparison of Australia's Four Largest Cities* – Research report 142, Canberra: Department of Infrastructure and Transport.

BMW Group, Landeshauptstadt München (2013) *Verkehrsprobleme Gemeinsam Lösen. Eine Initiative von BMW und der Landeshauptstadt München.* Available online at www.inzell-initiative.de.

Bose, M. (2001) Raumstrukturelle Konzepte für Stadtregionen. Chapter 19 in Brake, K., Dangschat, J. S., Herfert, G. (eds) *Suburbanisierung in Deutschland*. Aktuelle Tendenzen. Wiesbaden: Springer Fachmedien.

Boudreau, J. A., Hamel, P., Jouve, B., Keil, R. (2006) Comparing metropolitan governance: The cases of Montreal and Toronto. *Progress in Planning*, Vol 66, pp 7–59.

Bratzel, S. (1999) Conditions of success in sustainable urban transport policy – Policy change in 'relatively successful' European cities. *Transport Reviews*, Vol 19, No 2, pp 177–90.

te Brommelstroet, M., Silva, C., and Bertolini, L. (eds) (2014) *Assessing Usability of Accessibility Instruments.* The Netherlands: COST.

Burger, M. J., Van der Knaap, B., Wall, R. S. (2014) Polycentricity and the multiplexity of urban networks. *European Planning Studies*, Vol 22, No 4, pp 816–40.

Catalán, B., Saurí, D., Serra, P. (2008) Urban sprawl in the Mediterranean? Patterns of growth and change in the Barcelona Metropolitan Region 1993–2000. *Landscape and Urban Planning*, Vol 85, No 3, pp 174–84.

Cervero, R. (1998) *The Transit Metropolis. A Global Inquiry*. Washington DC: Island Press.

Cervero, R., Murakami, J. (2009) Rail and property development in Hong Kong: Experiences and extensions. *Urban Studies*, Vol 46, No 10, pp 2019–43.

Chakirov, A., Erath, A. (2012) *Activity Identification and Primary Location Modelling Based on Smart Card Payment Data for Public Transport* paper presented at IATBR, Toronto.

City of Melbourne (2011) *Melbourne Transport Strategy*. Melbourne: City of Melbourne.

Cowie, J., Asenova, D. (1999) Organisation form, scale effects and efficiency in the British bus industry. *Transportation*, Vol 26, No 3, pp 231–48.

Cullinane, S. (2003) Hong Kong's low car dependence: Lessons and prospects. *Journal of Transport Geography*, Vol 11, pp 25–35.

Cullinane, S., Cullinane, K. (2003) Car dependence in a public transport dominated city: Evidence from Hong Kong. *Transportation Research Part D*, Vol 8, No 2, pp 129–38.

Currie, G., Burke, M. (2014) Light rail in Australia – performance and prospects. *Transit Australia*, Vol 69, No 1, pp 4–6.

Curtis, C. (2008a) Planning for sustainable accessibility: The implementation challenge, *Transport Policy*, Vol 15, No 2, pp 104–12.

Curtis, C. (2008b) Evolution of the transit-oriented development model for low-density cities: A case study of Perth's new railway corridor. *Planning Practice and Research*, Vol 23, No 3, pp 285–302.

Curtis, C., Low, N. (2012) *Institutional Barriers to Sustainable Transport*. Aldershot: Ashgate.

Curtis, C., Punter, J. V. (2004) Design-led sustainable development: The Liveable Neighbourhoods Experiment in Perth, Western Australia. *Town Planning Review*, Vol 75, No 1, pp 116–50.

Curtis, C., Renne, J., Bertolini, L. (2009) *Transit Oriented Development: Making it Happen*. Aldershot: Ashgate.

Curtis, C., Scheurer, J. (2010) Planning for sustainable accessibility: Developing tools to aid discussion and decision-making. *Progress in Planning*, Vol 74, pp 53–106.

Curtis, C., Scheurer, J., Burke, M. (2013) Using accessibility tools to guide policy innovation. *Built Environment*, Vol 39, No 4, pp 454–72.

[DST] Danmarks Statistik (2010) *Statistisk Årbog 2009*. Available online at www.dst.dk.

Davison, G. (1978) *The Rise and Fall of Marvellous Melbourne*. Melbourne: Melbourne University Press.

Davison, G, Yelland, S. (2004) *Car Wars. How the Car Won Our Hearts and Conquered Our Cities*. Crows Nest (NSW): Allen & Unwin.

[DB] Deutsche Bahn (2013) *Die 2. Stammstrecke – Kernstück des Bahnknotens München. Untersuchte Alternativen*. Available online at http://www.2.stammstrecke-muenchen.de/das-projekt/untersuchte-alternativen.

[DoI VIC] Department of Infrastructure (2002) *Melbourne 2030. Planning for Sustainable Growth*. Melbourne: Department of Infrastructure.

[DoT WA] Department of Planning (2010) *Directions 2031 and Beyond*. Perth: Department of Planning.

[DPI NSW] Department of Planning and Infrastructure (2010) *Metropolitan Plan for Sydney 2036*. Available online at www.metroplansydney.nsw.gov.au.

[DoT WA] Department of Transport (1995) *Perth Metropolitan Transport Strategy 1995–2029*. Perth: Department of Transport.

[DoT VIC] Department of Transport (2012) *Annual Report 2011–12*. Melbourne: Department of Transport.

[DTRS] Department of Transport and the Regional Services (2003) *National Charter of Integrated Land Use and Transport Planning*. Canberra: Department of Transport and Regional Services.

Dowling, R., Kent, J. (2013) The Challenges of Planning for Autonomous Mobility in Australia. *6th State of Australian Cities Conference (SOAC)*, Sydney (NSW), Australia, November.

Dura-Guimera, A. (2003) Population deconcentration and social restructuring in Barcelona, a European Mediterranean city. *Cities*, Vol 20, No 6, pp 387–94.

Evans, R., Karecha, J. (2013) Staying on top. Why is Munich so resilient and successful? *European Planning Studies*, Vol 22, No 6, pp 1259–79.

Faber, C. (2003) *Governance-Regimes im Öffentlichen Verkehr*. PhD Thesis, Wirtschaftsuniversität Wien, Austria.

Filion, P., Kramer, A. (2012) Transformative metropolitan development models in large Canadian urban areas: The predominance of nodes. *Urban Studies*, Vol 49, No 10, pp 2237–64.

Flückinger, H., Koll-Schretzenmayr (2000) Das vernetzte städtesystem Schweiz. Eine schweizerische strategie, ein europäisches modell? *disP – The Planning Review*, Vol 36, No 142, pp 4–9.

Gallez, C., Kaufmann, V., Maxim, H., Thebért, M., Guerrinha, C. (2013) Coordinating transport and urban planning: From ideologies to local realities. *European Planning Studies*, Vol 21, No 8, pp 1235–55.

Garcia-López, M. A. (2012) Urban spatial structure, suburbanization and transportation in Barcelona. *Journal of Urban Economics*, Vol 72, No 2, pp 176–90.

Gauthier, M. (2005) La planification des transports et le développement durable à Montréal: quelles procédures de débat public pour quelles solutions intégrées? *Flux*, No 60-61, pp 50–63.

Gehl, J. (2014) *People-Oriented Strategies for City Planning*. Centre for Liveable Cities Singapore, Lecture Series, Singapore, 28 March.

Gehl, J., Gemzøe, L., Kirknæs, S., Søndergaard, B. S. (2006) *New City Life*. Copenhagen: Arkitektens Forlag.

Gleeson, B., Curtis, C., Low, N. (2003) Barriers to Sustainable Transport in Australia. Chapter 12 in Low, N., Gleeson, B. (eds) *Making Urban Transport Sustainable*. New York: Palgrave Macmillan.

Goodman, R., Coiacetto, E. (2009) Retail Form in Melbourne and Brisbane:

A Preliminary Investigation into the Differences Between the Two Cities. *4th State of Australian Cities Conference*, Perth, November 2009.

Greer, M. R., van Campen, B. (2011) Influences on public transport utilization: The case of Auckland. *Journal of Public Transportation*, Vol 14, No 2, pp 51–68.

Halden, D. (2002) Using accessibility measures to integrate land use and transport policy in Edinburgh and the Lothians. *Transport Policy*, Vol 9, No 4, pp 313–24.

Hale, C. (2010) The mega-project as crux of integrated planning: Insights from Munich's Central Corridor. *Planning Practice and Research*, Vol 25, No 5, pp 587–610.

Harris, C. (2007a) *Roads, Railways and Regimes: Why some societies are able to organise suburban public transport – and why others can't*. Research Paper 14, Urban Research Program, Griffith University, Brisbane (QLD), Australia.

Harris, C. (2007b) Buses last stand? Recent urban transit reform in New Zealand. *Urban Policy and Research*, Vol 25, No 1, pp 151–9.

Hemsley, W. (2009) The Commercial Reality of TOD in Australia, in Curtis, C., Renne, J., Bertolini, L (eds), *Transit Oriented Development: Making It Happen*. Aldershot: Ashgate.

Hillier, B., Hanson, J. (1984) *The Social Logic of Space*. Cambridge: Cambridge University Press.

Hillier, B. (1996) *Space Is the Machine*. Cambridge: Cambridge University Press.

[HVV] Hamburger Verkehrsverbund (2013) *HVV-Verbundbericht 2013*. Available online at www.hvv.de.

[IA] Infrastructure Australia (2009) *National Infrastructure Priorities. Infrastructure for an Economically, Socially and Environmentally Sustainable Future*. Canberra: Australian Government.

Kähler, G. (2012) Auto, Straße und Verkehr: Vom Freiheitsversprechen zum Stau. Part 1 in Frank H, Schwarz U (eds) *Die Stadt und das Auto. Wie der Verkehr Hamburg veränderte*. Hamburg: Dölling und Galitz Verlag.

Kamruzzaman, M., Baker, D., Washington, S., Turrell, G. (2014) Advance transit-oriented development typology: Case study in Brisbane, Australia. *Journal of Transport Geography*, Vol 34, pp 54–70.

Karou, S., Hull, A. (2014) Accessibility modelling: Predicting the impact of planned transport infrastructure on accessibility patterns in Edinburgh, UK. *Journal of Transport Geography*, Vol 35, pp 1–11.

Kasanko, M., Barredo, J. L., Lavalle, C., McCormick, N., Demicheli, L., Sagris, V., Brezger, A. (2006) Are European cities becoming dispersed? A comparative analysis of 15 European urban areas. *Landscape and Urban Planning*, Vol 77, pp 111–30.

Kenworthy, J., Townsend, C. (2009) Montreal's Dualistic Transport Character: Why Montreal Needs Upgraded Transit and Not More High-Capacity Roads. Chapter 1 in Gauthier, P., Jaeger, J., Prince, J. (eds) *Montreal at the Crossroads. Superhighways, the Turcot and the Environment*. Montreal: Black Rose Books.

Knowles, R. D. (2012) Transit-oriented development in Copenhagen, Denmark: from the Finger Plan to Ørestad. *Journal of Transport Geography*, Vol 22, pp 251–61.

Københavns Kommune (2014) *København Cyklernes By – Cykelregnskab 2012*. Copenhagen: Københavns Kommune.

[LTA] Land Transport Authority (2013) *Singapore Land Transport Statistics in Brief*. Available online at www.lta.gov.sg.

[LMRSB] Landeshauptstadt München, Referat für Stadtplanung und Bauordnung (2010) *Zentrenkonzept München. Fortschreibung mit Schwerpunkt Nahversorgung*. München: Landeshauptstadt München.

Lau, J. C. W. (1997) The performance of public transport operations, land-use and urban transport planning in Hong Kong. *Cities*, Vol 14, No 3, pp 145–53.

Lau, J. C. W. (2011) Spatial mismatch and the affordability of public transport for the poor in Singapore's new towns. *Cities*, Vol 28, No 3, pp 230–37.

Lee, R. (2010) *Transport: An Australian History*. Sydney: UNSW Press.

Lemon, J. T. (1996) Toronto, 1975: The Alternative Future. Chapter 7 in Lemon, J. T. (ed) *Liberal Dreams and Nature's Limits: Great Cities of North America since 1600*. Toronto: Oxford University Press.

Limtanakool, N., Schwanen, T., Dijst, M. (2009) Developments in the Dutch urban system on the basis of flows. *Regional Studies*, Vol 43, No 2, pp 179–96.

Majoor, S. (2008) Progressive planning ideals in a neo-liberal context: The case of Ørestad, Copenhagen. *International Planning Studies*, Vol 13, No 2, pp 101–17.

Manning, I. (1991) *The Open Street: Public Transport, Motor Cars and Politics in Australian Cities*. Sydney: Transit Australia Publishing.

Mares, P. (2012) *Can We Afford to Get Our Cities Back on the Rails?* Melbourne: Grattan Institute.

Margerum, R. D., Brody, S., Parker, R., McEwen, G. (2013) Metropolitan smart-growth centers: An assessment of incentive policies in four regions. *Journal of Transport and Land Use*, Vol 6, No 2, pp 21–32.

Mavoa, S., Witten, K., McCreanor, T., O'Sullivan, D. (2012) GIS-based destination accessibility via public transit and walking in Auckland, New Zealand. *Journal of Transport Geography*, Vol 20, pp 15–22.

May, A. D. (2004) Singapore: The development of a world class transport system. *Transport Reviews*, Vol 24, No 1, pp 79–101.

Mees, P. (2000) *A Very Public Solution. Transport in the Dispersed City*. Melbourne: Melbourne University Press.

Mees, P. (2010a) *Transport for Suburbia. Beyond the Automobile Age*. London: Earthscan.

Mees, P. (2010b) Planning for Major Rail Projects: The Melbourne Metro and Regional Rail Link. *33rd Australasian Transport Research Form* (ATRF), Canberra, September/October 2010.

Mees, P., Dodson, J. (2011) *Public Transport Network Planning in Australia: Assessing current practice in Australia's five largest cities.* Research Paper 34, Urban Research Program, Brisbane: Griffith University.

Mees, P., Dodson, J. (2007) Backtracking Auckland? Technical and communicative reason in metropolitan transport planning. *International Planning Studies*, Vol 12, No 1, pp 35–53.

Mees, P., Groenhart, L. (2013) Travel to work in Australian cities, 1976–2011. *Australian Planner*, Vol 51, No 1, pp 66–75.

[MVG] Münchner Verkehrsgesellschaft mbH (2014) *Tram Westtangente*. Available online at http://www.mvg-mobil.de/projekte/westtangente/index.html.

Murray, S. J., Walton, D., Thomas, J. A. (2010) Attitudes towards public transport in New Zealand. *Transportation*, Vol 37, No 6, pp 915–29.

Neal, Z. P. (2013) *The Connected City. How Networks Are Shaping the Modern Metropolis.* New York: Routledge.

Newman, P. (2001) Railways and Reurbanisation in Perth. In Williams J, Stimson R (eds) *Case Studies in Planning Success*. New York: Elsevier.

Newman, P. (2009) Planning for Transit Oriented Development: Strategic Principles. Chapter 2 in Curtis C., Renne J. L., Bertolini L. (eds), *Transit Oriented Development: Making It Happen.* Aldershot: Ashgate.

Newman, P., Kenworthy, J. (1999) *Sustainability and Cities. Overcoming Automobile Dependence*. Washington DC: Island Press.

Newman, P., Scheurer, J. (2010) *The Knowledge Arc Light Rail: A Concept for Delivering the Next Phase of Public Transport in Perth.* Curtin University Sustainability Policy Institute (CUSP), Perth (WA), Australia.

Nielsen, G., Nelson, J. D., Mulley, C., Tegnér, G., Lind, G., Lange, T. (2005) *Public Transport – Planning the Networks. HiTrans Best Practice Guide 2*, Oslo: Civitas Consultants.

Norley, K.(2010) The Role of the Rail System in the Sydney Journey to Work. *33rd Australasian Transport Research Forum (ATRF)*, Canberra, 29 Sep–1 Oct 2010.

Oliveira, V., Martins, A., Cruz, S.S. (2013) Evaluating Urban Policies from a Resilience Perspective: The Case of Oporto. Chapter 10 in Eraydin, A., Taşan-Kok. (eds) *Resilience Thinking in Urban Planning*. Dordrecht: Springer Science + Business Media.

Ordóñez, M., Arturo, A., Erath, A. (2013). Estimating dynamic workplace capacities by means of public transport smart card data and household travel survey in Singapore, *Transportation Research Record: Journal of the Transportation Research Board*, Vol 2344, pp 20–30.

Østergaard, J., Bendixen, M., Frederiksen, T. S., Erlandsen, H., Kampmann, N. (2013) Letbanen på Ring 3. Special Session, *Trafikdage på Aalborg Universitet 2013*, Aalborg, Denmark, August.

Ott, R. (1995) Conurbation transport policy in Zurich, Switzerland. *Proceedings of the Institution of Civil Engineers, Transport*, Vol 111, No 3, pp 225–33.

Paulhiac, F., Kaufmann, V. (2006) Transports urbains à Montréal: Evolution des référentiels et enjeux d'une politique durable. *Revue d'Economie Régionale et Urbaine*, Vol 1, pp 49–80.

Pernau, G. (2001) *Barcelona i el cotxe. Cent anys d'amor i odi*. Barcelona: Ajuntament de Barcelona, Lunwerg Editores.

Porta, S., Crucitti, P., Latora, V. (2006a) The network analysis of urban streets: A dual approach. *Physica A, Statistical Mechanics and its Applications*, Vol 369, No 2, pp 853–66.

Porta, S., Crucitti, P., Latora, V. (2006b) The network analysis of urban streets: A primal approach. *Environment and Planning B: Planning and Design*, Vol 33, pp 705–25.

Priebs, A. (2007) 60 Jahre mit dem Kopenhagener FingerPlan – Kontinuität und Wandel eines regionalen Siedlungsleitbildes. Norden, *Band 18*, pp 9–19.

Priemus, H. (1999) Dutch Experience with Compact City Policy and ABC Location Policy. In Brunsing, J., Frehn, M. (eds) *Stadt der kurzen Wege. Zukunftsfähiges Leitbild oder planerische Utopie?* Dortmund: Institut für Raumplanung, Universität Dortmund.

[PTA WA] Public Transport Authority (2013) *Annual Report 2012–13*. Perth: Government of Western Australia.

Pucher, J., Kurth, S. (1996) Verkehrsverbund: The success of regional public transport in Germany, Austria and Switzerland. *Transport Policy*, Vol 2, No 4, pp 279–91.

Punter, J. (2003) *The Vancouver Achievement: Urban Planning and Design*. Vancouver: UBC Press.

[QLD DIT] Queensland Department of Infrastructure and Transport (2009) *South East Queensland Regional Plan 2009–2031*. Brisbane: Queensland Government.

Richmond, J. E. D. (2008) Transporting Singapore: The air-conditioned nation. *Transport Reviews*, Vol 28, No 3, pp 357–90.

Schaeffer, K. H., Sclar, E. (1975) *Access for All. Transportation and Urban Growth*. Baltimore: Penguin Books.

Scheurer, J., Woodcock, I. (2011) Transforming Melbourne through Transit-oriented Intensification: Implications for public transport network performance, accessibility and development densities. *5th State of Australian Cities Congress (SOAC)*, Melbourne (VIC), Australia, November/December.

Schiller, P. L., Bruun, E., Kenworthy, J. R. (2010) *An Introduction to Sustainable Transportation. Policy, Planning and Implementation*. London: Earthscan.

Schwanen, T., Dieleman, F. M., Dijst, M. (2004) The impact of metropolitan structure on commute behaviour in the Netherlands: A multilevel approach. *Growth and Change*, Vol 35, No 3, pp 304–33.

Silva, C., Pinho, P. (2008) Structural Accessibility for Urban Policy: The case of Greater Oporto. *CITTA 1st conference on planning research: Evaluation in planning*. Oporto, Portugal, 30 May.

Silva, C., Reis, J. P., Pinho, P. (2014) How urban structure constrains sustainable mobility choices: Comparison of

Copenhagen and Oporto. *Environment and Planning B: Planning and Design*, Vol 41, pp 211–28.

Simpson, M. (2004) *On the Move. A History of Transport in Australia*. Sydney: Powerhouse Publishing.

Somenahalli, S., Sleep, C., Primerano, F., Wadduwage, R., Mayer, C. (2013) Public transport usage in Adelaide. *Procedia – Social and Behavioural Sciences*, Vol 104, pp 855–64.

[SCBCTA] South Coast British Columbia Transportation Authority (2013) *TransLink 2012 Annual Report*. Burnaby: TransLink.

Statistics Canada (2013) *2011 Census of Population*. Available online at http://www12.statcan.gc.ca/census-recensement/index-eng.cfm.

Stone, J. (2011) Can European Models of Public Transport Governance Help to Save Australian Cities? *5th State of Australian Cities Conference (SOAC)*, Melbourne (VIC), Australia, November/December.

Svensson, O. (1981) *Dansk Byplan Guide*. Copenhagen: Miljøministeriet, Planstyrelsen, Dansk Byplanlaboratorium.

Tang, S., Lo, H. K. (2008) The impact of public transport policy on the viability and sustainability of mass railway transit – The Hong Kong experience. *Transportation Research Part A*, Vol 42, No 4, pp 563–76.

Topp, H. (1989) Cooperation in transit delivery in West German metropolitan areas. *Transportation*, Vol 15, No 4, pp 279–95.

TriMet (2011) *TriMet Service and Ridership Information*. Portland: TriMet.

Tyson, W. J, (1995) Bus deregulation – The planning dilemma. *Transport Reviews*, Vol 15, No 4, pp 307–13.

Van den Boomen, T., Venhoeven, T. (2012) *De mobiele stad. Over de wisselwerking van stad, spoor en snelweg.* Rotterdam: nai010 uitgevers.

Van der Bijl, R., Hendriks, M. (2010) *Station Centraal. Over het samenbinden van station en stad*. Rotterdam: Uitgeverij 010.

Van der Burg, A. J., Dieleman, F. M. (2004) Dutch urbanisation policies: From 'compact city' to 'urban network'. *Tijdschrift voor Economische en Sociale Geografie*, Vol 95, No 1, pp 108–16.

Van Neste, S. L., Bherer, L. (2013) The spatial puzzle of mobilising for car alternatives in the Montreal city-region. *Urban Studies*, Special Issue 2013, pp 1–20.

Van Oort, F., Burger, M., Raspe, O. (2010) On the economic foundation of the urban network paradigm: Spatial integration, functional integration and economic complementarities within the Dutch Randstad. *Urban Studies*, Vol 47, No 4, pp 725–48.

Van Wee, B., Maat, K. (2003) Land-use and transport: A review and discussion of Dutch research. *European Journal of Transport Infrastructure Research*, Vol 3, No 2, pp 199–218.

[VOR] Verkehrsverbund Ost-Region (2012) *Zahlen und Fakten*. Available online at www.vor.at.

Vigar, G. (2002) *The Politics of Mobility: Transport, the Environment and Public Policy*. London: Spon, London.

Vuk, G. (2005) Transport impacts of the Copenhagen Metro. *Journal of Transport Geography*, Vol 13, pp 223–33.

Walker, J. (2012) *Human Transit. How Clearer Thinking about Public Transit Can Enrich Our Communities and Our Lives*. Washington DC: Island Press.

Ward, S. V. (2002) *Planning the Twentieth-Century City. The Advanced Capitalist World*. Chichester: Wiley.

White, P. R. (1997) What conclusions can be drawn about bus deregulation in Britain? *Transport Reviews*, Vol 17, No 1, pp 1–16.

Whitelegg, J. (1997) *Critical Mass: Transport Environment and Society in the Twenty-first Century*. London: Pluto Press.

Whitzman, C., Gleeson, B., Sheko, A. (2014) *Melbourne: What Next?* Melbourne: The University of Melbourne Sustainable Societies and Social Equity Institutes.

Wiener Stadtwerke (2012) *Spitzenplatz beim Modal Split*. Available online at http://www.nachhaltigkeit.wienerstadtwerke.at/daseinsvorsorge/oepnv/modal-split.html.

Willoughby, C. (2001) Singapore's motorisation policies 1960–2000. *Transport Policy*, Vol 8, No 2, pp 125–39.

Yago, G. (1984) *The Decline of Transit. Urban Transportation in German and U.S. Cities, 1900–1970*. Cambridge: Cambridge University Press.

[ZVV] Züricher Verkehrsverbund (2014) *4. Teilergänzungen S-Bahn*. Available online at www.zvv.ch.

Appendix 1
Methodological Annotations

DEFINITIONS FOR STRUCTURAL INDICATORS

Metropolitan Area

In defining the geographical extent of a metropolitan area, the key intent is to find the best fit for the daily commuter shed of the dominant centre of the agglomeration, while making allowance for the detrimental impact on commuter flows of controlled border crossings (such as between Singapore and Malaysia, or between Hong Kong and mainland China) or of financial disincentives (such as the typically quite steep fares on high-speed rail links into neighbouring cities where these exist, or across the bridge between Copenhagen and Malmö). Thus in the mostly free-standing agglomerations of Australia and Canada the metropolitan area definitions of the national statistical office are used (ABS, 2012; Statistics Canada, 2013). In Australia, however, we used the metropolitan area definitions from the 2006 (rather than the 2011) census since these are fully aligned with local government boundaries. In Perth, our metropolitan area definition also extends to the Peel region, connected to the core city by frequent rail. In the US, where there are several geographical layers of common metropolitan area definitions, those counties that presented a congruent public transit network at the SNAMUTS minimum standard to analyse were selected (King and Snohomish counties in Seattle; Clackamas, Multnomah and Washington counties in Portland). In Auckland, the metropolitan region was recently amalgamated into a single local government area or 'super council' which serves as a viable definition. In Hamburg, Munich, Zurich, Vienna, Oporto and Barcelona the metropolitan area definition is the jurisdiction of the regional public transport agency. In Copenhagen, where integrated ticketing stretches further than the commuter belt, an older definition of the Danish capital's 'Hovedstadsregion' is used. In Edinburgh, the geographical reach of the public transport network at the SNAMUTS minimum standard was used (while drawing a pragmatic demarcation line about halfway between the Scottish capital and Glasgow, with which it shares some commuter catchments as well as through public transport services). For the Dutch Randstad, there are numerous competing definitions, some larger, some smaller. Our definition includes the four provinces of Noord Holland, Zuid Holland, Flevoland and Utrecht with the exception of the island of Texel in Noord Holland and the Noordoostpolder region in Flevoland. For the component cities, our definitions of Zuid Holland (Rotterdam/Den Haag) and Utrecht are equivalent to the provinces of the same name, while Amsterdam includes the southern half of mainland Noord Holland and the municipality of Almere in Flevoland. Singapore and Hong Kong are defined by their respective administrative boundaries.

Residential and Employment Density

Data on the residential population and the number of jobs in the defined metropolitan region was collected at the smallest available geographical scale. Besides, the proportion of the defined metropolitan region's land area that can be counted as urbanised was determined. Statistics on residential population are generally straightforward to acquire and relatively unambiguous. For employment, however, there are varying definitions, especially with regard to how part-time jobs and the various forms of self-employment (including work-at-home arrangements) are counted, and how this data is collected. In Australia, the US, the Netherlands and Barcelona, geographical units used for the reporting of job data are larger and less detailed than for residential data. For instance, in the Netherlands residential data is available in the public domain at the very fine-grained level of six-digit postcodes while employment data is only released at the coarser level of the first four digits of each postcode. Such mixed databases may lead to modest overestimates of employment compared to the more precise representation of the distribution of the residential population, particularly near the fringes of settlement areas. In Canada, we resorted to using employment data from the 2006 census in conjunction with 2011 residential data, as the methodological rigour for collecting employment data had weakened between the two census years. Similarly, in Vienna the residential and employment census are done separately, in different years and with different frequency; as a result, residential data from 2011 coexists in our database with employment data from 2001. Minor inaccuracies might derive from these effects in all three cases. In Munich, Hong Kong and Singapore, both residential and employment data was only available for relatively large geographical units (Munich's 25 boroughs, Tertiary Planning Units in Hong Kong and Planning Subzones in Singapore). In these cases, the urbanised area of each statistical unit was identified and an average residential and job density calculated; this figure then also served as input for the determination of the residential and job numbers in activity node catchments. Since this procedure disregards any possible density gradient within each statistical unit and since in central areas, SNAMUTS activity node catchments are often smaller than these units, some distortion in the representation of land use concentrations is likely to remain. In Singapore, employment figures are not collected by the statistical office at a geographically differentiated level below the entire city-state. Here, we resorted to a methodology developed by Chakirov and Erath (2012) that estimates job numbers according to the floor space occupied by employment uses in different industries (and which is well documented at the scale of individual properties across Singapore). In Hamburg, employment figures for the small number of detailed geographical areas where a single employer provides for all or the majority of jobs were omitted from the data set by the statistical office due to privacy legislation; in these cases, estimates were made based on information gleaned from the web presence of these employers or failing that, by using typical job densities in the vicinity. In Hamburg, Munich and Vienna, reporting standards differ between the core city and the surrounding municipalities. Across the latter, both residential and job count in activity node catchments are usually based on average densities calculated from the population, employment and urbanised area figures of the municipality or county in question. In many cities, the results of these adjustments resulted in some inconsistency with the total employment figures reported for the metropolitan area by statistical agencies. In the German cities, this effect is exacerbated by the practice of the statistical offices to only collect geographically specific data for employment fully integrated in the social security system (*sozialversicherungspflichtige Beschäftigte*) but not for self-employment and the public service. In these cases, geographically detailed results were extrapolated in a linear fashion to concur with the metropolitan-wide figures. This procedure may lead to some geographical imbalances in our database where the spatial distribution of the non-reported jobs differs in practice from that of the reported jobs. Overall, considerable flexibility was exercised with the acquisition of employment data and some variation in the accuracy of its representation is likely to have remained. However, since the SNAMUTS analysis is more interested in the relative distribution of residents and jobs between the catchments of a limited selection of activity nodes in each case study city than their level in absolute figures, we do not consider these variations in data quality a make-or-break constraint to the robustness of the results in the contour catchment, network coverage, betweenness and resilience indicators which make use of the land use database.

The definition of what constitutes the urbanised area of each agglomeration is also sometimes problematic. Density figures are more meaningful if they are applied to urbanised land rather than the total land surface of the metropolitan region, since this can include agricultural land, nature reserves or other undevelopable areas. The urbanised area definition captures all built up land including land used for transport purposes (roads, rail yards, airports, seaports) as well as for parks or open spaces primarily used for urban recreation (but not agriculture or forestry). Water surfaces are excluded. Some cities, notably in the Netherlands, Germany and Switzerland, publish detailed statistics on land use that allow for these figures to be derived. In other cities, notably in Australia, New Zealand, the US, Portugal and Denmark, the small geographical units of the census were used to determine where residential or job density reached an urbanised threshold (defined as a minimum of 2 dwellings or 5 jobs per hectare). Elsewhere, urbanised areas were created from Google Maps satellite images. Given these issues of compatibility, the results serve as a general guide providing for the grouping of cities into rough density categories.

Public Transport Journeys Per Capita Per Year

The number of public transport journeys undertaken per person per year is usually derived from performance reports of the respective transport agencies or operators. Standards of such reporting vary. The intent is to capture linked public transport trips in this indicator, so to count each journey from origin to destination as a single trip, regardless of the number of transfers between vehicles or modes. Unfortunately, in many cases, especially where different operators do their own reporting, usage figures are only available for unlinked trips or boardings. In other cases, available patronage figures are linked for transfers as long as the transfers occur between lines of the same mode (such as within the controlled area of a metro system) but not if they occur to or from another mode, even where the fares are integrated. For the Dutch and Scottish railways, patronage figures were only available network-wide but not specific to our urban agglomerations so this proportion is estimated based on annual boarding figures for the stations within the study areas.

Additionally the methods by which the data is collected will lead to some variation. Electronic ticketing systems, introduced in several cities during the period of our investigations, have begun to enable transit agencies to compile 'big data' on the usage of their system by recording every journey, including transfers. The same is true for system components where fare gates are in place. In both cases, however, this only applies to passengers who actually pay for their trip, and who may or may not be a precise representation of the number of actual users. In agencies without electronic or fare-gated ticketing systems, trip making rates are usually calculated from travel surveys and often include generalised assumptions (e.g. 48 journeys per monthly travel card) which may or may not be accurate, or may not remain accurate as time passes and usage patterns change.

This indicator, then, should be taken with a degree of caution when comparing cities. It is legitimate to conclude from this data that public transport patronage in Vienna and Zurich (around 400 trips per person per year) is significantly higher than in Copenhagen (215), Hamburg (212) or Amsterdam (208), but it would be imprudent to read a meaningful message into the very small differences between the three latter cities.

Timetable Data

SNAMUTS endeavours to glean the timetable and other operational data required to build the databases from public domain material wherever possible. However, the standards at which such material is published vary from city to city. During the course of our investigations (2010–2014), many (but not all) case study cities initiated a process of sharing their timetable data with the Google Transit application, with the result that journey times and service frequencies can be found online in a universal format and queried according to the requirements of the SNAMUTS database. Many transit agencies also have home-grown travel planning software available for public use through their websites.

The practice of publishing timetables in printed format has survived only in some case study cities, with Vancouver, Portland, Hamburg, Munich and the Dutch railways offering the most comprehensive documents of this kind. However, not everywhere does such material contain the level of detail required for the SNAMUTS database. For example, in the majority of cities timetable brochures, particularly for surface lines, only show departure times for a limited number of stops along the route. In some cases, notably Barcelona, information on journey times was entirely absent and had to be calculated using average bus speeds in the core city and in suburban municipalities (a figure contained in the transport agency's annual report). Service frequencies, too, are occasionally not provided in exact terms but as a spread of values (e.g. every 8–13 minutes), in which case the average was used as input for the database. This practice is particularly prevalent in Barcelona and the Asian cities, and it should be noted that it might lead to a minor degree of imprecision in the representation of service intensity and impediment values compared to cities where this data is less ambiguous. In all cities, however, SNAMUTS relies on the assumption that published travel time and service frequency information is a more or less accurate representation of actual operational circumstances; in other words, our database does not account for possible effects of poor service reliability.

INDICATOR FORMULAS

Travel Impediment

$$d_{ij} = 4 * \sqrt{t_{ij} / f_{ij}}$$

where:

d_{ij} = Impediment value of route segment between nodes *i* and *j*

t_{ij} = Travel time between nodes *i* and *j* in minutes

f_{ij} = Service frequency in departures per hour per direction between nodes *i* and *j*

Closeness Centrality

$$C_i = \sum_{j=1, j \neq i}^{N} \frac{L_{min,ij}}{N-1}$$

where:

C_i = Closeness centrality of node i

$L_{min,ij}$ = Minimum cumulative impediment between nodes i and j

N = Number of activity nodes in the network

Degree Centrality

$$D_i = \sum_{j=1, j \neq i}^{N} \frac{p_{min,ij}}{N-1}$$

where:

D_i = Degree centrality of node i

$p_{min,ij}$ = Minimum number of transfers between nodes i and j

N = Number of activity nodes in the network

Network Coverage

$$Q_n = \frac{\sum_{j=1}^{N} act_j}{act_m}$$

where:

Q_n = Network coverage index

N = Number of activity nodes in the network

t_{ij} = Minimum travel time between nodes i and j

act_j = Number of residents and jobs in the catchment area of node j

act_m = Number of residents and jobs in the metropolitan area

Thirty-Minute Contour Catchment

$$Q_i(30) = \sum_{j=1}^{t_{ij} \leq 30} act_j$$

where:

$Q_i(30)$ = 30-minute contour catchment of node i

t_{ij} = Minimum travel time between nodes i and j

act_j = Number of residents and jobs in the catchment area of node j

act_m = Number of residents and jobs in the metropolitan area

Betweenness Centrality

$$B_k = \frac{\sum_{i=1,j=1,j\neq i}^{N(N-1)} \frac{P_{ij}(k) * act_i * act_j}{L_{min,ij}}}{1000 * \sum_{i=1,j=1,j\neq i}^{N(N-1)} \frac{act_i * act_j}{L_{min,ij}}} * B_g$$

where:

B_k = Betweenness centrality of node/segment k

$P_{ij}(k)$ = Paths between nodes i and j that pass through node/segment k

act_i = Number of residents and jobs in catchment area of node i

act_j = Number of residents and jobs in catchment area of node j

$L_{min,ij}$ = Minimum cumulative impediment between nodes i and j

B_g = Global betweenness index

N = Number of activity nodes in the network

Global Betweenness

$$B_g = \sqrt{\frac{\sum_{i=1,j=1,j\neq i}^{N(N-1)} \frac{act_i * act_j}{L_{min,ij}}}{1000 * N}}$$

where:

B_g = Global betweenness index

act_i = Number of residents and jobs in catchment area of node i

act_j = Number of residents and jobs in catchment area of node j

$L_{min,ij}$ = Minimum cumulative impediment between nodes i and j

N = Number of activity nodes in the network

Segmental Resilience

$$R_k = \frac{\sum_{i=1,j=1,j\neq i}^{N(N-1)} \frac{P_{ij}(k) * act_i * act_j}{L_{min,ij}}}{fk * ck * B_g}$$

where:

R_k = Segmental resilience index of segment k

$P_{ij}(k)$ = Paths between nodes i and j that pass through route segment k

act_i = Number of residents and jobs in catchment area of node i

act_j = Number of residents and jobs in catchment area of node j

$L_{min,ij}$ = Minimum cumulative impediment between nodes i and j

f_k = Service frequency along route segment k

c_k = Modal coefficient for route segment k

B_g = Global betweenness index

N = Number of activity nodes in the network

Nodal Connectivity

$$V_i = \left(\sum_{j=1,j\neq i}^{N(i)} a_{ij} - 1\right) * \left(\frac{3 * o_r * f_r(i)}{200} + \frac{3 * o_t * f_t(i)}{200} + \frac{3 * o_b * f_b(i)}{200} + \frac{3 * o_f * f_f(i)}{200}\right)$$

where:

V_i = Connectivity index for node *i*

a_{ij} = links converging in node *i*, with $j \in N(i)$ and $i \neq j$

$N(i)$ = network nodes adjacent (nearest neighbours) to node *i*

$f_r(i)$ = number of rail departures per hour per direction from node *i*

$f_t(i)$ = number of tram/LRT departures per hour per direction from node *i*

$f_b(i)$ = number of bus departures per hour per direction from node *i*

$f_f(i)$ = number of ferry departures per hour per direction from node *i*

o_r = average network-wide load factor rail (passenger-km divided by revenue train-km)

o_t = average network-wide load factor tram/LRT (passenger-km divided by revenue train/vehicle-km)

o_b = average network-wide load factor bus (passenger-km divided by revenue vehicle-km)

o_f = average network-wide load factor ferry (passenger-km divided by revenue vehicle-km)

Composite Accessibility Index

$$S_i = c_s * \frac{200}{C_i} + \frac{2.5}{D_i + 0.25} + \frac{\sqrt{\frac{Q_i(30)}{\sqrt{\text{act}_m}}}}{4} + \sqrt{\frac{B_i}{6}} + \log_3(V_i) - \sqrt{-R_i}$$

where:

S_i = Composite accessibility index for node i

c_s = Network benchmarking coefficient

C_i = Closeness centrality index for node i

D_i = Degree centrality index for node i

$Q_i(30)$ = 30-minute contour catchment for node i

act_m = Number of residents and jobs in the metropolitan area

B_i = Betweenness index for node i

V_i = If $V_i>1$: Connectivity index for node i

R_i = If $R_i<0$: Average resilience index for segments converging in node i, weighted by departures per hour

Network benchmarking coefficient

$$c_s = 0.84 * \sqrt[7]{\frac{10^7 * B_g * Q_n}{act_m * (30 - R_n) * c_d}}$$

where:

c_s = Network benchmarking coefficient

B_g = Global betweenness index

Q_n = Network coverage index

act_m = Number or residents and jobs in the metropolitan area

R_n = Average network resilience

c_d = Dispersion coefficient (ratio of average distance between activity nodes within conglomerates and average distance between all activity nodes on the network. 'Conglomerates' are defined as clusters of three or more activity nodes, each within a distance below the network average of at least one other node)

Index

Note: Page numbers in *italics* indicate illustrations and tables.